An Introduction to Phonetics and Phonology

Blackwell Textbooks in Linguistics

An Introduction to Phonetics and Phonology

Second Edition

John Clark and Colin Yallop

BLACKWELL
Oxford UK & Cambridge USA

Copyright © John Clark and Colin Yallop 1990, 1995

First published 1990
Reprinted 1991, 1992

Second Edition first published 1995
Reprinted 1996

Blackwell Publishers Ltd
108 Cowley Road, Oxford OX4 1JF, UK

Blackwell Publishers Inc.
238 Main Street
Cambridge, Massachusetts 02142, USA

British Library Cataloguing in Publication Data

A CIP catalogue record for this book is available from the British Library.

Library of Congress Cataloging-in-Publication Data
Clark, John (John Ellery)
    An introduction to phonetics and phonology / John Clark and Colin Yallop.—2nd ed.
        p.   cm.— (Blackwell textbooks in linguistics ; 9)
    Includes bibliographical references and index.
    ISBN 0–631–19452–5
    1. Phonetics.   2. Grammar, Comparative and general—Phonology.
I. Yallop, Colin.   II. Title.   III. Series.
P217.C65   1995
414–dc20   94–43128
                                                                 CIP

Typeset in 10 on 12pt Sabon by TecSet Ltd, Wallington, Surrey
Printed in Great Britain by Hartnolls Limited, Bodmin, Cornwall
This book is printed on acid-free paper

Contents

Figures

Tables

Preface to the Second Edition

This edition shows a number of improvements. An entire chapter on perception (chapter 8) has been added, and the information on anatomy and physiology has been rearranged so that most of it now comes much later in the book. There are other additions and amendments at various points throughout the text and the list of references has been substantially extended.

So many people have been kind enough to comment on the first edition that it is impossible to mention them all. We are grateful for their comments and have been encouraged and guided by them in the task of producing this revised edition.

We hope that this second edition proves useful to a wide readership.

John Clark and Colin Yallop

List of Abbreviations

cm	centimetre
cm^3	cubic centimetre
cm H$_2$O	centimetres of water
CNS	central nervous system
dB	decibel
DFT	discrete Fourier transform
DL	difference limen
F_0	fundamental frequency
F_1, F_2 etc.	first formant, second formant, etc
FFT	fast Fourier transform
IPA	The International Phonetic Association
JND	just noticeable difference
kHz	kilohertz
Hz	hertz
LPC	linear prediction coefficient
mm	millimetre
ms	millisecond
mV	millivolt
Pa	pascal
μPa	micropascal
PNS	peripheral nervous system
Psg	subglottal pressure
RMS	root mean square (value of sound pressure)
RP	Received Pronunciation
SPE	*The sound pattern of English* (Chomsky and Halle 1968)
SPL	sound pressure level
VOT	voice onset time

1 Introduction

1.1 Phonetics and phonology

Phonetics and phonology are concerned with speech – with the ways in which humans produce and hear speech. Talking and listening to each other are so much part of normal life that they often seem unremarkable. Yet, as in any scientific field, the curious investigator finds rich complexity beneath the surface. Even the simplest of conversations – an exchange of short greetings, for example – presupposes that the speaker and hearer make sense to each other and understand each other. Their ability to communicate in this way depends in turn on proper bodily functioning (of brain, lungs, larynx, ears and so on), on recognizing each other's pronunciation and on interpreting the sound waves that travel through the air. The fact that a total outsider, unfamiliar with the language, will find even a simple conversation a bewildering jumble of unpronounceable and unintelligible noise only underlines the extent of our organization and control of talking and listening within particular social and linguistic conventions.

Once we decide to begin an analysis of speech, we can approach it on various levels. At one level, speech is a matter of anatomy and physiology: we can study organs such as tongue and larynx and their function in the production of speech. Taking another perspective, we can focus on the speech sounds produced by these organs – the units that we commonly try to identify by letters, such as a 'b-sound' or an 'm-sound'. But speech is also transmitted as sound waves, which means that we can also investigate the properties of the sound waves themselves. Taking yet another approach, the term 'sounds' is a reminder that speech is intended to be heard or perceived and that it is therefore possible to focus on the way in which a listener analyses or processes a sound wave.

The study of these facets of speech is usually termed PHONETICS. Adopting the different perspectives suggested above, phonetics can be viewed as a group of phonetic sciences, separated as ANATOMY AND PHYSIOLOGY OF SPEECH, ARTICULATORY PHONETICS (which often tends to deal with the identification and classification of individual sounds), ACOUSTIC PHONETICS (sometimes restricted to instrumental analysis and measurement of sound waves) and AUDITORY or PERCEPTUAL PHONETICS. These different aspects of speech are of course integrated: speech sounds cannot be divorced from the organs that articulate them, a sound wave does not exist in isolation from the source that generates it, and so on.

Moreover, speech is a purposeful human activity: it is not just movement or energy or noise, but a systematically organized activity, intended – under normal circumstances – to convey meaning. The term PHONOLOGY is often associated with the study of this 'higher' level of speech organization. Thus phonology is often said to be concerned with the organization of speech within specific languages, or with the systems and patterns of sounds that occur in particular languages. On this view, a general description of how vowel sounds can be made and perceived might be the province of phonetics while the analysis and description of the vowels of English might be assigned to phonology. But both phonetics and phonology have been variously defined and it is impossible to consider such definitions without touching on fundamental questions about the nature of reality and its scientific exploration.

Let us consider some of the observations that phoneticians and phonologists have made about English. First, each English vowel can be said to have a characteristic length. It must be stressed here that we are talking about vowel sounds, not vowel letters; throughout this book, as generally in phonetics and phonology, we use the term VOWEL to refer to a sound, not a letter. Hence in our terms the words *limb*, *hymn*, *live* and *sieve* all contain the same vowel, despite the various spellings. On the other hand, *meat* and *great* contain two different vowels: despite the identical *ea* spelling, the two words do not have the same vowel, a fact which we recognize when we say that the words do not rhyme with each other. Turning now to vowel length in English, the vowel heard in words such as *lip*, *bit*, *miss* is rather short, the vowel of *lap*, *bat*, *lass* is somewhat longer (although its length relative to other vowels varies across different regions of the English-speaking world) and the vowel of *leap*, *beat*, *lease* is longer still. Secondly, whatever their intrinsic or characteristic length, vowels are longer before sounds such as [d] and [g] than they are before sounds such as [t] and [k]. (We follow the usual convention of writing phonetic symbols in square brackets.) If you listen carefully to the pronunciation of words such as *bead*, *greed* and *league*, it should be possible to hear that the vowel is longer than in words such as *beat*, *greet* and *leak*. (If the difference is not very clear, try imagining that you have to contrast two words over the telephone – 'I said *greet* not *greed*' – in which case you may find yourself cutting the vowel short in *greet* and exaggerating the length in *greed* as a way of distinguishing the two words.) This is a general pattern of English: any vowel, whatever its intrinsic length, will be longer before certain consonants than before others. Thus the vowel of *beat* is longer than the vowel of *bit*; but *bead* will be even longer than *beat* (as the vowel of *bid* will be longer than that of *bit*, even though it may still be judged a 'short' vowel). Thirdly, we can identify the consonants that have a shortening effect on the preceding vowel as 'voiceless' – sounds such as [p], [t], [k] and [s] – and those that trigger lengthening as 'voiced' – for instance [b], [d], [g] and [z]. Try hissing a lengthened [ssss] and compare it with a lengthened buzzing [zzzz]: the difference between the two is the 'voicing' of the [z], a vibration produced in the larynx which is perceived as a 'buzz'.

Observations such as these are merely the beginning of an account of English speech sounds, but they serve as illustrations. Research which has been concerned with, for example, the precise measurement of vowel length, or the behaviour of the larynx during voicing, or the acoustic consequences of voicing, has generally been considered phonetic research rather than phonological; while research concerned with, for example, identifying and characterizing the total number of distinctive vowels in English, or classifying the sounds of English according to distinctive properties such as voicing or voicelessness, or formulating rules to cover predictable patterns such as vowel lengthening before voiced consonants, has been considered phonological rather than phonetic. As these examples may suggest, phoneticians are likely to draw on methods and techniques used in the natural sciences – precise measurement (say of vowel duration), sampling and averaging (of some measurable value in an acoustic signal) and so on. Phonologists may profess to be more concerned with the mental organization of language – with the systematization of distinctions within a language, for instance, or with the modelling of a speaker's knowledge as a set of rules.

Unfortunately, what may appear to be a reasonable division of labour between phoneticians and phonologists is frequently discussed in the context of assumptions about the 'real' nature of speech. Thus the idea that phonetics is concerned with universal properties of speech, studied by scientific methods, may all too easily be read as a claim that phonetics deals with objective physical or concrete reality, while phonology is somewhat apologetically concerned with the linguistic organization of this reality. Or, more or less reversing the argument, phonology may be said to tackle the true mental reality behind speech, while phonetics handles 'merely' the concrete outworkings of this reality. Hence the relationship between phonetics and phonology becomes controversial and it is important to understand the reasons for this, rather than to attempt an oversimplified and divisive definition of the two terms.

In the first place, the frequent stress on the general or universal character of phonetics as opposed to the language-specific focus of phonology is not convincing. While it is true that phonetics often aspires to generalizations about speech organs and acoustics, phonology is often no less interested in generalizing across languages. Any endeavour, for example, to use uniform notation and terminology to describe the phonological organization of various languages suggests an interest in universality. On the other hand, much work in phonetics is quite language-specific – say, studies of the articulation of certain sounds in English – and it would be wrong to suggest that phonetics necessarily has a more universalist character than phonology.

Emphasis on the physical or concrete nature of phonetics must likewise be treated with caution. Of course, one might simply question the terms and ask in what sense a *movement* of the tongue or a sound *wave* is physical or concrete. But it is certainly true that speech organs and sound waves are amenable to observation and measurement in ways that mental organization is not. It is possible, for example, to take ciné X-rays of the speech organs, to measure muscular activity during speech and to record the complex sound waves of speech; and observation of this kind is an essential contribution to our understanding of speech. Nevertheless, a ciné X-ray film or a wave pattern traced on paper tells us very little unless it can be related to the speaker's and hearer's linguistic system. The relatively continuous flow of speech recorded in this way does not of itself display the speaker's organization in terms of syllables or words, or the hearer's perceptual decisions in terms of sounds or categories. Thus while it is true that certain aspects of speech are particularly amenable to certain kinds of quantitative measurement, it would be wrong to conclude that such measurement in itself is sufficient to capture the truth about speech.

On the other hand, talk of linguistic systems and mental organization is open to a different danger, to an assumption that the investigator is now free to speculate about speakers' intuitions and insights. To avoid any misunderstanding here, we stress that any scientific or theoretical investigation of any aspect of speech must be empirical, in other words must be properly based on observation. Empirical standards are perhaps more obvious in respect of articulation and acoustics, where guesswork and speculation defer to the results of properly conducted observation. The same standards nevertheless apply to phonology, where systems and structures need equally to be justified empirically. The techniques may be different – testing speakers' auditory judgements, for example, or observing agreed patterns of rhyme, or noting spelling preferences – but they are or can be none the less empirical.

Furthermore, if it is true that physical records need to be related to linguistic organization, the reverse is no less true. A speaker's intentions or a hearer's perceptual judgements, even when validated empirically, cannot be divorced from the spoken utterances themselves. My belief that I am saying the words 'how are you' on a particular occasion does not pass telepathically from my mind to the hearer's: the message is conveyed by articulated speech and rests on articulatory and acoustic functioning within a linguistic system.

It is not unreasonable, then, to say that phonology deals with the systems and structures of speech, while phonetics focuses more narrowly on articulation and acoustics. But the boundary need not be sharply drawn, nor should it be surreptitiously constructed on assumptions about the primacy of one kind of reality above others. In short, although we analyse speech by breaking it down into its several aspects, we should not forget that the true reality is one of integration.

1.2   Theory and analysis

It is impossible to investigate phonetics and phonology without confronting theoretical issues. In this, phonetics and phonology are no different from other fields of study. Indeed, it is part of the definition of a science – taking the word 'science' in its widest sense to include such areas as psychology and sociology as well as biology and physics – that it is characterized by theoretical reflection. This is not to say that human activities which require little or no theoretical thinking are worthless or inferior. The skills that humans can develop in, for example, dancing, cooking, gardening or carpentry are a valuable part of the riches of human culture: depending on one's criteria of judgement, they may be enjoyable, useful and, for that matter, well rewarded activities. But, characteristically, they reflect technical mastery, experience or practical wisdom rather than theoretical understanding.

If we apply this distinction to language and linguistics, it is clear that there are skills, such as mimicry of other accents or languages, which are not scientific in the sense we have outlined. We may, it is true, describe such skills as 'practical phonetics' or 'being a good linguist'. But we may also use the terms 'phonetics' and 'phonology' more narrowly to indicate the theoretically based exploration of spoken language. What is important of course is not so much the terms themselves, but the distinction between speaking, as we all do, with little or no deliberate attention to what we are doing, and analysing the nature of speech, consciously reflecting on the how and why of speaking.

It is significant for linguistic theory that speaking is normally unselfconscious. The integrated nature of language is such that we normally concentrate on meaning and purpose. We are not usually aware of the movements of articulatory organs, we do not keep count of the number of syllables we have uttered, nor do we register whether an utterance happens to have contained particular vowels or consonant clusters. Even when we are alert to speech – for example, when we are conscious of tripping over certain words or sounds in our own speech, or when we register the 'strange' accent of another's speech – our impressions almost always remain subordinate to questions of meaning. It is rare, and verging on the pathological if, for example, we are so selfconscious about our articulation that we lose track of what we want to say.

The theoretical significance of this point is that it puts both our everyday use of language and our scientific investigation of it into perspective and enables us to relate the two to each other. Speakers talk, say things, convey their meaning; they do not, from their own habitual perspective, make articulatory movements or initiate sound waves. But the linguist, as a scientist, is interested in precisely these constituent processes and activities which are not the speaker's focus of attention but which make it possible for speakers to say what they mean. In phonetics and phonology we analyse what goes on in everyday speaking, resolving the integrated complexity into its different aspects, breaking down the overall activity into its component details, explaining how the deceptive simplicity of the everyday is achieved. The analysis is neither better nor worse than the activity itself: it attempts to explain and explore.

What we have been saying so far is itself part of a theory (and therefore open to debate). Our view can be described as functional, in that we assume that language has the ultimate function of being meaningful and that the task of analysis is to investigate how that function is achieved through subsidiary functions. Thus speakers function characteristically in terms of meaning. They function also as biological mechanisms (using muscles to bring articulatory organs into place), as psychological subjects (perceiving and discriminating speech sounds) and so on. But these functions are harnessed to the overall goal of meaningful interaction with other humans.

Finally, it must be stressed that scientific knowledge and analysis are always provisional. As we shall see later, twentieth-century phonology has regrettably often been characterized by a polemical style in which certain insights or perspectives are proclaimed to the exclusion of all others. The inevitable consequence is that a distorted theory enjoys a brief spell as ultimate truth before falling prey to the next 'ultimate' alternative. To pursue absolute truth is one thing; to possess it quite another.

1.3   Relationships with other fields

Phonetics and phonology intersect with a number of interests, partly because of the theoretical connections between aspects of speech and other scientific fields of study, partly because of various practical motives that have drawn on or stimulated speech research.

Interest in recording and describing pronunciation has a long history. A concern to record dialect pronunciations, for example, was an important factor in the development of modern phonetic transcription. The consequent interest in the amount of detail that could be included in a transcription also contributed to phonological theory. Similar interest in recording hitherto unwritten languages, such as the indigenous languages of the Americas, was often combined with a desire to devise practical orthographies and to promote literacy. So strong was this motive that some linguists almost equated phonology with a set of techniques for reducing languages to writing. In fact the relationship between spoken and written language is not necessarily direct and the conception of phonology as the art of orthography design is far too narrow. Nevertheless, the study of phonetics and phonology is certainly relevant to questions of writing and spelling: it is probably fair to say, for example, that many teachers responsible for introducing children to reading and writing in English-speaking countries are insufficiently informed about actual pronunciations and often fail to appreciate the reasons for some of the problems experienced by children (such as confusion of spelling between *chain* and *train* or uncertainty about which vowel to write before *l* in *bolt* or *salt*). Moreover, many of the world's languages do have spelling systems that were deliberately designed to reflect pronunciation (sometimes misleadingly called 'phonetic spelling systems') and others have been reformed from time to time to keep them closer to actual pronunciation.

Language teaching has also contributed to and profited from phonetics and phonology. Many works on English phonetics and phonology have been written for the benefit of foreign learners, for example. The fact that English spelling is not a direct reflection of pronunciation has undoubtedly been an important factor here and has led to the publication of pronouncing dictionaries and other guides to pronunciations, both for native speakers of English and for learners. It is now customary for general-purpose English dictionaries to include some kind of transcription or guide to the pronunciation of each word (a practice which is by no means standard for other languages with more consistent spelling conventions). Debate about a standardized or 'correct' pronunciation of English has also played an important role, and much of the work on phonetics in Britain in the first half of the twentieth century was oriented towards the description and promotion of so-called Received Pronunciation (RP), a style of pronunciation more commonly and less precisely referred to as 'BBC English' or 'Oxford English'.

Information about speech and pronunciation is thus of some general interest to users of language and of specific importance to those engaged in recording, describing and teaching languages. Certain other professions are directly concerned with speech and hearing, notably audiology and speech therapy or speech pathology. A solid grounding in phonetics and phonology is normally an integral part of the training for these professions, and practice and research in these fields has also contributed to the development of phonetics and phonology.

Advances in technology in the twentieth century have opened up new ways of investigating the articulatory and acoustic properties of speech and have substantially enlarged the scope of phonetics. This continually widening field of instrumental research has not only made it possible to improve upon some of the earlier impressionistic observations about speech, but has also brought about interaction with other areas of research such as physiology, physics and electronics. There are now promising developments in, for example, the generation of synthetic speech ('machines that talk') and the conversion of speech to text ('machines that type what they hear'). Research of this kind has commercial potential as well as theoretical fascination and it brings phoneticians and phonologists together with experts in computing and artificial intelligence.

1.4   Outline of this book

We make no apology for devoting a large proportion of this book to what may seem to be technicalities. Chapters 2 and 3 are intended to provide a solid foundation of insight into the complexity of human speech, with detailed attention to the great diversity of speech sounds that can be found in the world's languages. Chapter 4 deals with some basic principles of phonological organization, in fairly traditional terms, while chapter 5 outlines the generative approach to phonology, which has rivalled more traditional concepts since the 1960s. Chapter 6 introduces relevant aspects of anatomy and physiology, exploring the structure and function of the organs of speech. Chapter 7 is a detailed account of the acoustics of speech and chapter 8 deals with the perception of speech. The two following chapters cover prosody (notably the phenomena of stress, tone and intonation: chapter 9); and the categorization of speech sounds into component features (chapter 10). Chapter 11 draws the book together by looking back over the theoretical issues that have been raised and by giving a historical survey of ways of thinking and talking about speech, from earliest times through to current attempts to refine theory and description.

Diagrams and small tables are included in the text wherever they help to illustrate a point. Phonetic symbols and features are also set out in the appendices, where they can be readily identified and referred to.

The organization of the book is somewhat unusual, and is deliberately intended to blur some of the boundaries which are often inflicted on phonetics and phonology. It might have been more in keeping with tradition to proceed through the 'phonetics' of speech (articulation and acoustics) to a review of schools of phonology and modern descriptive approaches in historical order. We have not done so precisely because we want to stress that there are no uncontroversial 'facts' of speech that are independent of questions about how to understand and describe them. Indeed, contrary to a common assumption, there is no simple theoretical progression from elementary and obvious truth to abstract and contentious theorizing, nor a straightforward historical progression from past ignorance to present or future omniscience.

To take just one example, it may seem obvious and indisputable that all speech sounds are either consonants or vowels. The moment one probes this statement, however, it turns out to raise all kinds of questions. Speakers of English first have to ensure that they distinguish between letters and sounds. Words such as *myth* and *hymn* certainly contain a vowel (the same vowel as in *pith* and *him*), despite the fact that they happen not to use the letter *i*, while words such as *union* and *usage* begin with a consonant (the same that begins *you* and *youth*), as is evident from the fact that we say *a union*, not *an union*. Having focused on pronunciation rather than spelling, we confront a series of questions: What criteria are actually used to classify sounds as consonants or vowels? Are there no other possibilities – sounds which are intermediate in nature between consonant and vowel or neither one nor the other? What of the consonant-like transition between the first two syllables of words such as *Diana*, *hyena* and *Guyana* – is there a consonantal y-sound here or not, and by what criteria can this question be answered? And so on. It is enough here to note that a simple assertion about consonants and vowels, if intended as part of a serious description of language, rests on assumptions about categories and criteria of description, assumptions which are theoretical in their import.

When challenging apparent simplicity and teasing out assumptions in this way, one could begin almost anywhere – with a detailed look at what makes a vowel a vowel, with a question about conventional spellings, with a particularly problematic example, among other possibilities. But because language itself is an integrated human activity the line of investigation will lead on into related questions and assumptions. And so it is with the entire domain of phonetics and phonology. Beginning with a broad theoretical framework would mean that essential detail has to be filled in later, while beginning with the details of how sounds are made would mean that other equally essential considerations are inevitably deferred. Thus we ask the reader not just to accept that the progression of this book may not seem ideally logical, but to enjoy the realization that there are limitations on our ability to cut up and neatly package a reality whose parts are interrelated.

Exercises

1 This chapter includes a few examples of discrepancies between spelling and pronunciation in English. For example, *limb* and *hymn* don't look as though they rhyme but they do in fact have the same vowel and final consonant. Add as many examples of such discrepancies as you have time for.

2 As a further exercise in distinguishing between spelling and pronunciation, consider English words which are often misspelled, either in error or for deliberate effect. For example, *separate* is often written as *seperate*, while in brand names *quick* may be written as *kwik*, *clean* as *kleen*, or *ease* as *eez*. Collect more examples of this kind, and in each case try to note whether the respelling seems to bring the written form closer to the pronunciation.

3 This chapter refers to a way of pronouncing English known as RP (Received Pronunciation), the accent that many readers may call 'BBC English' or 'Oxford English'. Of course this is not the accent of most people who speak English (even within Great Britain, let alone outside it) but it remains prestigious. For example, English speakers who have no desire to speak RP themselves may nevertheless expect foreigners to aspire to RP. Ensure that you can identify and recognize RP. In particular, try to note any major points of difference between RP and your own variety of English.

You may find it helpful to study Appendix 1.4 in this connection. But if the symbols used there prove troublesome, you may prefer to tackle it after having worked through later chapters. You will find a question about English vowels in the exercises at the end of chapter 4.

2 Segmental Articulation

This chapter gives a broad account of how speech sounds are made. After a brief introduction (2.1) the chapter begins with a functional overview of how speech is produced (2.2), a simple description of the various parts of the body used in speech (2.3) and some comments on the way in which we describe speech sounds (2.4).

The chapter then examines the means of producing a flow of air (2.5) and the role of the larynx in creating speech sounds (2.6). Subsequent sections turn more particularly to the articulatory nature of vowels (or vowel-like sounds, 2.7 and 2.8) and consonants (2.9).

Various aspects of articulation, concentrating on consonants, are then dealt with:

- the various places in the vocal tract at which consonants are made (2.10)
- the role of tongue position (2.11)
- different manners of consonant articulation (2.12)
- the shaping of constrictions (2.13)
- relative force of articulation (2.14)
- length (2.15)
- the timing of voicing (2.16).

2.1 Introduction

The human vocal apparatus is capable of producing a great variety of noises. Many of these do not count as speech sounds, such as coughs and snores and grunts, but we caution readers against being too narrow in their notion of speech sounds. It would be quite wrong to assume that English, or even Western European languages, are fully representative of phonological possibilities, and the range of sounds which we shall cover is far wider than occurs in any one language. In particular there are sounds, such as the kind of click sound which many English speakers use to express regret or disapproval (sometimes written as *tut* or *tsk*), which Europeans may well assume are not speech sounds, but which do occur in some languages.

In this chapter we will work towards developing a repertoire of all possible speech sounds and a framework in which to describe them – although, as we shall shortly see, we do better to think in terms of human ability to make distinctions or differences in sound, rather than in terms of an inventory of sounds. To this end, we shall examine the function of the vocal apparatus as a speech-producing mechanism, and in the process show how it can be used to make all kinds of sounds.

2.2   A functional overview of the speech production process

We begin with a general functional overview of the process of speech production, but its more technical aspects are dealt with in detail in chapter 6. The human vocal apparatus can be viewed as a kind of mechanism – it has measurable dimensions, such as the distance from the larynx to the lips, it has moving parts such as the tongue, and so on. Figure 2.2.1 gives a simple functional model of this mechanism which omits almost all anatomical detail, but should help the reader through the outline description of the following paragraphs.

To produce sound of any kind, a source of energy is needed. For speech, a flow of air makes it possible to generate sounds, and the volume and pressure of the air supply determine the duration and loudness of sound produced. The majority of speech sounds (in fact *all* in English and Western European languages), use airflow from the lungs for this purpose. As shown in Figure 2.2.1, the respiratory system therefore counts as the energy source, and the lungs form an air reservoir. The lungs are compressed by various respiratory forces, rather like a set of old-fashioned fire bellows. As the lungs are compressed, air flows out, and it is the periodic interruption, constriction and blockage of this airflow which results in the more or less continuous flow of sound which we identify as a sequence of speech sounds.

The airflow can be interrupted periodically by the vocal folds, which are situated in the airway above the lungs and form part of the air valve structure of the larynx. When airflow from the lungs through the windpipe is blocked by the closed vocal folds, air pressure below them builds up. This pressure momentarily forces the folds apart. As the air then flows out through the folds, the local air pressure is reduced and the folds can close again. Air is thus released in short puffs at a periodic rate. This process of vocal fold vibration, known as PHONATION, is similar to the process that produces noise when you inflate a balloon, stretch the neck into a thin aperture, and allow the air to escape through it. The puffs of air created by the vibration of the vocal folds occur at a certain rate or frequency. This frequency is variable and is determined by muscle forces controlling the tension of the vocal folds and by the air pressure below the folds. The frequency is perceived as the PITCH of the voice. Sounds

Segmental Articulation

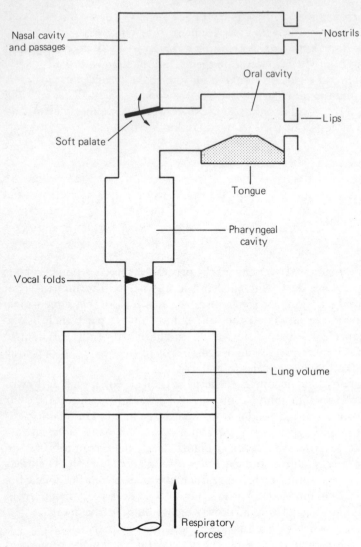

Nasal cavity
and passages

Nostrils

Oral cavity

Lips

Soft palate

Tongue

Pharyngeal
cavity

Vocal folds

Lung volume

Respiratory
forces

FIGURE 2.2.1   Functional model of the vocal tract

which are produced in this way, with air flowing from the lungs through vibrating vocal folds, include all vowels and vowel-like sounds.

These puffs of air constitute an effective sound source but are not in themselves sufficient to produce identifiable speech sounds. The essential additional ingredient is the contribution of the cavities above the vocal folds. These cavities can be opened or closed off and their size and shape can be manipulated in ways that modify the basic sound source, yielding a variety of individually identifiable speech sounds.

A simple example of this process is provided by the three vowel sounds heard in a typical southern English pronunciation of the words *heed*, *hard* and *hoard*.

(Appropriate phonetic symbols for the three vowels are [i:], [a:] and [ɔ:], where the colon is the convention for marking these vowels as relatively long.) In these vowels, the vocal folds vibrate as just described, releasing a periodic train of air puffs. The soft palate (which in normal quiet breathing hangs down to allow free airflow through the nasal cavity and nostrils) is raised, as it usually is during speech to stop or reduce airflow into the nasal cavity. Airflow therefore passes through the throat (pharyngeal cavity) and mouth (oral cavity). The shape, and hence the resonant properties, of these two cavities are controlled by the position of the tongue, the degree of jaw opening, and the shape of the lips. Thus for [i:] in *heed* the tongue is pushed forward and raised in the region just below the hard palate, while the lips are spread. For [a:] in *hard* the tongue is in a relatively neutral or slightly retracted position on the floor of the mouth, the jaw is opened further than for [i:], and the lips are opened in a neutral or natural position. For [ɔ:] in *hoard*, the tongue is retracted, the hump formed in it is raised some way towards the soft palate, and the lips are rounded. Each of these three articulatory positions alters the geometry of the pharyngeal and mouth cavities, and each position has its own characteristic resonant properties. The sound produced by the air puffs from the vibrating vocal folds is modified by these resonant properties, with the result that each vowel sound has a distinctive sound quality. Readers should be able to feel something of the change in articulatory setting if they say each of these three vowel sounds while paying attention to the position of the tongue, jaw and lips; it is also possible to verify the resonant effects of a cavity by producing an [a:] vowel while cupping and uncupping the hands around the lips.

Vowels and vowel-like sounds are made by varying the geometry of the pharyngeal and mouth cavities, but without any major obstruction or impediment to airflow. Consonantal sounds, on the other hand, are generally made by exploiting the articulatory capabilities of the tongue, teeth and lips in such a way that airflow through the mouth cavity is radically constricted or even temporarily blocked.

The [b] of the word *barn*, for example, is known as a STOP, produced as the name implies by transient blockage of the airflow. In this sound, the soft palate is raised to prevent airflow through the nasal cavity, the lips are closed for a fraction of a second, and, during this closure, air pressure builds up in the pharyngeal and mouth cavities. The lips are then parted, releasing the pressure behind them and allowing normal airflow for the vowel which follows. The characteristic sound of this articulatory action is largely due to the rapid changes in the resonant properties of the mouth cavity during the very short interval of time from the point when the lips begin to open to the point when normal vowel articulation has begun.

Other consonantal sounds rely on radical constriction of airflow within the mouth cavity, rather than transient blockage. Thus the [l] in the word *learn* is produced by holding the tip of the tongue against the ridge of flesh immediately behind the front teeth, and allowing airflow to be diverted around one or both sides of the tongue. Such sounds are known as LATERALS. This articulatory configuration again has its own particular resonant properties producing a characteristic quality of sound.

All sounds mentioned so far have relied on airflow through the pharyngeal and oral cavities. It is possible to block the oral cavity, so that air flows through the pharyngeal and nasal cavities, as in the [m] of the word *more*. Such NASAL consonants are produced with the soft palate lowered to allow airflow through the nasal passage, and with the mouth cavity blocked for the duration of the consonant. In this configuration, the unobstructed pharyngeal and nasal cavities and the blocked mouth cavity all contribute to the resonant properties of the sound.

Yet another way of producing consonantal sounds is by setting the articulatory organs in such a way that friction or turbulence is created. The simplest example of a FRICATIVE consonant is [h] as in *hard*. In this fricative, turbulence occurs both at the opening of the vocal folds and throughout the remainder of the airways and cavities through which air flows. In most fricatives, however, the sound is generated by air turbulence at some specific point. Thus the [v] in the word *vine* is produced with the lower lip held lightly against the edge of the upper front teeth, so that turbulence occurs when air is forced through.

In most of the sounds we have mentioned so far, vibration of the vocal folds continues through the sound. All such sounds are called VOICED. But some sounds are VOICELESS: they employ the same kinds of articulatory configurations that we have described for voiced sounds but the airflow is uninterrupted, as the vocal folds are not vibrating. There are now no periodic puffs of air to act as a sound source, and the constriction or interference somewhere in the airways and cavities above the larynx becomes the sound source. In a voiceless fricative, such as [f] in *fine*, for example, the turbulence created when the lower lip is held lightly against the edge of the upper front teeth is the sound source. Thus fricatives can be voiceless or voiced, and voiceless [f] is the counterpart of voiced [v], which uses both vocal fold vibration and the turbulence produced by localized constriction. Compare the words *fine* and *vine*, in which the principal distinguishing feature is the voicing, or vocal fold vibration, during the production of the [v].

Stops are also voiceless if vocal fold vibration does not begin until after the start of the release of the blockage in the mouth cavity. The major distinction between the initial sounds in the words *pat* and *bat*, as pronounced by most native speakers of English, is that in the former, vocal fold vibration begins after the lips have begun to part, and in the latter, the vocal folds are already vibrating when the lips part. (In fact there is more than one simple way of distinguishing between voiced and voiceless stops, but we shall return to this later.)

We have given only the briefest summary of some of the major types of articulatory processes involved in speech production. In normal continuous speech some of these processes occur very rapidly, and may interact with each other as a result. The sound output can show rapid changes of quality, and this dynamic aspect of speech is also important in providing cues that allow listeners to recognize a coherent sequence of speech sounds. And of course normal adult users of language are also aided by their knowledge of their language and their consequent expectations about what are, and are not, likely and acceptable sound sequences forming normal utterances.

2.3   The organs of speech

The term ORGANS OF SPEECH refers to all those parts of the human body which are concerned in various ways with the production of speech. Most of them are only secondarily concerned with speech production – their primary functions are to do with eating, chewing and swallowing food, and respiration. Figure 2.3.1 shows a section through the body indicating the major organs which contribute to the speech process.

The organs of speech shown in figure 2.3.1, namely the lungs, trachea, larynx, the pharyngeal and oral cavities with their component parts, and the nasal passages, constitute as a group what is termed the VOCAL TRACT. For functional and descriptive purposes, the tract is normally divided into two basic parts, one above the larynx, the other below it. Within the larynx itself are the vocal folds: the aperture between the folds is known as the GLOTTIS, and the tract above the glottis is therefore called the SUPRAGLOTTAL vocal tract, and that below it the SUBGLOTTAL vocal tract. The choice of

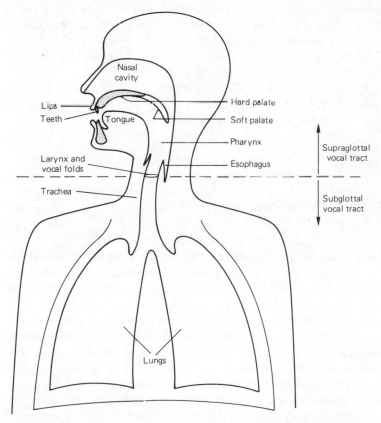

FIGURE 2.3.1   The organs of speech (greatly simplified and not to scale)

this point of division is based on a functional distinction. The respiratory system below the glottis provides the major energy source for producing speech sounds, while the tract above the glottis determines, in general, the phonetic quality of speech sounds. Most phonetic descriptions of speech sounds are primarily concerned with supraglottal activity.

2.4   Describing speech sounds

Despite the fact that speech is a relatively continuous flow, we are accustomed to thinking of it as sounds, or as sequences of sounds. Conceptually, we treat the flow of articulatory movement as a series of segments. Indeed, this is not just a matter of convenience, for the patterned organization of speech into systematic units and structures is fundamental to its nature, distinguishing speech from mere noise.

The rest of this chapter deals with the ways in which speech sounds can be described, using many of the traditional terms of articulatory phonetics, but showing how these terms often conceal considerable problems of description. The chapter explains the ways in which airflow is generated (2.5) and the role of the larynx as a sound source (2.6) before moving to what are usually thought of as the characteristic and distinctive qualities of vowels and consonants (2.7–2.16).

To a large extent, the segmental nature of speech will remain a convenient assumption in this chapter. Chapter 3 will take up the question of defining and delineating discrete segments and will show that many sounds defy simple segmental assumptions.

2.5   Airstream mechanisms

What Pike (1943) and a number of later writers have called 'airstream mechanisms' provide the sources of energy for generating speech sounds, using airflow and pressure in the vocal tract. Following Pike, we can distinguish three basic mechanisms, namely LUNG AIRFLOW, GLOTTALIC AIRFLOW, and VELARIC AIRFLOW.

LUNG AIRFLOW and the respiratory cycle are basic to speech production. In principle, air flowing either into or out of the lungs during the respiratory cycle may be used in generating speech sounds, and the nature of the sound produced will depend on what is happening in the vocal tract above the trachea – on the action of the larynx and on how the rest of the tract is constricted or modified in shape. The two mechanisms (outward and inward lung air) are often referred to as EGRESSIVE PULMONIC and INGRESSIVE PULMONIC. Outward lung airflow is the normal mode: it is easier to control and requires less overall articulatory effort in sustained speech, largely because speakers can exploit the relaxation pressure available when the lungs are relatively full, and can thus expel air in a slow, controlled fashion.

An egressive pulmonic airstream is the norm in all languages, and languages as diverse as English, Spanish, Indonesian and Chinese use no other mechanism. While it is possible to produce speech using ingressive lung airflow – readers will be aware of the possibility of uttering a gasp or groan or even intelligible vowels with air drawn inward into the lungs – no language in the world seems to use ingressive lung airflow as a distinctive feature of particular speech sounds during normal articulation. There are, however, languages that use glottalic and velaric mechanisms systematically.

The GLOTTALIC AIRFLOW mechanism (sometimes called 'pharyngeal') uses air above the glottis. The glottis is closed, and the larynx is moved up and down the pharynx, under the control of the extrinsic laryngeal muscles, to initiate airflow. Since the glottis is closed, subglottal air is not involved and the larynx thus acts rather like a plunger or piston in a cylinder. If the larynx moves upwards in this way, it can generate an egressive glottalic airstream; and moving downwards, an ingressive glottalic airstream.

Egressive glottalic sounds are commonly known as EJECTIVES, sometimes as 'glottalized stops'. The upward movement of the larynx, with the glottis closed, compresses the air above and forces airflow outward. Readers can attempt such sounds by taking a breath and holding it (thus shutting the glottis), then uttering [p], [t], [k] or [s] without opening the glottis, using only air compressed by raising the larynx. Some speakers of English sometimes produce word-final ejectives, for example at the end of the word *sick*. In the flow of articulation, sounds produced with an egressive glottalic airstream generally precede or follow sounds using normal lung airflow, since the airflow generated by the laryngeal movement is relatively weak and of short duration.

Sounds using an ingressive glottalic airflow are commonly known as IMPLOSIVES. The piston action of the larynx is generally less effective in producing ingressive airflow than egressive, partly because of the difficulty of maintaining a tightly closed glottis during the downward movement of the larynx. As a result, there is often some upward leakage of lung air sufficient to cause involuntary phonation or voicing. According to Ladefoged (1971) this upward leakage may offset the suction action of the downward larynx movement so that there is little or no inward airflow through the mouth, even to such an extent that the net airflow is actually egressive. The sounds can still be counted as implosives, since an important part of their sound quality is due to the effects of rapid larynx lowering during their production.

Ejective stops are found in languages of the Caucasus area, such as Georgian, as well as in a variety of languages of Africa and the Americas. Ejective fricatives are not as common. Implosives are found in a number of African and American languages. The West African language Hausa, for example, has an ejective velar stop (contrasting with pulmonic [k]), an ejective sibilant fricative (contrasting with [s]), and bilabial and alveolar implosives (contrasting with [b] and [d]). Maidu (from central California) has bilabial and alveolar ejectives and implosives (alongside pulmonic [p] and [t]) as well as a velar ejective stop and an ejective counterpart of the affricate [ts]. Basic discussion of sounds using glottalic airflow can be found in Ladefoged (1971); Greenberg (1966, ch. 2) and Maddieson (1984, ch. 7) give examples and some observations about the frequency of occurrence of glottalic sounds; and Pinkerton (1986) usefully combines an instrumental analysis of glottalic stops in some languages of Guatemala with a review of Greenberg's predictions about how glottalic sounds function in languages.

VELARIC (or oral) AIRFLOW is generated entirely within the oral cavity, by raising the back of the tongue to make firm contact with the soft palate. Air in front of this tongue closure may then be sealed off by closing the lips or by pressing the sides and tip of the tongue against the roof of the mouth behind the teeth. Although it is possible to generate both egressive and ingressive airflow using this oral air supply, only ingressive airflow is normally used in speech. Sounds produced in this way are commonly known as CLICKS. The simplest form of click is made with the lips, where the action of parting the lips will (with lowering of the jaw) increase oral cavity volume sufficiently to cause a drop in air pressure inside the mouth, causing air to flow in. The action is that of a light kiss. Alternatively, air is trapped in a small chamber created entirely by the tongue itself. The tongue is in effect sucked off the roof of the mouth. When the tongue is moved downwards, the air chamber above it is enlarged and the pressure drop in the trapped air generates a short but quite strong inflow of air as the closure is released. It is this rapid and rather turbulent inflow which causes the characteristic click sound. Click articulation requires complex interaction of the intrinsic and extrinsic tongue muscles, and the tongue can in fact be released in different ways, sufficient to create different click sounds. Readers will be familiar with the kind of click made when the tongue tip is reasonably forward, for the sound is commonly used to express regret or disapproval (usually repeated and sometimes written as *tsk tsk* or *tut tut*); a different click sound, sometimes used by English speakers to urge a horse, is achieved by pulling the tongue down at one or both sides rather than at the tip.

Click sounds are found in rather few languages (about 1 per cent of the world's languages according to Maddieson 1986, p. 115). They are characteristic of the Khoisan languages of the Kalahari area in southern Africa (of which the most famous is probably Hottentot) but are also found in Bantu languages such as Zulu and Xhosa (Westermann and Ward 1933, ch. 19; Ladefoged 1971, ch. 6). In these languages, clicks are consonants functioning as part of the speech sound system (unlike the *tsk tsk* used to express disapproval, which cannot be considered a speech sound in the same way).

We must also recognize COMBINATORY AIRFLOW PROCESSES, for the muscular systems used in the three airstream mechanisms are autonomous enough to function in partial combination. We noted above, for example, that egressive lung airflow in conjunction with ingressive glottalic airflow results in phonatory action while the larynx is descending. The egressive velaric and egressive pulmonic airstreams can also be activated simultaneously to produce, for instance, click sounds which have a velar nasal sound (as at the end of *sing*) imposed upon them. Such nasal click sounds do occur in languages that exploit the velaric airstream mechanism.

Finally, it should be noted that it is possible to use air from the stomach to generate sound, as in an audible belch. With considerable practice this mechanism, which can be described as egressive esophageal, can be used as a controlled substitute for egressive lung airflow. The technique, sometimes taught to those who have undergone laryngectomy, consists of swallowing air and then belching it out again.

Further discussion of airstream processes can be found in Pike (1943), Catford (1977) and Ladefoged and Traill (1980).

2.6 Modes of phonation

The term PHONATION refers principally to vocal fold vibration but can also be taken to include all the means by which the larynx functions as a source of sound, not all of which involve vibration of the folds in a strict sense. It is also important to bear in mind that besides this role as a sound source, the larynx has two other functions in speech: it can generate an airstream (yielding glottalic consonants, 2.5 above) and it can serve as an articulator (in glottal consonants, 2.10 below).

The complex laryngeal musculature is such that the vocal folds can be manipulated in highly diverse ways, but it is convenient to think in terms of a set of categories known as PHONATION MODES. These categories of laryngeal action are defined not just by observation of the physiology of the larynx, but by reference to distinctions that appear to be relevant in the world's languages. Thus the categories are not simple and direct reflections of different ways of using the larynx, and, as in many other areas of phonetic description, not all the details of physiology are relevant to the categories that are appropriate for describing speech.

Catford (1964, 1968, 1977) is responsible for a highly detailed set of categories: his emphasis is on what he terms 'anthropophonic' possibilities, that is on comprehensive coverage of all the articulatory possibilities. Laver (1968, 1980) offers a complete theoretical and practical descriptive system for laryngeal (and other) aspects of voice quality. Both accounts exploit combinations of a series of basic laryngeal settings. Catford, for example, defines some 13 phonation modes derived from four types of glottal stricture and three locations of phonatory activity. Other linguists (such as Halle and Stevens 1971 and Ladefoged 1971) work with rather fewer categories, as it is evident that real languages actually do not exploit all of the distinctions which a phonetician may recognize on articulatory or physiological grounds. The following account focuses on the distinctions that do seem relevant in language, and recognizes five phonation modes, namely VOICELESSNESS, WHISPER, BREATHY VOICE, VOICE and CREAK. The distinction between voiceless and voiced sounds applies in a high proportion of the world's languages (though it is certainly not universal); distinctive use of breathy voice and creak is much less common; and whisper could arguably be omitted as nonlinguistic, but it is included here both to underline its difference from voicelessness and breathy voice, and because of its widespread use (as in English) as a distinctive style of speech rather than as a feature of specific sounds.

VOICELESS means the absence of any phonation. The vocal folds are held far enough apart to allow a laminar (or non-turbulent) airflow through the glottis. If the airflow is more than moderate, even this open setting of the glottis will generate turbulence (which in fact allows the glottis to function as a sound source for a glottal fricative such as the [h] in English *hand* or *head*). Catford's figures (1977) suggest that voiceless articulation is maintained provided that airflow does not exceed 200–350 cm^3 per second (depending on the degree of glottal opening). Vocal fold abduction is largely a function of the posterior cricoarytenoid muscle action, and the opening of the glottis is usually greater in the voiceless mode than in any other mode used in speech. Ladefoged (1971) suggests that the opening for voiceless articulation is similar to that required in normal breathing. Voiceless sounds in English include the stops [p] (as in *pea*), [t] (as in *tea*), [k] (as in *key*) and fricatives [f] (as in *fee*), [θ] (as in *theme*), [s] (as in *see*). Many of the world's languages have similar sounds contrasting with their voiced counterparts: the distinction between voiceless [f] and [s] and voiced [v] and [z], for instance, is found in languages as diverse as French, Greek, Russian, Hungarian, Turkish, Vietnamese and Zulu.

WHISPER requires far greater constriction than the voiceless setting of the glottis, and it is generally achieved by adducting the ligamental vocal folds while maintaining an opening between the arytenoid cartilages, through which the bulk of airflow is forced. This setting can be created by the lateral cricoarytenoid muscles (contributing to medial compression of the ligamental folds) and the posterior cricoarytenoid muscle (contributing to abduction of the arytenoids). Adduction of the false vocal folds may also help to narrow the glottal airflow path, and to inhibit true vocal fold vibration (Sawashima et al. 1969).

The characteristic consequence of the whisper setting is that there is significant turbulence at the glottis. This functions as a sound source which can then be modified by articulatory activity in the supraglottal vocal tract. As the area of glottal opening is small, this mode can provide turbulence with relatively low airflow rates (from about 25 cm^3 per second according to Catford 1977). Whisper thus exploits a usable sound source without demanding a large air supply from the respiratory system; but it does also require considerable overall laryngeal tension. Readers should be able to verify the degree of tension by changing back and forth between whisper and quiet breathing.

In BREATHY VOICE, normal vocal fold vibration is accompanied by some continuous turbulent airflow. This occurs when glottal closure during the vibratory cycle is not complete (hence the term 'breathy'). Usually the arytenoid cartilages remain slightly apart while the ligamental folds vibrate; in some speakers, ligamental fold closure may also be weak or incomplete, accounting for part or even most of the turbulent air leakage.

There is some terminological inconsistency around this kind of phonation. We retain the term 'breathy voice', which is relatively widespread and has reasonably obvious relevance; but Heffner (1964) and Ladefoged (1971, 1982) use the term 'murmur', and Catford (1968, 1977) and Laver (1980) use 'whispery voice'. For

Catford, 'breathy voice' is a phonation mode with a very high rate of airflow, in which, according to his description, the vocal folds 'flap in the breeze'. See Sprigg (1978) for a general review of phonation description (including some criticism of Catford).

Several languages of South Asia make a systematic distinction between breathy voice and normal voiced phonation: in transliterations of Hindi and Urdu, for example, spellings such as *bh* and *gh* indicate plosives with breathy voiced release which are distinct from voiced *b* and *g*. In some languages, such as Tamang (a Sino-Tibetan language spoken in Nepal), vowels may have distinctive breathy voice. In English, breathy voicing is not exploited in the same way but is an identifiable feature of some speakers, either as part of their personal voice quality or as a result of some laryngeal disorder.

VOICE refers to normal vocal fold vibration occurring along most or all of the length of the glottis. Physiologically, there is a continuum of subtypes within this category (Ladefoged 1971). At one end of the continuum, approaching breathy voice, the muscles controlling vocal fold adduction are relatively relaxed; at the other end, tension in the musculature begins to limit the vibration of the folds and voice verges on laryngealized or creaky voice (described below). In a language such as English, individuals normally exploit a range of laryngeal muscle settings, constrained by such factors as the degree of vocal effort needed (e.g. shouting versus very quiet speech) and physiological and emotional state (e.g. tiredness or excitement). The consequent variation in voice quality can be described impressionistically as ranging from 'dark' or 'mellow' (the most relaxed end of the range of muscle settings), to 'bright' or 'sharp' or 'hard' (the most tense end of the muscle setting range).

All languages have voiced sounds, and voicing can be considered normal for sounds such as vowels and nasal and lateral consonants. In English, for example, vowels are always voiced, and nasal and lateral consonants are voiced unless devoiced by assimilation (as in e.g. *play* or *clay*, where the [l] may be voiceless by assimilation to the preceding voiceless stop). But the precise settings of the larynx that can be regarded as producing 'normal voice' depend not only on the language, or regional or social dialect, but also on the individual (Laver 1968, Laver and Trudgill 1979).

CREAK is a phonation mode characterized by low frequency vibration of the vocal folds. The folds open only for a very short time and often quite irregularly from cycle to cycle of vibration. It has also been variously described as 'laryngealization' (Ladefoged 1971, 1982), 'pulsation' (Peterson and Shoup 1966a), 'vocal fry' (Wendahl et al. 1963), and 'trillization' (Pike 1943, Sprigg 1978). There is some uncertainty among researchers about exactly how creak is produced, but the majority view is that the arytenoids are tensely adducted, and that only the anterior part of the ligamental folds vibrates. According to Catford (1977), subglottal pressure and airflow rates may be quite low, and the ligamental folds tightly closed but not greatly tensed.

In addition to these five phonation modes we must allow for COMBINATORY PHONATION MODES. These include BREATHY CREAK, in which creak is accompanied by some turbulent air leakage to produce breathiness, and VOICED CREAK, in which creak and normal voice are combined. Voiced creak is sometimes referred to as 'laryngealization', but this term should be treated with caution, as some writers use it to describe simple creak, and others use it to refer to a complex articulation in which complete glottal closure follows or accompanies some other articulatory gesture. For full details of the anatomy of the larynx and its various phonatory settings, see sections 6.5 and 6.6 below.

2.7 Vocalic sounds

What we commonly think of as vowel sounds are better described, when considering their articulation, as vocalic sounds. (It is often convenient to use the word 'vowel', but for some purposes it is necessary to distinguish between vowels and vocalic sounds, and we shall come to the reasons for that in chapter 3.) Vocalic sounds are produced by egressive pulmonic airflow through vibrating or constricted vocal folds in the larynx and through the vocal tract, and the sound generated at the larynx is modified by the cavities of the tract. The size and shape of the tract can be varied, principally by positioning of the tongue and lips; and as the tract is varied, so the perceived phonetic quality of the vocalic sound is altered. Thus the two most fundamental articulatory manoeuvres in producing various vocalic sounds are the shape and position of the tongue, and the shape and degree of protrusion of the lips. It is the tongue that largely determines the geometry of the oral and pharyngeal cavities, and the lips that control the shape and area of the front of the vocal tract. Lip protrusion also provides a means of extending the overall length of the vocal tract.

The major challenge in describing the articulation of vocalic sounds is to define the position of the tongue. The tongue moves within a spatial continuum without making any significant constriction in the area surrounding the midline of the oral cavity. As a result, we cannot locate a specific point of constriction or blockage, and phoneticians have had to struggle to devise a satisfactory way of plotting the position of the tongue (Ladefoged 1967, ch. 2).

Traditionally, vowels are plotted on a two-dimensional diagram representing the articulatory space: the vertical axis is tongue HEIGHT, and the horizontal axis is tongue FRONTING (or backness or retraction). There is no handy landmark on the tongue to serve as a point of reference in this mapping, but the traditional procedure has been to try to locate the highest point on the dorsum of the tongue. The height and fronting of this point are then plotted relative to some external reference point such as the atlas vertebra. An early example of the procedure is found in the frontispiece photographs in Jones (1960, first published 1918). The articulatory positions of some Australian English vowels, defined similarly, are shown in figure 2.7.1 (based on lateral X-ray photographs by Bernard 1970b). Both Bernard and Lindau (1978) describe this measurement procedure in detail; and Lindau extends it to account for other aspects of tongue posture.

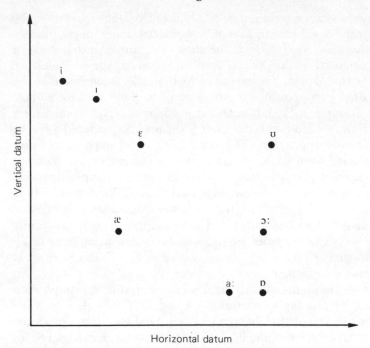

FIGURE 2.7.1   Articulatory positions of some Australian English vowels
Adapted from: Bernard 1970b.

Assuming that this method gives a valid measure of vocalic articulation, it is, however, impractical to take X-ray pictures for every vowel in every language and dialect that we would like to describe. As an alternative, we can use some form of acoustic analysis of the sound itself (chapter 7 below), but this may also be impractical because of the equipment needed for recording and analysis. Another possibility is to base the description on auditory impressions. The disadvantage here is precisely that it is to some degree impressionistic: the observer needs to be well trained in phonetics, and even then will still be influenced by conventional terminology and by linguistic experience, since none of us is ever entirely free of perceptual bias shaped by the language(s) which we happen to speak.

In an effort to bring accuracy and objectivity into impressionistic vowel descriptions, nineteenth-century phoneticians such as Alexander Melville Bell tried to define standard categories of vowel quality and associated articulatory positions. The most successful outcome of this idea, and one still in use for vowel description, is the set of CARDINAL VOWELS devised by Daniel Jones. These vowels are intended to serve as standard reference points, or 'cardinal' points in Jones's terminology.

The cardinal vowels are not drawn from any particular language or languages but are derived from a kind of grid imposed upon the space in which the tongue moves. There are 16 cardinal vowels in all, eight primary and eight secondary. In each set of eight there are two vowels which represent the outer limits of vocalic articulation, the boundaries beyond which vocalic sounds cannot be produced: if the tongue exceeds these boundaries, it will create constriction in the vocal tract sufficient to generate a consonant rather than a vowel. In the primary cardinal vowel set, the first reference vowel is cardinal 1, produced with the tongue as high and as far forward in the mouth (towards the hard palate) as it is possible to go without causing audible friction. (The nearest example in English is an extremely raised and fronted form of the vowel in *heed*.) The second reference vowel is cardinal 5, produced with the tongue as low and retracted as possible. (The nearest English example is an extremely lowered and retracted form of the vowel in *hard*.) The reason for choosing these two vowels as starting points is that they are the easiest (or perhaps least difficult) to locate by the feel of the tongue. From cardinal 1, Jones then defines cardinals 2, 3 and 4 as vowels for which the tongue is still fronted but is lowered in equal steps. Thus 1 and 2, 2 and 3, and 3 and 4 are supposed to be auditorily equidistant. The back vowels of the series are similarly formed, starting from cardinal 5 and raising the tongue in a retracted position such that 5, 6, 7 and 8 are again equally spaced from lowest to highest.

Cardinal vowels 1 to 5 are produced with the lips in a neutral or spread position (most spread for 1 and progressing to neutral for 4 and 5). Cardinals 6 to 8 are produced with the lips rounded. The eight secondary cardinal vowels are produced exactly as the primary set, except that the lip positions are reversed: cardinal 9, for example, has the same tongue position as cardinal 1, but with lips rounded instead of spread; cardinal 16 has the same tongue position as cardinal 8, but with lips spread instead of rounded.

The cardinal vowels are thus intended to represent the most peripheral tongue positions for vocalic sounds. They stand, so to speak, on the boundary of vocalic articulation, and it should be possible to locate any vowel in any language somewhere within the area encompassed by this boundary. Jones took the tongue positions for cardinals 1, 4, 5 and 8 from lateral X-ray photographs of his own productions of these vowels. He then constructed a quadrilateral with these four vowels at the corners (Jones 1960, pp. 36–7). The vowel quadrilateral is irregular – somewhat like a diamond tilting to the left – but a slightly simplified version of it (figure 2.7.2) is now standard.

The vowels of particular languages are commonly placed on a vowel quadrilateral to locate their phonetic qualities relative to the cardinal vowels, but this strategy of description must be treated with caution. The fundamental worry about the cardinal vowel system is that it confuses articulatory and auditory properties. Note that the two reference points in the system (cardinals 1 and 5) are established on physiological grounds – they are at the outer limits of tongue movement for vocalic articulation. On the other hand, intermediate vowels are determined by what Jones calls equal 'acoustic' (i.e. auditory) intervals along the continuum. Despite this, Jones implies that the tongue positions of the cardinal vowels also progress in equal steps, and he describes the cardinal vowel diagram itself in terms of tongue position (as do many linguists after him). Now it may seem reasonable to suppose that changes in articulatory setting and changes in

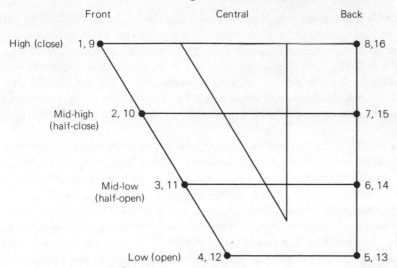

FIGURE 2.7.2   The cardinal vowel diagram

auditory quality go hand in hand; and that one can therefore judge articulatory position from auditory perception. In fact Ladefoged (1967) has shown that the assumption is not fully warranted. He examined X-ray photographs of a complete set of cardinal vowels (published in 1929, relatively soon after Jones's original work) and measured the tongue positions. His measurements reveal that the front vowels (cardinals 1–4) are indeed roughly equidistant, but not the back vowels (5–8): tongue height is actually identical for cardinals 6 and 7, which are also much farther from 8 than they are from 5. Lindau (1978) provides data to show that back vowels in natural languages similarly fail to conform to the cardinal idealization.

A second difficulty with the cardinal vowel system is that the specifications of tongue position suggest an invariant tongue position for each vowel quality. But, as Lindau (1978) has pointed out, X-rays of vowels in actual languages show that speakers generally have several possible ways of producing a given auditory vowel quality. Moreover, this is not just a matter of variation in tongue posture, for vowel quality is also affected by changes in jaw aperture and larynx height. Experimental investigations by Lindblom and Sundberg (1971), Ladefoged et al. (1972), Riordan (1977) and Lindblom et al. (1979) all clearly show that speakers are capable of a considerable degree of compensatory articulation to produce a single desired auditory result in vowel quality. There is thus no reason to assume a one-to-one matching of articulatory position and auditory quality.

A third problem concerns the definition of tongue position. In the classic formulation, tongue height is taken to mean the height of the point which is closest to the roof of the mouth. But tongue position could be measured in various ways, and there is no principled reason why the location of maximum tongue height should correspond directly and systematically to vowel quality (Lindau 1978, Wood 1979). Recent research suggests that it is the location of the major constriction formed by the tongue, rather than tongue height itself, which is a much more direct determinant of perceived vowel quality. Overall, it appears that the measures needed in vowel descriptions are rather more complex than the traditional one of tongue position; and this helps to explain some of the weaknesses in the supposedly physiological basis of the cardinal vowel system (Ladefoged 1967, Harshman et al. 1977).

Given these difficulties, the cardinal vowels are best taken to be auditory qualities rather than articulatory specifications. Understood in that way, they can serve a useful purpose in helping phoneticians to identify vowel qualities and in bringing some measure of objectivity into auditory judgements. The continuing use of articulatory labels for auditory qualities is unfortunate, but there is no easy alternative, since we lack a well-developed perceptual terminology. The fact that many phoneticians have used the system with a considerable degree of consistency is largely due to thorough training. Jones himself stressed 'ear training' and the importance of learning the cardinal vowels from a competent teacher, or at second best from a recording. The only 'standard' recording of the cardinal vowels is by Jones himself, and he trained a number of students at University College London, many of whom later became senior phoneticians in other British universities, so that something of a direct oral tradition has been maintained, at least in Britain.

The lip position of vocalic sounds raises far fewer difficulties than tongue location, if only because the lips are externally visible. We have already seen that cardinal vowels may have SPREAD, NEUTRAL or ROUNDED lips, and figure 2.7.3 illustrates these three settings. The difference between spread and neutral lip positions can generally be associated with vowel height: while a high vowel may have spread lips (as cardinal 1 does), a lower vowel will tend to have a more neutral lip posture, chiefly because the larger jaw aperture will tend to produce a more neutral lip position (unless the lips are deliberately rounded). For this reason, and because few if any languages actually exploit a distinctive difference between spread and neutral lips, the two positions are often united under the label UNROUNDED, which underlines the contrast with the ROUNDED lip position. Lip rounding may include some degree of lip protrusion, and there is commonly more protrusion in back rounded vowels than in front rounded vowels. According to Catford (1977), this may be motivated by the need to preserve the auditory impression of fronting in front rounded vowels.

Conventional symbols for the primary and secondary cardinal vowels are listed in table 2.7.1. It should be emphasized again that the cardinal vowels are not derived from English or any other language: the sample words are intended only as helpful approximations. Figure 2.7.4 shows the vowel symbols of table 2.7.1 on a cardinal vowel diagram. Figure 2.7.5 shows some English vowels as phonetic symbols mapped on to a cardinal vowel diagram. The vowels are based on Gimson (1980) and represent British Received Pronunciation (RP).

Some additional modifiers, or DIACRITICS, serve two functions: the first is to locate a vowel within the auditory space, relative to the cardinal vowel closest to it; the

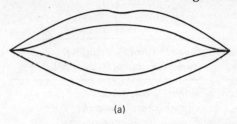

(a)

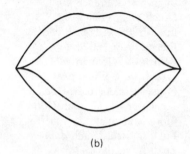

(b)

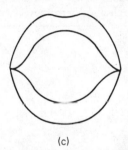

(c)

FIGURE 2.7.3 Lip positions in vowel articulation: (a) spread; (b) neutral; (c) rounded

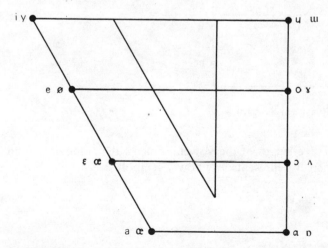

FIGURE 2.7.4 Cardinal vowel symbols located on the diagram of figure 2.7.2

Table 2.7.1   Cardinal vowel symbols

Cardinal vowel no.	Symbol	Lip position	Sample words illustrating approximate vowel quality
1	[i]	unrounded	English *beat*, French *si*
2	[e]	unrounded	French *chez*, Italian *che*
3	[ɛ]	unrounded	English *bet*, German *wenn*
4	[a]	unrounded	English *spa*, French *la*
5	[ɑ]	unrounded	Dutch *dam*, French *las*
6	[ɔ]	rounded	English *hawk*, French *côte*
7	[o]	rounded	French *beau*, Italian *lo*
8	[u]	rounded	French *ou*, German *gut*
9	[y]	rounded	French *tu*, German *für*
10	[ø]	rounded	French *eux*, German *Goethe*
11	[œ]	rounded	French *heure*, German *Götter*
12	[Œ]	rounded	(not distinctive)
13	[ɒ]	rounded	English *hock*, Dutch *dom*
14	[ʌ]	unrounded	English *but*, *luck*
15	[ɤ]	unrounded	Vietnamese *ờ*
16	[ɯ]	unrounded	Japanese *u*, Vietnamese *ừ*

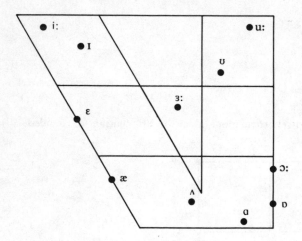

FIGURE 2.7.5   English vowels: typical RP values

second is to indicate the relative length of the vowel. Some of the commonly used diacritics are as follows (where V represents any vowel symbol):

V̬ or V^ – raised with respect to V

V̬ or V^ – lowered with respect to V

V̖ or V< – fronted with respect to V

V or V⟩ – retracted with respect to V

V̵   · – centralized with respect to V

V·   – half long, or slightly lengthened

V: – long

The use of symbols with diacritics to represent fairly precise estimations of vowel quality is sometimes known as NARROW phonetic transcription. It is not always necessary or possible to include all the detail of a narrow transcription, and it may be sufficient to make a BROAD transcription using the nearest appropriate cardinal symbols with few or no diacritics. For this reason many of the symbols have come to have conventional values in particular languages: cardinal 14, for example, is regularly used to represent the English vowel of *but* and *luck*, even though this vowel is central rather than back in many varieties of English, including RP. Cardinal 8 may likewise be used to transcribe the high back vowel of Japanese (which is actually unrounded rather than rounded) and the vowel of Australian English *boot* and *food* (which is rather more central than back).

The 16 cardinal vowel symbols have been supplemented by some additional symbols (table 2.7.2). These are technically redundant, since they could be replaced by cardinal vowels with diacritics; but they represent particular vowels for which it is judged convenient to have a distinct symbol. Contrary to the spirit of the cardinal system, some of them are conventionally understood to be inherently short or long.

In the description of languages, it is sometimes sufficient to represent the vowel sounds in a general auditory space without following the precise format of the cardinal system. Such displays may retain the quasi-articulatory dimensions of height and fronting, but are often intended to show relative differences in phonetic quality among members of a vowel *system* in a particular language or dialect. For this purpose, much of the phonetic detail can be judged irrelevant. Figure 2.7.6 displays the vowel system of Australian English in such a way.

Vowel systems vary greatly in their complexity from language to language. English happens to be relatively rich in vowel contrasts, with the added complexity that the vowel system is by no means uniform across the English-speaking world. Australian English, as shown in figure 2.7.6, represents one of the richer systems; note for instance that the distinction between the vowels of *look* and *Luke* is not universal, notably not in Scotland. RP (and the English of south-eastern England in general) is systematically comparable to Australian, although the precise quality of many of the vowels is quite different.

Most of the world's languages have rather fewer vowels, and some, including Classical Arabic and some Australian Aboriginal languages, have only three distinctive vowels. In a three-vowel system, the vowels are usually towards the outer edges of the vowel space, in the general region of cardinals 1, 4/5 and 8, i.e.

i   u
      a

Segmental Articulation

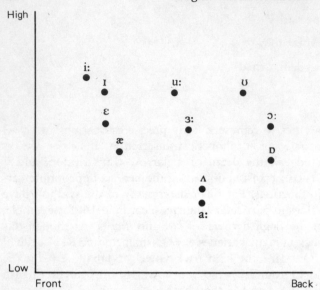

FIGURE 2.7.6   Australian English vowel system

Table 2.7.2   Additional vowel symbols

ɨ	high central unrounded vowel as in New Zealand English pronunciation of *pit* or *six*; value of Russian Ы
ʉ	high central rounded vowel as in Scottish pronunciation of *put*
I	centralized version of cardinal 1, usually understood to be a short 'lax' vowel, as in RP English *pit*
ɩ	alternative symbol for I
ʊ	centralized version of cardinal 8, usually understood to be a short 'lax' vowel, as in RP English *put*
ω	alternative symbol for ʊ
Y	centralized version of cardinal 9, usually understood to be a short 'lax' vowel, as in German *fünf*
æ	front unrounded vowel between cardinals 3 and 4, as in RP English *pat*
ə	central unrounded vowel, known as schwa: used in RP and similar varieties of English to represent the unstressed or 'indeterminate' vowel, as initial in *about* or final in *China*; also used to represent the (stressed) vowel of *cup* or *luck* as pronounced in North American English
3	long central unrounded vowel, equivalent to lengthened schwa, as heard in RP English *bird* or *hurt*

Five-vowel systems are widespread and are often similarly distributed. A common pattern (found, for example, in Spanish, Modern Greek, Maori and other Polynesian languages, and in Swahili and some of the other Bantu languages of eastern and southern Africa) can be represented as follows:

i   u
e   o
                a

Patterning is also revealed in other ways. For example, vowel length is often exploited in such a way that each short vowel is matched by a long vowel. In several Australian Aboriginal languages, for instance, we have

i   i: u   u:
        a   a:

So far as lip rounding is concerned, languages appear to favour unrounded lip position for front vowels and rounded for back vowels. (This serves to enhance the auditory difference between front and back vowels, although the rounding of back vowels is not always very prominent.) Few languages distinguish unrounded back vowels from rounded back vowels, and where rounded front vowels occur, they are normally found in addition to front unrounded vowels and not instead of them. German, for example, has the following long vowels (and some other Western European languages such as French and Dutch are broadly comparable in that they distinguish front unrounded, front rounded and back rounded vowels):

i: y: u:
e: ø: o:
                a:

Lindblom (1986) provides a brief but useful survey of 'some facts' about vowel systems as well as some discussion of how languages exploit the 'vowel space'. His paper includes references to both classic and recent work on universal aspects of vowel systems. Maddieson (1984, ch. 9) reviews data from a variety of languages to support the hypothesis that vowels tend to be evenly dispersed over the available 'space'.

In most languages vowels are normally voiced. Conventions for symbolizing other modes of phonation (2.6 above) are not well established, but breathy voice may be signalled by two dots beneath the main symbol – e.g. [a̤] – and creak by a tilde beneath the main symbol – e.g. [a̰] (cf. Ladefoged 1982, pp. 128–9, 256). A voiceless or whispered vowel may be symbolized by a diacritic used to indicate voicelessness more generally, namely a small subscript circle – e.g. [ḁ].

Vocalic sounds are normally produced with an oral airstream. That is, the velum is raised, preventing major airflow through the nasal cavities, although there may be some nasal 'leakage' if relatively little muscular effort is used to raise the velum. By contrast, a vowel may be distinctively NASALIZED when the velum is deliberately lowered to ensure substantial airflow through the nasal cavities. The nasal cavities are then said to be coupled to the oral and pharyngeal cavities, and the effect of the coupling is an audible nasalized quality. Nasalized vowels are found in a fair number of languages (French, Portuguese, Hindi and Burmese among others), usually as a subset of the oral vowels. French, for example, has four nasalized vowels alongside some twelve oral vowels: the four nasalized vowels are heard in the phrase *un bon vin blanc* 'a good white wine', and the contrast between oral and nasalized vowels is evident in pairs of words such as *beau* 'fine' versus *bon* 'good', and *bas* 'low' versus *banc* 'bench'. (For further remarks on nasalization see 3.3 below.)

There are other articulatory variables which affect vowel quality. One commonly cited is tenseness, although the notion that vowels can be validly described as tense or lax is controversial. Tenseness is generally described as an overall tightening of vocal tract musculature, associated with definite or forceful articulatory action. A tense vowel is therefore likely to be longer and more peripheral in quality than a corresponding lax vowel. Examples often quoted from English (especially American English) are the tense vowels in *beat* and *boot* compared with their lax counterparts in *bit* and *put*. Stevens et al. (1966) report instrumental evidence to support the nature of the distinction, and MacNeilage and Sholes (1964) note greater tongue muscle activity in tense vowels. Appealing to cine-radiographic evidence, Perkell (1969) suggests that the tongue attains a more stable and definite position in vowels that are judged to be tense. He also comments, however, that it is not clear that there is a distinct articulatory mechanism or strategy to account for what is impressionistically reckoned as tenseness. Ladefoged implies that tenseness may be a matter of pharynx width: if the tongue root is moved forward, it is possible to widen the pharynx without any effective alteration in tongue height. When the pharynx is widened in this way, the tongue is bunched along its length and therefore – on one interpretation of the term – 'tensed'. Ladefoged draws on data from Twi which, like a number of other West African languages, has two sets of vowels apparently distinguished by pharynx width (Ladefoged 1982, pp. 206–7; Lindau 1979). But he also notes that Twi speakers seem to use different methods of widening the pharynx: some advance the tongue root, others rely more on lowering the larynx.

We will avoid the simple labels 'tense' and 'lax' while noting that something like WIDENED PHARYNX or ADVANCED TONGUE ROOT is essential in the description of at least some of the world's languages. The labels 'tense' and 'lax' should be treated cautiously, given their apparent articulatory implications, for vowels that are often described as tense and lax may be distinct in several ways: the English vowels in *beat* and *bit* (in some varieties of English) may differ in pharynx width and perhaps also in tongue tension, but they also differ in length and tongue position. It may well be appropriate, in the description of a specific language, to subsume a number of differences under the tense–lax distinction. But in that case, 'tense' is likely to mean different things in different languages (or may even mean different things for different vowels within one language), and it becomes all the more unreliable as an articulatory label.

2.8 Duration and glide in vocalic articulations

We have already referred briefly to vowel LENGTH (or duration) in the preceding section. To some extent, length is dependent on, or conditioned by, other factors, in particular by the quality of the vowel and by consonants adjacent to the vowel.

All other things being equal, certain vowels tend to be longer than others. Lehiste (1976) speaks of the INTRINSIC duration of a vowel. Thus low vowels tend to be intrinsically longer than high vowels, because of the greater overall articulatory movement and biomechanical effort required to produce the lower vowels, particularly where major tongue and jaw movements are needed.

The effects of adjacent consonants on vowel duration are rather more complex, and it is not always easy to distinguish the influence of an adjacent consonant from a feature of pronunciation that is simply peculiar to the language concerned. In English, for example, vowels followed by voiced stops and fricatives are considerably longer than those followed by voiceless consonants: compare *feed* and *feet* or *fad* and *fat*. But while this may strike speakers of English as a natural and inevitable effect, lengthening before voiced consonants turns out not to be a universal feature – at least not to the same extent as in English. On the other hand, the point of articulation of neighbouring consonants does seem to have an inevitable effect on the duration of a vowel. If a consonant involves tongue movement, more time will be needed to establish the consonantal articulation, and the adjacent vowel will be longer. Thus vowels are likely to be longer before alveolars or velars than before bilabials, for example.

Length is not merely a conditioned feature of vowels, however, but can also function distinctively. Sometimes it works alongside other features. Thus in English – or at least some varieties of English – length is one of the factors differentiating *heed* from *hid* and *wooed* from *wood*. Sometimes length is the crucial distinguishing feature. Bernard (1967) has shown that the distinction between the long vowel of *calm* and *heart* and the short vowel of *come* and *hut* in Australian English is entirely a matter of duration. In some languages length is exploited rather more systematically than this. In languages such as Finnish and Hungarian, for example, there are two matching sets of long and short vowels: every short vowel has a long counterpart and every long vowel a short counterpart (although vowel quality may not be exactly identical across each pair of vowels).

Where vowel length is distinctive in this way, it is relative duration that matters rather than absolute duration. The length of any vowel will be in some measure dependent on its quality and context, and there is no minimum length for a long vowel or maximum length for a short vowel. If two vowels contrast with each other in length, what matters most is their duration relative to each other in comparable contexts. Thus the English short vowel in *hid* and *bid* is longer than in *hit* and *bit* (because of the effect of the voiced [d]) but it is still short relative to the long vowel of *heed* and *bead*; while the long vowel of *heed* and *bead* is shorter in *heat* and *beat* but still long relative to *hit* and *bit*. Bernard's studies (1967, 1970a) demonstrate this point for Australian English. Measurement of vowel duration thus reveals various degrees of length intermediate between the shortest and longest values. In general, however, the functional relativity of length is such that it is rarely if ever necessary to recognize more than two values in any particular language: functionally, vowels are either short or long (or neither if length is not distinctive in the language). Nevertheless, this simple conclusion about vowels must be set in a wider context, for syllabic organization and prosody also affect the way in which duration is exploited – in English, for instance, stressed syllables are normally longer than unstressed.

Simple vocalic sounds have a steady state articulation; that is, the tongue, lips and jaw are meant to achieve – however briefly – a stable configuration, commonly called the TARGET configuration. If produced in isolation, as in a demonstration of cardinal vowels in a phonetics class or in a singing exercise, a vowel can be prolonged without any appreciable change in quality. In normal connected speech, however, there is almost always some articulatory movement at the start and end of a vocalic sound. At the beginning of a vowel, the tongue and lips may be moving away from the configuration of the preceding consonant, and at the end, they may similarly be anticipating the gestures needed for a following consonant. For reasons such as these, the vowel target is normally preceded and followed by rapid TRANSITIONS. These transitions actually play a significant role, as they seem to be important cues in our perception of speech, but they do not disturb our impression that certain vocalic sounds have a single stable auditory quality. A vowel which meets this condition can be termed a PURE VOWEL.

It is also possible to make a deliberate movement of the articulators, particularly the tongue, during a vowel. Here the movement is not a direct response to the articulatory demands of adjacent consonants, but is usually somewhat slower, and constrained within the articulatory repertoire of the language concerned. The resulting change in auditory quality, either before or after the main vowel target, is known as an ONGLIDE or OFFGLIDE. The occurrence of such glides is quite language-specific, but the articulatory movement involved is often towards or from a generally centralized position. The range and direction of a glide, relative to the target, can be conveniently displayed on a cardinal vowel diagram. In transcription, an onglide can be represented as a superscript before the vowel, an offglide as a superscript after the vowel. For example, the vowel in *fee* has a noticeable onglide in many varieties of English and can be transcribed as [fᵊi]. The vowel in *four* may have an offglide (for example in conservative RP or in the southern USA) and can be symbolized as [fɔᵊ]. Figure 2.8.1 shows the two glides on a cardinal vowel diagram.

In some vocalic sounds, the glide component is so prominent that the vowel no longer has a single identifying vowel target value, even though it is still heard as a single sound. Such sounds are DIPHTHONGS. Articulatory movement, particularly of the tongue, occupies a substantial portion of a diphthong, which can be defined in terms of two vocalic targets that determine the range and direction of the glide between them. Diphthongs may be mapped on a cardinal vowel diagram, and are transcribed by a digraph consisting of the two vowel symbols which best represent the two targets.

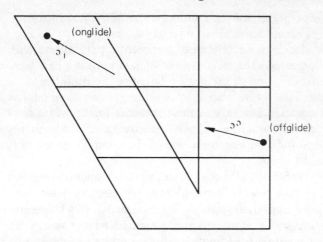

FIGURE 2.8.1 Vowel onglide and offglide

The vowels in *high* and *hear* are diphthongs in RP, which can be symbolized as [aɪ] and [ɪə]. (Many varieties of English have a comparable diphthong in *high* but not in *hear*: many Scottish and American speakers, for instance, will pronounce *hear* with a pure vowel followed by a consonantal *r*.) Traditionally in English phonetics, diphthongs such as [aɪ] produced with a tongue movement from a mid or low to a high position are known as CLOSING DIPHTHONGS (i.e. moving to a closer tongue position), while those like [ɪə], produced with a tongue movement from a peripheral to a central position, are known as CENTERING DIPHTHONGS. Figure 2.8.2 shows these two examples on a cardinal vowel diagram. Diphthongs vary widely in their total duration, and, like pure vowels, are influenced by their environment. Functionally, they count as long vowels, and just as the long vowel of *heat* is even longer before a

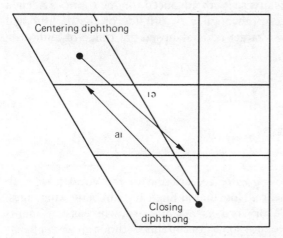

FIGURE 2.8.2 Closing and centering diphthongs

voiced stop in *heed*, so the diphthong of *height* is longer in *hide*. The measured duration of English diphthongs ranges from about 150 to 400 ms.

There is no simple way of deciding the difference between a pure vowel with onglide or offglide, and a diphthong. The two targets of a diphthong can have very unequal durations, and the duration of the glide relative to the total length of the diphthong is also variable. This means that two diphthongs can have similar targets and comparable total duration but vary in their auditory quality. One consequence of this is that the digraph notation is only approximate, although for greater accuracy it is possible to indicate length on one of the component symbols to convey its relative perceptual weight.

The durational structure of a diphthong also contributes to the distinction between a diphthong and a sequence of two vowels. If the glide component is quite short relative to targets of appreciable duration, the targets may be heard as two successive vowels. Readers may like to imagine a word *pawy* constructed from *paw* on the analogy of *handy* or *toey*. (Some speakers of English will be tempted to insert an *r* and to pronounce the word as *pory* but, for the sake of this illustration, they should resist the temptation.) Now by pronouncing *pawy* slower or faster and by adjusting the transition from one vowel to the next, it should be possible to vary the word from a distinctly bisyllabic word (*paw-ee*) to what sounds like a monosyllabic word containing a diphthong (*poy*). A simple exercise of this kind is useful in showing how we respond to variables in the flow of speech, but also points to the wider context of our judgements about syllables and other structural aspects of the organization of language which we shall treat further in the following chapter.

In summary, it is possible to produce an extraordinary range of different vowel sounds, although the repertoire of any one language will be confined within a system of relevant distinctions. Vowels can be described in terms of height and fronting (with suitable caution about the articulatory significance of these terms) and lip posture (rounded or unrounded); vowels are normally voiced but may in some languages have contrastive breathy voice or creak; vowels may also be nasalized (in opposition to normal oral vowels), tense (with advanced tongue root or widened pharynx) or long; and the presence of an onglide or offglide or the diphthongal combination of more than one vowel target adds a substantial range of auditorily distinct possibilities.

2.9   Consonantal sounds

In general, consonantal sounds show greater constriction of the vocal tract than vocalic sounds and have less prominence. Note that in English, as in many languages, a vowel can serve as an entire syllable (or word) as in *a*, *awe* or *I*, whereas consonants cannot. (It is certainly possible to produce some consonants without an accompanying vowel, as we do when we say *mm* or *sh*, but the structural organization of speech in most languages is such that vowels are normally central or nuclear in syllables, and consonants marginal or peripheral; see 3.1 and 3.11 below.)

There is a long tradition of drawing up inventories of symbols to represent all the various consonants of the world's languages, although the diversity of consonant articulation offers less scope for constructing a framework in the manner of the cardinal vowels (section 2.7 above). An early ambition of the International Phonetic Association (founded in 1886 and commonly referred to as the IPA) was to devise a universal phonetic alphabet, and the *Principles* of the IPA (1949) lists and illustrates a set of symbols (including a version of the cardinal vowel system) that are widely known and used. We prefer here to put the emphasis on the ways in which consonants are articulated rather than on an inventory of symbols; but we still need to use symbols and will follow many of the IPA conventions, without overlooking other systems of representation that supplement or challenge the IPA scheme.

So far as their articulation is concerned, consonants can be described in terms of where the constriction is made, how it is made, and what kind of phonation supports it. Traditionally, especially in the IPA scheme, this is taken to mean that consonants can be displayed in a chart in which PLACES OF ARTICULATION are listed from left to right (from the front of the vocal tract to the back), and MANNERS OF ARTICULATION from top to bottom (from stops, with maximal constriction, through fricatives to various consonants produced with less constriction); in addition some consonants need to be specified as voiced or voiceless. Thus a typical chart of this kind has in the top row voiceless stops, beginning with bilabial [p] on the left and moving through various stops made in the oral cavity towards glottal stop at the extreme right. Below them are voiced stops likewise beginning with bilabial [b] on the left, and below them voiceless fricatives, and so on. The scheme reflects its European origins, as it omits, for example, ejectives and implosives (2.5). Moreover, while it is diagrammatically convenient to treat place and manner as single dimensions, this sometimes means that some features of articulation (such as the posture of the tongue) have to be ignored or dealt with outside the main chart or compressed into one of the two dimensions.

An early and influential critique of the IPA's style of phonetic description was Pike's (1943), which has significantly influenced later approaches to phonetic description, including our own. Pike was conscious of the need to broaden the range of languages on which phonetic generalities were being based, and he wanted to account fully and consistently for all the articulatory mechanisms that were available to humans. His survey is impressively thorough, and is often pursued in a spirit of exploring the limits of human noise-making rather than describing sounds known to occur in languages. Thus in addition to a comprehensive range of articulatory mechanisms, he mentions such exotic possibilities as producing an 'ingressive stop' by sucking the tongue tip from the bottom lip (1943, p. 101) and twisting the tongue lengthwise so that the tip is upside down against the teeth (1943, p. 122). Pike's system consequently allows for detail that cannot be readily justified in phonetic description, and its value lies in its challenge to traditional approaches and its influence on later work.

Some later descriptive frameworks have incorporated the results of modern instrumental research. The earliest and most comprehensive of these is Peterson and Shoup

(1966a and b). This uses a primary articulatory description in terms of place and manner, but adds a series of secondary parameters to provide the necessary descriptive detail about airstream, airflow path, and phonation mode. The authors also specify acoustic and physiological correlates for many of the dimensions of their system. Their place and manner specifications differ from traditional IPA practice in that they rank manner of articulation according to degree of stricture (from greatest to least) and specify both horizontal (lip to glottis) and vertical (tongue height) places of articulation. The system not only divides these dimensions more finely than is usual, but also places both consonantal and vocalic sounds on a continuum using the one set of dimensions. Nevertheless, this treatment of vowels does not remove the difficulties of making accurate statements about tongue position in vowel sounds (2.7 above). In any event, despite Peterson and Shoup's logical and comprehensive approach, their system has not been widely used.

Among more recent contributions to general phonetic description, Catford (1977) is noteworthy: his objective is to account for all the articulatory possibilities of man – or 'anthropophonics' as he calls it, reviving a term used by Baudouin de Courtenay in the nineteenth century. Catford emphasizes the description of aerodynamic activity in articulatory processes, and offers more detailed categories for specifying articulatory locations (particularly on the tongue and lips) than are traditionally used. Catford also notes the inconsistency of using different descriptive systems for vowels and consonants, but concludes that the traditional method based on cardinal vowels remains the most practical. Other descriptive systems such as Jakobson, Fant and Halle (1952), Jakobson and Halle (1956), Chomsky and Halle (1968), and Ladefoged (1971; 1982, ch. 11), which explicitly address the question of 'features' as the ultimate components of speech, will be discussed in chapter 10.

The outline which follows is based on the traditional dimensions of manner and place of articulation. To refine these rather constraining dimensions, individual articulatory processes which implement the dimensions are defined in some detail. The level of detail is obviously controversial – the framework presented here goes beyond the IPA scheme but stops short of Pike's attempt to capture everything that is physically possible. Ultimately a framework must be realistic, in the sense that it is adequate to account for the diversity of sounds actually encountered in languages without encompassing mere possibilities that are linguistically irrelevant. The symbols used are basically those of the IPA, with some extensions and minor changes. A summary chart of the symbols can be found in Appendix 1.

2.10   Vocal tract place

The constriction that produces a particular consonantal sound is located at some point in the vocal tract. In traditional usage, a single value along the 'place of articulation' dimension defines *both* the area of the oral-pharyngeal vocal tract where the constriction is made *and* the part of the tongue used to form the constriction (if the tongue is the active articulator). In our scheme, VOCAL TRACT PLACE will refer only to location along the vocal tract. The posture of the tongue will be treated as a separate articulatory dimension, so that different tongue positions or gestures can be combined with different places of articulation. This approach is consistent both with Pike's method of description (1943) and with the spirit of much of the most recent work in phonetics.

The wall of the vocal tract, extending from the lips to the glottis, is a virtual continuum. There are some anatomical features – such as the teeth – which constitute boundaries or areas, but much of the tract, and especially the roof of the mouth, does not divide naturally and obviously into regions. Thus the phonetic conventions governing the definition and labelling of articulatory areas owe rather more to observation of where sounds tend to be made rather than to anatomy. Points or places of articulation should therefore be understood as approximately demarcated regions rather than as specific points in the vocal tract. Partly for this reason, the labels of places of articulation are not entirely standardized, and we shall draw attention to some ambiguities. Figure 2.10.1 shows a mid-sagittal section of the supraglottal vocal tract indicating the articulatory locations described below. Most of the locations can be identified by looking in a mirror or by feeling inside the mouth with fingers or tongue.

LABIAL refers to the upper and lower lips. For description of languages we need to distinguish between BILABIAL articulation (both lips involved) and LABIODENTAL (lower

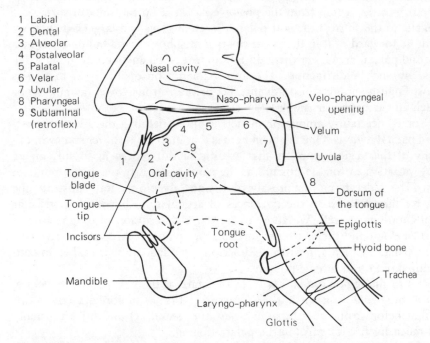

FIGURE 2.10.1   Mid-sagittal oral vocal tract showing major areas of articulation
Adapted from: Minifie, Hixon and Williams 1973, p. 173.

lip and upper teeth). In English, [p] as in *pea*, [b] as in *bee* and [m] as in *me* are all bilabial; [f] as in *feel* and [v] as in *veal* are labiodental.

DENTAL refers to the upper teeth. Apart from the involvement of the teeth in labiodental articulation (above), various sounds can be made by the tongue against the teeth. Examples are English [θ] as in *thin* and [ð] as in *this*; [n] may also be dental when it precedes one of these, as in *month* or *ninth*. Some phoneticians distinguish between the edges of the upper teeth and the posterior faces of the upper teeth. It is true that the tongue may make contact with the teeth in different ways, but this can be largely explained by the way in which the tongue is used.

ALVEOLAR refers to the gum ridge or alveolum, the thick membranous covering on the bone structure which joins the tooth-bearing bone of the upper jaw and the vaulted or arched bone structure of the hard palate. The alveolum begins immediately behind the upper teeth and extends to the corrugations on the membranous covering of the posterior part of the tooth ridge structure. Some writers, such as Heffner (1964), have suggested that the anterior part of this alveolar ridge be considered separately as the 'gingival' (gum) region, but there is no linguistic justification for a distinction of this kind. Alveolar sounds in English include [t] as in *toe*, [d] as in *doe* and [n] as in *no*.

POSTALVEOLAR refers to the region from the corrugations on the tooth ridge where the roof of the mouth has a convex contour, to the start of the smooth surface of the hard palate where the roof of the mouth begins to become concave. For many (but not all) English speakers [ɹ] as in *ray* and [ʃ] as in *shy* are postalveolar consonants.

PALATAL refers to the region from the postalveolar area on the smooth surface of the hard palate to the start of the soft palate or velum. This is a larger articulatory area than those forward of it in the vocal tract; some phoneticians subdivide it into pre-palatal and palatal areas, but there do not appear to be any sounds in language that depend on such a distinction. The approximant consonant [j] as in *you* is palatal; most English speakers also advance [k] before a front vowel (as in *keep* or *king*) to such an extent that it is palatal.

There is some uncertainty among phoneticians about defining the alveolar, postalveolar and palatal regions. One problem here is that individuals differ somewhat in the anatomy of this region, another that significant differences in sound can be achieved by variation in tongue posture at the same (or nearly the same) point of articulation. The older terms 'palato-alveolar' and 'alveolo-palatal' illustrate the difficulties, for they purport to specify places of articulation, but imply particular tongue configurations as well. We allow for separate description of tongue configuration (2.11 below) and prefer to limit articulatory place to three areas (alveolar, postalveolar, palatal) which appear to be descriptively adequate when taken in conjunction with variation in tongue posture.

VELAR refers to the region extending from the start of the soft palate, or velum, back as far as the uvula. In English, [k] as in *core* and [g] as in *gore* are velar stops (but note that before front vowels, as in *keep* and *geese*, [k] and [g] are usually articulated much further forward, in the palatal region).

UVULAR refers to the short projection of soft tissue and muscle at the midline of the posterior termination of the velum. It is possible to close the back of the tongue against the uvula, as in the voiceless uvular stop [q] found in Arabic; uvular fricatives and uvular trills are also possible, and the *r*-sound of French and German is often articulated in this way.

The boundary between the hard palate and the velum is reasonably clear, since it lies at the posterior end of the bony extension of the upper jaw. There is no such boundary between the velum and the uvula. Many phoneticians avoid any specific definition of this division, or simply imply that velar articulations may occur on all parts of the soft palate except the uvula. Catford (1977), without supporting evidence, suggests that velar articulations occur only in the anterior half of the region between the palatal–velar boundary and the uvula itself. The difficulty appears to be one of establishing the anterior limits of uvular articulation, which is affected by the nature of the articulatory activity concerned. Thus a uvular trill, which involves the uvular projection itself, occurs in the region of the posterior termination of the soft palate structure. A uvular stop, on the other hand, must be sufficiently far forward on the soft palate to ensure complete oral closure, and it does not require the uvular projection itself to serve as a dynamic articulator. The velar–uvular boundary is therefore not a sharp line, but rather an area slightly forward of the posterior termination of the velum.

PHARYNGEAL refers to the walls of the pharynx, including the root of the tongue. Pharyngeal consonants are not common but voiceless and voiced pharyngeal fricatives [ħ] and [ʕ] are found in several languages of which the best known is Arabic.

GLOTTAL refers to the glottis, which plays a central role in phonation (2.6 above) but can also function as an articulator. Closure and release of the vocal folds, for example, can constitute a stop analogous to a bilabial or velar stop. This glottal stop is a consonant in languages as diverse as Arabic, Vietnamese and Hawaiian. English speakers tend not to hear the sound as a stop – or to count it as 'a catch in the throat' – and its occurrence in English as a nonstandard substitute for other stops is usually reckoned as omission of the correct stop (as in the kind of London pronunciation popularly represented as *pu'* for *put* or *ma'er* for *matter*).

2.11   Tongue position

Different parts of the tongue may be used in combination with the above places of articulation. The combinations are constrained in obvious ways: it is impossible, for example, to bring the back of the tongue into contact with the anterior regions of the mouth, at least not in such a way that one can usefully control an articulatory process. As there are no real landmarks on the tongue, the naming of points or areas on the tongue is in any case a matter of convention, influenced by those combinations of tongue position and place of articulation which prove to be functional in actual languages. (Figure 2.10.1 above includes a sagittal section of the tongue indicating such functional locations.)

APICAL refers to the tip or front edge of the tongue; LAMINAL to the anterior part of the upper surface of the tongue, otherwise known as the blade; and DORSAL to the region from the blade of the tongue to the root. The boundary between the laminal and dorsal areas is a matter of convention, but is generally defined as the region lying below the tooth ridge when the tongue is at rest. SUBLAMINAL is a term suggested by Catford (1977) to identify the anterior part of the undersurface of the tongue, corresponding to the blade.

English alveolar sounds such as [t], [d] and [n] are normally apical; dental versions of these sounds (as the dental [ṉ] before [θ] in *month*) are also apical. On the other hand many Australian Aboriginal languages (such as Aranda from Central Australia) have a dental stop which is laminal: the tongue is pushed forward so that the tip is down and the blade bunched against the back of the upper teeth. Use of the dorsal area of the tongue is often predictable from place of articulation – a velar or uvular constriction will inevitably involve the dorsal area – but it is also possible to bring the tongue forward in such a way that the dorsal area of the tongue approaches the palatal area of the roof of the mouth. The fronted English [k] in *keep* or *keen* is of this nature. Australian Aboriginal languages again provide a contrast, since they employ a palatal stop which is laminal rather than dorsal. The auditory difference is noteworthy: English speakers tend to hear the lamino-palatal stop as something like [t] immediately followed by [j] (thus combining the stoppage of a [t] with the lamino-palatal articulation of [j]) rather than as a fronted [k]. The term 'sublaminal' is not widely employed but is useful in specifying tongue behaviour in so-called 'retroflex' consonants (found for example in some Australian Aboriginal languages as well as in many languages of India). In these consonants, the tongue may be curled up and back so that the undersurface of the front of the tongue makes contact with the roof of the mouth in the alveolar or postalveolar region.

Table 2.11.1 lists places of articulation in which various tongue positions are combined with various locations.

2.12   Manner of articulation

Manner of articulation covers both the degree or extent of a constriction and the way in which the constriction is formed in the vocal tract. Thus a category such as 'stop' implies both blockage of the airstream (total constriction) and a movement to create and then release the blockage (dynamic articulation). On the other hand, 'fricative' implies a lesser constriction and a kind of articulation which could, in principle, be prolonged as a steady state (stable articulation). In traditional descriptions (such as those following the IPA conventions), manner of articulation can sometimes also include a specification of constriction shape, for example in descriptions such as 'lateral fricative', where 'lateral' refers to tongue configuration against the roof of the mouth. But since it is possible to vary the shape of a constriction independently of

Table 2.11.1   *Places of articulation for consonants*

Name of place	Articulators used
Bilabial	Upper and lower lips (English *p*, *b*, *m*)
Labio-dental	Lower lip and edges of upper incisors (English *f*, *v*)
Apico-dental	Tongue tip and edges or backs of upper incisors (Spanish *t*, *d*, English *th* in *thin*)
Lamino-dental	Tongue blade and edges or backs of upper incisors (*th* in Australian Aboriginal languages)
Apico-alveolar	Tongue tip and alveolar region (English *t*, *d*)
Lamino-alveolar	Tongue blade and alveolar region
Apico-postalveolar	Tongue tip and postalveolar region (southern British English *r* in *trip*, *drip*)
Lamino-postalveolar	Tongue blade and postalveolar region (English *sh* as in *ship* may be apico-postalveolar or lamino-postalveolar depending on the speaker)
Sublamino-postalveolar	Tongue undersurface and postalveolar region (as in 'retroflex' sounds of Hindi or Urdu)
Apico-palatal	Tongue tip and palatal region
Lamino-palatal	Tongue blade and palatal region (English *y*)
Velar	Tongue body and soft palate (English *k*)
Uvular	Tongue body and uvula/soft palate (*r* in some varieties of French and German)
Pharyngeal	Pharynx walls
Glottal	Glottis (vocal folds)

the other aspects of manner of articulation, we deal with shape separately as STRICTURE (2.13 below).

Like most other articulatory variables, consonantal constriction is a continuum. It ranges from total closure of the vocal tract to fully open, vowel-like articulation. For linguistic description, a three-way distinction of stoppage, fricative articulation and a more open vowel-like articulation appears adequate. In English, [b] requires stoppage, [v] a fricative constriction, and [w] a still wider constriction. The distinction rests primarily on the effect of each degree of constriction on the airflow, and secondarily on the kind of articulatory manoeuvre that produces the constriction.

This relatively simple classification is complicated by the further distinction between dynamic and stable articulations. A stop is necessarily dynamic: it is characterized by the actions of forming and releasing the stoppage. Note that one cannot greatly prolong a stop such as [b] or [p] other than by maintaining the closure (in which case no sound is heard during the closure) or repeating the actions of closing and releasing the articulators. Readers may like to verify this by experimenting with a word such as *happen*. It is possible to hold the [p] closure for some time, but no sound is then heard; and it is possible to repeat the [p] a number of times as if stammering over the consonant; but there is no way to prolong the sound of a single [p]. On the other hand, the more open constrictions of sounds such as [v] and [w] are stable in the sense that they can be prolonged in a more or less steady state. It is possible, for instance, to hold the [v] in *ever* as long as one's breath lasts. The [w] in, say, *owing* can be similarly prolonged – and in keeping with its vowel-like character will sound much like a lengthened [u] vowel. (In normal running speech, of course, stable articulations are very brief and may not necessarily be perceived or identified as 'steady states'.)

Other manners of articulation extend this repertoire. Firstly, nasal consonants are in one sense stops, for the airflow is blocked at some point in the oral cavity; but since the velum is lowered to allow airflow through the nasal cavity, nasal consonants can be prolonged (and commonly are in what we call 'humming a tune'). Nasals are therefore classified not as stops but as a separate manner of articulation. Secondly, there are other kinds of dynamic articulation besides stops. Accordingly, we recognize seven manners of articulation: STOP, FRICATIVE and the vowel-like APPROXIMANT; NASAL; and three additional dynamic manners, FLAP, TAP and TRILL. These terms are standard, except that approximant consonants have been variously defined and labelled: terms such as GLIDE, FRICTIONLESS CONTINUANT, ORAL RESONANT and SEMIVOWEL are sometimes used for one or more kinds of approximant. And the term OBSTRUENT is commonly used to include both stops and fricatives.

A STOP is produced by the formation and rapid release of a complete closure at any point in the vocal tract from the glottis to the lips. The velum is raised to prevent airflow through the nasal cavity, and the oral airflow is thus interrupted. The durations of the phases of a stop are partly conditioned by phonetic context and therefore variable: the stoppage itself may last from 40 to 150 ms, and the closure and release phases may each last between 20 and 80 ms. The release of a stop is particularly complex, as several factors are relevant. Firstly, the nature of the airflow during release is largely dependent on the nature of the glottal airflow (defined by phonation, 2.6 above). Secondly, timing is also significant, as the moment of release need not coincide exactly with other articulatory gestures (such as the start or finish of voicing). Thirdly, the stoppage itself creates a change in pressure. If the airstream is egressive (whether pulmonic or glottalic), air pressure will build up in the oral cavity behind the occlusion; if the airstream is ingressive (whether glottalic or velaric), intra-oral air pressure is likely to be reduced during the occlusion. Egressive pulmonic stops are by far the most common type of stop and are sometimes identified by the label PLOSIVE.

In a typical voiced plosive, there must be airflow through the glottis to generate the voiced phonation. But the very nature of a stop is that airflow is blocked somewhere in the vocal tract. As pressure builds up behind this blockage, it will approach the level of subglottal pressure generating airflow through the glottis, eventually to the point where phonation cannot be sustained. At this point, of course, the stop is no longer a voiced stop, but voiceless. There are various linguistic responses to this aerodynamic problem. One is that voiced stops in many languages often are partially devoiced. In English, for instance, it is common for voicing to tail off in a word-final voiced stop (as in *rib* or *rid* or *rig*). It is also noteworthy that the occlusion phase is often shorter in voiced stops than in voiceless, so that the vocal apparatus is, so to speak, not put to the test of maintaining voicing for any length of time. And it is also possible to enlarge the space between the glottis and the point of stoppage during the occlusion, by lowering the larynx and distending the pharyngeal walls to increase cavity volume. In this way, intra-oral air pressure is not allowed to build up as quickly, and a pressure drop across the glottis can be maintained (Ohala 1978).

At the release of a stop, there is a very short sharp pulse of turbulent airflow through the (momentarily) narrow aperture of the parting articulators. During this pulse – known as the 'release burst' – the peak airflow rate can exceed 1.5 litres per second. After the release, the articulators move rapidly to the next required position. The actual phonetic quality of the release burst and what follows it, is dependent firstly on the place of articulation, and secondly on the phonation mode at the time. Figure 2.12.1 shows the formation, occlusion, and release of a bilabial stop with a normal pulmonic egressive airstream.

Readers can check some of these observations by producing an [a:] sound (*aah*) and then closing and releasing the lips at intervals to produce [a:ba:ba . . .]. Prolonging a closure will illustrate the devoicing which occurs as transglottal pressure falls; and a deliberate change of phonation mode from voiced [b] to voiceless [p] during the occlusion phase should enable the reader to sense the different demands of

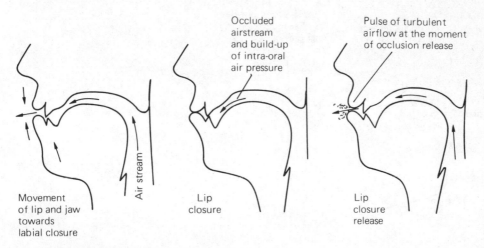

FIGURE 2.12.1   Phases of a bilabial plosive

voiced and voiceless stops. Many languages exploit the distinction of voiced and voiceless stops, but with considerable variation in the way the distinction is realized or implemented (especially in relation to the timing of voicing, 2.16 below). Only the glottal stop cannot be voiced, as the glottal occlusion obviously rules out any possibility of voiced phonation.

FRICATIVE is a potentially stable articulation produced by a constriction in the vocal tract that is narrow enough to create turbulent airflow. The noise of this turbulence (modified by the effects of the vocal tract shape) gives many fricative sounds a characteristic hissing or sibilant quality. Figure 2.12.2 illustrates the airflow pattern of the fricative [s].

The factors that make one fricative sound different from another are place of articulation, the shape of the constriction, and the aerodynamic forces of the airstream. Additionally, in the case of dental, alveolar and postalveolar fricatives, the front (incisor) teeth contribute to phonetic quality, since they deflect the airflow coming from the constriction, producing some additional turbulence.

There is a balance between the cross-sectional area of a fricative constriction and the rate of airflow through the constriction. The constriction must be relatively small to generate turbulence, but the air must also flow rapidly enough to exceed the threshold at which smooth or laminar airflow becomes turbulent. If the constriction area is enlarged, then the flow rate must be higher to achieve turbulence. Studies of fricative aerodynamics by Hixon (1966), Stevens (1972b), Warren (1976) and Catford (1977) indicate that fricative constrictions of up to around $30\,mm^2$ can produce turbulence, provided airflow is high enough. Flow rates vary between about 30 and $300\,cm^3$ per second. Models of fricative articulation as well as empirical data suggest that there is considerable room for variation and that individual speakers may have different articulatory habits. Air pressure in the oral cavity behind the fricative constriction seems to depend on the rate of airflow and size of

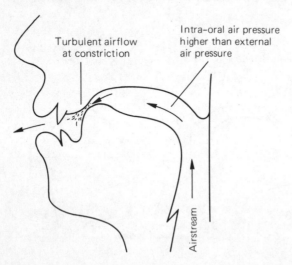

FIGURE 2.12.2   Articulation of a voiceless alveolar fricative [s]

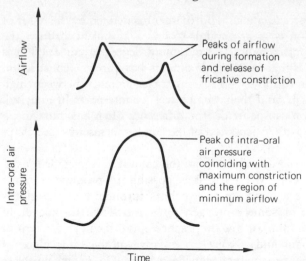

FIGURE 2.12.3   Pressure and airflow patterns for a voiceless alveolar fricative [s]

constriction, and is thus not a primary factor in determining the nature of a fricative. Reasonably typical pressure and flow patterns of a voiceless alveolar fricative are shown in figure 2.12.3 (Clark et al. 1982).

The peaks of airflow at the start and end of the fricative in figure 2.12.3 reflect the relatively large area of constriction during the formation and release of the fricative. Between the peaks, airflow falls to a minimum, corresponding more or less to the period of maximum constriction. The peak of intra-oral air pressure, as might be expected, also corresponds to the period of maximum constriction and maximum airflow resistance. Airflow rates are of course also affected by phonation. In a voiceless fricative, there is negligible resistance to airflow at the glottis, and airflow will be higher than in a voiced fricative. In voiced fricatives, not only is airflow resistance higher at the glottis, the flow is also interrupted at the rate of vocal fold vibration. This intermittent effect on the turbulence at the fricative constriction is largely responsible for the voiced quality of the sound (Klatt et al. 1968, Scully 1979).

To check the effects of fricative constriction on airflow, readers may like to produce a continuous [s] sound and then pull the tongue down from the alveolar ridge. Airflow will increase rapidly and fricative noise will suddenly cease as airflow through the constriction switches from turbulent to smooth or laminar flow, as shown in figure 2.12.3.

An APPROXIMANT is a potentially stable articulation in which the constriction is normally greater than in a vowel, but not great enough to produce turbulence at the point of constriction. Following Ladefoged, the term covers the traditional categories of 'frictionless continuant', 'semivowel' and 'oral resonant'. For Abercrombie (1967) and Catford (1977), approximant is a narrower class of sounds, excluding laterals. In English, the consonants [l], [w] and [j] as heard at the beginning of *law*, *war* and *your* are all approximants in the wider sense. The initial consonant in *raw* is also an approximant, at least for those speakers of English who do not trill or flap the *r*.

The maximum degree of constriction in an approximant is defined by the onset of turbulent airflow: if constriction is great enough to create turbulent airflow, the sound is a fricative, not an approximant. The minimum degree of constriction is less clear-cut. Even if we take it that most approximants have greater constriction than most vowels, we may find little or no articulatory difference between high (close) vowels such as [i] and [u] and their 'semivowel' counterparts [j] and [w]. While an articulatory distinction can be made, the difference often has more to do with syllabic organization than with articulation of the sounds themselves (see chapter 3 below, especially 3.11 and 3.13).

Approximants are normally voiced, and by definition cannot have turbulent excitation at the point of constriction. In theory, it is possible to produce voiceless approximants, but they require a noise source, such as turbulence at the glottis created by whisper phonation or some more generally distributed turbulence in the vocal tract created by high volume airflow. In practice, it is difficult to distinguish between a voiceless approximant and a voiceless fricative at the same place of articulation. Thus in English, approximants may be devoiced following voiceless consonants, for instance the [w] in *twin* or *twelve*. This voiceless approximant is in effect a voiceless bilabial fricative with lip rounding – or, more pertinently, it makes no difference to the English sound system whether the sound is regarded as an approximant or a fricative. And there is no evidence that any language in the world makes such a distinction crucial.

NASAL consonants have a stoppage at some point in the oral cavity; at the same time, the velum is lowered to allow airflow through the nasal cavity. The sounds are therefore perceived as potentially stable and continuous rather than as stops in the true sense. Common nasal consonants are [m] and [n] (as in English *more* and *nor*). English speakers should have no difficulty in verifying that a nasal consonant can be prolonged, as in a thoughtful *mmm*.

FLAP and TAP are dynamic articulations in which there is a very brief occlusion in the vocal tract. The terms are sometimes used synonymously, but it is possible to distinguish two kinds of action: in a flap, one articulator strikes another in passing, not so much to create a brief closure but more as the incidental effect of the articulatory gesture; in a tap, there is a single deliberate movement to create a closure, tantamount to a very short stop.

The most common flaps are ones in which the tongue strikes the alveolar ridge in passing. Many speakers of English use a flapped *r* in words such as *three* and *throw*, where the tip of the tongue strikes the alveolar ridge on its way from the dental position to a more retracted position for the following vowel. Some languages, including Hindi and the Central Australian language Warlpiri, have a flapped *r* articulated somewhat differently: the tongue tip may be curled back towards the palate and may then strike the posterior part of the alveolar ridge as it moves down towards its neutral or rest position. Ladefoged (1982, p. 155) also reports a labio-dental flap (from Margi, a language of Nigeria) in which the lower lip is drawn in and then allowed to flap against the upper teeth as it returns forward. The most commonly cited instance of a tap is from some varieties of English: some speakers, especially Americans but also younger Australians, pronounce the medial [t] in words such as *better* and *matter* as a tap. The pronunciation often strikes other speakers as converting a [t] into a [d] – and indeed a tap against the alveolar ridge is in one sense simply a very short [d]. But those who use a flapped *r* in English, such as Scottish speakers, may hear the sound as closer to the flap than to a stop. Moreover, it should be noted that speakers who use the tap do not normally confuse the tap with [d], and *matter* can still be distinguished from *madder* (although the length of the preceding vowel rather than the nature of the tap or stop may play the crucial role here).

TRILL is a dynamic articulation produced by vibration of an articulator. The articulatory setting is such that the articulator is not deliberately moved but vibrates as a consequence of the egressive airstream passing by it. The airstream is repeatedly interrupted at a rapid rate, rather in the way that voiced phonation is produced by vibration of the vocal folds. The most common trills use the tongue tip (held close to the alveolar ridge) or the uvula (by bringing the dorsum of the tongue into light contact with it). A trill is a series of vibrations and is described as a dynamic articulation because no single vibration can be lengthened significantly. But the trill itself can of course be lengthened by repeating the vibrations, in principle indefinitely, as long as the airflow lasts. But in normal speech, trills tend to be short and to use rather few vibrations.

Most readers will be familiar with the alveolar trill as a 'trilled r', even if they do not normally use it in their own speech. In fact, outside English many people will consider an alveolar trill to be the common or normal way of articulating an [r]. Speakers of Italian, Spanish and Indonesian, for example, readily trill the [r], particularly if speaking emphatically or clearly. (Other articulations, including tap or flap mechanisms, may be used in these languages; see Lindau (1985) for general discussion of 'r-sounds'.) The alveolar trill is not common in English, except in Scottish English, where it may be the normal articulation. Some speakers of French and German use a uvular trill as their 'r-sound' – but again other articulations may also be used, including a uvular fricative or approximant and, especially in stage pronunciation or in some rural dialects, an alveolar trill. Thus in many languages – English, French, German, Italian, and Indonesian among others – there is only one 'r-sound' and variations in the pronunciation of it are associated with regional, social or stylistic differentiation. On the other hand, Spanish distinguishes between a flap (as in *pero* 'but') and a trill (as in *perro* 'dog') while Warlpiri, from Central Australia, has three kinds of *r* – an alveolar flap or trill, a retroflex flap, and an approximant (similar to the *r* used by most English speakers).

2.13   Stricture

Stricture refers to the shape of a constriction. For many sounds, stricture is either irrelevant or determined by other aspects of the articulatory process. In a nasal consonant such as [n], for instance, the tongue makes a closure against the alveolar ridge

while air flows through the nasal cavity, which offers no option of varying constriction shape; or in a flap or trill, the stricture will simply be a consequence of the
vibratory movement of one articulator against another. In some articulations, however, the posture of the tongue can make appreciable differences in the shape of the
constriction and the resulting quality of sound. In the fricative [s], as in *saw*, the
tongue is grooved along its length in a way that contrasts with the flatter tongue
shape of the fricative [θ] in *thaw* or the approximant [ɹ] in *raw*; while in a lateral
sound such as the [l] in *law*, the tongue makes contact against the alveolar ridge but is
lowered at one or both sides so that air flows through relatively freely. Figure 2.13.1
shows schematic sections for the three stricture types CENTRAL, GROOVED and LATERAL.

CENTRAL can be taken in a general sense to be the neutral value of stricture,
applying to any constriction in which the tongue does not adopt a distinctively
grooved or lateral posture. The term is more narrowly justified in instances where
airflow along the centre of the vocal tract is in direct contrast with grooved or lateral
stricture. Compare the initial consonants of English *trip* and *chip*. In many varieties
of English the two words are auditorily and articulatorily quite similar. In the first
word, the initial [t] is followed by a voiceless fricative (a devoiced and fricative
counterpart of the common approximant value of English *r*); in the second word,
[t] is followed by a grooved fricative, more or less identical with the one written as *sh*
in *ship*. (Readers may like to pause over these examples. Comparison of *ship* and
chip and an attempt at pronouncing the beginning of *chip* very slowly should highlight the nature of the fricative component. It may then be possible to compare *trip*
and *chip* to verify that the shape of the tongue is different in the two fricatives,
although details of the articulation will be by no means identical for all speakers

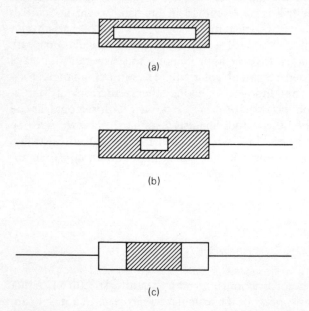

(a)

(b)

(c)

FIGURE 2.13.1   Stricture types: (a) central; (b) grooved; (c) lateral

of English. It may also be of incidental interest that young children sometimes have difficulty in grasping the spelling conventions and may produce written efforts such as *chrip* for *trip*.)

GROOVED refers to the tongue grooving already mentioned above, which yields a constriction of very narrow cross-sectional area along the vocal tract. Grooving is in fact common in fricatives which use the tongue tip or blade as the constricting articulator in the alveolar or postalveolar region. The grooved fricative [s] is found in many languages (but not in all – most Australian Aboriginal languages do not have it) and is far more common than flatter or more central fricatives of the kind heard in *trip*. Other quite frequent grooved fricatives are the voiced counterpart of [s], namely [z], and the voiceless postalveolar [ʃ] (as in English *ship*). English also has a voiced partner for [ʃ], namely [ʒ], heard in the medial position of words such as *measure* and *fusion*.

LATERAL refers to constrictions in which the airstream is diverted from the centre of the oral tract and flows to one or both sides. An alveolar lateral approximant [l] (English *law*) is widespread, but other points of articulation are possible (for instance the lamino-palatal lateral approximant [ʎ] represented as *gl* in Italian and as *ll* in standard European Spanish). A voiceless version of [l] is also possible, although as with other approximants, voicelessness is likely to imply fricative articulation. Thus the Welsh sound represented as *ll* (as in *llyn* 'lake' or *llan* 'church') is sometimes referred to simply as 'voiceless *l*' but probably is more strictly a voiceless lateral fricative, having turbulent airflow through the lateral stricture. If airflow is high enough, turbulence can be achieved in a voiced lateral, yielding a voiced lateral fricative (found in Zulu). Indeed, lateral stricture can combine with various other articulatory processes, even with a click mechanism (as in the sound known to most English speakers as the noise to urge a horse forward, 2.5 above).

2.14   Force

A distinction can be made between FORTIS articulation, relatively strong or forceful overall articulation, and LENIS or weak articulation. Our use of the terms follows Pike, who says that fortis articulation 'entails strong, tense movements . . . relative to a norm assumed for all sounds' (1943, p. 128). Fortis articulation is probably mainly a matter of greater subglottal pressure (and the term 'heightened subglottal pressure' has been used in some descriptions) but higher airflow and stronger and more definite supraglottal articulatory gestures are likely to accompany an increase in subglottal pressure.

Fortis articulation is sometimes described as 'tense' articulation: given the divergent uses of this term, we restrict it to vocalic sounds (and even there leave a question mark against it). Fortis articulation is also sometimes used to account for what we call 'aspiration' of stops: we deal with this as a matter of timing (2.16 below). We retain the fortis/lenis distinction because it is evident that a variable of force can be exploited in the articulation of certain consonants, alongside other variables such as phonation and timing. In Dutch, for example, the voiceless [p] heard at the beginning of words such as *pen* 'pen' and *pan* 'pan' is not aspirated but is typically articulated quite forcefully. (A similar kind of articulation may be heard from some English speakers from northern England; more commonly, English *pen* and *pan* will have initial stops that are voiceless, fortis *and* aspirated, 2.16 below.) But the exploitation of the processes and the precise way in which they are integrated for an overall distinctive effect varies from language to language. We urge caution in drawing conclusions about the universal nature of articulation from detailed phonetic investigation of sounds in a single language. (See also our comments on TENSE and LAX at the end of 2.7 above, the description of the STOP manner of articulation in 2.12 above, and discussion of VOICE ONSET in 2.16 below.)

2.15   Length

Like vowels (2.7, 2.8), consonants may be SHORT or LONG. Virtually any consonant can be made relatively longer or shorter, although in some cases the longer and shorter versions may count as different manners of articulation. Thus, one view of a flap is that it is a minimal trill, while a trill can be regarded as a series of flaps. Similarly, a tap may be considered a very short stop. Even voiced plosives, in which voicing will cease during prolonged closure, can be lengthened sufficiently to be noticeably different in duration from a shorter version.

Languages which distinguish long and short consonants of various kinds include Italian and Finnish. The spelling system of both languages uses double letters to represent the lengthened consonants, e.g. Italian *notte* 'night', *canne* 'canes' (versus *note* 'notes', *cane* 'dog'). Lengthened consonants are often treated as the uninterrupted succession of two identical short consonants (as implied by the Italian spellings), in which case they may be called GEMINATES.

2.16   Voice onset

This variable refers to the timing of the start of voiced phonation relative to the supraglottal activity. It is mainly relevant to stops, and we consider three simple possibilities. If voiced phonation begins at or before the formation of the occlusion, the stop will count as FULLY VOICED. If there is no voicing during the occlusion but voice onset is virtually simultaneous with the release of the occlusion, the stop can be regarded as VOICELESS. If voice onset is significantly delayed beyond the release of the occlusion, the release will be ASPIRATED because of the unobstructed flow of air through the abducted folds. The timing is obviously a continuum and can be varied between these three options, but the three are more than sufficient to account for what happens in many languages.

In many languages, the timing of voice onset is actually redundant with respect to phonation values. In English and German, for example, word-initial voiceless plosives [p] [t] [k] are generally aspirated, i.e. there is some delay in voice onset after the release. In these same two languages word-initial voiced plosives [b] [d] [g] may not be fully voiced, i.e. voice onset may be somewhat later than the start of occlusion. Under these circumstances, the voicing of voiced plosives may not be very prominent and the aspiration of voiceless plosives may be the major factor in identifying their voicelessness. Descriptions of the languages nevertheless refer to 'voiced' and 'voiceless' plosives on the assumption that voice onset is predictably delayed. On the other hand, there are languages in which voice onset is not significantly delayed, for example French and Dutch. In these languages, voiceless plosives are not normally aspirated, i.e. voice onset virtually coincides with the release of occlusion. As might be expected, the voiced plosives of these languages are fully voiced, i.e. voicing begins at or before the start of occlusion.

Languages are not restricted to a two-way distinction among stops. There are languages which distinguish three kinds of plosive, generally referred to as 'voiceless aspirated', 'voiceless unaspirated' and 'voiced'. These languages include a number of East Asian languages such as Thai and Burmese. Here voice onset cannot be regarded as a redundant or secondary factor, and the three options outlined above are relevant, namely: FULLY VOICED, where voice onset is at or near the beginning of the occlusion phase of the stop; UNASPIRATED, where voice onset occurs as the occlusion is released; and ASPIRATED, where voice onset is appreciably later than the release of the occlusion.

Finer differentiation is certainly possible, by the use of values such as PARTIALLY VOICED (for a word-initial plosive in which voicing begins during occlusion or for a word-final plosive in which voicing tails off well before release) or WEAKLY ASPIRATED and STRONGLY ASPIRATED (to distinguish between plosives with moderate delay in voice onset and those with considerable delay – which seems to be necessary in Korean, according to Kim 1965).

It should also be noted that plosives in most languages behave differently in different environments. In English, for example, voiceless plosives can be said to be noticeably aspirated; but this is most strikingly true of plosives standing word-initial before a vowel (as in *pea*, *tea*, *key*), less evident where a plosive stands between vowels (as in *happy*, *natty*, *lackey*) and generally not true at all of plosives following *s* (as in *spare*, *stare*, *scare*). In short, what appears to be a consistent distinction may be quite variable, and the precise cues that differentiate, say, *tie* from *die* may not be at all the same as those that distinguish between *matter* and *madder* or *mat* and *mad*.

Indeed, since variation in voice onset co-occurs with selection of various phonation types, of fortis or lenis articulation, and so on, a rich diversity of plosive types can be found in the world's languages. The voiced aspirated plosives of many South Asian languages, such as Hindi and Gujarati, for example, exploit breathy voice combined with some delay in the onset of normal voicing. Rarely, voicing delay

Segmental Articulation

can be observed in sounds other than plosives: a few languages have voiceless aspirated fricatives such as the [s^h] of Burmese.

The classic study of voice onset is Lisker and Abramson (1964). Ladefoged (1971) provides a useful survey. He distinguishes five values of voice onset for stops and fricatives, as follows:

1 voicing throughout (voiced);
2 voicing in part;
3 voicing starts immediately after (voiceless unaspirated);
4 voicing starts shortly after (slightly aspirated);
5 voicing starts considerably later (aspirated).

He also notes (1971, p. 20) that the five are merely points on a continuum and that no language seems to contrast more than three points.

Exercises

1 Check that you understand the meaning of the following terms used in describing speech sounds:

alveolar
apical
approximant
aspirated
fortis
glottal
palatal
sublaminal
uvular

2 What are airstream mechanisms?
3 What is phonation? Satisfy yourself that you can distinguish various modes (whisper, voicing, etc.) and that you understand the mechanics of producing them.
4 Explain the origin and use of cardinal vowels.
5 This chapter includes a suggestion (in 2.8) that readers play with the pronunciation of a word *pawy* to vary it from two syllables ('paw-ee') to one ('poy'). Experiment with this word and then check whether you pronounce each of the following as one syllable or two:

lion
ion
skier (someone who skis)
Leah
higher
buyer

Note any potential confusion with other words (e.g. *lion* and *line*, *higher* and *hire*, *buyer* and *byre*): do you distinguish these pairs and if so, what is the difference in timing or vowel quality?

6 Explain briefly what the 'place' and 'manner' of consonant articulations are. In particular, explain the differences among the following terms:

> labial, bilabial and labiodental;
> stop, plosive, fricative, obstruent, tap, flap.

7 What is a glottal stop? Give examples from (regional varieties of) English or other languages which you know.

8 This chapter includes the suggestion (in 2.12) that readers try producing a long [a:] vowel interrupted by either voiced [b] or voiceless [p], to see how voicing can be maintained during stop consonants. Revise the details of that suggestion and then try similar variations with the same vowel and [d] or [t].

9 What is stricture in the description of consonants?

3   Units of Speech

Introduction

This chapter brings us to a consideration of speech sounds as units. The chapter begins (3.1) with a discussion of what actually constitutes a unit of spoken language. It then introduces the concept of complex articulations, articulations in which gestures or settings overlap or are combined to produce what appear to be unitary sounds (3.2).

Specific complex articulations are then described:

- nasalization (3.3)
- labialization (3.4)
- palatalization (3.5)
- velarization and pharyngealization (3.6)
- affrication (3.7)
- double articulation, combining two places of articulation (3.8)
- vowel retroflexion (3.9)
- diphthongization (3.10).

This survey of complex articulation raises several questions about the distinction between consonants and vowels and about the ways in which languages organize syllabic structure. These questions are explained and addressed under the following headings:

- syllabicity (3.11)
- segmentation and structure (3.12)
- diphthongs and related phenomena (3.13).

The chapter ends with an account of how linguists have conventionally 'interpreted' the flow of speech as a linear structure appropriate to the language being analysed (3.14).

3.1 Identifying the units of speech

In describing language we need to refer to units of language. The fundamental reason for this is not just that it is traditional and convenient to refer to sounds and words and syllables and other such elements; it is that language itself depends on discrete and finite options. The point is a general one, not limited to phonology. Human beings can, for example, distinguish a vast number of colours, and frequently do make very fine distinctions when matching paints or dyes. Indeed, colour is a continuum (or in our usual experience of it, at least three intersecting continua, technically referred to as hue, saturation and brightness). These continua are infinitely divisible down to the limits of our perception, yet English represents only limited choices: a handful of colour terms, a few adjectives that can be combined with them (as in 'bright red', 'deep blue') and the general devices of English grammar that allow for relative judgements (as in 'this dress is a darker red than that one' or 'this is not very blue at all, more a grey'). Of course other languages have other words and other mechanisms, and they may divide the continua in quite different ways, but in principle they will all use limited options.

The point applies fully to speech and hearing. Pitch height is a continuum along which we can and do make fine distinctions (as in music, where we hear small variations as sharp or flat notes) but our linguistic systems exploit simple and relative contrasts, such as 'high' versus 'low', or 'high' versus 'mid' versus 'low' (Halliday 1970, p. 6). Vowels likewise (section 2.7 above) fall within a space that can be very finely subdivided, yet most languages exploit rather few contrasts with often no more than half a dozen contrasting vowel qualities.

Thus units point to the systemic nature of language. Wherever a finite number of elements forms a set of contrasting options, we may speak of a system (or a sub-system within a larger system). But the term also points to structuring, or linear arrangement, for a unit characteristically belongs to a particular level of linguistic organization. On one phonological level we may speak of speech sounds as units, on another level we may recognize syllables as units and on yet another, phonological words or phrases. On one level, the English word *conduct* is a sequence of seven sounds (which happen to be reasonably well indicated by the seven letters of the written form), on another level it is a sequence of two syllables, on another it is a single unit, a word.

These units are not ends in themselves but are justified by their descriptive validity. If we want to explain patterns of English stress, for example, we must recognize syllables as relevant units. Stress is a relative property and it must be defined over syllables – we hear a syllable as stressed because it stands out against something which counts as unstressed. In other words, a syllable is not stressed or unstressed in absolute terms, but is more stressed or less stressed than a neighbouring syllable or some other point of reference. Hence when we say, as part of the description of English, that English words such as *conduct, insert* and *produce* each have two patterns of stress (one signalling a verb, the other a noun) we need to refer not to properties of sounds but to relative values of syllables.

Moreover, the validity of units such as syllables can frequently be justified by appeal to the behaviour and judgements of native speakers of a language. English speakers, for example, can normally say how many syllables a word has, and make implicit use of this sense of syllabic structure when they construct verse or put words to a tune.

The units of a language are thus determined in relation to the system and structure of that particular language, although it is reasonable to assume that most languages will have comparable elements (such as sounds and syllables). But even if we can establish what the units of a language are, a further challenge arises when we try to determine the boundaries of those units – when we try to segment connected speech into a chain of sounds or syllables. In chapter 2 we assumed that discrete sound units could indeed be identified in any language (section 2.4), but we could not entirely avoid certain difficulties. It was apparent, for example, in the discussion of long vowels and diphthongs (section 2.8) that the distinction between a single segment and a succession of two segments was by no means straightforward.

Readers may have accepted fairly readily the assumption that speech consists of a sequence of individual units – perhaps too readily, and probably because of our alphabetic writing system, rather than because of any persuasion about the nature of spoken language. The custom of using sequences of discrete letters to write a language such as English does offer an immediate analogy for the segmentation of speech, and the conventional spelling of, say, *conduct* may make it seem obvious that the word consists of seven segmental sounds. But familiarity with alphabetic writing can be highly misleading, for the parallel between writing and speech is not exact. There are obvious examples in English spelling, where 'silent' letters (as in *psalm* or *knight*) and 'digraphs' (two letters for a single sound, e.g. *th*, *sh*) complicate the relationship between letters and sounds. Moreover, although written English is conventionally organized into various units (by spaces between words, punctuation marks between clauses or sentences, etc.), the units of written English do not necessarily match those of spoken English. There is, for instance, no regular indication of syllables in written English. Even when words are hyphenated at the ends of lines the hyphens often do not coincide with the boundaries of spoken syllables. Even more importantly, the organization of speech is *in principle* independent of orthography: languages without regular written form still have phonological system and structure, and persons who cannot read or write still use organized speech. It may well be true that knowledge of a writing system facilitates a certain analytical awareness of segments and structure, but the absence of written expression does not rob spoken language of its systematic nature (Halliday 1985b, especially ch. 7).

The experience of reciting and listing letters of an alphabet encourages the notion that segmental sounds have an independent existence, and literate speakers therefore tend to overlook the analytical process that is involved in segmentation and even to assume that individual letters prove the existence of individual sounds. But there are well-established nonalphabetic writing systems, such as the Chinese character system and the Japanese *Hiragana* and *Katakana* syllabaries, in which symbols stand for entire syllables (or even words), and this is sufficient evidence that orthography is not bound to represent discrete sounds. Moreover, conventional spelling too easily per-suades us to ignore the continuous nature of speech. Thus the natural transition between an |n| and a |z| in words such as *frenzy* and *bronze* could easily be taken as the consonant [d], but it is unlikely to be perceived as such by English speakers who are aware of the spelling; on the other hand, the [d] in, say, *friends* or *fronds* may be no more prominent than the transition in *frenzy* and *bronze* but will in this case be counted as a fully fledged consonant.

Realizing that speech and writing are different kinds or modes of expression, linguists have tried to establish phonetic segments from within the data of speech itself. This has not proved easy. Normal articulation does not consist of a series of discrete actions, each neatly separated from its neighbours. Acoustic records of speech as energy, obtained via a microphone, and articulatory records of the kind obtained by ciné X-ray film do not reveal tidily demarcated segments of speech; rather, they show a more or less continuous flow with various peaks and troughs of energy or movement. When listeners auditorily process this acoustic signal as speech, they are capable of interpreting it as a string of individually identifiable segments. Yet it is by no means obvious from an examination of this signal (and the articulatory activity which produces it) how the flow can be readily converted into a series of separate segments. We shall keep returning to this puzzle throughout this chapter, for the status of the segment as a unit has been questioned by some theorists. In the remainder of this section we shall be concerned particularly with ways in which phoneticians have tried to justify segmentation.

Even in investigations of articulation and perception it is impossible to ignore the units of speech. Of course, one could simply make measurements (of airflow rates or tongue movement or sound intensity) without any reference to units, but that would hardly constitute phonetics. In practice, phoneticians want to measure such things as tongue position in the production of certain kinds of vowels or consonants, or pressure variations during ejective stops. In so doing, phoneticians presuppose not only that there are indeed vowels and consonants of various kinds, but also that it is possible to tell where each segment begins and ends in the chain of speech. A simple working assumption is that, despite the continuous nature of speech, any sound can be identified as a stable state of the articulatory mechanism. This stable state is assumed to include all the articulatory settings that best characterize the sound in question, and is referred to by phoneticians as a TARGET.

Now some sounds, such as vowels, approximants and fricatives, can be fairly readily pronounced in isolation and prolonged indefinitely, subject to available air supply. For these sounds it does make sense to speak of a genuinely stable target – at least potentially, for the stable target will not necessarily be observable in running speech. Sounds such as stops, flaps, taps and trills, on the other hand, are inherently dynamic or transient in their articulation (section 2.12 above), and can be identified only by notional targets that relate to characteristic articulatory properties. Despite this limitation, the concept of target remains important in phonetics and it is com-monly used to justify canonical segments. Thus [k], for example, is said to represent a voiceless velar plosive without aspiration and with neutral lip position. This canonical definition may be convenient in an inventory of phonetic symbols and may also serve as a useful point of reference in studies of how velar plosives are actually articulated by speakers. It is none the less an idealization abstracted out of running speech, where the features of [k] – including even its voicelessness and point of articulation – may well vary considerably. However handy the concept of target may be, it remains important *not* to think of speech as a series of static targets linked by simple articulatory movements. If it has to be said that targets are rarely fully realized or are substantially modified in normal speech, then we must admit that the concept of target points beyond itself to assumptions about the organization of speech.

Besides making working assumptions, phoneticians have also tried to build analyses on the observable properties of the flow of speech. Since this flow does reveal some peaks of activity or prominence, it is theoretically possible to define units such as syllables and segments in terms of these peaks. A common approach proposes that a major peak of prominence represents the NUCLEUS of a syllable and that this nucleus will usually be a vowel or vowel-like segment; consonants will generally occur as MARGINS to these peaks, either as ONSET or as CODA. Other terms used in this kind of approach include CREST, with adjacent SLOPES (Jakobson and Halle 1956, p. 21), or PEAK, with adjacent TROUGHS (Jones 1960, pp. 55ff.). Authors using these terms concede that it is often difficult to locate the boundaries of segments and syllables on this basis; but, in a metaphor of Jespersen's (1922), one would not necessarily deny the existence of two adjacent hills simply because one cannot determine how much of the intervening valley belongs to either of them.

In general, there is no one physical variable which points unambiguously to segmental structure. Thus Stetson's contention that every syllable is initiated by a pulse of chest muscle activity – and that a syllable could therefore be defined by this criterion – was not substantiated by investigation of the muscles themselves (Stetson 1951, Ladefoged 1967).

Peaks of acoustic energy or of articulatory constriction are important in speech organization but again do not offer absolute criteria. As a rule, a peak of energy is likely to be identified as the nucleus of a syllable, and a trough of energy as the margin; while a peak (or trough) of constriction or stricture in the supraglottal tract is likely to be identified as the centre of a segment. In words such as *tot*, *tip-top*, *potato*, acoustic energy will be high at each vowel and sharply reduced during consonant articulation, supporting the impression of clear syllabic structure. At the same time, the degree of articulatory constriction which creates this variation in energy will obviously be highest during the consonants (which are all plosives, involving complete stoppage) and lowest during each vowel. Each segment can therefore be associated with a peak or trough of constriction (Pike 1943, pp. 107ff.). Nevertheless, there are instances where these criteria fail to produce the results expected by a native speaker. A word such as *gorilla*, for example, does not display the clear peaks and troughs that can be observed in *potato*. Apart from its initial consonant, the word *gorilla* contains only vocalic and vowel-like (approximant) sounds. It shows a relatively even acoustic output and little variation in the degree of constriction. More seriously still, a word like *extra*, with a cluster of medial consonants pronounced as [kstr], displays reduced constriction between the [k] and the [t]. It might be expected that the peak of energy at this point, relative to the adjacent plosives, would count as a syllabic nucleus. But it is clear that English speakers count *extra* as a two-syllable word, not three; within English, the peak of energy at this point *does* count as a segment [s] but *not* as a syllable peak.

Another strategy of description resorts to SONORITY. The term refers to energy relative to effort, or more informally to the 'carrying power' of a sound. A sonorous sound is one with high output relative to the articulatory effort required to produce it, and sounds can therefore be ranked according to their degree of sonority. The vowel in *hawk* is more sonorous than the vowel in *hook*, which is in turn more sonorous than a consonant such as *l* or *r*. We can say in general that the points of greatest sonority in an utterance will be interpreted as syllable peaks. But the concept is again not entirely satisfactory. To the extent that it remains a measurable property, derivable from the speech signal, it falls foul of the same difficulties raised by the medial peak in a word such as *extra*; to the extent that it is redefined in more impressionistic terms it merely raises the question of the criteria that language users actually employ in judging segments and syllables.

It must be clear at least that language users who perceive an utterance to have a certain number of syllables or segments are doing more than processing physical data in a purely mechanical fashion, and the customary use of the term PROMINENCE indicates that various factors are integrated within a linguistic system. Thus sonorous sounds can be made less prominent – and nonsonorous sounds more prominent – by variations in duration, pitch or loudness, for example. Moreover, native speakers of a language operate within the system of that language – so that, for example, an English speaker's perception of *extra* never takes the medial [s] to be sufficiently 'prominent' to count as a syllabic peak. For reasons such as these, some phoneticians have abandoned the notion of the syllable altogether (Heffner 1964, Kohler 1966).

It must indeed be recognized that segmentation cannot be based on the speech signal alone but must be responsive to the systematic organization of the language as a whole. Our ultimate assurance that the English word *extra* has only two syllables or that *gorilla* has three is the fact that native speakers perceive these words in just that way. Although much of this complex and abstract process of native speaker perception remains poorly understood, we are not thereby obliged to resort to impressionistic speculation about syllables and segments. English speakers demonstrate the reality of syllabic structure by the way they count the syllables in a line of verse, for example; and they show that they can respond to segmental composition by their assessment of rhyme and alliteration, which depend on shared segments or groups of segments (*mat, bat, fat*, etc. or *mat, mop, mud*, etc.). Ultimately it is this kind of analytical insight – rather than mere inspection of physical records of peaks of energy and stricture – that justifies breaking such words into three segments.

It does not follow from this that all utterances in all languages can be unambiguously segmented, nor that the location of boundaries between units is easily agreed. Given the continuous nature of speech and the overlap between successive articulatory events, it is usually easier to say how many segments or syllables an utterance has than to determine where exactly each unit begins and ends. Even in a simple case such as *door*, the transition from the [d] to the following vowel requires an articulatory movement of the tongue away from the tooth ridge, a movement which is simultaneously the end of the [d] and the beginning of the vowel. Comparable difficulties arise in determining syllable boundaries where, for example, medial consonants in words such as *falling* and *sugar* may be considered to belong both to the preceding syllable and to the following. Language users may or may not impose a sharp boundary, and may locate the boundary differently depending on the criteria to which they give priority. Thus when articulating the word *falling* slowly, as in shouting or singing, speakers may divide it as *fa-lling*, but when considering the grammatical structure, they may break it into *fall + ing*.

Our discussion so far has been almost entirely in terms of segments and syllables, reflecting the attention paid to these particular units in the literature, but other units are of importance in analysing speech. Larger units may be associated with patterns of stress, rhythm or intonation. The term PHONOLOGICAL WORD may apply not only to elements that also happen to be words in a grammatical or orthographical sense but more generally to closely knit clusters of syllables such as *an apple, at home, doesn't* or *shouldn't have*. Terms such as BREATH GROUP and PAUSE GROUP may refer to the 'chunks' into which we divide speech by pausing or taking a new breath, and TONE GROUP commonly refers to a unit defined within the intonational system (see further chapter 9 below).

In summary, segmentation and structural organization are crucial notions in phonological analysis but are not recoverable from orthographic practice or instrumental records of speech alone. Peaks (or troughs) of energy or stricture *tend* to be identified as the central points of units such as segments and syllables but are not absolute criteria in phonological analysis. The determination of phonological units – and in particular the location of boundaries between units – requires reference to the phonological system as a whole.

3.2   Complex articulations

Segmentation of the speech chain and identification of individual sounds is complicated by the way in which many languages use sounds involving combinations of articulatory values. Thus, for example, while oral airflow is the normal prerequisite for a vowel, certain vowels in some languages may have nasal air flow as well (section 2.7). These vowels are normally termed NASALIZED, suggesting that the nasalization is a secondary or superimposed articulation. There are also sounds which use two places of articulation simultaneously, a common example being the [w] heard in English *win* or *wet*, an approximant with narrowing at both lips and velum.

Phoneticians commonly make a distinction between so-called SECONDARY ARTICULATIONS (such as vowel nasalization) and other forms of complex articulation involving more than one place of articulatory activity in the vocal tract. Pike (1943), for example, defines secondary articulations as those associated with constrictions ranking lower than main articulations. But it is sometimes a matter of debate whether one articulator is subsidiary to another. Recognizing this, Ladefoged

(1971) suggested that secondary articulation could include other complex articulations if we arbitrarily assigned primary ranking to the stricture closest to the glottis.

Neither Pike nor Ladefoged deals satisfactorily with the dimension of time. Secondary articulations and other complex articulations may both show either simultaneous components or transitional modifications, and this further blurs the distinction between them. As there seems to be no adequate basis for a rigorous distinction between secondary and complex articulations, they are treated here as a single category under the heading of COMPLEX ARTICULATIONS, which is the more general and potentially less misleading term. We recognize two types of complex articulation: SIMULTANEOUS (separate but co-occurring articulatory activities which result in the production of a sound identifiable as a single segment) and TRANSITIONAL (separate and successive articulatory activities which together can be identified as a single segment).

There are special symbols for some complex articulations but in most instances either a digraph (composed of two appropriate symbols) or a diacritic is used. The digraph may if necessary be distinguished from a sequence of two segments by the use of a linking line above it, e.g. [t͡ʃ] in English *chop* or *much* versus [tʃ] in *hat-shop* or *hot-shot*. Diacritics for simultaneous complex articulations are placed on, above, or below the main symbol, as in [ã] for a nasalized [a]. Transitional complex articulations may use either a superscript or a digraph, where the choice can reflect the relative prominence of one or other aspect of the complex articulation, as in [tˢ] or [t͡s].

3.3   Nasalization

We have already noted that vowels can be nasalized by lowering the velum to allow air to flow through the nasal cavity as well as through the oral cavity (section 2.7 above). This is SIMULTANEOUS NASALIZATION. It is also possible to nasalize consonants such as approximants and fricatives but this seems to happen only as a response to context: for instance, a [w] standing between two nasalized vowels in the west African language Yoruba will normally be nasalized because the nasalization is continued through from one vowel to the next. Nasalization may often spread across several segments in comparable nonsignificant ways: in English, for example, a word such as *channel* may be pronounced with nasalization of both the vowel preceding [n] and the lateral following [n]. We indicate nasalization with the diacritic known as a tilde, thus: [ã], [ũ], [w̃].

Nasalization may be described as 'inherent' when speakers do not exert strong control over the raising of the velum, allowing nasalization to become an 'unintended' characteristic of all their vowels, even when not adjacent to nasal consonants. Nasalization may also be a general property of speech, for reasons of individual articulatory habit, dialect type, or pathological condition such as a cleft palate. Such nasalization is often described as 'pervasive'.

In PRENASALIZATION, a component of nasal articulation occurs before, or in the initial part of, the basic articulation of a segment. Most commonly this applies to stops, which can have nasal output during the initial part of the occlusion phase. Fijian *b* and *d*, for example, are prenasalized and may be represented in phonetic transcription as [m͡b] or [ᵐb] and [n͡d] or [ⁿd].

POSTNASALIZATION is the sequential reverse of prenasalization, with transitional nasal coupling at the end of the basic articulation. The central Australian language Aranda, for example, has stops that may be represented as [p͡m] or [pᵐ], [t͡n] or [tⁿ], and so on.

Note that the standard terminology is somewhat confusing. Nasal consonants (section 2.12 above) might be thought of as nasalized stops, since they have nasal airflow accompanying the articulation of a stop; but it is not usual to describe them in this way and the reader should be aware of the customary distinction between nasal consonants (i.e. nasal stops such as [m] and [n]) and nasalized sounds (especially vowels but also fricatives and approximants). Nevertheless, in stops which are traditionally described as 'prenasalized' and 'postnasalized', the so-called nasalization is in fact a brief nasal stop.

3.4 Labialization

Labialization is the addition of lip rounding or lip protrusion to any sound which is normally articulated with the lips in a neutral or spread position. Labialization modifies the basic articulation by extending the length of the vocal tract and altering its cross-section.

In SIMULTANEOUS LABIALIZATION, rounding or protrusion occurs during the basic articulation. In English (as in most languages) the lip setting of vowels is likely to be maintained through adjacent consonants, particularly where a consonant stands between two identical vowels. Thus the name *Lulu*, for example, may be pronounced with lip rounding persisting through the second [l] sound. This simultaneous labialization is marked by a subscript [w], as in [lʷ].

In TRANSITIONAL LABIALIZATION, the rounding or protrusion is most evident at the end of the main articulation as a part of the transition to the next segment. Not uncommonly, velar stops may have distinctive labialization of this kind, often shown by spellings such as *kw* or *qu*. The phonetic representation is with a superscript, e.g. [kʷ].

3.5 Palatalization

Palatalization involves raising the tip and blade of the tongue to a high front position close to the anterior part of the hard palate region, as for an [i] vowel.

In SIMULTANEOUS PALATALIZATION, the modification to tongue position occurs at the same time as the other articulatory gestures of the segment. An alveolar lateral, for example, can be produced with the body of the tongue (behind the lateral stoppage) raised toward the [i] vowel position. This yields what is often described as a 'clear l', as opposed to the 'dark l' with the body of the tongue lower and further back, as for an [u] vowel. The difference may be heard in comparing the standard German and English pronunciations of names such as *Helmut* and *Wilhelm*, in which the [l] sounds will normally be clear in German but dark in English.

Other sounds that can be palatalized in this way include [n] and [r]; some sounds, such as [k] and [g], cannot have simultaneous palatalization because of the requisite tongue position. We represent simultaneous palatalization by a subscript [j], as in [lⱼ].

In TRANSITIONAL PALATALIZATION, the constriction of the basic articulation is released through a palatal approximation of the tongue tip and blade, as part of the transition to the next segment. In the articulation of stops, the approximation may sometimes be so close that it causes a degree of airstream turbulence (and hence affrication) in the release. It is probably more common than simultaneous palatalization and occurs with a wide variety of consonants in Slavonic languages such as Russian and Polish. The phonetic representation of, for example, Russian or Polish palatalized [t] is [tʲ].

3.6 Velarization and pharyngealization

Velarization and pharyngealization involve moving the tongue body and root from their neutral vocal tract position towards the positions for the vowels [u] and [ɒ]. Since the tongue body posture is adjusted, these articulations always occur simultaneously with the basic articulatory gesture. The so-called 'dark l' referred to above in contrast with (simultaneously palatalized) 'clear l' is velarized to some extent. In Arabic, the so-called 'emphatic' consonants are either velarized or pharyngealized. There appear to be no languages which employ both velarization and pharyngealization. Ladefoged (1971) uses superscript vowels to distinguish between them (e.g. [lᵘ] versus [lᵅ]). A more common practice, followed here, is to place a tilde through the main symbol as a general marker for either of the two complex articulations, e.g. [ɫ].

3.7 Affrication

There is almost always some degree of air turbulence (and hence friction) at the release of a stop. This is normally of such short duration that it counts as part of the release burst of the stop itself. But when the release is strongly frictional and is extended in duration, it can be identified as a separate fricative phase of the articulation. A single complex segment of this kind, in which the articulators release an occlusion through a controlled fricative phase, is known as an AFFRICATE or AFFRICATIVE. The constriction of the fricative phase may be central, grooved, or lateral (section 2.13 above).

We can distinguish two kinds of affricate, according to the strength and duration of the frictional release. We use the term AFFRICATED STOP for the weaker kind, and reserve the term AFFRICATE for the stronger version. In London English, the [t] of e.g. *ten* or *time* may be heavily aspirated to the point of affrication (Gimson 1980, p. 160). The phonetic representation of this affricated stop is [tˢ]. This can be distinguished from a true AFFRICATE, such as the [t͡s] of German *zehn* or *zwei*.

3.8   Double articulation

Two stop articulations can be made simultaneously, creating a double stop. The most widely quoted instances are the labial and velar stops (sometimes called labio-velars) of west African languages such as Yoruba and Ewe, which can be represented as [k͡p] and [g͡b]. Note that these are true double stops, with simultaneous occlusion, not sequences as in English *crackpot* or *ragbag*. Other places of articulation can be combined, and while Ladefoged (1971) suggests that one of the two closures must always be labial, there seems to be no physiological basis for such a restriction. We include as double stops various stops with simultaneous glottal closure, such as [t͡ʔ] or [k͡ʔ]. In some varieties of English, speakers tend to produce syllable-final voiceless plosives (as in *sit* or *sick*) in this way. The replacement of the final [t] by a glottal stop (characteristic of some Londoners' speech, for example) can be regarded as an extreme development of this tendency to use glottal closure in stops: the tongue gesture of the double stop [t͡ʔ] disappears entirely. The mechanism of a double constriction is not limited to plosives and may apply also to nasals, e.g. [ŋ͡m] (the nasal analog of [k͡p] and [g͡b]).

3.9   Vowel retroflexion

In vowel retroflexion, the basic tongue posture of the vowel is modified to produce an 'r-colouring' of the auditory quality. Many American and Irish speakers will have 'r-coloured' vowels in words such as *far*, *four* and *fir*. The auditory effect is traditionally thought to result from curling the tip and blade of the tongue back from their normal vowel position without touching the roof of the mouth, while retaining the basic tongue root and body position for the vowel concerned. These 'r-coloured' vowels are sometimes described as RHOTACIZED vowels.

Ladefoged (1982, p. 78) suggests from X-ray evidence that there may be another way of producing rhotacization, by leaving the tongue tip down but bunching the tongue body upwards. He claims that both articulatory strategies cause the root of the tongue to retract, narrowing the pharynx. Vowel retroflexion is normally regarded as a simultaneous modification of the basic vowel articulation, but in many instances it occurs only in the coda of a vowel, and may thus be transitional in nature. We may represent all varieties of rhotacization by the same superscript symbol, e.g. [aˀ], [ɔˀ], but where the transitional effect is very prominent, it may be more appropriate to interpret the articulation as an approximant consonant following the vowel, i.e. [aɹ], [ɔɹ].

3.10   Diphthongization

We have already referred to diphthongization as a complex articulation combining pure vowels (section 2.8 above). The timing of articulatory movement between two endpoints of pure vowel quality can be finely varied, but three categories appear adequate to account for auditory distinctions. ONGLIDE refers to a relatively brief onset leading into a dominant vowel quality, as in, for example, the [əi] heard from many Londoners and Australians in the words *sea* and *me*. OFFGLIDE refers to a comparable effect at the end of a vowel, moving away from the dominant vowel quality. Some speakers of conservative RP and some from the southern USA have [ɔˀ] in words such as *pore* and *lore* (as opposed to *paw* and *law* without the offglide). The term DIPHTHONG is then reserved for a glide between two vowel qualities, neither of which dominates, e.g. [ɔɪ] as in *toy* or *coy* (in virtually every variety of English).

This categorization of glides and diphthongs is based on the major auditory distinctions that divide the continuum of articulatory timing. In the following sections, we shall see that diphthongs – in common with most of the complex segments mentioned in this chapter so far – need further assessment in the light of the functional role which they play in particular linguistic systems.

3.11   Syllabicity

A syllable commonly consists of a vocalic peak, which may be accompanied by a consonantal onset or coda. In some languages, *every* syllabic peak is indeed a vowel. But other sounds can also form the nucleus of a syllable. In English, this generally happens where a word ends in an unstressed syllable containing a nasal or lateral consonant, as in the following examples, where syllabic consonants are marked by the conventional subscript:

sudden [sʌdən] or [sʌdn̩]
medal   [mɛdəl] or [mɛdl̩].

To take another example from English, the word *and* may often be pronounced as a syllabic nasal (as reflected in the informal spelling '*n*). In fast colloquial speech, the nasal consonant may be assimilated to [m] before a bilabial consonant or [ŋ] before a velar, although this is often condemned as slovenly or careless:

bread 'n butter: 'n may be [n̩] or [m̩]
cash 'n carry: 'n may be [n̩] or [ŋ̩]

In German, unstressed final –*en* is frequently pronounced as a syllabic nasal. Here, the nasal may assimilate to the point of articulation of the preceding consonant, although again the pronunciation is often condemned (e.g. Siebs 1961, p. 43):

haben	('to have')	[ha:bən] or [ha:bm̩]
geben	('to give')	[ge:bən] or [ge:bm̩]
sagen	('to say')	[za:gən] or [za:gŋ̩]
danken	('to thank')	[daŋkən] or [daŋkŋ̩]

Syllabic consonants can be identified as such by their relative length and in some instances by the lack of any audible vocalic release of the preceding stop. (Compare the [d] in the two pronunciations of *sudden*.) In the majority of cases in English, there is variation between syllabic and non-syllabic forms of these consonants. Where they occur medially, there may even be variation in the number of syllables in the word: *fiddler*, for example, can be three syllables (*fidd-l-er*) or two (*fidd-ler*). Ladefoged (1971) suggests, however, that the difference may sometimes be distinctive. His example is *coddling* (three syllables, from 'coddle') versus *codling* (two syllables, meaning 'baby cod').

Syllabic nasals are reasonably common in African languages. In Swahili, for instance, the word for 'man' is *mtu* [m̩tu], in Yoruba, 'big' is *ńlá* [ń̩lá]. Both words are pronounced as two syllables. (The accents in Yoruba mark tone, which occurs on the syllabic nasal as well as on vowels.)

Less commonly, other consonants besides nasals and laterals may have a syllabic value. Syllabic fricatives are reported from languages of the Pacific Coast of North America, such as Bella Coola, a language of British Columbia in which the word for 'bad' is [ʃx] and 'northeast wind' is [s̩ps̩] (Hoard 1978, p. 67).

Syllabicity is sometimes treated as an additional articulatory quality – so that nasal consonants, for example, are specified as either nonsyllabic or syllabic. While this may be convenient in description, it should be noted that perception of syllabicity is shaped by the perceiver's linguistic system. English speakers take the word *spots* to be a single syllable; Bella Coola speakers, on the other hand, might well take it to be a three-syllable word, since it has three phonetic crests, with the initial and final fricatives forming peaks relative to the adjacent plosives.

In the case of some sounds, syllabic and nonsyllabic counterparts tend to be identified as vowels and consonants. This is particularly true of the vowels [i] and [u] and the corresponding approximants [j] and [w]. The term SEMIVOWEL, used for approximants such as [j] and [w], points to the fact that the distinction between a syllabic high vowel and a nonsyllabic semivowel is not always clear-cut. Orthographic practice is often confusing. Classical Latin orthography, for example, used *i* to represent both [i] and [j] and *u* to represent both [u] and [w]. Although the Romans themselves considered the possibility of introducing a distinction in spelling, it was not until the Renaissance that the custom of using *i* and *u* for the vowels and *j* and *v* for the consonants was introduced into the writing of Latin, e.g. *major* 'greater' for earlier *maior*, *pluvium* 'rain' for earlier *pluuium*, etc. (The variants *i/j* and *u/v* were originally different styles of the same letters; see Allen 1978, p. 37.) In English, there are alternative pronunciations of words such as *piano* and *fiasco*, depending on whether they are pronounced with the vowel [i] in the initial syllable (making them three-syllable words) or with the semivowel [j] following the initial consonant (in which case they have only two syllables).

Other semivowels in addition to the widespread [w] and [j] include a labio-palatal [ɥ], which is the approximant counterpart of the front rounded vowel [y], and a velar [ɰ], which is effectively an unrounded [w], corresponding to the back unrounded vowel [ɯ]. French has both [w] – as in *oui* [wi] 'yes' or *loi* [lwa] 'law' – and [ɥ] – as in *nuit* [nɥi] 'night' or *puis* [pɥi] 'then'. The velar [ɰ] is rather rare but occurs in Karen (Burma) and in some Australian Aboriginal languages (where it sometimes seems to have been derived from [w] by a process of derounding or from [ɣ] by loss of friction).

Certain kinds of approximant *r* can be also viewed as semivowels corresponding to retroflexed vowels (section 3.9 above). As in other instances mentioned above, there is often doubt as to the true status or value of these segments. In some varieties of American English, for example, sequences of *r* + vowel and sequences of vowel + *r* merge into a single syllabic sound which could be regarded as either a retroflexed vowel or a syllabic approximant [ɹ]. Thus the words

pretty   prevent   purpose   pervert

may all be pronounced with an identical initial syllable [pɹ-]. Note that spellings such as *purty* or *prevert* represent the typical spelling mistakes of a speaker who makes no distinction in pronunciation between *pre-* and *per-* (although these 'misspellings' are often deliberate and jocular nowadays, rather than genuine errors).

3.12   Segmentation and structure

The segmental organization of some languages can be relatively easily described. In Walmatjari, for example, an Aboriginal language spoken in the north of Western Australia (Hudson 1978, pp. 4ff.), every word begins with a single consonant; consonants may be adjacent to each other only at the junction of two syllables; and the boundaries of segments and syllables are fairly easily determined. Thus for each of the following words we can show the separate syllables and their structure in terms of C (consonant) and V (vowel):

ngapa ('water')   [ŋa pa]   CV CV
kurrapa ('hand') [ku ra pa]   CV CV CV
ngarpu ('father') [ŋaɹ pu]   CVC CV.

We stress that the description is *relatively* easy and that there are some problems (which will be mentioned later). But it is generally possible to identify units such as segments and syllables and to give a relatively straightforward account of their patterning. Thus we can say that a Walmatjari syllable is realized as either CV or CVC, that words must end with a CV syllable, and so on.

The term DISTRIBUTION is often used in such contexts and a description of phonological structure is sometimes known as a DISTRIBUTIONAL STATEMENT (i.e. a statement specifying how segments are distributed within syllables, and syllables within words, etc.). The term PHONOTACTICS is also widely used to refer to the general description of sequences and combinations. In particular, PHONOTACTIC CONSTRAINTS express limitations on the free combination of units. In English, for example, a word-initial syllable can begin with various consonant sequences (such as *sp, st, sk, pl, bl, kl, gl*) but there are systematic constraints that exclude *zb, zd, tl* or *dl*. Sequences of three consonants are even more severely constrained in English: in initial position we have, for instance,

spr as in spring, sprat
str as in string, strap
skr as in script, scrap

but not *smr, zbr, fpr*, etc. (See Gimson 1980, pp. 237 ff. for a detailed account.)

Accounts of distribution or phonotactics sometimes suggest an unduly mechanical picture, as if segments were building blocks put together to form syllables, and syllables in turn put together to form larger units. In fact phonotactic description cannot be divorced from the process of segmenting speech and establishing units, and there are often difficulties even in distinguishing between a single segment and a sequence of segments. This is particularly true of complex articulations such as prenasalized plosives or affricates (sections 3.3 and 3.7 above), where we seem to be talking about single segments even though the articulation indicates a sequence of two elements or components.

In some cases a language may actually distinguish between one-segment and two-segment articulation. Most English speakers will probably regard the initial consonant of *chip, chain, chop* as a single consonant, even though it is an affricate 'consisting of' a stop and a fricative. Certainly there is no possibility in English of distinguishing between a word-initial affricate and a word-initial sequence of stop + fricative. But in cases such as *he cheats* versus *heat-sheets* or *what can each add?* versus *what can eat shad?* there is, at least potentially, a distinction (Chao 1934,

p. 40). Readers may like to consider whether and how they distinguish between the medial consonants in such pairs of words as

lychee	light-ship
ketchup	pet-shop
urchin	(a) hurt shin

A direct contrast among such words in connected speech is of course unlikely, but many speakers of English will sense a difference, principally in the timing of the transition from the stop to the following fricative.

More commonly, there is no distinction within the language: some languages have affricates, others may have sequences of plosive plus fricative. In such cases what appears to be identical in articulation proves to be differently valued in different languages. The sequence [ts], for instance, occurs in English – *cats, fatso, Betsy* – Dutch – *fiets* ('bicycle'), *etsen* ('to etch') – and German – written *z* or *tz* in *zehn* ('ten'), *bezahlen* ('to pay'), *salzen* ('to salt'), *witzig* ('funny'). In English and Dutch this sequence is not an affricate but simply a sequence of [t] and [s]; in German, however, [ts] is normally counted as a single-segment affricate, just as [tʃ] is in English.

Affricates of this general type (plosive plus sibilant fricative) are reasonably common and are often represented as single letters within the spelling system of the relevant language, e.g.

[ts]   Polish and Czech *c* in *co* (what) *cena* (price)
       Italian *z* in *zio* (uncle) *marzo* (March)
[dz]   Italian *z* in *zona* (zone) *zero* (zero).

Russian script also has a single letter for [ts], while in ancient Greek the letter zeta seems to have represented [dz]. (In modern Greek, zeta represents [z], but it is thought that the Ancient pronunciation was [dz], metathesized to [zd] early in the Classical period; see Allen 1987, pp. 56–9.)

Affricates similar to English [tʃ] (*chip, chess*) and [dʒ] (*jump, jeep*) are also widespread, but with variation in the precise point of articulation. In the Pinyin romanized spelling of Chinese, for example, *q* and *j* represent palatal affricates, and *ch* and *zh* postalveolar affricates, as in *qiang* ('rob'), *jian* ('build'), *chuanghu* ('window'), *zhui* ('chase'). In Indonesian, *c* and *j* represent sounds that are sometimes described as palatal plosives but are normally articulated with a clear fricative release, as in *cari* ('search'), *jari* ('finger') or in names such as *Cilacap, Jawa* (Java), *Jakarta*.

Other less common types of affricate include [pf] as in German *Pferd* ('horse') or *pflanzen* ('to plant') and [kx], a velar affricate which occurs in some Swiss German dialects where the standard language has initial *k* (Russ 1978, p. 46). An affricate with lateral fricative release is found in a number of indigenous American languages, represented as *tl* in names such as *Nahuatl* and *Tenochtitlan*. In all such instances, the definition of these complex sounds as affricates depends upon the single-segment value assigned to them within the particular phonological system (section 3.14 below).

Similar remarks can be made about prenasalized stops. Many languages allow sequences of nasal plus plosive (English *amber*, *under*, *anger*) but it is only in certain languages that such sequences have the status of single segments. A clear instance is Fijian, where [mb], [nd] and [ŋg] count as single consonants within the phonological system. Voiced plosives are always prenasalized in Fijian and [b], [d] and [g] do not occur other than in prenasalized form. Note, for example, the Fijian spellings *Nadi* (place name) and *noda* 'our' for [nandi] and [nonda].

Lengthened sounds are also open to interpretation as single or double sounds. In English, there is no particular reason to take long vowels to be sequences: some vowels are relatively long (as in *beat* and *boot*) and others are short (as in *bit* or *but*). Depending on the variety of English, some long and short vowels can be paired as vowels distinguished by length alone, but others cannot. In Australian English, for example, the long vowel of *calm* and *psalm* can be matched with the short vowel of *come* and *sum*: the two vowels are distinguished by length alone. But the long vowel of *bead* and *fees* has no short partner. (If there is a long counterpart of the short vowel of *bid* and *fizz*, in typical Australian pronunciation it is the long vowel of *beard* and *fears* rather than that of *bead* and *fees*.) On the other hand, in Japanese, there are five short vowels and five matching long ones. Not only do the long vowels count as double vowels in written Japanese, they are also reckoned as two vowels in the rhythmic organization of verse (Comrie 1987, p. 868).

3.13   Diphthongs and related phenomena

At first sight diphthongs seem to be another instance of two phonetic segments functioning as one. They are, in a sense, two vowels forming a single entity (sections 2.8 and 3.10 above) and are analogous to affricates or prenasalized plosives in that they are generally regarded as single but complex segments. Nevertheless, the interaction of syllabicity and segmentation can be intricate. We may begin by distinguishing two simple categories, namely diphthongs and sequences of two vowels. English vowels heard in the RP pronunciation of the following words are undoubtedly diphthongs:

how, bough, cow
eye, high, buy, tie
hay, bay, cay
owe, hoe, toe
boy, toy, coy.

All of these words count as single syllables in English. On the other hand, there are languages in which sequences of vowels are clearly not diphthongs. In Komering, for example, a language of southern Sumatra, words such as *mait* ('corpse'), *tuot* ('knee') and *kuah* ('sauce') are articulated and perceived as two-syllable words (Yallop and Abdurrahman 1979, pp. 11–12). Note that syllabicity is crucial in distinguishing the English diphthongs from the Komering two-vowel sequences.

Now in the case of diphthongs, the first or second target is often a vowel of [i] or [u] quality. In some languages, especially where the [i] or [u] target is clearly not the dominant component of the diphthong, the possibility arises of treating the [i] or [ʊ] as a nonsyllabic semivowel. Thus diphthongs such as [oi] and [au] might be represented as [oj] and [aw]. In fact notations of just this kind have been widely used in English transcription, particularly in the USA, e.g. *high* as [haj] and *how* as [haw].

With sequences of two vowels, transcription is complicated by the fact that an intrusive glide may be heard between the two vowels. Thus in many languages, words such as [mei] or [mou], articulated as two syllables, may well be heard as [meji] or [mowu].

It may be necessary to make a further distinction here, as there are also 'triphthongs' in some languages, vowel sequences in which three components can be heard but which none the less count as a single vowel. In some varieties of English (notably those without postvocalic *r*) words such as *hire*, *lyre* and *our*, *cower* contain triphthongs, often transcribed as [aɪə] and [auə]. Here too, however, intrusive glides may occur, and some speakers may distinguish between, e.g.

one syllable:	hire	lyre	flour	cowered
two syllables:	higher	liar	flower	coward.

But many authorities, including Jones and Gimson, do *not* recognize any distinction between these pairs, treating every one of these eight words as a monosyllable containing a triphthong.

It is also possible to analyse long vowels as vowel + semivowel. Hence [i:] or [u:] may be transcribed as [ij] or [uw], particularly if there is a change in quality during the articulation of the vowel, or if a transitional glide becomes prominent before a following vowel, that is, if [i:] followed by [a] is pronounced as [ija]. Note, for example, the English tendency to insert a [j] glide after the first vowel of words such as *piano*, *Fiona* and *Seattle*. Again, there is a tradition, notably in the USA, of transcribing English long vowels in this way.

In some Aboriginal languages, phonological structure suggests an interpretation which is the mirror-image of the above. That is, [i:] may be interpreted as [ji]. In Walmatjari, for example, we saw (in section 3.12 above) that words regularly begin with a consonant. There are apparent exceptions to this pattern, specifically words beginning with [i:] and [u:], such as [i:nja] 'gave' and [u:lju] 'good'. But these words are not exceptions if they are taken to begin with [ji] and [wu]. If so, then [i:nja] is [jinja] and [u:lju] is [wulju]. While this may seem a surprising equation, it is important to see how such interpretations make sense within a particular system. Unlike English, Walmatjari has no contrast of the type found in English *east/yeast*, *ooze/woos* and no words beginning with a vowel (other than the 're-interpretable' instances of initial [i:] and [u:]). Hence the predominant pattern of

Walmatjari – that words regularly begin with a consonant – may be sufficient to make speakers of the language 'feel' that [i:nja] and [u:lju] do also begin with a consonant.

We can therefore distinguish, potentially at least, a number of distinct structural possibilities:

1   DIPHTHONG, i.e. a single vowel, but one in which two targets or components can be discerned. The term is warranted only if the vowel genuinely counts as a single vowel in the language in question. In English, for example, *high*, *how* and *hoe* are judged by speakers to be monosyllables and their vowels can justifiably be called diphthongs.

2   TRIPHTHONG, i.e. a single vowel with three discernible targets. As with diphthongs, the term presupposes some justification for treating the complex as a single vowel.

3   VOWEL PLUS SEMIVOWEL, e.g. [ej] [aj] [ow] [oj]. In many languages such sequences are simply alternative ways of transcribing diphthongs, i.e. [ej] = [ei]; but there are Australian Aboriginal languages in which the second component of a diphthong such as [ai] has a consonantal value, and is therefore analysed as [j]. Where a high vowel is followed by an appropriate semivowel (high front vowel followed by palatal semivowel, high back vowel followed by velar semivowel) it is unlikely that the sequence will be distinct from a long vowel. Hence [ij] = [i:] and [uw] = [u:].

4   SEMIVOWEL PLUS VOWEL, e.g. [ju] [wa] [ji] [wu]. As with vowel plus semivowel, these sequences may be alternative transcriptions of diphthongs or (where appropriate) long vowels.

5   VOWEL SEQUENCE, i.e. a sequence of two (or more) vowels which is *not* a diphthong. If such a sequence is genuinely distinct from the other possibilities listed above, it is highly likely that the constituent vowels will constitute separate syllabic peaks.

6   VOWEL PLUS SEMIVOWEL PLUS VOWEL, e.g. [aji] [uwa]. In some cases these will simply be part of the phonotactic possibilities of the language; in others the semivowel may be regarded as an intrusive transition. Compare English words like *leeway* and *blow-wave*, where the semivowel [w] readily counts as the initial consonant of the second syllable; and words like *booing*, *cluey*, *blowy* and *Joey*, where a medial [w] may be taken to be intrusive.

The ways in which these six possibilities are exploited and equated with each other vary enormously from language to language, and it is important to avoid generalizations based on one or two languages. Thus the tendency to link adjacent vowels via a semivowel is strong in some varieties of English (as in *seeing* with intrusive [j], *suing* with intrusive [w]); and the consequence of this is to blur the distinction between [i:] and [ij]. In German, however, there is a quite different tendency, namely to separate adjacent vowels by a glottal stop: compare German *Hiatus*, pronounced [hia:tus] or [hiʔa:tus], with the English pronunciation of *hiatus*.

Such tendencies are by no means predictable from general phonetic principles and may reflect complex linguistic patterns. Thus some speakers of English extend the pattern of intrusive semivowels to include insertion of an r-sound between certain vowels – the so-called 'intrusive r' in e.g. *law(r) and order, the idea(r) of it, draw(r)-ing*, etc. This r-transition applies only after certain vowels, namely [ɜ:] [ɔ:] [a:] [ə] and centering diphthongs such as [ɪə] and [ɛə], and is restricted to varieties of English in which *r* is not normally pronounced unless followed by a vowel. In such varieties (e.g. south-eastern England, Australia, New Zealand, north-eastern USA) we find:

r is not pronounced at the end of an utterance,
   e.g. two plus two equals fou(r);
r is likewise not pronounced before a consonant,
   e.g. fou(r) books; fou(r) tables;
but r is pronounced before a vowel,
   e.g. four apples; four eggs.

This pattern sets up a powerful analogy for *all* words ending in an appropriate vowel, including those in which there is no *r* in the spelling, such as *law* and *idea*. The 'intrusive r' is thus a consequence of the historical loss of word-final and pre-consonantal *r* in certain regions of the English-speaking world. The 'intrusion' is quite unnatural for those who retain the *r*, including most Scottish and Irish and many North American speakers of English. Hence judgments about diphthongs, semivowels and transitions must in general take careful note of the particular phonological system within which the phenomena are found.

3.14 Interpretations

Questions of the kind that have arisen in this chapter – whether two consonants truly constitute an affricate or whether a vowel is really a semivowel – have generally been treated as questions of interpretation. The assumption here is that certain sounds (or combinations) will need to be interpreted within the linguistic system of which they are part. The concept of interpretation has a long history. De Saussure, for example, proposed a phonetic classification that allowed certain sounds to function as either vowels or consonants (more strictly, in his own French terminology, as *sonantes* or *con-sonantes*). In his illustration from French, the *i* in both *pied* and *fidèle* is a single phonetic 'species' but [j] in *pied* is *consonante*, [i] in *fidèle* is *sonante* (1916, pp. 87–8). Some years later, Sapir suggested various criteria by which one might determine what he calls 'the place of a sound in a phonetic pattern over and above its classification on organic or acoustic grounds' (1925, p. 19). The criteria hinted at by Sapir and later exploited in the phonological description of many different languages include the following.

Combinatory possibilities or phonotactic patterning

For example: English [tʃ] and [dʒ] (as in *chin, chart, gin, jump*) are single-segment affricates because of their occurrence in word-initial position. In general, English words cannot begin with a combination of stop followed by fricative. (Note that where English spelling appears to allow word-initial stop plus fricative, the pronunciation is of a fricative alone, e.g. *ps* pronounced [s] in *psychology, pseudo*, *x* pronounced [z] in *xylophone, xenophobia*.) Now if English [tʃ] and [dʒ] were sequences of two consonants, they would violate this general pattern; but if they are taken to be affricates, the generalization that English words do not begin with stop plus fricative remains valid.

Patterns of stress or other prosodic regularities

For example: in Alyawarra, a central Australian language (Yallop 1977), words may contain sequences such as [pmp] or [tnt] e.g. *apmpima* ('burn'), *atntirrima* ('run'). The nasal in these sequences appears to form a syllabic peak, but the stress system overrides this impression and suggests a nonsyllabic interpretation. The general rule in Alyawarra is that words which begin with a vowel are stressed on the second syllable, e.g. *a'tirra* ('cicada'), *a'nima* ('sit') etc. Now in words such as *apmpima*, the stress falls not on the syllabic nasal but on the following vowel, i.e. *apm'pima*, *atn'tirrima*. Hence within the Alyawarra phonological system, the nasal consonants do not count as syllabic peaks and are better interpreted as release features of the preceding plosive. In other words, *pm* and *tn* are complex segments rather than sequences of two consonants.

Symmetry and parallelism

For example: Moba, a language spoken in Togo, west Africa, has a number of short and long vowels, illustrated in the following:

[bil]	to put	[biː]	to be spoilt
[pel]	to hurry	[kud]	to prepare porridge
[tud]	to push	[tuːd]	to trip over
[pal]	to clean	[kod]	to slaughter
[pɔl]	to plug	[kaːd]	interrogate the dead.

Now there is an asymmetry in the vowel system, for there are no long vowels matching short [e] [o] [ɔ]: we have

long vowels   iː   aː   uː
short vowels   i   e   a   o   ɔ   u

There are, however, diphthongal vowels [ie], [uo] and [ua], as in

[piel]	to harvest peanuts		[miel]	nose
[puod]	to cross		[kuod]	to diminish
[pual]	to pluck		[kuad]	to sell.

If these diphthongs are interpreted as long vowels – [ie] = [e:], [uo] = [o:] and [ua] = [ɔ:] – the gaps in the system are filled. It must then be assumed that Moba does have long mid vowels (in a functional or systemic sense), but that these vowels are realized as diphthongs with a high onglide (Russell 1980).

Morphological or grammatical patterning

For example: in many Australian Aboriginal languages, there are often phonotactic reasons for interpreting certain vowels as semivowels. In some instances such interpretations are supported by the rules or patterns of affixation. In Dyirbal, for example, words can end in [ui], which is probably best interpreted as [uj], e.g. [walguj] 'brown snake' rather than [walgui]. An important criterion here is the affixation: the locative suffix in Dyirbal takes the form [ŋga] after a vowel but [ɟa] after a palatal consonant, e.g.

[jaɹa]	man		[jaɹaŋga]	on a man
[biɲɟiriɲ]	small lizard		[biɲɟiriɲɟa]	on a lizard

Now the locative form of 'brown snake' is [walguiɟa], not [walguiŋga]. Even though the root-final [i] may strike the hearer as clearly vocalic, it seems reasonable to say that, from the Dyirbal perspective, the root ends in a consonantal [j] (Dixon 1972, p. 42).

The most highly formalized statements of criteria such as these can be found in Trubetzkoy (1939, ch. 2) and Pike (1947, ch. 12). Trubetzkoy proposes a series of rules for what he calls 'monophonematic' interpretation (i.e. interpretation of complex articulations as single segments) and 'polyphonematic interpretation' (i.e. interpretation of a single segment as more than one). His two most important rules or conditions are

1 If two segments are to be interpreted as one, they must fall within the same syllable;
2 If two segments are to be interpreted as one, they must involve a unitary articulatory movement, e.g. [ts] and [kx] are potential affricates, but [ks] and [tf] are not.

Although these two rules have an air of common sense about them, they are not entirely satisfactory. A recurrent theme of this chapter has been that the definition of the syllable and the determination of segmental boundaries interact with each other, and it will not always be self-evident that two sounds fall within the same syllable. Furthermore, while there are obviously limits on the phonetic nature of potential diphthongs and affricates, these limits are not easily defined. We know, for instance, that [pf] and [tʃ] count as affricates in some languages, and we must presumably define 'unitary articulatory movement' in such a way as to include these complex sounds. But it is not clear whether the definition may then include other sequences (say [ps] and [ks]) and whether there is really any property of the articulation itself that can settle this question independently of particular phonological systems.

Trubetzkoy's further rules 3–7, which he himself describes as subordinate or secondary to 1 and 2, draw on various other phonetic and systemic criteria, such as the duration of a complex segment in relation to that of simple segments in the given language (rule 3) or the occurrence of elements of a complex segment elsewhere in the language (rule 6; cf. [mb] as a single segment in Fijian, where [b] does not occur on its own, section 3.12 above).

Pike (1947, ch. 12) provides a highly detailed listing of the kinds of phonetic phenomena which are open to interpretation. Under segments which may be either consonant or vowel, he includes not only semivowels but also voiceless vowels (which he suggests need not be syllabic) and a weak velar fricative (which is in effect the semivowel [ɰ]).

His list of sequences of two segments which may be interpreted as one includes:

> stops with various kinds of release phenomena (aspirated, labialized, affricated, nasally released, etc.);
> homorganic nasals plus stops, i.e. prenasalized stops;
> vowel glides, i.e. diphthongs;
> double stops, such as [k͡p] and [g͡b]; and
> sequences of voiced and voiceless equivalents, such as word-final [zs] which may simply be a [z] without full voicing throughout.

He has a separate category of complex segments which may be interpreted as a sequence of two, including long vowels and consonants, vowels with various kinds of secondary articulation (e.g. nasalized [ã] interpreted as [an]) and syllabic consonants (e.g. [m̩] interpreted as [əm]).

Pike's treatment is impressive for its comprehensive attention to phonetic detail and analytical procedure in a field situation. Pike's appeal is to the weight of predominant structural patterning, which he calls 'structural pressure'. More precisely, 'characteristic sequences of sounds exert structural pressure on the phonemic interpretation of suspicious segments or suspicious sequences of segments' (1947, p. 128). Pike operates with a firm distinction between the phonetic level and the phonological. Thus the terms 'contoid' and 'vocoid' are phonetic terms defined independently of any particular language, while 'consonant' and 'vowel' are (phonological) terms applying within specific languages. For example, an affricate is a sequence of two contoids but a single consonant; a semivowel is a vocoid functioning as a consonant; and so on. Pike's routine, then, is one of assessing phonetic ambiguities in the light of structural patterns. In a language in which all words begin with a single contoid, except that some words begin with [ts] or [dz], the predominant pattern would exert pressure on the linguist to interpret [ts] and [dz] as (single) consonants. This routine has undoubtedly proved useful to field linguists struggling to transcribe and analyse previously unwritten languages. In such situations the linguist often has to decide whether to write [ai] or [aj], [an] or [ã:], and so on.

Some of Pike's exercises and examples may give the unfortunate impression that it is the field linguist's task to impose organization on raw data. Such misgivings are not allayed by Pike's remark to the effect that 'phonetics gathers raw material' while phonological analysis 'cooks' the raw material (1947, p. 57). Nevertheless it is clear from the wider context of Pike's work that he was concerned to analyse language in ways that accorded with native speaker intuitions, and that he was interested in the development of spelling systems that would be efficient from the native speakers' point of view. At the same time Pike was undoubtedly well aware that phonetic raw material is a questionable concept: even highly trained phoneticians cannot transcribe an unfamiliar language in such a way as to provide objective phonetic data for analysis.

It is worth dwelling on this point because linguists such as Pike have been accused of being obsessed with 'taxonomic' analysis and field procedures. In a sense the charge is valid. But it should at least be clear that Pike's 'cooking' of the data is not an exercise in the arbitrary pursuit of regularity or symmetry or notational convenience. Rather, his (and others') work should be judged in the light of the ambition to reduce languages to writing and to correct the natural tendency to interpret all phonological systems against the background of one's own language.

The most serious objection to the formulation of an interpretative routine is that it may give the impression that each doubtful case can be submitted to a decision-making procedure. In fact different criteria may point in different directions, and alternative solutions may simply reflect differing but equally valid perspectives. Frequently, the routine of interpretation is successful only because one criterion, say phonotactic regularity, is pursued to the exclusion of others.

Consider, for example, the [ju] in English *unicorn, unity, due, assume, module*. There are at least two reasons for arguing that this complex vowel is a sequence of [j] followed by [u], namely:

1   The [j] can affect a preceding consonant in exactly the same way as any other occurrence of the consonant [j]. Thus the initial consonant of *due* may be [dʒ] while *ss* in *assume* may be [ʃ]. This is parallel to the effect of [j] on a preceding [d] or [s] in sequences such as *could you* and *this year*.
2   Where [ju] begins an English word, we treat it as beginning in a consonant. We say, for example, *a unicorn*, not *an unicorn*.

There are also at least two reasons for arguing that [ju] is a single diphthongal vowel, namely:

3   If [j] is a consonant, then we must allow that English has sequences of consonants such as [dj] and [sj] (as in *due* and *assume*). But these sequences

occur only before the vowel [u]. There are no words in English containing sequences such as [dja] or [sji]. This irregularity would not exist if [ju] were interpreted as a diphthong, with [j] understood as part of the complex vowel.

4 The vowel [ju] alternates with the undeniably simple vowel [ʌ]: compare *assume* and *assumption* or *induce* and *induction*. This shift of vowel quality is parallel to other shifts in English: note for example the long vowels in *convene* and *concede* corresponding to short vowels in *convention* and *concession*.

Readers may care to review these four reasons and to consider whether – and why – any of them should take priority over the others.

Exercises

1 Which of the following words do you pronounce identically?

cents, scents, sense, sends
wince, wins, winds (plural of 'a wind')

Check your own perception by saying the words in random order and asking others to judge which you are saying. Where there is a difference in articulation try to state exactly what it is.
2 How many syllables are there in the following words? How would you break the words into spoken syllables? (For example, 'banana' has three syllables: 'ba-na-na'.)

above, music, window, extra, betray, longer, interest,
camera, horrible, atrocious, delightful, yesterday,
ferocity, perforation, approximately, secretarial

Note that some words are much easier to deal with than others and try to identify the reasons for this. Note also any differences among speakers, either in pronunciation or in judgments about syllabic structure.
3 The following words rhyme (at least for many speakers of English). What exactly is it that makes us count them as rhymes?

weight, mate, bait
peril, feral, Meryl

4 The following words illustrate alliteration. What exactly is alliteration?

soothing, psychic, cell, scene
cool, chemical, company, king

5 The following words illustrate assonance (at least for many speakers of English). What exactly is assonance?

meant, deck, said
walk, taunt, lawn

6 What is the difference between:

– simultaneous and transitional palatalization?
– onglide, offglide, diphthong and triphthong?
– affricated stop and affricate?

7 Check that you understand the following terms:

sonority
prenasalization
labialization
velarization
double stop
rhotacized vowel
syllabic consonant
semivowel
phonotactics

8 At the end of this chapter a question is posed about the interpretation of English [ju] (as in *few* and *cue*). Note the criteria mentioned in the text and discuss the interpretation.

Consider any other examples of interpretation. Can you, for instance, justify the claim that the words *catch* and *cadge* end in affricates, whereas *cats* and *adze* end in a sequence of stop + fricative?

9 Misspellings such as *chrane* for *train* and *jragn* for *dragon* have been recorded from children who are just beginning to read and write. What do the misspellings suggest about the children's perception of the initial consonant sequences in these words?

4 The Phonemic Organization of Speech

Introduction

This chapter explores a long-standing and fundamental insight into spoken language – that it can be understood as the realization of a system of phonemes. The chapter begins by placing the phoneme in the context of the inherent variability of speech (4.1). It then explains and illustrates what is meant by 'phoneme' (4.2) and by the related concept of 'allophone' (4.3).

This basic introduction is followed by a series of topics which are a necessary part of conventional phonemic description but which also need to be addressed as theoretical issues:

- the notion of phonemic norms (4.4)
- pattern and symmetry in phonemic systems (4.5)
- the question of phonological reality (4.6)
- the relevance of units and boundaries in speech (4.7)
- phonemic invariance and overlap (4.8)
- biuniqueness in phonemic analysis and the neutralization of phonemic distinctions (4.9)
- morphophonemic alternation (4.10)
- free variation (4.11).

The chapter ends with a review of the kinds of phonemic systems that are found across the languages of the world (4.12).

4.1 Phonetic variability

In chapters 2 and 3 we have seen how various articulatory gestures and processes can be used to generate speech sounds and how particular languages organize the flow of speech within structured patterns. Putting it very simply, we can say that a language selects from the human articulatory potential, and that it systematizes that selection. In consequence individual languages (and dialects) are normative, in the sense that speakers operate within the limits imposed by such selection and systematization. This phonological normativity is not of course a matter of legal obligation or moral duty, nor in most cases does it emerge from formal training or instruction in pronunciation; rather it unfolds in the process of our growing up in a particular speech community, and acquiring and maintaining the speech habits of that community. We show our response to such normativity in dozens of ways – often quite informally or even subconsciously – whenever we identify a particular pronunciation as strange or foreign, when we recognize and warm to a familiar regional dialect, or when we dismiss a foreign word or name as 'unpronounceable'.

This is not to imply that we are all loyally attached to a single local dialect or language. Speakers of a language such as English, spread across a large and diverse population around the world, may be familiar with many different norms and may themselves exploit different norms according to circumstance, shifting, say, between a local or informal style of pronunciation and one that would be considered more standardized or formal. Nevertheless, while such versatility may complicate the status and application of phonological norms, it does not deny the existence and strength of the norms themselves.

If we do not acknowledge this normative character, we have little justification for talking about and investigating 'normal' pronunciation. If we do acknowledge it, we have a basis at least for describing pronunciation against a background of what counts as normal. For pronunciation is in fact highly variable, even within the limits of what may be agreed as normal. This is hardly surprising, given the nature of the articulatory mechanism, the precision and coordination needed to control it, and the fineness of auditory discrimination.

A problem for phoneticians, but not for the average user of language, is that there are considerable physical differences among speakers. Variations in the size and shape of the vocal tract and articulators are sufficient to yield substantial and persistent differences between one speaker and another. (As we shall see later, in chapter 7, it is a challenge to explain how it is that we can discount such differences – how we manage to hear 'the same words' being uttered by two quite different speakers, and yet at the same time respond to the differences by identifying the two voices as particular individuals.) An obvious and striking example is the difference between a child and an adult in, among other things, the overall length of the vocal tract. The difference in length – far greater in adults than in children – has major effects on the sound quality of speech, yet we are able to allow for this in our hearing of children's speech.

Another relatively permanent cause of differences is that individuals learn or become accustomed to habitual settings in the underlying postures of articulators – in much the same way that individuals have habitual body postures of which they are barely conscious but which affect the way they characteristically sit and stand and walk. There are also wide variations in habitual rate of articulation, and differences in the laryngeal settings used for 'normal' voiced phonation. A speaker may, for example, always use somewhat breathy phonation, or always articulate with the lips slightly protruded, or always use a relatively slow rate of articulation. Such differences usually do not affect the articulation of individual speech sounds in a particular or selective way, but are global properties that contribute to a total impression of voice quality. (See Laver 1980 for a comprehensive discussion of the phonetics of voice quality.)

Apart from these global differences among individuals, many speakers have a characteristic way of articulating certain sounds. For example, a particular speaker of English may, regularly and systematically, produce alveolar plosives with unusual fronting, almost as dentals. This is likely to be a noticeable feature of the individual's speech, the kind of thing a mimic might fasten on to. Among English speakers there are sizeable minorities who pronounce [s] and [z] sufficiently unusually to be noticed (and sometimes to be described as 'lisping') or who use an r-sound with a high degree of lip protrusion (which may lead to the accusation that they 'say *w* instead of *r*').

Variability such as we have mentioned so far is often described as pervasive. But speakers may also vary their articulatory behaviour, consciously or unconsciously, in a way which is often unpredictable and certainly not pervasive. This sort of idiosyncratic variation may often go unnoticed or be dismissed as trivial oddity, and it is generally tightly constrained by the demands of the phonological system. Thus a speaker of English who happens in one particular utterance to devoice the initial consonant of the word *zip* is likely to be heard as having said the wrong word, namely *sip*. While context may make it perfectly clear that *zip* was intended, a systemic error of this kind is more likely to attract attention than, say, devoicing of the [z] in *adze* or *adds*, where both words are normally pronounced identically and the voicing is not distinctive. In general, the phonological system of any language will make some variations far more tolerable than others.

Certain aspects of speech may vary according to the speaker's social environment and emotional state. Speakers will generally exercise considerably more articulatory care when making a speech on a formal occasion than when chatting casually with friends. The articulatory consequences of such deliberate attention to speech cannot always be easily distinguished from the involuntary effects of the speaker's emotional state. Anxiety or fear or anger can noticeably affect articulation rate, phonation mode or articulatory forcefulness, and we are all accustomed to reading emotions from an overall impression of these properties of speech. Similarly, articulation may change quite radically as a speaker makes special efforts to be heard intelligibly in adverse circumstances, such as against a background of noise. Effects such as these are often described as 'affective' or 'paralinguistic', implying that they are a matter of general background, peripheral to the main communicative function of language, but it is in fact not at all easy to quantify and predict these factors in such a way as to separate them off from 'truly linguistic' functions. Consider, for example, the difficulty of distinguishing between anger as a communicative strategy – with features of articulation deliberately adopted and under control for persuasive or threatening purposes – and anger as an uncontrolled and involuntary emotion. In any case, so-called paralinguistic features do contribute significantly to variability in articulation, both within the speech of an individual and from one speaker to another.

Traditionally more central to linguistic description is CONTEXT-SENSITIVE VARIATION. Speech does not consist simply of a string of target articulations linked by simple movement between them (section 3.1 above). Instead, the articulation of individual segments is almost always influenced by the articulation of neighbouring segments, often to the point of considerable overlapping of articulatory activities. As a consequence, the notional or 'ideal' way of articulating a particular sound is subject to modification in running speech. This phonetic variability is due not just to differences among individual speakers, but also to the phonetic context. The general effect is known as CONTEXT-SENSITIVITY.

Context-sensitive variation has complex and interacting causes which are not yet completely understood. Two basic types can be distinguished: (1) the effects of the biomechanical performance properties of the vocal tract, and (2) the effects of the nature and organization of the neuromuscular control mechanisms which actuate articulator movements. Both types may reflect genuine limitations on what the vocal tract can achieve – there are, after all, limits to the speed with which the tongue can move from one position to another, or to the rate at which the vocal folds can vibrate. But the other side of the coin is that both types may reflect the level of articulatory performance that is sufficient to produce adequate phonetic distinctiveness in the language in question. In many instances what is required for the language makes it irrelevant to ask what the limits of articulatory potential are – linguistic organization is such that articulation does not, so to speak, stretch the machinery to its limits. It is context-sensitivity that accounts for much of the complexity and indirectness in the relationship between the acoustic output of articulatory activity and the linguistic structure which it represents. As a result, the way in which linguistic structure is encoded in the acoustic speech signal is rather opaque. Despite that, listeners can decode it with apparently unconscious ease.

Nevertheless, the pressure of context may have quite noticeable effects. We do not normally think of English as having nasalized vowels – in the way that French and Portuguese have a distinction between oral and nasalized vowels. But vowels preceding nasal consonants in English, as in *sand* or *can't* or *bend*, may well be nasalized because of the following consonant. Even more radically, many English segments may be articulated in certain contexts as sounds from which they are normally distinguished. Thus [s] is distinct from [ʃ] in English, but [s] may nevertheless be articulated as [ʃ] in an appropriate context, as for example when the [s] immediately precedes [j], as in *this year* or *tissue*. While effects of this kind may still go unnoticed if they are common enough in the community, they may also attract attention, especially if there is a division between speakers who tolerate the context-sensitivity and others who try to suppress it.

The causes and mechanisms of context-sensitivity have been the subject of a fair amount of research, contributing to our understanding of articulatory dynamics and raising new questions about the high-level neural representation and organization of muscular commands and the transformation of these commands into articulatory movements. The vocal tract, including the articulators within it, forms a biomechanical system which is subject to the laws governing all mechanical systems, from can-openers to space shuttles. Specifically, the mass and size of articulators constrain their movement in relation to the muscle systems that actuate them. Articulators have mass and are subject to inertia: they resist being set in motion. There is therefore some inherent delay between a neuromuscular command and the intended articulatory gesture. The greater the mass, the greater the inertia and hence the greater the delay.

A common example of this effect is the tendency for peripheral vowels in short syllables to become centralized, particularly when the speaker is talking rapidly. In simple terms, the tongue may not have time to reach the target position before the next sound has to be articulated. While the tongue is moving towards the peripheral target position determined by the neuromuscular commands, conflicting commands for the following segment are already arriving, initiating movement towards a different position. The result of this conflict is a general tendency for the tongue to assume a more central or neutral position, effectively smoothing or summing the mechanical consequences of the individual movement commands. In effect, the average or long-term 'context' of tongue position is central, and biomechanical inertia heightens the tendency to centralization as the speaker attempts a faster rate of movement. But this tendency is not just a matter of yielding to the constraints of biomechanical performance, for the speaker may also impose limits on the muscular activity used to overcome mechanical inertia. In other words, a speaker may, to varying degrees, either make efforts to operate the articulatory system to the upper limits of its performance or lower the performance to accommodate to the system. Whatever its cause, the effect is known as target UNDERSHOOT: the principal articulator fails to reach the target position defined in the canonical description of the segment. The centralization of peripheral vowels by undershoot is commonly known as VOWEL REDUCTION (Stevens and House 1963, Lindblom 1963, Stevens et al. 1966, Tuller et al. 1982).

The effect of delay on articulator movement can be seen in English words such as *more* and *now*, where the (beginning of the) vowel is nasalized, partly because of delay in raising the velum at the end of the nasal consonant. The nasality of the initial consonant thus overlaps on to the following nominally oral vowel. A similar effect tends to nasalize the voiced fricative following [n] in words such as *burns* and *bronze*. Comparable effects of delay can be observed in words such as *paws* and *jaws*, where the lip rounding of the vowel is likely to persist into the alveolar fricative at the end of the words. By comparison, the same fricative has spread or neutral lip position in words such as *bees* or *haze*.

The organization of neuromuscular commands may also produce the very opposite effect. To compensate for inherent delay, neuromuscular commands may be initiated well before the segment for which they are required; articulatory properties of that segment may then appear on an earlier segment. This, then, is an anticipatory form of overlap. A simple example is provided by the nasalization of the vowel in words such as *sand* and *can't*, where the velum may be lowered during the vowel in anticipation of the following nasal consonant. Anticipation likewise affects the point of articulation of velar plosives in English, in words like *key*, *car* and *core*: the stop closure is most forward in *key* and most retracted in *core*, because the tongue body anticipates the position required for the following vowel. A third example is the lip rounding on alveolar fricatives in words such as *saw* and *sue*, which anticipates the demands of the following rounded vowel.

Amerman and Daniloff (1977) have shown that when a speaker articulates a CCV sequence, the tongue body may begin to move towards the vowel even during the first consonant. Similarly, in VCC sequences, anticipatory movements towards the second consonant can start during the vowel. According to Benguerel and Cowan (1974), lip protrusion may be evident several consonants in advance of the rounded vowel for which it is required, while Amerman et al. (1970) note that speakers may likewise anticipate a relatively open vowel by beginning to lower the jaw during preceding consonants.

These context-sensitive effects underline the danger of assuming that individual segments (and their articulatory properties) have any real autonomy within connected speech. Features of articulation interact and overlap, in both anticipatory and perseverative fashion, sometimes extending over several segments.

Context-dependent overlap of the kind we have been describing is often known as COARTICULATION. The reader should note, however, that this term is not used consistently. Some writers use it in the narrow and rather literal sense of simultaneous movement of two different articulators. Under this definition, the lip rounding of a consonant, anticipating the rounding of the following vowel (as in *saw* or *sue*) is coarticulation, but the adjustment of the tongue position for a velar consonant, anticipating the tongue posture of the following vowel (as in *key* and *core*) is not. The second kind of phenomenon may be described as 'adaptation' or 'accommodation' – the articulator (in this example the tongue) is, so to speak, reaching a compromise with the demands of an adjacent articulation. Our own usage is to describe both types of context-dependent overlap as coarticulation, without reference to the number of articulators involved.

Perseverative coarticulation effects are known as LEFT-TO-RIGHT COARTICULATION (in short, L > R). Thus in the string . . . AB . . . , sound A influences sound B (or beyond). L > R coarticulation is thought to be largely due to lag in articulatory movement, induced by inertia. The relevant ingredients are the biomechanical properties of the articulators (their size and mass, and the nature of the muscles involved); the speaker's rate of articulation; and the extent to which the speaker is exercising voluntary neuromuscular effort in the control and movement of the articulators.

Anticipatory coarticulation effects are known as RIGHT-TO-LEFT (L < R) COARTICULATION. In the string . . . CD . . . , sound D influences sound C (or earlier sounds). L < R coarticulation is thought to be due to deliberate high-level organization of the neuromuscular commands for the relevant sounds. This high-level planning is complicated by the differences in innervation latencies among the various articulatory muscle systems.

Again, if we think of speech as a series of autonomous segments, we are in danger of dismissing coarticulatory overlap as a sort of needless complication, interfering with the ideal properties of speech. But, on the contrary, coarticulation is an essential characteristic of speech. Speech production depends on very rapid, highly coordinated articulatory movements, and it is doubtful whether we could achieve anything like the articulation rates of normal running speech if we did not make extensive use of overlap. Daniloff (1973) claims that the tongue tip – the fastest of the articulators controlled by muscles – can perform only about eight closures per second. We are nevertheless able to produce from 12 to 18 segments per second in running speech. Thus coarticulatory overlap enables us to work very effectively within the constraints on our performance. As a consequence, the quasicontinuous fluidity of speech can be thought of as efficient encoding, rather than as degradation of the signal.

It is not always easy to determine how far speakers are simply constrained by the limits of the biomechanical system and how far they are actually setting a level of articulatory performance that is just sufficient to meet the demands of their language – just sufficient, that is, to be adequately intelligible in the immediate circumstances. Lindblom (1983) argues strongly that distinctiveness and communicative effectiveness are primary motives in speech production. It is certainly true that general tendencies such as vowel reduction and anticipatory nasalization are not uniform in their effect on different languages. For example, although it is generally true that a faster rate of articulation is likely to increase the amount of vowel reduction, a comparison of speakers of English from different parts of the world would show different responses to this tendency. At a given rate of articulation, speakers of RP probably reveal appreciably more examples of reduction than, say, northern English or Australian speakers, well before any biomechanically imposed limit is reached. Consider, for instance, the variability in words such as *hostel*, *synod* and *bursar*, where the second vowel may or may not be reduced: the choice of the reduced form is likely to be influenced more by the speaker's sense of a correct or natural pronunciation within the relevant community than by rate of articulation. (More general observations about the reduced vowel in English can be found in Gimson 1980, pp. 126–7 and 224–5). A similar point could be made about nasality, since the occurrence and extent of both anticipatory and perseverative nasality varies considerably among speakers and languages. Such examples suggest that language-specific phonological norms and patterns play a major role in determining the nature of speech. The term PHONOLOGICAL CONDITIONING is widely used to explain variability which seems to be a matter of language-specific 'rules of pronunciation' (section 4.3 below).

The term ASSIMILATION has a longer tradition than coarticulation, and is sometimes used in a rather general way, more or less synonymously with coarticulation. Quite often the term refers only to those cases of context-sensitive articulatory overlap which are reflected in phonetic transcription. In this usage, the term becomes rather too dependent on ill-defined conventions about the nature of transcription. Thus assimilation may include instances of overlap which happen to generate a change from one common sound to another (as when the alveolar [n] of *un-* becomes velar [ŋ] before a velar plosive in *unkind* or *ungainly*) but exclude instances that give rise to a less common sound for which there is no well-known phonetic symbol (as when the initial consonants of *saw* or *sue* are lip-rounded in anticipation of the following rounded vowels). In other words, what counts as assimilation tends to depend on the availability of symbols to indicate it and on conventional judgments about its auditory or linguistic salience. Many effects, such as changes in the tongue body posture of alveolar stops in the context of different vowels, are not even allowed for in conventional phonetic transcription, and so are likely to be ignored in accounts of assimilation.

Assimilation is often mentioned in connection with historical changes, and many of the sound changes that languages have been observed to undergo can appropriately be described as assimilatory. Thus English words such as *mission, passion, special, crucial, nation* and *lotion* were once pronounced with a medial [sj] or [si] but in modern English have [ʃ]: by a process of assimilation, the [s] has been retracted in anticipation of the following [j] or [i] (which has then disappeared, or been 'swallowed up' in the assimilatory process). We must, however, distinguish between historical processes and processes that are still current or operative in the modern language. We know, for example, that words such as *ship* and *shall* are derived from older forms (in Old English or even earlier) beginning with [sk]. Here a sound change has had its effect on the language, and we have no access to the earlier pronunciation other than by historical investigation and comparison with other related languages. (Part of the evidence for the change, for example, is that Old English records reveal the spellings *scip* and *sceal*, while other old Germanic languages, notably Old Norse and Gothic, show *skip* and *skal*.) Note that this change is in a real sense over and done with. There is no tendency in modern English speech to repeat the process in words such as *skill* or *sky*, for instance. On the other hand, there are processes which can be observed within the current state of the language. The assimilation of alveolar [n] to velar [ŋ] before velars, for instance, is demonstrable within modern English. There are forms such as the prefix *un-* which clearly have [n] in non-velar contexts (*untidy, unsettled*, etc.) but which may have [ŋ] before a velar (*unkind, ungainly*, etc.); and the process can be seen to apply to many words that normally have alveolar [n], as when unstressed *can* precedes a word beginning with a velar (*they can* [ŋ] *keep it, you can* [ŋ] *go now*) or when words like *pan* and *sun* are compounded in *pan*[ŋ]*cake* or *sun*[ŋ]*glasses*. In describing the system and structure of pronunciation in the current language, we need take no account of historical changes that are over and done with; indeed, it would be inappropriate to do so, for from the point of view of a speaker of the modern language, these changes have disappeared over the horizon. But assimilatory processes that can be observed at work within the modern language certainly are part of the modern speaker's organization of pronunciation and are relevant to our description of the language.

It is also important to note here that English spelling, taken without other evidence, is no sure guide to either historical or current processes of assimilation. Thus it happens to be true that the spelling *ssi* in *mission* or *passion* suggests an earlier pronunciation with [si]; but the spelling *sh* in *ship* and *shall* does not indicate a previous pronunciation as [s] followed by [h] (as in *mess-hall* or *doss-house*). Moreover, English spelling abounds in oddities that make it quite unreliable in this regard: for example, the *l* in *should* and *would* is indeed a pointer to an earlier pronunciation with [l], but the *l* in *could* is there by analogy with the other two forms, and the word has never been pronounced with [l]. If we want to demonstrate relationships among sounds in the modern language, we must appeal not to spelling but to pronunciations that can be recorded, checked and compared. Thus the spelling of *mission* is in itself no reason to connect the [ʃ] of its pronunciation with an [s]. But we can show a relationship between the [ʃ] and [s] by appealing to the forms *sub-mission* and *submissive* or *permission* and *permissive*. (In fact appeals of just this kind are central to the generative approach to phonology, which we shall outline in chapter 5.)

Traditional use of the term assimilation focuses on the more obvious or more easily symbolized consequences of coarticulatory effects, and for this very reason the term is widely known, especially with reference to consonants. In a non-technical way, three types of assimilation can be identified. ASSIMILATION OF PLACE is exemplified by English *ratbag* or *oatmeal* pronounced with [p] instead of [t] in rapid or informal speech, by assimilation of the alveolar stop to a following bilabial. ASSIMILATION OF MANNER refers to instances such as *Indian* pronounced as *Injun*, where the stop [d] and approximant [j] merge to form an affricate. (While *Injun* is generally considered substandard in modern English, the same assimilation has applied historically in *soldier*, in which the affricate is now normal.) ASSIMILATION OF VOICING is illustrated by *have to* pronounced with [f] rather than [v], by assimilation of the voiced fricative to a following voiceless consonant.

ELISION refers to the special case of loss or omission of segments or syllables. Sounds may be so weakly articulated that they no longer have auditory significance, or they may be omitted altogether in the stream of running speech, particularly – but not exclusively – in casual or rapid speech. Like other phonetic variations we have looked at, elision is constrained by the phonological system and often applies to segments and weakly stressed syllables whose absence does not seriously impair intelligibility for native speakers of the language. In English, elision is often found in consonant clusters, as in *facts* and *chests* pronounced without [t], or *fifths* and *sixths* pronounced without [θ]. When unstressed, the word *and* often loses the [d], and an entire unstressed syllable is often elided from longer words such as *February* and *library*. In many languages, word-final unstressed vowels may be elided, either in general or when the next word begins with a vowel. In French, instances of such elision are standard and are marked in orthography by an apostrophe, as in *j'ai* 'I have' or *l'air* 'the air', where an unelided *je ai* or *le air* would be simply incorrect.

The question of context-sensitive effects and their causes continues to cause lively debate among speech researchers. We conclude this section with a conservative summary of what is known. In the first place, coarticulation effects seem capable of spreading across several segments, and are often not checked unless they are in direct conflict with other articulatory demands, or unless they run up against the contrastive requirements of the language. Secondly, observable assimilations seem to be caused more often by anticipatory coarticulation effects than by perseverative effects, at least in English if not in most languages. Thirdly, even if we restrict our attention to vocal tract performance alone, coarticulation effects are not yet fully understood: it is not clear to what extent we can explain them by assuming that high-level commands associated with specific segments are confounded by biomechanical 'sloppiness' and the unequal latencies of the neuromuscular innervation system; or to what extent high-level commands are quite deliberately planned to optimize transitions between targets and to yield the best possible vocal tract performance in running speech. In general, it does seem that the limitations of vocal tract performance are not predominant in influencing context-related variability. Fourthly, there is often no simple way of distinguishing between those assimilation effects which are due to the inherent properties or limitations of speech production and those which are not, unless the latter are very obviously language-specific. Assimilation often appears to be motivated by ease of articulation, but what seems easy and natural in one language often turns out to be less so in another. Thus ease of articulation needs to be assessed within the constraints of differing languages, each with its own system and structure.

4.2 The phoneme

The constant background to our discussion of variability in the previous section has been the observation that in any language some differences in pronunciation are crucially distinctive. It is these distinctions or contrasts that are recognized by speakers of the language as 'making different words' and acknowledged by linguists as systemically functional. In English, for example, we must differentiate words such as *led*, *red* and *wed* from each other if we are to achieve acceptable pronunciation; and similarly *allay*, *array* and *away*, and *click*, *crick* and *quick*. Abstracting the individual sounds from the normal flow of speech, we can say that in English the three consonants *l*, *r* and *w* are CONTRASTIVE or DISTINCTIVE.

The phonological system of English is such that each of these sounds may vary considerably in its articulation. The *r* in *tree* and *train* may be a voiceless fricative, the *r* in *dream* and *drain* a voiced fricative, and the *r* in *three* and *throw* a tap or flap, all three of these variants being phonetically quite different from the *r* in *red* or *array*. Not all speakers of English pronounce *r* in the same ways, of course, but the general point is that what counts as a single sound within a system may be articulated in various ways provided that contrasts are maintained (i.e. provided that *train* is still distinct from other words such as *twain* or *chain*, and that *drain* is still distinct from *Jane*, and so on).

To avoid any misunderstanding about the 'English phonological system', we should stress that it is actually not one system but many, for dialects as well as languages can differ in their system of phonological contrasts. In English, though certainly not in all languages, it is the vowel contrasts that differ most; readers may care to check their own pronunciation of the following words, arranged in five columns:

(1)	(2)	(3)	(4)	(5)
spa	spar	saw	spore	spoor
Pa	par	paw	pore	poor
Ma	mar	maw	more	moor

For some speakers of English (including the authors) only two contrastive vowels are represented here, a rather central long [a:] in columns (1) and (2), and a rather more back and rounded [ɔ:] in columns (3), (4) and (5). This is a version of English in which final *r* is not pronounced, and in which the words adjacent to each other in columns (1) and (2) are therefore identical. Those who do have a final *r* (many American and Scottish speakers, for example) may distinguish the vowel of column (4) from that of column (5); on the other hand, at least some of these speakers may use the same somewhat rounded vowel for columns (1) and (3). Thus the number of contrasts, as well as the nature and variability of individual sounds, may certainly differ from dialect to dialect within a language.

The extent to which variant pronunciation counts as 'saying the same sound in a slightly different way' will obviously depend on the linguistic system. A number of the world's languages (including Classical Arabic and some Australian Aboriginal languages) have only three contrastive vowels, which can be represented as *i*, *a* and *u*. In such languages, the quality of the *a* vowel may vary considerably, say from a back rounded [ɒ] in the neighbourhood of consonants such as [w] to a front [æ] in the neighbourhood of [j] or other palatal consonants. Such variation cannot be systematically tolerated in a language in which [ɒ] and [æ] are distinct phonemes.

Contrastive systems range in complexity from languages with less than 20 distinctive consonants and vowels to languages with 60 or more. English, depending on the particular dialect, has up to 24 consonants and up to about 20 vowels. English has a rather high number of vowel contrasts, especially in comparison with a typical Australian Aboriginal language. On the other hand, most Aboriginal languages have a contrast between at least two and sometimes three kinds of r sound. For example in Warlpiri, from central Australia, we have:

marru house	*rr* represents trilled [r]
tjarra flame	
maru black	*r* represents approximant [ɹ]
tjara fat	
mardu wooden bowl	*rd* represents retroflex flap [ɽ]
tjarda sleep	

It is difficult to formulate comparisons of this kind without adopting the perspective of one particular language system: we are inclined to say that Warlpiri has 'three r-sounds' but from the Warlpiri point of view the three sounds are not three versions of one sound, but three distinct consonants, as crucially different from each other as *l*, *r* and *w* are in English.

A common way of conceptualizing such phenomena in modern linguistics is through the notion of the PHONEME. Although the notion remains controversial, it rests ultimately on the recognition of functional differences. English speakers take *led* and *red* to be different words, as Warlpiri speakers take *marru* and *maru* to be different words. A phoneme can thus be described as a contrastive or distinctive sound within a language. [r] and [ɹ] and [ɽ] are separate phonemes in Warlpiri but not in English; [ɒ] and [æ] are separate phonemes in (most varieties of) English but not in Warlpiri.

Sounds which count as alternative ways of saying a phoneme may be termed VARIANTS or ALLOPHONES. A common convention is to use slant lines to indicate phonemes and to retain square brackets for the phonetic notation of allophones, e.g.

English /r/ may be realized as [r], [ɹ], etc.
Warlpiri /a/ may be realized as [ɒ], [æ], etc.

For any of the world's languages, then, it is possible to draw up an inventory of phonemes, each of which will have one or more variants or allophones. Although this will by no means exhaust what can be said about the phonological system of a language, it will in effect be a list of the significant or contrastive sounds of the language with a specification of major phonetic variants for each phoneme.

In most cases, allophones will fairly evidently be governed by processes or patterns of the language concerned (many of them due to coarticulatory effects of the kind discussed in section 4.1 above). This implies that each allophone occurs in a particular phonetic environment or specifiable context. The phoneme /n/ in English, for example, may have three allophones as follows:

Phoneme   *Allophones*
/n/   [n̪] before a dental fricative
             [n:] before a voiced obstruent in the same syllable
             [n] elsewhere

Thus /n/ is dental by assimilation in e.g. *tenth* or *month*, and is lengthened before [d], [z] or [dʒ] in e.g. *tend*, *tens* or *lunge*. Where neither of those two conditions applies, the phoneme has its 'normal' English value of [n], as in *net*, *ten* or *tent*.

An inventory of phonemes can be viewed in two directions. Seen from the point of view of the language system, it represents those sounds which are significant in the language: the phonemes are those sounds which serve to differentiate words. From this perspective, what matters about a phoneme is not so much the precise ways in which it may be pronounced but rather the fact that it is different from the other phonemes of the language. Hence the importance attached to pairs of words differing in only one phoneme, such as English *red* versus *led*, *red* versus *wed*, *real* versus *zeal*. These pairs, known as MINIMAL PAIRS, provide solid evidence of phonemic contrasts, of the differences that matter in a language, and they are of interest not just to the phonological analyst but also in such fields as language teaching and hearing testing.

We can, however, also view phonemes from the point of view of their actual pronunciation. In this case we are, so to speak, looking upwards from the level of a narrow phonetic transcription. Seen from this angle, a phoneme is a set of related sounds or phones. Allophones are similar sounds occurring in complementary environments: English [n̪] is found only before a dental fricative, never in any other environment, lengthened [n:] occurs only before voiced obstruents and never elsewhere, and so on. Hence, where a phoneme has more than one variant, it may be said to consist of a set of allophones standing in COMPLEMENTARY DISTRIBUTION or in MUTUALLY EXCLUSIVE ENVIRONMENTS.

These two perspectives on the phoneme have sometimes been set against each other as, say, a 'functional' view of the phoneme as opposed to a 'phonetic' view of the phoneme. We take the two notions of the phoneme to reflect two different aspects of the same phonological reality. To the native speaker, this reality means on the one hand, 'functionally', that certain differences in pronunciation are genuine or real; and on the other hand, 'phonetically', that a good deal of phonetic variability may be tolerated within a phoneme.

4.3   Allophones

In general, allophones can be described as CONDITIONED variants of a phoneme, generated by PHONOLOGICAL CONDITIONING. Phonological conditioning is usually understood to be a matter of language-specific 'rules of pronunciation', although we have already noted that it is often difficult to draw a clear boundary between the effects of the biomechanical system and the effects of the linguistic system (section 4.1 above). There are observable universal tendencies in pronunciation, but languages differ enormously in the extent to which they constrain or suppress these tendencies. Moreover, some instances of phonological conditioning have little or no apparent biomechanical justification. In such instances, the habitual pronunciation of a language may be strikingly odd to speakers of other languages (and far from easy for others to imitate). Certainly, phonemic analysis customarily describes as allophones only those major variants that can be categorized and represented in a segmental transcription, and these tend to represent variation which is not universal, even if found in a substantial number of languages; variability that is revealed only by instrumental analysis is ignored. Some examples follow.

/a/   [ã] before a nasal consonant
         [a] elsewhere.

Redundant or nonsignificant nasalization of vowels is observed in many languages, including at least some varieties of English (nasalized vowels in *can't*, *sand*, but not in *cat*, *cart*, *sad*).

/k/   [g] between two voiced sounds
         [k] elsewhere.

Conditioning of this kind occurs in many Australian Aboriginal languages and other languages in which there is no phonemic contrast between voiced and voiceless sounds: the plosive is voiced in a fully voiced context but not otherwise (e.g. not in word-initial position).

/n/   [ŋ] before a velar consonant
           [n] elsewhere.

This applies for instance to Italian and Spanish, in which there is no phoneme /ŋ/.
Wherever /n/ immediately precedes /k/ or /g/ it is assimilated to the velar position, e.g.
in words such as *banca* and *mango*. A comparable assimilation is found in English,
with a velar nasal preceding the velar stop in words such as *sink*, *bank*, *anger*; but /n/
and /ŋ/ are in contrast in English in minimal pairs such as *sin/sing*, *run/rung*, *sinner/
singer*, etc. There are, however, varieties of English in which this contrast does not
exist, namely those in which words such as *sing*, *rung*, *singer* are pronounced with
[g] following the velar nasal (e.g. *sing* is [sɪŋg]). These varieties of English (chiefly
found in the Midlands and north of England) are like Italian and Spanish in that [ŋ]
occurs only immediately before a velar consonant and can therefore be analysed as a
conditioned variant of /n/.

/d/   [ð] between two vowels
           [d] elsewhere.

In this instance the plosive is 'weakened' or 'lenited' to a fricative when between
vowels. A process of this kind is observable in Spanish and Portuguese, where the
medial *b*, *d*, *g* in words such as *Cuba*, *Toledo* and *Diego* are generally articulated as
voiced fricatives rather than as plosives.
    Processes of conditioning are not always obvious from a segmental transcription;
imagine that the following are words of a language, phonetically transcribed:

[kimu]   [komo]   [komu]   [mini]   [mito]   [møki]
[muko]   [nipu]   [nytil]   [piti]   [puko]   [pymi]
[tito]   [tonu]   [tøni]   [tøpi]   [tunu]   [tyki]

Note that the vowels are high front unrounded [i], high front rounded [y], mid
front rounded [ø], high back rounded [u] and mid back rounded [o]. Now [y] and [u]
are in complementary distribution, as are [ø] and [o]. [y] occurs only in the first
syllable where the following syllable contains [i], whereas [u] occurs only in other
positions, namely in the second syllable or in the first syllable if the following syllable
does not contain [i]. A parallel distribution can be noted for [ø] and [o]. The phonetic
explanation is that the high front position of [i] is anticipated in the preceding vowels
[u] and [o], which are fronted to [y] and [ø]. The vowel phonemes of this artificial
language are thus

/i/   [i]
/u/   [y] before a syllable containing [i]
           [u] elsewhere
/o/   [ø] before a syllable containing [i]
           [o] elsewhere

Phenomena of this general type are known variously as VOWEL HARMONY, UMLAUT or MUTATION, and are vivid demonstration of coarticulation effects. The German term *Umlaut* and its English equivalent 'mutation', taken in their narrow sense, refer specifically to certain processes operative at earlier stages of Germanic languages. The difference in vowels in English *foot/feet*, *mouse/mice* or German *hoch/Höhe* ('high/height'), *Kuh/Kühe* ('cow/cows') is in fact due to a process of precisely the kind exemplified in our artificial data. Both English and German have undergone subsequent sound changes which have obscured the original conditioning, but, inasmuch as earlier pronunciation can be reconstructed, *foot* and *feet* are derived from something like [fo:t] and [fø:ti], *hoch* and *Höhe* from [ho:x] and [hø:xi].

In most of the above examples it is relatively easy to point to CONDITIONING FACTORS, features of the context that are responsible for the allophonic variation – the nasal consonant that conditions nasalization of a preceding vowel, the voicing of vowels that conditions voicing of an intervocalic stop, and so on. In these cases, the processes affecting the phonemes seem general or 'natural' tendencies of speech. But it is obviously not true that these tendencies yield identical consequences in all languages. Furthermore, some instances of allophonic variation are relatively difficult to explain in phonetic terms, and it is not at all easy to find plausible conditioning factors. Some examples follow.

In Korean, [l] and [r] are allophones of one phoneme, with [r] standing word-initial and between two vowels, and [l] elsewhere. The notion that [l] and [r] are really 'the same sound' is of course quite contrary to the expectations of speakers of many other languages. The 'similarity' of [l] and [r] is not easy to justify, although it is worth noting that even in a language such as English, in which *l* and *r* are distinct phonemes, the two consonants are prone to confusion, witness the way in which even fluent native speakers may stumble over words containing *l* and *r* in 'awkward' combinations, e.g. *meteorological*, *corollary*, *irrelevantly*, etc. The similarity that allows these two consonants to be identified or confused must be understood systemically: in many languages *l* and *r* are the only two continuant consonants which are neither fricative nor nasal.

In a few Australian Aboriginal languages, a lamino-dental stop and a lamino-palatal stop are allophones of a single phoneme. Although both consonants are articulated laminally (with the blade rather than the tip of the tongue), the auditory effect is quite different, at least to those who are not native speakers. The details are often complicated (see e.g. Glass and Hackett 1970, pp. 109–10 for a description of what happens in one dialect of Pitjantjatjara or Western Desert) but the general pattern is that lamino-palatal [c] occurs before a front vowel [i], whereas lamino-dental [t̪] occurs before other vowels, i.e. [a] and [u]. While it is normal for vowel quality to cause some kind of modification to a preceding consonant, variation from dental to palatal articulation is unusual among the world's languages.

In standard Indonesian, the phoneme /k/ has a glottal stop allophone occurring word-finally, as in *duduk* ('sit'), *tarik* ('pull') pronounced with final [ʔ]. While the adjustment can be explained as substitution of a glottal closure for the velar closure of a [k], it is certainly not a substitution that comes easily and naturally to speakers of most other languages.

Finally, as an instance of an allophonic adjustment which happens in many varieties of English but is far from universal, we note the distinction between clear and dark laterals. (The 'dark *l*' is velarized by raising of the back of the tongue towards the soft palate; see section 3.6 above.) The clear variant normally occurs before a vowel (*lend, alight, believe*) and the dark before a consonant or word-finally (*wild, halt, will, hall*). The velarization is extreme in some varieties of English, notably in the speech of many Londoners and South Australians, who may even fail to make the lateral occlusion. As a result, the raising of the back of the tongue virtually creates an [u] vowel (cf. *hall* pronounced as [hɔːu], *halt* as [hɒut]). Far from being a common and natural assimilation, this variation in the pronunciation of /l/ is not found in many of the world's languages. Thus German *kalt* ('cold') and Italian *caldo* ('warm') are pronounced with clear [l].

In considering the diversity of allophonic adjustment, we should also not forget that languages undergo sound changes, with the consequence that what seems a natural pronunciation to one generation becomes less so to the next. It is fairly clear from the history of the French language, for example, that /l/ had a dark allophone in medieval French. Indeed, the velarization of this allophone was so extreme that it eventually became a [u] vowel (compare the London and South Australian pronunciation mentioned above). We find *u* for earlier *l* in modern French *chevaux* ('horses') (singular *cheval*, earlier plural form *chevals*); and note also *paume* ('palm'), *loyauté* ('loyalty') and *faute* ('fault'). (In all of these instances, the vocalized [u] formed a diphthong with the preceding [a], which has been reduced to a simple [o] vowel in modern French pronunciation.) But with the vocalization and loss of the medieval occurrences of the dark variant, modern French no longer has clear and dark allophones of /l/, and the London English pronunciation of words such as *halt* and *will* does not come easily to French learners.

The range of allophonic variation encountered in natural languages means that it is not easy to predict which sounds can or cannot be allophones of a single phoneme. Some attempts have been made to draw up charts or tables of similar or 'suspicious' sounds. Pike (1947), for example, includes a chart designed as a guide to field workers engaged in transcription and analysis of hitherto unwritten languages. Pike's chart is so complex, however, with circles enclosing sounds judged to be phonetically similar, that it is unlikely to be of much help to any field worker who is not already familiar with the articulatory and auditory character of the sounds referred to. At any rate, there is no mechanical procedure by which one can determine, for any two sounds, whether or not there is at least one language in the world which counts them as variants of a single phoneme. A few general remarks are nevertheless appropriate.

In the first place, it is evident that complementary distribution is not of itself a guarantee that two sounds are allophones of one phoneme. In other words, allophones must show *some* degree of phonetic similarity as well as being in complementary distribution. In some varieties of English, for instance, [h] and [ŋ] are in complementary distribution, since [h] occurs only at the beginning of a syllable (*hat, ahead, behind*, etc.) whereas [ŋ] is never syllable-initial but always syllable-final or before a consonant (*sing, sink*, etc.). (Some speakers of English may have a different patterning, if, for instance, they pronounce *dinghy* with [ŋ] beginning the second syllable.) But even if [h] and [ŋ] are in complementary distribution, they are quite dissimilar in their phonetic nature and it would seem to fly in the face of any sensible description of English to suggest that these two sounds are variants of one phoneme simply because they are in complementary distribution. There are thus limits on the sounds which can be allophones, even though we need to be cautious in giving a universally valid specification of these limits. (See, for instance, Gudschinsky et al. 1970, for a description of a Brazilian Indian language, Maxakalí, in which plosives appear to have vowel allophones.)

Secondly, failure to take account of degrees of phonetic similarity among sounds could lead to patently ridiculous statements. Especially where a language displays general phonetic processes such as nasalization of vowels before nasal consonants, or voicing of plosives between vowels, there will be a number of allophones in complementary distribution with a related set of allophones. Consider, for example, a language in which voiceless [p] [t] [k] occur only word-initially and word-finally, while voiced [b] [d] [g] occur only word-medially. Such a language might have words such as

[pabat]   [tadak]   [kadap]   [pagap]   [tabat]   [kagak] etc.

Imagine now a computer instructed to scan these words for complementary distributions. The computer would in fact register nine such distributions:

[p] with [b], [p] with [d], [p] with [g];
[t] with [b], [t] with [d], [t] with [g];
and   [k] with [b], [k] with [d], [k] with [g].

The correct pairings are of course [p] + [b], [t] + [d] and [k] + [g], but the computer would have no way of recognizing this without some appeal to the kind of phonetic process involved or some insight into the fact that [b] is the voiced counterpart of [p], not of [t] or [k], and so on.

Thirdly, even when the notions of complementary distribution and phonetic similarity are properly combined, there is still room for doubt in some instances about the correct phonemic analysis. Italian, for instance, has three nasal consonant phonemes: /m/ as in *amore* ('love'), *ramo* ('branch'); /n/ as in *anello* ('ring'), *vano* ('futile'), *sano* ('healthy'); and palatal /ɲ/ written *gn* in *agnello* ('lamb'), *ragno* ('spider'), *bagno* ('bath'). Italian also has occurrences of the velar [ŋ] but this sound is found only before velar consonants, written as *n* in e.g. *banca* ('bank'), *lungo* ('long'), *cinque* ('five'). Now although the spelling identifies this [ŋ] as an *n*, it could in fact also be an allophone of /m/ or /ɲ/, as none of the nasal consonants other than [ŋ] ever precedes a velar. Judged by its articulatory position, [ŋ] is actually closer to palatal [ɲ] than it is to [n]. Nevertheless, the solution implied by the standard orthography, namely that [ŋ] is an allophone of /n/, is widely accepted, even by those whose phonetic interests make them relatively sceptical of phonological analysis (see e.g. Jones 1962, p. 63 on Italian and Spanish [ŋ]). For an instance of alternative solutions in German, see Trim's note (1951) on the fricatives [ç] [x] and

[h] in that language: the usual view of German is that [ç] and [x] are allophones of /x/, distinct from /h/, but it is also possible to take [x] and [h] to be allophones of /x/, distinct from /ç/.

There are thus certain indeterminacies about phonemic analysis. For some linguists, this means that the concept of the phoneme needs refinement, and we turn to some of the issues later in this chapter. For others, as we shall see in chapter 5, the very concept becomes questionable.

4.4 Phonemic norms

If allophones, at least in a large number of cases, are conditioned by their phonetic environment, it seems reasonable to maintain the perspective adopted in section 4.1 and to speak of allophones as variations from a norm. If English /w/ is actually voiceless after voiceless plosives (as it usually is in e.g. *twin*, *quit*), we may say that voiced [w] is the norm but that the normal [w] is 'devoiced' or 'becomes voiceless' under the influence of a preceding voiceless plosive. It thus seems natural to call the phoneme /w/ rather than /w̥/.

It will frequently be the case that one of the allophones of a phoneme readily suggests itself as the normal value in this fashion. The phoneme may then be labelled or transcribed with the symbol representing this normal allophone. In somewhat more technical language, the phonemic symbol should be the symbol of the allophone which is least restricted in its distribution (Pike 1947, p. 88). Two simple examples of the application of this principle are: (1) if the two allophones of a single phoneme are [ŋ] before a velar consonant, and [n] elsewhere, then the phoneme is /n/ rather than /ŋ/; and (2) if the two allophones of a single phoneme are [ã] before a nasal consonant, and [a] elsewhere, then the phoneme is /a/ rather than /ã/. The very use of the term 'elsewhere' of course suggests that the second allophone has the less restricted distribution.

It should, however, be noted that from the perspective of the language in question a phoneme is not necessarily identified with any of its allophones. Moreover, decisions about how to symbolize phonemes are frequently tied up with orthographic issues, not all of which relate directly to phonology. For example, Australian Aboriginal languages in the southern half of the continent usually have no contrast between voiced and voiceless plosives: each plosive phoneme has voiced and voiceless allophones. If these allophones are more or less equally distributed, say voiced allophones word-medially and voiceless allophones word-initially, there may be no particular reason to take either allophone as the norm. Certainly so far as a practical orthography is concerned, it makes little difference whether the spelling employs voiced or voiceless symbols provided it uses one or the other consistently. Indeed, some Australian languages are usually written with voiceless symbols, others with voiced. (The real complications arise where Aborigines who have learned to read and write English introduce into their own language the convention of distinguishing between voiced and voiceless symbols, or where English speakers have transcribed Aboriginal words using both voiced and voiceless symbols on the assumption that there must inevitably be such a distinction. Thus alternative spellings of tribal names such as *Pintupi, Bindubi* and *Pindubi,* or *Warlpiri* and *Warlbiri,* continue to compete with each other.)

In some parts of the world, new orthographies have been deliberately designed in ways that conform to an already widely known spelling system. In areas of Latin America where Spanish is the national language, indigenous languages may follow Spanish orthographic conventions even where this is not necessary on phonemic grounds. The phoneme /k/, for instance, may be written as *c* before *a, o, u,* but as *qu* before *i* and *e,* simply because this follows a Spanish spelling rule with which many readers will already be familiar. Hence, although the selection of a basic allophone or phonemic norm may be important for a phonemic analysis and transcription, orthography is likely to be constrained by other factors.

4.5   Pattern and symmetry

In discussing vowels (section 2.7 above) we noted that systems tend to be symmetrical. Other phonemes may likewise form symmetrical patterns when charted according to their articulatory characteristics. Thus the English plosives (excluding affricates) form a 3×2 set, as shown in table 4.5.1(a). In general, languages appear to favour this kind of symmetrical exploitation of contrasts. German, for example, has the same plosive contrasts as English; French and Italian have a similar pattern, except that the voiceless plosives are normally unaspirated and the alveolars tend to be articulated further forward, i.e. as dentals. Some languages distinguish more than just voiced and voiceless plosives, and more than three points of articulation. Some examples are given in table 4.5.1(b)–(d) (again excluding affricates and affricated stops).

Allophones are often similarly patterned. If one voiced stop has a partially devoiced allophone in word-final position, it is highly likely that other voiced stops are subject to the same general phonetic process. Thus in English not only /b/ but also /d/ and /g/ may be partially devoiced at the end of an utterance. If one alveolar consonant is fronted or retracted in certain environments, it is highly likely that other alveolars will behave in the same way. In English, not only /t/ but also /d/ and /n/ are fronted to dental position when immediately preceding a dental fricative. This simply means that allophones tend to be governed by general rules or strategies of pronunciation rather than by idiosyncratic adjustments to individual phonemes.

It is sometimes argued that symmetrical patterning is a target towards which phonological systems keep moving. Certain processes of sound change indeed seem to favour symmetry. It seems fairly clear, for example, that in Old English voiced fricatives were not separate phonemes but allophones of the voiceless fricatives: fricative phonemes were voiceless in some contexts, voiced in others. Changes

Table 4.5.1   *Plosive phonemes*

(a) ENGLISH

	Bilabial	Alveolar	Velar
Voiceless (aspirated)	p	t	k
Voiced	b	d	g

(b) KOREAN[a]

	Bilabial	Alveolar	Velar
Strongly aspirated voiceless	ph	th	kh
Weakly aspirated	p^h	t^h	k^h
Glottalized	p	t	k

(c) HINDI

	Bilabial	Dental	Retroflex	Velar
Voiceless aspirated	p^h	t^h	$ʈ^h$	k^h
Voiceless	p	t	ʈ	k
Voiced aspirated	b^h	d^h	$ɖ^h$	g^h
Voiced	b	d	ɖ	g

(d) ANCIENT GREEK

	Bilabial	Dental or alveolar	Velar
Voiceless aspirated	p^h	t^h	k^h
Voiceless	p	t	k
Voiced	b	d	g

[a] For the terms used, see Chomsky and Halle 1968, p. 327.

in the language have led to the emergence of separate voiced and voiceless fricative phonemes, namely /f/ /v/ /θ/ /ð/ /s/ and /z/. (Even though the Old English conditioning no longer applies, modern English does still show traces of the earlier pattern, with voiceless fricatives word-final in e.g. *knife, half, bath, south, house,* but corresponding voiced fricatives in *knives, halves, baths, southern, houses.*) But by the time the voiced fricatives had achieved phonemic status in English, another voiceless fricative /ʃ/ had also arisen, for example by coalescence of /s/ with a following consonant (compare Old English *scip, sciell* with modern *ship, shell*). This fricative was potentially without a voiced partner, but occurrences of /ʒ/ have in fact been supplied either by new words of French origin (*beige, rouge*) or by assimilation of /zj/, as in *measure, treasure,* etc. Thus the /ʒ/ has filled what might otherwise have been a 'gap' in the phonemic pattern, as shown in table 4.5.2(a).

Similar arguments to the effect that languages tend to fill 'holes in the pattern' or to maximize symmetrical exploitation of contrasts have been based on various data. Table 4.5.2(b) gives the fricative phonemes of modern German (assuming that [h] is an allophone of /x/). Each of the voiceless fricatives now has a voiced counterpart, but from different origins: /v/ results from a change in pronunciation of earlier /w/; /z/

Table 4.5.2   Fricative phonemes

(a) ENGLISH (excluding /h/)

	Labiodental	Dental	Alveolar	Postalveolar
Voiceless	f	θ	s	ʃ
Voiced	v	ð	z	ʒ

(b) GERMAN

	Labiodental	Alveolar	Postalveolar	Palatal	Uvular
Voiceless	f	s	ʃ	ç	x
Voiced	v	z	ʒ	j	ʁ

is from earlier /s/; /ʒ/ occurs only in borrowings such as *Journal*, *Manege*; /j/ is the palatal semivowel but is often pronounced with friction so that it virtually becomes a voiced palatal fricative; and /ʁ/ results from the relatively recent adoption of a uvular articulation for earlier /r/. Hence it can be argued that various shifts in pronunciation, some of them ostensibly independent changes to individual consonants, are part of a systemic trend. The classic discussion of this topic is found in Martinet (1955); Fischer-Jørgensen (1975, pp. 44–8) provides a useful overview and additional references.

It is evident, however, that phonemic systems are not always symmetrical. (Indeed, the historical discussion of English and German presupposes that some sound changes destroy rather than create symmetry, otherwise there would never be 'gaps' to be filled.) Voicing contrasts, for example, are not always exploited as systematically as one might expect from simple assumptions about symmetry and economy. In Dutch there is no voiced velar stop: orthographic *g* represents a uvular fricative, and [g] occurs only as an allophone of /k/, whereas /p/, /b/, /t/ and /d/ are separate phonemes. In standard Arabic there are voiced and voiceless sounds in contrast, such as /t/, /d/, /s/, /z/, but no /p/ in contrast with /b/, and no /g/ alongside the /k/.

Moreover, there is always a danger that discussion of phonological symmetry will be more concerned with patterns on paper than with genuine insight into the phonological system. It may well be convenient to represent vowel systems as squared arrays, as in table 4.5.3 (cf. section 2.7 above); but while these diagrams have some merit in displaying the number of vowel contrasts, they have serious drawbacks so far as the nature of the contrasts is concerned. The apparently equivalent systems of Spanish, Russian and Japanese, for example, are rather different in detail. Japanese /u/ is noticeably unrounded, whereas Spanish /u/ and Russian /u/ *are* rounded; Russian /i/ is subject to considerable allophonic conditioning and in many environments is central rather than front, whereas this is not true of Spanish or Japanese; moreover, the effects of such phenomena as stress are quite different among the three languages (with Russian, for example, reducing some unstressed vowels to something like the English indeterminate [ə]); and so on.

Table 4.5.3   Vowel phonemes (squared arrays)

(a) THREE-VOWEL SYSTEM (e.g. Warlpiri, central Australia)

	Front		*Back*
High	i		u
Low		a	

(b) FIVE-VOWEL SYSTEM (e.g. Spanish, Russian, Japanese)

	Front		*Back*
High	i		u
Mid	e		o
Low		a	

(c) SEVEN-VOWEL SYSTEM (e.g. Italian)

	Front		*Back*
High	i		u
High mid	e		o
Low mid	ɛ		ɔ
Low		a	

(d) EIGHT-VOWEL SYSTEM (e.g. Turkish)

	Front unrounded	*Front rounded*	*Nonfront unrounded*	*Nonfront rounded*
High	i	y	ɨ	u
Nonhigh	e	ø	a	o

Even more seriously, a neatly arranged diagram does not necessarily reflect neatly arranged pronunciation. The plosive, fricative and nasal consonant phonemes of French, for instance, can be set out as in table 4.5.4. The arrangement shows that there are three distinctive points of articulation for each kind of consonant; it does not show that each of the three columns represents an identical point of articulation. /f/ and /v/ are labio-dental whereas /p/ /b/ and /m/ are bilabial, and /k/ and /g/ are velar whereas /ʃ/ /ʒ/ and /ɲ/ are palatal. The heading 'Back' above the third column is legitimate in so far as it indicates that all the consonants in this column are articulated further back than alveolar, but certainly not accurate as a precise articulatory label.

Table 4.5.4   Plosive, fricative and nasal consonants of French

	Labial	*Dental/alveolar*	*Back*
Voiceless plosives	p	t	k
Voiced plosives	b	d	g
Voiceless fricatives	f	s	ʃ
Voiced fricatives	v	z	ʒ
Nasals	m	n	ɲ

For further discussion of labels of this kind, see the treatment of phonological and phonetic features in chapter 10 below. In addition to Martinet's work mentioned above, Trubetzkoy (1939, especially ch. 4) and Hockett (1955, especially pp. 82–126) give detailed comparative discussion of phonological systems. Section 4.12 below comments further on surveys of sounds across the world's languages. See also Ladefoged's evaluation of vowel charts (1982, ch. 9) and other discussion of vowel systems in Liljencrants and Lindblom (1972), Lindau (1978) and section 2.7 above.

4.6   Phonological reality

Enough has been said already to demonstrate that phonological organization is more than a matter of how sounds are articulated. The judgment that English [tʃ] is an affricate but [ts] is not is not based simply on observation and measurement of the way in which these sounds are pronounced or perceived but requires reference to English sequential patterning and to the phonological system within which these sounds function (section 3.12 above). Likewise, the recognition that clear and dark variants of /l/ are allophones of the one phoneme in English but [h] and [ŋ] are not (section 4.3 above) also depends on more than just articulatory and acoustic observation.

Nevertheless, especially in the English-speaking world, where empiricism and pragmatism are powerful philosophical currents, some linguists have remained suspicious of ascribing any kind of reality to phonological analyses. Some of the scepticism is framed in terms that suggest that articulatory and acoustic phonetics deal with the 'real' or 'objective' nature of speech, while phonology is 'speculative' or 'metaphysical' or 'merely concerned with orthography'. An example is chapter 29 of Jones 1962, where a 'physical' view of the phoneme is defended against a 'superphysical' view. But it is worth noting that few if any of us are totally consistent on such issues. Daniel Jones announces his scepticism about phonemic theory but none the less resorts to an appeal to native speakers' 'feelings' in the case of the Italian velar nasal (1962, p. 63; cf. section 4.3 above).

It is now generally agreed that the classic attempt to produce phonological descriptions that would make no reference to the meanings of words, let alone to native speakers' intuitions or insights, is indeed inconsistent. Z. S. Harris's *Methods in structural linguistics* (1951) represents the claim that it is possible to discover phonemes purely by examining the distribution of phonetic segments: 'The present survey is thus explicitly limited to questions of distribution' (p. 5). But Harris's analysis in fact assumes the investigator's ability to judge whether two utterances in a language are intended to be different words or whether they count as alternative ways of saying the same word. It can be argued that Harris's and others' efforts to define 'objective' analytical procedures constantly presuppose access to native speakers' intuitions into their own language (Chomsky 1964).

Our own view is that it is valid to appeal to the reality of a phonological analysis provided that it is supported by empirical evidence. Empirical evidence can be gathered not only by instrumental means (for example in the spectrographic analysis of sound waves in the electromyographic analysis of speech organs) but also by the observation of speakers' intuitions. Of course 'intuitions' does not refer here to idiosyncratic or speculative comments about language but rather to what underlies speakers' abilities to count the number of syllables in a word, to say whether two words are pronounced identically or differently, to select rhyming words, and so on. In this sense, the phonological system of a language is open to empirical validation, inasmuch as speakers demonstrate, implicitly or explicitly, their awareness of phonemic differences in their own language. Sapir was particularly intrigued by evidence of this general kind, as for example in the case of a speaker of southern Paiute who pronounced a word as [pa:βah] but then separated it into the two syllables [pa: pah]. This evidence that the native speaker counts [β] as a realization of /p/ (provided that it is not merely an idiosyncratic response on the part of an individual) is just as empirical as the evidence of spectrography or radiography (Sapir 1933).

Admittedly the status of such evidence may be complicated by various factors, including the existence of conventionalized spelling systems, traditions of grammatical terminology and so on. Thus when English speakers say that English has five vowels they are referring to the five letters A E I O U and not to the phonological system. On another level, however, the same English speakers operate with more than five vowels when they construct or assess rhyming verse (in which case they respond to phonemic contrasts rather than spellings). Similarly, English speakers may claim that the words *cent*, *sent* and *scent* are different because they have different spellings and meanings. But they will agree that they are pronounced identically – or, putting it in an empirical context, they will be unable to distinguish the words when given only the pronunciation and not the spelling or meaning.

We have already referred to such evidence in connection with interpretations and phonemic analysis (sections 3.14 and 4.2 above) and we stress that the variety of available evidence points not only to different levels of analysis but also to interaction and integration among these levels. Even without access to instrumental findings about the articulation and acoustics of speech, speakers are aware of interrelationships in their language, say between words which differ in meaning but not in spelling and pronunciation (*football matches*, *box of matches*) or between different spellings of the 'same' word (*Catherine*, *Katherine*; *judgment*, *judgement*) and so on. One could imagine a language in which all of this was maximally simple: each phoneme would have a single allophone, with minimal variation in articulation and acoustic properties, the spelling would have a perfectly consistent one-to-one mapping of visual symbols on to phonemes or syllables, there would be no synonymy or homonymy, and so on. In practice, although some languages are simpler or more consistent in certain respects than others, maximal simplicity seems to be so remote from the truth that it is artificial.

4.7   Units and boundaries

Many phonological processes apply within certain domains. For example, the lengthening of English /n/ before a voiced stop or fricative (as observed in words such as *sand*, *bend*, etc.) does not apply where the nasal and obstruent belong to different syllables. There is no lengthening of the /n/ in *undo* or *indecent* compared with *until* or *intelligent*. We may say that this lengthening is 'intrasyllabic', i.e. it applies within a syllable. On the other hand, some English processes clearly have a larger domain. The assimilation of /n/ to the point of articulation of a following consonant is in no sense blocked by a syllable or word boundary, and the /n/ in *ten boys* or *ten miles*, for instance, may often be pronounced as [m].

In fact a proper account of phonology, including intonation, stress and assimilatory processes as well as phonemic contrasts, requires reference to units at various levels. Many linguists recognize an ascending hierarchy of units such as: syllable, phonological word, tone group, breath group, etc. (See section 3.1 above and remarks on the organization of intonation in section 9.8 below.) Note that the boundaries of these units do not necessarily coincide with grammatical boundaries. It can be argued, for instance, that an English article plus a noun form a single phonological word, even though there are two distinct grammatical elements written as two words. The article is normally unstressed and is phonologically indistinguishable from a prefix: compare *a head*, *a way* with *ahead*, *away*. Actually the history of certain English words makes it quite clear that the boundary between article and noun is not a strong one: *adder* (snake) and *apron* are derived from earlier forms *nadder* and *napron*, by a process in which *a nadder* and *a napron* were taken to be *an adder* and *an apron*. Common reduced forms such as *I've*, *he's*, *she'll*, *don't* also demonstrate that grammatical and phonological units need not coincide: each of these forms is a single syllable but two grammatical elements (MORPHEMES).

This is not to say that phonological and grammatical units never coincide. There are certain languages (and certain phenomena within particular languages) in which grammatical units have special relevance to phonology. A simple instance is the Javanese glottal stop occurring as an allophone of /k/ in morpheme-final position. (This differs from Indonesian, in which /k/ has the glottal stop allophone in *word*-final position, as described in section 4.3 above.) Note the following Javanese words, where hyphens have been added to the normal spelling to show the morphemic composition:

anak	[anaʔ]	child
anak-e	[anaʔe]	the child
mangan-ake	[maŋanake]	cause to eat
temok-ake	[təmɒʔake]	cause to meet

To interpret /k/ correctly as [k] or [ʔ], one must know whether it is at the end of a morpheme.

In Turkish, a process of vowel harmony extends through the word. In general outline, it is the vowel of the first syllable that is distinctive, and the vowels of subsequent syllables are constrained within the rules of the language. As a consequence, suffixes have different phonemic shapes, depending on the vowels of the roots to which they are attached. Some suffixes, such as plural, have a front *e* vowel if preceded by a front vowel; otherwise the suffix has the *a* vowel. Other suffixes, such as the genitive, have four different vowels, again depending on the nature of the preceding vowel in the root: these suffixes have front unrounded *i* after *i* or *e*, back rounded *u* after *u* or *o*, and so on. Table 4.7.1 gives some examples in standard Turkish spelling, in which front rounded vowels are shown by a diaresis above the *u* and *o* and a high central or back unrounded vowel is represented by an undotted *i*.

Turkish actually has two vowel systems, effective at different points of the structure. In the first syllable of a root, any of a full set of eight vowels can occur. In subsequent syllables (including suffixes, of course) there is systemically only a two-way choice between a relatively low vowel (which has two variants according to context) and a relatively high vowel (which has four variants according to context). Table 4.7.2 shows these systems. One consequence of this is that Turkish suffixes – units recognized in the grammar of the language – are not fully specified for vowel quality but depend on the root to which they are affixed.

Table 4.7.1   Examples of vowel harmony in Turkish

Root	Meaning	Root + plural	Root + genitive
kedi	cat	kediler	kedinin
ev	house	evler	evin
kız	daughter	kızlar	kızın
adam	man	adamlar	adamın
gün	day	günler	günün
göz	eye	gözler	gözün
ulus	nation	uluslar	ulusun
kol	arm	kollar	kolun

Table 4.7.2   Turkish vowels

(a) FULL SYSTEM (in first syllable of a root)

	Front		Central/back	
	Unrounded	*Rounded*	*Unrounded*	*Rounded*
High	i	ü	ı	u
Low	e	ö	a	o

(b) SUBSYSTEM (in noninitial syllables, including suffixes)

High	I
Low	A

I is realized as /i/, /y/, /ɨ/ or /u/ according to harmony
A is realized as /e/ or /a/ according to harmony

Thus phonological description must sometimes take account of grammatical units, such as morpheme or suffix; and grammatical description may sometimes need to recognize the phonological properties of grammatical units. (For more general remarks on the interaction between phonology and grammar, see section 4.10 below.)

4.8   Invariance and overlap

A rigid model of phonemic organization can give the impression that every phoneme has certain invariant characteristics. Thus it might be supposed that English /p/, despite some allophonic variation in the degree of aspiration and the nature of the plosive release, will be invariably bilabial, voiceless and plosive in character. While this may be reasonable for the specific case of English /p/, it is simplistic to assume that comparable invariant features can be specified for every phoneme in all languages.

In the first place, it is sometimes extremely difficult to specify precisely what features are common to all allophones of a phoneme. English /r/ may have allophones ranging from a voiced tap or flap, to a voiced (frictionless) approximant, to a voiceless fricative. If there are common characteristics shared by all of these allophones, they are more easily defined in negative terms (non-lateral, non-nasal, non-velar, etc.) than in precise phonetic terms. Indeed, this is one reason why phonological description frequently resorts to terminology which is language-specific, if not *ad hoc* (sections 4.5 above and 10.7 below).

In the second place, linguistic distinctions are relative rather than absolute. For the sake of simple illustration we take an artificial example, which is nevertheless based on the kind of phenomena encountered in a number of natural languages. The following words reveal four phonetic vowels but only three contrasts in any particular environment:

[tip]	[tɪk]	[pit]	[pɪk]
[tɪp]	[tek]	[kɪp]	[kek]
[tep]	[tɛk]	[ket]	[pɛk]

Minimal pairs demonstrating the three vowel phonemes are contained in the first two columns. The reasonable explanation of this language is to say that there are three vowel phonemes, each of which is lowered before [k], i.e.

/i/   [ɪ] before [k]
        [i] elsewhere
/ɪ/   [e] before [k]
        [ɪ] elsewhere
/e/   [ɛ] before [k]
        [e] elsewhere

The phonemes overlap with each other, in that one allophone of /i/ is identical with one allophone of /ɪ/, and one allophone of /ɪ/ is identical with one allophone of /e/. But distinctions are maintained, because the contrast is one of *relative* vowel height in the relevant context: whether before a [k] or not, /e/ is always lower than /ɪ/, and /ɪ/ always lower than /i/. Vowel systems often show shifted contrasts in this manner, and data of this kind are attested for various languages (see Jones 1962, ch. 19, for examples from French and Russian, and Stokes 1981, especially pp. 149ff., and Waters 1979, pp. 69ff., for the Australian languages Anindilyakwa and Djinang). Examples of this kind obviously defy any attempt to specify the *absolute* values of each phoneme.

In the third place, contrasts are not always localized strictly within one segment. The contrast between English /t/ and /d/, for example, is often more a matter of the length of the preceding segment than of the nature of the plosives themselves. Compare pairs like *seat* and *seed*, or *bent* and *bend*, and note that in certain circumstances (say over a bad telephone line) the length of the preceding vowel or nasal consonant is likely to be a more crucial factor than the quality of the plosive ('I said seeeed, not seat'). Phonological systems do not appear to be constrained by a principle that distinctions must be firmly anchored within segmental boundaries, and there are many other examples which may raise doubts about too narrow a concept of the segment as a basic unit (section 3.1 above). In Javanese, for example, the distinction between voiced and voiceless plosives often seems to be signalled by the nature of voicing in the following vowel (breathy voice after a voiced plosive). And in many varieties of German (especially in the north of the country) the presence of a final *r* is indicated by the quality of a preceding vowel (mimicked by other Germans as *bessa* instead of *besser*, *guta* instead of *guter*, etc.).

The historical developments which many languages have undergone further demonstrate the relativity of phonemic distinctions. There is ample evidence of quite radical shifts in the nature of these contrasts. A system of long and short vowel contrasts may at some later stage of the language become a system of pure and diphthongal vowel distinctions. Or if consonants are dropped or elided, vowel allophones that were conditioned by the lost consonants may become contrastive vowel phonemes; and so on. Many tonal languages, for instance, can be traced back to an earlier stage at which pitch was a redundant feature associated with certain adjacent consonants (Hyman 1975, pp. 228–9, and section 9.4 below).

One of the reasons for the diversity of modern English pronunciation is that the vowel system has undergone major shifts over the last few hundred years, with different consequences in various regions. Some five to six hundred years ago the English vowels of e.g. *time* and *tame* were approximately [i] and [a]. (Compare the values of the letters *i* and *a* which persist in other European languages such as French and German.) In modern English pronunciation these vowels are commonly diphthongs, although the extent and nature of diphthongization vary considerably. At the same time, the loss of final /r/ in south-eastern England has led to modification of preceding vowels, e.g.

here   earlier /hiːr/   modern /hɪə/   (cf. *he* /hiː/)
hire   earlier /hair/   modern /haɪə]   (cf. *high* /hai/).

The forms given here as 'earlier' are in fact maintained in some parts of the English-speaking world (notably south-western Britain and much of North America). But areas where English has spread from Britain subsequent to the elision of final /r/ or where closer connections have been maintained with British English (such as Australia and New Zealand) show the same kinds of contrast as modern south-eastern British English.

These examples show that different historical stages and regional varieties of a language may have different phonological organization, and they underline the point that a phonemic system is a network of relative contrasts. They do not, however, rule out the possibility of unambiguous phonemic analysis for any language taken as a particular regional version at a particular point of time. In the following section, however, we turn to phenomena that can create serious ambiguity in the analysis itself.

4.9   Biuniqueness and neutralization

A phonemic description is said to be BIUNIQUE if phonemes and allophones are unambiguously mapped on to each other. The analysis of the three vowel phonemes in the artificial data in section 4.8 above is biunique, despite some overlap, because environments can be clearly specified: [ɪ] before [k] is unambiguously an occurrence of /i/ whereas [ɪ] before consonants other than [k] is equally clearly an allophone of /ɪ/. Admittedly, where there is linear realignment of a contrast, reanalysis may be necessary in order to preserve biuniqueness. Suppose that English pronunciation actually changed to the point where the only distinction between final /t/ and /d/ (and other voiceless and voiced sounds) was in the length of the preceding segment, i.e.

send pronounced as [sɛnːt], *seed* as [siːt];
sent pronounced as [sɛnt], *seat* as [sit].

Now it is difficult to contrive a statement of phonemes and allophones to the effect that /t/ is [t] but that /d/ also has an identical allophone [t] provided that the preceding segment is lengthened. Moreover, a simple statement that both /t/ and /d/ are sometimes indistinguishable as [t] would violate the principle of biuniqueness. It would therefore be more realistic to recognize that words no longer end in /d/ and that the language now has new phonemic contrasts such as /n/ versus /nː/.

For any particular system, then, biuniqueness is a requirement that phonemes and allophones can be unambiguously assigned to each other. A problem in this connection is that contrastive systems are often unequally exploited. This means, for example, that two phonemes may be distinguished in some structures but not in others. Following Trubetzkoy (1939) we may say that some phonemic oppositions are suspended or NEUTRALIZED under certain conditions. Trubetzkoy distinguishes three kinds of neutralization and we give examples of each.

Firstly, a language has a certain contrast but only one of the relevant phonemes occurs under neutralization. Suppose a language has a contrast of voiced and voiceless plosives in word-initial and word-medial positions, but only voiceless plosives occur word-finally. Since the word-final plosives are not in contrast with voiced plosives, the contrast of voicing is inoperative or neutralized word-finally. This pattern of neutralization is found in a number of languages, including Dutch, German and Russian. In Dutch, /t/ and /d/ are in contrast, e.g. in *toen* ('then'), *doen* ('to do'), *teken* ('sign'), *deken* ('blanket'). Although written forms show both final *t* and *d*, there is no such thing as a final voiced plosive in pronunciation. Thus both *bond* ('association') and *bont* ('fur') are pronounced identically, with final [t], as are *pond* ('pound') and *pont* ('ferry'). Comparable illustration of the same pattern of pronunciation can be found in German and Russian, although the details of how the neutralization applies and how it intersects with assimilatory processes of voicing and devoicing vary from language to language. (In particular the concept of 'word-final' neutralization needs refinement, since the neutralization may apply, for example, at the end of the first element of a compound as well, as in Dutch *bondgenoot* 'ally, confederate'.)

Secondly, neutralization may be represented by some kind of variation or alternation among the otherwise contrasting phonemes. In Indonesian, for example, there are four nasal consonant phonemes (bilabial /m/, alveolar /n/, palatal /ɲ/ and velar /ŋ/); but sequences of nasal plus other consonant are homorganic, that is the nasal and following consonant are at the same point of articulation. Thus we find clusters such as /mb/ and /nd/, but not /md/ or /nb/. (Borrowing from other languages has brought some exceptions to this pattern, but we ignore these for the sake of illustration.) This means that there is no contrast of nasal consonants preceding a plosive. It would be possible to represent the preconsonantal nasal with a single symbol (say *n* or *N*): the value of *N* would be entirely predictable from the point of articulation of the following plosive. Other languages in which nasal consonant clusters are similarly homorganic include Japanese and Spanish.

Alternatively, neutralization may be represented by free variation (section 4.11 below) of the phonemes in question. Some varieties of English have a contrast between /aʊ/ and /aʊə/ in e.g.

cow   [kaʊ]   cower   [kaʊə]
bow   [baʊ]   bower   [baʊə]

This contrast is neutralized before /r/ (and often also before /l/), where there may be indeterminate variation between the diphthong and triphthong. For example, Australian students beginning to learn to transcribe English are often uncertain whether they say the place name *Cowra* as /kaʊrə/ or /kaʊərə/. Similar indecision usually affects words such as *dowry*, *cowering*, *towel* and *owl*.

Thirdly, neutralization may be represented by a sound which is distinct from both of the otherwise contrasting phonemes. One of the most common instances of this kind of neutralization is where vowel contrasts are reduced under certain conditions, say before certain consonants or in unstressed syllables. The English tendency to reduce all vowels to the so-called 'indeterminate' [ə] is one illustration of the principle. Compare the capitalized vowels in e.g.

legAlity [æ]   legAl [ə]
irOnic [ɒ]   irOny [ə]
torrEntial [ɛ]   torrEnt [ə]

In varieties of English such as RP, [ə] never occurs as the vowel of a fully stressed syllable (other than as the offglide of centering diphthongs). It can therefore be seen as representing neutralization of the usual range of vowel contrasts.

It should be noted that neutralization sometimes creates alternate forms of a morpheme: English *torrent* has two different phonemic forms depending on whether it is unsuffixed or carrying the suffix *–ial*. In this case, the phenomenon may be described as morphophonemic (section 4.10 below).

In terms of a phonological analysis, there are three ways of treating neutralizations. The first is to insist that sounds representing neutralizations must be treated as allophones of a phoneme – which means in effect not recognizing neutralization. Thus if a language has both voiced and voiceless plosives but only voiceless plosives in word-final position, the word-final voiceless plosives are simply taken at face value. It must then be said of this language that voiced plosives do not occur word-finally. While this reflects a phonetic truth and may seem perfectly obvious, some cases will require an arbitrary choice. For instance, where the distinction between /aʊ/ and /aʊə/ is neutralized before /r/ in English, it is not clear by what criterion one can insist that the vowel is phonemically one or other of the two alternatives.

A second possibility, which avoids this arbitrariness, is a strategy proposed by Trubetzkoy himself, namely that of recognizing an ARCHIPHONEME. Thus English [ə] might be judged to be an archiphoneme representing the neutralization of vowel contrasts exhibited in stressed syllables: it is not identified with any of the other vowel phonemes but represents the suspension of the relevant contrasts. In this tradition of analysis, archiphonemes are often indicated by capital letters to show their special status. Applying this convention to a language in which the voicing opposition is neutralized word-finally, we might write final plosives as /P/ /T/ and /K/. We have also mentioned the possible use of /N/ for a nasal consonant that takes the point of articulation of the following consonant. An archiphoneme is in effect an underspecified segment. Thus /N/ stands for 'nasal consonant', without point of articulation features, /P/ for 'bilabial plosive' without specification of voicing, and so on.

A third possibility is to forgo biuniqueness. If we do this, we seem to introduce ambiguity into the analysis. If we suggest, for instance, that English [ə] is indeed an allophone of *any* other vowel, then we may have no way of determining, for any particular occurrence of [ə], to which of the vowel phonemes it is to be assigned. But there are often related forms which do provide a means of making a choice. The very fact that the form *torrent* (with [ə]) is related to the form *torrential* (with [ɛ]) provides a reason for allocating [ə] to the phoneme /ɛ/ in this instance; while a comparison of *irony* and *ironic* allows us to say that the [ə] in *irony* 'belongs to' the phoneme /ɒ/. Now there are indeed multiple sources or origins for [ə], and each case will be decided by related forms. From a strictly phonemic perspective, the analysis is ambiguous, for there is nothing in the phonological context that tells us that one [ə] belongs to /ɛ/, another to /ɒ/, and so on. But there is no indeterminacy once the appeal to grammatical or semantic relationships is allowed. To return to the example of word-final neutralization of voicing in languages such as Dutch and German, we can distinguish between voiced and voiceless plosives, even though they are pronounced identically. Here too there are related forms to appeal to, e.g.

pond [pɒnt] pound   *ponden* [pɒndən] pounds
pont [pɒnt] ferry   *ponten* [pɒntən] ferries
bond [bɒnt] association   *bonden* [bɒndən] associations
bont [bɒnt] fur   *bonten* [bɒntən] furs.

It is important to note that *pond* and *pont* are not distinct in pronunciation – but once we know the meaning, or specifically affixed forms such as the plural, then we can relate [t] to either /t/ or /d/.

It is interesting to measure biuniqueness in phonemic analysis against the orthographic practice of written languages. Generally speaking, a spelling system that matches or reflects a biunique phonemic analysis is an attractive one. It is the kind of spelling system that is commonly but misleadingly termed 'phonetic': there will be no orthographic ambiguities, so that any letter or symbol will have a unique value (i.e. pronunciation) and any sound will have a unique orthographic representation (letter or symbol). Of course, the pronunciation of some letters will be relative to the environment in which they stand, because some phonemes have various allophones, but the correct pronunciation will be governed by the 'allophonic rules' of the language. Thus it may be necessary to know that word-final *k* is pronounced as a glottal stop in Indonesian or that *l* is dark before a consonant in English, but these are matters of unambiguous rule. Native speakers who have already learned to speak their own language will not need to be instructed in what they take to be the normal way of pronouncing phonemes.

There is none the less a case *against* biunique spelling systems. It can be argued, for example, that a spelling system ought to distinguish homonyms (*knight* and *night*, *right*, *rite* and *write*, etc.) or that a conservative and even difficult spelling system may be justified as a common orthography for speakers of different dialects. Furthermore, there are few if any current orthographic systems that are truly biunique. Even those often praised for their consistency and simplicity, such as Dutch, Italian and Indonesian, have some ambiguities. For example, Dutch *nog* and *noch* are pronounced identically, Italian *e* represents both /e/ and /ɛ/, and Indonesian *e* represents both /e/ and /ə/. The fact remains, however, that most spelling systems approach phonemic biuniqueness much more closely than the notoriously conservative orthographies of English and French.

Few orthographies have special letters corresponding to the archiphonemes of phonological analysis. One possible case is the apparently redundant use of special letters in Ancient Greek to represent the sequences /ps/ and /ks/. Ancient Greek actually had a contrast of three kinds of plosive, namely voiceless aspirated, voiceless and voiced (table 4.5.1(d) above). /pʰ/, /p/ and /b/ were represented by the letters known as *phi* φ, *pi* π and *beta* β, and /kʰ/, /k/ and /g/ by the letters known as *chi* χ, *kappa* κ and *gamma* γ. (We restrict our attention here to the labial and velar instances, and should also note that Modern Greek does not preserve this three-way distinction, some of the plosives of Ancient Greek now being pronounced as fricatives.) The contrasts of aspiration and voicing were, however, neutralized before /s/. Numerous consequences of this pattern of neutralization can be observed in Ancient Greek. In verb forms, for example, the verb root is followed by /s/ in future forms, as in /lu–/, verb root meaning 'undo' or 'loose', /luo:/ 'I undo', /luso:/ 'I will undo'. Where the verb root happens to end in a plosive, the neutralization will be evident before the /s/ in future forms:

/grapʰo:/ I write	/grapso:/ I will write
/blepo:/ I see	/blepso:/ I will see
/tʰlibo:/ I press	/tʰlipso:/ I will press
/arkʰo:/ I rule	/arkso:/ I will rule
/dio:ko:/ I chase	/dio:kso:/ I will chase
/anoigo:/ I open	/anoikso:/ I will open.

The neutralization means of course that one cannot tell from a future form what the root is – whether /k/ before /s/ corresponds to a root-final /k/, /kʰ/ or /g/. What is noteworthy for our purposes is that the Greek spelling system uses single letters for the sequence of a neutralized plosive and following /s/, namely *xi* ξ for /ks/ and *psi* ψ for /ps/. These special letters can be taken as orthographic signals of the neutralization (cf. Allen 1987, pp. 59–60). Traces of the spelling conventions can be found in English. The flower *phlox* takes its name from the Greek for 'flame', with the letter *x* representing /ks/, where the final /s/ is a suffix; the root actually ends in /g/ (when not affected by a following /s/) as seen in words such as *phlogistic* and *phlogiston*. The occasional use in German of spellings such as word-final *dt* (*Stadt, Brandt*) is also a minor instance of special orthographic recognition of a loss of contrast. But in most spelling systems there are few if any special devices to represent neutralization.

It seems rather more common that orthographic practice reponds to related forms. Thus in Dutch, German and Russian, the orthography does distinguish between final voiced and voiceless plosives, depending on how the consonant is pronounced in non-final position. Dutch *pond* is written with a *d*, *pont* with a *t*, even though both end in [t] and are therefore indistinguishable in pronunciation: the spelling is justified by appeal to other forms such as the plurals *ponden* (pronounced with [d]) and *ponten* (pronounced with [t]). Likewise, English [ə] is written with various vowels, often depending on a related form: thus we write *e* in *torrent* (compare *torrential*), *a* in *legal* (compare *legality*), and so on. Nevertheless, many users of English are evidently not always sensitive to related forms. Common spelling mistakes include errors like *grammer*, even though a knowledge of the pronunciation and spelling of *grammatical* would suggest the spelling *grammar*. In some instances users may simply not know the related forms, such as the word *sentential* (justifying the use of *e* rather than *a* in the second syllable of *sentence*). And it must also be recognized that in many cases in English, there is no related form with a full vowel: spellings such as *o* in *button*, *a* in *defendant* and *e* in *apparent* cannot be justified by appeal to other forms.

A brief but useful explanation of neutralization, based on Trubetzkoy's exposition, can be found in Sommerstein (1977, pp. 49–53); see also section 11.6 below.

4.10   Morphophonemic alternations

If a morpheme has two or more phonemic shapes, the different forms are sometimes referred to as ALLOMORPHS (compare the term 'allophone', section 4.3 above). Allomorphs are not necessarily closely similar to each other. In Dutch, for example, the plural suffix is

-en in e.g. *ponden* ('pounds'), *bonen* ('beans')
-eren in e.g. *kinderen* ('children'), *eieren* ('eggs')
-s in e.g. *tafels* ('tables'), *zoons* ('sons').

Even more remote from each other are English forms such as *go* and *went*, where, arguably, *went* (or *wen-*) can be regarded as the allomorph of the verb that occurs in the past tense.

Some allomorphs, however, belong within a general pattern of phonemic alternation. In this case the allomorphs may be said to be in MORPHOPHONEMIC ALTERNATION with each other. We have already met some examples earlier in this chapter, such as the neutralization of final voiced and voiceless plosives in languages such as Dutch and German. In German, words such as *Hunde* ('dogs') and *Hände* ('hands') contain /d/; but the singular forms *Hund* and *Hand*, although written with *d*, are pronounced with /t/. Forms such as *Bund* ('federation') and *bunt* ('colourful') are therefore indistinguishable in pronunciation: it is only suffixed forms such as *Bundes* and *buntes* that show an opposition between /d/ and /t/. Not only are /t/ and /d/ phonologically close, differing only in voicing, but the pattern is a highly regular one: any final /d/ will be devoiced but will be recoverable from related forms in which the /d/ is not final. Moreover, the pattern is not just an alternation of /t/ and /d/ but extends to all voicing contrasts in German. Thus *Laub* ('foliage') has final /p/, but the /b/ is recoverable from e.g. *laubig* ('leafy').

In English, voicing contrasts are also neutralized, giving rise to morphophonemic alternations, although under different conditions from German. English /s/ and /z/

are separate phonemes (*seal/zeal*, *fuss/fuzz*) but the plural suffix is /s/ in words such as *maps*, *cats*, *socks*, and /z/ in words such as *tubs*, *lids*, *dogs*, even though the conventional spelling does not show the difference in pronunciation. This is again part of a wider pattern, applying also, for instance, to the possessive suffix (as in *the cat's food* and *the dog's food*) as well as to the past suffix (*rubbed*, *sagged* ending in /d/, *ripped*, *sacked* ending in /t/).

Contrasts among English nasal consonants are likewise neutralized under certain circumstances. Notice, for example, that /m/ and /n/ are separate phonemes (*meat/ neat*, *sum/sun*) but the prefix in words such as *improbable*, *imbalance*, *indecent*, *insolvent*, ends in /m/ or /n/ depending on the following consonant. (Here English spelling does show the difference in pronunciation, whereas written *–s* and *-ed* stand for alternative phonemic forms.)

English also has a number of vowel alternations. The following examples show five pairs of alternating vowels: in each case the forms on the right show a different vowel from the forms on the left, in the syllable immediately preceding the suffix *-ic*:

state, mania	static, manic
esthete, academe	esthetic, academic
analyse, type	analytic, typic(al)
cone, microscope	conic, microscopic.

Phonemically, each pair of vowels is distinct, as shown by minimal pairs such as

mate / mat	main / man	fate / fat
seat / set	dean / den	steam / stem
type / tip	sight / sit	lime / limb
own / on	coat / cot	toast / tossed.

Despite such instances of contrasts, the occurrence of one vowel rather than the other is often predictable from the grammatical context. Thus the same vowel that occurs before *–ic* also occurs under other conditions: for instance, the alternation evident in *esthete* and *esthetic* is also seen in e.g.

obscene	obscenity
convene	convention
keep	kept.

This predictability is often not thought of as an instance of neutralization, for neutralization in the classic sense is peculiar to some specific phonological environment (such as word-final position, or preceding a consonant). In this case, while we can predict the change of vowel when /t/ is suffixed, in forms such as

keep, kept   sleep, slept   weep, wept

it is not true that the distinction between the two vowels is neutralized before /pt/ (or comparable consonant sequences). Note, for instance, forms such as *heaped* and *reaped* and the minimal pair *steeped/stepped*. Indeed, even particular suffixes do not guarantee that the alternation will apply. Thus *-ic* is preceded by /ɒ/ in e.g. *conic* and *tonic*, but the word *rhotic* is often pronounced with /oʊ/, possibly because it is not perceived to contain the suffix *-ic*; the words *phonemic* and *morphemic* are often pronounced with the same vowel as in *phoneme* and *morpheme*, rather than rhyming with *endemic*; and some Australians pronounce *basic* with the same vowel as *base*, others rhyme it with *classic*.

Phonological analysis in narrowly phonemic terms has often relegated these apparent violations of phonemic consistency to a special category of description intermediate between phonology and morphology: hence the blended term MORPHOPHONEMICS, replacing earlier MORPHONOLOGY or MORPHOPHONOLOGY (Martinet 1965). The allomorphs or variant forms of specific morphemes may then be described under this heading. For instance, the English plural suffix has (among others) the allomorphs

/-s/   occurring after roots ending in /p/ /t/ /k/ etc. (as in *cups*, *pots*, etc.)
/-z/   occurring after roots ending in /b/ /d/ /g/ etc. (as in *clubs*, *heads*, etc.).

Or *telephone* may be said to have (among others) two different allomorphs, depending on whether the stem is unsuffixed or carries the suffix *-ic*.

Generalizations about patterns of alternation can be expressed as MORPHOPHONEMIC RULES. Thus there is a morphophonemic rule of devoicing final stops and fricatives in languages such as German and Dutch; and in English the processes of vowel alternation such as we have illustrated above are sometimes covered by general rules of 'tensing' and 'laxing'. The status and validity of such rules became a key issue in the 1960s, as part of a wider debate about the nature of phonological description (chapter 5 below).

Martinet's classic discussion of morphophonemics (1965) includes a brief review of the origins and early uses of the terminology in the writings of Trubetzkoy (1939) and Bloomfield (1933) (see also sections 11.5 and 11.6 below). A helpful summary of modern perspectives can be found in Sommerstein (1977, pp. 41–4).

4.11 Free variation

The notion of free variation or free fluctuation is intended to account for random interchangeability in language. Suppose that an English speaker pronounces the initial consonant of *then*, *this*, *there*, etc., as either a dental fricative or a dental plosive and is unaware of the variation or apparently indifferent to the choice. The two sounds can be described as FREE VARIANTS or freely fluctuating allophones of the phoneme. The allophones are ostensibly *un*conditioned by their phonetic environment (section 4.3 above). The usual notation, implying random variation in any environment, is

/ð/ [ð] ~ [d].

Alternatively, if the free variation applied only in word-initial position, we would then show it as follows:

/ð/ [ð] ~ [d] word-initially
    [ð] elsewhere.

In practice, a great deal of free variation will be of the kind that is not noticed even by trained phoneticians, let alone by the average speaker or learner of the language, such as minute variations in tongue position or timing that are a natural part of articulatory processes (section 4.1 above).

Other apparent cases of free variation may be as much due to uncertain hearing on the part of the linguist recording the language as to indifference on the part of the speaker. Still other 'free' variants turn out to be associated with specific regions or styles. English speakers may say that it does not matter whether you pronounce the /r/ phoneme as an approximant or as a flap or trill; but in fact there are strong regional and stylistic associations. Scottish speakers favour the flapped or trilled articulation far more than, say, English or Australian speakers do, and use of the flap is the kind of evidence that enables people to identify regional origins. English and Australian speakers may, however, adopt a flap or trill in certain circumstances, including operatic singing or other kinds of highly deliberate or careful speech. Thus it would be quite wrong to suggest that differences in the articulation of /r/ are a matter of free variation in English: it is true that such differences are not functional within the phonological system of contrasts, but they are not randomly disregarded and certainly are communicative in signalling speech styles or regional identity. Allophonic variation that is truly free probably occurs rarely, if at all, unless it is below the threshold of normal perception.

The concept of free variation may also be applied to phonemes themselves. Consider, for example, the possibility of pronouncing the English word *economics* with either /ɛ/ or /i:/ as the first vowel, or *either* with /i:/ or /aɪ/. The vowels are separate phonemes (compare *head*, *heed* and *hide*, or *men*, *mean* and *mine*) and are not interchangeable in most words. Cases of this kind are more likely to constitute genuinely free variation, especially where neutralization is involved: Australian English speakers, for example, may be undecided between /aʊ/ and /aʊə/ in words like *dowry* and *cowering* (section 4.9 above). Once again, regional and stylistic preferences are often involved. In the case of the word *either*, pronunciation with /i:/ is widely regarded as 'American' and with /aɪ/ as 'British', although this is something of an oversimplification, since both pronunciations can be heard in Australia. Some readers may conclude that this merely confirms that Australia is torn between British and North American models. Certainly, speakers are likely to be more conscious of differences among phonemes than of allophonic variation, and they may indeed be torn between competing norms. Readers will be familiar with the phenomenon of a speaker with a shifting pronunciation, say someone who moves from one area to another and seems to have partially and inconsistently changed pronunciation as a result, or someone who seems sometimes to be 'putting on' a different accent. Such phenomena are of considerable social significance – people are often alert to what they perceive as oddities or signs of an 'outsider's' accent, and may be quick to condemn those who 'betray' their native accent, for example. A simple concept of free variation is inadequate to explain the complexities of speech communities and the norms towards which individuals aspire.

For further remarks on free variation, see Pike (1947, ch. 11), Harris (1951, pp. 29ff.) and Sommerstein (1977, pp. 18–19). The social and regional significance of speech variation is a large subject in its own right: a general introduction to the sociolinguistic study of variation – including summary accounts of particular studies of phonological variables – can be found in Wardhaugh (1986, especially ch. 6 and 7); and Wells (1982) is thorough survey (in three volumes) of regional diversity in English pronunciation.

4.12   The sounds of the world's languages

If it is possible to list an inventory of phonemes for any language, then it is also possible to look for generalizations across these inventories, by asking questions such as

- What are the most common kinds of phoneme?
- What is the average number of phonemes in a language?
- Are some phonemes found only in some regions of the world?

Questions such as these have been pursued by a number of linguists, often in connection with an interest in 'universals of language' and more recently in the context of compiling databases of 'phonological segment inventories' such as the one created at the University of California at Los Angeles, known as the UCLA Phonological Segment Inventory Database, or UPSID for short (see the introduction to Maddieson 1984).

Such questions are nevertheless not as easy to answer as one might hope. In the first place, we have to decide what we mean by 'all languages'. There are many languages which we know were once spoken but are no longer in living use. While we have no particular reason to believe that any of these extinct languages was radically different in its phonology from modern languages, it would certainly be unwise to generalize too confidently. In fact, not even all the living languages of the world have been analysed in sufficient depth to allow us to say what their phonemes are, making it all the more necessary to be cautious.

In the second place, statements about what kinds of phonemes all or most languages have – or don't have – may overlook the difficulties of determining what counts as one language. To take a simple illustration from English, most phonologists would say that English has three nasal consonant phonemes: the /m/ of *sum* or *ram*, the /n/ of *sun* or *ran*, and the /ŋ/ of *sung* or *rang*. If we were trying to make some generalizations about how many and what kind of nasal phonemes languages have, we would thus count English as one of the languages which has three nasal consonants. But in fact, as we noted in 4.3 above, there are regional varieties of English, in the Midlands and north of England, in which there is no velar nasal phoneme: words like *sung* and *rang* are pronounced with a final /g/ following the velar nasal consonant, and the nasal consonant is therefore an allophone of /n/ conditioned by a following velar consonant. It is clear that any generalizations about how many languages have three nasal consonant phonemes, and how many have two, will be affected by whether we count English as a single language and ignore its regional variation, or whether we begin to recognize regional varieties as (potentially) different phonological systems, and therefore as different languages. There are many examples of this kind, especially in parts of the world where what is commonly referred to as a single language (such as Chinese or Arabic) has many speakers over a wide area and is phonologically diverse.

In the third place, this chapter (as well as comments at the end of the previous chapter) should have made it clear that a phonological analysis of a language is often open to debate. In some instances, linguists may disagree about the number and nature of phonemes in a language. One example already mentioned (in 3.14) is that of the vowel heard in words like *cue* and *few*: if we do indeed take this to be a vowel, the diphthong /ju/, then we must count it as one of the vowel phonemes of English; if we take it to be a sequence of /j/ and /u/, then there is no vowel phoneme /ju/. Another example mentioned earlier in this chapter (4.3) is the question of whether German has /ç/ and /x/ as phonemes, rather than /x/ and /h/ as is usually assumed. There are similar alternative analyses for many languages, which will affect both the total number of phonemes in a language and the nature of the phonemes themselves.

In the fourth place, the very notion of the phoneme makes it difficult to make simple statements. The phoneme is better understood as a point in a system of oppositions, rather than as an item in an inventory. Suppose, for example, that we observe that most, if not all, of the world's languages, including languages as diverse as Aranda, English, Indonesian and Japanese, have a phoneme /t/. What does this actually mean? The apico-alveolar /t/ of Aranda is in contrast with other plosives such as a lamino-dental and a retroflex (or apico-postalveolar); but Aranda has no opposition of voicing, so /t/ is not in contrast with /d/ (and /t/ may sometimes be realized as [d]). On the other hand, English /t/ is opposed to /d/, and its voicelessness is therefore a relevant feature (although in many environments it may be the aspiration of /t/ that is more significant than its voicelessness); but, again unlike Aranda /t/, English /t/ is not in opposition to dental or postalveolar plosives, and, indeed, English /t/ has an apico-dental allophone in a word like *eighth*. Indonesian /t/, like English /t/, is opposed to /d/, but without significant aspiration. Japanese /t/ is different again: it has allophones not found in the other three languages, namely a palatal plosive or affricate before the vowel /i/ and the affricate [ts] before the vowel /u/. In what sense then can we say that these four languages have the same phoneme /t/? It would be more accurate to say that all of these languages exploit – to some extent – a plosive manner of articulation in conjunction with an apico-alveolar place of articulation. But the languages differ in the extent to which they maintain this particular articulatory setting against other options (such as dental articulation) or allow it to be adapted in context (as when English /t/ is realized as dental rather than alveolar, or Japanese /t/ is realized as affricate rather than plosive); and the languages differ also in the way they combine this articulatory setting with other features such as voicing.

With reservations like these in mind, and without trying to compare phonemic inventories that cannot really be compared, it is still possible to make some tentative generalizations.

A pulmonic airstream mechanism (with air coming from the lungs) is normal in the sense that all languages seem to make use of it and some languages use no other airstream. Sounds using other mechanisms – ejectives, implosives, clicks – are relatively uncommon among languages which have been well documented, although they are common in some areas. Ejectives are found among the indigenous languages of the Americas, Africa and Caucasia (in languages such as Armenian and Georgian) and rarely elsewhere. Implosives seem to be relatively common in some parts of Africa but are quite rare elsewhere. Clicks are common in the languages of southern Africa (including Xhosa and Zulu as well as the linguistically distinct Khoisan languages of the Kalahari region) but are virtually unknown outside that area.

All languages seem to make some kind of distinction between consonants and vowels, and most languages have at least a dozen consonant phonemes and at least three vowels. (The smallest phonemic systems in the UPSID database are those of Rotokas, a language spoken on the island of Bougainville, and Mura, one of the indigenous languages of Brazil: Rotokas has six consonants and five vowels, Mura eight consonants and three vowels.)

As mentioned in 4.2, quite a few languages have relatively simple vowel systems. Classical Arabic, Inupik (formerly Eskimo), and many Australian Aboriginal languages have just three vowels, although, as often, it is necessary to qualify this statement. Classical Arabic, for example, has only three vowel qualities, usually represented in Roman transcription as /i/, /a/ and /u/; but vowel length is also distinctive, so that if we include long and short vowels, there are actually six vowels; moreover, the vowel /a/ also combines with a following /w/ or /j/ to create what are in effect the diphthongs /au/ and /ai/; and, in a further elaboration of the basic three-vowel system, modern speakers of Arabic may pronounce these diphthongs as simple vowels (/ai/ as /e/, and /au/ as /o/).

Vowel systems of between five and eight phonemes are common, with five probably the most frequent. Among the better-known languages, Hebrew, Japanese, Modern Greek, Maori, Russian, Spanish and Swahili can all be considered to have a five-vowel system; Indonesian and Romanian have six; Bengali and Italian seven; Javanese and Turkish eight. But again, some of these languages have other distinctive features as well, such as vowel length and nasalization – each of the seven vowels of Bengali, for instance, may be distinctively oral or nasalized – so that it is unwise to dwell on a simple count of vowel phonemes. It is probably fair to say that if a language distinguishes more than about ten vowels, it is likely to be exploiting diphthongal combinations and additional features, such as length or nasalization, in conjunction with vowel quality. RP English, for example, can be said to have 21 vowel phonemes (as listed in Appendix 1.4). But nine of these are clearly diphthongs rather than simple vowels, and five are distinctively long (although not necessarily in contrast with a short vowel of precisely the same quality). Similarly, Thai can be described as having 21 vowel phonemes: but three of these are diphthongs and the other 18 are actually nine pairs of long and short counterparts.

Turning to consonantal articulation, plosives seem to be universal, and fricatives and nasals almost so. Rotokas and Mura, mentioned earlier as UPSID's smallest inventories, both demonstrate that nasal consonants are not universal. The consonants of Rotokas are three voiceless plosives, one voiced plosive, a fricative and a tap; Mura has six plosives (including a glottal stop) and two fricatives. Most languages have fricatives, except in Australia, where the majority of Aboriginal languages do not have any fricative phonemes.

Most of the world's languages seem to have one or more other consonants, using approximant articulation or some other manner such as trill or flap, but no one sound is universal. A trilled or flapped [r], for example, is common but by no means universal: the /r/ phoneme of English (in most of its realizations in most regional varieties) is not a trill or flap; while languages as diverse as Chinese, Inupik and Luganda have an /l/ phoneme but no consonantal r-sound. Many languages have at least one lateral consonant, but Japanese and Tahitian are examples of languages which do not use contrastive lateral articulation, while Korean has [l] and [r] as allophones of a single phoneme. Questions about the occurrence of approximants such as [w] and [j] are particularly difficult to answer because of the scope for alternative analyses (3.11–3.14 above). Taking [w] as an example, we can say that it does occur in English (as in *west* and *woe*) but not in German (orthographic *w* represents [v], not [w] in German); but a language like Spanish has vowel sequences which may or may not be interpreted as containing [w], as in *huevo* 'egg' and *continuo* 'continuous' which may be phonemically represented as /wevo/ and /kontinwo/ (Comrie 1987, pp. 245–6). The status of /w/ is likewise arguable in Italian and Portuguese.

Even the smallest phonemic systems make some use of place of articulation contrasts, and a large number of the world's languages seem to distinguish bilabial and velar from some kind of dental or alveolar place of articulation: thus it is quite common for a language to distinguish /p/ from /t/ from /k/ (where /t/ may be apico-alveolar or apico-dental depending on the language and the phonetic context).

A good number of languages have additional places of articulation for plosives. Probably the most common of these are those usually called retroflex (including apico-postalveolar or sublamino-postalveolar) and palatal. Retroflex plosives are found in many Australian Aboriginal languages and in most of the languages of South Asia (such as Bengali, Pashto, Punjabi, Tamil, Hindi and Urdu). In some languages, including Dutch, Norwegian and some varieties of American English, some speakers may use postalveolar or retroflex plosives after a preceding r-sound. Some Dutch speakers, for example, pronounce the word *hart* 'heart' with a final apico-postalveolar plosive and with little or no articulatory gesture to correspond to the *r* of the spelling: for such speakers, the postalveolar place of articulation may serve as the phonetic realization of alveolar following an (elided) r-sound.

Palatal plosives are very widespread, being virtually universal among Australian Aboriginal languages and occurring elsewhere in languages as diverse as Basque, Hungarian, Indonesian, Thai and Vietnamese. This is again a point for special caution, however, as many languages do not differentiate between palatal plosives and affricates, and there is a close relationship between palatal articulation and affrication. (Notice in English that some occurrences of the affricate /tʃ/ have arisen from assimilation of /t/ to a following lamino-palatal /j/, as in *nature* and *picture*.) Some descriptions of Indonesian or Malay, for example, refer to the initial consonant of words such as *cantik* 'pretty' and *cepat* 'quick' as a voiceless palatal plosive while others identify it as an affricate.

The exploitation of places of articulation is often not uniform across different manners of articulation. English illustrates the point by having, for example, bilabial plosives /p/ and /b/ (but no labiodental plosives) and labiodental fricatives /f/ and /v/ (but no bilabial fricatives). Indeed, in the UPSID database there is no record of any language with labiodental plosives. On the other hand, labiodental fricatives are very common, much more so than bilabial fricatives. A similar asymmetry is observable with palatal articulation. There are languages, such as Italian and Spanish, which have no palatal plosive phoneme but do have a palatal nasal and a palatal lateral. Nevertheless, some languages are more symmetrical than others (4.5 above). It is a striking feature of Australian Aboriginal languages that they tend to have exactly the same places of articulation for plosives and nasals: languages that have five places of articulation for plosives usually have five corresponding nasal consonants, for example.

Voicing is a widespread feature of articulation, although it must be remembered that what appears in a phonemic inventory as /t/ versus /d/ may be realized in various ways: /t/ may be aspirated in some or all environments, /d/ may be only partially voiced, and so on. While a high proportion of languages make some kind of differentiation of this kind, there is a substantial minority of languages in which voicing is not a distinctive feature at all. In the Australian language Warlpiri, for example, there is a single series of plosives (at five points of articulation) which are usually voiceless in word-initial position but may be (partially) voiced in other environments. All other consonants – nasals, laterals, approximants and flaps – are characteristically voiced. Most other Australian Aboriginal languages, at least in the southern half of the country, are similar to Warlpiri in this regard. Other languages which do not exploit voicing can be found among the indigenous languages of the Americas, including Inupik.

There are, of course, languages which distinguish more than two kinds of plosive. Ancient Greek and Thai and some other south-east Asian languages have voiceless aspirated plosives as well as voiceless and voiced. Korean also has a three-way distinction among plosives, but of a somewhat different nature, while many south

Asian languages, such as Hindi and Urdu, exploit breathy voicing to create a fourth series of plosives (sometimes referred to as voiced aspirates) alongside voiceless aspirated, voiceless and voiced plosives. (See table 4.5.1. for more details.)

Again, some languages are less consistent or symmetrical than others, and it is not uncommon for a language to have a 'gap' in the way it exploits voicing. Arabic has no /p/ in contrast with /b/, although it does distinguish /t/ from /d/. Dutch has no /g/, although it does distinguish between /p/ and /b/ and between /t/ and /d/. (The *g* of Dutch words such as *gast* 'guest' and *goed* 'good' represents a fricative, and the voiced plosive [g] occurs only as a conditioned variant of /k/, as in, say, [zagduk] for /zakduk/, *zakdoek* 'handkerchief'.)

Turning to the question of an average number of phonemes, it seems likely that a majority of the world's languages have somewhere between 20 and 40 phonemes. But, as we have said before, the number of phonemes in a language can be altered quite radically by analytical decisions. Suppose, for example, a language has 12 obstruent phonemes, each of which may be distinctively labialized. (Thus we might have /p^w/ in contrast with /p/, /t^w/ alongside /t/, and so on, making a total of 24 obstruent phonemes.) But suppose that this language also has the phoneme /w/ and that we decide to analyse the labialized consonants as realizations of obstruent followed by /w/. The number of obstruents is now brought back from 24 to 12. The analysis affects the statistics.

We have already mentioned languages with as few as 11 phonemes. English has 40 or so, the exact number depending on the regional variety being described and on the phonemic analysis itself. Languages can have far more phonemes than this, however, and the largest inventory in the UPSID database has 141 phonemes (Maddieson 1984, p. 7). This is a Khoisan language from southern Africa which has a relatively large number of obstruents and click sounds: among other distinctions, it differentiates voiceless aspirated plosives from voiceless and voiced; it also has distinctively ejective stops; it distinguishes both ejective and aspirated affricates from 'ordinary' voiceless affricates; and achieves a large array of click sounds by complex articulations such as simultaneous nasalization of clicks and affricated release of clicks.

The examples given above indicate that there are some regional tendencies. Clicks are virtually limited to southern Africa (but they do occur elsewhere, in the secret language of at least one Australian Aboriginal people, and as paralinguistic signs, as in the English use of the click represented as 'tsk tsk' or 'tut tut'). Languages using several implosive consonants seem to be confined to Africa, while languages without any fricative phonemes seem to be found only in Australia. Regional generalizations of this kind are nevertheless rather few in number and of doubtful significance. There are many other cases where similar sounds or patterns of contrast can be found across a range of diverse languages.

In general it is difficult to establish a significant relationship between a language's genetic affiliation and its phonological characteristics. The mere fact that a language's phonological system can change quite substantially over time is enough to show that families of historically related languages do not necessarily share phonological characteristics. To take the example of English, Old English as spoken around a thousand years ago differed phonologically from modern English in a number of ways: it had, for instance, a voiceless velar fricative and front rounded vowels of the kind still heard in German but no longer in modern English; it had no distinction between voiceless and voiced fricatives (the voiceless phonemes having voiced allophones in some environments); and it had distinctive length for both consonants and vowels (with, for instance, a difference in pronunciation between the long [n] of *sunne* 'sun' and the short [n] of *sunu* 'son'). Thus the phonemic system of Old English looks rather different from that of modern English. To take another example, Ancient Greek had three series of plosives, voiceless aspirated, voiceless and voiced (see table 4.5.1 above), and it had only sibilant fricatives and affricates; changes in pronunciation have been such that modern Greek now has only voiceless and voiced plosives, but has a much richer series of fricatives than Ancient Greek, including voiceless and voiced labiodental, dental, palatal and velar fricatives, as well as sibilant /s/ and /z/. Such changes in pronunciation mean that one cannot count on historically related languages to retain phonological similarities.

In summary, generalizations about phonemic inventories should never be taken as bare facts. Hidden behind them lie decisions about which languages have been included and which dialect(s) of the languages have been described, and judgments within the process of making a phonemic analysis and representing the phonological system as a set of phonemes. It is possible to say, tentatively, that some kinds of articulation seem more common than others: vowels and plosives, produced with a pulmonic airstream, seem fundamental, with fricative and nasal consonants also very widespread; many languages also seem to have at least one lateral approximant and some kind of r-sound. Among places of articulation, differentiation of bilabial, dental or alveolar, and velar is very common for plosives, with palatal articulation also widespread. Among fricatives, labiodental /f/ and a dental or alveolar grooved sibilant /s/ are probably the most common. Far less common – at least among the best studied languages – are sounds produced other than with air from the lungs, notably ejectives, implosives and clicks, and places of articulation such as uvular and pharyngeal. Voicing (or aspiration) is probably relevant in a majority of languages, but by no means a universally distinctive feature.

The UPSID database, mentioned earlier as a careful sampling of the world's phonemic systems, is explained in Maddieson 1984. Maddieson includes detailed discussion of what inferences can be drawn from the 317 phonemic systems in the database.

Exercises

1 Check that you understand the following terms and can explain any debate or controversy that surrounds them:

   coarticulation
   elision

allophone
minimal pair
complementary distribution
phonological conditioning and conditioning factors
phonemic overlap
biuniqueness
neutralization
archiphoneme
allomorph
morphophonemics

2   Consider a few people whom you judge to have an unusual or distinctive voice quality, such as film stars or television or radio personalities. Can you mimic the voice quality? What are the articulatory mechanics that generate the voice quality?

3   Note examples of context-sensitive variation in your own English. Examples may include

– the effects of /l/ and /r/ on a preceding vowel
  (compare the first vowel of *Betty*, *belly* and *berry* and other such examples)
– variations in the consonant /r/ according to its position
  (try the /r/ in *red*, *tread*, *dread*, *thread*)

4   List the vowel phonemes of your own variety of English. You may find it helpful to refer to Appendix 1.4 and you should make careful use of minimal pairs to justify your listing. Give as much detail as you can, including if possible the inherent length of each vowel and conditions under which vowels are noticeably modified (for example before a lateral consonant, before voiced obstruents, and so on).

5   Some Japanese names are listed below in the standard romanized spelling, in which *f* represents [ɸ], *sh* [ʃ] and *ch* the affricate [tʃ]. Note that some consonants occur only before certain vowels and are in complementary distribution with other consonants. List all the consonants and vowels which are illustrated in the sample and show the complementary variants as allophones where appropriate.

Fuse	Himi	Misumi	Soto
Futatsume	Hitachi	Motomachi	Susa
Futami	Hofu	Mutsu	Tamana
Hachinohe	Matsushima	Numata	Tate
Hamamatsu	Mine	Setana	Tsunami
Hashimoto	Minamata	Shinichi	

6   English *adds* and *adze* are pronounced identically. Explain this in terms of phonological neutralization.

Various speakers may not distinguish *Welsh* from *Welch*; or *merry* from *marry*; or *Kelly* from *Calley*; or *ferry* from *fairy*. Describe the phonological neutralizations suggested by these examples (and any others you may be aware of).

7   The speech of very young children can be analysed phonemically, generally revealing a much simpler phonemic system than adult speech. For example, a child who is growing up in an English-speaking community and who has not yet acquired the alveolar–velar distinction will have only two voiceless plosives, /p/ and /t/, and will pronounce *keep* as /tip/, *car* as /ta/ or /tar/, *key* as /ti/, and so on. From the child's perspective, of course, a word such as /ti/ has two meanings: 'tea' and 'key'. If you have opportunities to listen to a young child, try to record a sample of utterances and to note some of the phonemic distinctions which the child does appear to be making, and some of those which have not yet been acquired.

5   The Generative Approach to Phonology

Introduction

This chapter deals with an approach to phonology which represents an influential alternative to the phonemic view of the previous chapter. After a brief account of the origins of generative phonology (5.1) and of Chomsky and Halle's major work *The sound pattern of English* (5.2), the heart of the chapter is devoted to explaining and illustrating the basic notation and principles of generative phonology:

- rule notation (5.3)
- formalism and evaluation (5.4)
- abbreviatory devices (5.5)
- rule order (5.6).

The final part of the chapter treats critical issues that have arisen in the elaboration of generative phonology:

- functional considerations (5.7)
- the notions of naturalness and markedness (5.8)
- abstractness in phonological description (5.9).

5.1   The origins of generative phonology

The 1960s saw increasing discontent with orthodox phonemics in North America. A series of publications by Halle (1959, 1962, 1964), a vigorous attack by Chomsky on phonemics and structuralist linguistics in general (1964), a book by Postal (1968), and a large-scale treatment of English phonology jointly authored by Chomsky and

Halle (1968) marked the emergence of generative phonology as a new theory and framework of description.

Halle had been involved in research and publication on phonological features or components (chapter 10 below) and went on to devote attention to the function of features within phonological systems. In assessing phonological description – and particularly in formulating phonological rules – Halle argued that plausible general rules were better expressed in terms of features. A phonological process whereby all plosives are voiced between vowels is a plausible rule: it is known to operate in some languages and it seems to reflect a probable pattern of voicing assimilation. It is a more likely rule than one which says, for example, that [p] is voiced only between [a] and [u], [t] is voiced only between [u] and [i], and [k] is voiced only between [e] and [o].

Most phoneticians and phonologists readily agree that there are 'normal' tendencies in speech and that certain processes seem more common or more plausible than others – although their universality should not be exaggerated (section 4.1 above). Halle's point, however, concerns description and explanation: when expressed in segments, plausible rules do not necessarily appear simpler. The two rules suggested above might appear as

(5.1.1) $\begin{matrix} [p] \rightarrow [b] \\ [t] \rightarrow [d] \\ [k] \rightarrow [g] \end{matrix} \Bigg\}$ between $\begin{Bmatrix} [i] \\ [e] \\ [a] \\ [o] \\ [u] \end{Bmatrix}$ and $\begin{Bmatrix} [i] \\ [e] \\ [a] \\ [o] \\ [u] \end{Bmatrix}$

(5.1.2)   [p] → [b]   between   [a]   and   [u]
        [t] → [d]   between   [u]   and   [i]
        [k] → [g]   between   [e]   and   [o].

Of course the first rule can be expressed as a general statement, such as

> any voiceless plosive is voiced between any two vowels.

In this wording, it is the use of features (voiceless, plosive, and so on) that captures the generality of the rule. If we adopt the same style with (5.1.2), our use of features now makes the rule much more cumbersome than (5.1.1):

> a voiceless bilabial plosive is voiced between a low vowel and a high back vowel; a voiceless alveolar plosive is voiced between a high back vowel and a high front vowel; and a voiceless velar plosive is voiced between a mid front vowel and a mid back vowel.

This, according to Halle, is precisely what we want – the more plausible general rule looks simpler, the less plausible looks more complex. In other words, phonological description should employ feature-based rules as a proper means of reflecting the complexity of the description. This does not mean, of course, that rules such as (5.1.2) are said to be impossible, only that they are far less likely than rules such as (5.1.1) and that it is therefore proper to signal their complexity.

The use of rules and features as the elements of phonological description meant that the concept of the phoneme was under threat. Indeed, Halle claimed that the phoneme was often a hindrance to description. In his treatment of Russian phonology (1959), he cited an example which has been quoted in subsequent literature repeatedly (*ad nauseam*, according to Sommerstein 1977, p. 116). In brief, Halle points out that there is a general rule in Russian that an obstruent (plosive or fricative) is voiced when preceding a voiced obstruent. Thus a word-final voiceless plosive will be voiced if the following word begins with a voiced plosive: [t] + [b] is pronounced as [d] + [b], [p] + [g] as [b] + [g], and so on. Now, in orthodox phonemic terms Russian has distinct voiced and voiceless plosive phonemes. We find, for instance, /bil/ ('was') versus /pil/ ('blaze', glow'), /djenj/ ('day') versus /tjenj/ ('shade, shadow') as minimal pairs. But Russian does not have voiced and voiceless affricates as separate phonemes: there is no phonemic contrast between [tʃ] and [dʒ] or between [ts] and [dz], and the voiced affricates are simply allophones of their voiceless counterparts. Hence, in a phonemic account, when a word-final /t/ is voiced preceding a voiced obstruent, we are dealing with the substitution of /d/ for /t/, of one phoneme for another. On the other hand, when a word-final /ts/ affricate is voiced in the same context, /ts/ is realized as its voiced allophone [dz]. But, Halle argues, the phenomenon of voicing assimilation in Russian is surely a single process, and not one of phonemic substitution in some cases and allophonic conditioning in others. We should be suspicious of a framework of description which leads us to an awkward account of such an apparently straightforward phenomenon. We ought to be able to say that Russian simply has a phonological rule that obstruents are voiced when preceding voiced obstruents.

Postal (1968, pp. 36–37) gives another example designed to undermine the centrality of the phoneme. In Mohawk, it can happen that /t/ or /k/ precedes /j/ across a morpheme boundary, but both sequences are realized as [dʒ]. Postal argues that it should be legitimate to say that [dʒ] is derived, by rule, from two different sources, namely /tj/ and /kj/. This of course makes [dʒ] phonologically ambiguous, in violation of the biuniqueness principle (section 4.9 above). And it is not clear how a phonemic account can satisfactorily avoid this violation. It would be possible to say that [dʒ] unambiguously represents /tj/ and that /kj/ becomes /tj/ by morphophonemic rule, but Postal points to the arbitrariness of this decision. Why doesn't [dʒ] realize /kj/, with /tj/ becoming /kj/ by morphophonemic rule? Postal's solution, in the spirit of generative phonology, is to dispense with the phonemic level and morphophonemic rules altogether. If we regard /tj/ and /kj/ as rather deeper or more abstract than a phonemic transcription, then we can state relatively neat and general phonological rules which derive the phonetic forms from these underlying representations.

Arguments of this kind led generative phonologists to abandon the concepts of phoneme and allophone, and to talk in terms of a relatively abstract or morphophonemic underlying level of phonological representation from which the phonetic output could be derived by application of a set of phonological rules. The elaboration of this new conception of phonology was part of the development of the transformational–generative theory of language in general, pioneered by Noam Chomsky. Although he is sometimes thought of as a grammarian with a particular interest in syntax, Chomsky himself contributed to the development of generative phonology. His *Current issues in linguistic theory* (1964) is generally critical of modern linguistics: the nineteenth century narrowed 'the scope of linguistics to the study of inventory of elements' (p. 22), and de Saussure and 'structural linguistics' were preoccupied with 'systems of elements rather than the systems of rules which were the focus of attention in traditional grammar . . .' (p. 23). Against this background he dismisses much of modern phonology as 'taxonomic phonemics', having referred to 'a curious and rather extreme contemporary view to the effect that true linguistic science must *necessarily* be a kind of pre-Darwinian taxonomy concerned solely with the collection and classification of countless specimens' (1964, p. 25). He criticizes in detail (pp. 75–95) the 'taxonomic' phonologists' concern with segmentation, contrast, distribution and biuniqueness (chapter 4 above) and puts forward the view that phonological description is not based on 'analytic procedures of segmentation and classification' (p. 95) but is rather a matter of constructing the set of rules that constitute the phonological component of a grammar.

5.2   The sound pattern of English

Chomsky and Halle's major contribution to phonology, *The sound pattern of English* (1968), is on the one hand an alternative to 'taxonomic' phonemics, and on the other an ambitious attempt to build a description of English phonology on a transformational–generative theory of language. The book (henceforth, as widely, referred to as SPE) begins with a theoretical foundation, arguing that a grammar is a system of rules that relate sound and meaning (p. 3). There are several components of such a grammar, including a phonological component which relates grammatical structures (i.e. grammatically organized strings of morphemes) to their phonetic representations. The heart of SPE (chapters 3 to 5) deals with how such a component of English grammar can be formally expressed.

Chomsky and Halle call attention to numerous alternations in English – what their predecessors would have called morphophonemic rules (section 4.10 above). They classify as 'tense' the vowels in the final syllables of words such as

insane, prostate, explain
obscene, esthete, convene
divine, parasite, divide
verbose, telescope, compose
profound, pronounce, denounce.

Each of the five tense vowels has a corresponding 'lax' vowel, as in

> insanity, prostatic, explanatory
> obscenity, esthetic, convention
> divinity, parasitic, division
> verbosity, telescopic, compositor
> profundity, pronunciation, denunciation.

Noting the patterns of such alternations, Chomsky and Halle propose various rules which 'tense' and 'lax' vowels in appropriate environments. This means that a word like *convene* can be assigned an underlying form containing a vowel which is lax or tense according to its environment – lax, for instance, before two consonants (as in *convention*) and tense when no suffix is present (as in *convene*). The rules are intended to encompass all the relevant conditioning environments (before CC, before *-ic*, etc.) and include changes to tense vowels such that they are realized as the appropriate long vowel or diphthong. The tense counterpart of [æ] must surface as the diphthong [eɪ] (as in *sane*); the tense counterpart of [ɛ] as the long vowel [iː] (as in *convene*), and so on. The 43 rules finally presented (summarized in SPE chapter 5) are not only complex but include some formal intricacies to do with the abbreviation and ordering of rules (sections 5.4 to 5.6 below). A separate chapter (SPE chapter 8) summarizes and explains the formal apparatus.

Students of the history of the English language will note that the rules of tensing and laxing correspond fairly closely to changes that have taken place in the pronunciation of English. In the fifteenth century, English vowels were subject to a substantial shift known as the Great Vowel Shift. Before this change, for example, the current diphthong [aɪ] in words such as *time*, *wide* and *dine* was almost certainly a long [iː], while the vowel now pronounced [iː] (as in *green* and *meet*) was a long [eː]. Since short (or lax) vowels were not affected in the same way, alternations of the kind mentioned above are largely a consequence of the Great Vowel Shift. It is therefore no coincidence – given the highly conservative conventions of English orthography – that Chomsky and Halle's pairs of tense and lax vowels appear in English spelling as 'long' and 'short' values of the five vowel letters. (In terms of articulation and perception, they are by no means long and short counterparts; see section 10.7 below for consideration of this point in the context of feature systems.)

While Chomsky and Halle are careful not to base their analysis on historical forms – the phonological rules of today's English cannot be justified by appeal to past sound changes – they do include in SPE a chapter on the historical development of the English vowel system (chapter 6) and they do note that 'underlying lexical forms in English contain vowels in pre-Vowel-Shift representation' (p. 332). Elsewhere in SPE, they argue that conventional English spelling is in fact 'a near optimal system for the lexical representation of English words' (p. 49). Their justification for this view – one which is surprising both to those who espouse a phonemic view of phonology and to those who know the struggle of mastering English spelling – is that 'the fundamental principle of orthography is that phonetic variation is not indicated where it is predictable by general rule' (p. 49). Thus wherever speakers know a rule, say that an underlying tense vowel is laxed before the suffix –*ic*, they ought to prefer a spelling convention that presupposes operation of that rule.

The implication that SPE envisages rules applying to segments such as [i] or [o] is actually misleading. Although Chomsky and Halle, and most generative phonologists following them, frequently quote rules containing segmental symbols, they insist that any such symbols are merely convenient shorthand for arrays of features. Thus the symbol [i] is really shorthand for something like

$$
\begin{bmatrix}
+ \text{ syllabic} \\
- \text{ consonantal} \\
+ \text{ voiced} \\
+ \text{ high} \\
.. (\text{etc.}) ..
\end{bmatrix}
$$

where the segment is specified as a set of phonetic feature values. A string of segments in comparable notation is sometimes referred to as a matrix, since each segment can be viewed as a set of values entered against the features. The word *deep* [di:p] might be displayed as

$$
\begin{bmatrix}
\text{d} & \text{i:} & \text{p} \\
- \text{ syllabic} & + \text{ syllabic} & - \text{ syllabic} \\
+ \text{ consonantal} & - \text{ consonantal} & + \text{ consonantal} \\
+ \text{ voiced} & + \text{ voiced} & - \text{ voiced} \\
- \text{ high} & + \text{ high} & - \text{ high} \\
.. (\text{etc}) .. & .. (\text{etc}) .. & .. (\text{etc}) ..
\end{bmatrix}
$$

Chapter 7 of SPE gives details of the features, which Chomsky and Halle consider to be the elements of a 'universal phonetic framework' (chapter 10 below). Rules are in principle expressed in terms of these features (as argued by Halle), so that a rule derives one feature specification from another. According to SPE, features are binary at the underlying level (i.e. they take the value + or −) but may have more than two values at the phonetic (surface output) level. (The final chapter of SPE – chapter 9 – does, however, recast feature specifications in a way that has caused major discussion; see section 5.8 below.)

5.3   Basic rule notation in generative phonology

Typically, a phonological rule states that a certain class of segments undergoes a change in some particular environment. For example, a rule may state that obstruents are voiced following any voiced segment. Using the features of SPE (which are listed in Appendix 2.2 and further discussed in chapter 10 below), we can write this rule as

(5.3.1) [− sonorant] → [+ voiced] / [+ voiced] __.

The slash comes before the environment specification and the bar on the line indicates the position of the affected segment. A precise but cumbersome reading of the rule is: 'Any segment which is, among other things, nonsonorant is also voiced when standing after any segment which is, among other things, voiced'.

For comparison, here are two rules which state that obstruents are voiced under slightly different conditions:

(5.3.2) [− sonorant] → [+ voiced] / [+ voiced] __ [+ voiced];
(5.3.3) [− sonorant] → [+ voiced] / __ [+ voiced].

Rules refer to classes of segments. Some classes can obviously be specified by a single feature value, such as

sonorants   [+ sonorant]
laterals   [+ lateral]
voiceless segments [− voiced].

Other classes may require several feature values (again using Chomsky and Halle's features):

$$\left[\begin{array}{l} + \text{syllabic} \\ - \text{consonantal} \end{array} \right] = \text{vowels}$$

$$\left[\begin{array}{l} + \text{syllabic} \\ - \text{consonantal} \\ + \text{high} \end{array} \right] = \text{high vowels}$$

$$\left[\begin{array}{l} + \text{syllabic} \\ - \text{consonantal} \\ + \text{back} \\ + \text{round} \end{array} \right] = \text{back rounded vowels.}$$

Any feature not mentioned immediately to the right of the arrow is assumed to be left intact. Thus by rule (5.3.1), which voices obstruents, a voiceless bilabial plosive becomes a voiced bilabial plosive, a voiceless velar fricative becomes a voiced velar fricative, and so on. The exception to this principle is that there are certain incompatibilities in the feature system. For instance, it is universally impossible for a vowel to be both [+ high] and [+ low], and a rule which makes a vowel [+ high] ought therefore to make it [− low] at the same time, without any need to state this in the rule itself (see section 5.8 below).

It is a principle of generative phonology that phonological rules may refer to grammatical information, specifically that a rule may apply in a particular grammatical domain. The notation includes symbols indicating boundaries, commonly # for the lowest level boundary, # # for the one ranking above it, and so on. By this convention, English morphemes might be separated by #, words by ## and phrases by # # #, e.g.

# #dog# #	dog
# #laugh#ing# #	laughing
# # #the# #laugh#ing# #dog# # #	the laughing dog

Rule (5.3.4) states that consonants are voiceless at the end of a morpheme, (5.3.5) that vowels are high at the end of a word:

(5.3.4) [+ consonantal] $\rightarrow$ [− voiced] / __ #

(5.3.5) $\begin{bmatrix} + \text{syllabic} \\ - \text{consonantal} \end{bmatrix}$ $\rightarrow$ [+high] /__ # #.

This notation has the virtue of making it clear that some boundaries are implied by others: a rule that applies in the context −# will also apply in the context −# # or −# # #. An alternative convention uses + for a morpheme boundary, in which case # indicates a word boundary.

The environment of a rule may include several segments, including boundary symbols, e.g.

(5.3.6) $\begin{bmatrix} + \text{syllabic} \\ - \text{consonantal} \end{bmatrix}$ $\rightarrow$ [+nasal]/__ [+nasal] # #

(a vowel is nasalized before a word-final nasal segment);

(5.3.7) [− sonorant] $\rightarrow$[+ voiced] / # # $\begin{bmatrix} + \text{cons} \\ + \text{nasa l} \end{bmatrix}$ __ $\begin{bmatrix} + \text{syll} \\ - \text{cons} \end{bmatrix}$

(an obstruent is voiced if between a word-initial nasal consonant and a vowel).

Other lexical and syntactic information can also be included in the environment, e.g.

(5.3.8) [− sonorant] $\rightarrow$ [+ voiced] / __ # #][verb]

Rule (5.3.8) states that an obstruent is voiced when word-final in a verb; in case this seems improbable, note that some English verbs differ from a cognate noun or adjective in just this way, e.g. *wreath, wreathe, safe, save.*

Classical generative phonology has no symbol for a syllable boundary, and relevant contexts must be specified in other terms – for example, 'in an open syllable' may be equivalent to 'before a single consonant followed by a vowel'. More recently, the need to indicate syllable boundaries has been recognized, and the symbol $ is often used.

Many generative descriptions contain rules which are not worked out in detail. Segmental symbols, including C and V for any consonant or vowel, are often written into rules, e.g.

(5.3.9)   C → [+ voiced] / V __ V
(a consonant is voiced between two vowels);
(5.3.10) i → e / __ r C
(the vowel [i] is lowered to [e] before a sequence of [r] plus consonant).

Such rules are informal and it must be assumed that symbols such as C, V, r and so on, would be fully worked out in feature notation in a formal description.

The symbol Ø has a semi-formal status as the representation of zero. It appears frequently in the literature but can be regarded as an abbreviation for a feature specification containing [− segment]. The zero symbol appears in rules of deletion and epenthesis or insertion, e.g.

(5.3.11) V → Ø/ / V __ # #
(a vowel is deleted if word-final after a vowel);
(5.3.12) Ø → t / n __ s
(the consonant [t] is inserted between [n] and [s]).

The zero symbol never appears in the description of the environment. Irrelevant components of the environment are simply omitted, so that C__ means 'after a consonant and before anything whatsoever'. But it is sometimes necessary to indicate that something is present, even though its composition is irrelevant. For this purpose dots may be used, or more commonly capital X, Y, Z, W, etc.

(5.3.13a)   V → Ø / __ C]^{root} . . .]^{verb};

(5.3.13b)   V → Ø / __ C^{root}X]^{verb}.

(5.3.13) gives two versions of a rule stating that a vowel is deleted if it precedes the root-final consonant of a verb. The dots or X specify that the root will be followed by something, perhaps a suffix or an auxiliary element, which falls within the verb but whose composition is of no relevance to the operation of the rule. Actually, notational practice varies: some writers will include boundary symbols whenever they refer to categories such as verb or root, and some seem to prefer to include both opening and closing brackets. The following rules are taken, with some simplifications, from different sources to illustrate notational variety:

(5.3.14)   V → Ø/ / V + C __ ##]^{verb}
(within a verb, a suffix of the shape CV loses its vowel if it follows a vowel and stands word-final)

(5.3.15) $\quad \emptyset \rightarrow \text{ə} / \left[\#\ X\ C \ \underline{\quad} \ \begin{bmatrix} + \text{ consonantal} \\ + \text{ sonorant} \end{bmatrix} \# \right]$

(a schwa vowel is inserted between two consonants at the end of a word, where the second consonant is a sonorant, e.g. [lm] becomes [ləm], [gl] becomes [gəl]; the rule is formulated so as not to apply across a word boundary, i.e. the two consonants must be within the same word);

(5.3.16) $\quad V \rightarrow \emptyset / \left[[X \ \underline{\quad} \ ]^{\text{ stem}} \ V\ Y \quad ^{\text{verb}} \right]$

(within a verb, a stem-final vowel is elided if before another vowel);

(5.3.17) $\quad \begin{bmatrix} V \\ -\text{high} \end{bmatrix} \rightarrow [+\text{low}] / \underline{\quad} \begin{bmatrix} V \\ +\text{low} \end{bmatrix}^{\text{stem}} V\ldots \Big]^{\text{verb}}$

(within a verb, a nonhigh vowel is low if it precedes a low vowel which is both stem-final and before another vowel);

(5.3.18) $\quad \begin{bmatrix} + \text{ consonantal} \\ - \text{ coronal} \\ + \text{ high} \end{bmatrix} \rightarrow \emptyset / \underline{\quad} + [\text{PLURAL}]$

(a velar consonant is elided before the plural suffix)

All rules dealt with so far are of the format A → B / C __ D, but rules of coalescence and metathesis require special comment. Consider processes such as the coalescence of a vowel and nasal consonant into a nasalized vowel (e.g. [an] → [ã]) or the metathesis of a fricative and plosive (e.g. [sp] → [ps]). Rules expressing such processes apparently do not fit the format. But A → B / C __ D is actually another way of writing CAD→CBD, and this second format is in fact the more general one, allowing us to include more possibilities. In other words, the basic format of a generative rule is one which rewrites one string of symbols as another. For rules of coalescence and metathesis we can retain this format (e.g. ABCD → ACBD); but other rules can be abbreviated into the format we have been using so far, on the understanding that this is a special case of rewriting. Thus a rule of vowel nasalization, with loss of the following nasal consonant, can be written as

(5.3.19) $\quad \begin{matrix} \begin{bmatrix} + \text{ syllabic} \\ - \text{ consonantal} \end{bmatrix} & \begin{bmatrix} + \text{ consonantal} \\ + \text{ nasal} \end{bmatrix} & \rightarrow [+\text{ nasal}]\ \emptyset. \\ 1 & 2 & \quad\quad 1 \quad\ 2 \end{matrix}$

Metathesis of a fricative and plosive can be written as (5.3.20a) or more concisely as (5.3.20b):

(5.3.20a) $\quad \begin{matrix} \begin{bmatrix} - \text{ sonorant} \\ + \text{ cont} \end{bmatrix} & \begin{bmatrix} - \text{ sonorant} \\ - \text{ cont} \end{bmatrix} & \rightarrow & \begin{bmatrix} - \text{ sonorant} \\ - \text{ cont} \end{bmatrix} & \begin{bmatrix} - \text{ sonorant} \\ + \text{ cont} \end{bmatrix} \\ 1 & 2 & & 2 & 1 \end{matrix}$

(5.3.20b) $\begin{bmatrix} - \text{ sonorant} \\ + \text{ cont} \end{bmatrix}$ $\begin{bmatrix} - \text{ sonorant} \\ - \text{ cont} \end{bmatrix}$ $\rightarrow$ 2 1
                        1   2

The following rule of metathesis reverses the order of a glottal stop and consonant when between vowels (e.g. [aʔna] → [anʔa]):

(5.3.21) $\begin{bmatrix} + \text{ syll} \\ - \text{ cons} \end{bmatrix}$ $\begin{bmatrix} - \text{ cons} \\ - \text{ cont} \\ - \text{ distrib} \end{bmatrix}$ $\begin{bmatrix} - \text{ syll} \\ + \text{ cons} \end{bmatrix}$ $\begin{bmatrix} + \text{ syll} \\ - \text{ cons} \end{bmatrix}$ $\rightarrow$ 1 3 2 4.
         1   2   3   4

The following rule says that if a sequence of nasal consonant and plosive occurs between two vowels, then the first vowel is nasalized, the nasal consonant elided and the plosive voiced, e.g. [ampa] → [āba]:

(5.3.22a)

$\begin{bmatrix} + \text{ syll} \\ - \text{ cons} \end{bmatrix}$ $\begin{bmatrix} + \text{ cons} \\ + \text{ nas} \end{bmatrix}$ $\begin{bmatrix} - \text{ son} \\ - \text{ cont} \end{bmatrix}$ $\begin{bmatrix} + \text{ syll} \\ - \text{ cons} \end{bmatrix}$ $\rightarrow$ $\begin{bmatrix} + \text{ syll} \\ - \text{ cons} \\ + \text{ nas} \end{bmatrix}$ $\emptyset$ $\begin{bmatrix} - \text{ son} \\ - \text{ cont} \\ + \text{ voic} \end{bmatrix}$ $\begin{bmatrix} + \text{ syll} \\ - \text{ cons} \end{bmatrix}$

or

(5.3.22b)

$\begin{bmatrix} + \text{ syll} \\ - \text{ cons} \end{bmatrix}$ $\begin{bmatrix} + \text{ cons} \\ + \text{ nas} \end{bmatrix}$ $\begin{bmatrix} - \text{ son} \\ - \text{ cont} \end{bmatrix}$ $\begin{bmatrix} + \text{ syll} \\ - \text{ cons} \end{bmatrix}$ $\rightarrow$ [+ nas] $\emptyset$ [+ voic] 4.
    1   2   3   4   1   2   3

Of particular interest within generative phonology is the interplay of the notational apparatus and the system of rules taken as an integrated whole. For the sake of simple illustration, the examples given above have been taken in isolation, but in fact any rule will have to be formulated appropriately for a specific language. In languages in which there are no syllabic consonants, for example, the label [+ syllabic] will be adequate to refer to vowels; in other languages the specification may have to include [− consonantal] as well as [+ syllabic]. Moreover, alternative rules may be possible. For example, a single rule that coalesces vowel plus nasal consonant into a nasalized vowel may be better expressed in two rules: instead of

(5.3.23)   V N → Ṽ   e.g. [an] → [ã]

we might have

(5.3.24)   V → Ṽ / __ N   e.g. [an] → [ãn]
(5.3.25)   N → Ø / Ṽ __   e.g. [ãn] → [ã]

But in postulating rules (5.3.24) and (5.3.25) we are assuming of course that forms will undergo both rules – that (5.3.24) will 'feed' (5.3.25). This raises the question of how rules may interact with each other and of how we might choose between a series of relatively simple interacting rules and a set of more complex but independent rules. We turn to the formalism and its part in evaluating descriptions before going further into questions of rule interaction and rule order later in the chapter.

5.4   Formalism and evaluation

It is possible to distinguish in a very general way between formal and informal approaches to description and explanation of a variety of phenomena. There is a kind of question that asks for the next number in a series such as

       1, 3, 6, 10, 15, 21, 28, . . .
or   2, 5, 11, 23, 47, 95, 191, . . .

Those of us familiar with these questions (whether or not we believe they test any-thing worthwhile) will look for a pattern or rule so that we can generate the next number. If we cannot state a formal rule (say, $k = 2j + 1$) or at least produce an answer from a tacit understanding of such a rule, we have failed to explain the series.

   On the other hand, if we were asked to identify paintings by famous artists, we would expect to adopt a far less formal approach. We might be able to identify a Rembrandt by general similarity with other Rembrandts which we have seen, and by attention to such characteristics as contrast between light and dark, predominance of certain colours, details of the subject itself, and so on. But we are not likely to think of our criteria as formal rules, let alone express them in formal terms.

   It is an intriguing question whether these two kinds of task are as different as they seem. If the brain works always with finite possibilities, then the identification of the authorship of a painting may be just as 'rule-governed' as the identification of the next number in a series: it may only be that the rules or procedures are so much more intricate that we are scarcely able to make them explicit. With a series of numbers we deal with reality in a single dimension, as it were; with paintings we have to consider various scales and values, such as colour, brightness, shape and texture, which are integrated in complex ways as design or imagery or style. Whatever the nature of our mental processes and knowledge, it is customary practice to expect relatively formal description and explanation in some fields (such as mathematics and physics) and to expect it much less in others (such as esthetics or the study of art or literature).

   In phonology, generative linguists are firmly on the side of a formal approach. The very term 'generative' draws on a mathematical concept of definition by the applica-tion of rules or operations. Thus in generative linguistics, a set of rules may be said to 'define' a language by generating all and only the correct possibilities. A language in which every word consisted of one or more occurrences of [m] followed by one or more occurrences of [a] would be defined by a rule that generated any number of [m]s preceding any number of [a]s. Despite the simplicity and artificiality of a language of this kind, it is worth noting that the number of words is infinite, if there is no upper limit on the number of occurrences of [m] and [a]. The rule is therefore powerful, in the sense that it generates an infinite number of possibilities, but also restrictive, in the sense that it generates only sequences of the language and not impermissible sequences like [aa], [m] or [aaammm]. Indeed, rules are too powerful if they generate not only what is required but also a lot more besides. Hence the predictive or explanatory value of a model of language cannot be equated with generative power: the model needs to be constrained, not open-ended. And one of the challenges facing generative linguistics has been to restrict or constrain its rule-based model of language in principled ways that are appropriate to explain what we find in natural languages.

A concern with formal and explicit description as such is not unique to generative linguists, and it can be argued that the concern itself was inherited from pregenerative North American linguistics (Anderson 1985, p. 316). In general, language is not only amenable to formal investigation but also demands some degree of descriptive formality to convey its true nature. While there may be some value in attempting global characterizations of the phonology of a language, the risk of vagueness and inaccuracy is high. A claim that Dutch or German is a 'guttural' language, for example, means little unless perhaps refined into a statement about the perceptual quality of velar or uvular fricative articulation; likewise a comment that English consonants 'tend to assimilate to a following consonant' again needs to be made more precise, for example by specifying which consonants assimilate, what features are changed in the process and under what conditions. Without such refinement, the comments are tantamount to explaining a series of numbers by saying that each number is 'a lot higher than' the one before it. And refinement and precision bring with them the need for a formal apparatus with which to specify sounds and features and their patterning. What is characteristic of the generative approach, then, is not so much formality and explicitness in themselves but the way in which these goals have been debated and expressed in a rule-based conception of language.

The fundamental reason for formality is the requirement for precision and accuracy. But from this follow further principles, which have been strongly emphasized within generative phonology. Firstly, if the formalism is relatively strict, it limits what can be said. Since models can be too powerful, formal limits are a descriptive strength: the limits make claims about what is possible and therefore make the formal apparatus an expression of a theory of language. If, for instance, there is no limit to the kinds of sounds or rules that can appear in a phonological description, then there may indeed be no reason to constrain the formal apparatus. But if it is true, as most of us believe, that there are limits, then these limits can be expressed or implied by specifying an inventory of features or a set of parameters or a format for rules. Our formal apparatus may then prove to be wrong – if, for example, it turns out to be inadequate for some of the world's languages – but this is precisely what we want, namely that the apparatus makes a claim about the nature of language which can be disproved. If disproved, the claim can be revised and the formal apparatus amended accordingly. In this way, formalism functions as part of the model-building and hypothesis-testing which are characteristic of modern science.

Secondly, a strict formalism of the type favoured by generative phonology provides its own inbuilt measure of what is the simplest and best description. Halle's point about the use of features in rules (section 5.1 above) is central here. If phonological rules are expressed in ordinary English, with few if any constraints on the wording, it is hard to judge what counts as a simple or plausible rule. But if rules follow a certain format, using features and a limited number of notational devices, then we can measure the complexity of a rule by the complexity of its expression. Here, according to Chomsky (1964), other models of phonology are weaker than the generative model: other phonologies may offer 'descriptive adequacy' but they fail to achieve the 'explanatory adequacy' of a model in which evaluation of the description is inherent in the description itself.

The analogy with explaining a series of numbers may again be helpful. The requirement that such explanation be formulated as a rule implies a framework that both limits the possible answers and provides a measure of simplicity. A rule $k = 2j + 1$ conforms to the format, has explanatory power which can be checked against the series, and can be easily evaluated against an alternative formulation such as $k = 4(j/2 + 1/4)$.

5.5 Abbreviatory devices in rule notation

In previous sections we have touched on two assumptions: that rules may apply in a certain order (section 5.3) and that a rule can be evaluated by counting the number of features in it (sections 5.1 and 5.4). While the arguments for these assumptions are clear enough, the implications are not straightforward. In particular, the notation of orthodox generative phonology includes a number of so-called abbreviatory devices, which have the effect of (partially) amalgamating some rules that come next to each other in the sequence of application. The amalgamated rule then counts more cheaply, by virtue of having fewer features.

Consider, for example, the deletion of /r/ in many varieties of English, where /r/ is not pronounced before a consonant (as in *ear-lobe* or *ear-muff*) nor at the end of a word when nothing follows (*ear*) and is retained only before a vowel (*ear-ache*, *my ear is . . .*). The deletion applies in two environments, suggesting two rules:

(5.5.1) $r \rightarrow \emptyset$ / __ C;
(5.5.2) $r \rightarrow \emptyset$ / __ # #.

Assuming that these two rules are ordered next to each other, are they really distinct or can we take them as variants of a single r-deletion rule? If the two can be collapsed, as

$$(5.5.3) \quad r \to \emptyset \, / \, \underline{\quad} \left\{ \begin{matrix} C \\ \# \# \end{matrix} \right\}$$

then the number of features is clearly reduced, by mentioning /r/ and Ø only once. This abbreviation is legitimate in orthodox notation. It is signalled by the use of BRACES (curly brackets) and applies only to adjacent rules and only where environments can be (partially) combined. (Where it might seem possible to use braces on the left-hand side of a rule, the expectation is that one could achieve the necessary generalization by choice of features; thus instead of bracketing, say, [l] and [r], one should be able to specify non-nasal sonorants). A condition attached to the use of braces is that the abbreviated rules are taken to be CONJUNCTIVELY ordered. That is, if two rules, collapsed by use of braces, can both apply to a particular string, then both of them *must* apply, one after the other.

Adjacent rules may be similar in a different way if the environment of one is equivalent to part of the environment of the other. Suppose that vowels undergo a certain process both before a single consonant (followed by a vowel) and before certain sequences of consonant, say nasal plus other consonant. The two environments __ C V and __ N C V can be combined as __ (N) C V. (Processes conditioned by environments of this kind are quite common and in most cases are best explained as applying in open syllables, where the nasal consonant does not close the preceding syllable but begins the following syllable; since orthodox generative phonology does not recognize syllable boundaries, it has to formulate the environment in terms of sequences of consonants and vowels.) In Javanese, for instance, /a/ is rounded to a low back rounded vowel (sometimes written /â/) in certain open syllables: the rounding applies in the last two syllables of words such as *râjâ* ('king') and *negârâ* ('country'), and also in *kândâ* ('tell') and *tâmpâ* ('receive'), where the *n* does not close the first syllable but counts as part of the second syllable; on the other hand, rounding does not apply to the first (closed) syllable of words such as *warnâ* ('colour') or *jalmâ* ('human being'). The Javanese rule can be written as

$$(5.5.4) \quad a \to [+ \text{ round}] \, / \, \underline{\quad} \, ([+ \text{ nasal}]) \, C \, V.$$

As with the previous abbreviatory device, the assumption is that a rule of this kind is actually two or more rules collapsed into one. The conditions attached to the convention, marked by PARENTHESES or round brackets, are firstly that the longer rule (including the elements in parentheses) is presumed to precede the shorter, and secondly that the component rules are ordered DISJUNCTIVELY, meaning that once one has applied, any subsequent rules are skipped, whether applicable or not.

In rule (5.5.4) the disjunctivity of the two abbreviated rules is irrelevant, but consider the following rules of stress assignment. Suppose for simplicity's sake that we are dealing with a language in which every syllable is of CV shape and that [+ stress] can be regarded as a value assigned to any stressed vowel. The stress in this language is antepenultimate, i.e.

monosyllables are stressed: 'CV;
two-syllable words have stress on the first syllable: 'CVCV;

words of three or more syllables have stress on the third syllable from the end: 'CVCVCV, CV'CVCVCV, etc.

As a first approximation we might have three rules:

(5.5.5) V → [+ stress] / __ # # (monosyllables)
(5.5.6) V → [+ stress] / __ CV# # (two-syllable words)
(5.5.7) V → [+ stress] / __ CVCV# # (longer words).

If we amalgamate these into one rule, using parentheses, we have

(5.5.8) V → [+ stress] / —— ((CV) CV) # #.

By convention, the expansions of (5.5.8) apply in descending order of size, i.e. in the order (5.5.7), (5.5.6), (5.5.5), and once one of these applies, no other may apply. This is precisely what is necessary to obtain the correct results in this instance. In the case of a two-syllable word, rule (5.5.7) will not apply, (5.5.6) will, assigning stress to the first syllable, and (5.5.5) could apply but should not, as it would assign an additional stress to the final vowel.

A deceptively simple notation in which, for instance, C_1^3 is used to mean 'at least one and not more than three consonants' is actually equivalent to the use of parentheses. Given the formality of generative notation, the conditions that apply to the use of parentheses must be understood to apply to the use of subscript and superscript numbers. Thus C_1^3 is shorthand for $(((C)C)C)$, which will expand into CCC, CC and C, applied disjunctively in that sequence. Further examples of the notation are

C_0^2 two consonants, one consonant or none
V_1^2 two vowels or one
C_1 at least one consonant.

Examples such as the last imply an infinite series of expansions without any principled limit on the maximum number of segments. The notation avoids the problem of having to specify the longest expansion (which should of course be first in the sequence of expansions). This is probably more relevant to syllables than to segments, since the number of syllables per word is likely to be less constrained than the number of consonants or vowels in a cluster or sequence. Hence abbreviations such as $(CV)_1$ or $(CVC)_0$ may be useful in rules that need to skip over an indefinite number of syllables. Anderson (1974, p. 101, appealing to data from Tryon 1970) suggests that Tahitian has just such a rule of stress assignment, in which it would be arbitrary to fix an upper limit on the number of syllables that a word can contain.

A further extension of the parentheses notation is the use of ANGLED BRACKETS to enclose two optional elements that are either both present or both absent. Thus the environments C __ C and VC __ CV could if necessary be combined as

$< V > C \_\_ C < V >$. As with parentheses, the longer expansion applies first and ordering is disjunctive. A more realistic example of angled brackets is a rule such as

(5.5.9) $\begin{bmatrix} +\text{syllabic} \\ < +\text{high} > \end{bmatrix} \rightarrow [+\text{stress}]/ \_\_ < CV > \# \#.$

The rule states that a high vowel receives stress before CV## or, if this condition is not met, any vowel is stressed before ##. Disjunctive ordering ensures that final vowels will not be stressed in words that have already received stress on a penultimate high vowel.

It is possible to combine different brackets where appropriate. In some varieties of Indonesian, a vowel is 'tense' if it precedes a consonant plus vowel, or if it precedes a nasal consonant plus consonant plus vowel, or if it is word-final:

(5.5.10) $V \rightarrow [+\text{tense}] / \_\_ \begin{Bmatrix} ([+\text{nasal}]) \; CV \\ \# \# \end{Bmatrix}$

Here the ordering conventions happen to have no relevance, but it is important to realize that they are implied by the notation. Generative phonology hypothesizes that rules that show relevant formal resemblances must be amalgamated and applied in accordance with the conventions. The hypotheses include the claim, for instance, that two rules are disjunctively ordered if and only if they can be combined using braces.

A further notational device is suggested by the existence of complementary rules. A common kind of assimilation simply adjusts a feature to the same value as that of the following segment. In Dutch, for instance, fricatives are as a rule voiceless before voiceless consonants and voiced before voiced consonants: in the plural noun *hoofden* ('heads'), the fricative is voiced to [v] before voiced [d], but in the singular *hoofd* (where the word-final plosive is devoiced) the fricative is voiceless in agreement with the following voiceless plosive. In cases such as these, we may appear to have two rules, one of voicing and one of devoicing:

(5.5.11) $\begin{bmatrix} - \text{ sonorant} \\ + \text{ continuant} \end{bmatrix} \rightarrow [- \text{ voiced}] / \_\_\_ [- \text{ voiced}];$

(5.5.12) $\begin{bmatrix} - \text{ sonorant} \\ + \text{ continuant} \end{bmatrix} \rightarrow [+ \text{ voiced}] / \_\_\_ [+ \text{ voiced}]$

But the two rules are actually opposite sides of the same coin and may be combined into a single rule. As with other abbreviatory devices, amalgamation into a single rule amounts to a hypothesis that two related rules count more cheaply in the evaluation system. In this case, the notation allows (5.5.11) and (5.5.12) to be combined as

(5.5.13) $\begin{bmatrix} - \text{ sonorant} \\ + \text{ continuant} \end{bmatrix} \rightarrow [\alpha\text{voiced}] / \_\_\_ [\alpha\text{voiced}]$

The alpha symbol is sometimes referred to as a FEATURE COEFFICIENT and is, technically, a variable ranging over the values + and − (and any other values that may be assigned to a feature, if such there be). The variable must occur at least twice in a rule, and any rule which contains alphas has only two expansions, one in which every occurrence of the alpha is plus, the other with alpha as minus throughout.

The alpha variable has an obvious use in assimilation rules, but the features marked as agreeing in value need not be one and the same feature. Rule (5.5.14) says that obstruents are voiced before sonorants but voiceless before obstruents:

(5.5.14)   [− sonorant] → [αvoiced] / __ [αsonorant].

As a further example, rule (5.5.15) states that back vowels are rounded and other vowels are unrounded when before a consonant:

$$(5.5.15) \quad \begin{bmatrix} + \text{ syllabic} \\ - \text{ consonantal} \\ \alpha\text{back} \end{bmatrix} \rightarrow [\alpha\text{round}] \text{ / \_\_ } [+ \text{ consonantal}].$$

The use of a minus sign in front of one alpha allows reference to features which are opposite in value. Thus (5.5.16) and (5.5.17), expressing a dissimilatory process whereby [l] becomes [r] before [l] and [r] becomes [l] before [r], can be abbreviated as (5.5.18):

$$(5.5.16) \quad \begin{bmatrix} + \text{ sonorant} \\ - \text{ nasal} \end{bmatrix} \rightarrow [- \text{ lateral}] \text{ / \_\_\_ } [+ \text{ lateral}];$$

$$(5.5.17) \quad \begin{bmatrix} + \text{ sonorant} \\ - \text{ nasal} \end{bmatrix} \rightarrow [+ \text{ lateral}] \text{ / \_\_\_ } [- \text{ lateral}];$$

$$(5.5.18) \quad \begin{bmatrix} + \text{ sonorant} \\ - \text{ nasal} \end{bmatrix} \rightarrow [\alpha\text{lateral}] \text{ / \_\_\_ } [-\alpha\text{lateral}].$$

Or consider rule (5.5.19), which says that a word-final [n] is syllabic if it follows a nonsyllabic segment (such as a plosive) but is otherwise nonsyllabic:

$$(5.5.19) \quad \begin{bmatrix} + \text{ consonantal} \\ + \text{ nasal} \end{bmatrix} \rightarrow [\alpha\text{syllabic}] \text{ / } [-\alpha\text{syllabic}]. \text{ \_\_\_ } \# \#$$

Where more than one variable is needed, successive letters of the Greek alphabet are used. Assimilation rules often require that segments agree in a number of feature values. In Indonesian, the final nasal consonant of certain prefixes agrees in point of articulation with the following plosive; this is evident in, for example, the agent noun prefix, which is *pem-* before a bilabial, *pen-* before an alveolar, and so on:

bantu (help)   *pembantu* (helper)
duduk (sit)   *penduduk* (inhabitant)
jahit (sew)   *penjahit* (tailor)
guna (use)   *pengguna* (user).

Indonesian *j* is described sometimes as an affricate, sometimes as a palatal plosive, but we assume in any case that the *n* preceding *j* is palatal by assimilation and equivalent to the consonant otherwise written as *ny* in Indonesian. There are thus four points of articulation, which, in the SPE system, can be captured by the features [anterior], [coronal], [high] and [back] (described in Appendix 2.2). Hence the feature specifications are:

bilabials (m,b) $\begin{bmatrix} + \text{ anterior} \\ - \text{ coronal} \\ - \text{ high} \\ - \text{ back} \end{bmatrix}$

alveolars (n,d) $\begin{bmatrix} + \text{ anterior} \\ + \text{ coronal} \\ - \text{ high} \\ - \text{ back} \end{bmatrix}$

palatals (ny,j) $\begin{bmatrix} - \text{ anterior} \\ - \text{ coronal} \\ + \text{ high} \\ - \text{ back} \end{bmatrix}$

velars (ng,g) $\begin{bmatrix} - \text{ anterior} \\ - \text{ coronal} \\ + \text{ high} \\ + \text{ back} \end{bmatrix}$

The rule of assimilation must therefore specify that the nasal consonant agrees in each of these four features, as shown in rule (5.5.20):

(5.5.20) $\begin{bmatrix} + \text{ consonantal} \\ + \text{ nasal} \end{bmatrix} \rightarrow \begin{bmatrix} \alpha\text{anterior} \\ \beta\text{coronal} \\ \gamma\text{high} \\ \delta\text{back} \end{bmatrix} / \_\_\_ \# \begin{bmatrix} \alpha\text{anterior} \\ \beta\text{coronal} \\ \gamma\text{high} \\ \delta\text{back} \end{bmatrix}$

Note that each Greek letter variable is independent of the others: the two alphas must have the same value as each other (+ or −) but need not agree with the other variables, and so on.

In general the question of how rules like these are to be expanded and applied is of no importance, for only one subpart of the rule can apply in any relevant environment. There are, however, some rules which seem to be candidates for the Greek letter notation but which do raise a problem of ordering, namely EXCHANGE RULES. Exchange rules yield an interchange of values (e.g. i → e and e → i) and, to say the least, they are extremely rare. Anderson (1974, pp. 92–7) and Zonneveld (1976) mention examples. One of those quoted by Anderson concerns the formation of plurals in Dinka, a language of the Sudan in which plurality is indicated by a reversal of the vowel length of the singular form: thus the plural of [pal] 'knife' is [paːl] 'knives', while the plural of [tʃiːn] 'hand' is [tʃin] 'hands'. The rule must be something like this:

$$(5.5.21) \quad \begin{bmatrix} V \\ \alpha\text{long} \end{bmatrix} \rightarrow [\alpha\text{long}] \, / \, \_\!\_ \, X \,]^{\text{noun plural}}$$

Such a rule cannot be taken to be an abbreviation of two conjunctively ordered rules, for the second would simply undo the effects of the first. On the other hand, imposition of disjunctive ordering is arbitrary, since it would make no difference which of the two subrules came first, as long as the other subrule was blocked from applying after it. In fact Anderson (1974, p. 94), appealing to the spirit of Chomsky (1967), proposes that rules abbreviated by the use of feature coefficients are a special exception to the principle of rule ordering. The rules apply not sequentially but simultaneously.

5.6   Rule order

In the earliest orthodoxy of generative phonology, rules applied in a fixed order, one after the other. There were exceptions to this principle, namely the special cases signalled in the notation by parentheses and Greek letter variables, which indicated disjunctive or simultaneous application (section 5.5 above); but apart from these well-defined exceptions, rule order was LINEAR, TRANSITIVE and CONJUNCTIVE. The rules of a language could be listed in a numbered sequence; each rule would appear only once in the list; and the output of each rule was the input to the next applicable rule in the numbered order. This early orthodoxy is discussed by Chomsky (1967).

Implicit in these principles of rule order is the assumption that the order must be determined empirically, that the rules of a language take whatever order yields the correct outputs in the most economical way. In other words, order is EXTRINSIC, imposed by the description and not derived from general principles or from the nature of the rules themselves. Indeed, examples have been quoted to show that two dialects might share certain rules but differ in the ordering of them. Sommerstein (1977, pp. 159–61, based on Newton 1972) illustrates the point from Modern Greek. Some dialects share rules which, among other things

1   turn mid vowels into high when next to a low vowel;
2   turn high vowels into semivowels when next to a vowel;

3   turn semivowels into voiced fricatives under certain conditions (e.g. [w] →
    [v]);
4   delete voiced fricatives between vowels.

The order of these rules does appear to differ among the relevant dialects. In most of
the dialects a form such as /aloγas/ 'horsedealer' is pronounced [aloas], which suggests that the rules apply in the order given above: the voiced fricative is deleted by
(4), but, at this point in the sequence, rule (1) has already been skipped and cannot
apply to the mid vowel standing next to a low. In one dialect spoken on Rhodes,
however, 'horsedealer' is [alvas]: (4) has applied and the output has then undergone
(1), (2) and (3), i.e. [aloas] – [aluas] – [alwas] – [alvas]. Other facts argue that all four
rules are present in all the dialects. Their order is therefore crucial.

It has always been apparent, however, that there are difficulties with the orthodox
view of rule order. An early attempt to allow some rules to be repeated (ostensibly
violating linear transitive order) was the postulation of CYCLICAL RULES. Certain rules
were assumed to form a block which could be repeated in a series of CYCLES. In
keeping with the generative penchant for constraining the model, only some rules
qualified for cyclical application, namely those which were both deep (i.e. 'early' in
the total set of ordered rules) and sensitive to syntactic information. Hence successive
cycles are not arbitrary but correspond to increasingly larger syntactic domains. A
set of cyclical rules might apply first of all within morphemes; on the second cycle the
same rules would apply again within words; on the third within phrases; and so on.
Thus the cycle was not a means of repeating any rule at random, and linear conjunctive order was still the norm. In SPE it is only the stress rules of English which are
cyclical, and other rules are postcyclical (Chomsky and Halle 1968, chs 2, 3, especially pp. 15–24; some details can be found in the treatment of English prosody in
chapter 9 below.) It has been suggested that stress is also assigned cyclically (either
entirely or partly) in other languages, including Russian (Halle 1973), Japanese
(McCawley 1968) and Spanish and Arabic (Brame 1974). Brame goes so far as to
hypothesize that stress rules are cyclical in all natural languages.

An example of cyclical rule application other than stress assignment is given by
Harms (1968, pp. 99–100). In Komi, a Finno-Ugric language spoken in the USSR,
the vowel [ɨ] is inserted between consonants to avoid clusters of three consonants.
But in a word such as *pukśɨnɨ* the vowel is inserted between *ś* and *n*, whereas in
vundiśnɨ the vowel is inserted between the *d* and *ś*. The correct form can be predicted, according to Harms, if the insertion rule is applied cyclically. The structure of
the two words can be represented as

puk + ś + nɨ   i.e. [[[puk][ś]] nɨ]
vund + ś + nɨ   i.e. [[[vund][ś]] nɨ]

and the insertion rule can be written as

(5.6.1) Ø → ɨ / [X C C __ C Y].

Now the rule will 'search' for a string that meets its requirements, working upwards from the smallest constituents. On the first cycle, searching within the innermost brackets, the rule will fail to apply. On the next cycle, the innermost brackets are now ignored, and insertion applies to the three consonants within the string [vund ś]; but it is not applicable to [puk ś] since the CC __ C environment is still not to be found. On the next cycle [vund i ś ni], having undergone the insertion rule, no longer has a CCC sequence; but [puk ś ni] does now trigger insertion, at the appropriate point in the string. Cyclical treatment of other segmental phenomena in North American Indian languages was proposed by Kisseberth (1972, for the language Klamath) and Kaye and Piggott (1973, to account for palatalization in Ojibwa).

A very simple summary account of conjunctive and disjunctive order as handled in the early days of generative phonology can be found in Schane (1973, pp. 89ff.). Chomsky and Halle's own treatment of English stress rules, accompanied by some discussion of the ordering conventions, is in chapter 2 of SPE. For more general evaluation of the hypotheses themselves and their validity, see Anderson (1974, chs 6 and 7), and Sommerstein (1977, ch. 7).

Even with these various exceptions or qualifications, the principle of linear transitive order has faltered in the face of various examples of ORDERING PARADOXES (Anderson 1974, pp. 141ff., Sommerstein 1977, pp. 174–6). In Icelandic, for instance, there are two rules, one of which is an umlaut rule converting /a/ to a front rounded /ö/ before an /u/ in the following syllable, the other an elision rule deleting unstressed vowels in certain environments. Slightly simplified, the two rules are

(5.6.2) $a \rightarrow \ddot{o} \; / \; \_\_ \; C_o \; u;$

(5.6.3) $\begin{bmatrix} V \\ -\text{stress} \end{bmatrix} \rightarrow \emptyset \; / \; C \_\_ C \; \# \; V$

Thus in the nouns *jökull* ('glacier') and *jötunn* ('giant') the first vowel is an underlying /a/ which has become /ö/ because of the /u/ in the following syllable. Now the dative form of 'glacier' is *jökli*, from underlying /jakuli/: the /u/ triggers assimilation of the /a/ in the first syllable but is then deleted by the elision rule. Thus the two rules seem to apply in the order given above. But the dative plural of 'gods' is *rögnum*, from underlying /raginum/. Here – and in comparable forms such as *kötlum* ('kettles'), from underlying /katilum/ – the rules must apply in the reverse order: the unstressed /i/ is elided, which then allows the /u/ of the last syllable to trigger rounding of the preceding /a/.

Paradoxes such as these prompted a number of suggestions about principles of rule order. One proposal envisaged PARTIAL ORDER: rules would be unordered and could apply whenever and wherever their conditions were met, but some of the rules might be specified as preceding certain others, or as blocking the subsequent application of certain others. Or, most rules might fall into an ordered set, but some, termed PERSISTENT RULES or ANYWHERE RULES (Chafe 1968; Anderson 1974, p. 191) would be capable of applying as often as they could. Or, under a principle known as

LOCAL ORDER, the order of precedence might be specified only for pairs of rules at a time. (See Sommerstein 1977, pp. 176–88 for an overview.)

5.7   Functional considerations

Debate about rule order led to reconsideration of functionality in language. The question arose whether rule order might not in fact be determined by functional or natural principles – whether rule order might be INTRINSIC, i.e. determined by the nature and function of the rules themselves.

In 1968 Kiparsky had already drawn attention to the effects of alternative orders and had distinguished between FEEDING and BLEEDING. If two rules (call them A and B) are such that A generates forms which will undergo B, then A feeds B. If the order of these two rules is reversed (nonfeeding or counterfeeding order), there will be apparent exceptions to B, since A now generates forms that escape the effects of B by virtue of the ordering. Assuming that language is characteristically regular and averse to exceptions, feeding order seems more likely or more natural than counterfeeding. To take a simple example, rule (5.7.1) feeds (5.7.2), since it creates additional occurrences of /r/ to undergo (5.7.2):

(5.7.1) $l \rightarrow r$ / — # #
(5.7.2) $r \rightarrow$ [− voiced] / — # #

It seems unlikely that the order of these two rules would be the reverse. Counterfeeding would mean that those occurrences of /r/ which resulted from (5.7.1) – and only those – would remain voiced in word-final position, violating the pattern implied by (5.7.2).

If two rules (C and D) are such that C robs D of some of its inputs, then C bleeds D. If the order of these two rules is reversed (nonbleeding or counterbleeding) then the application of D will be maximized instead of constrained. Here counterbleeding seems the more natural order. For example, rule (5.7.3), which raises /a/ to /e/ before any palatal consonant, bleeds (5.7.4), which nasalizes the low vowel before any nasal.

(5.7.3) $a \rightarrow e$ / $\begin{bmatrix} - \text{ anterior} \\ + \text{ coronal} \end{bmatrix}$

(5.7.4) $a \rightarrow$ [+ nasal] / — [+ nasal].

Bleeding order means that an /a/ standing before a palatal nasal is raised to /e/ and then fails to undergo low vowel nasalization. This seems the most plausible state of affairs, given that rule (5.7.4) applies only to /a/ and therefore would not apply to any occurrence of /e/, whether generated by (5.7.3) or not. The reverse (counterbleeding) order would mean that /a/ standing before a palatal nasal would be nasalized and then raised to become /ẽ/, violating the general pattern that vowels other than /a/ are not nasalized before nasal consonants.

Feeding and bleeding are related to the notions of TRANSPARENCY and OPACITY (Kiparsky 1971). A rule is transparent if its effects are obvious from the phonetic forms of a language. Suppose a language has a rule that underlying word-final [o] becomes [u]. If the language has no instance at all of word-final [o], no instance of [u] other than word-finally, and no instances of word-final [u] other than those derived from [o] by this rule, then the rule is as transparent as can be. If on the other hand the language has some instances of word-final [o] that somehow escape the effect of the rule, some instances of word-medial [u] and even instances of final [u] which are not derived from [o], then the rule is highly opaque. Many rules will of course fall between these two extremes. In English, the reduction of unstressed vowels to [ə] is relatively transparent, at least in varieties such as RP: there are few if any occurrences of unreduced vowels in unstressed syllables, and arguably few instances of [ə] other than those derived by the reduction process (although it is a controversial question whether the [ə] in the final syllable of words such as *carrot*, *summon* or *opal* is in any sense derived from a full vowel). On the other hand, what Chomsky and Halle (1968) call the laxing of vowels is relatively opaque. The generative treatment of English predicts, for example, that a vowel will be 'lax' before a consonant cluster (section 5.2 above): hence the change of vowel in e.g. *mean*, *meant*, *sleep*, *slept*, *wide*, *width*. But there are certainly instances of 'tense' vowels before clusters (*fiend*, *heaped*, *pint*, *heights*) and some 'lax' vowels before clusters are not derived from 'tense' vowels (*dent*, *adept*, *crypt*, *lint*).

Kiparsky's discussion of feeding and bleeding was actually in a historical context. He observes that, over time 'rules tend to shift into the order which allows their fullest utilization in the grammar' (1968, p. 200), and he quotes instances of languages in which rules have evidently been reordered in line with this tendency. In other words, the historical development of languages seemed to favour feeding and eliminate bleeding. Other historical tendencies have been noted: in a study of Spanish, Harris (1973) suggests that rules tend to shift into the order that favours PARADIGMATIC UNIFORMITY, i.e. rules will occur in whatever order reduces irregularity in the morphology of the language. In Spanish, some verb paradigms are not regular: note the alternation of *c* and *g* in

hacer	[aθer]	to do
hago	[aɣo]	I do
hacemos	[aθemos]	we do.

Now, non-uniform paradigms such as these are, as Harris puts it, a 'vanishingly small minority of Spanish verbs', and it seems that many verbs which once had variable stems have been made regular by the reordering of rules. The stem-final consonant of *cocer* ('to cook'), for instance, must once have appeared as an affricate in some forms of the verb and as a velar plosive in others. In modern Spanish, however, the stems end consistently in [θ] (or [s] in much of the Spanish-speaking world) and it is possible to explain this regularization as the result of reversing the order of two particular rules. But Anderson (1974, p. 208) points out that natural principles may conflict with each other. He points to the SELF-PRESERVATION of rules, noting that counterbleeding may be natural where bleeding order would mean that the first rule would actually be lost from the language. But these various historical tendencies are no more than that: they do not preclude exceptions and it is clear, for example, that notwithstanding paradigmatic uniformity, languages may tolerate a high degree of morphological irregularity, and that notwithstanding self-preservation, rules do sometimes disappear from languages (Anderson 1974, pp. 209–18, Kisseberth 1973, Thomason 1976).

While some of this discussion in the 1970s seemed to concentrate on formal mechanisms, attention returned from time to time to functional goals or targets. It was noted, for instance, that rules which appear formally unrelated may nevertheless serve a common functional target, such as elimination of consonant clusters, preservation of distinctiveness or maintenance of a generalized stress pattern.

Kisseberth (1970) argued that a number of rules in Yawelmani (a language of California) had the net effect of severely constraining consonant clusters: 'There are a variety of phonological processes which, it may be said, "conspire" to yield phonetic representations which contain no word-final clusters and no triliteral clusters' (1970, p. 293). Studies of RULE CONSPIRACIES, as they came to be called, included one of the Australian language Yidiny, in which stress and vowel length are subject to intriguing constraints (Dixon 1977). Briefly, long vowels cannot occur in adjacent syllables, and in words with an odd number of syllables, at least one even-numbered syllable must contain a long vowel. Stress falls on the first syllable containing a long vowel (or on the first syllable if all the vowels in the word are short); and, counting outwards from this stressed syllable, stress is also assigned to every even-numbered syllable. For example:

yatjí:rringál
wúngapá:tjinyúnta
tjámpulángalnyúnta.

There are various rules, including even some determining the sequence as well as the forms of affixes, which conspire to maintain the phonotactic constraints. Dixon concludes that the details of affixation and vowel length 'must surely indicate that the development of Yidiny morphology has been in part oriented to the language's overriding phonological targets – that every long vowel should occur in a stressed syllable, and that stressed and unstressed syllables should alternate in a phonological word' (1977, pp. 33–4).

In fact functional targets of this kind are not necessarily captured in a subset of the rules. It can be argued (Kiparsky 1972, p. 216) that English tends to avoid repeating /l/ or /r/ within the same word, but that this is revealed in a variety of phenomena, including the general phonological patterning of words as well as morphological alternations that can be expressed in rules. Consider firstly words such as *prattling*, *sprinkling*, *trampling*, *trickling*, *fluttering*, *glimmering*, *glittering*, *spluttering*. These may contain a cluster containing /l/ and a cluster containing /r/, but not two containing /l/ or two containing /r/. There are few if any words (and certainly none of this semantic type) that have a shape such as *flickling* or *sprittering*. Secondly, an apparently quite different phenomenon in English is that while many adjectives end in *-al* (*educational, occasional, cultural, dental, natural*), *-ar* appears where there is an /l/ in the stem (*cellular, circular, vulgar, lunar, alveolar*). This constraint – which actually reflects a pattern of Latin – is not absolute in modern English (cf. *laminal, laminar*) and in any case loses some of its force in those varieties of English that no longer pronounce final *r*, but nevertheless seems to tend in the same direction as the patterning of words such as *flickering* and *sprinkling*. Thirdly, it may be noted that while *-al* can also mark nouns in English (*betrayal, burial, dismissal, denial*) there are no such nouns with stems containing /l/ (such as *applial, dispellal* or *recoilal*). Conspiracies and functional targets are a problem for a model of phonology that relies on formal devices such as bracketing to unite or relate rules. Indeed, Sommerstein takes the Yawelmani example and others like it as evidence for the traditional recognition of phonotactic constraints as a separate component of phonological description (1977, pp. 194–9).

Kisseberth (1973) had also noted that phonological rules often seemed to operate not according to some arbitrarily imposed order but in a way that was sensitive to the consequences of rule interaction. One of his examples is from Dayak (a language spoken on the island of Kalimantan), as reported by Scott (1964). In Dayak vowels are nasalized following a nasal consonant, e.g.

[mãta]	eye
[nãŋãʔ]	straighten
[nãŋgaʔ]	put up a ladder.

Optionally, a voiced plosive following a nasal can be deleted – but this rule does not feed vowel nasalization. Hence 'put up a ladder' may be pronounced [nãŋgaʔ] or [nãŋaʔ], but not [nãŋãʔ]. This is in one sense unnatural, since we would expect feeding order, making vowel nasalization more transparent. But it also makes functional sense, since the lack of nasalization is what keeps 'put up a ladder' distinct from 'straighten'. In other words, vowels are nasalized after a nasal consonant, provided that the nasal is not derived from a cluster of nasal and voiced plosive. Following Kisseberth's formulation, a constraint of this kind is known as a GLOBAL CONSTRAINT or TRANSDERIVATIONAL CONSTRAINT, as it makes reference to derivational history, carrying out, so to speak, a check on the effect of rules.

As Kiparsky puts it (1972, p. 217), phonological rules tend to avoid the universally complex and to maintain what is distinctive in the language. All languages, for instance, put limits on the clustering of consonants. Some, like Japanese and Polynesian languages, allow few or none at all; in Japanese, for example, no consonant cluster of any kind is tolerated word-initially or word-finally, and word-medial clusters are restricted to lengthened plosives and nasals plus plosives. Other languages, like English, are far more tolerant of consonant clusters but are nevertheless prone to processes of simplification: many speakers of English will elide the bracketed consonants in e.g.

Did you sen(d) my letter?
They kep(t) quiet.

But distinctiveness is not ignored in such processes. The lengthening of nasals before voiced plosives in English is such that the [n] in *sen(d)* may still be significantly long, even when the [d] is dropped, and therefore distinct from the shorter [n] that would signal a following [t]. Of course, distinctiveness is not an absolute requirement, and there is ample evidence that distinctions do sometimes disappear from a language – modern English has, for example, lost the distinction between *ail* and *ale* or *hail* and *hale*. But sociolinguistic studies suggest that speakers may be less likely to apply elision where a crucial distinction is lost. Thus in some varieties of English, elision of the final consonant of *fist* is extremely common – and nothing is really lost, for there is no potential confusion with a word such as *fiss*. Elision of the [t] in *kept* is less frequent: here the [t] is a signal of past tense and perhaps therefore more likely to be retained (although the change of vowel from *keep* serves to maintain distinctiveness). But elision is even less frequent in a form such as *passed* (or *past*), where without the [t] the form is phonetically indistinguishable from *pass*. If it is legitimate to speak of a rule of consonant elision applying to these forms, it is a rule constrained not arbitrarily by its priority in a sequence but in its frequency of application and by its effect on communicativeness (Kiparsky 1972, p. 197; Wardhaugh 1986, p. 178–81). A useful review of rule order and feeding and bleeding, with copious examples, can be found in Kenstowicz (1994, pp. 90–100).

5.8 Naturalness and markedness

Chomsky and Halle begin chapter 9 of SPE with an honest if irritating admission that they are dissatisfied with their treatment of features in the book. They point out that the use of features is intended to provide an inbuilt evaluation of naturalness. Generative phonology implies, for instance, that a natural class of sounds will be characterized by relatively few features. Indeed, the fewer the features needed, the more natural the class of sounds: hence obstruent consonants (which can be characterized simply as [−sonorant]) constitute a more natural class than, say, voiced consonants other than laterals (which might require the specification [+voiced, +consonantal, −lateral]). But SPE's approach to such evaluation is, in Chomsky and Halle's own words 'overly formal' (1968, p. 400). That is, merely to count the number of features overlooks the 'intrinsic content' of the features. Thus the feature specification [−voiced, −sonorant] (= voiceless obstruents) indicates a more common category of description than, say, [−voiced, +nasal] (= voiceless nasals), yet both need only two features. A similar point can be made about rules, undermining

Halle's contention about simplicity (section 5.1 above). Even when expressed in features, the simpler rules do not always appear simpler.

For reasons such as these, Chomsky and Halle proposed that feature values be revised to clarify the extent to which certain rules or combinations of features were expected or natural. They appealed to the terms MARKED and UNMARKED, which had been used by some European phonologists (section 11.6 below) to refer to phonemes which showed the presence or absence of a particular feature. In this usage, voiced phonemes might be described as 'marked' by voicing, in opposition to 'unmarked' voiceless phonemes which lacked the feature. But the unmarked member of an opposed pair was often the one to appear in a position of neutralization (section 4.9 above), and the term 'unmarked' sometimes carried the sense of 'neutral' or 'natural' (what the computer-literate might call the 'default value'). This concept has not been confined to phonology and it is sometimes said, for example, that in an adjective pair such as 'long' and 'short', 'long' is the unmarked term because it is the one used in neutral contexts such as questions. (The question 'How long is that string?', without stress on 'long', need not imply that the string is either long or short, whereas the question 'How short is that string?' does imply that the string is short; hence the choice of 'short' in this context is 'marked'.)

Now strictly speaking, the feature system of SPE is incompatible with the notion of markedness: if features are binary (having only the two values, + and −) then there is no room for a third value, 'unmarked'. In fact, phonologists have experimented with such possibilities, abandoning the binary assumption and allowing three values. For instance, if English /m/ is [+labial] and /n/ [−labial] (among other things, of course), we might allow that the nasal consonant of the prefix *in-* is [0labial], meaning that it is unspecified for this feature: here the nasal consonant takes the feature value of the following consonant and will be [+labial] in e.g. *impossible* and *impertinent*, but [−labial] in e.g. *indecent* or *intolerable*. But Chomsky and Halle kept a binary system, while still attempting to exploit a concept of markedness. They proposed that the binary values of underlying features should be 'marked' and 'unmarked' (abbreviated as *m* and *u*) instead of + and −. These new values would reflect expectedness or naturalness, and would be converted into + and − by UNIVERSAL MARKING CONVENTIONS. Thus if it is more usual or natural that sounds are voiced, a universal convention will specify that [*u*voiced] → [+voiced]. In fact the marking conventions are not quite as simple as this, and many of them are sensitive to context. It is assumed, for instance, that [+voiced] is the natural status of vowels, since they are voiced in most languages and vowel qualities are less audible in voiceless vowels; but plosives are more likely to be [−voiced], since it is physiologically easier to switch off voicing during occlusion (see STOPS in section 2.12 above). To allow for this, a marking convention may specify that [*u*voice] is interpreted as [−voiced] in obstruents, but otherwise as [+voiced]. Similarly, since it seems to be the case that consonant followed by vowel is a natural syllabic structure, another of Chomsky and Halle's marking conventions specifies that [*u*vocalic] is [+vocalic] following a consonant. Universal implications are also incorporated into the conventions, including some which simply reflect the incompatibility of certain values, e.g. [+low] → [−high].

Chomsky and Halle add to these conventions the concept of LINKING (1968, pp. 419ff.), which allows the marking conventions to monitor phonological rules. In effect, marking conventions are not only a set of initial interpretations, applying before phonological rules go to work, but conditions on the output of rules, so that they may also be triggered by appropriate rules. This is a way of simplifying some rules (and hence enhancing their naturalness) by omitting from them details which can be tidied up by the application of relevant marking conventions.

Chomsky and Halle's concept of markedness has been rejected by most of their successors, on the grounds that it still fails to do justice to naturalness. Concern with naturalness has proved a strong motive in recent phonology, so much so that two 'schools' of phonology have enshrined the term in their titles (sections 11.10 and 11.11 below). Classical generative phonology is, however, less famous for its regard for naturalness than for the degree of abstractness which it allows in phonological analysis.

5.9   Abstractness

Orthodox generative phonology is mentalist, in that it implies mental storage of underlying representations which are converted into surface representations by the application of rules. Chomsky and Halle speak of 'mental construction' by speaker and hearer (1968, p. 14). And in connection with access to underlying representation in the process of reading aloud and with the development of such representation in children's acquisition of language, they refer to the 'fundamental importance of the question of psychological reality of linguistic constructs' (1968, pp. 49–50; see also Chomsky 1964, chs 1, 5, and 1968, for Chomsky's views on the relationship between linguistics and psychology). Much of the early argument for generative phonology (in Chomsky 1964, for instance) was devoted to showing that a traditional phonemic transcription was an unjustifiable level of representation, intermediate between underlying and surface representations. The new underlying level (termed 'systematic phonemic') corresponded to the speaker's storage of phonological representations, while the surface level ('systematic phonetic') remained comparable to a traditional phonetic transcription of the speaker's utterances.

Underlying representation was now 'deeper' or 'more abstract' than a conventional phonemic transcription and could be as abstract as the phonological rules would allow. Thus the underlying form of the morpheme common to the English words *telephonist* and *telephonic* should be such that the appropriate surface vowels can be derived by rules. For convenience (and following the example of most generative phonologists) let us represent the underlying form in segments rather than features as *tElEfOn*: this form now depends for its validity upon the fact that English has phonological rules deriving unstressed [ə] from underlying E in appropriate environments (as in the first syllable of *telephonist*), and [ɒ] from underlying O (again in appropriate contexts, such as in the syllable preceding the suffix *-ic*), and so on. The question that then arose was whether there were principled limits on this strategy of description. Thus a single form may underlie *south*, *south(ern)* and *sou'(west)*, provided that English includes rules to voice a dental fricative in appropriate places and to delete it in others. But these rules might be regarded as *ad hoc*, devised not to reflect general processes but purely to cater for one or two words. (Note that the final dental fricative can be dropped in *north* and *south* but not in other words such as *mouth*, *birth* and *hearth*). And if this case seems worrying, what of *go* and *went*? If *went* is grammatically the past form of *go*, could it be derived from *go+ed* by application of rules that turn the underlying initial consonant into [g] or [w] according to context, an underlying vowel into [oʊ] or [ɛ], and so on?

In fact generative phonology recognized this problem quite early, and various restrictions on abstract analyses were formulated. Totally abstract segments were ruled out, for example. This meant that both underlying and surface representations were expressed in standard features, and it was not considered legitimate to postulate abstract features or segments that had no genuine phonetic value. Postal (1968) makes this point in the form of the NATURALNESS CONDITION, which states that a (systematic) phonemic representation implies identical phonetic representation unless the phonological rules determine otherwise. In other words, an underlying representation must be such that it would surface as a pronounceable item in the language without the intervention of any rules. The condition forbids any totally abstract segment that is phonetically invalid until altered or fleshed out by the rules of the language.

A further early proposal was to exclude ABSOLUTE NEUTRALIZATION. (Kiparsky's paper on this subject circulated from 1968 but was published only in 1973.) This exclusion meant that if two segments were distinguished at the underlying level, then they must also be distinct in at least some contexts in surface representation. It should not be possible for phonological rules to turn all occurrences of both segments into identical surface segments. Consider, for example, those varieties of English in which the distinction between voiced and voiceless /w/ has disappeared, so that there is no longer any distinction in pronunciation between *which* and *witch* or *whale* and *wail*. Historically, these versions of English have undergone a sound change which has indeed absolutely neutralized the distinction. There would be no justification for postulating two underlying segments, one voiced and one voiceless, for there would then have to be a rule that turned voiceless semivowels into voiced, to ensure the output of forms as pronounced. In short, we need no underlying distinctions that have no phonetic reflex whatsoever. Of course the constraint on absolute neutralization does not exclude the possibility that distinctions are neutralized under some conditions, nor that segments are radically altered by rules; it does require that the distinction survive in surface representations in *some* way under at least *some* conditions.

Limitations such as these still left room for a degree of abstractness in underlying forms that many phonologists found alarming. Indeed, the potential to offer abstract analyses was defended as a virtue of generative phonology, and SPE proposed that English had, among its underlying segments, a front rounded vowel /œ/ (which surfaces as the diphthong [ɔɪ] as in *coin*, SPE pp. 191–2) and a velar fricative /x/

(which never appears on the surface but triggers certain changes in adjacent segments before it is deleted; SPE pp. 233ff.). The reader will notice that neither of these two segments is readily pronounceable by most speakers of English, and the postulation of an English velar fricative became something of a cause célèbre.

Chomsky himself chose his analysis of the word *righteous* to illustrate the possibility that surface structures might be quite surprisingly remote from what underlay them. Pointing to examples such as

expedite	expeditious
ignite	ignition
delight	delicious

Chomsky suggests that we might expect the adjective *righteous* to follow the same pattern, i.e. *ritious*, rhyming with *delicious*. The actual form *righteous* is in fact unexpected in two ways: it shows [tʃ] instead of [ʃ], and [aɪ] instead of [ɪ]. Now there are other forms which show [tʃ] where [ʃ] might be expected, e.g.

suggest	suggestion
Christ	Christian.

These apparent exceptions can be explained by the presence of the fricative [s] before the [t]. The general rule converting [t] to [ʃ] before the relevant suffixes can be modified to ensure that [t] preceded by a fricative becomes [tʃ] and that [t] otherwise becomes [ʃ]. If the underlying form of *righteous* is assumed to contain a fricative preceding the [t], it will undergo this rule.

There are also instances in English where a velar consonant triggers a change in a preceding vowel and is then deleted. Compare

paradigm	paradigmatic
resign	resignation.

In the generative treatment of English, these forms are assumed to contain an underlying [g] which is preserved in the suffixed forms but is lost before the word-final nasal after conditioning a change of the preceding vowel. If the fricative just postulated in *righteous* is now taken to be a velar fricative, then the rules applying to *paradigm* and *resign* can be extended to *right(eous)*. The various rules of English to which we have now referred will derive the initially unexpected pronunciation. By postulating an underlying velar fricative in *righteous*, we make the form accessible to rules which will not only generate the correct diphthong and affricate but also delete the fricative into the bargain. Moreover, the rules applying to this form have not been invented specially or arbitrarily for this purpose but are already required elsewhere in the description of English phonology. In generative terminology, they are 'well motivated' rules.

Acknowledging that a single example such as this may be less than convincing, Chomsky nevertheless claims that careful investigation of sound structure 'shows that there are a number of examples of this sort, and that, in general, highly abstract underlying structures are related to phonetic representations by a long sequence of rules . . . Assuming the existence of abstract mental representations and interpretive operations of this sort, we can find a surprising degree of organization underlying what appears superficially to be a chaotic arrangement of data . . . ' (1968, p. 36). Thus within the early orthodoxy of generative phonology, a high degree of abstractness, within an explicitly mentalist perspective, was regarded as a cornerstone. Sommerstein reviews the early debate about abstractness in some detail and lists major references (1977, pp. 211–25); Lass (1984, ch. 9) also gives a thorough overview; and Kenstowicz (1994, pp. 103–14), gives a useful account of the debate about alternants and underlying forms. Not surprisingly, the permissible extent of abstractness remained a matter for discussion and became a key feature of modifications to generative phonology, which are reviewed in chapter 11 below (sections 11.10 onwards). The approach to phonology represented by SPE, taken as a formal apparatus of description, scarcely survived the 1970s; but the concept of a generative model of phonology and the assumption that theory must be expressed in explicitly formal terms amount to a still powerful tradition. Many phonologists still proclaim themselves generativists, and, in that sense, the spirit of SPE lives on.

Exercises

1   What is a 'plausible general rule' (5.1)? Suggest some plausible and implausible rules.
2   Check the examples of 'tense' and 'lax' vowels in 5.2 (*insane, insanity*, etc.). Add as many more examples as you can.
3   Using the notation outlined in 5.3, write rules to express the following phenomena. Try to note any assumptions you make about the phonological system – for example if you capture vowels as simply [+syllabic] you may be assuming that there are no syllabic consonants in the language being described.

    a   low vowels are nasalized between nasal consonants
    b   fricatives are voiced before nasal consonants
    c   sibilant fricatives are voiced between vowels
    d   plosives are voiceless if word-final
    e   vowels are lax at the beginning of a morpheme
    f   any vowel is deleted before another vowel
    g   velar fricatives are deleted between vowels
    h   [h] is inserted between a vowel and a voiceless plosive
    i   sonorants are deleted at the end of noun roots provided that the root is not carrying a suffix
    j   a sequence of vowel plus [r] is metathesized before a plosive

The Generative Approach to Phonology

Suggest at least two ways of writing rules to account for:

k   a sequence of [s] + [i] becomes [ʃ]
l   a sequence of [a] + [u] becomes [o]

4   Explain the use and implications of the following devices:

braces (curly brackets)
parentheses (round brackets)
angled brackets
Greek letter variables

5   What do Chomsky and Halle mean by 'marked' and 'unmarked' values of features?
6   If the English word *right* contains an underlying velar fricative, why don't *delight* and *night* also have one?
7   Ensure that you understand the following:

feature coefficient
exchange rule
cyclical rules
Postal's naturalness condition
a rule conspiracy
a global constraint

8   Explain the following distinctions:

conjunctive versus disjunctive order
transparent versus opaque rules
extrinsic versus intrinsic rule order
feeding, counterfeeding, bleeding, counterbleeding

Referring to these distinctions, discuss the notion that some rule orders are more natural than others.

6 The Anatomy and Physiology of Speech Production

This chapter provides a comprehensive anatomical background to the book's account of speech sounds. The first two sections set the scene for a technical account using the conventions of anatomical description (6.1 and 6.2).

The bulk of the chapter reviews the various organs of speech in a logical order, moving from the broad underlying structures and functions of the nervous system and respiratory system to the details of specific articulators such as tongue and lips. Given the complex functions of the larynx in speech, the section dealing with the larynx is followed by a separate section on how the larynx functions in phonation. The sections are:

- the nervous system (6.3)
- the respiratory system (6.4)
- the larynx (6.5)
- phonation (6.6)
- the pharynx (6.7)
- the velum and the nasal cavity (6.8)
- the oral cavity (6.9)
- the tongue (6.10)
- the lips (6.11)
- the mandible (6.12).

6.1 Introduction

In chapter 2 we outlined the speech production process from a functional perspective with sufficient detail to allow us to describe the speech sounds of language, but deliberately avoiding much discussion of the underlying technical detail. In this chapter we now provide a more technical examination of the anatomical and physiological processes of speech production. Some readers may choose to skip this and the ensuing chapter on speech acoustics, but for others, and especially those whose interests lie in experimental phonology and phonetics, speech and hearing science, communication disorders, cognitive science, artificial intelligence and speech technology, these two chapters provide an essential foundation. Moreover, these more physical and empirical perspectives on the subject have been basic to the development of some of the more theoretical and abstract units and categories of phonological description and analysis.

6.2   Conventions of anatomical description

We shall confine technical detail to essentials, but an understanding of some basic conventions of anatomical description is necessary. Figure 6.2.1 shows the basic division of the body into three planes (for sections through the body) and the five basic aspects from which anatomical features are viewed.

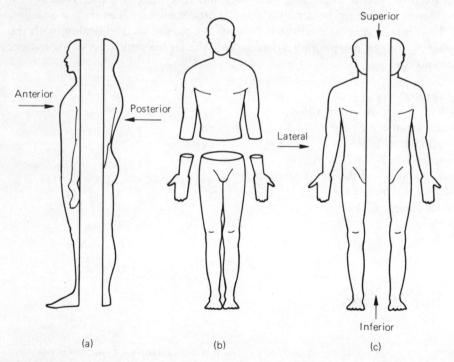

FIGURE 6.2.1   Sections and viewing aspects in human anatomy: (a) coronal; (b) transverse; (c) sagittal
Adapted from: Zemlin 1968, p. 9.

The following terms will be found in many anatomical descriptions:

CRANIAL	: nearest or towards the brain
CAUDAL	: away from the head
PROXIMAL	: near the source of attachment
DISTAL	: away from the source of attachment
AFFERENT	: conducting towards the brain or spinal cord
EFFERENT	: conducting from a central to a peripheral region
SUPERFICIAL	: towards the surface
DEEP	: away from the surface
PROCESS	: projection or elevation on a bone

The organs of speech are all bodily structures composed of a variety of tissue types (such as bone, cartilage and skin) which are specific to their biological (rather than linguistic) function. Such tissue is in turn composed of cells, and the inner structure of these need not concern us further here. Bodily organs are generally grouped into systems which have particular functions in the life of the organism. These include the respiratory system, digestive system, the reproductive system and so on. While it can be argued that the organs of speech form a system, they do not contribute to life support in the same way as other systems, and they are generally not thought of as performing their primary biological function when they are used in speech production.

In terms of bodily structure, humans are vertebrates – they have a backbone or vertebral column and their bodily structure is a mirror image either side of the backbone. Many parts of the body (such as muscles) are therefore PAIRED.

There are several ways of classifying the various tissues that make up the organs of the body. A common categorization recognizes five basic types, the first of which is of little relevance in the study of speech organs but is included here for completeness:

1 EPITHELIUM is the technical term for the layers of cells that constitute the outer skin of the body and the various membranous linings inside the body, including the so-called mucous membranes that are capable of secretion.

2 SCLEROUS or SKELETAL TISSUE refers to the dense tissues that provide the relatively rigid structure of the body. There are two subtypes, BONE, which is the most dense and rigid of all the tissues, and CARTILAGE, which also constitutes stiff supporting material but is more flexible than bone. Cartilage varies in its elasticity: the most flexible type (generally termed simply ELASTIC CARTILAGE) is not widely distributed through the body but is important in determining the structure and function of the larynx. Most other cartilage, as found in joints for example, is termed HYALINE CARTILAGE.

3 CONNECTIVE TISSUE is a rather loose category (which can be taken in a wider functional sense to include skeletal tissue). It includes adipose or fatty tissue and other tissues which are not particularly relevant in speech. Connective tissues which *are* relevant are the fibrous tissues that constitute TENDONS (which connect muscles to bones and are commonly known as 'sinews'),

LIGAMENTS (which connect bones or cartilages to each other) and APONEUROSES (flat sheets of fibrous tissue functioning in the same way as tendons).

4   MUSCULAR TISSUE consists of bundles of fibres. The significant characteristic of muscular tissue is that it can contract, either voluntarily or involuntarily.

5   NERVOUS TISSUE is composed of nerve cells and supporting tissue and is characteristically capable of carrying electrochemical impulses through the nervous system.

The organs of speech, no less than other parts of the body, depend on the nature and function of these tissues. In particular, movement of the speech organs depends on the intricate structure of the body, in which muscles are anchored and interconnected within the skeletal structure, and on the complex operation of these muscles under nervous stimulation. The next section deals with the nervous system and its role in muscular control.

6.3   The nervous system

The nervous system is usually considered to have two parts, the CENTRAL NERVOUS SYSTEM (CNS), consisting of the brain and the spinal medulla, and the PERIPHERAL NERVOUS SYSTEM (PNS), consisting of the nerves distributed through the body.

The CNS begins with the spinal cord in the vertebral column and its extension, the brain stem. Within the brain stem are located the nuclei of the cranial nerves (which are vital to speech production). Posterior to the top of the spinal cord is the CEREBELLUM or 'little brain', whose function is the precisely coordinated muscular control of movement. Above the brain stem are the two cerebral hemispheres, which are fundamentally responsible for complex functions such as speech and vision. Figure 6.3.1 shows this area in sagittal section.

From birth, human development shows increasing evidence that one of the two cerebral hemispheres is dominant in the functioning of spoken language (usually the left, even in left-handed persons). According to Lenneberg (1967) this process of hemispheric lateralization is essentially developmental, and largely complete by the time puberty is reached. More recently, it has been suggested that lateralization is present from birth, and that specific language-related hemispheric function is rather more complex and not primarily developmentally determined (Bryden 1982, Springer and Deutsch 1985). Investigation of the functioning of the brain in language is actually very difficult, and only limited conclusions can be drawn from case studies of persons who have suffered damage to the brain or who undergo brain surgery. In fact little is known about the ways in which the brain and its various neural structures actually initiate and control the complex and integrated activities of speech (see Lenneberg 1967, Kinsbourne 1980, Abbs and Welt 1985).

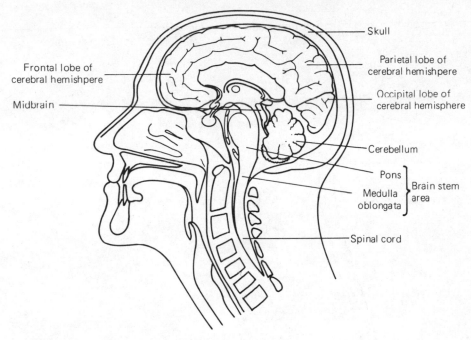

FIGURE 6.3.1   The central nervous system
Adapted from: Tribe and Eraut 1977, p. 4.

The PNS consists of three components: the CRANIAL NERVES, which arise from the brain stem and the head and neck area (much of which is involved in speech production), the SPINAL NERVES, which innervate the trunk and lungs, and the AUTONOMIC NERVOUS SYSTEM, which is responsible for involuntary activities such as blood flow and breathing.

The cranial nerves innervating the vocal tract consist of mixed nerves – that is, they contain both efferent (motor) fibres sending muscle control signals from the CNS, and afferent (sensory) fibres sending information to the CNS from receptors in the skin, mucosa and muscles.

The functional unit of the CNS is the NEURON, which consists of a nerve cell and its nerve fibre extensions (or processes). Figure 6.3.2 shows a motor neuron, consisting of a cell body, the axon (a nerve fibre which conducts impulses to muscles, as shown here, or to other nerves) and dendrites (which are similar to axons but are shorter and may conduct impulses to the neuron). On the cell body and dendrites are connecting points or SYNAPSES, which allow connections with other neurons. Hence the nervous system consists of a complex interconnecting network of neural pathways which can conduct nerve impulses. Muscle commands initiated in the CNS do not travel to their destination via single nerve cells. Rather, they may pass across many synaptic junctions with nearby cells interacting with and modifying the original command impulse before it reaches the muscle.

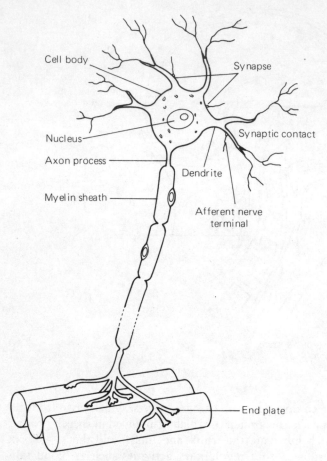

FIGURE 6.3.2   Motor neuron
Adapted from: Tribe and Eraut 1977, p. 109.

Neural signals travelling along nerve fibres take the form of short impulses of electrochemical energy caused by the firing of the associated nerve cell. The magnitude of nerve activity is determined not by the strength or amplitude of the pulse but by the number of pulses per unit of time travelling down the axon. A nerve cell can fire only if the impulse energy arriving at one or more of its synapses is above a threshold level. Beyond that level any increase will have no further effect. This 'all-or-none' principle is reflected in the behaviour of muscle fibre.

After a cell has fired there is a short refractory period (typically 0.5 ms) when no further firing can occur. Firing may require several impulses at a synapse, and there are also inhibitory synapses which can inhibit cell excitation. Thus both summation and inhibition of impulses contribute to the complex and selective control of muscles. The cranial nerves for muscle control in speech are listed in table 6.3.1.

Table 6.3.1 Cranial nerves for muscle control in speech

Number and name of nerve		Function	Latency
V	Trigeminal nerve	Jaw	Short
VII	Facial nerve	Lips	Short
X	Recurrent laryngeal nerve	Larynx	Long
XI	Accessory nerve	Pharynx	Short
XII	Hypoglossal nerve	Tongue	Short

Two types of muscle occur in the body: striated (striped) muscle which is capable of rapid contraction under voluntary control, and smooth muscle, capable of involuntary contraction (as found in the blood supply system). Only the first of these is of concern in speech production.

Voluntary muscle is made up of bundles of fibres from 10 to 100 microns in diameter and up to 10 cm long. The main fibres are termed EXTRAFUSAL and a smaller group of fibres (which are separately innervated) termed INTRAFUSAL fibres. Figure 6.3.3 shows typical muscle fibre arrangements. As previously noted, muscle fibre contraction is controlled by impulses from motor neurons, and these are supplied to the muscle fibres by connections at regions called motor end plates. The extrafusal fibres are supplied via large myelinated (alpha) nerve fibres and some smaller (gamma) fibres. The latter also contribute to innervation of intrafusal muscle fibres.

When a nerve impulse arrives at a motor end plate, a complex electrochemical action occurs at the neuromuscular junction, and an action potential, in the form of a

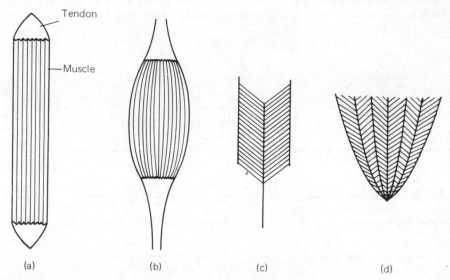

FIGURE 6.3.3 Muscle fibre patterns: (a) strap; (b) fusiform; (c) bipennate; (d) multipennate
Adapted from: Tribe and Eraut 1977, p. 107.

wave of depolarization, moves along the outer sheath (the sarcolemma) of the fibre, causing it to contract or twitch once only, about 2 ms after the arrival of the nerve impulse. The resting potential of the outer sheath is −70 mV with a depolarization spike of +30 mV, as shown in figure 6.3.4. To reach maximum contraction, a fibre will usually require several such stimuli. Thus to remain shortened or tensed, a muscle must receive repeated stimulation from nerve impulses. Such sustained shortening is known as TETANIC contraction.

It is the inner structure of muscle fibres that allows them to contract. A fibre consists of thin threads called MYOFIBRILS which in turn are composed of units called SARCOMERES (which are responsible for the striated appearance of voluntary muscle). Within these are fine MYOFILAMENTS which slide between each other to cause fibre contraction, their actual length remaining unchanged (Huxley 1958, Tribe and Eraut 1977, Mill 1982).

Muscle activity is of three basic types:

- ISOTONIC contraction, or the dynamic shortening of muscles;
- ISOMETRIC tension, or increased tension, without shortening; and
- LENGTHENING, where an opposing force is greater than the muscle's active contraction force.

The overall control of muscle can be considered in terms of MOTOR UNITS. Each unit consists of a nerve cell (motor neuron), its axon, and the muscle fibres controlled by the branches of the axon (figure 6.3.2 above). A single impulse in the axon will thus reach all the motor end plates, causing the associated fibres to contract simultaneously. The number of muscle fibres in a motor unit (the INNERVATION RATIO) varies from muscle to muscle, depending on their roles. Muscles involved in delicate movement, such as eye muscles or intrinsic tongue muscles, have low innervation ratios

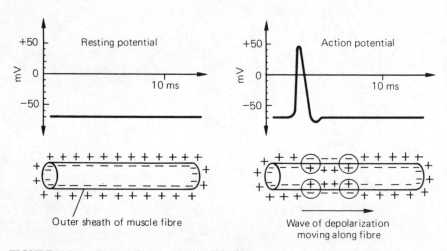

FIGURE 6.3.4   Potentials across a muscle fibre
Adapted from: Tribe and Eraut 1977, p. 53.

(less than 1 to 10). Muscles involved in larger and less precise forms of movement, such as limb muscles, may have much higher innervation ratios (up to 1 to 700). The degree of contraction or tension is determined by the rate of firing of motor units and the number of units firing. The 'all-or-none' principle of contraction is determined by the nerve impulses themselves rather than by the contractile properties of the muscle structure.

So far we have been considering the efferent or motor component of the nervous system. The afferent, or sensory aspect, of the nervous system is also vital to speech production, sending back information from various parts of the vocal tract to the CNS and thereby contributing to appropriate control of the various articulators and their movements. This is one form of the general process known as FEEDBACK.

Most of the sensory receptors for speech are found in the oral and respiratory areas. There are also receptors in the muscles and joints which respond to their movement (muscle spindles and joint receptors). Primary afferent endings in the muscle spindle (at the intrafusal fibres) respond to the degree and rate of stretch of the muscle spindle. These afferent neurons make direct synaptic connections with motor neurons in the same muscle, and thus cause the main extrafusal fibres to contract. This is known as STRETCH REFLEX. It has been suggested that stretch reflex contributes to muscular control in speech (in conjunction with direct efferent control to both the main muscle fibres and the muscle spindle itself).

The continuous sensory feedback which is needed for coordination of articulatory movement in speech can be divided into three kinds of feedback:

- AUDITORY (by hearing the consequences of an articulation);
- TACTILE (by the feel or touch of the articulators); and
- PROPRIOCEPTIVE (by signals from the muscle spindles and joint receptors which provide information on joint movement and position, and muscle contraction).

Researchers are investigating the question of which feedback is primary, but there appears to be no simple answer. From what happens when a speaker is deprived of feedback, it appears that each of the three types of feedback is related to different aspects of speech control. The relationship is more or less what one would expect from the nature of the feedback. Thus when tactile feedback from the tongue is suppressed, sounds such as [iː] and [s] are inadequately articulated, whereas when auditory feedback is interfered with, it is the overall intensity and pitch of speech that is affected, and so on. Normal feedback mechanisms are clearly important, both in the development of articulatory motor skills in childhood and in the preservation of these skills in adulthood. This is sadly evident in the development of children who are born profoundly deaf: without adequate auditory feedback, these children have great difficulty in acquiring fluent and intelligible speech. Feedback is thus crucial to the acquisition of spoken language (Borden 1980; see also Borden and Harris 1980, MacNeilage 1981, Clark and Palethorpe 1982, and Lieberman and Blumstein 1988 for further details of feedback processes in speech).

More extensive general accounts of the anatomical and physiological principles of speech production can be found in Hardcastle (1976), Daniloff et al. (1980), Zemlin (1981), Dickson and Dickson (1982) and Perkins and Kent (1986); and more detailed information on nerve and muscle mechanisms can be found in Mann (1981) and Ottoson (1983).

6.4   The respiratory system

We begin our detailed examination of the vocal tract with the subglottal respiratory system. The respiratory cycle not only provides the major source of airflow for speech sound sources, but is also important in the sequential organization of speech. For this reason, most accounts of the articulatory processes of speech begin with a categorization of the so-called AIRSTREAM MECHANISMS which provide the sources of energy in the production of speech sounds (2.5).

The respiratory system (aside from the upper airways in the supraglottal vocal tract) is contained within the chest, or THORAX. It consists of the barrel-shaped rib structure which forms the sides of the thoracic cage itself, the associated muscles, and the lung structure contained within it. There are 12 (paired) ribs, roughly U-shaped, flexibly attached posteriorly to the VERTEBRAL COLUMN, and anteriorly to the breast-bone, or STERNUM, by muscle and connective tissue. (But the two lowermost ribs have no anterior attachments.) The upper limit of the thoracic cage is formed posteriorly by the shoulder blades, or SCAPULAE, and anteriorly by the collar bones, or CLAVICLES. The floor of the cage is formed by the dome-shaped DIAPHRAGM muscle (unpaired). In conjunction with the rib cage, the movement of the diaphragm plays an essential role in the respiratory cycle. Figure 6.4.1 shows the general structure of the thorax.

Within the thoracic cavity are the lungs, which provide the reservoir for airflow in much of speech. In the process of inspiration and expiration in the normal respiratory cycle, they perform the vital function of replenishing oxygen and removing unwanted carbon dioxide from the blood. They consist of soft spongy material which is roughly cone-shaped, with the base resting on the diaphragm and the peak reaching towards the base of the neck. The lungs are connected to the windpipe, or TRACHEA, by two bronchial tubes which join at the base of the trachea. Within each lung the bronchial tubes divide into smaller and smaller tubes, or BRONCHIOLES, which distribute the air supply throughout the lung. These end in tiny air sacs, or ALVEOLI, which make up the bulk of elastic or spongy tissue in the lung structure. Figure 6.4.2 shows the general arrangement of the lungs, bronchial tubes and trachea. The two lungs actually form a single mechanical unit, for they are connected by the PLEURAL LINKAGE, an interface of fluid between the outer lining of the lungs and the inner lining of the thoracic cage. It is through this linkage that changes in the thoracic cavity volume cause changes in lung volume during the respiratory cycle. Since the lungs tend naturally to contract and the thorax to expand (when

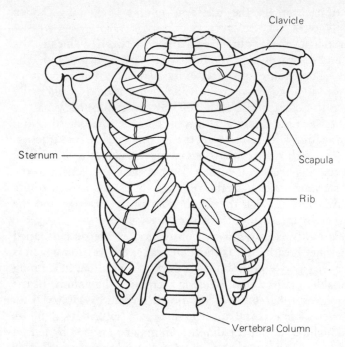

FIGURE 6.4.1   Structure of the thorax
Adapted from: Zemlin 1968, p. 60.

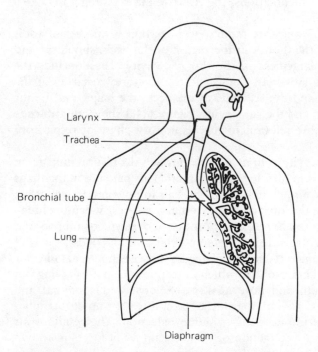

FIGURE 6.4.2   Lungs, bronchial tubes and trachea: general arrangement
Adapted from: Minifie, Hixon and Williams 1973, p. 78.

considered independently of each other), the quiescent volume of the lung–thorax system is the result of a balance of forces.

During inspiration, the thoracic cavity volume is enlarged by two basic means: the rib cage is lifted upwards and outwards, and the floor of the cavity is lowered. The balance between the two is a function of posture, individual habit and respiratory demands. Direct control of rib cage movement during inhalation is principally effected by the EXTERNAL INTERCOSTAL muscles which fill the spaces between the ribs. They are connected between the upper and lower edges of adjacent ribs, and as a group run upward and outward relative to the sternum. Their contraction shortens the distance between each rib causing the rib cage structure to be raised. Because of the U-shape of the ribs and the flexible nature of their attachment to the vertebral column and the sternum, raising of the rib cage causes the ribs to rotate relative to their posterior attachment, such that both sides of the rib cage and the sternum move outwards, thereby increasing thoracic cavity volume.

The floor of the thoracic cavity is lowered by contraction of the dome-shaped diaphragm muscle. During quiet breathing it is this diaphragm contraction which is largely responsible for thoracic cavity volume changes during inspiration. In running speech the diaphragm probably retains a major role in increasing the volume of the thoracic cavity during inspiratory phases. Investigations described by Hixon et al. (1977) suggest that the external intercostal muscles may not contribute quite as much as was previously thought, and that the diaphragm may be assisted by tensed abdominal musculature, which optimizes the effect of the diaphragm on thoracic cavity volume by allowing it to work against a taut abdominal wall. These investigations also suggest that under such conditions, the effort of the diaphragm may also contribute to rib cage movement.

In very deep inspiration, as during extreme physical exertion, a number of additional muscles associated with the thorax in the region of the back, shoulders and neck also contribute to the enlargement of the thoracic cavity. These include the serratus posterior superior, the latissimus dorsi, and the levatores costarum in the back, the sternocleidomastoid and the scalenus in the neck, the major and minor pectorals, the anterior serratus, and the subclavius. Figure 6.4.3 shows the rib cage and some of the muscle structure relevant to the inspiratory phase of respiratory activity.

Enlargement of the thoracic cavity volume results, through the pleural linkage, in an increase in lung volume. This in turn lowers the internal air pressure in the lungs relative to external atmospheric air pressure and allows air to flow into the lungs via the nose and mouth to equalize the internal and external pressures. When the lung–thorax system is enlarged, the resultant expansion and movement of muscle and other tissue in the lung–thorax structure also sets up ELASTIC RECOIL FORCES.

For expiration, the lung volume is reduced, causing an increase in internal lung air pressure relative to the external atmosphere, which in turn results in air flowing out of the lungs through the mouth and nose airways to equalize the internal and external pressures. In normal exhalation, the elastic recoil forces set up during inhalation are sufficient to achieve the necessary volume reduction. The resultant air pressure produced in the lungs by the action of these elastic recoil forces is known

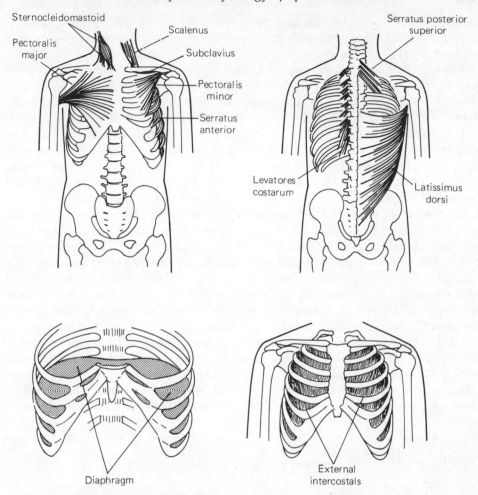

Sternocleidomastoid

Pectoralis major

Scalenus

Subclavius

Pectoralis minor

Serratus anterior

Serratus posterior superior

Levatores costarum

Latissimus dorsi

Diaphragm

External intercostals

FIGURE 6.4.3   Muscles used in inspiration
Adapted from: Minifie, Hixon and Williams 1973, pp. 84, 86, 87.

as RELAXATION PRESSURE. Research into respiratory behaviour during speech described by Ladefoged (1967, although carried out about a decade earlier) has shown that for an appreciable part of the expiratory phase, relaxation pressure produced by the elastic recoil forces is rather greater than required for normal conversational speech. As a result, muscles primarily associated with inspiratory activity, particularly the external intercostals, are used to resist the effects of the elastic recoil forces, until relaxation pressure has lowered to the appropriate level for speech. Hixon (1973) and Hixon et al. (1977) suggest that the effectiveness of the external intercostals in lowering the rib cage to offset excess relaxation pressure is optimized by abdominal forces pulling downwards on the undersurface of the diaphragm. Otherwise, the diaphragm would have a greater tendency to be pulled upwards when relaxed in the expiratory phase. This would decrease thoracic volume and, as a consequence, reduce the effectiveness of rib cage control in offsetting the effects of relaxation pressure.

When relaxation pressure can no longer satisfy the aerodynamic demands of speech production, the true muscles of expiration provide the necessary forces to continue reducing lung volume and thereby maintain the required air pressure in the lungs.

The principal muscles which compress the lung–thorax system and therefore reduce its volume are located in the region of the thorax and the abdomen. Certain back muscles also assist under conditions of extreme expiration, such as when shouting, or in producing extremely long continuous utterances, but do not normally make a significant contribution. The principal thoracic muscles involved in exhalation are: the internal intercostals (which lie in the spaces between the ribs approximately at right angles to, and below, the external intercostals); the subcostals; and the transverse thoracic. All of these function to pull the rib cage downwards. The abdominal muscles used in exhalation are: the transverse abdominal; the internal oblique; the external oblique; and the rectus abdominis. All of these function to compress the abdomen, causing upward pressure on the lung–thorax system; in some cases they also assist in compression of the rib cage. Figure 6.4.4 shows some of the muscle structure concerned with exhalation.

The level of respiratory activity required in speech production is greater than in normal quiet breathing, but will vary with the degree of overall vocal effort used. Stetson (1951) proposed that the muscular activity of respiration was to some extent related to the syllabic organization of speech. He claimed that each syllable had an associated 'ballistic chest pulse' initiated by the internal intercostal muscles, but data

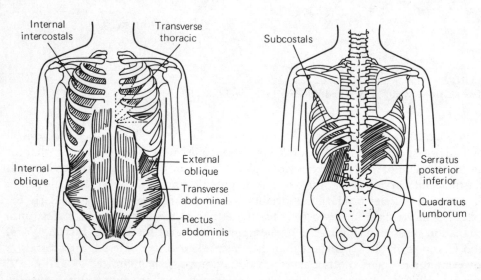

FIGURE 6.4.4   Muscles used in expiration
Adapted from: Minifie, Hixon and Williams 1973, pp. 91, 92

from physiological experiments (Ladefoged 1967) seem not to support the claim. The general tendency during speech is for the respiratory system musculature to maintain a relatively consistent level of pressure below the glottis, known as SUBGLOTTAL PRESSURE (Psg). Psg is relative to the overall level of vocal effort being employed at the time. Rises in Psg tend to occur on strongly stressed syllables, and falls are often associated with sudden reductions in resistance to airflow at the glottis, as occur in voiceless fricatives. But such changes rarely amount to more than 20 per cent of the average value of Psg. When rapid compensatory activity is required of the respiratory musculature – because of short-term changes in Psg requirements or because of air-flow resistance – it appears to be supplied largely by the action of the intercostal muscles, with some contribution from abdominal muscles (Sears and Newsom-Davis 1968, Bouhuys 1974). Fine control of respiratory muscle function in speech is not completely understood, but the available evidence suggests that the role of the diaphragm is not as great as some traditional accounts suggest.

Respiratory capacities vary with posture and bodily size, with a typical TOTAL LUNG CAPACITY in a male adult being 5–7 litres. The maximum volume of air that may be exhaled following maximum inspiration is known as the VITAL CAPACITY; it ranges from about 3.5 to 5 litres. In normal quiet breathing approximately 0.5 litres is inspired and expired. This is known as the QUIET TIDAL VOLUME, representing about 10–15 per cent of vital capacity. During speech, demands on respiratory capacity are somewhat greater, with actual tidal volume depending on the overall degree of vocal effort involved and, to some extent, on the durational demands of the particular utterance. Normal quiet breathing and speech operate in the lower midrange of vital capacity, with minimum respiratory volumes of 30–40 per cent of vital capacity at the end of the exhalation phase. (The figure applies to a speaker standing up and may be slightly different in other postures.) The tidal peak at the end of the inspiratory phase may range from around 45 per cent of vital capacity in quiet breathing to 80 per cent of vital capacity in loud speech. Figure 6.4.5 illustrates typical use of respiratory capacity during quiet breathing and speech.

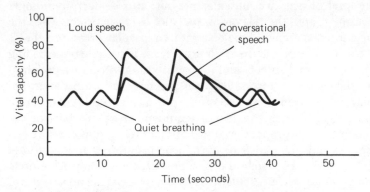

FIGURE 6.4.5   Respiratory volumes and normal breathing patterns in speech and quiet breathing
Adapted from: Minifie, Hixon and Williams 1973, p. 115.

The aerodynamic demands of speech on the respiratory system vary according to the type of articulation involved, overall vocal effort, and the habits of the individual speaker. Psg provides a measure of the overall articulatory effort being used in a sequence of speech and therefore varies widely between quiet talking and very loud shouting. The perceived loudness of speech is proportional to Psg but in a nonlinear way: it follows a power function law which shows appreciable variability (Isshiki 1964, Ladefoged 1967). In normal conversational speech during phonation (with vocal folds vibrating for voiced sounds) Psg will be in the region of 4–8 cm H_2O, with a minimum differential pressure drop of around 4 cm H_2O needed to initiate vocal fold vibration for voiced sounds (Baken 1987). Airflow rate, while also affected by the general level of vocal effort, varies much more directly according to changes in the resistance to glottal and supraglottal vocal tract airflow caused by individual articulatory configurations. Investigations by Isshiki and Ringel (1964), van Hattum and Worth (1967), Klatt et al. (1968), Gilbert (1973), Clark et al. (1982), Stathopoulos and Weismer (1985) and others, suggest that typical flow rates during normal phonation are in the region of 100–200 cm^3 per second for vowels, 200–600 cm^3 per second for voiceless fricatives with the glottis open, and transiently up to 1 litre per second or more at the release of voiceless aspirated stops. Airflow figures of the kind quoted are measured at the lips and nostrils and represent total airflow through the vocal tract (predominantly but not exclusively through the oral cavity).

Some of the basic relationships between respiratory forces and aerodynamic performance are shown in figure 6.4.6, which illustrates the roles of muscular pressure and relaxation pressure in meeting the demands of Psg during a simple sustained vowel sound over most of the range of vital capacity. At point *a* on the graph, which represents the start of expiration after deep inspiration, the positive value of Psg produced by relaxation pressure far exceeds the requirements of the articulation: muscular forces need to work against the excessive relaxation pressure, to bring the net value back to that required for the level of articulatory effort being used. As the available air supply diminishes, the lung volume is reduced, and the relaxation pressure falls; and the level of negative muscular pressure can be correspondingly reduced. At point *b* on the graph, the relaxation pressure curve intersects with the constant Psg value for normal speech and the respiratory muscular pressure value is zero. Relaxation pressure at this point in the expiratory phase is capable of providing the necessary Psg value for normal speech, and no contribution, offsetting or otherwise, is required from the muscular forces. Between points *b* and *c* on the graph, there is a positive contribution from both relaxation pressure and muscular forces since the former is no longer able to supply Psg requirements in this part of the expiratory phase. At point *c* on the graph, the contribution of relaxation pressure has fallen to zero and Psg demands are satisfied by the true inspiratory muscle forces acting to compress the lung–thorax system. Beyond point *c*, the respiratory muscle forces must supply more pressure than is actually required, to offset the now negative effects of relaxation pressure resulting from the compression of the lung–thorax tissue. As can be seen, the negative effects of relaxation pressure become quite large as the expiratory phase approaches zero vital capacity, demanding substantial

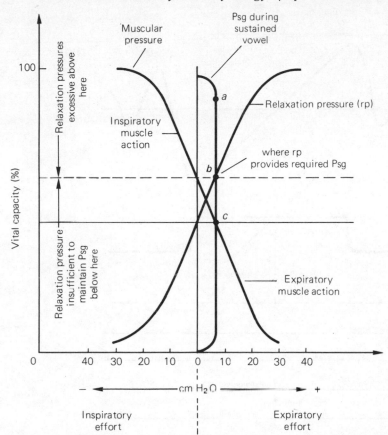

FIGURE 6.4.6   Respiratory forces producing constant Psg

counter-forces. For this reason, speech does not exploit this part of the expiratory phase except under extreme conditions such as prolonged shouting.

How the data of figure 6.4.6 relate to the relevant muscle functions can be studied in figure 6.4.7, which is derived from work by Ladefoged and his colleagues. Here, lung volume, Psg, relaxation pressure, and measurements of muscle activity are plotted on a common time scale. It can be seen that at the point where the relaxation pressure curve intersects with the value of Psg, there is a changeover of muscle activity from the inspiratory external intercostals to a number of true expiratory muscles. The data were obtained from a subject counting from 1 to 32 at a reasonably constant level of loudness. Ladefoged and his colleagues are careful to point out that the data come from a single subject and that individuals vary in the way they use their respiratory musculature during speech.

Extensive discussion of respiratory function and the aerodynamics of speech can be found in Hixon (1973, 1987), Warren (1976) and Weismer (1985). Baken (1987) provides a comprehensive literature review, and a detailed account of methods of measurement.

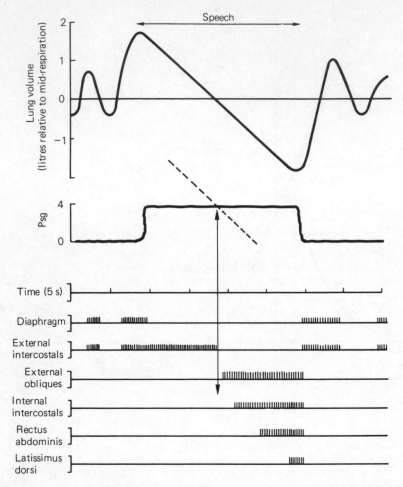

FIGURE 6.4.7   Respiration and associated muscle activity during speech
Adapted from: Ladefoged 1967, p. 12

6.5   The larynx

The basic function of the larynx is as a valve in the respiratory system. Thus in the process of swallowing, the larynx is automatically shut to ensure that food or drink pass through the pharyngeal cavity into the esophagus and not into the windpipe. We all know the uncomfortable results when this process fails. The valve action of the larynx is also important in short-term physical exertion as a means of stiffening the thorax when we inhale deeply and hold our breath. In speech, the larynx is important as a source of sound and as an articulator.

The larynx connects to the lungs via the windpipe or TRACHEA, which consists of a series of roughly horseshoe-shaped cartilaginous sections held together by membranous tissue. It is typically around 11 cm long and 2.5 cm in diameter. The larynx has a skeletal frame formed by a series of cartilages (figure 6.5.1). Some of these cartilages are able to move with respect to each other in ways which affect both the larynx's valving action and its functions in speech production. Figure 6.5.2(a) shows a lateral view of the CRICOID and THYROID cartilages which make up the major part of the cartilaginous laryngeal structure. The cricoid cartilage forms the base of the larynx, and is also the last cartilaginous section of the trachea. It is a complete ring whereas those below it are completed by flexible connective tissue. The cricoid cartilage extends upwards posteriorly to form a plate, or lamina, while anteriorly it is comparable in height to the other tracheal rings. The thyroid cartilage consists of two flat plates forming an angle anteriorly which, among other things, acts as a shield for the vocal folds. The THYROID ANGLE is about 90° in males and about 120° in females. Because the angle is more acute in males, the protrusion can often be seen and felt as the 'Adam's apple'. Posteriorly each plate of the thyroid cartilage has two horns, or CORNUA. The inferior horns form a joint with the cricoid cartilage on its posterior lateral part at matching facets on the two cartilages. This allows the cricoid to tilt over a range of about 15° in an anterior–posterior sense with respect to the thyroid cartilage. The tilting motion plays an important role in controlling vocal fold tension. The superior horns connect to the hyoid bone, which provides the upper suspension of the larynx by muscle connection to the main skeleton structure.

The other important cartilages in the larynx are the small pair of ARYTENOIDS located on the upper posterior lateral part of the cricoid cartilage. The arytenoids move with respect to the cricoid in a rotational and sliding motion which controls

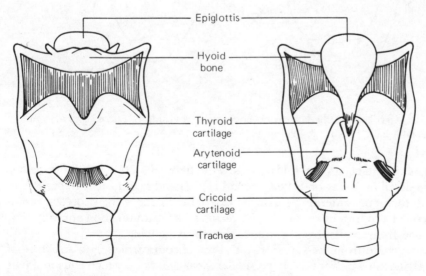

FIGURE 6.5.1   The larynx: anterior and posterior views

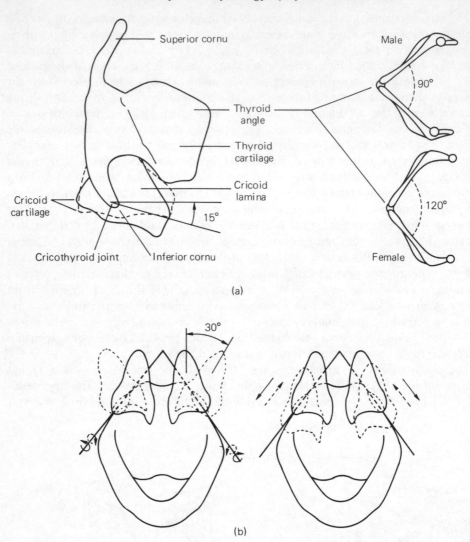

FIGURE 6.5.2   Cartilages of the larynx: (a) cricoid and thyroid; (b) cricoid and arytenoid
Adapted from: (a) Minifie, Hixon and Williams 1973, pp. 130, 133; (b) Sonesson 1968, p. 53.

positioning of the attached vocal folds, as shown in figure 6.5.2(b). This movement is described in detail by Sonesson (1968), Broad (1973) and Perkins and Kent (1986).

Hinged to the upper anterior part of the thyroid cartilage is the EPIGLOTTIS, commonly described as a leaf- or spoon-shaped cartilage. Its main function appears to be to deflect food from the laryngeal entrance during swallowing.

Extending upward from the superior rim of the cricoid cartilage is a structure of ligamental tissue known, from its shape, as the CONUS ELASTICUS, which ends in a pair of thickened edges called the VOCAL LIGAMENTS. These form part of the VOCAL FOLDS proper (sometimes a little misleadingly called 'vocal cords'). The folds are roughly triangular in cross-section and they include the upper part of the conus elasticus, the vocalis muscle, and the mucous membrane lining in the laryngeal airway. The vocal folds run from the inferior edge of the thyroid angle to the anterior part of the arytenoid cartilages. The arytenoid cartilages and the vocal folds together form the long slit-like laryngeal valve aperture known as the GLOTTIS. The edges of the glottis (i.e. the length of the vocal folds) are typically about 17 to 22 mm long in males and about 11 to 16 mm long in females. At birth, the length is around 3 mm, and there is no developmental difference between the sexes below the age of 10. Differences in length do appear after 10 years, although there appears to be little evidence that there is any rapid change in the length of the folds accompanying the change in voice pitch in males around puberty. In adults the length of the membranous portion is from four to six times that of the cartilaginous portion; in children the ratio is much lower.

The anatomy of the vocal folds has been well studied, with a view to understanding the behaviour of the folds during speech. The folds are now generally described in terms of cover and body components. These components have distinctive mechanical properties and to some extent move independently of each other; and they may respond differently to the same muscular forces. The general structure of the vocal folds and the glottis is shown in the anterior view and coronal section of the larynx in figure 6.5.3. Hirano et al. (1981) and Kurita et al. (1983) give detailed descriptions of vocal fold structure.

Above the vocal folds is a similar structure known as the FALSE VOCAL CORDS or VENTRICULAR FOLDS (figure 6.5.3(a)). These make no significant contribution to normal vocal fold vibration as such, but they may help lubricate the true folds during

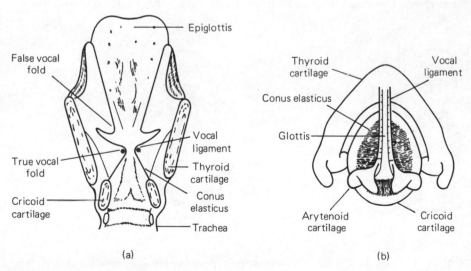

FIGURE 6.5.3   Vocal fold structure: (a) anterior view; (b) coronal section
Adapted from: (a) Zemlin 1968, p. 131; (b) Minifie, Hixon and Williams 1973, p. 137.

phonation, and may assist the glottal valve action when holding high pulmonary (subglottal) pressures.

The various functions of the larynx – valving and phonatory and articulatory activity – depend on a quite complex muscle system. Functionally the muscles fall into two groups, the INTRINSIC laryngeal muscles, which have their attachments within the larynx and are concerned with the control of vocal fold behaviour, and the EXTRINSIC muscles, which are largely concerned with overall movement of the larynx itself.

The intrinsic muscles control the ABDUCTION (opening), ADDUCTION (closing), and TENSIONING of the vocal folds. The posterior CRICOARYTENOID muscle runs from the posterior lamina of the cricoid cartilage to the posterior part of the arytenoid cartilages. When contracted, it pulls the arytenoids back and downwards while at the same time causing them to rotate, thus abducting the vocal folds and opening the glottis. This action is illustrated in figure 6.5.4. Under normal conditions of speaking and breathing it is the only muscle responsible for vocal fold abduction, and it is therefore most active during the inspiratory phase of respiration and during the production of voiceless speech sounds.

The LATERAL CRICOARYTENOID and the INTERARYTENOID (or transverse arytenoid) muscles (unpaired) are the principal ones controlling adduction of the vocal folds. The lateral cricoarytenoid muscle runs from the anterior lateral part of the cricoid cartilage to the lateral part of the arytenoid cartilages; it pulls the arytenoids forward and rotates them, thus contributing to vocal fold adduction and overall vocal fold stiffening. The interarytenoid muscle contributes to fold adduction by pulling the arytenoids together, and it tends to reduce vocal fold tension slightly. The actions of both these muscles are shown in figure 6.5.5.

Vocal fold tension, which is important in phonation, is controlled by the THYROARYTENOID, VOCALIS and CRICOTHYROID muscles. The thyroarytenoid muscle

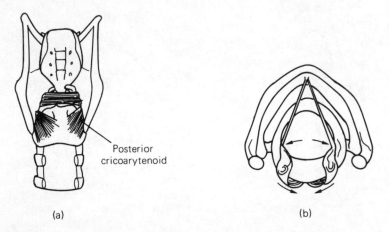

(a)   (b)

FIGURE 6.5.4   Posterior cricoarytenoid muscle: (a) posterior view; (b) superior view showing action
Adapted from: Schneiderman 1984, p. 70.

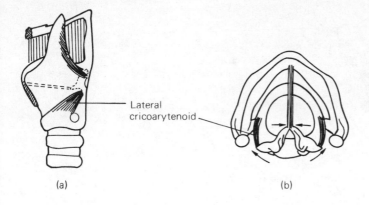

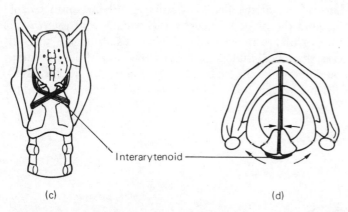

FIGURE 6.5.5 Lateral cricoarytenoid and interarytenoid muscles: (a) lateral view; (b) superior view showing action; (c) posterior view; (d) superior view showing action *Adapted from*: Schneiderman 1984, p. 72.

runs from the inner part of the thyroid angle to the anterior and lateral surfaces of the arytenoids. Although its exact function in speech production is not fully understood, the muscle appears to shorten and reduce tension in the vocal folds by pulling the arytenoids forward, thus acting as an antagonist to the cricothyroid muscle; but it may also support the action of the vocalis muscle in maintaining tension in the folds. The vocalis muscle, which is sometimes considered simply as a medial component of the thyroarytenoid muscle, runs parallel to the vocal ligaments as part of the vocal fold structure proper. Its function is in general to control tension in the vocal folds, and although the exact nature of this control during speech is still a matter of debate, it appears to stiffen the body while slackening the cover of the folds. The vocalis is generally thought to contribute to quite fine tension control, and possibly to shortening of the vocal folds. Figure 6.5.6 shows a superior view of the muscles.

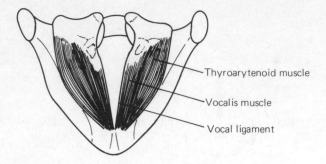

FIGURE 6.5.6   Vocalis and thyroarytenoid muscles
Adapted from: Zemlin 1968, p. 149.

The cricothyroid muscle runs between the anterior lateral part of the cricoid cartilage and the lower lateral part of the thyroid cartilage. When contracted, it tilts the cricoid cartilage around the pivot formed by the cricothyroid joint, with the result that the arytenoid cartilages move away (backwards) from the thyroid cartilage. This action lowers, stretches, thins and stiffens the vocal fold structure, increasing both the length and tension of the folds. The tilting action of the cartilages can be seen in figure 6.5.2(b) above; figure 6.5.7 shows the same action in relation to

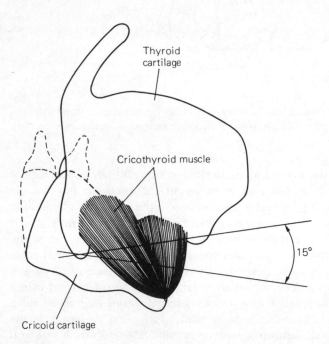

FIGURE 6.5.7   Cricothyroid muscle: vocal fold tension control
Adapted from: Minifie, Hixon and Williams 1973, p. 158.

the cricothyroid muscle. For an overview of the role of the intrinsic laryngeal muscles, see Hirano and Kakita (1985).

The extrinsic laryngeal muscles control overall movement and positioning of the larynx, and may be divided into two groups, INFRAHYOIDAL and SUPRAHYOIDAL; the former contribute to lowering the larynx and the latter to raising it. Larynx lowering is largely controlled by the STERNOHYOID, STERNOTHYROID, OMOHYOID and THYROHYOID muscles. The sternohyoid is a long strap muscle which runs from the upper posterior part of the breast-bone to the anterior part of the hyoid bone. Its contraction pulls the hyoid bone downwards and forwards, thus lowering the larynx. The sternothyroid muscle runs from the upper posterior part of the breast-bone to the lateral part of the thyroid cartilage. When contracted it pulls downwards on the thyroid cartilage, contributing to lowering of the larynx. The omohyoid muscle runs from the upper part of the shoulder blade to the lower part of the hyoid bone. When contracted it pulls downward on the hyoid bone and contributes to lowering the larynx. The thyrohyoid muscle runs from the thyroid cartilage to the hyoid bone, and when contracted may help to move both the hyoid bone and the thyroid cartilage, and to lower the larynx, depending on what other extrinsic laryngeal muscles are doing at the same time.

The muscles mainly responsible for raising the larynx are the DIGASTRICUS, GENIOHYOID, MYLOHYOID, STYLOHYOID and HYOGLOSSUS. The digastricus (literally 'two-bellied') is a long thin muscle having two components: the anterior component runs from the lower inner face of the jawbone to connective tissue attached to the hyoid bone, and the posterior part runs from the base of the skull to the same connective tissue. When both components are contracted, they will pull the hyoid bone, and hence the larynx, upwards. The geniohyoid muscle runs from the upper anterior part of the inner face of the jawbone to the anterior surface of the hyoid bone, and when contracted will pull the hyoid bone upwards and forwards (provided that the jawbone remains stable). The mylohyoid is a thin sheet of muscle which is part of the structure of the floor of the mouth. It runs from around the inner face of the jawbone via connective tissue to the hyoid bone and (among other functions) aids the action of the geniohyoid and other muscles in raising the larynx. The stylohyoid is a long thin muscle running between the base of the skull and the greater horns of the hyoid bone. When contracted it pulls the hyoid, and thus the larynx, upwards and backwards; its function is therefore similar to that of the posterior component of the digastricus. The hyoglossus (which also functions as a tongue muscle) may contribute to raising the larynx: when the tongue is stabilized by its own extrinsic musculature, the hyoglossus can pull the hyoid bone upwards. The extrinsic laryngeal muscles and the general direction of the laryngeal movements they control are shown in figure 6.5.8.

The extrinsic laryngeal musculature is responsible for positioning and stabilizing the larynx, with infrahyoidal muscles acting as antagonists to suprahyoidal. The potential movement of the larynx is mainly vertical, and up–down movement is important in the action of swallowing, as well as in airstream generation for certain sounds that do not use air from the lungs (2.5 above). In addition, specific positioning of the larynx can alter the shape and volume of the pharynx, and can indirectly

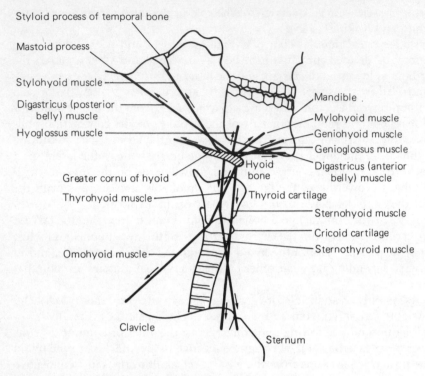

FIGURE 6.5.8   Laryngeal strap muscles and their actions
Adapted from: Hardcastle 1976, p. 68.

affect the tension of the vocal folds themselves. As a consequence, particular relatively stable settings of the larynx may contribute to voice quality both in speech and in singing.

6.6   Phonation

Phonation (vocal fold vibration, 2.6 above) is the single most important function of the larynx as a sound source, and the mechanics of phonation have been the object of scientific inquiry for over 250 years. The hypothesis that vocal fold vibration is directly controlled by neural impulses, known as the NEURO-CHRONAXIC theory, is given some credence in older works on phonetics, but the theory finds no support from neurophysiological evidence and in any case presumes a rapidity of muscular control which cannot be substantiated. The explanation of phonation that is now generally accepted is known as the AERODYNAMIC MYOELASTIC theory. This theory takes into account not only the effects of aerodynamic forces, muscle activity and tissue elasticity (van den Berg 1958, 1968), but also the mechanically complex nature of the vocal fold tissue structure (Broad 1979, Hirano and Kakita 1985).

In its simplest form, the aerodynamic myoelastic theory is as follows. When the glottis is closed (i.e. the vocal folds are adducted), expiratory airflow will build up pressure until the vocal folds are forced apart, allowing airflow through the slit of the glottis. Now when a gas or fluid flows through a narrow opening, it accelerates and its pressure drops; the phenomenon is known as the BERNOULLI EFFECT. Thus as air flows through the narrow glottis, the air pressure will be reduced. This in turn will mean that the vocal folds close again, as the pressure reduction sucks them together. The elasticity of the folds assists the entire process, as the folds will part under pressure but will tend to push back once they are apart. The actual opening and closing of the folds has been described as a rippling action: the folds open first at the bottom and the opening moves upward; then the folds close first at the top and the closure moves downward. The action is due to the combined effects of the aerodynamic forces and the flexible structure of the folds themselves, in which the cover and body components have some independence of movement. Figure 6.6.1 shows the vibratory cycle (including this effect) as revealed in X-ray studies.

The actual sound produced by the larynx during phonation is created not by the vibration itself, but by the periodic train of puffs of air emitted through the vibrating folds, generating a modulated stream of air. Figure 6.6.2(a) shows the nature of the airstream generated during normal phonation, in the form of what is known as a

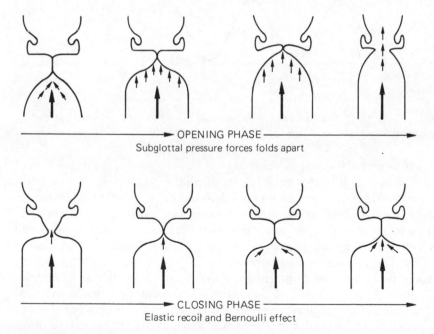

OPENING PHASE
Subglottal pressure forces folds apart

CLOSING PHASE
Elastic recoil and Bernoulli effect

FIGURE 6.6.1   Vibratory cycle of the vocal folds
Adapted from: Schneiderman 1984, p. 76.

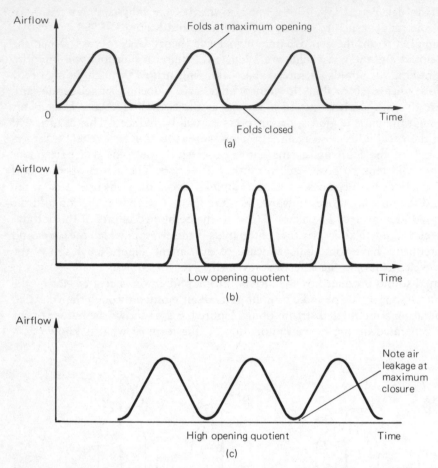

FIGURE 6.6.2   Phonation airflow waveform: (a) normal (modal) voice; (b) loud (bright) voice; (c) breathy voice

volume-velocity output waveform. (Details of such waveforms and the techniques of investigation will be found in chapter 7 below, especially 7.11.)

It is possible to distinguish three auditory dimensions or parameters of phonation: loudness, pitch, and a quality of sound that is sometimes called 'timbre'. Normally there is some interaction among the three. Perceived loudness is related to subglottal pressure (6.4 above). Pitch is the perceptual correlate of the frequency of vibration of the vocal folds. The frequency is determined by subglottal pressure (Psg) and by laryngeal adjustments governing the length, tension and mass of the vocal folds themselves. Although these control mechanisms do not normally function independently, the logarithm of the frequency of vibration is more or less proportional to Psg for a given laryngeal setting (Ladefoged 1967; see also Ohala 1970 for details of the relationship between frequency and Psg). As already noted, Psg tends to remain relatively constant during a sequence of speech, except for slight rises occurring on strongly stressed syllables. Since pitch contours do not generally follow such a simple pattern, it seems reasonable to suppose that laryngeal adjustments arc mainly responsible for controlling the frequency of vocal cord vibration in normal speech (Ohala 1978). On the other hand, Lieberman and Blumstein (1988) maintain that Psg is the primary determinant of frequency, continuing a view long held by Lieberman. It may well be that individual speakers vary in the way that they use laryngeal musculature in relation to Psg to control pitch, but the primacy of laryngeal control is widely accepted.

What we have called 'timbre', a quality of sound sometimes reflected in such impressions as the 'mellowness' or 'sharpness' of the voice, is largely determined by the mode of vocal fold vibration during phonation. A simple measure is the OPENING QUOTIENT, the proportion of each vibratory cycle during which the vocal folds are open. The opening quotient is thus the duration of glottal opening during one cycle, divided by the duration of the entire cycle. In normal speech the quotient is typically around 0.5 (see figures 6.6.1 and 6.6.2 above). With increasing loudness, the folds will be closed for longer periods and the opening quotient will fall below 0.5. The explanation for this is that an increase in Psg and in the force of the Bernoulli effect will cause the vocal folds to be forced further apart and pulled together again more rapidly. As the increased kinetic energy must be dissipated, the folds will remain closed longer during the vibratory cycle. The consequent 'sharpness' or 'brightness' of the tonal quality of the voice is due to the additional upper frequency acoustic energy generated by the very rapid changes in the volume-velocity of the airflow. The reverse occurs in soft speech with low vocal effort. Here the opening quotient may become greater than 0.5, giving a 'mellow' tonal quality. With even less vocal effort, the folds do not completely close, and there is some continuous airflow, causing the voice to become 'breathy'. While variation in voice almost always accompanies significant changes in loudness, the reverse is not necessarily true. It is possible to alter the quality without greatly altering the loudness of the voice, by trading Psg and the various muscle forces affecting laryngeal adjustments against each other. Figure 6.6.2 includes volume-velocity waveforms for high and low opening quotients. Finer phonatory distinctions are dealt with under the heading of MODES OF PHONATION (2.6 above); see also Lindqvist (1970) and Monsen (1981) for more examples of laryngeal waveforms under varying conditions of vocal effort, showing a variety of opening quotients.

Phonation is never perfectly regular in its periodicity, but (in normal voice) shows a small degree of random variation in both frequency and amplitude from cycle to cycle. Variation in frequency is known as JITTER and variation in amplitude as SHIMMER. These variations are not generally noticeable in the healthy adult voice, but both do increase with ageing, and if the variation is considerable, because of age or vocal or neurophysiological disorder, it may be perceived as a significant component of voice quality. For details, see Heiberger and Horii (1982); for methods of extracting, measuring and analysing laryngeal waveforms, see Baken (1987).

The complex nature of laryngeal control of phonation makes it hard to offer any brief and simple summary. As van den Berg puts it, 'the mean adjustment of the larynx depends mainly on the mean adjustment of the laryngeal muscles' and 'the number of adjustments is infinite' (1968, p. 296). Reviewing the research literature on laryngeal function and control, Ohala notes: 'there is thus much redundancy in the muscular system regulating pitch such that if one or two muscles are lost, the others can take over and pitch regulation is not thereby completely lost, although it may be drastically reduced in range' (1970, p. 19). It must also be recognized that information about laryngeal muscle function during speech is quite limited, because the electromyographic techniques of investigation are both invasive and technically demanding.

Most researchers agree that cricothyroid muscle activity correlates well with pitch control, predominantly in the raising of pitch (by tilting the cricoid cartilage backwards and thereby increasing tension on the vocal folds). At the same time, there may be some decrease in the effective mass of the vibrating part of the folds (due to tissue tension) which will augment this action. There is also an accompanying increase in the length of the folds which may offset the rise in pitch, but tension and its consequences are predominant. The vocalis muscle is also active during pitch rises, although the exact nature of its function is more controversial. It appears to contribute to tensioning and stiffening of the body of the folds; some researchers are of the opinion that it may be responsible for fine incremental control of pitch. The thyroarytenoid and lateral cricoarytenoid muscles also appear to contribute to pitch rises by medial compression of the folds, which may add to their stiffness; when the lateral cricoarytenoid functions as an adductor, it may reduce the effective length of the folds (i.e. reduce the length which is free to vibrate). Such shortening, with a concomitant reduction in effective vibrating mass, will also contribute to a rise in pitch. Other adductor muscles may also play a lesser role in this process. (See van den Berg 1968, Ohala 1970, 1978, Hirose and Gay 1972, Hardcastle 1976, Zemlin 1981 and Honda 1983.)

Although less well understood, pitch lowering is associated with reduced tension in the vocal folds; the vocalis and thyroarytenoid muscles may act as antagonists to the cricothyroid muscle to shorten and reduce vocal fold tension, thereby lowering the rate of vibration. The extrinsic laryngeal muscles also contribute to pitch control, but the relationships between their activity and pitch changes appear to be rather indirect (Sawashima 1974, Honda 1983). There is, however, evidence from Erikson et al. (1983) that infrahyoidal strap muscle activity may complement relaxation of the cricothyroid in pitch lowering. The positioning of the larynx (by extrinsic muscle forces acting on the external cartilaginous structure of the larynx) also has some indirect effect on vocal fold tension: in general, raising of the larynx is associated with raising of pitch, and larynx lowering with lowering of pitch.

The intrinsic laryngeal muscles also control the timing of laryngeal action relative to supraglottal articulatory activity. The posterior cricoarytenoid muscle, as already noted, is active in abduction of the vocal folds during voiceless sounds. During a voiced sound, it may anticipate the end of voicing by 20–30 ms, cutting off phonation by abduction of the vocal folds. It may also show some activity during voiced fricatives, indicating that the vocal folds are slightly abducted to create a mode of phonation with a higher rate of airflow. The transverse arytenoid muscle appears to function reciprocally with the posterior cricoarytenoid, and may prepare for phonation by adducting the vocal folds 40–50 ms before the start of voicing (Hirose and Gay 1972, Flanagan et al. 1976).

Beyond the normal or modal phonation we have considered so far, and particularly during singing, it is possible to extend pitch range by switching among distinct modes of control known as REGISTERS. Normal speech and the normal range of pitch control operate in CHEST REGISTER. Above the highest pitch which can be attained within chest register, it is possible to enter a higher pitch range by switching abruptly to FALSETTO REGISTER. One of the objectives of voice training for singing is to overcome the abruptness of this change and to control a transitional mode of pitch control known as MIDDLE VOICE REGISTER. According to van den Berg (1968), the pitch control and phonation characteristics of the three registers differ chiefly in tension adjustments in the vocal folds: he describes chest register as having relatively short, thick vocal folds and large amplitude vibrations, and falsetto register as having long, thin vocal folds and much smaller amplitude vibrations. It is difficult to make a smooth transition between registers because the vocal folds have to be considerably elongated and tensed for falsetto, and because the pitch ranges of the two registers may also overlap. To make the transition it is thus necessary to reset the laryngeal musculature. Broad (1973) likens this to shifting gears in a car to suit the speed required. Figure 6.6.3 illustrates the general state of the glottis during the inspiratory phase of respiration, whispered speech, and several phonation modes, including falsetto. Details of various aspects of pitch control and phonation mode can be found in van den Berg (1968), Sawashima (1974), Ohala (1978), Hollien (1983) and Lieberman and Blumstein (1988).

6.7   The pharynx

The pharynx is a tube of muscle shaped rather like an inverted cone. Typically around 12 cm long, it lies between the glottis and the base of the skull. It acts as an air passage for respiration, aids in the ingestion of food, and provides drainage for the nasal passages. It makes a passive contribution to speech production by forming part of the length of the supraglottal vocal tract, but its geometry and volume can also be adjusted to vary this contribution or for other articulatory effects. For descriptive purposes it is commonly divided into three functional areas, as shown in figure 6.7.1.

The lowest section is the LARYNGO-PHARYNX, bounded inferiorly by the glottis and superiorly by the hyoid bone (but some writers take the laryngo-pharynx to extend to the tip of the epiglottis). Because of the muscular linkages between the hyoid bone and the body of the tongue, tongue movement can change the diameter of the laryngo-pharynx quite considerably, particularly in a lateral direction. Up and down movement of the larynx also substantially alters the length (and hence volume) of the laryngo-pharynx.

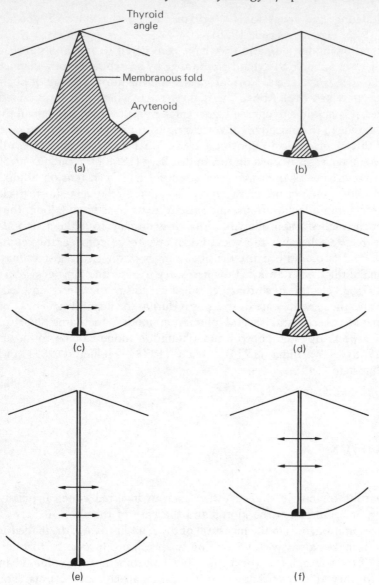

FIGURE 6.6.3   Glottal state in six common modes: (a) inspiration; (b) whisper; (c) normal phonation; (d) breathy voice; (e) falsetto; (f) creaky voice

The mid section is the ORO-PHARYNX, bounded inferiorly by the hyoid bone and superiorly by the soft palate. Since the anterior face of this section is formed by the back of the tongue and the upper part of the epiglottis, it also undergoes considerable changes in volume and geometry as the tongue moves. The diameter of the pharynx at the tip of the epiglottis, which has membranous links to the back of the tongue,

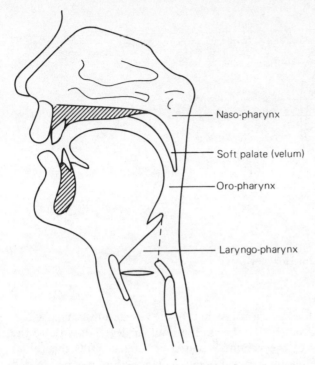

FIGURE 6.7.1   The pharynx

may vary from 20 mm or more during the articulation of front vowels (as in *heed* or *head*) to 5 or 6 mm during back vowels (as in *hoard*). Further details can be found in Zemlin (1981).

The upper section is the NASO-PHARYNX, bounded inferiorly by the soft palate and extending to the nasal passages. It can be sealed off from the lower sections of the pharynx by raising the soft palate (figure 6.7.1 above; and section 6.8 below).

6.8   The velum and the nasal cavity

The soft palate or VELUM is a continuation of the roof of the mouth, posterior to the bony structure of the hard palate. It consists of a flexible sheet of muscular tissue covered in mucous membrane ending at the UVULA, a small tip of muscle and flexible tissue. When raised, the velum serves to seal off the nasal cavity by closing the entrance to it, known as the VELOPHARYNGEAL PORT. Three classes of muscle are relevant to the velum and its functions: those which raise the velum, those which enhance velopharyngeal closure, and those which lower the velum. Figure 6.8.1 shows an anterior view of the velum and uvula through the oral cavity.

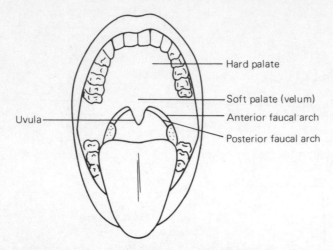

FIGURE 6.8.1   Oral vocal tract: anterior view
Adapted from: Zemlin 1968, p. 254.

The most important muscle for raising the velum is the LEVATOR PALATINE, which runs from the temporal bone at the base of the skull (about ear level) down into the medial part of the aponeurosis of the velum. When contracted it pulls the velum upward, tending to close off the velopharyngeal opening. This action may be assisted by the UVULAR MUSCLE which runs from the posterior part of the aponeurosis of the velum to the mucous membrane of the uvula. When contracted, the uvular muscle will shorten and raise the uvula.

Velopharyngeal closure can be enhanced by the PALATAL TENSOR. This muscle runs from the sphenoid bone at the skull base to connective tissue which passes around a projection of the same bone to insert into the aponeurosis at the sides of the velum. When contracted, the muscle serves to stretch the velum laterally, helping to press it against the oropharyngeal wall. In addition, the PALATOPHARYNGEAL SPHINCTER, a single muscle which runs around the pharyngeal wall, may further improve sealing of the velopharyngeal port by forming a bulge, known as 'Passavant's ridge', which presses against the velum. But not many speakers seem to exploit this mechanism in normal speaking, although it may contribute to the pharyngeal wall movement that occurs in some vowels.

The velum is lowered by the action of the PALATOGLOSSUS and PALATOPHARYNGEAL muscles. The palatoglossus, which also counts as an extrinsic tongue muscle, runs from the aponeurosis of the velum to the posterior lateral edges of the tongue. When contracted, it will pull the velum downwards if the tongue is steady. Conversely, it raises the tongue if the velum is stabilized. The palatopharyngeal muscle, which is posterior to the palatoglossus, runs from the inferior aspect of the aponeurosis of the velum to the pharyngeal walls in the area of the posterior part of the thyroid cartilage. When contracted with the larynx stabilized, it may contribute to pulling the velum downwards, and conversely may assist in raising the larynx if the velum is stable. These two muscles and their associated tissue form the ANTERIOR and POSTERIOR FAUCAL ARCHES, shown in figure 6.8.1 above. Figure 6.8.2 shows a sagittal section view of the velum and its associated muscle structure.

In the production of vowels, the velum may be raised to direct airflow through the oral cavity, in which case the vowel is said to be oral; or it may be lowered to allow air to flow out through the nasal cavity as well as through the oral cavity, in which case the vowel is said to be nasalized. In some languages, such as French and Portuguese, the difference is systematically exploited, so that some of the vowels are oral and some are nasalized. In other languages, such as English and German, there is no such distinction and all vowels are oral. But in oral vowels it is quite common for some flow to occur through the nasal cavity as well, because of incomplete velopharyngeal closure. This nasal flow may be due to persistent or anticipatory velum movement (because of neighbouring nasal consonants), or to the habitual articulatory patterns of the individual, or to the linkage between the velum and the tongue such as that formed by the palatoglossus muscle. According

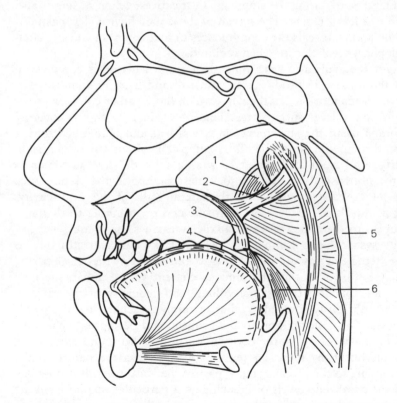

FIGURE 6.8.2 Supraglottal vocal tract showing soft palate musculature: 1 palatal tensor muscle; 2 levator palatine muscle; 3 uvular muscle; 4 palatoglossus muscle; 5 palatopharyngeal sphincter; 6 palatopharyngeal muscle
Adapted from: Zemlin 1968, p. 299.

to Moll and Shriner (1967), this linkage or 'mechanical coupling' could account for the fact that the velopharyngeal port tends to be more open during a vowel with low tongue position (as in *hard*) than during a vowel with a high tongue position (as in *heed*). But Lubker (1975) disagrees with Moll and Shriner, and the question of muscle function in velum control (particularly the roles of the palatopharyngeal sphincter and the palatopharyngeal muscle) is not fully resolved. Part of the problem is that there appear, once again, to be marked differences among individual speakers in the way they use the musculature to control the velopharyngeal port. Specific muscular activity also appears to be influenced by phonetic context. Whether there is in fact a greater degree of inherent nasality in low vowels (as Ladefoged (1971) suggests) seems to depend in part on the way in which nasality itself is defined and measured. (See Bell-Berti (1980) for an extensive discussion of velopharyngeal function, and Baken (1987) for a review of acoustic and aerodynamic techniques for estimating port size, velum height and movement, and nasality.)

In the articulation of stops, the velum must be fully raised to allow adequate buildup of intra-oral air pressure during the stoppage. In fricatives, velum raising is also important, though to a lesser extent. The speech of those who have a cleft palate or related structural deficiency reveals the consequences of inability to create a reasonable degree of velopharyngeal closure when required.

In some languages, the uvula also has a function as an articulator, in conjunction with the body of the tongue, in producing certain trill and fricative sounds.

The naso-pharynx leads into the nasal cavity, which has a rather complex cross-sectional shape, giving it a large surface area. The size of the area and its covering of mucous membrane mean that incoming air is warmed and humidified during normal respiration through the nose. The cavity is typically about 10 cm long from pharynx to nostrils, and is divided into two passages by the SEPTUM, which is cartilaginous at the nostril end and joined to bone structure in the skull. Three bony protrusions, or CONCHAE, extend from the lateral walls of the nasal cavity, partially dividing it into three passages on each side and contributing to the large surface area. Coupled to them is a series of auxiliary cavities, or SINUSES.

The nasal cavity system has a complex shape, but lacks muscular structure to vary this shape. External factors do affect the size and shape of the nasal cavity, however: as Fant (1960) points out, the mucous content varies, and tissue may swell, causing considerable variation in the volume and geometry of the cavities. These variations are obviously involuntary but certainly affect the nasal cavity's resonant properties and its contribution to the acoustic and perceptual characteristics of speech. Voluntary control of the cavity's contribution to sound quality can be achieved only indirectly, by muscular tensions which affect the nature of the nasopharyngeal coupling to the oropharyngeal part of the vocal tract. It is possible, for example, that the nasalized vowels of French gain a particular quality from the kind of nasal coupling which occurs when the velum is lowered and tension is maintained on associated muscles.

6.9   The oral cavity

The oral cavity is the single most important part of the vocal tract in determining the phonetic qualities of speech sounds. Its importance rests on our ability to control the geometry and volume of the cavity, by shaping and positioning the tongue and by moving the lips, jaw and soft palate (2.10 above).

The limits of the oral cavity are defined anteriorly by the lips, and posteriorly by the arch-shaped entry formed by the palatoglossus muscle (the ANTERIOR FAUCAL PILLARS). Inferiorly, the floor of the mouth is formed by the tongue, flexible connective tissue, and the (extrinsic laryngeal) mylohyoidal muscle. Superiorly, the oral cavity is divided from the nasal cavity by the roof of the mouth, the front of which is defined by the edges and inner surfaces of the upper teeth. Just behind the upper teeth is the ALVEOLAR RIDGE, the thick membranous covering on the bone structure which joins the tooth-bearing bone of the upper jaw and the vaulted or arched bone structure of the hard palate. At the meeting point of the tooth ridge and the hard palate, the membranous cover has a series of distinctive ridges or corrugations across it. These and the shape of the palatal arch itself vary widely from individual to individual. The hard palate ends approximately level with the rearmost molars and the partition between the nasal and oral cavities is continued by the soft palate or velum (6.8 above). Laterally, the oral cavity is delimited by the teeth and associated bone structure in the jaws, extending to the flexible tissue and muscle structure of the checks when the mandible is lowered. For reference, the figure used in 2.10 above to illustrate the principal areas of articulation is repeated here as figure 6.9.1.

6.10   The tongue

Within the oral cavity is the tongue, which makes the greatest contribution to changes in the volume and geometry of the cavity. The tongue consists largely of muscle, with an outer covering of mucous membrane and a fibrous septum dividing it longitudinally. It is anchored anteriorly by some of its extrinsic muscles to the hyoid bone. For purposes of phonetic description, the upper surface of the tongue is usually divided into functional areas (2.11 above). Actually, as Hardcastle (1976) points out, there is no anatomical basis for such subdivision. Probably for this very reason, writers on articulatory phonetics differ in their use of terms (see Heffner 1964, p. 32; Abercrombie 1967, p. 53; Daniloff 1973, p. 175, and Zemlin 1981, p. 318; a detailed account of tongue anatomy is found in Fucci and Petrosino 1981).

The extrinsic muscles of the tongue make for highly versatile positioning of the tongue, while the intrinsic muscles work with the extrinsic to give control over

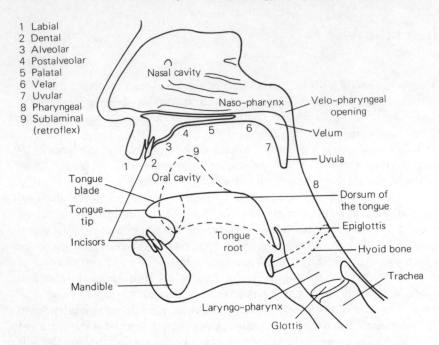

1 Labial
2 Dental
3 Alveolar
4 Postalveolar
5 Palatal
6 Velar
7 Uvular
8 Pharyngeal
9 Sublaminal
   (retroflex)

Nasal cavity

Naso-pharynx

Velo-pharyngeal
opening

Velum

Uvula

Tongue
blade

Oral cavity

Tongue
tip

Incisors

Dorsum of
the tongue

Epiglottis

Tongue
root

Hyoid bone

Trachea

Mandible

Laryngo-pharynx

Glottis

FIGURE 6.9.1   Mid-sagittal oral vocal tract showing major areas of articulation
Adapted from: Minifie, Hixon and Williams 1973, p. 173.

tongue shape. The consequent mobility and plasticity of the tongue are fundamental
to speech production.

The extrinsic muscles of the tongue are the PALATOGLOSSUS, STYLOGLOSSUS,
GENIOGLOSSUS and HYOGLOSSUS (figure 6.10.1). When contracted, the palatoglossus
(see 6.8 above) assists in raising the back part of the tongue. The styloglossus runs
from the base of the skull down and forward to the back edges of the tongue,
dividing and distributing into the hyoglossus and (intrinsic) inferior longitudinal
muscle running towards the tongue tip. Its contraction will pull the tongue upwards
and backwards. The genioglossus is a bulky muscle which runs from the medial part
of the posterior surface of the jawbone, fanning out upward into the tongue from
the tip to the root and extending downward towards the hyoid bone. The fibres in
the anterior and posterior parts of this muscle are capable of independent contraction, which enables the muscle to perform a variety of functions in the control of the
tongue. When the anterior part is contracted, it may pull the tip back and down
within the jawbone trough. When the posterior part is contracted, it may pull the
tongue forward, causing the tip to protrude. The hyoglossus (mentioned in 6.5
above) runs upward and forward from the greater horns and anterior lateral part
of the hyoid bone to the root of the tongue, blending with other tongue muscle
fibres from the back to the tip of the tongue. When contracted, it may pull the
tongue downwards. With its anterior fibres it aids the action of the genioglossus in

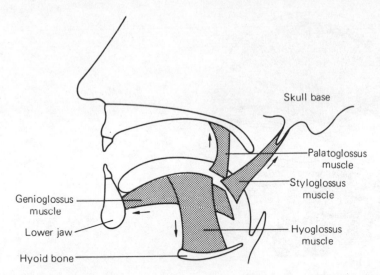

FIGURE 6.10.1   Extrinsic muscles of the tongue
Adapted from: Sonesson 1968, p. 67.

depressing and pulling back the tongue tip, and also functions as an antagonist to the palatoglossus and styloglossus.

The intrinsic muscles of the tongue mostly lie above the extrinsic, and are configured in three planes at right angles to each other (Sonesson 1968, Zemlin 1981). The SUPERIOR and INFERIOR LONGITUDINAL muscles run along the tongue. The superior longitudinal is directly under the surface of the dorsum, and runs from the tongue root to the tip and lateral edges of the tongue. Its contraction can shorten the tongue and contribute to raising the tip and edges. The inferior longitudinal runs from the root of the tongue, blending with the genioglossus and hyoglossus muscle fibres, to the lower surface of the tongue tip. When contracted, it may lower the tip and contribute to shortening the tongue. The TRANSVERSE muscle, which forms a significant part of tongue body bulk, runs from the fibrous septum towards the lateral edges of the tongue, blending with other muscles in this region. When contracted, it may narrow and elongate the tongue and contribute to grooving the tip and blade. The VERTICAL muscle runs from the mucous membrane of the dorsum downwards towards the lower side of the tongue, blending with the inferior longitudinal and transverse muscle fibres. When contracted, it may flatten and widen the tongue. Figure 6.10.2 shows the location of the intrinsic muscles.

In completing this summary of the role of individual muscles in tongue control, we should not lose sight of the way in which the muscles work together to create an enormous diversity of tongue shape and position during speech. Cooperation between extrinsic and intrinsic muscles is made clear, for example, in a study by MacNeilage and Sholes (1964) of tongue muscle activity in vowels. Studies designed to capture the complex positioning and posture of the tongue include the famous and early example of Daniel Jones, who used lateral X-ray photographs as evidence in his

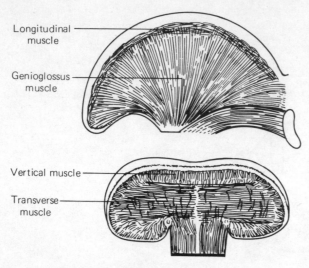

FIGURE 6.10.2   Intrinsic muscles of the tongue
Adapted from: Sonesson 1968, p. 68.

theory of vowel description (2.7 above). Lindau (1978) and others have undertaken similar analyses in a more modern context. Perkell (1969) analysed the dynamic behaviour of the tongue during articulation by using sophisticated ciné X-ray film measurements. He suggests that the extrinsic tongue muscles are responsible for the relatively slow positional adjustments required mainly in vowel production, and that the intrinsic muscles control the more rapid localized movement and shaping required mainly in consonant production. The slower positioning includes, for example, raising and retracting the tongue, using muscles such as the styloglossus, for a back vowel as in *hoard*. The faster and more localized kind of activity includes blockage of the vocal tract by placing the tongue tip just behind the upper teeth, followed by rapid release of the blockage (as in the stop [d] at the beginning of *deal*). This action uses muscles such as the superior and inferior longitudinals to control the requisite rapid movement of the tongue tip.

   As with most of the articulatory system, the relationship between muscular activity and articulatory function is not simple. As Abbs (1986) has observed, individual muscle activity in the vocal tract is meaningful only when understood within the overall articulation and its goals and context.

6.11   The lips

The lips are the anterior termination of the oral cavity and thus also of the entire vocal tract. They consist of two fleshy folds which are richly supplied with muscles and are formed externally of skin and internally of mucous membrane. The muscle arrangements are such that the lips and mouth show considerable plasticity and mobility and therefore contribute significantly to the range of vocal tract configurations possible in the articulation of speech.

Muscles associated with the lips allow control over opening and closure, raising and lowering of the upper and lower lips, rounding and protrusion of the lips, and vertical or lateral movement of the angles or corners of the mouth (figure 6.11.1).

The major muscular component of the lips proper is the ORBICULARIS ORIS, a sphincter muscle consisting of an oval band of fibres, some of which are shared with other facial muscles which pass into the lips. The muscle is thus capable of providing a range of different movements associated with lip control. When the muscle is contracted, movements include lip closure, pursing, rounding and protrusion, drawing the upper lip down and the lower lip up, and pressing the lips against the teeth. Lip protrusion is also assisted by the MENTALIS muscle, which runs from the anterior part of the mandible below the lower incisors down to the lower part of the chin. When contracted, it may contribute to raising and protruding the lower lip.

Raising of the upper lip is controlled by a series of levator muscles, which have insertions in the region of the upper lip. These are the ZYGOMATIC MINOR, and the two LEVATOR LABII SUPERIOR muscles. The zygomatic minor runs from the cheekbone of the skull to the upper lips and orbicularis oris fibres. The levator labii superior muscles run from the maxilla bone to the medial part of the upper lip around the nasolabial groove. All these muscles contribute to lip raising when contracted.

Lowering the lower lip is controlled by the DEPRESSOR LABII INFERIOR muscle which runs from the anterior face of the jawbone to the lower lip, blending with the orbicularis oris.

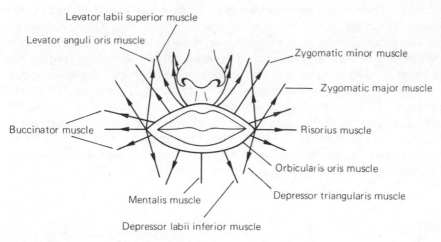

FIGURE 6.11.1   Labial muscles
Adapted from: Hardcastle 1976, p. 113.

Lateral movement of the mouth angle is controlled by the BUCCINATOR, RISORIUS and ZYGOMATIC MAJOR muscles. The buccinator, or bugler's muscle, is a thin sheet of muscle which runs via connective tissue from the lateral parts of the maxilla, jaw-bone and skull in the region of the back molars to blend with the orbicularis oris at the mouth angle. When contracted, it will draw the mouth angle back, spreading the lips. It also has an important function in maintaining tension in the cheeks during oral activity, including speech production. The name 'bugler's muscle' points to its role as an antagonist to distension of the cheeks during blowing or bugling. The risorius, which runs from the region of the lateral part of the jawbone to the lateral part of the lips and mouth angle, also contributes to the action of spreading the lips. The zygomatic major runs from the outer cheekbone to blend with the orbicularis oris at the mouth angle. When contracted, it contributes to drawing the mouth angle back and upwards.

Longitudinal mouth angle movement is controlled by the LEVATOR ANGULI ORIS, the ZYGOMATIC MAJOR (described in the preceding paragraph) and the DEPRESSOR TRIANGULARIS. The levator anguli oris runs from the lateral part of the maxilla and blends with the orbicularis oris at the mouth angle. When contracted, it will raise the mouth angle, as in laughing; the zygomatic major also contributes to this function. The depressor triangularis, so called because of its triangular shape, runs from the anterior lateral part of the mandible and blends with the orbicularis oris at the mouth angle.

Like the tongue muscles, the lip muscles operate in various combinations to yield a considerable range of lip configurations. Precise, rapid closure and release of the lips, as required in the articulation of labial stop sounds such as [p] and [b], may involve the action of the orbicularis oris to close and hold the lips together, and the levator and depressor muscles to open the lips rapidly at the release of the stop. For a sound such as the fricative [f], it is necessary to draw the lower lip against the upper teeth and to spread the lips. This may require the orbicularis oris to pull the lower lip inwards, and the buccinator, risorius and zygomatic major muscles to spread the lips by retracting the mouth angle. Certain vowels, as in English *hoard* or *talk*, have lip rounding and protrusion as part of their articulatory configuration, which may involve the orbicularis oris and the mentalis. Other vowels, as in *heed*, require the lips to be spread, which may involve the buccinator, risorius and zygomatic major muscles for lip spreading and the triangularis to maintain lip opening. These and other functions of the lip muscles during articulation are discussed in Hardcastle (1976) and Zemlin (1981). Kennedy and Abbs (1979) give a detailed account of labial musculature, and Abbs et al. (1984) offer some evidence that sections of the orbicularis oris may be activated independently. This independence would certainly contribute to the extent and versatility of labial movement control.

6.12   The mandible

The jaw or MANDIBLE does not play the same kind of role in speech production as the lips and tongue. If the lips or tongue are immobilized, speech is seriously impaired; by contrast, it is possible to produce quite intelligible speech with an object such as a pencil clenched between the teeth. The mandible does nevertheless function both as a moving articulator and as an important anchor point for a number of muscles which affect and are affected by its movement. It is approximately U-shaped with vertical extensions known as RAMI at each end of the U; these are heavy bone structures at the ends of which the mandible has joints with the skull base. The mandible is capable of movement in vertical, longitudinal and lateral directions. It may be lowered to produce a typical aperture of around 40 mm, protruded about 10 mm and moved laterally about 20 mm to either side (Heffner 1964, Zemlin 1981). Of these adjustments, vertical movement is the most important in speech; forward longitudinal movement plays a minor part; and lateral movement seems to make no significant contribution to normal articulatory processes.

In vertical movement, the mandible is lowered by the action of the mylohyoid, geniohyoid and digastricus muscles (6.5 above) and the genioglossus muscle (6.10 above). All of these muscles have attachments in the posterior face of the anterior part of the mandible and, if the hyoid bone is stable, will pull the mandible downwards when contracted. In addition, gravity will also contribute a downward force, as can be seen when the muscles relax and the jaw drops. Raising of the mandible is controlled by the INTERNAL PTERYGOID, TEMPORAL and MASSETER muscles. The internal pterygoid runs from the lateral part of the skull to the posterior of the ramus of the mandible. The temporal muscle runs from a wide area of the upper lateral part of the skull to the front of the upper end of the ramus of the mandible, while the masseter muscle runs from the lateral part of the cheekbone to most of the outer surface of the ramus of the mandible. Contraction of these muscles will raise the mandible, with the masseter being the most powerful of the three. Longitudinal movement or protrusion of the mandible is effected by the EXTERNAL PTERYGOID muscle, with some contribution from the internal pterygoid and masseter muscles just described. The external pterygoid runs from the area of the cheekbone to the posterior part of the extremity of the ramus of the mandible. Contraction of these muscles will pull the jaw forward, although in the case of the masseter and internal pterygoid muscles, forward movement is combined with vertical movement. Figure 6.12.1 shows the mandible and the muscle structure related to its movement during speech production.

Given an abnormal condition in which mandible movement is resisted or fixed, most speakers are able to make rapid and adequate compensatory manoeuvres in lip and tongue articulatory movements to produce highly intelligible speech, as Folkins and Abbs (1975) have shown. Under normal conditions, however, mandible movement and positioning are an important adjunct to certain classes of lip and tongue articulatory activity. Thus in vowel articulation, an increase in jaw

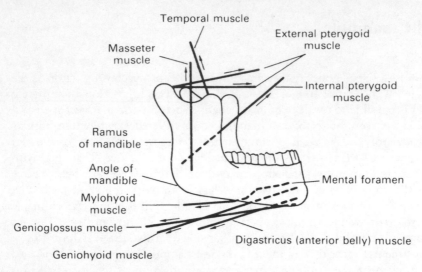

FIGURE 6.12.1   Muscles of the mandible
Adapted from: Hardcastle 1976, p. 107.

aperture normally accompanies the lowering of the tongue for production of relatively low or open vowels (as in *ban* or *barn*). The role of jaw aperture in speech
production is quantified in models of articulatory processes outlined by Lindblom
and Sundberg (1971) and Coker (1973).

There is a connection between mandible movement and lip movement, particularly
in such articulatory gestures as lip closure or constriction for stops and fricatives.
Photographic studies by Fujimura (1961) have shown that mandible movement
normally accompanies the opening of the lips at the release of a stop such as [p]
(as in *pay*). Lindblom (1967) has also made indirect photographic measurements of
the relationships between lip and jaw movement. Investigations of this sort show that
mandible movement does not correspond directly with lip movement, but may lead
or lag depending on the phonetic context. This is partly a matter of inertia, as the
mandible has a greater mass than the lips. Since mandible movement is generally
involved in setting the tongue position for low vowels, the mass of the mandible may
help to explain why low vowels tend to be longer than high or close vowels.

Labial and mandibular movement have been extensively studied, not least because
the lips and jaw can be fairly easily observed. Again Baken (1987) provides a useful
review of the techniques of investigation.

Readers wishing to consult more technical works on the anatomy and physiology
of speech production are reminded of works already cited, notably Hardcastle
(1976), Daniloff et al. (1980), Zemlin (1981), Dickson and Dickson (1982) and
Perkins and Kent (1986). The colour photographs of relevant anatomical sections
and specimens in McMinn and Hutchings (1988) may also be helpful.

Exercises

1   Check that you understand the meaning of the following:

Bernoulli effect
glottis
innervation ratio (of a muscle)
neuron
subglottal pressure
synapse
thyroid angle
trachea
velum

2   Give a broad outline of the 'apparatus' with which we produce speech, including the lungs, the vocal folds, and the supraglottal cavities.

3   It is debatable whether the various organs used in generating speech can be described as a 'system'. Taking a biological perspective, list the 'primary' functions of as many of these organs as you can. In what sense do these functions remain primary?

4   Give a brief account of the relevance of the nervous system to speech. Ensure that you understand the following:

CNS and PNS
cranial nerves
spinal nerves
autonomic nervous system

5   What is feedback and what kinds do we use in monitoring speech?

6   Describe how air is drawn into and out of the lungs, noting the relevance of factors such as how much air is already in the lungs, how fast the air is being moved, and so on. Then explain figure 6.4.6.

7   What are the cartilages of the larynx and how do they move?

8   What is the 'aerodynamic myoelastic theory of phonation'?

9   What does the 'opening quotient' of the vocal folds tell you about the vibration of the folds?

10   What muscles are used to close off the nasal cavity in the production of oral sounds?

11   Give a brief description of the tongue, including its structure and the muscles used to position and shape it.

12   How could you demonstrate the following to an introductory phonetics class, without resort to complex equipment?

– that jaw movement is less important in speech than tongue or lip movement?
– that air flows out through the nose during the production of nasal consonants such as [m] and [n]?
– that vowel qualities are affected by the size and shape of the cavities through which the sound passes?

7   The Acoustics of Speech Production

Introduction

This chapter provides a thorough account of the acoustics of speech. The first eight sections are a basic introduction to the nature of sound and sound waves, laying a foundation for the understanding of speech as sound:

- the nature of sound (7.1)
- the propagation of sound (7.2)
- simple harmonic motion (7.3)
- complex vibrations (7.4)
- resonance (7.5)
- amplitude (7.6)
- duration in sound waves (7.7)
- frequency components in sound waves (7.8).

The chapter then addresses the relevance of these basic acoustic insights to the analysis of speech:

- perceptual properties of sound waves (7.9)
- acoustic modelling of speech production (7.10)
- phonation considered as a source of sound (7.11)
- frication considered as a source of sound (7.12)
- the vocal tract considered as a filter in vowel production, and the significance of formants (7.13).

The next sections explain how and why spectrographic analysis has played a major role in modern phonetics:

- spectrographic analysis (7.14)
- acoustic properties of vowel quality (7.15)

– the vocal tract as a filter in consonant production (7.16)
– the acoustic properties of consonants in syllables (7.17).

The chapter ends with comments on the relationship between articulation and acoustics (7.18) and the acoustic analysis of prosody, with particular attention to fundamental frequency as a measure of pitch (7.19).

7.1   The nature of sound

As sensory beings we see, touch, taste, smell and hear. What we hear, we call sound. More technically, the scientific study of sound and how we hear it is ACOUSTICS. In this chapter we examine some of the acoustic properties of speech sounds, to complement the physiological, articulatory and phonemic accounts of previous chapters.

All sound results from vibration of one kind or another. In turn, vibration depends on some source of energy to generate it. Fry (1979) takes the example of a symphony orchestra: the players perform such actions as moving their arms or blowing, and their work (under skilful control) generates various kinds of vibration which we hear as sound.

Vibration alone is not enough to produce audible sound, and three accompanying criteria must be satisfied as well. In the first place, there must be a PROPAGATING MEDIUM, something the sound can travel through. Most commonly this medium is air, but any other physical substance, including wood, metal, liquid, or living tissue such as bone, can, with varying degrees of efficiency, serve as the propagating medium. If there is no medium – in a vacuum, that is – no sound can be heard. A classic experiment is used to demonstrate this. If an electric bell or buzzer is placed inside a bell-jar and the air is pumped out of the jar, the sound of the bell fades away. (Some faint sound usually remains because the mounting of the electric bell in the jar still provides a connection to the outside air.)

The two other criteria that must be satisfied concern properties of sound relative to the sensitivity of the ear. Much more will be said about these properties later in this chapter, but we must note here that vibrations vary in their rate or FREQUENCY from very rapid to very slow. The ear detects only a certain range of these frequencies, commonly down to about 20 vibrations per second and up to about 20,000 vibrations per second, although this varies among individuals and is certainly affected by ageing. Thus the second criterion is that a sound must be within the normal audible frequency range.

Thirdly, a vibration has not only a frequency, but also an AMPLITUDE – a measure of the size of vibration or the extent of movement in the vibration. Amplitude relates to what we normally call loudness, and as the amplitude of a vibration diminishes, it becomes less audible. Thus the third criterion is that a vibration must have an amplitude great enough to be detectable. This is not just a matter of the level of vibration at the sound source itself, for audibility also falls rapidly as the distance between the sound source and the listener increases. In addition, the general level of sound in the surroundings can have a masking effect, and the connection or coupling between the source of vibration and the propagating medium may also be inefficient. The effect of inefficient coupling is easily demonstrated with a tuning fork. If the fork is struck and held between finger and thumb in the air, it is scarcely audible because its vibrating prongs are not coupled efficiently to the air. If the same fork is placed on a wooden table top, the sound can be clearly heard at greater volume because the fork's vibrations are transmitted to the air far more efficiently by means of the larger surface area of the table.

Sounds are not all perceived as identical in quality. For a broad categorization, we can make two basic distinctions. The first of these distinguishes between continuous and impulse-like sounds. A jet plane and an electric power drill are examples of essentially continuous sounds, whereas a door slamming shut or a gunshot are examples of impulse-like sounds. Continuous sounds involve vibrations which last for some time, from seconds to hours. In impulse-like sounds, the vibrations start very suddenly and build up to their maximum amplitude very rapidly (usually in a fraction of a second). The vibrations die away relatively quickly, but mostly not as rapidly as they build up.

The second distinction separates what are often called musical sounds from noise-like sounds. Almost all musical instruments produce PERIODIC sounds, so called because their vibration follows a certain pattern which is repeated regularly. (We shall see below what kinds of patterns vibrations may show.) The number of times the vibration pattern is repeated per second will determine whether we perceive them as high or low pitched sounds. Thus a tuba, a foghorn and a bass guitar all generate low pitched sounds, with a small number of repeated vibration patterns per second, while a violin, a kettle whistle and a piccolo all generate high pitched sounds with a large number of repeated vibration patterns per second. By contrast, noise-like sounds are APERIODIC and result from vibrations which are much more random and do not repeat their pattern regularly. The hiss of a steam pipe and the steady roar of a large waterfall are good examples of sound sources which have continuous yet quite random patterns of vibration.

Although these distinctions are useful, they are not quite as tidy as they may seem. A single explosion, for example, will have the character of an impulse-like sound, but if a series of explosions is rapid and sustained (as in a fast-running internal combustion engine) the effect may be that of a continuous sound. In fact many sounds have a quite complex nature. For instance, when compressed air or steam is suddenly released from a valve (as in an espresso coffee machine) the initial impulse sound decays into a continuous sound. Furthermore, there are both musical and noise-like elements in the sound, because some of the vibration which produces it is repeated regularly and some is quite random in pattern.

A further important way in which sounds differ is in their quality or TIMBRE. Consider a violin and a flute each playing the same note. Both instruments produce a continuous periodic set of sound vibrations repeated at the same rate – if this were not so, they would not be heard as playing the same note. Yet there is a distinct difference in the quality of their sound, which enables us to hear that different instruments are being played. This difference, commonly described as a difference in timbre, can be judged in impressionistic terms – the violin is perhaps 'sharp edged' whereas the flute is 'rounded and smooth' – but, as we shall see below, it is possible to analyse and explain the difference in terms of patterns of vibration.

These comments on the nature of sound are relevant to speech, which is a very complex form of sound. Speech includes impulse sounds (as in stops, such as [t] or [k]) and continuous sequences (as in vowels, such as [i] or [a]). It has periodic components (again in vowels), aperiodic components (as in fricatives, such as [f] or [s]), and mixes of both (in voiced fricatives, such as [v] or [z]). Differences among the vowels (for instance [i] versus [a] versus [u]) are heard in much the same way that we discern a violin from a flute. It is therefore important to understand the nature of sound itself if we are to have some grasp of the acoustics of speech.

7.2 The propagation of sound

When sound travels from its source to a hearer, vibration is transmitted or propagated, through some medium. This transmission is of course invisible, but we do see something comparable (though by no means identical) when vibration is propagated through water. If a small stone is thrown into the centre of a pool of water, it will start the water vibrating by temporarily displacing water at this point; the vibration is then propagated outwards as a series of ripples of displacement, moving in ever increasing concentric circles until they reach the edge of the pool. Because a single stone thrown into a pool cannot sustain vibration, these ripples will die away, but if a stick or paddle is used to produce repeated displacement of the water at the centre of the pool, the vibration will keep on spreading outwards from this point.

While rippling water offers a simple and easily observed illustration, it is important to realize that the propagation of sound is rather more complicated. Unlike water, air is an elastic medium. Hence, when a sound is produced, the air immediately around the source is compressed. Being elastic, the air will tend to expand again after being compressed, and as it does so, it compresses the air next to it, which will in turn expand again and propagate the compression outwards. Thus when water ripples, the displacement is at right angles to the direction of the wave – the water ripples upwards and downwards from its normal surface plane. But a sound wave travelling through air varies the local air pressure in the same plane as the direction of the wave (figure 7.2.1). In both cases the wave motion amounts to a succession of local displacements. In the case of water, however, the wave is transverse (the plane of displacement is at right angles to the plane of propagation) while in air, the wave is generally longitudinal (displacement and propagation are in the same plane). The velocity of propagation of sound in air at normal temperature and pressure is around 345 metres per second.

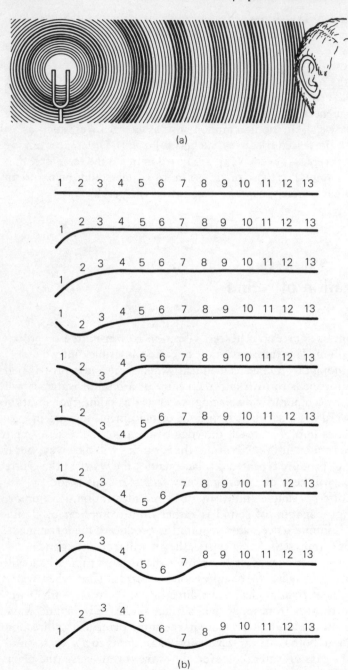

FIGURE 7.2.1   Propagation of a sound wave: (a) longitudinal; (b) transverse

7.3 Simple harmonic motion

Sound consists of mechanical vibrations transmitted to the ear through a physical medium, usually air. The simplest form of mechanical vibration is found in systems of the kind shown in figure 7.3.1. When the pendulum (a) is set in motion, or the spring-mass (b) is pulled into oscillation, or the tuning fork (c) struck, each system will vibrate in a similar fashion. We can show the nature of the vibration by plotting the displacement of the vibrating object from its rest position, measured in relation to time. In the case of the pendulum, this means measuring the distance that the pendulum weight moves from right to left relative to its rest position. For the spring-mass, it is the distance the mass moves up and down. For the tuning fork, it is the movement of the fork prongs either side of their rest position, in this case a very slight movement requiring extremely delicate measurement. When plotted against time, the vibration (displacement) of each of these systems will have the pattern shown in figure 7.3.2. Vibration represented as a graph of this kind is known as a WAVEFORM.

Vibration with a pattern like the one shown is the simplest kind found and is known as SINUSOIDAL vibration, or simple harmonic motion. The term 'sinusoidal wave' is generally abbreviated as SINE WAVE. If idealized, these simple mechanical systems would keep vibrating indefinitely once set in motion. In practice, energy is lost because of factors such as friction and air resistance. As a result, the amplitude of displacement in the vibrations will decrease over time. The vibration is therefore said to be 'damped'. Damped vibration is normal (unless the energy is replenished) and common in speech.

The waveform of figure 7.3.2 is characteristic of undamped vibration. Though idealized, this simple harmonic motion can usefully be taken to be the basic building block of most other more complex forms of vibration.

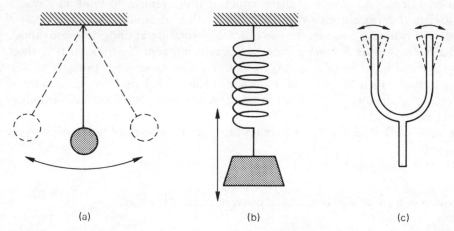

      (a)   (b)   (c)

FIGURE 7.3.1   Simple vibrating systems: (a) pendulum; (b) spring-mass; (c) tuning fork

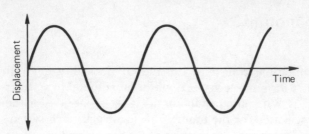

FIGURE 7.3.2   Simple vibration waveform

For purposes of measurement and calculation, it is helpful to rethink the graph. Let us first be clear about the wave pattern of the graph itself. If we trace the waveform of figure 7.3.2 from the left, the line of displacement curves up and over, returning to the rest point, then curving down to register the displacement in the opposite direction before returning to the axis. At this point, when we meet the axis for the second time, the wave has completed one CYCLE; the rest of this particular idealized wave is simply a repetition of the same pattern for an indefinite number of cycles. Now in acoustic phonetics several values are of significance:

A   the maximum amplitude of vibration: the distance between the axis and the highest (or lowest) point on the wave;
D   the instantaneous amplitude of vibration at some point of time: the distance between the axis and some selected point on the wave;
T   the period of vibration: the time taken by one complete cycle;
f   the frequency of vibration: the number of cycles per second, usually expressed as Hertz (Hz); hence 5 Hz is five cycles per second, 10 kHz is 10,000 cycles per second, and so on.

For many calculations involving these values, it is convenient to think in terms of the rotation of a wheel rather than the wave motion of figure 7.3.2. Any point X on the wave is now a point on the rim of a wheel rotating at uniform speed, and D is still the distance of X from a base line drawn horizontally through the wheel. But by thinking in terms of rotation, we can now also express the position of X as an angle (theta, θ) relative to the base line. Figure 7.3.3 provides a diagram of rotation alongside a wave. With this in mind we can note the following methods of deriving values.

The value of D (expressed as a fraction of A) at any instant of time t is given by:

(7.3.1) $D = A \sin 2\pi t / T$.

The common form of this equation is given in physics texts as:

(7.3.2) $D = A \sin \omega t$

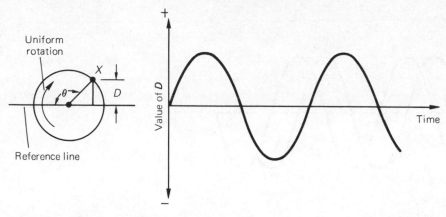

FIGURE 7.3.3   Simple harmonic motion

where

(7.3.3) $\omega = 2\pi f$.

Since f is the frequency of vibration (or, equivalently, the frequency of rotation of the wheel) it can be derived from T, the time it takes to complete a single rotation:

(7.3.4) $f = 1/T$ (expressed in Hz).

Making use of the angle θ (as shown in figure 7.3.3) we can also calculate displacement as ANGULAR DISPLACEMENT:

(7.3.5) $D = A \sin \theta$

To take simple examples, when point X is on the axis, $\theta = 0$, $\sin \theta = 0$ and $D = 0$. When point X is farthest from the axis, $\theta = 90°$, $\sin \theta = 1$, and $D = A$.

Most waveforms – including those studied in acoustic phonetics – are not sinusoidal but can be analysed as the sum of two or more sine waves. To approach this analysis, we need to understand the time relationship between two or more waveforms, known as their PHASE relationship. Consider the two sinusoidal waveforms in figure 7.3.4. Each has the same frequency (or period), and each has the same maximum amplitude, but they are displaced from each other such that they pass through their maximum and minimum values at different points of time. The phase relationship between two or more waveforms is always relative: we have to take one of the waveforms as the point of reference for measurement. The phase relationship can be expressed as the time displacement between two waveforms, as in figure 7.3.4, but this has the disadvantage of giving an absolute measurement, a value that will vary according to the frequency of the vibration involved. What is more significant is the

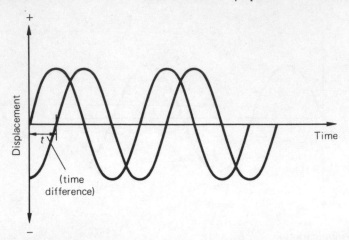

FIGURE 7.3.4   Time displacement between two waveforms

relative relationship between the cycles of vibration of the two (or more) waveforms. This can then be used in defining the properties of complex vibrations made up of several sine wave components. This relative relationship is based on angular displacement, instead of time. Figure 7.3.5 shows the PHASE ANGLE between two sine waves, in this case 90°. The phase angle between two waveforms is normally expressed as a value between 0° and 360° relative to the waveform used as the reference. This range of values represents one full vibration cycle of the reference wave.

Consider now two sine waves which have the same frequency and amplitude and which are also perfectly in phase (their phase difference is 0°). Add the two waves together, and the amplitude of the combined wave will be double that of the two constituent waves at every point in the cycle, as shown in figure 7.3.6. The addition

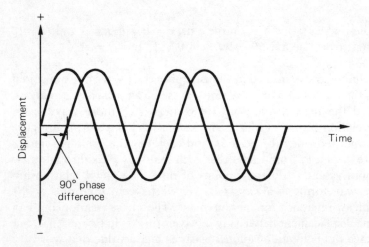

FIGURE 7.3.5   Phase relationship between two waveforms

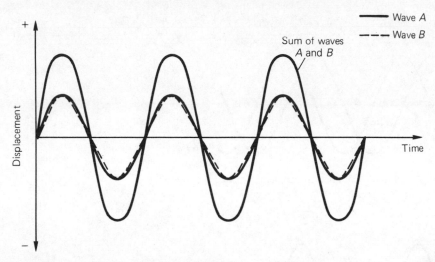

FIGURE 7.3.6   Effect of combining two waves in phase

shows how one wave can be composed of two waves. But when these same two sine waves are out of phase, say by 90°, the situation is not as simple. In some parts of the vibration cycle the values of the waves have to be added to each other, in others subtracted from each other. Figure 7.3.7 shows the result. In this case, the resultant wave has greater amplitude and is shifted in phase relative to the two component waves. (In practice, calculations are done by trigonometrical methods based on the phase angle between the waveforms, rather than by the time-consuming addition implied by figure 7.3.7.#)

Readers wanting a more detailed account of simple harmonic motion may find Small (1973) helpful, and, for a more rigorous mathematical approach, should consult any standard work on acoustics, such as Wood (1964 or 1966).

7.4   Complex vibrations

Sine waves are the building blocks of all forms of vibration, and figure 7.4.1 shows how a complex vibration may consist of the combined effect of three simple sinusoidal vibrations of 100 Hz, 200 Hz and 300 Hz. The result is a complex wave which is not sinusoidal, and which will have a timbre different from that of any simple sine wave. Its frequency of vibration is defined as that of the lowest frequency of the sine waves which compose it. This frequency (100 Hz in the case of figure 7.4.1) is known as the FUNDAMENTAL FREQUENCY (often just as the FUNDAMENTAL). The three sine waves are the COMPONENTS of the complex wave.

If the same three waves are combined with different phase relationships among them (figure 7.4.2), the resultant complex vibration can be seen to have a different

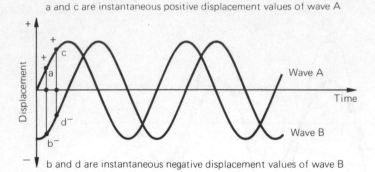

a and c are instantaneous positive displacement values of wave A

b and d are instantaneous negative displacement values of wave B

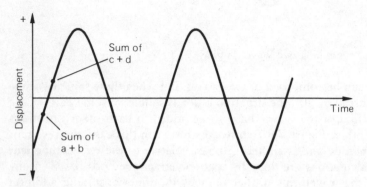

FIGURE 7.3.7   Effect of combining two waves displaced by 90°

shape. Although the waveshape is different, the fundamental frequency is the same, and, perhaps surprisingly, the timbre or quality of the sound will strike a listener as almost the same, if not identical. Thus waveshape alone does not reflect the quality of perceived sound, because the human ear is not particularly sensitive to phase. It was once thought that the ear was completely deaf to phase; this is not strictly correct, but it is true that we will hear an appreciable difference in sound quality only if there are changes in the frequency and amplitude of the component waves.

So far we have assumed that the component sine waves are at frequencies which are integral multiples of, and have a fixed phase relationship to, a fundamental. As we have seen, if these component sine waves are shifted statically in their phase relationships, the shape of the complex wave will vary, but the sound quality will generally not change appreciably. If, however, the component sine waves are not integral multiples of the fundamental, their phase relationships will keep changing, as will the resultant complex waveshape. More importantly, the timbre or sound quality will be dissonant and unmusical, even though the hearer can perceive a note or pitch. The larger bells in a carillon are a reasonably good example of the sound of this sort of waveform. This sort of complex vibration reaches its limit when all of the components have randomly varying frequencies and randomly varying amplitudes.

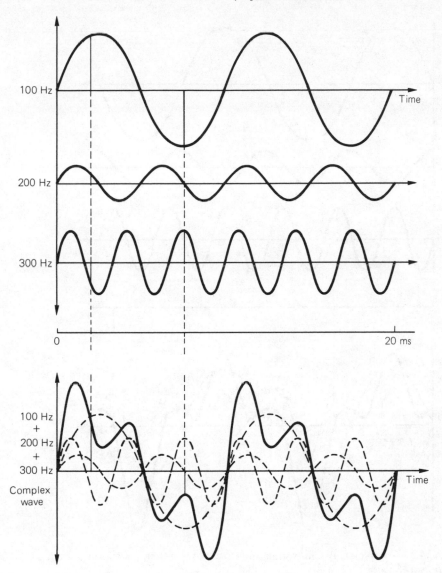

FIGURE 7.4.1 Complex wave with three sinusoidal components (100 Hz, 200 Hz, 300 Hz)
Adapted from: Ladefoged 1962, p. 35.

The result is a complex waveshape that is constantly and rapidly changing, with no general pattern. The sound produced will no longer be periodic in nature, but noise-like. The more truly random the variations in frequency and – to a lesser extent – in amplitude, the more truly noise-like the sound will be. A typical example of a noise waveshape is shown in figure 7.4.3.

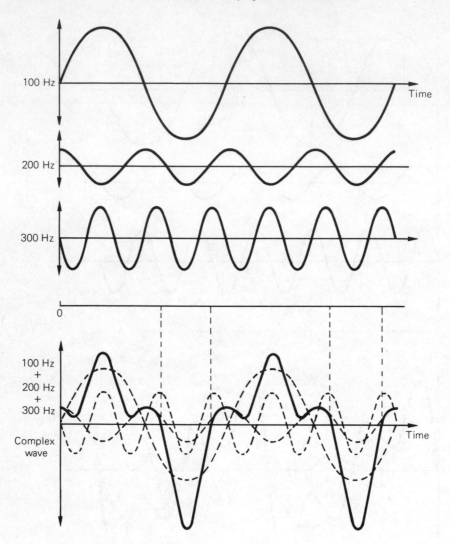

FIGURE 7.4.2   Complex wave illustrating the effects of phase on waveform pattern
Adapted from: Ladefoged 1962, p. 40.

The most completely noise-like sound is one in which all possible frequencies in the range of hearing are randomly present, at random amplitudes and in random phase relationships. This is known as WHITE NOISE.

FIGURE 7.4.3   Noise waveshape

7.5   Resonance

If we were to take the pendulum of figure 7.3.1(a) above and give it a single push, it would swing for a time and the displacement on each swing would get smaller until the pendulum came back to rest. The graph of displacement against time would be as shown in figure 7.5.1. The period of each complete vibration is easily measured, and would be found to be approximately the same, for the pendulum moves more slowly as the distance it travels decreases. In fact the pendulum has a natural frequency at which it vibrates, known as its RESONANT FREQUENCY. If the string on the pendulum were lengthened, the period of vibration would be longer and the resonant frequency lower. Thus the resonant frequency is a function of the length of the pendulum string. All resonant mechanical systems behave much in the same way, and the waveshapes they produce are known as damped vibrations. For reasons that will become apparent later, these damped vibrations are in fact complex vibrations.

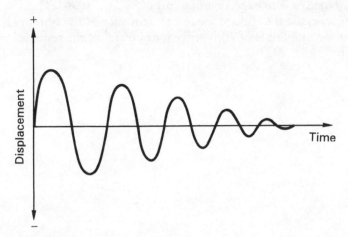

FIGURE 7.5.1   Pendulum vibration pattern

An important property of mechanical systems is that they respond selectively to vibrations of different frequencies. A simple illustration of this is the spring-mass system of figure 7.3.1(b) above. Imagine that we wish to transmit periodic vibrations through this system, by vibrating the anchoring point. There will be input vibration at the top of the spring and output vibration at the bottom of the mass (figure 7.5.2). If the input vibration is at a frequency very much higher or lower than that of the natural resonance frequency of the system, the input vibrations will be transmitted to the output with very weak displacement amplitude. Assume now that the input vibrations start much lower than the resonant frequency of the system but are gradually increased. Then, as the input frequency approaches the natural resonance frequency of the system, the output vibration amplitude will steadily increase and reach a maximum when the input frequency is equal to the resonance frequency. At this point, the output vibration amplitude may actually exceed the input vibration amplitude.

If we keep the amplitude of the input vibrations constant while varying their frequency from well below to well above the resonant frequency of the spring-mass system, we can plot the response of the system. Figure 7.5.3 represents this response as a graph of output vibration amplitude against frequency. The display is known as a RESONANCE CURVE. The resonance curve illustrates the extremely important principle that a resonant system transmits the energy of input vibration with selective efficiency, reaching its peak at the resonant frequency of the system. Resonance and its selectivity are important characteristics of the vocal tract.

The degree of selectivity exhibited by a resonant system is determined by its degree of damping. Recall that when a pendulum or spring-mass is given a single impulse of input energy, it will vibrate at its natural (resonant) frequency, with the amplitude of vibration gradually dying away. The duration of this decay in amplitude, relative to the period of the resonance, reflects the effect of losses in the resonant system, and hence its degree of damping. Figure 7.5.4 shows the resonance curves, or frequency responses, of (a) lightly and (b) heavily damped systems.

It is not always convenient to define the selectivity of a resonant system in terms of its damping; a common alternative is to express it in terms of its BANDWIDTH. This is defined as the range of frequencies either side of the centre frequency of the system's resonance curve which have an amplitude of 70.7 per cent or greater of the resonant frequency amplitude (figure 7.5.5).

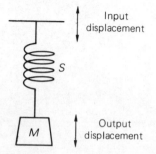

FIGURE 7.5.2   Transmission of vibration through a spring-mass system

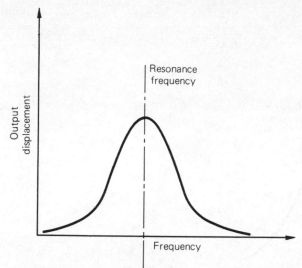

FIGURE 7.5.3   Resonance curve

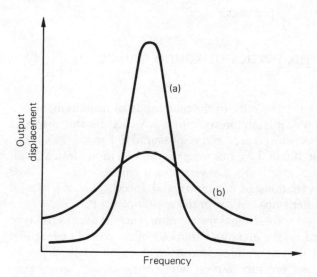

FIGURE 7.5.4   Resonance curves of damped vibrating systems: (a) lightly damped; (b) heavily damped

The selectivity implications of a given bandwidth figure make it necessary to know the resonance frequency as well. Selectivity as an independent property may also be defined by the Q factor of the resonant system, given by:

$$Q \text{ factor} = F_{\text{resonance}}/\text{bandwidth}.$$

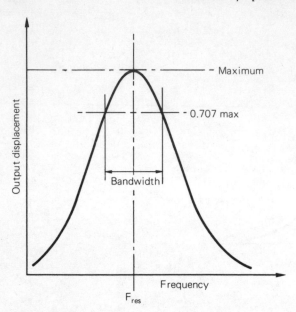

FIGURE 7.5.5   Method for determining bandwidth

7.6   Basic amplitude properties of sound waves

Amplitude is the term normally used to refer to the magnitude of displacement in a sound vibration. Most commonly, it is air pressure that is varied by this displacement. Pressure is defined as force per unit area and is measured in Pascals (Pa). Static air pressure at sea level is about 100,000 Pa, but the pressure variations which result in audible sound at normal listening levels are very much smaller than this. For example, the sound pressure variations of conversational speech at a distance of about one metre from the speaker's lips will be in the region of 0.1 Pa.

When a sound is picked up by a conventional microphone, such as the electret type provided with many tape recorders, the pressure variations of the sound propagated in air are transformed into a corresponding electrical voltage. This gives us an electrical representation of sound pressure waves, which then raises the question of what is the most appropriate way to measure and portray this representation.

Consider the sinusoidal and complex waves shown in figure 7.6.1. A simple measure of amplitude is to take the maximum values of displacement in the wave. This is useful if we wish to know the peak or peak-to-peak values of a periodic waveform, or if we need to measure the peak values of impulse sounds. This is the kind of measure we need to know to avoid overload when recording sounds or processing them in some form of computer analysis. Unfortunately, however, this measure tells us little about the rest of the waveform. To account for an entire waveform, we need measurements all the way along a cycle, a series of instantaneous

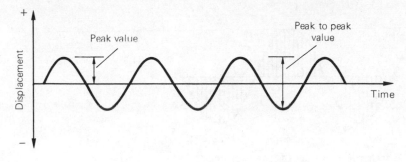

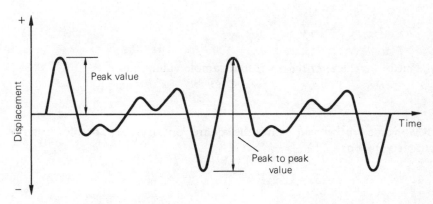

FIGURE 7.6.1   Waveform amplitude

values, as shown in figure 7.6.2. Note that values above the axis line will be positive, those below the axis will be negative. These sample values can give us a picture of the behaviour of the wave, and it would be useful to summarize or average them in some way. But note what happens if we simply add and average a series of values taken along a sine wave: the positive and negative values cancel each other out when added, leaving a sum of zero. We could avoid this by making all the signs of the samples positive, but it is even more useful to turn to another kind of calculation.

We can derive from amplitude a property called INTENSITY. Intensity is power per unit area, or the way power is distributed in a space. Power itself is a measure of the rate at which energy is being expended – for our purposes, in producing sound. Now it can be shown that intensity is proportional to the square of pressure. Hence, if we take our sample values (as in figure 7.6.2), square them, and then add them and find the average, we have a measure of amplitude over the cycle that relates well to effective intensity. If we then take the square root of this average, we can express pressure rather than pressure squared. This value is known as the ROOT MEAN SQUARE or RMS value. The method of calculation, using samples as shown in figure 7.6.2, is as follows.

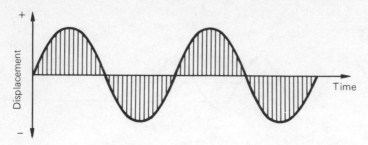

FIGURE 7.6.2   Instantaneous values of wave amplitude

Assume we have a set of N samples of the instantaneous values of a waveform defined as X_1, X_2, X_3 ... X_n. Let Z = the sum of the squared values of the N samples, i.e.

$$Z = (X_1)^2 + (X_2)^2 + (X_3)^2 + (X_n)^2.$$

Let A = the mean (average) of these squared sample values, i.e.

$$A = Z/N.$$

Then the RMS value for the waveform is the square root of A. Suppose, for instance that the sample values are

$$1, 3, 5, 3, 1, -1, -3, -5, -3, -1.$$

The squared values are 1, 9, 25, 9, 1, 1, 9, 25, 9,1 and their sum Z is 90. There are 10 values ($N = 10$) and A is therefore equal to 90/10. The RMS value is the square root of A, namely 3.

For sine waves, the RMS value of amplitude over the period of the wave is actually 0.707 of the peak amplitude. For any other complex waveshape, the RMS value must be calculated from samples, as above. With the benefit of any of the modern general-purpose computer-based speech waveform editing and analysis packages, the calculation is quite straightforward.

The RMS value of sound pressure is thus proportional to sound intensity. In fact, when measured under plane wave conditions (i.e. with pressure variations in one plane only) and using 20 microPascals as a reference pressure, the RMS pressure may be equated with intensity. (20 µPa is the usual threshold value of sound pressure which can be detected by a normal adult listener.) It is indeed commonly assumed that intensity and RMS pressure are equivalent, although the assumption is accurate only when a sound is picked up close to the microphone with minimum interference from reflected sound.

It is often useful to know the intensity of a sound over more than one period of vibration. For example, it may be of interest to know the intensity of a whole syllable or word or clause relative to another. The RMS intensity of an entire word may be readily calculated from a stored speech waveform of any defined length using an appropriate number of samples from the speech waveform. Most speech analysis software allows the user to set cursors or markers on the time axis of the speech waveform and to calculate the RMS intensity over the period within the markers. Figure 7.6.3 gives two examples of marked waveforms. The intensity of a speech wave can be expected to vary over time – during a syllable or longer utterance – but can be calculated on a continuous basis. Effectively, the method determines intensity over a defined window and thus deliberately provides no detail of intensity variation within the period of the window.

Such output can be obtained from a traditional pitch and intensity meter of the stand-alone analog electronic type found in most phonetics laboratories, as well as by means of computer analysis packages. The period over which intensity is instantaneously and continuously calculated is known as the INTEGRATION TIME of the instrument and is usually adjustable from about 5 ms to about 50 ms. Commonly, integration times of from 10 to 20 ms are used, being short enough to detect any significant fluctuations within a syllable, but long enough to avoid including any effects of the period or fundamental frequency of the speech wave itself. Figure 7.6.4 shows the intensity envelope calculated from the waveform of figure 7.6.3(b) by means of a computer speech-processing package.

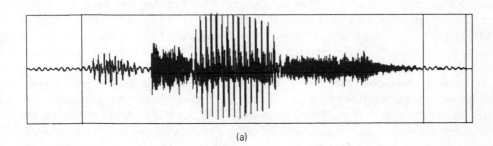

(a)

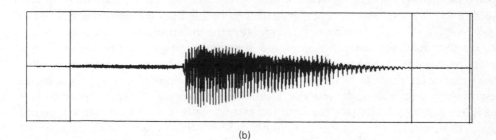

(b)

FIGURE 7.6.3 Waveforms marked for computation of RMS intensity: (a) *juice*; (b) *farm*. The overall intensity of waveform (a) between the markers is approximately 1.5 times that of (b)

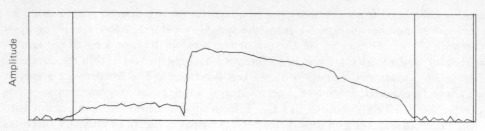

FIGURE 7.6.4   Intensity envelope for the waveform of figure 7.6.3(b)

7.7   Time domain properties of sound waves

When we analyse sound waves, we can consider them to have various properties, some of which are related to time and some to frequency. All the examples we have so far considered in this chapter are in fact time domain waveforms: they display changes (e.g. in the value of pressure) over time. In this section we will focus on time itself as a property.

The duration of a speech sound or an utterance is often phonetically important (sections 2.8 and 2.15 above). Durations we need to consider may be as small as a fraction of one cycle of a periodic waveform, or may be one complete period of vibration, or may be far longer. In some instances we want to know the duration of a whole word or utterance, or even the duration of a silence such as may occur in the closure phase of a voiceless stop.

To measure duration from a speech waveform we must be able to set reference markers on that waveform which have some meaningful relationship to the phonetic structure of the speech signal being measured. This normally means displaying the waveform on a computer screen (usually using a speech editing and analysis package) or on graph paper (most commonly using an inkjet recorder or similar device). The computer usually offers greater accuracy, especially if it allows the experimenter to replay the section of waveform between the markers. The experimenter can then place the markers accurately and confirm by ear that the phonetically appropriate section of the waveform has been marked. Figure 7.7.1 shows the waveform of the word *seat* /si:t/, marked to identify and measure the duration of the vowel nucleus. If larger durations are being measured and very high accuracy is not required, it is more practical to use a time-varying intensity graph to identify the start and end of the word or utterance to be measured. The major problem with this technique lies in establishing a reliable and consistent means of determining the appropriate thresholds of intensity which mark the start and end of the speech to be measured. Figure 7.7.2 shows an example of segmentation based on intensity (applied to the sentence 'I said "pen", not "pan"').

It is possible to become quite skilled at reading time domain waveforms and relating these to the phonetic structure of which they are realizations, but much of speech cannot be segmented and labelled as easily as the straightforward example of

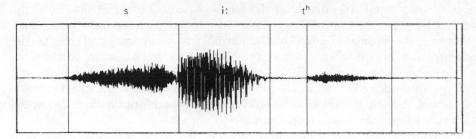

FIGURE 7.7.1   Segmentation of the waveform for /siːt/ (*seat*)

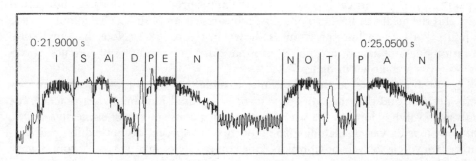

FIGURE 7.7.2   Segmentation of the intensity envelope of a sentence: *I said 'pen', not 'pan'*

figure 7.7.1. In fact, the most accurate method of measuring duration and of segmenting and labelling the time course of the acoustic speech signal, involves the combined use of time and frequency domain information. The techniques are discussed in the following sections.

7.8   Frequency domain properties of sound waves

If we are interested in the frequency-related properties of sound waves, it is possible, at least in the simplest cases, to take a fixed section of the waveform (extracted from the time course) and to analyse it without reference to the time domain.

As we have seen, sinusoidal vibrations are the simplest form of vibration, and they can be taken to be the components which are added together to constitute all other forms of vibration. The mathematical technique of breaking a complex wave down into its sinusoidal components is known as FOURIER ANALYSIS, after the nineteenth-century French scientist who developed its mathematical basis. The example given earlier as figure 7.4.1 illustrates a complex periodic vibration consisting of three sinusoidal components. The lowest frequency sine wave component is the FUNDAMENTAL frequency and the two higher frequency components are the second and third HARMONICS. All three form the harmonic components of the wave, the fundamental frequency being the first harmonic. Note that in periodic waves such as this one, the frequency values of the harmonics are integral multiples of the fundamental. Aperiodic vibrations may also be analysed into sinusoidal components but there will not be any simple arithmetic relationship among the components, which are then referred to not as harmonics but as OVERTONES or simply FREQUENCY COMPONENTS. Among speech sounds, vowels are characteristically periodic, while fricatives are examples of aperiodic sounds.

The frequency distribution and amplitudes of the harmonic components of a complex wave may be represented as its line SPECTRUM. For this display, the horizontal axis represents frequency and the vertical axis amplitude: each harmonic appears as a single vertical line located at the appropriate point along the horizontal axis, and the height of the harmonic line indicates its amplitude. The complex wave of figure 7.4.1 has a line spectrum as shown in figure 7.8.1. Note that this representation does not include any phase information. More examples of common waveform shapes are shown in figure 7.8.2.

The spectral analyses in these examples assume that the complex waves are perfectly periodic and that the same waveform is repeated indefinitely. In practice, the analysis is valid as long as the waveform remains consistent over successive cycles. Many sounds, however, including some of those in speech, do not exhibit this continuity from cycle to cycle of vibration. One commonly occurring type of sound wave is that known as QUASIPERIODIC. Imagine that a pendulum is given a push, then allowed to swing freely for several cycles before being given another push. The cycles following each push will decrease in amplitude at a rate dependent on the degree of damping in the system; and it remains for the next push to restore the amplitude of

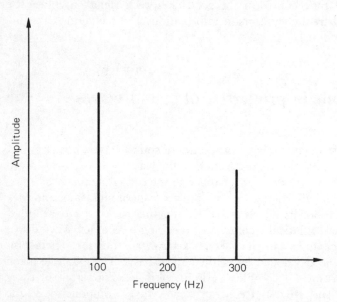

FIGURE 7.8.1   Line spectrum for figure 7.4.1

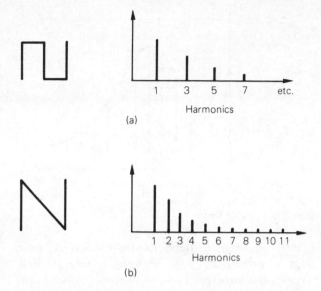

FIGURE 7.8.2 Line spectra of two common waveforms: (a) square wave; (b) sawtooth wave

swing to its initial value. If the pushes occur at uniform intervals, the resultant wave will have an effective period set by this interval, with a damped train of sine waves occurring in between. Two examples are shown in figure 7.8.3, where (a) has only a small amount of damping, and (b) substantial damping. The spectral properties of such waves are determined by three factors:

1   the natural resonant or oscillation frequency of the system;
2   the degree of damping (or losses) in the system;
3   the period / frequency of the external energy input.

Figure 7.8.4 gives line spectra for the waveforms of figure 7.8.3. The spacing of the harmonic lines is determined by the frequency with which the energy is restored (which is the effective fundamental frequency); the frequency of maximum amplitude of harmonic energy is set by the natural resonant frequency of the vibrating system;

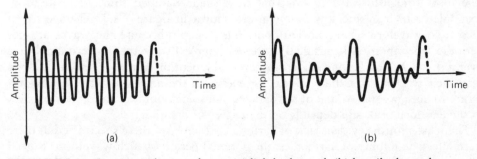

FIGURE 7.8.3   Quasiperiodic waveforms: (a) lightly damped; (b) heavily damped

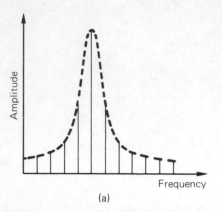
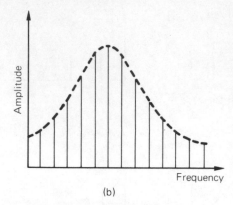

FIGURE 7.8.4   Line spectra: (a) figure 7.8.3(a); (b) figure 7.8.3(b)

and the pattern of the amplitude peaks (forming a shape usually referred to as the ENVELOPE) is determined by the degree of damping in the vibrating system. In these examples, the only difference between the two spectra is in their environ shape, since it is only the degree of damping in the resonant systems that varies.

If, on the other hand, the damping is kept constant, and only the frequency of energy restoration is changed, the resultant spectra have amplitude envelopes with the same shape and same centre frequencies; only the frequency spacing between their harmonic lines differs. Figure 7.8.5 shows examples of such waveforms and their corresponding spectra. Finally, if the damping and energy-restoring frequency remain constant, and only the oscillation frequency is altered, then the only significant change will be the centre frequency of the spectral envelope amplitude peak. Waveforms and spectra to illustrate this are shown in figure 7.8.6.

The shape of the spectral envelopes shown above can be seen to depend on the frequency and damping properties of the resonant system alone, and not on the frequency of energy restoration. A comparison of these spectral envelopes with those of the resonance curve in figure 7.5.3 will show that they correspond in shape quite directly. This is exactly as it should be: such spectra effectively display the frequency-selective properties of resonant vibrating systems.

Aperiodic sounds have more complex spectra than any of the preceding examples. The most straightforward case is that of a single damped sinusoidal vibration. Examples with high and low damping are shown in figure 7.8.7. The spectra of these two waveforms have no harmonic lines, simply because the waves are not periodic. The vibration (sinusoidal in these examples) converges to zero amplitude over a number of cycles and there is no cyclical repetition of the waveform. Despite this, their spectra still exhibit a peak of energy in the amplitude envelope with a centre frequency equal to that of the damped sinusoidal vibration, and the sharpness of the envelope peak still depends on the degree of damping.

The reason for the evident lack of harmonic structure in these spectra is that there is, in effect, an infinity of harmonics; the notional period of such waveforms is itself infinite. As a result, there is uniform density of spectral energy throughout the

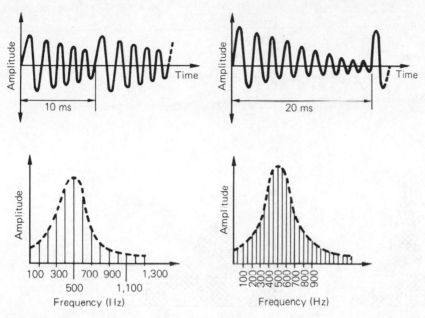

FIGURE 7.8.5   Waveforms with constant damping and differing energy restoration rates, with their line spectra

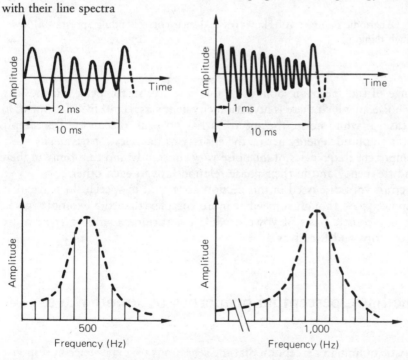

FIGURE 7.8.6   Waveforms with constant damping and energy restoration rates, and differing oscillation frequencies, with their line spectra (harmonics at 100 Hz intervals)

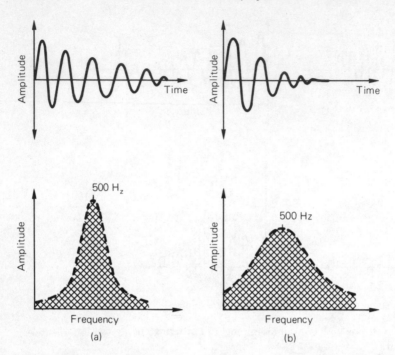

FIGURE 7.8.7   Aperiodic damped 500 Hz waves and their corresponding spectra: (a) low damping; (b) high damping

frequency range of the spectrum. Sounds of this sort are, so to speak, on the way towards pure noise, in which there is no periodicity in any aspect of the waveform. In the extreme case of white noise, the spectrum has no peak of energy, but simply reveals uniform amplitude energy across the entirety of the relevant frequency spectrum. The component frequencies of the noise vary constantly and randomly in their amplitude and frequency and in their phase relationships to each other.

All the spectral types discussed in this section are found in speech. In particular, the quasiperiodic type – though somewhat more complex than the examples given here – forms the acoustic basis of vowels, while the various aperiodic spectra are fundamental to stops and fricatives.

7.9   Some basic perceptual properties of sound waves

It is characteristic of human perception that the sensations we experience in response to stimuli rarely correspond directly with the values we derive from measurement of those stimuli. Our perception of light and dark, for instance, is not like the operation of a light meter but is highly sensitive to context: grey looks lighter against a dark background, sunshine seems even brighter when you emerge from a dark building, some colours under certain lighting are much easier to distinguish than others, and so on. Similar considerations apply to the perception of sound, studied under the heading of PSYCHOACOUSTICS. Here we are concerned particularly with the perception of loudness, pitch and what we have previously called timbre (section 7.1 above).

The human auditory system is capable of responding to an enormous range of sound intensities, and the upper end of this range is more than a million times greater than the lowest perceivable intensity. Not only does this lead to some very inconvenient numerical values, but, given the nature of perception, the figures do not relate very well to the perceptual effects of differences in intensity. If the intensity of a sound is doubled in numerical value on a simple linear scale, it does not necessarily mean a doubling in the sensation of loudness. The relation between perceived loudness and acoustic intensity is more nearly logarithmic. In a logarithmic scale increments are powers of ten, i.e. 2 corresponds to 10^2 ($= 100$), 3 to 10^3 ($= 1,000$), and so on. Hence the most convenient way to express intensity so that it relates to perceived loudness is as a logarithmic ratio, comparing the sound to a reference intensity. In honour of Alexander Graham Bell (the inventor of the telephone) the term BEL was given to a unit of this logarithmic scale: one Bel represents a ratio of 10:1, two Bels a ratio of 100:1. It turned out that this unit was too large for practical purposes, and one tenth of it, the DECIBEL (dB), was adopted as the usual measure. Thus one decibel is ten times the logarithm ($\log_{10}$) of the measured intensity (I_a) divided by the reference intensity (I_b):

$$1\,dB = 10\log_{10}(I_a/I_b).$$

Note that any sound intensity expressed in dB is always relative to some reference level of intensity. When dB values are expressed without explicit indication of this reference level (as they often are), it can usually be assumed that the reference level is the threshold of hearing. This threshold can be taken to be an intensity of 10^{-16} Watts per cm^2, which corresponds to a sound pressure of $20\,\mu Pa$, the statistically normal threshold of absolute hearing for a 1 kHz sinusoidal tone (section 7.6 above).

Since intensity is proportional to the square of sound pressure, a decibel is also equivalent to 20 times the logarithm ($\log_{10}$) of measured pressure (P_x) divided by the reference sound pressure level (P_y):

$$1\,dB = 20\log_{10}(P_x/P_y).$$

Intensity calculated in terms of sound pressure in this way, using the threshold of hearing as a reference level, is known as SOUND PRESSURE LEVEL or SPL. Some typical sound pressure levels are:

130 dB very loud sounds, such as the note of a trumpet at the bell of the instrument, or heavy metal music;

100 dB a brass band or ambulance or police siren;

80 dB noise in the cabin of a jet aircraft;

70 dB normal speech;

60 dB the background noise of a quiet office;

40 dB very quiet speech;

20 dB residual noise in a sound-treated room such as a recording studio;

0 dB threshold of hearing.

Although the logarithmic dB scale relates intensity to perceived loudness far better than a simple linear scale, there are substantial differences in the perceived loudness of sounds at different frequencies. The auditory system of a young healthy adult will respond to sounds at frequencies ranging from about 20 Hz to about 20,000 Hz, but the system is by no means equally sensitive to sounds at all frequencies within this range. Even simple sinusoidal tones of different frequencies may vary by 40 dB or more in their intensity to yield the same perceived loudness. This is particularly true of low-frequency sounds below 200 Hz; it also applies, to a lesser extent, to sounds above 5,000 Hz. (But most of the useful information in speech lies within the 200–5,000 Hz range.) The loudness of complex sounds is a more difficult matter, which will not be considered in detail here. In general terms, loudness is a function of the range and energy distribution of the frequency components in the sound concerned.

Pitch is the perceived period or frequency of a sound wave. Perceived pitch is largely determined by the fundamental frequency of the sound, and to a minor extent by the intensity of the sound, but the relationship between pitch and fundamental frequency is again nonlinear and varies with the frequency involved.

Our sensitivity to changes in the frequency of a sinusoidal tone – in other words our pitch discrimination – varies enormously as we move up the audible frequency scale. Below 1,000 Hz, listeners can readily hear frequency changes of 4 or 5 Hz; above this frequency our ability to perceive small absolute changes in frequency decreases progressively and substantially. By about 8,000 Hz listeners may have difficulty in discriminating changes that are below 40 or 50 Hz. Figure 7.9.1 shows just noticeable differences (JND) in pitch plotted against test frequency, illustrating this characteristic.

Since the relationship between frequency and pitch is not linear, a perceptual unit called the MEL has been devised to represent equal increments of pitch and relate them to frequency. Figure 7.9.2 shows mel values plotted against frequency: below 1,000 Hz there is a fairly direct correspondence between perceived pitch and frequency, and above this point the relationship becomes essentially logarithmic. Readers interested in the calculation may like to note the formula given by Fant (1968):

$$P = (1,000/\log_{10} 2)\,(\log_{10}(1 + f/1,000))$$
where P = pitch in mels and f = frequency in hertz.

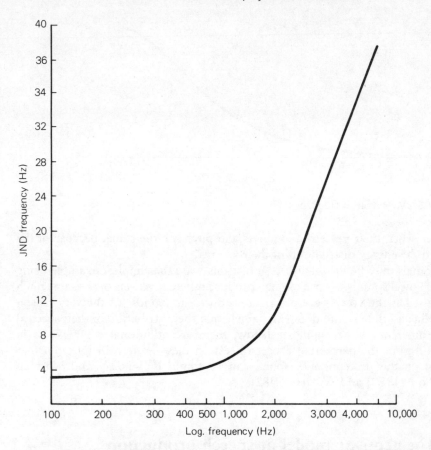

FIGURE 7.9.1   Just noticeable differences in frequency (JND) against frequency

Alternative transformations from frequency to mels are given by Beranek (1949), Lindsay and Norman (1977) and O'Shaughnessy (1987).

Complex sounds pose a curious problem. The pitch perceived depends on the fundamental, or lowest frequency component in the spectral composition of the sound. It does not matter what the amplitude of that fundamental is in relation to the other harmonic components of the sound. Indeed, even if the fundamental is removed by some form of electronic processing such as filtering, a pitch corresponding to the fundamental, known as the 'phantom fundamental', will still be perceived. (Recall that it is the fundamental frequency which determines the harmonic spacings.) It appears that essential pitch information can be decoded by listeners from the harmonic structure of the complex sound, at least for frequencies up to around 5,000 Hz.

Finally, we return to timbre and the example of a violin and a flute, playing the same note but sounding very different (section 7.1 above). In essence, timbre is a quality perceived in complex sounds: we hear differences of timbre in complex

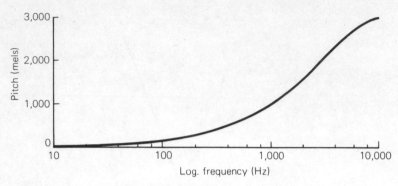

FIGURE 7.9.2   Mels against frequency

sounds, even when their perceived loudness and pitch are the same, because of the difference in the energy distribution of their spectra.

Speech sounds may be distinguished in just this way, the simplest example being that of pure vowel sounds. A speaker may produce different vowels of the same pitch and loudness, but the vowels are perceived as different sounds for the very reason that the violin and flute sound different, namely that the distribution of their spectral energies is different. As we shall see below, there are additional complexities in speech sounds, but the perceptual processes rest on these basic principles. Further information on the perception of sound can be found in Lindsay and Norman (1977), Moore (1982) and Warren (1982).

7.10   The acoustic model of speech production

The acoustic behaviour and properties of the human vocal tract in speech production are traditionally considered in terms of a source and filter model of the general type shown in figure 7.10.1. In the light of this model, the speech signal can be viewed acoustically as the result of the properties of the sound source, modified by the

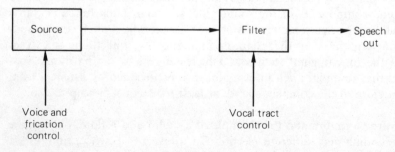

FIGURE 7.10.1   Source and filter model of speech production

properties of the vocal tract functioning as a frequency-selective filter. Both the properties of the source and those of the vocal tract can be varied – and are varied continuously – during speech.

A description of speech should of course relate the acoustic properties of the speech signal to the phonological information which the signal conveys. This is by no means a simple task, but the source and filter model provides a convenient functional division of the mechanisms that are active in the process of generating speech sounds.

7.11 Phonation as a sound source

The periodic vibration of the vocal folds known as PHONATION (sections 2.6 and 6.6 above) provides the most important and acoustically efficient sound source in the vocal tract. The expiratory airflow from the lungs is interrupted or modulated in a periodic vibratory cycle, and muscular tension settings and aerodynamic forces regulate the frequency and intensity of the output. An idealized form of the phonation airflow waveform is shown in figure 7.11.1(a), corresponding to the waveform of figure 6.6.2. The waveform displays the amount of air flowing through the glottis, plotted against time, and can be described as a volume velocity waveform. Being a form of periodic vibration, the waveform has a harmonic spectrum, as shown in figure 7.11.1(b). The slope of the energy profile of the spectrum for this idealized waveform is −12 dB per octave, which means that the intensity of the harmonics falls away quite rapidly at high frequencies. In normal speech, the slope of the spectrum varies considerably, depending on the phonatory setting being used. To some extent, this setting will be a matter of the individual's choice of speaking style; to some extent it will reflect the speaker's personal voice quality and habitual long-term phonatory setting.

Figure 7.11.2 shows volume velocity waveforms for two varieties of phonatory setting, with their harmonic spectra. Example (a) is breathy voice: the waveform results from relatively slow closure of the folds for quite short periods during the total cycle, such that there is almost continuous airflow. Although not shown here, there is usually some accompanying turbulence (especially in the region of vocal fold closure and minimum airflow). By contrast, example (b) represents quite forceful phonation, usually in the context of high overall articulatory effort, which results in very 'bright' voice quality. In this case, the folds remain closed for more than half the total cycle and the closure action is quite rapid, causing a very sharp fall in airflow rate before the airflow stops altogether in the closed phase of the cycle.

Several aspects of phonation waveforms contribute to their spectral shape. The property which affects voice quality as much as any other is the slope of the spectrum, as described above. This slope is controlled largely by the rate of change of airflow during the phonatory cycle, usually its fall from peak to closure in the pitch pulse. The faster the rate of change, the smaller the spectral slope and the greater the

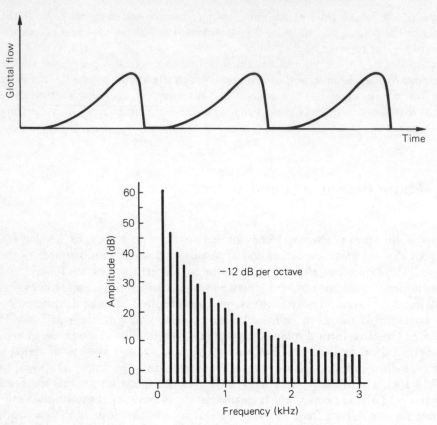

FIGURE 7.11.1   Phonation waveform and (idealized) spectrum
Adapted from: (b) Pickett 1980, p. 64.

amount of high frequency energy available as input to the vocal tract filter. Thus phonation which results in a rapid rate of change in the airflow is generally more efficient as a vocal tract sound source, because of its overall greater distribution of acoustic energy. The number of phonatory settings is of course virtually infinite, and the examples above merely illustrate one or two possibilities and their acoustic consequences.

Apart from its long-term variability, phonation also shows minor inconsistencies from cycle to cycle, which may have some effect on voice quality. All speakers seem to exhibit some inconsistency in duration from cycle to cycle of phonation. This constitutes variation in frequency, known as pitch JITTER. The greatest degree of jitter is usually evident at the start of phonation following a voiceless consonant, after which it reduces greatly in the syllable peak. If jitter is more pervasive, it is likely to be perceived as 'roughness' or 'harshness' in voice quality. Inconsistencies in the amplitude of phonation from cycle to cycle, known as SHIMMER, may also contribute to perceived voice quality.

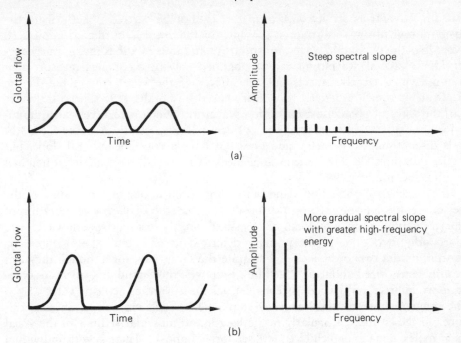

FIGURE 7.11.2 Phonation airflow (volume velocity) waveforms and their corresponding spectra: (a) breathy voice; (b) bright voice

More regular or periodic changes from cycle to cycle are also common. The perceptual effects are generally covered by the labels 'creak', 'creaky voice' and 'vocal fry' (cf. section 2.6 above). These changes occur most often at or below the bottom of a speaker's normal pitch range. The phonation waveform may show either a regular pattern of a pitch pulse of high amplitude followed by one of low amplitude, or pairs of pitch pulses close together with a longer interval between successive pairs (sometimes known as double pulsing).

Vocal creak is pervasive in some speakers, but may also be used deliberately. It is not uncommon for English speakers to switch into creaky voice as they reach the end of an utterance on low pitch, where, functionally, creak may be said to serve as a kind of extension of low pitch into a yet lower range. Flanagan (1958), Miller (1959), Lindqvist (1970), Fant (1979), Sundberg and Gauffin (1979) and Ananthapadmanabha (1984) provide extensive discussion of the acoustic properties of phonation, and Laver (1980) and Nolan (1983) offer useful accounts of how these properties contribute to overall voice quality and its linguistic functions. Ladefoged's review of the phonation process (1971, ch. 2) includes examples of contrasts from a variety of languages, including the breathy (or 'murmured') voicing of south Asian languages such as Gujarati, and the creaky voicing of West African Chadic languages such as Margi.

The phonation waveforms and spectra shown so far in this section have all been idealizations of natural speech, for the sake of simple illustration. But, in a sense, all phonation waveforms are idealizations: they cannot be derived directly from the acoustic output of the vocal tract at the lips, for the vocal tract filter (section 7.10 above) alters the phonation waveform spectrum and thus modifies the output wave-form. Hence 'actual' waveforms can be obtained only by a complex measurement technique which largely cancels out the effects of the vocal tract filter. Figure 7.11.3(a) shows such a derived waveform, based on Sondhi (1975) who describes one of the ways of obtaining a phonation waveform which is relatively uncontami-nated by vocal tract filter effects. The corresponding spectrum in figure 7.11.3(b) reveals discontinuities of energy and does not have a constant spectral slope, but these 'irregularities' do contribute in some measure to overall voice quality, often in a quite idiosyncratic way.

Two properties of phonation stand out as important in our understanding of the voice source: firstly, FUNDAMENTAL FREQUENCY (F_0), i.e. the frequency of vibration of the larynx in phonation, which can be measured directly from the speech waveform; and secondly, INTENSITY, as the primary determinant of overall speech intensity. Phonation modes cannot be included in quite the same way, for although they can be readily categorized auditorily (section 2.6 above), they stand in a far more com-plex, more indirect and less consistent relationship to various acoustic values.

The range of fundamental frequency employed by speakers reflects physical dif-ferences in the larynx, particularly in the length and muscular settings of the vocal folds in males, females and children (see section 6.5 above). There is wide individual variability, but the general ranges of F_0 for English speakers are:

Adult males   80–200 Hz
Adult females   150–300 Hz
Children   200–500 Hz.

Average values suggested by Peterson and Barney (1952) are around 130 Hz (males), 220 Hz (females) and 270 Hz (children). We should, however, be wary of general-izing about the characteristics of adult male, adult female and children's voices.

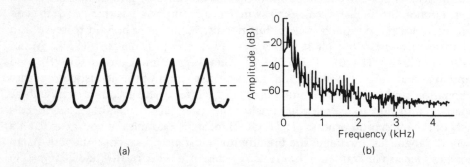

(a)   (b)

FIGURE 7.11.3   Waveform and spectrum of typical phonation in natural speech:
(a) waveform; (b) line spectrum
Adapted from: Sondhi 1975, p. 230.

Peterson and Barney's figures derive from linguistically restricted material, and do not reflect the dynamics of intonation. Moreover, it is especially difficult to generalize from the data on children because of the additional variation due to the process of maturation. It is also clear that there is appreciable overlap in the ranges used by the three groups, and that frequency range alone does not distinguish among them. There is much to be explored in this area, a point which is underlined by the fact that most research in speech acoustics has used male voices, partly for reasons of convenience in spectrographic analysis (section 7.14 below).

7.12   Sources of frication

Fricational sounds depend on air turbulence (sections 2.6 and 2.12 above) which creates aperiodic acoustic energy (sections 7.1 and 7.8 above). Unlike phonation, fricational sound may be generated at any location in the vocal tract, from the larynx to the lips, provided that it is possible to satisfy the minimum aerodynamic conditions for turbulent airflow: a constriction must be formed between two articulators, and sufficient airflow initiated to meet the aerodynamic conditions required to change laminar into turbulent airflow. These conditions will depend on the cross-sectional area and geometry of the constriction in question, and the acoustic properties of fricational sound are less predictable than those of phonation.

The intensity of fricational sound sources is essentially determined by the aerodynamic conditions and the relevant constriction geometry. Catford (1977) presents some evidence that intensity increases with increasing airstream velocity (which is not to be confused with volume velocity). Arkebauer et al. (1967) have shown that intensity is a function of the differential air pressure across the constriction. Stevens (1972b) and Scully (1979) provide quantitative treatments based on model studies which show that the turbulent noise sources of frication are determined by both the differential pressure across the constriction and its cross-section. The relationship between the two is shown in figure 7.12.1.

For some constrictions, where the fricative constriction area is much smaller than the glottal area, the differential pressure is effectively the subglottal pressure (Psg); but if the two areas are of comparable magnitude, the differential pressure will be defined by the actual pressure drop across the constriction. In general, it appears that the intensity of the sound source is essentially controlled by Psg during the dynamics of articulation, just as with phonation. The constriction area itself has much less influence, and cannot readily be varied systematically for a given fricative sound. As with phonation, we have no direct way of measuring frication sources, and the overall intensities measured for fricative consonants are in many instances strongly influenced by the vocal tract configuration.

Little quantitative information is available on the spectral properties of fricational sound sources. Both Fant (1960) and Stevens (1972b) suggest that the energy distribution is relatively uniform over the frequency range 500–3,000 Hz (within which

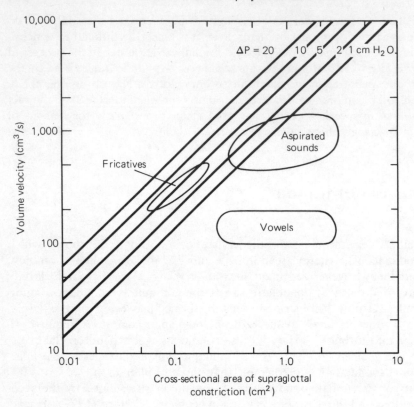

FIGURE 7.12.1   Relationship between constriction area, differential pressure (ΔP) and airflow
Source: Stevens 1972b, p. 1188.

fricative consonants are distinguished), with a falling slope of 6 dB per octave at both the high and low frequency ends. Figure 7.12.2 is an approximation to the typical fricational spectrum, based on the general characteristics of analogous turbulent airflow.

Voiced fricational sound sources introduce a further complexity. Since phonation occurs simultaneously, the pulses of phonation affect the differential pressure across the fricational constriction. This effect, known as MODULATION, causes regular variation in the pattern of airflow. According to Stevens (1972b), a Psg of 8 cm H_2O will result in a variation of 2–6 cm H_2O across the constriction over each phonatory cycle, causing modulation of around 15 dB at the fundamental frequency. Overall intensity will again be largely controlled by Psg, and the spectrum of this sound source will contain both periodic and aperiodic components.

For descriptive purposes, using categories or parameters of description, two properties of fricational sound sources are significant: their intensity, as reflected in the overall intensity of the speech sounds produced with this source; and their

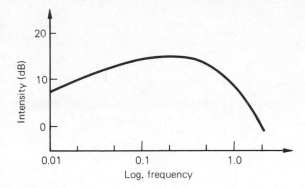

FIGURE 7.12.2   Fricative source spectrum (based on model studies)
Adapted from: Stevens 1972b, p. 1183.

categorization as either voiced or voiceless, determined by the presence or absence of any periodic (harmonic) structure in their spectra.

7.13   The vocal tract filter in vowel production

The source and filter model (section 7.10 above) treats the vocal tract as a filter: the filter is frequency-selective and constantly modifies the spectral characteristics of sound sources during articulation. The properties of the filter vary from moment to moment, for they are determined by the geometry of the vocal tract, which is itself varied as the speaker moves and positions articulatory organs such as the tongue and lips.

We begin with the acoustics of vowel production – consonants are rather more complicated – and take one of the simplest instances, a long central vowel [ɜ] such as is heard in RP *bird* or *fur*. This vowel is formed with the tongue, lips and jaw in a relatively neutral open position, and the cross-section of the supraglottal vocal tract is more or less uniform along its length, as seen in figure 7.13.1(a). In this vowel setting, the configuration of the vocal tract approximates a parallel-sided tube which is closed at one end (the larynx) and open at the other (the lips), as shown in figure 7.13.1(b). With one end closed, the tube acts as a resonator (section 7.5 above); in this case, the resonance is in the air column within the tube, resulting from the reflection of air pressure from one end of the tube to the other in what is known as a STANDING WAVE or stationary wave. Provided that the length of the tube is much greater than its diameter, air pressure will be reflected when a minimum of pressure occurs at the open end of the tube and a maximum of pressure at the closed end. This condition will be met at one quarter of a complete cycle of a sinusoidal vibration and at every half cycle thereafter, as shown in figure 7.13.2. As a result, the air column in the tube will resonate at a basic frequency corresponding to four times the length of

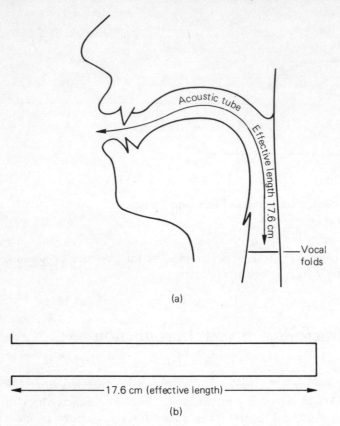

FIGURE 7.13.1   Resonator configuration for the central vowel [ɜ]: (a) actual vocal tract; (b) simple tube equivalent to (a)

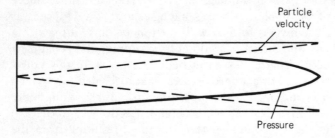

FIGURE 7.13.2   Quarter wave resonant frequency pressure and particle velocity patterns in a simple tube resonator

the tube (because of the quarter cycle of vibration) and at frequencies corresponding to every successive half cycle – in other words, at frequencies which are three, five, seven (and so on indefinitely) times the basic resonant frequency.

If we take s to stand for the relevant multiples 1, 3, 5, 7, etc., and C to be the speed of sound in air (about 340 m/s at sea level), then s multiplied by C, divided by 4 times the length of the tube, will give the resonant frequency:

$$F_{res} = sC/4l.$$

The equation is actually not quite accurate, for the standing wave does not stop precisely at the end of the open tube. In other words, the 'acoustic end' of the tube is slightly beyond the physical end of the tube. The equation therefore needs an 'end correction', which is partly related to the diameter of the tube; further details can be found in Wood (1964). It should also be noted that the reflections in the air column are not perfect, and some acoustic energy is radiated. It is of course desirable that this happens – so that sound is propagated – but it does produce losses in the column which are manifested as damping of the oscillations of resonance (section 7.8 above).

Thus the fundamental difference between the closed tube resonator just described and the resonating systems introduced in section 7.3 is that in the former resonance occurs at a succession of frequencies. This more complex mode of multiple resonance is crucially important in speech production.

We now return to the vowel of figure 7.13.1 and its tube resonator equivalent. The length of this resonator is the length of the vocal tract from the lips to the glottis. Human vocal tracts are of course not all of identical length, and there are appreciable differences, depending on whether the person is male or female, physically mature, and so on. With those reservations in mind, we can nevertheless take a typical male vocal tract to be 17.6 cm long (Fant 1960). According to data in Pickett (1980), the length of a woman's vocal tract is about 80–90 per cent of a man's, while a child's, depending on age, may be around 50 per cent of a man's.

Using the tube resonator equation above – including end-effect corrections – we can show that a vocal tract of 17.6 cm will resonate at 500 Hz, 1,500 Hz, 2,500 Hz, and so on to infinity. Figure 7.13.3 shows the frequency response of this tube

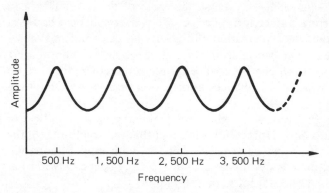

FIGURE 7.13.3   Frequency response of tube resonator approximating male vocal tract for the vowel [ə]

resonator. The figure reveals that the frequency-selective characteristics are similar to those of the simple resonator shown in figure 7.5.3, except that a series of resonant peaks now appears at the frequencies predicted by the tube resonator equation. Of these peaks, the three lowest play a major part in determining vowel quality. Higher peaks contribute more to personal voice quality, and become progressively less significant above about 5 kHz.

These resonance properties of the vocal tract must of course be considered in conjunction with the sound source, which for vowels is normally phonation at the larynx (section 7.11 above). In fact speech output from the lips actually reflects the combined acoustic properties of phonation, tract resonance and the acoustic radiation properties of the human head. Figure 7.13.4 shows these components for the vowel [ɜ], namely

a   the spectrum of laryngeal phonation;
b   the resonant frequency response of the tract;
c   the phonation spectrum resulting from the effects of tract resonance;
d   the spectrum of the final radiated acoustic sound pressure wave;
e   the time domain sound pressure wave itself.

In this idealized example, the phonation spectrum (a) is assumed to have a slope of -12 dB per octave, and the resonance peaks in the tract (b) have equal amplitudes. The result is a spectrum (c) with peaks of energy caused by the resonance. These peaks of energy, produced by selective enhancement of the source by tract resonance, are known as FORMANTS. The tract resonances themselves are sometimes referred to as formants, but this is technically imprecise. Formants are a consequence of resonance, not resonance itself. The information-bearing formants of the speech spectrum are conventionally numbered upwards from the lowest in frequency (F_1, F_2, etc.); the three lowest formants are essential parameters in the description of vowel quality.

The final spectrum (d) of the radiated sound pressure wave has a high-frequency slope only half that shown in (c). This is because sound emerges from the lips, and the lips constitute a single point relative to the surface area of the head. The head functions as a kind of reflecting surface, or, more precisely, as a spherical baffle of about 9 cm radius. This favours the propagation of high-frequency sound and causes output to rise by about $+6$ dB per octave from the region of several hundred Hz upwards. The -12 dB per octave slope of the voice source is thereby reduced to an effective -6 dB per octave, which also enhances information-bearing aspects of the signal.

Our example of the vowel [ɜ] assumes that there is equal damping (or bandwidth) on each of the resonances. It is only if this condition is met that the amplitudes of the resonant peaks are equal. In fact under normal conditions, with modal phonation providing the sound source, there is usually greater damping (wider bandwidth) at the higher resonances, yielding unequal formant amplitudes.

Having looked at frequency characteristics, we can also consider the process of vowel production in the light of the time domain waveform shown in figure

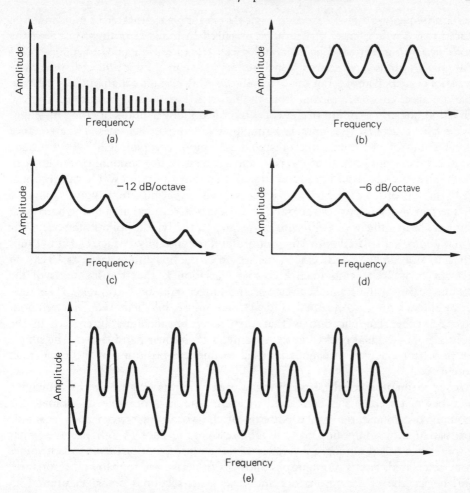

FIGURE 7.13.4   Acoustic properties of the vowel [ɜ]: (a) harmonic spectrum of phonation source; (b) resonant response of vocal tract; (c) spectral envelope from filtering of source by vocal tract resonance; (d) spectral envelope of radiated sound pressure wave; (e) time domain sound pressure wave

7.13.4(e). This is a damped quasiperiodic wave similar to that shown above in figure 7.8.3 (waveform) and figure 7.8.4 (line spectrum). In both cases, there is a single peak in the line spectrum, and the harmonic energy lines are determined by the repetition rate of the energy restoration. But the vowel waveform is more complex: because of the multiple resonances of the vocal tract, there are several damped sine waves superimposed on each other, and only the one occurring at the lowest frequency is clearly seen. From this perspective, vowel production may be seen as a series of impulses from the larynx which shock the multiple resonator into a series of simultaneous damped sinusoidal vibrations at different frequencies. This gives us an alternative view of the speech production process, a view no less valid than that based on frequency. It is another reminder that reality is multifaceted and cannot be reduced to a single aspect. We must be prepared to think in both ways about the speech signal to understand how phonological structure is encoded in it.

All vowel sounds have spectra which reflect the source, filter and radiation characteristics described above, but other vowels are more complex than our [ɜ] example. Once the articulators are moved from the more or less neutral posture of a vowel such as [ɜ], the cross-section of the vocal tract is no longer uniform along its length and the tract ceases to approximate a simple tube with parallel sides. The resonance characteristics of the tract are correspondingly more complex. Change of tongue position, vertical movement of the jaw, and protrusion or rounding of the lips can all contribute to variation in cross-sectional area. For the [ɜ] vowel, cross-sectional area is of the order of $6\,cm^2$; but some vowels, especially high vowels, involve extreme narrowing in part of the tract, and the cross-sectional area at the narrowest point may be as little as one-fifteenth of the area at the widest point in the tract. For the vowel [uː], articulated with lips rounded and tongue fully retracted, Fant (1960) quotes areas as small as $0.32\,cm^2$ in the region of the lips and as large as $13\,cm^2$ in the front cavity. The consequence of such variation is that the locations of the resonant peaks on the frequency scale are no longer equally distributed. Their relative amplitudes are also unequal, and are determined by their frequency relationships. A further complication is that there may be absolute differences in the amplitude of individual peaks, caused by differences in their bandwidths. The simple tube resonator calculation cannot be used to find the positions of the vocal tract resonances.

To approximate a vocal tract varying in area along its length, we could imagine two tubes of different size connected to each. And it is possible to estimate the unequally distributed resonance patterns of the vocal tract from such a simple approximation, a compound pair of tube resonators. Fant (1960) provides what are sometimes called nomographs, diagrammatic representations from which values can be calculated. Fant's nomographs allow us to derive the four lowest resonances from the lengths of the resonators and their cross-sectional areas. Figure 7.13.5 shows such compound resonators for various vowels with the approximate positions of their resonant peaks.

It is nevertheless essential to note that the two-tube representation is only a crude approximation of the complex resonant cavity system of the human vocal tract during vowel production. The approximation can be improved by using more than two resonators – indeed, the more tubes the better the approximation – but the calculations also become more complex as the number of tubes increases (cf. section 7.18 below).

Early theories of the acoustics of vowel production did in fact attempt to explain the resonance patterns of vowels in terms of a vocal tract made up of two resonant cavities coupled together. It would indeed be convenient if we could associate resonances (and hence formants) with specific cavities formed by the vocal tract shape characterizing a particular sound. The model does work tolerably well for high vowels such as [iː] where the tongue does divide the tract into a small front cavity and a large back cavity. In this case the first resonance is correspondingly

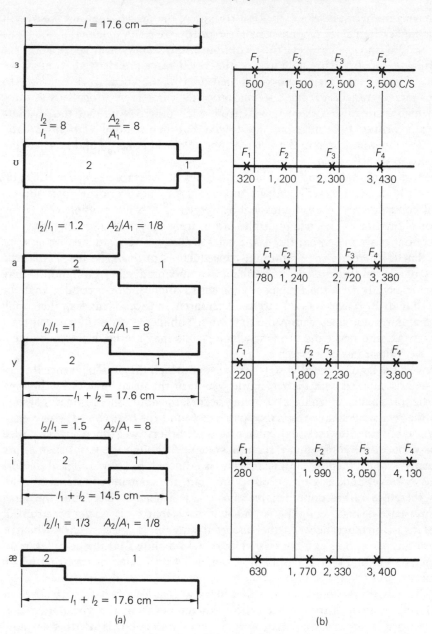

FIGURE 7.13.5   Two-tube resonators approximating the vocal tract for various vowels: (a) resonator dimensions; (b) formant pattern
Adapted from: Fant 1960, p. 66.

quite low and the second quite high. Unfortunately, the model does not work well either for higher-frequency resonances or for open vowels in general.

Figure 7.13.6 shows the vocal tract configurations and typical spectra for the vowels [i], [a] and [u]. The diagrams of the vocal tract are derived from X-ray data and represent the varying cross-sectional area of the vocal tract from lips to glottis. As already noted, it is the distribution of the three lowest formants in these spectra which distinguishes these vowels from each other. Note that the absolute values of the formant frequencies are not crucial, but their relative relationships are, reflecting the inherent systemic character of phonological contrast and its encoding in the acoustic speech signal.

It is important to understand that the frequencies of the tract resonance peaks do not necessarily coincide exactly with harmonic energy lines from the voice source. They will coincide only when the resonance frequency is some multiple of the frequency of phonation (F_0); since both phonation frequency and resonance patterns change continuously in speech, the frequencies will not be consistently or systematically related. There are two important consequences of this. The first is that the frequency of a given formant (i.e. its frequency of maximum energy amplitude) may not coincide exactly with the frequency of tract resonance. The second is that for voices with high F_0 ranges (notably those of children and some females), there may be very few harmonic lines within the amplitude-enhancing range of a given tract resonance peak, and hence the formant which results may not be distinctly defined. Figure 7.13.7 illustrates two extremes.

So far we have ignored nasal vowels – vowels in which the oral–pharyngeal resonator system is coupled with the resonator system of the nasal cavities by the lowering of the soft palate. When nasal coupling occurs, the additional resonator system modifies the relatively simple resonance patterns found for oral vowels: some resonances, notably the lowest, are enhanced and others weakened by so-called ANTIRESONANCES in the compound resonator system. Although the nasal cavities are anatomically stable, their overall geometry is affected by physiological factors (section 6.8 above) and, as Fant (1960) points out, the contribution of nasal resonance is therefore rather unpredictable. From the listener's viewpoint, the most important aspect of nasal coupling is that it distorts that basic vowel spectrum. It is the relative difference between the distorted and undistorted spectra which is relevant in the perception of a contrast. Figure 7.13.8 shows (a) the complex resonant cavity system of a typical nasalized vowel, and (b) the kind of spectrum which may result.

Finally, it is worth reminding readers that for vowels at least (whether nasalized or not), it is the relative distribution of the resonant peaks in the vocal tract that matters. Thus if whisper rather than normal voice phonation is used as a sound source, vowel identity can still be preserved. In whispered vowels, the formants are peaks of aperiodic energy, demonstrating that it is the energy peaks themselves which reflect tract filter characteristics and which allow the hearer to discern the identity of the vowels.

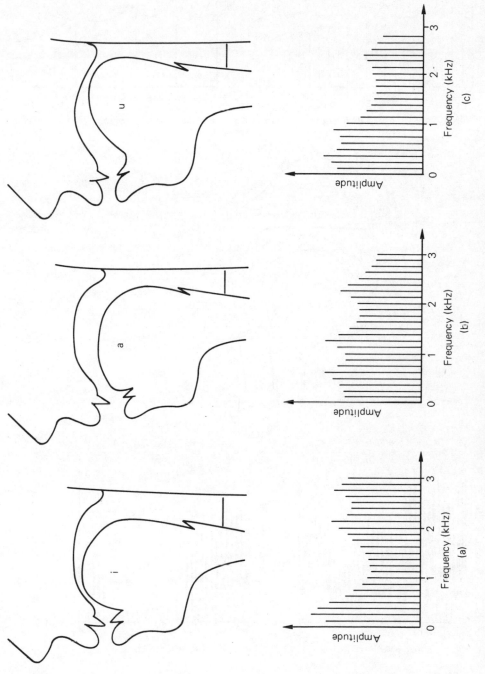

FIGURE 7.13.6 Vocal tract configurations and spectra for the vowels (a) [i]; (b) [a]; (c) [u]

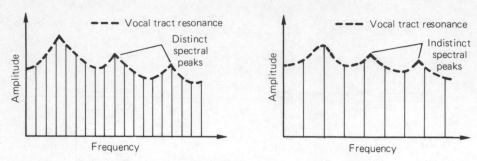

FIGURE 7.13.7   Effect of harmonic spacing on spectral peak structure

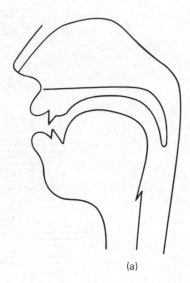

(a)

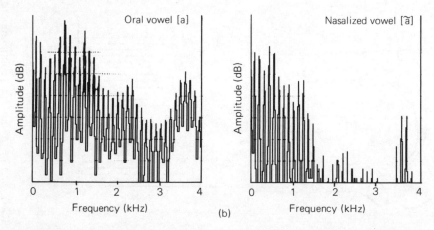

(b)

FIGURE 7.13.8   Nasalized vowel: (a) vocal tract resonance system; (b) comparative oral and

7.14   Spectrographic analysis of speech

Our account so far has been concerned with static vowel sounds: all the spectral information we have presented has been in the form of SPECTRAL SECTIONS. In effect we have taken slices of speech, to show the distribution of acoustic energy across the frequency spectrum in a specific portion of time. Such an analysis gives no information about any changes during the time course. Single spectral sections are certainly very useful, but given that speech is a dynamic process, it is essential to have a spectral analysis which also displays the changes in the speech spectrum over time. Indeed, the development of the first instruments which could do this, at the end of the Second World War, proved to be one of the great landmarks in experimental phonetics.

There are several ways in which time-varying spectral energy can be displayed, the challenge being that of portraying three continuously variable dimensions on a flat (two-dimensional) display. The classic format is known as the SPEECH SPECTROGRAM: frequency is represented on the vertical axis of the display, and time on the horizontal axis, while the magnitude of acoustic energy is shown by the intensity (darkness or brightness) of the display. Figure 7.14.1 shows such a display for the central vowel [ɜ], produced with a constant fundamental frequency of 100 Hz. The frequency axis usually has variable scaling but is commonly set to 0–8 kHz or less. The time axis is usually fixed to display a stretch of 2.5 seconds. In this particular spectrogram, the harmonic structure of the speech signal can be seen very clearly, the darkest harmonic lines indicating the peaks of energy of the formants.

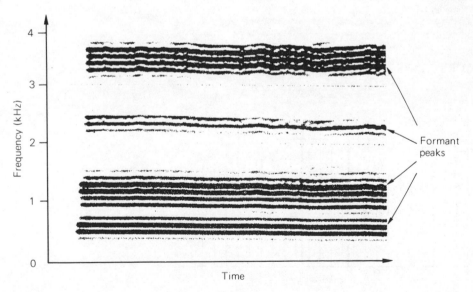

FIGURE 7.14.1   Spectrogram of the vowel [ɜ]

The instrument traditionally used to produce an analysis of this sort is the SPEECH SPECTROGRAPH. First described by Koenig et al. (1946), it has been refined technically over the years but with little change in principle. The machine has been commercially available for many years and most phonetics laboratories contain at least one. Figure 7.14.2 shows how the instrument is organized. The stretch of speech which we wish to analyse is first recorded on a magnetic drum, or in some machines on a loop of magnetic recording tape. Usually no more than 2.5 seconds of speech can be recorded. To perform the analysis, the sample is repeatedly replayed by rotating the drum or running the tape loop. To save time and to minimize certain technical limitations in the analysis, this replaying is at a much higher speed than normal speech. During each rotation of the drum or tape loop, the replayed speech is passed through a bandpass filter to achieve a spectrum analysis. This filter allows only the energy from the range of frequencies within its bandwidth (or bandpass) to pass through. Figure 7.14.3 illustrates the principle of bandpass filtering.

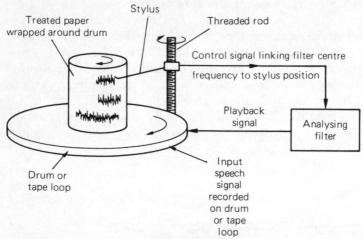

FIGURE 7.14.2   The speech spectrograph

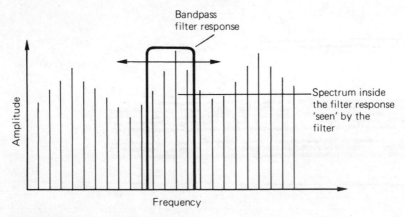

FIGURE 7.14.3   Bandpass filtering

The key property of the filter is that it can be electronically moved across the range of frequencies to be analysed. On the very first replay of the recorded speech, it is effectively located so that the centre of its band is at the lowest frequency to be analysed. The output from the filter is thus only the energy in the speech sample that falls within that small range of frequencies. Mechanically linked to the rotating drum or tape loop is a smaller drum around which is wrapped a sheet of specially treated paper. The paper is actually a sandwich with an inner layer of a carbon-based powder between two layers of paper. Beside the magnetic drum and paper drum assembly is a tall threaded metal rod, also mechanically linked to the rotating magnetic drum, usually via a rubber drive belt. Mounted on the threaded rod is an assembly, also threaded, containing a wire stylus. When the threaded rod rotates, this stylus assembly moves up the rod, just as a nut moves along a bolt if the bolt is rotated.

The output of the bandpass analysing filter is processed to yield a signal representing the overall intensity of the energy from the filter. The signal is transformed into a high voltage and fed to the wire stylus, which rests on the paper wrapped around the drum. The voltage at the stylus, representing the intensity of the energy in the speech sequence, burns into the carbon-loaded paper: the greater the stylus voltage, the greater the degree of burning and the blacker the paper at that point on the rotating drum. With each rotation, the stylus assembly moves up the paper and marks a new section. As the bandpass filter is linked electronically to the stylus position, it too moves to a higher frequency range with each rotation.

Thus the stylus and the analysing bandpass filter spiral continuously up the frequency scale, while the paper is synchronized so that the speech recorded on the drum is repeatedly passed through the filter, but always at a new band of frequencies. The stylus marks on the paper the relative intensities of all the frequency components in the speech sequence, and does so in correct timing, matching the pattern of the speech signal itself.

Although the time scale is not ordinarily changed, the frequency scale may be expanded or contracted to display as much or as little of the overall range of speech frequencies as may be required. In the analysis of vowels the frequency range is commonly set at 0–5 kHz, as there is little of phonological interest above this range. For fricatives, which often exhibit substantial high frequency aperiodic energy, the full frequency scale of 0–8 kHz may be more appropriate.

The other important variable in this form of analysis is the frequency resolution of the spectral analysis, which is set by the bandwidth of the analysing filter. If the filter has a very narrow bandwidth it will be able to pinpoint the energy from the individual harmonics, but if the bandwidth is wide in relation to harmonic spacing, the filter will not reveal comparable detail. Figure 7.14.4 shows how a signal with an F_0 of 100 Hz is 'seen' by bandpass filters of 50 Hz and 300 Hz.

From Figure 7.14.4 it is evident that the 50 Hz filter easily resolves the individual harmonics of the signal, and would do so down to an F_0 of 50 Hz. Below this frequency, the harmonics would become too closely spaced for them to be identified individually. (In fact very few speakers have F_0 values below this in their speech.) The 300 Hz filter will obviously be unable to resolve the harmonics unless F_0 exceeds

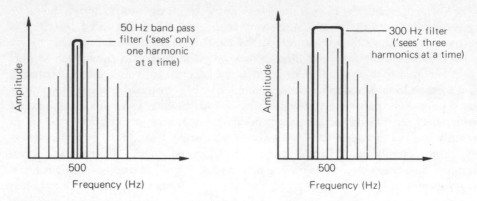

FIGURE 7.14.4   Effects of narrow (50 Hz) and broad (300 Hz) bandpass filters

300 Hz, which confines the analysis to relatively high pitched voices, higher than most adult males.

In most applications of an analysis, attention will be focused either on the formant structure of the speech or on the F_0 patterns. For this reason conventional spectrographs are usually provided with at least two analysis filters, known simply as narrow and wide, usually with the bandwidths cited, namely 50 Hz and 300 Hz. The narrow band filter is used for analysis of F_0, and the wide band filter is for formant analysis. The wide band filter effectively smears the harmonic structure so that only the overall energy seen by the filter across any span of 300 Hz is detected and marked on the paper. This enhances the visual display of the formant structure. See figure 7.14.5 for narrow and broad band analyses of the vowel of figure 7.14.3; but note that in this case F_0 falls from the region of 140 Hz to around 90 Hz.

There is another effect of varying the filter bandwidth, which influences the time domain aspect of the analysis. All filters take a finite time to respond at the output to

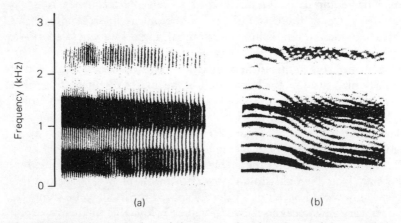

FIGURE 7.14.5   (a) Wide and (b) narrow band analyses of the vowel [3]

energy at the input; this response time T_r, in seconds, is approximately the reciprocal of the filter bandwidth:

$T_r = 1/$filter bandwidth.

Thus the response times of 50 Hz and 300 Hz filters will be about 20 ms (one fiftieth of a second) and 3.3 ms (one three-hundredth of a second).

This means that there is a direct trade-off between frequency resolution and time resolution. Fortunately, this works largely to our advantage in speech analysis, because F_0-related analysis does not usually involve the examination of rapid changes of spectral energy in the time course of the speech; in particular, changes occurring over less than 20 ms are unlikely to be of interest. On the other hand, rapid changes are often relevant in formant-related analysis, where the wide band filter is able to respond far more quickly (to energy changes occurring over greater than 3.3 ms). The time and frequency resolution properties of the analysis are easily seen in figure 7.14.5. In the narrow band analysis, the harmonics are clearly visible and come closer together on the frequency scale as F_0 falls; in the wide band analysis, no harmonics can be seen but the location of formant energy is distinct. In addition, the wide band display shows vertical lines which correspond to the individual pulses of phonation, and these can be seen to be more widely separated on the time scale as F_0 falls.

A comparison of the representation of F_0 in these two displays is another reminder of the importance of balancing different perspectives: no one view can be singled out as the sole objective representation. The point is even further emphasized by the choice of 50 Hz and 300 Hz for the filters. The two values are actually optimized for low pitched voices, although more modern instrumentation sometimes provides 450 and 600 Hz filters as well, to enhance the analysis of higher pitched voices.

Spectral displays of the sort shown above provide easily quantified and quite accurate information about the general pattern of energy distribution in the spectrum over time. In particular they highlight the location of formant peaks and other high amplitude energy, and for many purposes this is all that is required. But they do not provide readily quantified data on the amplitude and shapes of energy distribution. This applies especially to wide band spectrograms because of the filter's smearing effect on harmonic structure. Most spectrographs include a facility for making SPECTRAL SECTIONS which do give detailed amplitude information – based on the narrow band analysis filter – about any given point on the waveform.

The use of computers and special purpose digital hardware has overtaken much of the traditional analog instrumentation in speech research, although it remains true of spectrum analysis, as of other areas of speech technology, that the underlying principles and aims often do not change. The essential characteristic of digital signal analysis is that it is based on discrete samples. Most forms of spectral analysis relevant to our concerns perform a Fourier analysis (section 7.8 above): what is distinctive about digital analysis is only that it uses discrete samples. That is, analog instruments process a continuous speech waveform, but digital systems perform an analysis on discrete samples of that waveform. The general procedure is known as the DISCRETE FOURIER TRANSFORM or DFT.

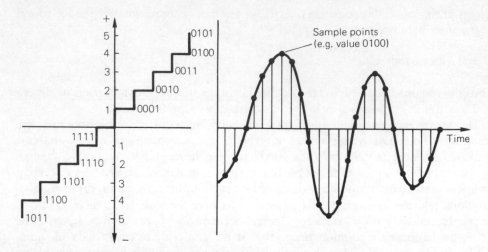

FIGURE 7.14.6   Waveform sampling: digital values for the magnitude of the waveform at each sample point may be read from the quantization scale

Figure 7.14.6 shows the process of DIGITIZING a waveform: the sampling is discrete on both the amplitude axis and the time axis. The accuracy of the digital representation depends on the number of discrete steps or samples taken on each axis. The digital encoding of amplitude is known as QUANTIZATION. Since each amplitude value is represented as a number made up of bits (binary digits, i.e. zeros or ones), the total number of steps on the amplitude axis will always be a power of two (2, 4, 8, 16, 32, 64 and so on). Sufficient steps must be used to ensure that we do encode the range of amplitudes in the waveform being analysed. In speech, we are normally interested in frequency components of the spectrum of a given speech waveform over an amplitude range between 40 dB and 60 dB, and the amplitude quantization must contain 1,024 steps to encode a 60 dB range. The figure 1,024 corresponds to a 10-bit binary number, and we thus need a 10-bit word per sample. (If this seems large, it is worth noting that hi-fi music is usually encoded on compact discs using 16 bits per sample.) The digital encoding of the instantaneous values of the amplitude at regular discrete intervals of time along the speech time domain waveform is known as the process of SAMPLING. The number of such samples taken per unit time is known as the SAMPLING RATE.

The maximum frequency (F_{max}) encoded is directly determined by the sampling rate. If T is the time in seconds between successive samples, then F_{max} is the reciprocal of $2T$:

$$F_{max} = 1/2T.$$

In other words, the frequency of the sampling rate must be double that of the highest frequency component which we wish to encode digitally. For example, to include all the frequency components up to 5,000 Hz we must have a sampling rate of 10,000 samples per second, so that $T = 10$ microseconds. Again, this is quite a modest level of accuracy compared to the sampling rates in excess of 40,000 per second used for compact discs and hi-fi digital tape recording.

The properties of the DFT spectrum analysis are directly related to sampling rate. To obtain a spectral section of the kind shown in figure 7.14.7, we select the place of interest in the waveform and use a set of samples on the time axis giving amplitude values around that point to make the spectral analysis (DFT) calculations. A single sample obviously cannot be used, because the Fourier analysis must have access to properties of the waveform over time. For this reason, a WINDOW on the time axis is needed to capture a precisely known interval of the waveform information. This yields a set of samples. To avoid introducing artifacts into the analysis, the samples in the window either side of its centre can be amplitude weighted in one of several ways. The most common of these, known as the HAMMING WINDOW, progressively reduces the amplitude of the samples either side of the centre, using a cosine law. The width of the window is defined by the number of samples it contains. Where no amplitude weighting is used the window is said to be rectangular.

A commonly used version of the DFT algorithm is the FAST FOURIER TRANSFORM (FFT), so called because it provides a rapid method of calculating DFTs. These normally work with windows with numbers of samples which are a power of two, and hence are known as 64, 128, 256, 512 or 1,024-point FFTs.

The effective time resolution (T_r) of the DFT is the number of points in the DFT multiplied by the time in seconds between successive samples; and the frequency resolution (F_r) is the reciprocal of T_r. If N is the number of points, and T the time in seconds between successive samples, then

$$T_r = N \times T$$
and $\quad F_r = 1/T_r.$

Thus for a 512-point FFT (DFT), performed on a sample digitized at 10,000 samples per second, the width of the window will be 51.2 ms, which will also be the worst case time resolution. The frequency resolution will be 19.5 Hz consisting of 256 equally spaced points. (The reason why the analysis contains only 256 points and not 512 is that only the points in the lower half of the transform contain information related to the frequency spectrum below half the sampling frequency, i.e. 0–5,000 Hz, the actual encoded frequency range of signal.) Figure 7.14.7 shows 512-point FFTs for the vowels [iː], [aː] and [ɔː], with the Hamming windowed waveform samples on which the analysis was performed.

There are two major advantages of digital analysis of speech signals. The first is that once the signal has been digitally encoded and stored, it can be edited, processed, measured and manipulated and filed with far greater efficiency than is possible with analog instruments and an ordinary tape recorder. The second is that the analysis itself can be more easily varied to give optimum time and frequency resolution properties.

The FFT example in figure 7.14.7 shows a very narrow band spectral analysis. If less frequency resolution is required in a spectral section, the simplest procedure is to

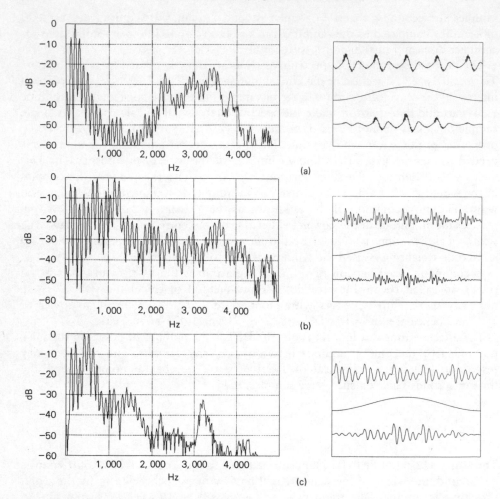

FIGURE 7.14.7 FFT analyses (512-point) of the vowels (a) [iː], (b) [aː]; (c) [ɔː], together with their windowed waveforms used in the analysis

reduce the number of points in the FFT. As the trading relationship between time and frequency resolution in the analysis applies to the DFT just as it does to the analog spectrograph, reducing the number of points will reduce the width of the analysis window. Time resolution will then become finer, which may or may not be an advantage. If the window becomes shorter than the pitch period of the waveform, the location of its centre will become more critical, and may markedly affect the spectral shape yielded by the analysis. It is also important to understand that as the number of points in the DFT is reduced, the interpolation on the frequency scale becomes coarser.

If all that is needed is a smoothed outline of the spectral energy, and time resolution is not critical, a CEPSTRALLY SMOOTHED narrow band DFT may be more desirable.

In this process, further spectrum analysis and processing are performed on the spectrum itself by treating it as though it were yet another signal waveform. This yields a smoothed spectral envelope undisturbed by voicing ripple, and preserves more frequency domain detail and interpolation than is possible by merely reducing the number of points of analysis. Figure 7.14.8 shows spectral sections for the vowel [iː], with (a) a 512-point FFT, (b) a 128-point FFT, and (c) a cepstrally smoothed 512-point FFT. All these FFTs were produced by a signal editing and processing package operating at 10,000 samples per second, and greater than 10 bit quantization.

DFT techniques can also be used to generate spectrograms by taking a large number of spectral sections side by side and overlapping them. This procedure of course differs from that of the traditional analog spectrograph, in which each sweep (or drum rotation) covers a small frequency range but the whole of the time occupied by the speech being analysed; here, each analysis covers the whole frequency range. The case of the narrow band spectrogram is simple enough: a 512- or 256-point FFT is taken every 5 or 10 ms along the waveform (giving reasonable overlap) and then displayed in the conventional way with frequency on the vertical axis and time on the horizontal axis. The amplitude of the spectral energy is given by intensity of blackness, or in some cases by colour (either in hard copy or on a visual display screen). The broad band spectrogram presents more of a problem, because a simple reduction of the number of FFT points results in a frequency axis with rather poor interpolation. This is overcome by performing equivalent narrow band FFTs of, say, 512 points, but actually using only the centre of the sample window for data and filling the outer parts of the window with zeros. The result provides the excellent frequency interpolation of the 512 point analysis, yet has the fine time resolution and broad frequency resolution of an analysis with many fewer points. Figure 7.14.9 shows examples of narrow and broad band DFT spectrograms of the vowels [iː], [aː] and [ɔː], which were produced on a commercial digital spectrograph having all the analysis functions of a traditional analog spectrograph (and many more, given the much greater flexibility of the digital signal processing technology).

Although Fourier-based spectrographic analysis of speech is the most common technique for examining the properties of the speech spectrum, linear prediction coefficient analysis (LPC) has proved increasingly popular in recent years. LPC analysis represents the speech signal in terms of a set of coefficients which aim to predict the signal from its past time domain values with minimum error. These coefficients may be used to produce a spectral representation of that signal. In essence this takes the form of a vocal tract filter frequency response, including the effects of the slope of the voice source spectrum and radiation, which would produce a time domain speech waveform the same as that of the waveform being analysed. The result is a pseudo-spectral section rather similar in appearance to a cepstrally smoothed DFT section, which can show the formant structure of the speech very clearly (figure 7.14.10).

Although very useful for the analysis of vowels (and some approximants) because of the clarity with which it can identify formant locations, LPC analysis must be treated with some caution. In its conventional form, it is based on resonances only in

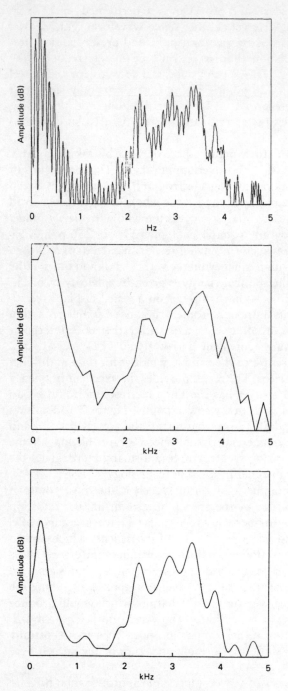

FIGURE 7.14.8   Spectral sections of the vowel [iː]: (a) 512-point FFT; (b) 128-point FFT; (c) cepstrally smoothed 512-point FFT

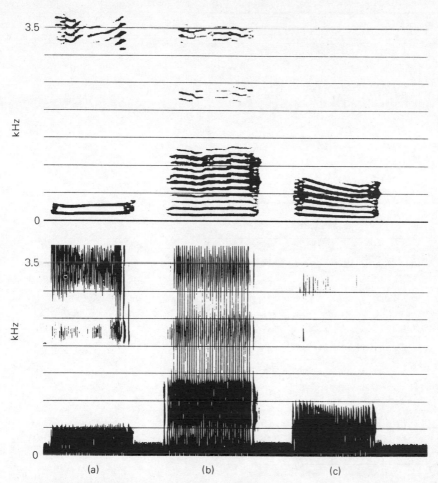

FIGURE 7.14.9   Narrow (top) and broad (bottom) band DFT spectrograms of the vowels
(a) [iː]; (b) [aː]; (c) [ɔː]

the vocal tract, and some sounds such as nasals and fricatives have more complex
tract frequency response properties which are not properly accounted for by some
forms of LPC analysis. There may be some occasions when the LPC analysis will
generate a spectrum which does not correspond to a DFT-calculated spectrum, even
though it is a computationally valid alternative tract frequency response for the input
waveform.

Much more could be said about the details of spectral analysis, and readers
wishing for more information should consult Fry (1979) or Pickett (1980) on the
analog spectrograph, and Witten (1982) on digital signal analysis. Those with a
mathematical background will find further material on speech signal analysis in
Markel and Gray (1976), Wakita (1976), Rabiner and Schafer (1978) and
O'Shaughnessy (1987).

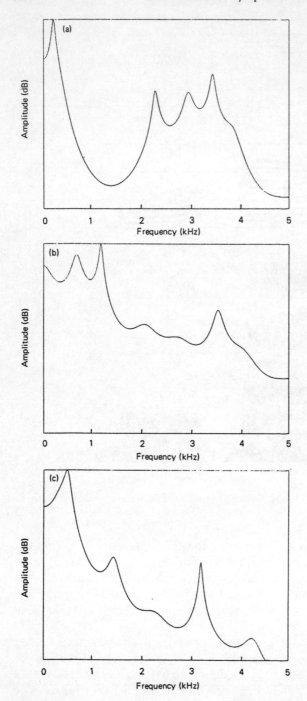

FIGURE 7.14.10   Linear prediction coefficient sections (P = 15) for the vowels (a) [iː]; (b) [aː]; (c) [ɔː]

To avoid complexity, we have concentrated on spectrographic analysis of simple static vowels. But one of the important properties of the spectrogram is its dynamic portrayal of the time-varying spectrum, and we include here (figure 7.14.11) a spectrogram of the phrase *human speech* segmented to show the parts of the spectrum which characterize its phonological structure (in so far as a simple serial segmentation is capable of doing this). Further information about the acoustic properties of speech sounds in the context of the spectral dynamics of the speech signal can be found in following sections of this chapter.

The conventional spectrographic display is not the only means of providing amplitude information on a time-varying spectrum. An alternative sometimes used in speech research is a geometric projection of spectral slices. This can provide very useful detail over short periods of time, but is somewhat difficult to read for long stretches of speech. Rabiner and Schafer (1978, p. 314) and Lieberman and Blumstein (1988, p. 194) provide typical examples.

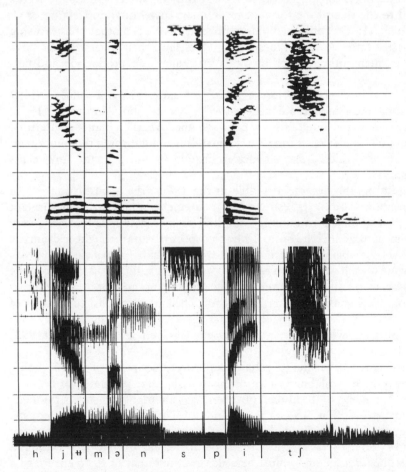

FIGURE 7.14.11 Segmented and labelled spectrogram of the phrase *human speech*

7.15   Acoustic properties of vowel quality

It has long been recognized that the auditory distinctions in individual vowel quality which enable us to give them phonologically distinct labels are predominantly determined by the frequency distributions of the first three formants (section 7.13 above). In the nineteenth century, researchers such as Willis and Helmholtz recognized the role of tract resonance and formant structure – although the term 'formant' was not then current – as did Miller, Stumpf, Paget and others in the first half of the twentieth century. Stewart (1922) succeeded in demonstrating the validity of the source and filter model for speech acoustics with a primitive electrical analog of the vocal tract. This used a buzzer as a periodic electrical impulse generator for a voice (larynx) source, and simple resonant electrical circuits (each with a single resonance peak) for the tract filter, to produce identifiable synthetic vowel sounds. Stewart's success pointed to the role of the formant in defining vowel quality. Delattre et al. (1952) and Miller (1953) confirmed this with extensive perceptual studies using much more sophisticated vowel synthesis techniques, and their investigations have been followed by many others, using methods involving both production and perception.

Vowel quality is, however, not just a matter of static formant values. Miller (1953), Lindblom and Studdert-Kennedy (1967), Millar and Ainsworth (1972) and others have shown that we also depend on the overall dynamic pattern of syllable structure to supplement formant information in establishing the phonological identity of vowel sounds. Relevant factors include F_0 and formant movements next to consonants.

Before the spectrograph became available in the 1940s, the acoustic analysis of speech was so laborious and so restricted by equipment limitations that formant structure and its relationship to auditory qualities of speech sounds had been very little explored in natural speech. From 1946 the spectrograph brought a dramatic change. It was soon recognized that if the first two formant frequencies of vowels were plotted against each other on axes with appropriate scaling and direction, the result was a vowel map which bore a remarkable resemblance to that of a traditional auditory map of vowel quality (section 2.7 above). The earliest published account of this mapping relationship seems to be that of Essner (1947), although work by Joos (1948) is probably more widely known. Ladefoged (1967, ch. 2) and Catford (1981) provide some details of this history.

Given the problems of providing a reliable auditory description of vowel quality (section 2.7 above), the availability of an ostensibly objective technique of acoustic analysis, free from the bias of the human observer, was an important step in phonetic and phonological description. The basic technique for obtaining such an acoustic map of vowel quality is to plot F_2 on the horizontal axis, with values increasing from right to left, and F_1 on the vertical axis, with values increasing from top to bottom. In addition, the frequency scale of F_1 must be at least double that of F_2 to ensure that the resulting map has an appropriate aspect ratio. Figure 7.15.1 shows plots of the

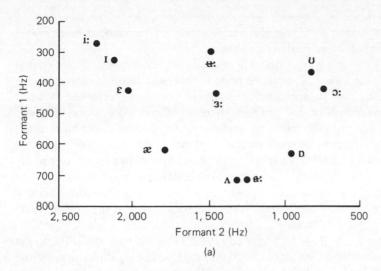

(a)

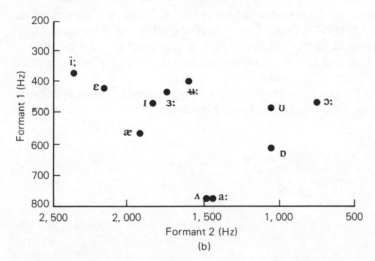

(b)

FIGURE 7.15.1   Acoustic mapping of vowels to correspond to auditory map: (a) Australian English; (b) New Zealand English

so-called pure (monophthongal) vowels of Australian and New Zealand English, using formant data from Bernard (1985).

Figure 7.15.1 reveals the vowels in a standard auditory arrangement, distributed from front to back horizontally and from high to low vertically. In this diagram, vowel fronting is represented as proportional to the value of F_2, while vowel height is inversely proportional to the value of F_1. Thus back vowels are seen to have lower F_2 values, and high vowels are seen to have lower F_1 values. The diagram incidentally shows some characteristics of Australian English, in particular the acoustic similarity of [a:] (as in *calm* or *heart*) and [ʌ] (as in *come* or *hut*): this is part of the evidence for the assertion that these two vowels are distinguished purely by duration in Australian English (Bernard 1967). It also shows the very substantial front vowel shift that has occurred in New Zealand English.

Although plots of this kind are extremely useful, they do not match a cardinal vowel diagram quite as closely as might be hoped. This was recognized even in the 1940s and Joos (1948) used logarithmic scales for the formant axes, while Delattre (1951) commented at length on the problem of relating articulatory and auditory vowel descriptions to acoustic descriptions, in the context of logarithmic plots of the kind used by Joos. In his extensive study of vowel quality Ladefoged (1967) converts formant data to the mel or pitch scale in an attempt to move closer to a perceptually oriented and hence auditorily realistic acoustic map. Ladefoged notes that, even with this transformation, a two-formant plot does not adequately display the auditory differences between vowels at the extreme high and back areas of the vowel space; elsewhere it is reasonably satisfactory.

More recently Lindau (1978) and Ladefoged (1982, especially pp. 177–80), on the strength of quite sophisticated statistical analyses, replace the F_2 dimension by the difference between F_2 and F_1 (i.e. $F_2 - F_1$). The claim is that this difference is more directly related to the auditory concept of 'frontness' or 'backness' than F_2 alone. They also retain a pitch (mel) scaling of the frequency values on both axes. Figure 7.15.2 shows the vowels of figure 7.15.1(a) replotted in this way, and it can be seen that the front to back scaling is now a little more like an auditory plot, particularly for the back vowels.

Catford (1981) has proposed another solution to the problem. He warps the frequency scaling and angular axis relationships of the formant plot to fit a traditional

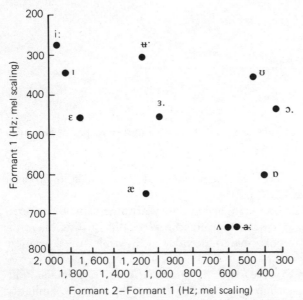

FIGURE 7.15.2 Alternative form of vowel mapping

cardinal vowel chart (in which all the vowels are either unrounded or rounded, thus removing one variable from the mapping problem). Although this is a very interesting idea, and provides quite a good fit between Catford's acoustic and auditory data, it rests on the assumption that a cardinal vowel diagram is a consistent and (presumably) reasonably linear map of auditory quality which can be taken as a standard. Given an inevitable component of arbitrariness in the choice of the original cardinal vowels, and the somewhat apostolic nature of their subsequent preservation and use, a scientific defence of this assumption is likely to be difficult. The separation of vowels into rounded and unrounded categories has some merit acoustically, but is not without drawbacks, as it is often of phonological interest to map all the vowels of a language in a single plot which portrays their systemic relationships. The reality is that most languages exhibit a mix of unrounded and rounded vowel sounds, and that lip position is often intermediate between fully rounded and fully unrounded.

Ladefoged (1967) has rightly observed that any kind of two-dimensional vowel map will encounter difficulties, particularly where vowels having similar height and fronting values but different lip positions are involved. The underlying acoustic problem for the two-formant plot is that it does not account for F_3, which also contributes to vowel quality. For example, in moving from cardinal vowel 5 to cardinal vowel 6, there may be a fall in F_3 of several hundred Hz, but this is not shown on a normal two-formant plot. Vowel qualities between 5 and 6 may well require more than the first two formants to provide an adequate mapping of their real auditory relationships. Fant (1968, 1973) has addressed this problem, partly from the perspective of speech synthesis, and proposed the use of a weighted F_2, which would take account of F_3 as F_2 increases in frequency; but this approach also has its limitations and is not commonly used. It is also important to note that none of these schemes takes account of the normalization of vocal tract length. Auditory maps of vowel quality appear to generalize across a number of speakers and thus imply some such normalization; but it is not clear how data from diverse voices (males, females, children) are actually to be reconciled.

For practical purposes, it is often most useful to accept the basic formant plot as it stands, and to add to it an F_3 axis as an extension of the F_1 axis, thus making a dual plot which will show the relative importance of the contributions of all three formants in any set of distinctions. As will be seen later, this strategy is also of value in consonant mapping. Figure 7.15.3 shows the vowel data of figure 7.15.1 replotted in this fashion, and it can be seen that F_3 does indeed provide useful additional information (note in particular the central and back vowels). A true three-dimensional representation of the vowel space based on this principle is described by Broad and Wakita (1977).

We return to the dynamic aspects of the continuous speech spectrum. The formant data used in figure 7.15.1 are taken from the targets of nominally pure vowels, that is, vowels having a single stable articulatory and auditory target value (section 2.7 above). The acoustic target of a vowel can be recognized on a spectrogram by the stable spectral structure in a syllable nucleus – although this is not always an entirely simple matter. Figure 7.15.4 provides an example that is relatively straightforward, using the word *hard* [ha:d] to illustrate the principle. The word [ha:d] happens to

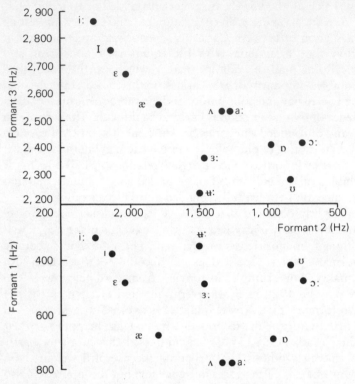

FIGURE 7.15.3   Vowel mapping using three formants

have a long, low vowel with a stable target of substantial duration. The target is identified by the spectral sequence in which the formants are parallel to the time axis and thus not changing. It is usual to take the target formant values from about the centre of this sequence. (In this spectrogram there are other spectral changes relating to the consonants in the peak and coda, but these will be ignored for the moment.) Making accurate target estimations is less straightforward when the syllable peak is of short duration and there is insufficient time for a stable target to be established by the articulators, which usually results in target undershoot; or it may be that the effects of preceding and following consonants hinder a stable target. Figure 7.15.5 shows spectrograms of two words, *kit* and *bag*, which illustrate some of the problems in identifying vowel targets.

In the spectrogram of *kit* it can be seen that the formants move towards a peripheral vowel position, but never stabilize there. The best estimate of the vowel target is taken as shown, at the (acoustically) most peripheral position. In *bag*, the consonant influence again prevents a stable target, and the area shown is in the middle region of the syllable nucleus, where the effects of the two consonants merge into a vowel target region. Comparable problems of analysing vowel targets within the dynamic spectra of syllables have been extensively discussed by Stevens et al. (1966).

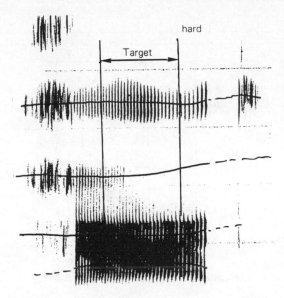

FIGURE 7.15.4   Acoustic vowel target in the word *hard*

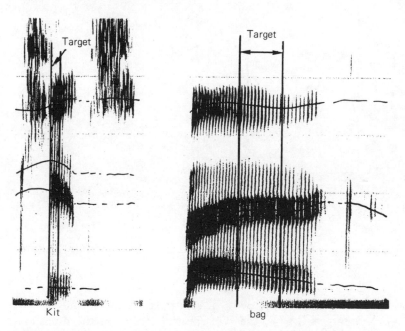

FIGURE 7.15.5   Acoustic vowel targets in the words *kit* and *bag*

Acoustic mapping of vowels need not be confined to static information in the spectrum. Glides and diphthongal vocalic movements can be shown very clearly using a formant plot. Figure 7.15.6 shows (a) spectrograms of the diphthongs in

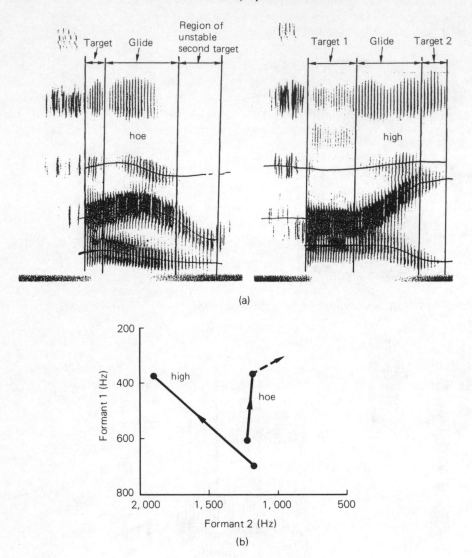

FIGURE 7.15.6   Diphthongs in *high* and *hoe*: (a) spectrograms; (b) two-formant plots of targets

the words *high* and *hoe* articulated slowly in Australian English, and (b) two-formant plots of their targets. In (a), the two spectral targets of the diphthongs can be seen, as can the smoothly changing spectrum between targets which characterizes these diphthongs both articulatorily and acoustically. In (b), these targets have been plotted and lines drawn between them to show the direction of their spectral movements. This suggests a useful general correspondence with auditory impressions of these sounds.

The classic study of vowel mapping was done quite soon after the appearance of the speech spectrograph, by Peterson and Barney (1952), who analysed a set of ten monophthongal vowels from each of 76 men, women and children. The two-formant plots of these vowels showed an appreciable amount of overlap between adjacent vowels, suggesting that the absolute acoustic discrimination between some vowels was not particularly good.

The explanation for this is twofold. Firstly, speakers do vary in the phonetic (acoustic) realizations of their vowels, but they normally maintain their systemic contrasts. Thus two speakers may vary substantially in the shape of their vowel space, and the formant values for, say, [ɛ] in one speaker may be close to those for [æ] in another; but both speakers will make adequate acoustic distinction between [ɛ] and [æ] within their own vowel system. Secondly, speakers differ substantially in the length of their vocal tract (section 7.11 above), and these variations have an inherent influence on the patterns of formant values in ways which speakers cannot really control. There is therefore no absolute acoustic discrimination among adjacent or nearby vowels that applies to a number of different speakers. As language users we have little difficulty in coping with this, as we are able, with only a very small speech sample from an individual, to normalize to the vowel system of that speaker. In other words we are accustomed to adjusting the map from speaker to speaker.

Indeed our ability to cope with different systems is not confined within a relatively homogeneous group, but may extend to quite radically different regional varieties or dialects. Despite many jokes about misunderstandings within the English-speaking world, the number of genuine confusions is relatively small. This is all the more impressive given that there are substantial discrepancies and overlaps among the regional varieties of English: the vowel in a New Zealander's *catch*, for example, may be close to the vowel of a Londoner's *ketch*; when an Australian says *clerk*, many North Americans may hear the vowel quality as equivalent to their own *clock*. But the point is of course that speakers maintain their own patterns of distinctiveness: a New Zealander distinguishes *catch* from *ketch*, and so does a Londoner, but they do so in different ways, with a different contrast of vowel quality. Thus normalization reflects the general principle that phonological distinctiveness is a matter of relative contrast within a system rather than a matter of absolute or universal phonetic values (cf. section 4.8 above). Ladefoged and Broadbent (1957) demonstrated the capacity for normalization with a rather ingenious experiment involving synthesized speech: in effect, they showed that the same sound could be perceived as different vowels, depending on the listener's normalization triggered by what was uttered immediately before the sound in question. Taking an anecdotal instance of the principle, we may say that one and the same utterance may be heard as *clock* if listeners are expecting North American speech but as *clerk* if they are expecting Australian speech. It is thus inadvisable to combine the formant data from a variety of speakers, as Peterson and Barney did.

A number of algorithms have been proposed for performing mathematical normalizations of formant data to remove some of the sources of variance. One of the earliest is Fant's (1966) scaling of formant data in relation to vocal tract size. A number of other techniques have been developed since, of which Gerstman (1968) and Nearey (1977) are well known examples. An extensive appraisal and review of several normalization procedures can be found in Disner (1980). Disner observes that mere reduction of data variance does not of itself have any value if it does violence to the vowel quality relationships within or between languages.

Much of the research into the acoustic aspects of vowels has focused on the use of the linear time–frequency space properties of vowels, as provided fairly directly by conventional spectrographic analysis. In the past few years, there has been increasing interest in a more listener-based approach to analysis procedures and acoustic representations of vowel quality. Specifically, it is well known that the human auditory system has rapidly decreasing frequency resolution above 1 kHz, and that as a consequence our ability to discriminate individual peaks of formant energy becomes poorer at these higher frequencies. It is likely that current research will generate standard techniques for both mapping and normalizing vowel data, based on transformation of the data into a spectral representation which models that in the human auditory system itself (see Chistovich et al. 1979, and Bladon and Lindblom 1981). Such procedures aim to focus our attention on the most perceptually relevant aspects of the data, but they are as yet controversial and incompletely understood, as Bladon (1987) points out.

To end this section, we offer an example of spectrographic analysis and mapping, dealing with the back vowels of Australian English and their context-sensitivity to a following velarized lateral. Figure 7.15.7 is a comparative two-formant plot of data from Bernard (1985): it demonstrates the strong retraction effect of the lateral on the entire target and glide structure of the diphthong in the word *hole* compared with the word *hoe*.

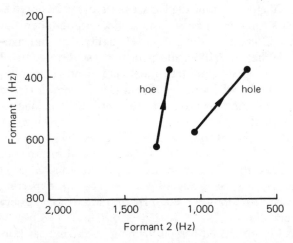

FIGURE 7.15.7   Two-formant plot showing effects of [l] on preceding [oʊ]
Adapted from: Bernard 1985, p. 328.

7.16 The vocal tract filter in consonant production

The articulation of consonants is generally characterized by the constriction and partitioning of the oral–pharyngeal vocal tract, with the addition, in the case of nasal or nasalized consonants, of coupling of the nasal cavity system (sections 2.9 and 6.8 above). Approximant consonants are in many ways comparable to vowels, but other consonants have a more complex tract resonance system (although mention of nasalized vowels in section 7.13 above has anticipated some of the complexity). In this section we will consider static aspects of vocal tract filter properties in consonant production; in section 7.17 we will then relate these to the dynamic spectral patterns which encode the phonological features of consonants within the syllable.

The most vowel-like tract filter properties are found in approximants, which fall into two groups. The first, needing no further treatment here, consists of certain central approximants which have acoustic properties little different from very high vowels; they are classified as consonants more by their functional role in syllabic structure than by their acoustic properties. The most common examples are [w] and [j] (sections 2.12 and 3.11 above). The second group consists of those which partition or constrict the tract more radically than vocalic sounds, resulting in demonstrably different resonance properties. Common examples of these are laterals such as [l] and central approximants such as [ɹ].

Laterals divide the oral cavity into two around the location of the tongue occlusion. The oral cavity remains undivided both in front of and behind this point of occlusion. The analysis by Fant (1960) of [l] suggests that this complex divided resonator system yields a spectrum with low values for both F_1 and F_2, and a marked dip of energy in the spectrum in the region surrounding 2,000 Hz, caused by an antiresonance in the tract filter. Figure 7.16.1(a) shows a spectral section for [l] taken from the nonsense syllable *lah*.

An example of a central approximant is English [ɹ], as in *rag* or *ruck* (as pronounced by, say, Londoners or Australians rather than by Scottish speakers, who may use a flap or a trill). Central approximants have resonance patterns that deviate markedly from vocalic sounds. The principal feature of these sounds is a very low F_3, resulting from resonance associated with the anterior cavity formed by tongue tip and blade constriction. Figure 7.16.1(b) gives an example of a spectral section taken from [ɹ] in the nonsense syllable *rah*. The difference in F_3 value is often an important means of discriminating [ɹ] from other approximants such as [w] and [l].

The constrictions of fricative articulation produce tract resonance properties which differ even more from those of vowels. An important difference from other sounds is that the excitation source of a fricative is not necessarily at the glottis. The vocal tract cavity is effectively divided into two parts at the point of fricative constriction. Alveolar and postalveolar fricatives provide typical examples of this form of resonator system: according to the analysis of Heinz and Stevens (1961), the cavity anterior to the constriction acts as a short closed pipe (quarter wave)

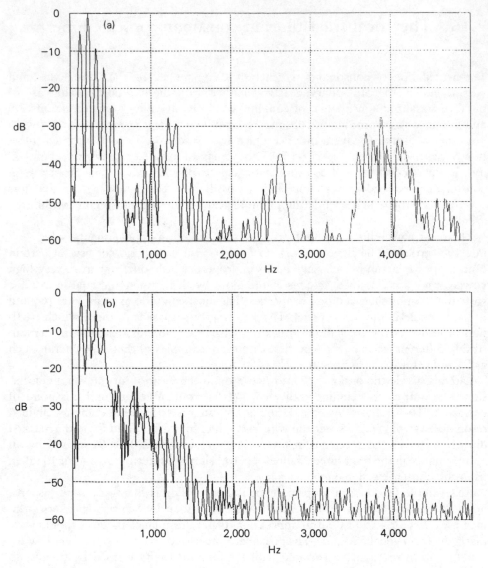

FIGURE 7.16.1   Spectral sections (512-point FFT) of the approximant consonants: (a) [l] in *lah*; (b) [ɹ] in *rah*

resonator, coupled to the frictional constriction which acts as an open pipe (half wave) resonator. Figure 7.16.2 shows a model of this system. The entire fricative source and filter system is quite short, typically less than 4 cm long for places of articulation anterior to the palate; and the large oral–pharyngeal cavity system behind the constriction is largely decoupled from the source and filter system. In voiceless sounds, the lowest resonance will also be heavily damped by the open

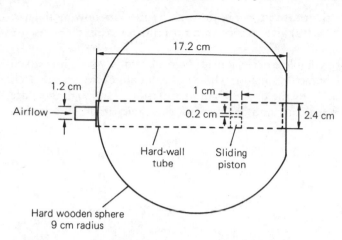

FIGURE 7.16.2   Model of fricative resonator system
Adapted from: Heinz 1958, p. 147.

glottis. Overall, when the effects of constriction antiresonance are taken into account, there is little resonance effect in voiceless fricatives below that resulting from the anterior system. The resultant fricative spectra generally exhibit a band of high-frequency, high-intensity energy, and very rapid energy attenuation at frequencies below those that are due to the anterior cavity resonance.

Although the cavity resonance effects in fricatives are more complex than those in vowels, the resultant high-frequency formant energy shows continuity with its associated syllable peak structure, as Heinz and Stevens (1961) point out. This reflects the principle of resonance continuity in the vocal tract, whatever the dynamic changes in its geometry during articulation. Where there is a marked step in fricative energy amplitude in the spectrum, the frequency region at which it occurs provides a strong static cue to the place of articulation of the fricative (see Strevens 1960, Heinz and Stevens 1961, Clark et al. 1982, and Karjalainen 1987). Figure 7.16.3(a) gives a spectrum for [s] taken from the nonsense syllable *sah*. The shape of the spectrum is also influenced by the effect of the upper front teeth, which deflect the fricative airstream, as Catford (1977) has shown.

What we have said about fricatives so far applies most clearly to fricatives with constrictions posterior to the teeth, because of the stronger spectrum-shaping influence of the anterior resonator on the frication noise source. It is less easy to characterize the static spectra of dental and labial fricatives, whose resonant cavity effects are weaker in shaping the output of their frication source spectrum. The property of resonance continuity is of general importance to the perceptual integration of syllables, and will be mentioned again in the next section.

Voiced fricatives are more complex, because there are now two excitation sources, the phonating larynx and the frication constriction. As the glottis is not open, the lowest resonance will be less damped. Furthermore, phonation produces maximum energy at low frequencies, and predominantly periodic energy will be observed in this region, with characteristic fricative noise in the high frequencies now modulated by the phonation. Figure 7.16.3(b) gives a spectrum for [z] taken from the nonsense syllable *zah*.

Nasal consonants involve complete occlusion of the oral cavity, which is coupled to the nasal cavity as a side branch resonator. The nasal resonant cavity system itself cannot be systematically varied by the processes of articulation – although there are individual variations in the structure and geometry of the cavity itself, and various

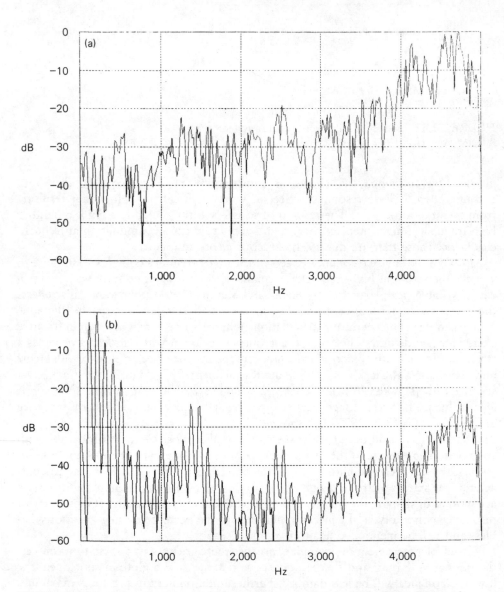

FIGURE 7.16.3 Spectral sections of fricative consonants: (a) [s] in *sah*; (b) [z] in *zah*

physiological effects (see sections 6.8 and 7.13 above). According to Fant's data (1960), the nasal passages in a male speaker form a resonator system about 12 cm long which couples into the oral–pharyngeal system some 7 cm from the glottis. The oral cavity thus forms a closed resonating chamber with a length determined by the place of nasal articulation. Figure 7.16.4 shows a simple model of the system.

The static spectral properties of this complex resonator system are a set of relatively stable nasal tract formants with generally greater damping than those of the open oral tract. These formants are said to occur in the regions of 250 Hz, 1,000 Hz, 2,000 Hz and 3,000 Hz. (See Fant 1960, Minifie 1973, Pickett 1980, O'Shaughnessy 1987, and Lieberman and Blumstein 1988 for reviews of nasal formant characteristics.) The formants are not always clearly visible in standard displays and may be generally or selectively weakened by the coupling of the oral cavity resonator, which contributes both resonance and antiresonance effects to the spectrum. The overall result is a nasal consonant spectrum with a broad peak of low-frequency energy and rather weaker upper formant energy which provides quite strong spectral cues to the nasal manner of articulation, but rather weaker cues to the place of articulation. The point of articulation is also cued by the spectral dynamics of the syllable in which the nasal consonant occurs. Figure 7.16.5 gives (a) the spectrum of [m] in the nonsense syllable *mah*, and (b) the spectrum of [n] in *nah*.

Stop consonants, by the nature of the articulation, do not have the same kind of stable constriction phase as approximants, fricatives and nasals. They are therefore characterized not so much by the typical spectrum of a 'steady state' as by the dynamic spectral properties of the formation and release of the oral occlusion (discussed further in section 7.17 below). There is in a sense a stable state for stops, namely the occlusion phase itself, but the vocal tract is of course very strongly damped in this phase. In voiced stops, where there is some airflow to generate voicing during occlusion, a broad peak of low-frequency energy is seen as a 'voice bar' in spectrograms. Far more importance attaches to the release burst of a stop, which is the result of the momentary frication between the articulators as they part at the release of the occlusion. For a very brief period (typically less than 20 ms), the vocal tract is effectively producing a fricative. As with fricatives, occlusions anterior

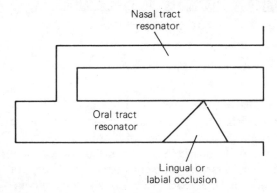

FIGURE 7.16.4   Model of nasal consonant resonator system

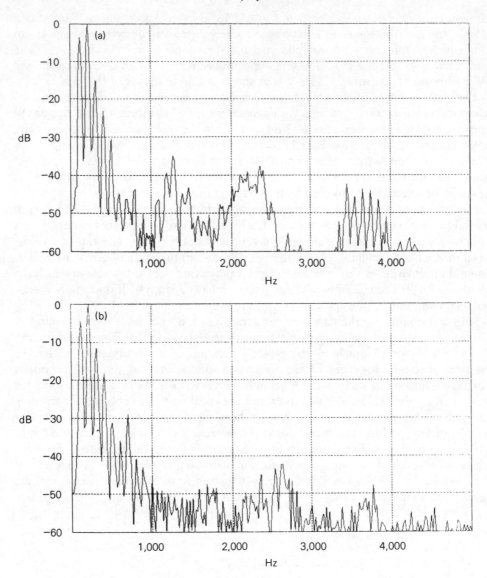

FIGURE 7.16.5   Spectral sections of nasal consonants: (a) [m] in *mah*; (b) [n] in *nah*

to the teeth have the least clearly defined spectra, with the weight of energy at the low end of the spectrum. It has been suggested that this is due, in part at least, to some contribution from the large anterior tract. Alveolar stops, and stops at locations posterior to this, produce noise spectra with energy distributions predominantly influenced by the length of the anterior cavity at the moment of release. Thus, not surprisingly, we find that the release burst of an alveolar stop has a spectrum comparable to that of the fricative [s], with the major energy occurring above 3 kHz. The velar stop burst has major energy distribution in the mid frequency range 1.5–2.5 kHz. Figure 7.16.6 shows the spectra of release bursts of the initial stops in *bah*, *dah* and *gah*.

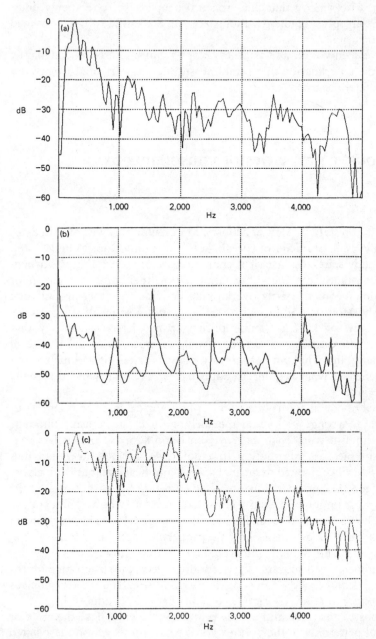

FIGURE 7.16.6   Spectral sections (256-point DFT) of release burst of plosives: (a) [b] in *bah*; (b) [d] in *dah*; (c) [g] in *gah*

The spectral properties of release bursts are significant cues to the place of articulation of stops, and have been described in detail by Halle, Hughes and Radley (1957) and Fischer-Jørgensen (1954), and by Blumstein and Stevens (1979) and Kewley-Port (1983), who suggest that their spectral properties are relatively uninfluenced by context. Perceptual studies by Blumstein and Stevens (1980) have tended to confirm these conclusions.

The differences between voiced and voiceless stops require reference to dynamic characteristics and the coordination of glottal and supraglottal articulatory activity (section 7.17 immediately below).

7.17   The acoustic properties of consonants in syllables

In concentrating so far on static aspects of acoustic representations, we have tried not to lose sight of the dynamic character of speech. While it is important to understand the properties of 'steady state' displays, it is characteristic of speech that the articulatory organs are constantly moving, often anticipating their next movement or adjusting to the simultaneous or partly overlapping activities of other articulators. As a consequence, the acoustic output is, by and large, not a series of steady states but a continuously varying signal. Oversimplifying somewhat, we can say that human hearing is attentive to changes in the signal, as much as to the nature of the signal at any point; and what we hear at any point may tell us as much about what has just happened or what is going to happen next as about what is actually happening at that point.

This brings us back of course to the question of phonological encoding. Often our expectations are simply wrong: we look at the spelling, or even the usual phonetic transcription of an English word such as *sent* [sɛnt] and suppose that it has four sounds, four successive pieces of information. In so doing we overlook the possibilities which are characteristically exploited in normal speech and hearing: that the nasality of the consonant [n] may be anticipated in, and even conveyed by, nasalization of the preceding vowel; that the timing of the nasal consonant itself may be a significant cue to the hearing of a following [t]; and so on. In short, it is useful to look at larger units of speech – in particular at syllables – to see how the properties of the vocal tract system, viewed as static properties, are actually integrated into a linear flow.

Syllabic organization, studied acoustically, naturally reflects the structural patterns discussed in section 3.1 and other sections of chapter 3 above. The peak or nucleus may display the strong and relatively simple formant patterns produced by vocalic resonance in an unobstructed tract, and the onset and coda usually have the more or less complex spectral patterning of the various vocal tract configurations associated with consonants. Syllables vary in their structure of course, but a CV syllable is the most useful starting point for description (figure 7.17.1).

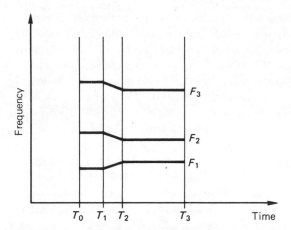

FIGURE 7.17.1 Idealized structure of a syllable

Figure 7.17.1 has the format of a spectrogram in which only the first three formants (or comparable properties) are displayed. It is divided into two major components, the second of which is further divided into two, making three sections in all. The first of these, marked T_0 to T_1 in the figure, is a quasistationary complex spectrum consisting of formants or noise components or both (depending on the manner of articulation). Its precise nature is determined by the particular consonant constriction and excitation source(s) used. It is quasistationary in the sense that the formants are, in principle, constant over time, but actually vary with both manner and context of articulation. The sequence T_1 to T_2 is the first part of the syllable peak or nucleus, and is characterized by formant movement from the point of consonant constriction release at T_1 to the vowel target values at T_2. The formant movements in this sequence are known as the FORMANT TRANSITIONS, and they play an important role in encoding consonant-related information. Formant transitions are a classic illustration of the overlapping of acoustic encoding of phonological information: although located in the syllable peak, they provide important information about adjacent consonants. The formant movements reflect the rapid shift of articulatory position from consonant to vowel, in which the tract changes its consonant constriction shape to become an unobstructed resonant system, often creating rapid resonance changes during the process. Sequence T_2 to T_3 is the vowel target proper, with a nominally stable spectrum as described in 7.15 above (unless of course the syllable nucleus is occupied by a diphthong).

Figure 7.17.1 shows that the formant structure is quite continuous through the coda and peak, which illustrates the principle of resonance continuity mentioned in section 7.16 above in connection with fricatives. Nevertheless, complex spectra such as those of nasals and fricatives are such that the continuity will not be observed for all resonances. Figure 7.17.1 also illustrates the detail with which durational analyses can be made on the speech signal using a spectrographic display (section 7.14 above). T_0–T_3 gives the total syllable duration, and T_1–T_3 gives the vowel duration, which normally includes the transition and target components of the nucleus.

The frequency changes occurring in the formant transition provide important information about the place of articulation of the preceding consonant and may contribute to information about its manner of articulation. The actual frequency values in the transition are usually determined both by the consonant place of articulation and by the acoustic target (i.e. formant patterns) of the following vowel. This is a classic example of context-sensitivity, in the form of coarticulation.

The pioneering work in exploring the dynamic spectral patterns of speech was undertaken during the Second World War by a research team at Bell Laboratories in the USA, and later published in a comprehensive form by Potter, Kopp and Green (1947). The context of their work was an attempt to make it possible to read speech from spectrographic displays (hence 'visible speech' in their title). Potter and his colleagues tried to deal with context-dependent variability by the notion of the HUB, which they defined as the characteristic position of F_2. Recognizing that the position of the hub varied according to the strength of coarticulation effects, they included appropriate allowances in their recognition rules. Thus velars exhibit more hub variability than alveolars, and so on.

The next important step in understanding spectral structure was taken in perceptual studies initiated by Cooper et al. (1952) at the Haskins Laboratories in the USA. In this research, representations of speech spectrogram patterns were hand painted on clear acetate sheets, which were then used to generate synthetic speech. The researchers could thus manipulate the values and shapes of formant patterns and replay them on a special machine called a 'pattern playback'.

In a development of this work, Delattre et al. (1955) showed that F_2 in particular appears to 'point' towards a notional characteristic frequency for a given place of articulation, whatever the associated vowel. This observation was later extended by Liberman et al. (1959) to include F_3. These notional frequencies were called the consonant LOCI, and the Haskins group demonstrated that once the dynamic spectral properties of syllable structure were understood, it was possible to formulate rules by which spectral patterns for any given utterance could be constructed. Using their pattern playback machine, they demonstrated that simple utterances could be produced using these rules without having to copy the corresponding spectral patterns of a human speaker. This was an important development, which has been followed by research designed to extend our understanding of rules relating phonological strings to the acoustic structures which realize them. The pioneering pattern playback experiments also illustrate the importance of relating the dimensions of production to those of perception in studying the phonological properties of speech.

Figure 7.17.2(a) contains spectrograms of the CV syllables *lee* [liː], *lah* [laː] and *law* [lɔ]. In figure 7.17.2(b) the three F_2 patterns of part (a) have been combined in a single display to show how all three point towards a locus. The choice of [l] as the initial consonant in the three examples ensures a reasonably stable spectrum during the consonant constriction, and a strong formant structure illustrating the resonance continuity principle. Plotting formant movements in the time domain, as illustrated in figure 7.17.2(b), is a common and useful technique for the display and analysis of speech spectrum dynamics. It is, however, not always the best way of explaining how phonological distinctiveness is conveyed. The locus theory is a case in point. The

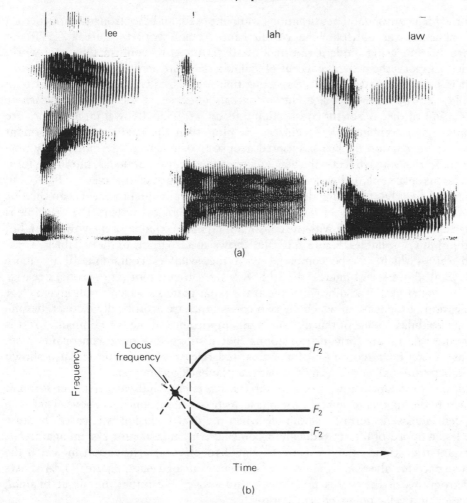

FIGURE 7.17.2   (a) Spectrograms of *lee, lah, law*; (b) locus effect of coarticulation on F_2

theory assumes that each formant transition for a given sound points towards a specific frequency locus. In effect, the locus frequency is a notionally invariant point, mostly never reached because of coarticulation. Unfortunately, in the case of velar stops, investigation has shown that it is impossible to determine a single locus frequency for each formant and for all vowels. To overcome this problem, proponents of the theory have argued for two locus frequencies – one associated with front vowels, and one with back vowels – but this pragmatic solution has little in the way of true explanatory value.

In his fundamental study of coarticulation, Ohman (1966) argued against the locus theory on the grounds that it was impossible to reconcile a single invariant acoustic 'target' with the observable phenomena of coarticulation. He proposed instead that the speech signal should be regarded as a sequence of vocalic structures upon which consonantal perturbations were imposed; and the strongest influence on a consonant was the following vowel. More recent work by Purcell (1979) on coarticulation using modern statistical analysis tends to confirm Ohman's work, which supports the general concept of syllabic structure centred on a vocalic peak.

It is from this vowel-based perspective that an alternative form of spectral data display has been developed. If the formant frequencies at the point of release or formation of the consonant constriction and the associated vowel target values are plotted on a combined F_1/F_2 and F_2/F_3 plot, then the true consonant formant patterns, in relation to their associated acoustic vowel space, are more easily portrayed. In this way we retain the general concept of consonant locus, but in the form of a 'locus space', plotted within a general frequency space whose axes are F_1, F_2 and F_3 independently of the time domain. The data for individual segments can then be seen in the context of associated sounds in the phonological system. The principle is illustrated in figure 7.17.3 with the consonant [ɹ] in the context of the vowels [iː], [aː] and [ɔː] in CV syllables. Figure 7.17.3(a) shows spectrograms of the syllables *re, rah* and *raw* – which can be compared with the syllables containing [l] in figure 7.17.2(a) above – and figure 7.17.3(b) shows a formant plot (at consonant release and vowel target). The distinctive spectral spatial patterns which result give a clear indication of the ways in which the two consonants are acoustically distinct, despite their variability. None of this discounts the importance of the time domain, for it is also the rate of the formant transitions that distinguishes these consonants from stops, which have more rapid formation and release of occlusion (as also shown by Liberman et al. 1956, using the pattern playback technique).

Nasal consonants show strong low-frequency energy and weaker upper formant structure during their oral occlusion phase, as noted in section 7.16 above. There is a sudden increase in formant amplitude when the oral occlusion is released, because the less damped oral tract suddenly becomes the main resonator system again. The formant transitions exhibit a pattern related to place of articulation in which the locus space for alveolars is much smaller than that for velars. Figure 7.17.4 shows spectrograms of the words *timer, finer* and *singer*, illustrating nasals at bilabial, alveolar and velar points of articulation.

Fricatives show complex periodic spectral properties during their constriction (section 7.16 above). Spectrographic analysis reveals how the integration of glottal with supraglottal activity meets the aerodynamic demands of frication yet allows a rapid switchover to phonation. This is shown in its simplest form in figure 7.17.5(a) for the fricative [h] in *who*: here the constriction is at the larynx, so that the fricative uses the full vocal tract resonator system, giving it a formant structure very similar to that of the following vowel. Only the source differs – aperiodic in the fricative, periodic in the vowel. Since no supraglottal articulators are involved in producing the [h] fricative, there are no appreciable formant transitions. Contrast this with figure 7.17.5(b), which shows the two fricatives [s] and [ʃ] in the word *seashore*. The [s] shows little energy below 4,000 Hz because of the short anterior resonator system (section 7.16 above). The formant transitions from the [s] into the following [iː] vowel are clearly seen, and are similar in pattern to those of other alveolar sounds. Resonance continuity is preserved largely in F_4 and F_5. A similar structure

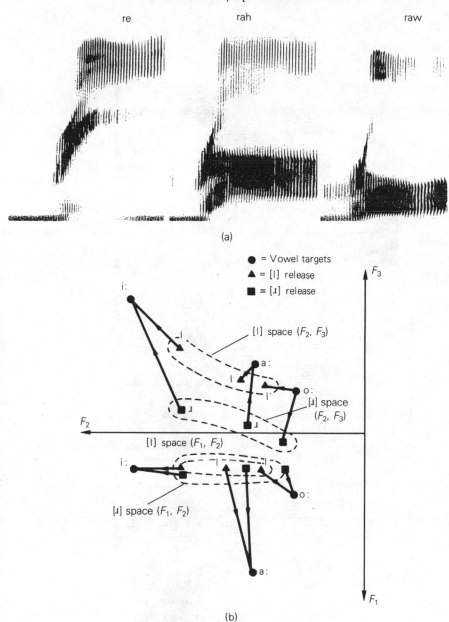

FIGURE 7.17.3   (a) Spectrograms of *re, rah, raw*; (b) locus space for [l] and [ɹ] with [i:], [a:] and [ɔ:]

can be seen in the intervocalic [ʃ] except that the fricative energy now extends down to around 2,500 Hz. As noted in section 7.16 above, the frequency at which the fricative noise is sharply attenuated is an important cue to place of articulation. In

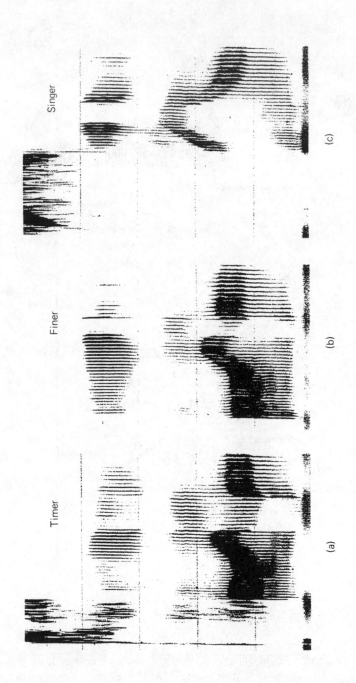

FIGURE 7.17.4   Spectrograms illustrating nasal consonants: (a) *timer*; (b) *finer*; (c) *singer*

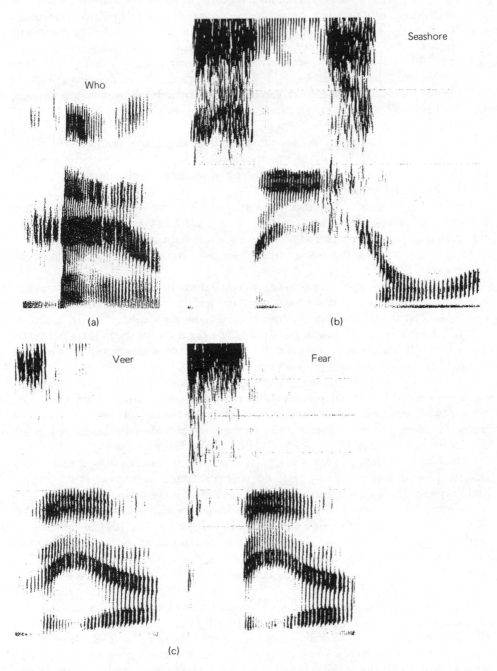

FIGURE 7.17.5   Spectrograms illustrating fricatives (a) *who*; (b) *seashore*; (c) *veer* and *fear*

the example shown, the noise attenuation frequency is relatively stable for [s], but in [ʃ] it falls appreciably between the vowels because of their coarticulatory influence. The demands of the vowels are such that during the articulation of the [ʃ], the tongue and lips are already moving towards their positions for the following vowel.

Figure 7.17.5(c) shows the words *veer* and *fear*, illustrating the voicing contrast in fricative spectra. The low-frequency periodic voicing, and its modulating effects on the upper-frequency noise spectrum, can be seen clearly in [v]. Formant structure and spectrum shaping are not very apparent in fricatives such as these, since their constriction site is very close to the front end of the tract. It is also evident that there is less formant movement in the vocalic nucleus than in the examples of figure 7.17.5(b). This is due in part to the anterior location of the constriction, which causes less perturbation of vowel-related tract resonance properties than would occur with lingual fricatives.

The last major class of sounds to be considered here are stops. These have three basic spectral components: an occlusion (which is silent in voiceless stops); a release burst composed of a short period of relatively stable fricational energy (section 7.16 above); and, if a vowel follows, a transition into it characterized by rapid formant movement.

Stops generally exhibit strong coarticulation effects in their formant transitions, and it is the combination of the burst spectrum and the transitions which identifies their place of articulation. Their manner of articulation is identified by the relatively low frequency of F_1 at occlusion release, and the rapid rise of spectral energy thereafter. Fant (1973) includes an extensive analysis of stop acoustics, with a good example of the formant mapping described at the beginning of this section.

Figure 7.17.6(a) shows the stop [d] in the word *ordeal*, illustrating the three spectral components. The coarticulation influence on formant transitions at closure and release (where the consonant is flanked by different vowels) is analogous to that of figure 7.17.5(b). The low values of F_1 at the start and end of occlusion are also easily seen, as is the low-frequency 'voice bar' during the occlusion. Figure 7.17.6(b) shows the syllables [tʰa], [ta] and [da]. These three kinds of stop (voiceless aspirated, voiceless unaspirated, and voiced) are phonologically distinctive in languages such as Thai and Burmese. The spectrograms illustrate the effects of voice onset time (section 2.16 above): in [tʰa], phonation does not start until after the release of the occlusion, [ta] shows phonation beginning at about the point of release, and [da] has phonation starting during the occlusion. The timing of voice onset in stops is of great importance in the recognition of stops as voiced, voiceless or voiceless aspirated. Both our productive control of this timing and our perception of it have been studied extensively by Lisker and Abramson (1964, 1971), Slis and Cohen (1969) and Ladefoged (1971). There is ample evidence from the research that languages differ in the values of voice onset time used to signal voicing contrast. In languages such as English and German, for example, aspiration is often a crucial feature of voiceless stops distinguishing them from voiced stops (at least in some contexts) whereas in languages such as French and Dutch the contrast may be more truly one of presence or absence of voicing during the occlusion itself. In yet other languages, such as Hindi, stops may also have voiced aspiration (in contrast to voiceless aspiration), which demonstrates

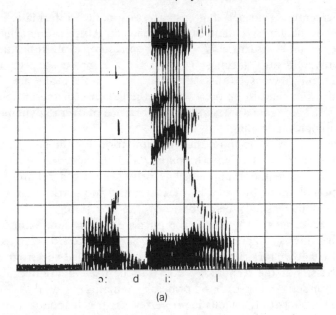

(a)

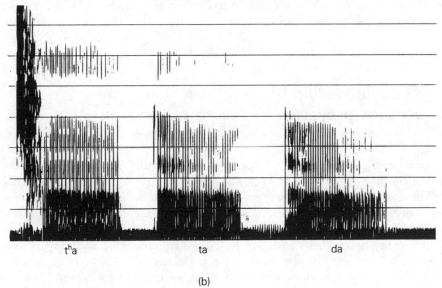

(b)

FIGURE 7.17.6   Spectrograms of (a) *ordeal*; (b) [tʰaː], [taː], [daː]

that speakers can exploit very complex coordination of laryngeal behaviour in relation to the supraglottal articulation to achieve phonological distinctions.

Phenomena such as we have been describing point to the danger of trying to locate
acoustic features within discrete segments, and underline the importance of the
syllable as a whole. It is worth repeating the point made in section 7.15 above:

there is good perceptual evidence that just as consonantal information is partly specified by the coarticulatory dynamics of formant structure in the syllable peak, certain aspects of syllable structure as a whole contribute to the robustness of the perception of vowel identity (Strange et al. 1976). It has also been found by Lindblom (1963) and Stevens et al. (1966) that as syllable peaks are shortened, the formant transitions tend to be preserved at the expense of the more spectrally stable vowel target. This again argues for the importance of overall dynamic spectral patterns in phonological encoding.

This section has provided no more than a foundation for the study of complex spectral and temporal aspects of speech sounds, and the spectrographic examples have illustrated the segmentation and labelling process in a general and basic way. What was traditionally done by hand, by measurement and marking of hard copies of spectrograms, is increasingly being done by multipurpose speech editing and analysis software packages designed for the purpose, or on stand-alone and purpose-built speech analysis equipment using digital signal processing chip technology. Some systems also allow storage of the segmented and labelled spectrographic data for further analysis. But the technology does not of itself guarantee insight and analysis, and the understanding of basic principles remains essential.

More detailed accounts of the acoustic properties of speech sounds may be found in Fant (1960), Minifie (1973), Shoup and Pfeiffer (1976), Fry (1979), Pickett (1980), O'Shaughnessy (1987) and Lieberman and Blumstein (1988).

7.18   The relationship between articulatory and acoustic properties of speech production

Phonological description has always tended to be articulatory in orientation, for the obvious reason that the gestures and settings of articulatory organs are more easily observed than sound waves. Certainly it was possible to describe articulation – even if impressionistically – without much recourse to modern technology. Once spectrographic analysis became available, a natural and immediate step was to try to relate what were already known as articulatory properties to what were now being investigated as acoustic or spectral properties (see e.g. Delattre 1951).

We can think of the relationship between articulation and acoustics in terms of transformations which will derive acoustic properties from articulatory properties. The basic method of obtaining such transformations is by modelling the vocal tract, treating the supraglottal resonator system as a series of very short tube sections of fixed length and variable cross-sectional area. Before computers, this analog was realized as an electrical transmission line consisting of coils, capacitors and resistors which modelled each short section, including losses due to damping. These AREA FUNCTION ANALOGS, described in detail by Dunn (1950) and Fant (1960), typically had from 18 to 40 separate sections, each of adjustable area. In more recent times it has been possible to simulate a transmission line on computer, or to use models based on reflection coefficients, although there are limitations as some models do not deal well with tract losses (Kelly and Lochbaum 1962; Wakita 1976). The articulatory to acoustic transformation is achieved by adjusting each section of the model to an appropriate area value, to approximate the vocal tract shape for a particular sound. To do this, of course, researchers really need accurate articulatory information (from X-rays or other such sources) to make the model approximate the cross-sectional area of the actual vocal tract shape as closely as possible. Figure 7.18.1 shows how the vocal tract can be analysed to this end.

It is then possible to compute the effective frequency response of the vocal tract shape to which the model has been adjusted, and to obtain the corresponding formant frequency data. The process is reasonably accurate, but laborious. Researchers soon looked for more economical articulatory specifications, preferably in the form of a parametric articulatory model, a model with discrete articulatory values that could be, so to speak, overlaid on the vocal tract. The parameters or categories of this model should ideally be related to those of conventional phonetic description, and should at the same time be capable of specifying the cross-sectional areas of all sections of the area function model.

Stevens and House (1955) approached the task by treating the vocal tract as a tube with adjustable lip and tongue hump geometry. Fant (1960) used two- and three-tube compound resonator tubes as rudimentary approximations of vocal tract configurations. In both approaches, nomographs were supplied, from which one could predict formant values for a large combination of the input parameters to the models.

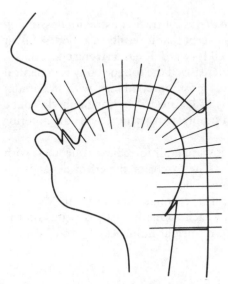

FIGURE 7.18.1   Derivation of vocal tract area function characteristics, showing cross-sections of the vocal tract at equal intervals between glottis and lips, used to specify the overall vocal tract area function which can then be used to determine the effective vocal tract filter frequency response

The limitation in these two approaches is that both used articulatory parametric overlays which were somewhat removed from phonetically valid measurements of the human vocal tract shape. Lindblom and Sundberg (1971) took the essential further step of devising an economical set of parametric measures specifying lip and tongue shape, and jaw and larynx height. This meant that a recognizable vocal tract could be defined. Like their predecessors, they provided nomographs which predicted formant frequency values for any combination of the parametric values defining vocal tract state. Again as in previous research, they used an area function analog to obtain the primary formant data with which they constructed their nomograms.

Lindblom and Sundberg's work suggests the following general relationships between articulatory and acoustic factors:

1 Jaw opening causes F_1 to rise quite markedly (all else being constant), usually in the context of controlling vowel height. It will cause F_2 to rise if the tongue is retracted up towards the soft palate: this effect is strongest when the lips are spread, but minimal in other articulatory positions. F_3 may rise sharply at moderate jaw apertures when the tongue is raised towards the palate region.

2 Tongue body movement in a general anterior to posterior direction causes a modest rise in F_1 (typically around $200\,\text{Hz}$) if the jaw is kept at a fixed opening (but the jaw is *not* normally kept in one position). Movement from anterior to neutral position results in a large drop in F_2 in all cases. From neutral to posterior position, F_2 will tend to rise with small jaw openings, but continue to fall with larger jaw openings.

3 Tongue body shape, which controls the degree of tract constriction (assuming a constant jaw position), has little effect on F_1 except that it results in a modest fall at maximum constriction if the tongue body is well forward. It has a strong effect on F_2, causing it to fall substantially as constriction increases if the tongue body is in neutral or posterior position. An anterior tongue body position combined with maximum constriction results in a sharp rise in F_2. F_3 is little affected by tongue body shape except for a modest fall at neutral and maximum constriction with an anterior tongue position.

4 Lip rounding has the general effect of lowering all formant frequencies, with the strongest effects observable on F_2 and F_3. The extent of the effect depends on what the tongue and jaw are doing at the same time.

5 Lowering of the larynx makes the vocal tract longer and tends to lower all formant frequencies; the degree of lowering of each formant partly depends on the overall state of the vocal tract. In general, larynx height influences F_2 and F_4 more than F_3.

Lindblom and Sundberg conclude that tongue height (maximum height of the tongue hump), despite its traditional importance in the description of vowels, does not relate directly or usefully to acoustic properties. In general agreement with Lindblom and Sundberg, Wood (1979) shows that formant frequency patterns in vowel production relate more directly to the location and degree of tongue constriction within the vocal tract.

Stevens (1972a) takes a more overtly phonological view of articulatory–acoustic relationships in his QUANTAL THEORY. He maintains that there are general states or regions of articulatory activity, within whose natural boundaries little change in the acoustic output of the tract can be achieved. On the other hand, a small shift beyond the boundary will produce a large (discontinuous) acoustic change. This argues that the relationship between vocal tract state and spectral properties is not linear. It is these 'step-wise' spectral changes which contribute to phonological distinctiveness, and Stevens suggests that articulation is organized to make optimum use of the vocal tract's ability to produce such changes. Discrete manners and places of articulation are located inside insensitive regions, which means that the acoustic properties of specific sounds are relatively tolerant to minor articulatory variability, but that large acoustic changes occur when we cross the boundaries of the regions.

An example of this principle is the sudden change from laminar to turbulent air-flow when a constriction reaches a critical cross-sectional area and the sound thereby moves from vocalic or approximant mode to fricative mode. The way in which a shift of articulation from [s] to [ʃ] produces a sudden lowering of the fricative noise cut-off frequency is another illustration of the same principle. Similarly, it can be argued that the quasi-universal vowel triangle of [i], [a] and [u] is the preferred three-way vowel system because these vowels represent three stable and acoustically non-critical articulatory positions. Wood's X-ray studies (1979) appear to confirm the quantal hypothesis.

The difficulty of obtaining comprehensive data about dynamic articulation in speech – the research methods are often invasive and costly – makes it attractive to try to predict articulatory details from acoustic information. There is indeed continuing interest in acoustic-to-articulatory transformations and it is possible to predict the vocal tract shape for a given acoustic signal sample; but in many cases the prediction is not a unique solution. This is regrettable but hardly surprising, for it is an important attribute of the vocal tract that it can compensate for one or another articulatory constraint and still generate a required acoustic output. It is, for instance, possible to produce intelligible speech with a fixed mandible, as when holding a pencil between the teeth. Although attempts have been made to produce acoustic-to-articulatory models (Ladefoged et al. 1978; Ladefoged and Harshman 1979), the fact that transformations cannot be guaranteed to be unique has remained an underlying limitation.

7.19 Acoustic features of prosody

Prosodic features – such as pitch and loudness – are reviewed in detail in chapter 9 below, but some basic acoustic aspects merit attention here. Of particular importance is the fundamental frequency (F_0), which carries a wealth of information, much of it describable as prosody or personal voice quality.

A gross but useful dimension of speech is its long-term spectral energy profile. This is derived simply by averaging a large number of spectral slices over a long sample of speech, usually at least several minutes. Obviously this measure gives no information about segmental details or even about intonation patterns, but it does provide some insight into voice quality and vocal effort. Standard data for English can be found in Dunn and White (1940). Figure 7.19.1 shows relevant long-term spectra.

In general, when speakers increase their vocal effort, there will be more high-frequency energy in their long-term spectrum, while reduced vocal effort means less. Often such a change in energy distribution will be revealed as a change in the high-frequency spectral slope (or rate of attenuation). Speakers do in any case differ from each other in the distribution of spectral energy within their speech, largely because they manage their phonatory and other vocal tract settings in different ways. The differences may be evident over relatively long stretches of speech, as in the case of voice quality and speaker identity characteristics described by Laver (1980) and Nolan (1983); or differences may be relatively short-term, reflecting the speaker's response to a specific communicative situation. Figure 7.19.2 is an example from Clark et al. (1987) showing the difference in voice quality between speech produced in a quiet environment and speech produced with considerable extra effort.

Long-term spectra are probably most useful in a comparative form, as shown in figure 7.19.2. They may also be of sociolinguistic interest where voice quality is characteristic of a regional or social group. In this connection, there may also be value in measures such as the mean value of F_0, which may have a typical range and distribution in particular communities.

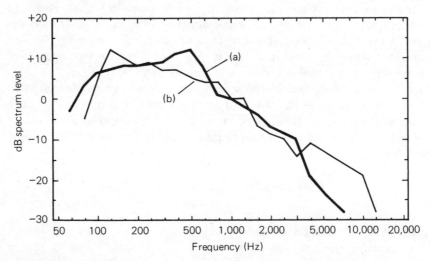

FIGURE 7.19.1   Long-term speech spectra: (a) data from six male American speakers; (b) data from five male Australian speakers
Source: (a) Dunn and White 1940.

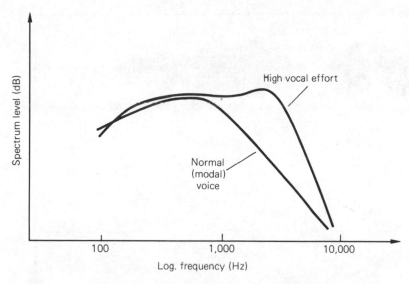

FIGURE 7.19.2   Long-term speech spectrum showing changes due to vocal effort

Most useful of all is the F_0, or pitch contour. (The two terms are often used interchangeably, but 'pitch contour' is strictly speaking a perceptual measure only.) Measuring F_0 is not always easy, for several reasons. Firstly, the effects of vocal tract resonance in some speakers may make it hard to detect the F_0 pattern in the waveform by automatic methods. Secondly, speakers rarely produce 'ideal' phonatory patterns: in particular, the onset and offset of voicing is often weak and may have erratic periodicity, so that it is not always clear precisely where the F_0 pattern starts and finishes. Thirdly, certain segments, such as initial stops, may produce short term perturbations in periodicity (section 9.2 below) which may not be accurately detected in F_0 measurement.

The techniques for measuring F_0 may be broadly divided into two types: time domain and frequency domain. In the first of these, the speech waveform is usually passed through a low bandpass filter to remove much of the high-frequency information which could obscure the periodic pattern. The resulting time domain waveform is then processed to identify the period of the speech wave, by detecting either the recurrent zero crossings or the peaks. F_0 is then easily determined as the reciprocal of the period. To display a continuous pitch trace, the cycle by cycle measures of F_0 are often smoothed, unless information on jitter or individual perturbations is required. An example of an unsmoothed trace is shown in figure 7.19.3. (See figure 9.2.2 for a smoothed version of the same contour, in which these perturbations are absent.)

The traditional equipment for this type of measurement used simple analog electronics. Computer-based methods are now being used, except where continuous real time displays are needed. Some of the more sophisticated computer-based time domain analyses incorporate decision-making processes, in which alternative

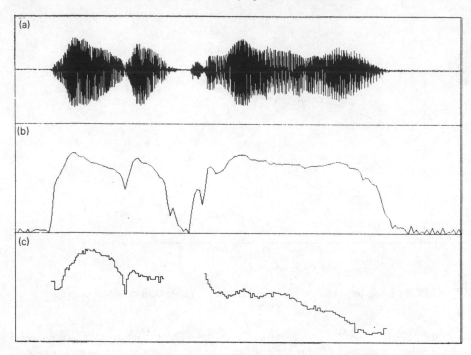

FIGURE 7.19.3 F_0 derived by analysis of time domain waveform *We went to Woolloomooloo*; (a) time domain waveform; (b) intensity contour; (c) F_0 contour

estimates of the pitch period can be checked against the estimates of adjacent pitches, to avoid anomalous decisions. A well-known and very successful example is Gold and Rabiner's time domain pitch algorithm (Gold and Rabiner 1969). With powerful algorithms such as this, there is far less need to prefilter the signal before making pitch estimates, and the analysis can track rapid perturbations in F_0 much more accurately.

Frequency domain methods make the pitch estimates from the harmonic structure of the spectrum. They are inherently accurate, within the limits of the frequency resolution of the spectral analysis. If the resolution is too broad, the harmonic structure of the spectrum will not be adequately resolved, and if it is too narrow, its response time will be too slow to track rapid F_0 changes. The simplest form of frequency domain F_0 measurement uses a narrow band spectrogram. The technique is to pick a suitably clear harmonic (say between the third and seventh) and measure its frequency values. The F_0 value is then simply the harmonic frequency divided by the harmonic number. Figure 7.19.4 shows an example with some values calculated by hand.

Frequency domain methods are laborious, but provide relatively unambiguous pitch estimates (using the method shown in figure 7.19.4). They are computationally demanding, which makes them less popular than time domain approaches. Digital signal analysis methods for F_0 are discussed in a general review of pitch measurement techniques in Hess (1983) and in Rabiner and Schafer (1978).

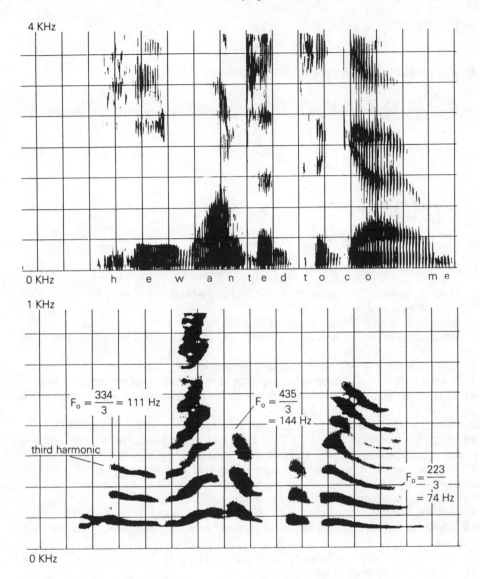

FIGURE 7.19.4 F_0 derived from a narrow band spectrogram with equivalent segmented and labelled broad band spectrogram of the utterance *He wanted to come*

Intensity and time are also important in prosody. For gross measures of intensity and time, see sections 7.6 and 7.7 above; and for detailed time measures, see the account of spectrographic segmentation in section 7.17. The broader phonological role of duration and intensity is taken up in chapter 9 below.

Exercises

1   Ensure that you understand the following terms:

   frequency and amplitude of a vibration
   periodic vibration
   waveform
   sinusoidal vibration
   white noise
   damped vibration
   fundamental frequency
   resonant frequency
   bandwidth
   line spectrum
   spectral envelope
   formant

2   What is meant by the phase relationship of two waves?
3   What does a resonance curve measure?
4   What is a 'discrete Fourier transform'?
5   What is a decibel and how does it relate to sound pressure level and acoustic intensity?
6   What is a mel and how does it relate to frequency?
7   What is the phantom fundamental and what does it tell us about the nature of hearing?
8   Outline the source and filter model of speech production. Why is a central unrounded vowel the easiest to deal with in a source and filter model?
9   Why is it difficult to record phonation waveforms directly with a microphone?
10   Explain the analytical process involved in producing a speech spectrogram. What are the uses and limitations of the narrow and wide band filter resolution?
11   Explain the terms 'digitization', 'quantization' and 'sampling rate'. What is the maximum frequency encoded by a sampling rate of 16 kHz?
12   How can acoustic vowel plots be related to cardinal vowels?
13   Why is normalization such a challenge to phoneticians?
14   Describe the acoustic properties of approximants, voiceless and voiced fricatives, nasals and stops.
15   Explain the role of the formant transitions in figure 7.17.1.
16   Explain the concept of locus.

8 Speech Perception

Our ability to perceive – and understand – speech is quite remarkable. This chapter begins by drawing attention to the complexity of the perceptual task (8.1). It then describes the structure of the human ear (8.2) and the basic perceptual functioning of the ear (8.3).

The chapter then gives a brief account of research into speech intelligibility (8.4) and the perception of speech sounds (8.5) before dealing with particular phonological aspects in more detail: the perception of vowels is treated in 8.6 and the perception of consonants in 8.7, while section 8.8 reviews discussion among researchers about the basic unit of perception, for example about whether the phoneme can be taken as a unit of speech perception. Section 8.9 turns to the perception of prosodic information, such as stress and pitch.

The chapter includes mention of work on word recognition – much of it usually considered to be research in psychology rather than phonetics (8.10). A brief overview of the principal models of speech perception that have been proposed by researchers (8.11) and concluding remarks (8.12) complete the chapter.

8.1 Introduction

Our recognition of linguistic units such as syllables and words and clauses depends on a number of factors. These include the acoustic structure of the speech signal itself, the context, our familiarity with the speaker, and our expectations as listeners. There is substantial evidence that much of our understanding of continuous speech involves a component of 'top-down' linguistic processing which draws on our personal knowledge base, and does not necessarily demand segment-by-segment processing of the acoustic signal to establish the phonological structure and arrive at its identity and meaning.

There are two central problems which are as yet not fully resolved in our total understanding of the processes leading to the perception of phonological structure in speech. The first is the highly variable and contextually sensitive relationship between the phonological structure and the acoustic cues embedded in the spectral time-course of the acoustic signal (sections 7.15 to 7.17 above). This is sometimes referred to in the literature as the invariance problem because of the capacity of listeners to perceive an invariant phonological structure from extremely variable speech signals which are rich with multilayered information. Lindblom (1986) provides a stimulating discussion and overview of this issue, particularly in relation to the perception and production of vowel sounds.

A simple example of this richness and variability which can nevertheless produce an invariant phonological percept is a phrase such as 'is that your ticket?' uttered by four speakers, say a young adult female, a young adult male, a very young child and a very old male. As listeners we are not only able to perceive the phonological structure of this phrase as produced by four quite different voices; and even without seeing the speakers we can usually identify their age and sex as well, at least to the point of distinguishing female speakers from male, very young from elderly, and so on. But, more than that, if our four speakers were to repeat this phrase several times, we can probably judge, from the speech signal alone, whether they are now getting angry or remaining patient or becoming over-polite, and we achieve this without undermining our perception of the phonological structure. Yet these 'repetitions' of the same phonological structure by different speakers under different conditions will actually vary substantially in their acoustic signal and its spectral time-course.

The second problem has already been alluded to above, namely the rather fluid relationship between our reliance on high-level linguistic and contextual knowledge and our response to the acoustic cues in the acoustic signal itself. Despite some uncertainty here, we do know that listeners can determine phonological structure when relying almost entirely on the acoustic speech signal alone: all of us are, after all, able to write down recognizable representations for the pronunciation of nonsense words or proper names which we have not heard before; and with training, professionals can make reasonably accurate phonetic transcriptions of unfamiliar speech patterns in linguistic fieldwork or clinical sessions.

The preceding chapter (section 7.9) has already introduced some of the basic perceptual properties of sound waves to explain the psychoacoustic basis for the units of measurement used to quantify amplitude and frequency. In this chapter we examine the perception of speech more generally, concentrating on acoustic-phonetic aspects of the processes which underlie our capacity to identify the phonological structure of speech.

8.2   The auditory system

The human auditory system is generally considered to consist of two broad components, the peripheral and central systems. Our concern is mainly with the peripheral

system and its properties in processing the acoustic signals of speech. Figure 8.2.1
shows the structure of the peripheral system.

The peripheral system has three parts, the outer, middle and inner ears. The
outer ear comprises the PINNA or AURICLE and the auditory MEATUS or outer ear
canal. The pinna makes little or no contribution to our basic hearing acuity, but
serves to protect the entrance to the ear canal and does seem also to contribute to
our ability to localize sounds, especially at higher frequencies. (The topic of auditory localization lies outside our linguistic concerns here, but it is worth noting that
our ability to localize a source of sound is important in enabling us to be selective,
for example in a crowded room where many people are talking and we are trying
to listen to one speaker only. This ability is of course greatly enhanced by our
having two ears.)

The pinna connects to the outer ear canal, a short tube of variable shape between
25 and 53 mm long which provides the pathway for acoustic signals to the middle
ear. The canal has two major functions. The first is the obvious one of providing
physical protection to the complex and not very robust mechanical structures of the
middle ear. The second is to act as a tube resonator (section 7.13 above) which
favours the transmission of high-frequency sounds between 2,000 and 4,000 Hz.
This function is important to speech perception and particularly supports the perception of fricative sounds, as their identity is often encoded in aperiodic energy in
this region of the acoustic spectrum. The resonance in the auditory meatus also

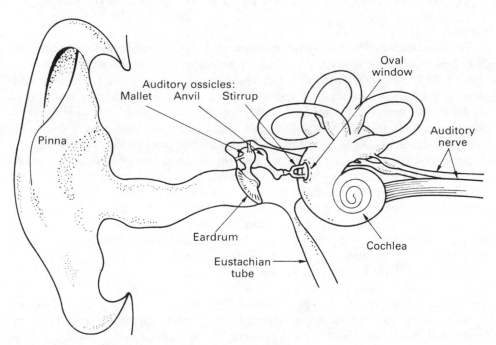

FIGURE 8.2.1   The structure of the peripheral auditory system

contributes to our general hearing acuity between 500 and 4,000 Hz, which is the range of frequencies containing the major cues to phonological structure.

The middle ear consists of a cavity within the skull structure containing the EARDRUM (a membrane at the inner end of the outer ear canal), a set of three inter-connected bones, known as the mallet, the anvil and the stirrup (together termed the AUDITORY OSSICLES), and associated muscle structure. The purpose of the middle ear is to transform the sound pressure variations in air that arrive at the outer ear into equivalent mechanical movements. This process of transformation begins at the ear-drum membrane, which is deflected by air pressure variations reaching it via the canal. The resulting movement is transmitted to the auditory ossicles, which act as an ingenious mechanical lever system to convey these movements to the oval window at the interface to the inner ear and the cochlear fluids beyond.

The lever action of the ossicles, and the fact that the eardrum has a much larger surface area than the oval window, ensure efficient transmission of acoustic energy between 500 and 4,000 Hz, effectively maximizing the sensitivity of the ear in this frequency range. The musculature associated with the auditory ossicles also works to protect the ear against damage from excessively loud sounds by an action known as the acoustic reflex mechanism. This mechanism comes into action when sounds of around 90 dB and greater reach the ear: the musculature contracts and repositions the ossicles to reduce the efficiency of sound transmission to the oval window (Borden and Harris 1980, Moore 1989).

The middle ear is connected to the pharynx by a narrow tube known as the EUSTACHIAN TUBE. This provides an air pathway which opens when necessary to equalize background air pressure changes between the outer and middle ear struc-tures.

The inner ear is a complex structure encased within the skull, and our discussion here will focus on the COCHLEA, which is responsible for converting mechanical movement into neural signals: the mechanical movement conveyed to the oval win-dow by the auditory ossicles is transformed into neural signals that are transmitted to the central nervous system. Essentially, the cochlea is a coil-like structure termi-nating in a window with a flexible membrane at each end. Figure 8.2.1 shows the general form of the cochlea, and figure 8.2.2 shows a cross-section through it.

Internally, the cochlea is divided by two membranes, one of which, the BASILAR MEMBRANE, is central to hearing. When movements (caused by sound vibrations) occur at the oval window, they are transmitted through the cochlear fluid and cause displacement of the basilar membrane. The basilar membrane is stiffer at one end than the other, and this means that the way in which it is displaced depends on the frequency of the incoming sound. High-frequency sounds will cause greater displacement at the stiff end; with decreasing frequency, maximum displacement moves progressively towards the less stiff end.

Attached along the basilar membrane is the ORGAN OF CORTI, a complex structure containing many hair cells. It is the movement and excitation of these hair cells which transforms basilar membrane displacement into neural signals. Because the mem-brane is displaced at different places depending on frequency, the cochlea and its inner structures are able to transform sound intensity and frequency into neural

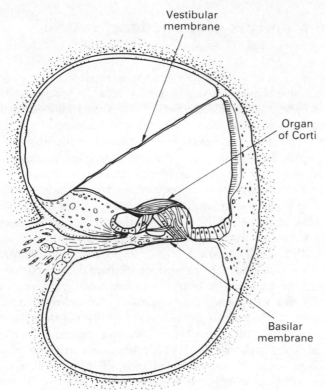

Vestibular membrane

Organ of Corti

Basilar membrane

FIGURE 8.2.2   Cross-section through the cochlea
Adapted from: Denes and Pinson 1963, p.71.

signals. But it must be emphasized that the ultimate neural representation of frequency information is not dependent on the location of maximum basilar membrane displacement alone, and our understanding of the way in which frequency is encoded through the auditory system is incomplete.

Early research on speech perception took little account of the basic perceptual properties of the ear. Rather, it tried to correlate the perceptual properties of the speech signal with the kind of representation of a linear time-varying spectrum of the kind we have already examined in chapter 7, especially section 7.14. By about 1980 researchers had realized that it was important to understand the analytical effects of the human auditory system on speech signals and that it was unwise to treat listeners as though they were simply processing information in the same way as a conventional spectrograph.

For this reason, the following section offers a brief review of the basic psychophysical properties of the auditory system in respect of frequency, time and amplitude, as they affect speech signals. For each of these three aspects of the signal, the most striking property of the human auditory system is that it is nonlinear.

8.3 Psychophysical properties of the auditory system

In section 7.9 above we showed that the auditory system is capable of making discriminations between successive changes in the frequency of an acoustic signal of about 0.5 per cent below about 1,000 Hz (figure 7.9.1). This ability is very important for our detection of cues to intonation and word tone encoded in speech signal fundamental frequency patterns. The magnitude of the just noticeable difference (JND) also depends upon the way in which the test stimuli are presented. See Zwicker and Fastl (1990) for a review of work in this area.

Our ability to discriminate differences in the centre frequencies of formants in speech signals is about an order of magnitude poorer, with JNDs at around 5 per cent. This reflects the more complex nature of the signal. Nevertheless, this level of discrimination is substantially better than that required to encode and distinguish phonological contrast between acoustically similar vowels and sonorant consonants. O'Shaughnessy (1987) provides a useful overview of work on formant discrimination.

A further important property of the auditory system is its frequency selectivity – its capacity to resolve the contiguous frequency components of a complex acoustic signal such as speech. This aspect of the auditory system was first investigated in the 1920s and has been a continuing object of inquiry since. The most common method of measuring this property is to use a constant amplitude stimulus consisting of a narrow band of noise which is progressively increased in bandwidth until the listener can detect a change in loudness. As long as the listener hears no loudness change with bandwidth change, it is assumed that the auditory system is unable to resolve the increase in noise bandwidth; but when the bandwidth exceeds the limits of the auditory system resolution, this is detected as a loudness change. This psychophysical measure of frequency resolution is known to correspond with the neurophysiological frequency resolving capability of the cochlea.

As with other psychophysical measures, frequency resolution data vary somewhat with stimulus structure and presentation methods. Moore (1989) describes these and the results obtained. Most commonly, frequency resolution is expressed in terms of critical bands (or Bark), specifying the limiting bandwidth of acoustical energy which can be resolved at any frequency. Figure 8.3.1 shows the most commonly cited results of Zwicker (1962).

Figure 8.3.1 shows that the auditory system has quite fine frequency resolution to about 500 Hz; above this, the resolution broadens approximately logarithmically. In terms of speech signals, this means that we are able to resolve harmonic information in sounds such as vowels and sonorant consonants up to about 500 Hz, and phonologically relevant spectral peaks up to about 3,000 Hz. Broadband fricative noise information in the range 3,000 to 5,000 Hz (which encompasses all the essential information in the speech signal spectrum) is more crudely resolved. As might be expected, these resolution characteristics correlate well with the progressively broader frequency domain encoding of phonologically contrastive information for non-resonant sounds.

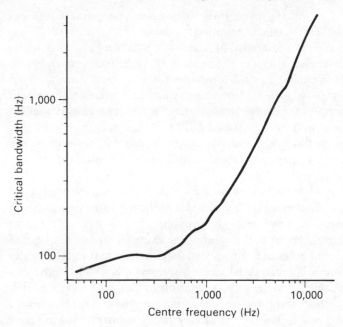

FIGURE 8.3.1 Critical bandwidth dF plotted against its centre frequency
Adapted from: Zwicker 1962.

Frequency is interwoven with time in speech signals: we respond to phonological encoding in the spectral time-course of the speech signal which reflects its characteristically dynamic nature. Time is important both in the encoding and perception of short-term acoustic events in stops and affricates and in the much longer-term encoding of prosodic information.

Temporal processing may be considered from two perspectives. The first concentrates on the interval over which the auditory system integrates information, and the second is concerned with the ability of the auditory system to detect gaps in otherwise apparently continuous acoustic signals. We have noted that the frequency resolution of the auditory system increases nonlinearly with increasing frequency; but there is no simple relationship between filter bandwidth and temporal resolution as is found in the electronic or software filters used in speech signal analysis (section 7.13 above).

The temporal integration of short-term signals by the auditory system is of direct relevance to the detection of very weak acoustic information. It appears that the threshold of audibility for sounds decreases progressively up to 200 ms and is unchanged thereafter, which suggests that stop bursts and other rapid onsets make substantial demands on the auditory system. But this generalization needs to be treated with caution because different test stimuli and protocols used by a number of investigators have yielded varying data in investigations of temporal integration.

Temporal acuity – demonstrated by the ability of listeners to distinguish between two successive acoustic events – also varies depending upon the stimuli and test protocols used. Pisoni (1977) found listeners able to distinguish temporal differences between 500 Hz and 1,500 Hz signal at minimum relative differences of 20 ms. Moore et al. (1993) investigated the ability of listeners to detect gaps in a signal consisting of a sinusoidal wave. The just distinguishable gap (or 'gap detection threshold') was roughly constant at around 6 to 8 ms for test signals in the range 400 to 2,000 Hz: outside this frequency range the gap detection threshold rises to around 18 ms. Other techniques for measuring gap detection threshold have yielded figures as low as 2 ms at test frequencies around 8,000 Hz. Overall, it appears that whatever the measurement methods, the auditory system is capable of resolving the rapid onsets and acoustic energy gaps associated with obstruent consonants in running speech.

Another important form of temporal performance is the detection of spectral change in complex signals. The most common and significant form of change in speech occurs in the transitional movements of formants at the onset and coda of syllables (section 7.17 above). Perceptual experiments using complex synthesized speech-like signals with varying rates of frequency change suggest that rapid changes below about 30 ms are temporally integrated in the auditory system and heard as a single broader bandwidth signal. Extensive investigation of this area indicates that the ability to discriminate short duration frequency transitions is greater where a contiguous steady state signal follows. The relatively rapid formant transitions of around 50 ms for voiced stops in speech are, in perceptual and phonological terms, close to the relevant limits of the auditory system's processing ability. There are also suggestions by Jamieson (1987) that 50 ms may be close to an optimal level of salience for formant transition rates.

Turning to the amplitude of the speech signal, we note that the auditory system accommodates an extremely wide range of sound intensities. The system responds to differences in intensity logarithmically, a fact recognized by the development of the decibel scale as described earlier in section 7.9. The minimum JND depends as always on the measurement methods and stimuli, but data from Florentine et al. (1987) indicate figures of around 1 dB for high intensity stimuli at frequencies below 10 kHz, and 3 to 4 dB at more moderate intensities and frequencies above 10 kHz. These levels of acuity are well beyond those required to decode speech signals.

The actual perceived loudness of sound for a constant intensity stimulus varies considerably with frequency. The threshold of intensity at which sound can be detected varies by about 70 dB between 20 Hz and 15,000 Hz. This is why some stereo systems have a so-called loudness control to boost up very low and very high frequencies when the system is being played at low sound levels. Some of this variability in auditory system acuity is a consequence of the frequency selective propagation of sound in the auditory canal. Fortunately, over the range 500 to 5,000 Hz, which contains most of the phonologically relevant information for speech, the auditory system has its lowest threshold of detectable intensity and thus is relatively uniform in sensitivity.

8.4   Speech intelligibility

The three basic dimensions of acoustic signals which we have been considering –
frequency, time and intensity – and the related performance of the human auditory
system have often been investigated by task-specific test signals designed to probe
performance limits in the one dimension under investigation. In our everyday perception of normal speech signals, however, we attend to the totality of a complex
signal encoding actual language and we can use some top-down processing as well as
bottom-up. This is, of course, highly relevant to our capacity and performance as
listeners, and a brief review of this area follows. Most of the literature examining
general speech intelligibility has focused either on whole words and syllables or on
consonants, because of the interest in communication which has motivated the
research. Vowels, the most intelligible component of syllables, have received more
attention in later and more phonetically oriented studies.

In the first half of the twentieth century, telecommunications engineers embarked
on extensive testing of the intelligibility of speech. One question of primary interest
was to find out what band of frequencies had to be transmitted to ensure that speech
was intelligible. An extensive set of investigations using filters to attenuate frequencies above and below a defined cut-off showed that most of the phonologically
important information that ensures intelligible speech is contained in the band of
frequencies between 300 Hz and 3,500 Hz. This is the typical passband used for
telecommunications systems. The telephone system is a good example of an effective
trade-off: the provision of a wider passband would have little cost benefit other than
improving general fidelity and making speaker identification easier.

Differences in acoustic encoding among segments are such that not all sounds
require even this passband, while some sounds will benefit from transmission of
an even wider band of high frequencies. For example, back vowels such as /u/
gain little from frequencies above 2,500 Hz, whereas fricatives such as /f/ and /s/
would be more intelligible if telephones passed frequencies up to 5,000 Hz.
Fletcher (1953) and O'Neill (1975) are useful summaries of the classical work
in this area.

In addition to frequency passband, the effects of the intensity of presentation on
intelligibility were also extensively studied in the same period. Typically these studies
have shown that the intelligibility of monosyllabic words moves from about 10 per
cent intelligibility to about 90 per cent intelligibility with an increase of 40 dB in
stimulus presentation level (figure 8.4.1). These figures should be taken as a general
guide only, because, as always, the actual figures obtained depend upon the particular stimuli chosen and the experimental protocol used.

The choice of stimuli is indeed crucial to the nature and results of speech intelligibility tests. If the speech materials used to test intelligibility are, for example, meaningful sentences, we do not rely on acoustic information alone to identify words. For
instance, in a sentence such as 'the baker burned the bread', the word 'bread' is fairly
predictable from the context and it is unlikely we would confuse it with similar

sounding words such as 'bed' or 'pet' or 'brad'. On the other hand, if an intelligibility test asks us to identify nonsense syllables such as 'gup', 'dar' and 'oosh', there is little opportunity to use top-down linguistic knowledge to complement the available acoustic information. It is therefore not surprising that tests which include a linguistic context and offer substantial predictability produce higher scores for a given set of conditions (such as filtering or masking) than those involving meaningless syllables. Much of the earlier work in studying intelligibility failed to take real account of these effects. Similarly, tests which use forced choice answers also result in higher scores than those which leave the listener without any options for a potentially correct response.

Figure 8.4.1 shows a typical graph (known as a Performance Intensity Function) of the progressive increase in the intelligibility of monosyllabic words with an increasing level of intensity. As with studies of the effects of a reduced frequency passband, intensity studies reveal different outcomes for different classes of speech sounds. The absolute intensity level at which the speech is presented can markedly affect intelligibility. Kent et al. (1979) examined the phonetically selective effects of intensity of presentation in some detail, and showed that sonorant and strong fricative consonants such as /w/ and /s/ require a markedly lower intensity level to be reliably recognized than do weak fricatives such as /v/ and voiceless stops such as /k/ and /t/.

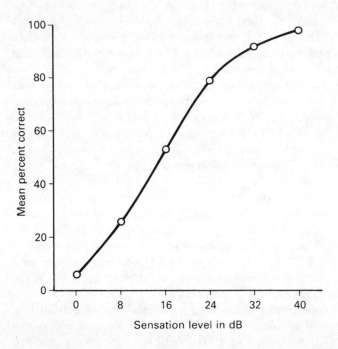

FIGURE 8.4.1   Performance Intensity Function for a set of monosyllables
Source: Robert Mannell, Macquarie University. Based on data in Kopra et al. 1968.

Another method of investigating the effects of intensity on speech intelligibility is by the use of a competing signal to mask the speech. This has a practical merit, because it removes the artificiality of simply manipulating intensity. Instead it introduces the sort of competing signal which listeners encounter in the real world. Such competing signals may be as varied as the background noise in a jet aircraft cabin, the propagation noise of a radio communications link, or the babble of voices at a party.

In investigations of this kind, the masker is most commonly a broadband noise signal with either a uniform frequency–intensity distribution, or a profile approximating the long-term averaged frequency–intensity spectrum of a number of speakers (of the kind shown in figure 7.19.1 above). The noise and the speech signals are mixed in precisely computed signal-to-noise ratios and presented to listeners. The classic investigation in this area is by Miller and Nicely (1955) whose very comprehensive data have been extensively quoted and reanalysed in the literature of experimental phonetics. They showed, as might be expected, that voiceless sounds generally, and fricatives in particular, show greater losses in intelligibility than voiced sounds, especially sonorant sounds such as nasals. This demonstrated that nasality and voicing were the most robust phonetic features under masked listening conditions and that features such as place of articulation, duration and affrication are much less robust.

A series of later investigations, of which Pickett (1957), Pickett and Rubenstein (1960), Busch and Eldridge (1967), Williams and Hecker (1968) and Clark (1983) are examples, demonstrate that the effects of masking are generally explained by the relationship of the frequency–intensity profile of the masker to that of the speech sound under examination. Figure 8.4.2 illustrates the phonetically selective nature of band limited uniform noise on various consonant classes in English.

Duration, reflected in the timing of the components of a syllable, is phonologically important. Early investigations of duration showed that rapid periodic interruptions to a continuous speech signal – by turning it on and off in rapid succession for equal intervals of time – affect intelligibility. When interruptions to the speech signal approach intervals of 500 ms, intelligibility falls to near zero; but when the duration is reduced to 200 ms or less, intelligibility approaches 100 per cent. Predictably, when the duration of the interruptions exceeds 500 ms, the effects on intelligibility are confounded by the nature of the test materials and by listeners' ability to use top-down sensitivity to the context being established by continuous speech.

Simple signal interruption is, of course, a relatively crude measure of the contribution of duration to intelligibility. Studies of the effects of time compression on speech indicate that the formant transitions in the onset and codas of syllables tolerate very little compression, but that the effects are quite variable on other parts of syllabic structure. Duration as part of the phonological structure of speech naturally plays a role in intelligibility: words of longer duration are typically more intelligible than shorter ones. In monosyllables, this is a function of the overall perceptual salience of the phonological structure of the syllable itself. Thus the word *hoof* is likely to be less intelligible than the word *rage*. The first word not only has a much shorter syllabic nucleus, it also has consonants at the onset and coda which are acoustically weak

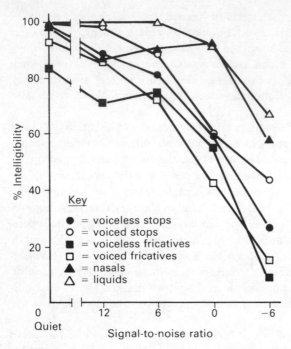

FIGURE 8.4.2   Effects of masking on consonant identification
Source: Clark 1983.

and relatively easily masked. Polysyllabic words are more complex, because the prediction of their intelligibility will depend on a mixture of duration, phonological structure, and lexical familiarity. Consider for example the word *secretary*: there are not many English polysyllabic words beginning with similar sounds and having a similar stress pattern (such as *secondary*, *secular* and *sacrament*). Put any of these similar words into a reasonably genuine context (such as 'who's the departmental secretary?' or 'what kind of secondary school did you attend?') and the chances of mishearing them are quite low. Our familiarity with particular words in particular contexts thus introduces a significant top-down component into the recognition process. Data illustrating some of these effects can be found in Rubenstein et al. (1959) and Schultz (1964).

8.5 Acoustic-phonetic perception

Many general speech intelligibility studies have been motivated by what might be described as global interests in the properties of the speech signal in the context of the adequacy of communications systems or the impairment of hearing. As facilities for

acoustic analysis, synthesis and signal processing have improved, researchers
investigated the detailed phonetic aspects of speech perception with the objec
discovering how the cues to perceived phonological structure are encoded in
acoustic signal itself.

The pioneering studies of acoustic cues to the perception of phonological structure
were undertaken at the Haskins Laboratories, using the painted spectrogram technique described earlier in section 7.17. These studies showed some of the ways in
which formants and other spectral patterns encode the phonetic identity of segments
in the time and frequency structure of the syllable. For details see Cooper et al.
(1952) and Delattre et al. (1955). These early experiments demonstrated, among
other things, the value of speech synthesis as a tool in the investigation of speech
perception. With synthetic speech, the spectrum can be manipulated in a controlled
fashion to check the perceptual significance of its dynamic spectral parameters.

Using synthesized speech, researchers from the Haskins group and elsewhere have
shown that if a parameter is changed in equal increments from a value encoding a
reliable percept of one segment, to a value encoding a reliable percept of another,
listeners reach a point of sudden change in their perception from one segment to the
other. There is no significant region of indecisiveness in the perception of sounds
synthesized in the region of intermediate values. In other words, listeners do not
gradually change their opinions on the identity of the stimulus in line with the
progressive changes in the signal, but make a quite sudden changeover. The most
striking form of this effect occurs when voice onset time (VOT) is delayed in stop
consonants. If the delay is increased in small steps (say 10 ms) from around zero to
about 100 ms after the release of the occlusion, English speaking listeners continue to
hear the stop as voiced up to about 20 or 30 ms (and perhaps up to 40 ms for velar
stops), always depending on the particular stimulus properties. The next 10 ms
increment then brings a switch in judgment and the stop is heard as voiceless.
Figure 8.5.1 shows the effect, using idealized data.

This effect is known as CATEGORICAL PERCEPTION. Its presence in speech perception is
not surprising, given that phonological organization is a matter of discrete options;
in the context of acoustic and auditory analysis, it is appropriate to describe such
perception as categorical. A further illustration emerges when listeners are asked to
identify pairs of stimuli from a continuum as 'same' or 'different'. In general, we are
not sensitive to differences within a series of values which we commonly count as
occurrences of the same sound. As shown in figure 8.5.1(b), it is only around the
VOT value at which listeners identify a change from voiced to voiceless that they can
reliably hear a difference between pairs of stimuli. In other words, discrimination is
weaker within the boundaries of a perceptual category, and sharper at or near the
boundary. This again demonstrates the fundamental principle of functional contras-
tiveness. The effect has also been illustrated for formant transition frequencies and
durations. (See Studdert-Kennedy 1976, Pickett 1980, and Lieberman and Blumstein
1988 for further discussion of this field of research.)

Category boundaries are of course language-dependent, at least to some extent.
Thus English commonly has marked aspiration (delayed VOT) on stops, serving as a
cue to their voicelessness, and shows larger VOT categories than languages like

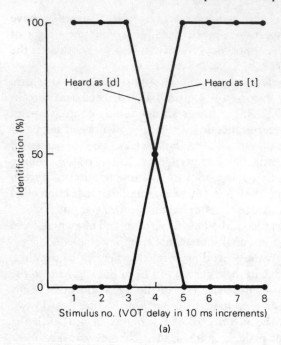

(a)

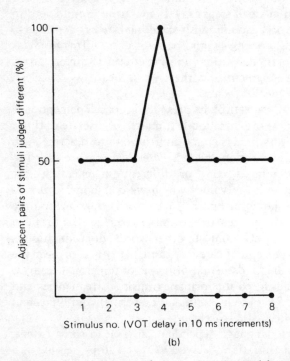

(b)

FIGURE 8.5.1   Perceptual responses to VOT delay: (a) identification; (b) discrimination

French (in which voiceless stops are generally not aspirated) or Thai (in which there is a three-way phonological distinction of voiceless aspirated, voiceless and voiced stops). There is also evidence that where more than one cue determines a category choice, trading relations may exist among the cues. For example, Repp (1979) has shown that aspiration, duration and intensity may be traded against each other in establishing the boundary of the voicing category in English.

Studies of animal perception suggest that categorical perception is not specific to human speech and hearing, but perhaps partly a consequence of general psychophysical boundary effects. If so, categorical perception need not be taken to be uniquely phonologically motivated: it may be that language capitalizes, as it were, on a basic psychoacoustic capability to optimize the phonetic processing of stimuli.

8.6 Vowel perception

The prime importance of the values of the first three formants in the encoding of vowel quality was confirmed in the early Haskins experiments (section 7.15 above). It has also been shown by Carlson et al. (1975) that accurate percepts can be obtained from synthetic vowels using only two formants, where F_2 is adjusted upwards to compensate for the absence of the high-frequency energy of the upper formants. Peterson and Barney (1952) recorded natural vowels in words beginning with /h/ and ending with /d/ from a range of speakers (men, women and children), analysed the formant structure of these, and conducted perceptual studies using the same recordings. Their analysis, and later work by Shepard (1972), showed that where perceptual confusions occurred, they were generally well correlated with acoustic proximity as defined by the three lowest formants. Their data also show a remarkable degree of variability among supposedly identical vowels and overlap between apparently different vowels. Work on Australian English by Bernard and Mannell (1986) demonstrates comparable variability and overlap. Figure 8.6.1 shows the variability of a number of Australian English vowels and the overlap among them when their formants are plotted against each other.

These data reveal an important aspect of vowel perception, namely the crucial importance of the systemic nature of the formant specified acoustic relationships: we distinguish vowels from each other, and are less concerned with their absolute values. We have already had cause to note that there is significant diversity in the acoustic properties of the vowels of children, women and men, arising from differences in vocal tract length, as well as further diversity due to differences among individuals in their vocal tract and in the habitual settings of their speech organs (section 7.15 above). As a consequence, researchers have formulated mathematical algorithms for normalizing data variance, particularly that which results from variations in vocal tract length.

Ladefoged and Broadbent's experiment demonstrated that formant frequencies only determine phonological identity within a vowel system (Ladefoged and

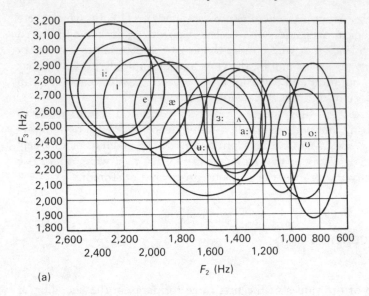

(a)

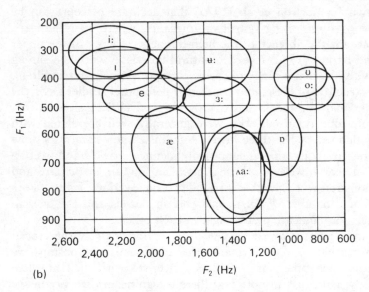

(b)

FIGURE 8.6.1   (a) F_2/F_3 plot (2 standard deviation ellipses) of the monophthongs produced by 172 adult male speakers of Australian English (b) F_1/F_2 plot (2 standard deviation ellipses) of the monophthongs produced by 172 adult male speakers of Australian English

Broadbent 1957, and section 7.15 above). Using synthetic speech they showed that if the complete vowel system in a sentence was shifted except for the test vowel, listeners would reliably normalize if the systemic shift effectively placed the vowel within the bounds of the acoustic specification of a phonologically distinct vowel.

Thus the vowel of *head* could be made to be heard as the vowel of *hid* if the formant frequencies of all the other vowels were lowered. It seems that listeners can normalize to a new speaker within the first few words that they hear. (See further discussion in Holmes 1986.)

Nevertheless, vowels also seem to differ from many consonants in being identified along a continuum of values rather than categorically. Fry et al. (1962) used synthetic speech and the labelling and discrimination techniques previously applied to consonants to generate a continuum of vowels with precise increments in formant values. They were unable to find the same categorical shift in labelling or the same peaks in discrimination. This suggests some justification for the tradition of describing most consonant sounds in terms of a discrete set of production categories, but characterizing the acoustic and articulatory possibilities in vowel production in terms of continua.

Our discussion here has followed most researchers in concentrating on the first few formants as the acoustic determinants of vowel identity. But it has been persuasively argued by Strange et al. (1983) that when listeners identify the vowels of natural speech, as opposed to experimentally constrained synthetic stimuli, they also depend upon the dynamic coarticulatory transitional information in the formant structure of the syllable. While this has been challenged by some, it seems highly likely that listeners do, in normal situations, gain extra information in this way.

8.7   Consonant perception

As discussed earlier in section 7.17, the work by the Haskins group using painted spectrograms to synthesize stimuli provided basic evidence of the principal acoustic cues to place of articulation in stops, and to the voiced–voiceless distinction. Extensive work at Haskins and elsewhere using synthetic speech has provided detailed knowledge of most of the acoustic features of consonants. This includes the notion of the formant locus, and the role of noise bursts as cues to voicing and place of articulation in stops. Figure 8.7.1 illustrates the role of the noise burst spectrum and its coarticulatory relationship with the following vowel in CV syllables, in well-known data from Cooper et al. (1952). The Haskins work also showed that transitions and the rate of change of formant transitions at the onset and coda of a syllable had a significant role in distinguishing stops from sonorant consonants (Liberman et al. 1956), in identifying approximants (O'Connor et al. 1957), and in identifying nasals and stops (Liberman et al. 1954). Harris (1958) also showed that the spectral structure of the noise in fricatives provides a major cue to their perception.

Since this early work, the technology of speech analysis and synthesis has become far more sophisticated, accurate and flexible, and there is now a large body of literature on the acoustic cues to a variety of consonants. In general, these studies accord with the consonantal acoustic properties described from the point of view of

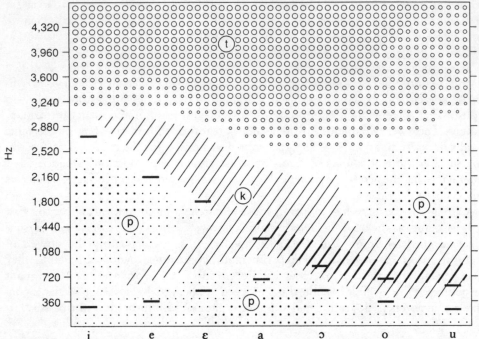

FIGURE 8.7.1   The role of the noise burst spectrum. Twelve different noise bursts (their centre frequencies shown along the vertical axis) were combined with seven different vowels and presented to 30 listeners. The zones show the dominant perceptions of the burst as [p], [t] or [k] according to its frequency and the following vowel
Adapted from: Cooper et al. 1952.

production in chapter 7 above. Fant (1973), Shoup and Pfeiffer (1976), Pickett (1980) and O'Shaughnessy (1987) provide extensive reviews of the work on perceptual features of consonants.

8.8   Units of perception

The phoneme as a unit of linguistic processing generally, and of perceptual processing in particular, continues to be defended by many researchers. Work by Warren (1970, 1984), for example, has demonstrated that when segments are excised from the stream of speech and replaced by noise, listeners will report hearing the correct missing segment. They presumably restore the segment by top-down contextual prediction.

Much of the classic work in speech perception has chosen to focus on investigating cues in the acoustic signal which encode the identity of phonological segments. Yet, as even the very early Haskins work showed, these cues are not generally discrete or invariant. Nor does the syllable simply consist of a concatenation of discrete, isolated phonological features and segments. Rather, the features and segments may overlap with each other, and are materially influenced by the phonological structure and context of the syllables in which they are produced. (See section 4.1 above, Fant 1973, and Fowler and Smith 1986.)

This has led some researchers to consider the syllable as the primary unit of production and perception. (Compare the argument in section 7.17 above that the acoustic structure of segments can be properly understood and described only within the context of the acoustic syllable.) Studdert-Kennedy (1976) describes the syllable as a 'symbiosis of consonant and vowel' which acts as the effective vehicle for the transmission of linguistic information. The greater salience of the syllable than the segment is also suggested by a speech error experiment by Tent and Clark (1980), in which listeners detected syllable level errors far more readily than segment errors. Crompton (1982) also argues from speech error data that the syllable is the primary unit in which articulatory patterns are stored; if, as many researchers believe, there are direct links between production and perception, this also has implications for perception.

By contrast, Blumstein and Stevens (1979, 1980) sparked a major debate by arguing, on evidence from both production and perception, that in certain segments, notably stops, there were invariant spectral cues in the acoustic signal. Other researchers have argued for the existence of subsegmental units of perception in the form of phonological features. Such work has often used multivariate statistical data reduction to obtain the necessary supporting evidence. The work of Miller and Nicely (1955) is an early example of this approach. Their primary data were presented segmentally in confusion matrices, of the kind shown in figure 8.8.1: here the test segments presented to listeners are shown in the rows of the matrix and the sounds heard by the listeners in the columns. Such forms of presentation are useful in allowing an immediate view of the pattern of perceptual errors. Simple visual inspection may, however, fail to reveal important underlying patterns.

Further analysis of these data suggests that there are regular underlying relationships between the listening conditions and the intelligibility of certain phonological features, as shown in figure 8.8.2.

Researchers using computer-based statistical analysis techniques, such as multidimensional scaling and hierarchical clustering, have conducted further analyses of intelligibility data to provide visualizations of the perceptual properties of features and segments in relation to listening conditions. Shepard (1972), Wang and Bilger (1973) and Singh (1975) provide detailed accounts of such studies, including the statistical methods used. Other approaches include that of Wickelgren (1966), who undertook feature-based analyses of short-term memory error in consonant recall. He concluded that feature-based analyses had greater explanatory power for the data than segments alone, and that the explanatory power of some feature sets was greater than others.

Other researchers have sought evidence for the existence of specific perceptual feature detection mechanisms, prompted by the more general evidence of functionally specific neural auditory detectors in cats and other animals. Eimas and Corbit

		p	t	k	b	d	g	ɡ	dʒ	f	θ	s	ʃ	h	v	ð	z	ʒ	m	n	ŋ	l	r	w	j
															SPOKEN CONSONANT										
	p	3		3						1															
	t	1	3	6				4		1		2													
	k	10	7	4						2															
	b		1		1												1								
	d					9				2	1						1								
	g			1		2	1		2																
	ɡ							3						11											
	dʒ				3	3	9		8																
	f	1	2					1		9	7														
	θ									1							1								
	s		1					2		2	1														
	ʃ							2			1														
	h				1																				
	v				10					1					15		1						1	1	
	ð									1							1					1			
	z					1				2							4						1		
	ʒ					1																			
	m																		13						
	n																		2	15					
	ŋ																								
	l																					12	1		
	r							1									5					2	10	7	5
	w																						1	7	
	j					4		5															1		10
	null		1		1			2									1								
	%	20	20	27	7	60	7	20	53	60		13	7		100		27		87	100		80	67	47	67

FIGURE 8.8.1 Confusion matrix for consonants in a CV frame heard in noise of equal intensity. The data are from 15 subjects listening to masked natural speech (−6 dB S/N white noise)

Source: Robert Mannell, Macquarie University.

(1973) conducted a series of experiments which demonstrated that it was possible to shift phonetic category boundaries by repeatedly presenting a stimulus at one end of a feature continuum (such as VOT). Their hypothesis was that this effect might be explained by the fatiguing of the relevant feature detector and the increased sensitivity of the contrasting feature detector, causing a shift in category boundary. Research since then has not revealed substantial evidence to advance this claim, which is now regarded with some caution.

SPOKEN MANNER					
	ST	AF	FR	NS	AP
ST	58	20	15		
AF	13	37	15		
FR	22	17	63		7
NS				100	
AP	4	20	7		93
null	2	7	1		

(left axis: PERCEIVED MANNER)

SPOKEN VOICING		
	+V	−V
+V	93	10
−V	4	88
null	2	3

(left axis: PERCVD VOICING)

SPOKEN PLACE		
	LD	AL	VL
LD	75	15	10
AL	3	66	53
VL	20	10	20
null	2	9	17

(left axis: PERCEIVED PLACE)

Key
Manner (all consonants)
ST = Stops
AF = Affricates
FR = Fricatives
NS = Nasals
AP = Approximants and semi-vowels

Voicing (stops, affricates and fricatives only)
+V = Voiced
−V = Unvoiced

Place (Stops, affricates and fricatives only)
LD = Labial and dental
AL = Alveolar and post-alveolar
VL = Velar

FIGURE 8.8.2 Effective intelligibility of selected features. The figures are percentages of inter-class confusions (intra-class confusions are not included)
Source: Robert Mannell, Macquarie University.

Much of the investigation of the perceptual units of speech described so far has relied on manipulation of the spectral time-course of the speech signal, either by reprocessing natural speech or by parametric manipulation of formant coded synthetic speech. A different approach has been to present listeners with a natural speech recording in which the time-domain waveform has been 'gated' so that only a precise fraction of the signal is heard by the listener. The duration of this gated fraction is usually progressively increased to a point at which the signal is likely to be reliably identified by most listeners. In its simplest form such an experiment might align the start of the gate with the start of the consonant stimulus in, say, a CV syllable, and then lengthen the duration of the gate incrementally until the consonant is reliably identified. For initial stops it has been shown that the first 10 to 15 ms of the release burst is often all that is needed for accurate identification. Studies of various classes of consonants reveal that sounds such as fricatives, which have less rapid changes of spectrum after release, require longer gate times for reliable identification; although for most sounds the required duration remains well under 80 ms. Interestingly, these results indicate that identification of consonants does not always rely on formant transition from the acoustic nucleus of the syllable, although in some instances it does improve the reliability of identification.

What then is the basic perceptual unit of speech? No simple answer can be given, because there is no clear evidence pointing to just one unit. It is clear that we can perceive some features, such as voicing, without correctly identifying the segment in which that feature is present. On the other hand, in some instances, cues to segment identity are distributed across the entire syllable, or at least across more than one segment; for example, the voicing of postvocalic fricatives in English is often detected from the length of the preceding vowel, not from any strong presence of periodicity caused by phonatory modulation of the fricative noise. In general, we may say that the syllable provides the normal acoustic structure of the continuous speech. Cues to phonological structure may be distributed across the syllable in various ways that allow us to perceive both phonological features and segments. But the syllable is not always an absolutely essential structure for the communication of all information about phonological features or segments.

8.9   Prosodic perception

The term 'prosodic' is used here to refer to linguistic information of the kind often described as rhythm and intonation (which will be dealt with in detail in chapter 9 below). The chief acoustic parameters of relevance here are duration, fundamental frequency and intensity. As we have already seen, these features may also encode phonological information within segments and syllables, but we are now concerned more with their functions across longer stretches of speech. (This is another reminder that acoustic cues often serve more than one function: the encoding of speech is complex and multilayered.)

Duration illustrates the point, for it signals various things. As indicated in sections 8.6 and 8.7 above, it contributes to segmental contrasts in English, in the distinction between long and short vowels, in the VOT distinction between voiceless and voiced stops, and in the encoding of postvocalic consonant voicing in the length of the preceding segment. Across longer stretches of speech, duration is a measure of speaking rate. There is, however, no direct relationship between the overall rate of utterance and the durations of syllabic and segmental structures within the stream of speech. A number of studies of speaking rate have shown that as the rate increases, the speaker preserves those aspects of the acoustic structure which are valuable for encoding segmental and prosodic structure; at the same time, listeners are able to compensate for increased coarticulatory effects and for the spectral and temporal contraction of less important information. See O'Shaughnessy (1987) for a useful overview of this topic.

The speech rhythm of a language such as English is perceived in the durational interplay of prominent (or 'stressed') syllables and weaker or less prominent ones. English has traditionally been considered to have an isochronous pattern of rhythm, that is a pattern in which prominent syllables seem to occur at roughly equal intervals, regardless of the number of weak syllables occurring between the prominent ones (see section 9.3 below). Buxton (1983) suggests that despite this perceptual effect, the speech production evidence for isochrony in English is rather weak. She concludes that it is likely that other factors, such as distributed coarticulatory acoustic cues, may contribute to the strength of the isochrony percept.

In investigating temporal patterning, phoneticians have tried to identify the point or points (so-called P-CENTRES) in a stream of speech which are perceived to be the location of prominence or stress. Experimental evidence suggests that these perceived locations depend on syllable duration and total syllabic structure, rather than on the particular segmental constituents of the syllable. Morton et al. (1976) showed that if a series of syllables is spaced so that there is equal time between successive syllable onsets, listeners do perceive a pattern of isochrony. But if the spacing is based on p-centres, a much stronger effect of rhythmicality is perceived.

Our sensitivity to small changes in pitch, its consequent strong perceptual salience, and our capacity to control pitch in speech production are discussed in some detail in sections 7.9 and 7.19 above and 9.2 below. As with duration, pitch provides several layers of information to the listener. It is a major contributor to voice quality, it helps us to identify the sex and age of a speaker, and it can in some cases be a means of distinguishing among individual speakers. It even seems to be the case that listeners make judgments about the personality, attitude and even truthfulness of speakers on the basis of pitch information; Cooper and Sorenson (1981) give a useful overview of studies that have investigated these global (and largely nonlinguistic) aspects of information which listeners derive from fundamental frequency.

Despite the significance of fundamental frequency as a cue, Brown et al. (1980) report that even trained listeners have difficulty in making accurate estimates of the magnitude of pitch movement in prominent syllables. In fact, the experience of many introductory classes in phonetics and phonology shows that some students are initially unable to consistently identify the direction of perceived pitch movement in a prominent syllable, much less its magnitude relative to other points of pitch-based prominence in the same speech sequence. This limited ability to make accurate judgments about local detail in pitch patterns is, of course, unsurprising given the enormous variability among speakers in their production of fundamental frequency patterns. What has long been established is that listeners do make very effective use of the dynamics of fundamental frequency patterns as the basis for judgments about contrasts that are relevant within the particular language (such as stressed versus unstressed or querying tone versus determinate). Further details can be found in chapter 9 below and in overviews such as Lehiste (1970) and Gandour (1978).

8.10　Word recognition

This chapter has so far concentrated on phonetically motivated approaches to under-standing the perception of speech, based on our bottom-up processing of the acous-tically encoded cues in the spectral time-course of speech. Less central to phonetics and phonology and of more significance in cognitive psychology is work on the cognitive processes involved in the recognition of words – how listeners process phonological structure sequentially and how they access lexical information from memory.

We have already noted earlier in this chapter the effects of top-down influences such as context and word familiarity in mediating reliable perception. Warren's phonemic restoration effect, described in section 8.8, is an example of top-down processing making use of context and the listener's linguistic knowledge base. More recent work by Samuel (1981) also shows that words in common use show a stronger restoration effect and that the effect is stronger for word-final segments than for word-initial segments.

One well-known way of investigating this question as a matter of cognitive pro-cessing is a speech shadowing task in which subjects repeat what they hear as quickly as possible after it is spoken. Marslen-Wilson (1985) and Marslen-Wilson and Welsh (1978) have shown that skilled listeners are able to shadow a speaker so closely that words can be recognized as little as 200 ms after their onset. In such rapid shadow-ing, the listener has generally had too little time to respond to the acoustic cues alone and must therefore be making top-down predictions as well.

Some further insight into this process comes from Aitchison and Straf (1982) who compared adults' and children's errors in retrieving words. Although this experi-mental work investigates retrieval rather than direct perception, it suggests that children rely far more on macrophonetic aspects of the word being recalled (such as rhythm and the location of the stressed syllable) but that adults rely more on initial consonants (perhaps implying that adults have more recourse to their exten-sive mental lexicon). There remains considerable debate about the processes involved in lexical access, and about the roles of top-down and bottom-up processing, and the way in which these are integrated in the overall perceptual task. In a discussion of evidence from the literature, Marslen-Wilson (1989b) concludes that linguistic con-textual information does not necessarily override or unreasonably constrain the use of bottom-up information from the speech signal itself.

8.11　Models of speech perception

Research into speech perception still awaits the development and verification of a comprehensive explanatory model, although several models have been proposed. We concentrate here on those constructed from an essentially phonetic and phonological perspective.

The MOTOR THEORY is one of the oldest, best-known, and most widely criticized of the phonetically based models of perception. Its basic hypothesis is that we decode the perceived acoustic signal in terms of stored articulatory patterns which can generate an acoustic signal with the same linguistic percept. The theory gained currency through the proposals of Liberman et al. (1967). A more recent version (Liberman and Mattingly 1985) maintains that stored articulatory patterns have a more abstract status as underlying forms representing articulatory intentions which are directly perceived by the listener. Defenders of this theory have yet to provide an explanation of how the model works in detail, and of how the storage and accessing of the underlying articulatory information is accomplished.

An early version of the ANALYSIS BY SYNTHESIS model is described by Stevens and Halle (1967). The model is far more computational in approach than the motor theory and assumes, in essence, that listeners perform a spectral analysis of the incoming speech signal, resolving it into features and parameters which are then stored. The acoustically analysed information is then further analysed to provide an estimate (which may also be mediated by higher order information) of the phonological structure of the input. This estimate or trial form of the phonological structure is operated on by a phonological rule system to generate a hypothesized utterance which is compared with an appropriate neural auditory representation of the analysed input. If the match is good, the hypothesis is taken to be correct and accepted. If the match is poor, the process is iterated until an acceptable match is obtained.

Klatt (1979, 1981) has proposed a model which is even more oriented to the speech signal, called LAFS (Lexical Access From Spectra). This model assumes a very large store of spectral patterns or templates as the basis for identifying all familiar words held in the listener's memory. It avoids any postulation of stored segmental representation or of segmentally organized analysis of incoming speech, and thus bypasses many of the problems of context-sensitive variability in the spectral representation of segmental sequences, both within words and across word boundaries. Decisions about phonetic identity are made using spectral distance metrics which allow the match between the input spectrum and competing spectral templates to be scored, the candidates compared and a choice made. This model presupposes very powerful analysis, storage, access and decision processes in any computational realization of it. It does, however, address in a direct way some of the realities of dealing with natural speech which are swept away by various forms of cognitive or linguistic abstraction in other models.

The TRACE model is probably the best known of the models of speech perception and recognition inspired by work on connectionist models of cognition. The model, described by Elman and McClelland (1986), depicts a procedure that begins by generating spectral slices from the input signal every 5 ms. These form the input to a set of interconnected processing elements, known as nodes within connectionist models, which act as feature detectors. Connections to the nodes are either excitatory or inhibitory, and the features themselves are defined in terms of spectral properties.

Progressive slices of analysed speech will either inhibit or cumulatively excite a given node and so identify a particular feature. The feature nodes are in turn connected to a set of segmental detection nodes, and the same basic process is repeated to accumulate a decision which will identify a particular segment. In turn, the outputs of the segmental nodes are connected to a set of word detection nodes. Interconnections between nodes are weighted to adjust their level of contextual influence on node output.

Other perceptual models can be found in the literature, but none can claim to have won wide acceptance, and some have never been computationally implemented or extensively tested. For a comprehensive critique of well-known models, see Klatt (1989).

8.12   Conclusion

A very large body of information about speech perception has been collected since the 1950s, and our knowledge of the basic acoustic correlates contributing to many phonological features and segments is now quite extensive. The failure to establish an unassailable case for a particular basic unit of perception probably reflects the fact that linguistic information is encoded in the speech signal at various levels and in ways that exploit interdependence and redundancy. It is evident, for example, that some features and segments can be reliably identified within tens of milliseconds from the onset of the syllable, while others rely on information distributed across the entire syllable, and even beyond.

The array of models of speech perception reflects the lack of a unified understanding of perceptual processes and of the complex interaction of its top-down and bottom-up aspects. None of the models of perception which have been computationally implemented has been demonstrated on more than a very limited set of test materials. These limited materials do not really put the models to the test of dealing with the enormous variability among speakers and the complexities of rapid continuous speech which are the everyday reality of actual discourse.

Exercises

1   Give a broad outline of the structure of the human ear (including the outer, middle and inner ears) noting how each part of the structure contributes to the process of hearing.

2   Why would you expect, when receiving a message by telephone, to be more likely to confuse the names *Flack* and *Slack* than the names *Goode*, *Godde* and *Goad*?

3   What does it mean to say that the auditory system is 'frequency selective'?

4 Explain briefly what is meant by the distinction between 'top-down' and 'bottom-up' speech processing.

5 What do you understand by the term 'categorical perception'?

6 What evidence could you appeal to if you wanted to support the claim that we can understand what someone is saying without hearing every detail of the speech signal?

7 Why is it difficult to specify a particular unit of language (such as phoneme, syllable or word) as the basic unit of perception?

8 'We hear with the brain, not with the ear.' Does this chapter support this statement? What is the relevant evidence?

9 Prosody

This chapter deals with prosodic features of speech of the kind commonly described as tone, stress and intonation. After a general introduction (9.1) the chapter explains the chief phonetic correlates, notably pitch, duration and loudness (9.2).

Prosodic features may be systematized in various ways in language (9.3). Many of the world's languages can be described as tone languages (9.4); a less common type of systematization can be found in so-called pitch-accent languages (9.5).

The latter part of the chapter focuses mainly on English and discusses

- the phenomenon of lexical stress (9.6)
- the extent to which stress patterns are governed by rules (9.7)
- the description of intonation (9.8).

9.1 Introduction

Features of spoken language which are not easily identified as discrete segments are variously referred to as PROSODIC FEATURES, NONSEGMENTAL FEATURES or SUPRASEGMENTALS. The terms imply a difference between segmental sounds (traditionally consonants and vowels) which are commonly thought of as entities, and features such as pitch and tempo which are likely to be perceived as features extending over longer stretches of speech. The distinction is reinforced by many writing systems (including that of English) which have an alphabet of consonant and vowel symbols but no comparable indication of prosody, other than through the use of punctuation marks and devices such as italicization. The distinction is by no means clear-cut, however. Prosodic features *can* be just as discrete as consonants and vowels; and, as we have noted in looking at the details of acoustics and articulation, consonants and vowels are not always identifiable outside the context of speech in which they appear. And the implication that *supra*-segmentals are somehow superimposed on a basic message of consonants and vowels is decidedly misleading, given that prosody is an integral part of speech production and often a fully meaningful contribution to the message itself. After all, no one utters stretches of English consonants and vowels in an absolutely even-measured monotone – or if they do, the result is perceived as highly marked speech, perhaps as a comic affectation of extreme boredom or as an imitation of a robot. But if these qualifications are borne in mind, the distinction is a convenient one, principally because prosodic phenomena *tend*, much more than consonants and vowels, to be directly related to higher levels of linguistic organization, such as the structuring of information. This in turn means that prosody cannot always be readily separated from other long-term settings and adjustments, such as voice quality and rate of articulation.

We can take prosody to be a continuum of functions and effects, ranging from the nonlinguistic or extralinguistic at one end, through the paralinguistic, to the essentially linguistic. At the nonlinguistic end, for example, are features of voice quality that reflect the nature of the speaker's larynx and vocal tract; at the linguistic end are features such as stress and tone, which are functional within specific linguistic systems and often vary widely in their systematization from language to language. But note that the term PARALINGUISTIC points to a grey area in between the two reasonably uncontroversial extremes: it is not at all easy, for instance, to determine whether a particular style of speech delivery is an unconscious habit, perhaps related to the speaker's anatomy or physiology, or a deliberate – and therefore communicative – attempt to project a certain personality. An obvious example is the effect of nervousness. We are all familiar with certain features of speech that tell us that the speaker is nervous, often despite the speaker's best efforts to disguise the nervousness; but it is also possible for a speaker to adopt some of these features deliberately, whether as a long-term style of speech, or to gain sympathy on a particular occasion. Readers will probably be able to think of various comparable examples, noting their ambiguous status – the affected stammer, the characteristic languid drawl or the constant nervous giggle, for instance.

Features at the least linguistic end may be thought of as a substratum of underlying properties of the signal, including the phonation quality determined by the anatomy and tensions of the larynx, the pitch range determined by management of the larynx, and long-term articulatory settings such as tongue root posture and articulation rate, among others. Some of these factors may be a function of anatomy, others may be acquired as habitual characteristics. While they are generally not considered to form part of the functional system of language – since they do not reflect genuine options exercised by the speaker – they may still be communicative to the extent that they enable us to identify a particular speaker or type or class of speaker. (See Laver 1980, pp. 3–7, for comments on the way in which features such as nasality and phonation quality may characterize social or regional groups.)

Physical illness such as respiratory tract infection may of course have a profound and pervasive effect on speech, and emotions such as fear or anger may alter pitch range, phonation quality, loudness and articulation rate. Laughter, sighing and sobbing may all cause complete interruption to the normal processes of articulation. These phenomena are in one sense common to all human beings and outside language, but they are by no means beyond functional control. English speakers often use a deliberate laugh or sigh as a meaningful comment or reaction, and, in general, the conventions governing such behaviour as laughing and sighing vary sharply among societies and social settings.

More closely related to linguistic functioning is the speaker's use of such features as overall voice quality, pitch range, pitch movement and articulation rate to indicate a general attitude. Again conventions vary widely, but it is probably safe to say that most speakers in most languages have ways of signalling authoritativeness or submissiveness, seriousness or lightheartedness, excitement or calmness, even though these 'states' or 'attitudes' will certainly not be identical across cultures.

Strategies such as tempo may also be used to demarcate stretches of speech within discourse. Crystal, for example, refers to the way in which accelerated tempo may serve to indicate an embedded phrase or clause in English (1969, pp. 152–3). Note the underlined sections in the following examples:

It's one of those reply-immediately-in-five-lines-or-less memos!
Is the How to Write English course on this year?

In examples such as these, a clause constituting a unitary description or title may be spoken distinctly faster than the rest of the utterance, as a signal of its shifted status. This mechanism may be coupled with pauses at the boundaries of the unit. The functions of tempo and pause here are clearly linguistic, as much part of the grammar as any other device signalling relations among clauses.

At the most linguistic end of the continuum are systems such as stress, intonation and tone. Typically, features of pitch, loudness and duration are relevant here, contributing to the organization of discourse and even to lexical distinctions. Since languages vary in their systematic exploitation of these features – and are often categorized accordingly, as 'tone languages' or 'intonation languages' and so on – we shall return to these systems in more detail below (sections 9.3–9.8).

While the continuum described above indicates the range of information carried by the speech signal, it leaves an incomplete picture of what is really happening, for all kinds of information may be encoded simultaneously in the speech signal, and listeners abstract what they judge relevant to the communication context. Note, for example, that listeners may be perceiving emphasis on certain words or phrases, and responding to the speaker's organization of the message, at the same time that they are forming a judgment about the speaker's regional background and emotional state. Communication is also inherently interactive. There is after all some reason for speaking, and usually a listener or audience, even if at some remove via a telephone or other such communication system. Even in public speaking, the audience is a collective listener whose reactions (real, imagined or anticipated) are likely to influence the speaker. Thus both speakers and listeners operate in a context of (largely) shared assumptions about the significance of prosody, ranging from expectations about the effects of tiredness and nervousness and sore throats, and conventions about appropriate levels of loudness and speeds of delivery, to knowledge of systematic ways of structuring discourse.

In summary, a simple taxonomy of phonological features, isolated from contextual function, is not enough to account for linguistic prosody, and much of what is written about suprasegmental phonology provides only a point of departure for analysis. Here there is some justification for a distinction between segmental and suprasegmental phonology, in that the phonetic resources underlying segmental distinctions can be more easily and directly related to indisputably linguistic organization and are more amenable to taxonomic treatment.

Against this background, it is not surprising that much of the traditional literature on the analysis and description of suprasegmentals tends to concentrate on generalized abstractions (for example, about typical intonation melodies or the functions of tones) rather than on the complex and highly variable phonetic detail. Research in information technology, however, has stimulated much closer scrutiny of phonetic aspects of the suprasegmental structure of the speech signal. A notable example is the strong interest in the development of intonation models ('t Hart 1979, Pierrehumbert 1981) and durational rule models (Klatt 1979) for use in text-to-speech systems.

Laver (1980) deals with voice quality, taking a broad view of what is involved and commenting helpfully on the problem of deciding what is or is not part of language. Detailed discussion of the ways in which phonetic resources are used for 'affective' and 'attitudinal' functions, with some spectrographic analysis, can be found in Crystal and Quirk (1964). Crystal (1969) offers a thorough taxonomy of English prosodic features in the context of a wide-ranging survey of relevant literature, including a useful review of the linguistic status of prosodic and paralinguistic features (pp. 179–93). Many writers, however, forgo comprehensiveness and make the working assumption that there is a limit to what is linguistically conventional. For a general overview of prosodic features and the issues raised in this section, see Cruttenden (1986, especially chs 1, 6).

9.2   The phonetic basis of suprasegmentals

The principal phonetic correlates of the more linguistic aspects of prosody are the dynamic patterns of pitch, duration and loudness. All three of these are both overlaid on, and influenced by, the less dynamic substratum of voice quality as determined by the state of the vocal tract. These dimensions of the speech signal, interacting with each other and with the segmental structure, are fundamental to our perception of emotion, attitude and other such information conveyed in speech.

VOICE QUALITY and VOCAL TRACT STATE are treated by Laver (1980), who uses the concept of 'articulatory settings' of the vocal tract (pp. 12ff.) These long-term settings are the underlying articulatory positions or postures upon which all the dynamics of articulation – both segmental and suprasegmental – are superimposed. The settings have articulatory – and hence acoustic – consequences which pervade the whole stream of speech.

Very importantly, he notes that the time domain of these settings may vary. A setting contributing to personal voice quality may be for all practical purposes a permanent feature, while another setting may be controlled contrastively. Thus a speaker may talk with habitually rounded and slightly protruded lips, which will influence the overall frequency range of formant patterns and be judged part of his personal characteristics. On the other hand, laryngeal tension settings may be changed to produce a voice quality associated with a particular attitude: many speakers of English, for example, may use vocal creak to indicate boredom or dismissiveness.

Laver's system has two basic divisions, supralaryngeal and phonatory settings. Supralaryngeal settings describe the vocal tract state longitudinally (larynx height and labial protrusion) and latitudinally (labial, lingual, faucal, pharyngeal and mandibular settings); they also include velo-pharyngeal settings, affecting the coupling of the nasal tract and perceptions of nasality. Phonatory settings describe phonation types relative to normal or modal phonation, and allow for compound phonation types.

Acoustically, supralaryngeal vocal tract settings are reflected primarily in formant distribution. Thus, a raised larynx may shorten the vocal tract and raise formant frequencies, although not always in a simple linear relationship to larynx height. The speech production model of Lindblom and Sundberg (1971) provides a theoretical basis for estimating some of the acoustic correlates of the supralaryngeal settings defined by Laver. The acoustic properties of phonatory settings are rather more difficult to establish independently, since phonation provides the excitation source for the vocal tract and is therefore always modified by the current vocal tract filter function. Special measurement techniques do exist for cancelling out the effects of vocal tract resonance, such as the reflectionless tube (Sondhi 1975) and computer-based antiresonance filtering (section 7.11 above). The overall effects of changes in phonatory setting can be seen in the spectral slope of voiced speech spectra, and in the degree of periodicity of phonation, as revealed in speech spectrograms. A general measure of long-term vocal tract setting differences can also be obtained from long-term spectrum measurements of the kind described in section 7.19 above. These measurements will show average changes in the energy distribution of the speech spectrum caused by both phonation and vocal tract settings. (See chapter 2 for the phonetic background to these settings, and chapter 7 for the relevant acoustic information.)

PITCH is widely regarded, at least in English, as the most salient determinant of prominence. In other words, when a syllable or word is perceived as 'stressed' or 'emphasized', it is pitch height or a change of pitch, more than length or loudness, that is likely to be mainly responsible (see, for example, Fry 1958, Gimson 1980, pp. 222–6, Lehiste 1976, Fudge 1984, ch. 1). Pitch is the perceived correlate of fundamental frequency. It is commonly measured on the mel scale, since changes of perceived pitch are proportional to, but not the same as, changes of frequency (section 7.9 above).

Fundamental frequency (F_0) – the number of times per second that the vocal folds complete a cycle of vibration – is controlled by the muscular forces determining vocal fold settings and tensions in the larynx, and by the aerodynamic forces of the respiratory system which drive the larynx and provide the source of energy for the phonation itself (sections 6.4 and 7.11 above). It has been argued by Lieberman (1967) that aerodynamic forces, specifically subglottal pressure (Psg), are primarily responsible for pitch control and that laryngeal adjustments are a secondary or alternative form of control. He maintains that Psg patterns have an archetypal shape in utterances, and that Psg variations are superimposed on them. Ohala (1970) refutes Lieberman's evidence and (1978) reviews the 'larynx versus lungs' controversy in general. It seems that for the majority of languages, laryngeal adjustments are primarily responsible for pitch control. In particular, the cricothyroid muscle is always active during pitch raising by its direct tensioning of the vocal folds. Vertical movement of the larynx, controlled by its extrinsic strap muscles, correlates well with corresponding rises and falls in pitch. In general, pitch raising is better understood than pitch lowering, which appears to involve relaxation of the cricothyroid muscles, and contraction of the infrahyoidal strap muscles (Erikson et al. 1983). In the lowest portion of the pitch range, these mechanisms seem to be supplemented by other muscles such as the lateral cricoarytenoid and the thyro-arytenoid and vocalis, which shorten, slacken and thicken the folds.

Although less significant than laryngeal muscle action, Psg does show a positive correlation with pitch movement. Data for English suggest that Psg is responsible for about 5 to 10 per cent of the total range of pitch change in normal speech. But it is not clear how far this generalization extends to all languages: in at least some dialects of Chinese, for instance, it does seem that Psg provides the primary form of pitch control (Rose 1982). Detailed discussion of pitch regulatory mechanisms can be found in Sawashima (1974), Ohala (1978) and Hollien (1983), and there are relevant data in Ladefoged (1967).

Our ability to discriminate pitch has been investigated in various studies, many of them focusing on the threshold of minimal perceivable difference, or 'difference limen' (DL). A change in pitch of as little as 0.3–0.5 per cent may be perceivable, at least in vowels synthesized to simulate a male voice (Flanagan 1972). Studies by 't Hart (1981) and Harris and Umeda (1987) show that the DL may be substantially higher in running speech, the actual value depending on the average fundamental frequency, the speaker and the complexity of the speech signal concerned. Rietfeld and Gussenhoven (1985) also report data suggesting, surprisingly, that perceptual judgments of the magnitude of prominence tend to match frequency values rather than a pitch scale.

DURATION as a property of sounds or units cannot be separated from the larger context of time and timing in speech production. The duration of individual speech segments varies enormously, depending on both segment type and the surrounding phonetic context. A vowel, for example, may last 300 ms or longer, while the release of a voiced stop may be only about 20 ms. Duration is also constrained by bio-mechanical factors: part of the reason why the vowel in English *bat*, for example, tends to be relatively long is that the jaw has to move further than in words like *bit* or *bet*.

In the context of prosodic distinctions, overall syllable duration is more important than segment duration, and relative duration more important than absolute duration.

Vowel duration is obviously the most significant component of syllable duration, but maintenance of appropriate durational relationships within the whole structure of the syllable is very important if segmental relationships and distinctions are to be preserved.

Overall syllable duration is influenced by many contextual factors. These include the rate of articulation, the placement of prominence or stress, the position of the syllable within a word or other larger unit and the structure of those larger units themselves. Although syllable duration is quite elastic – and the actual duration is an important contribution to the perceived prominence of the syllable – not all components of duration are equally elastic. Studies of vowel target reduction and undershoot by Lindblom (1963), Stevens and House (1963) and Stevens et al. (1966) have shown that as syllable length is reduced, consonant transitions tend to be preserved at the expense of vowel target length (although not absolutely so). Consonant durations vary with the number of consonants in the syllable, and are also influenced by overall syllable duration. Pickett (1980) reviews the general properties of durational structure in syllables. The way in which the temporal components of the syllable can be varied differentially is shown in the phonological rules set out by Allen et al. (1987), where the variability is expressed quantitatively for a text-to-speech system.

The way in which each language exploits durational relationships within the syllable for phonological purposes will also influence its internal temporal structure. In English, for example, vowel length is substantially increased when the vowel is followed by consonant voicing, and the length of the vowel becomes a significant perceptual cue to the voicing contrast (see, for example, Lisker 1978, p. 134). The effect is also clearly seen in the data from a fricative consonant study by Clark and Palethorpe (1986), and there are other examples reviewed by Lehiste (1970).

From a much larger suprasegmental perspective, it is important to note that the way in which rhythmic structure and stress placement are integrated in a given language will also influence duration patterns. Languages such as English and German, sometimes described as 'stress-timed' languages (section 9.3 below), make a relatively large difference between stressed and unstressed syllables, in such a way that stressed syllables are generally much longer than unstressed (see, for example, Gay 1978). Other languages, especially where stress is less important than other prosodic features such as tone, may exhibit more even duration from syllable to syllable.

Finally, we should not forget silence: pauses are an important ingredient of our total communicative resources. Crystal (1969, pp. 166–72) reviews the ways in which pauses function in English and refers to relevant literature; Cruttenden (1986, pp. 36–9) also gives a useful overview, noting the role of pauses in signalling structural boundaries as well as what are usually called 'hesitation phenomena'. Allen et al. (1987) have proposed rules for pause durations in which the length of pause increases with the size of the syntactic or informational units which the pauses demarcate.

LOUDNESS is the perceptual correlate of intensity, which is usually expressed as magnitude of sound pressure variation in the speech signal (section 7.6 above). Intensity is primarily controlled by subglottal pressure (Ladefoged 1967, Lehiste

1970, Ohala 1970) but is also influenced by the natural sonority of the segments or sequences of segments in the relevant syllables. For example, the vowel of the English CVC syllable *shack* is more sonorous relative to its neighbouring consonants than the vowel in, say, *wool*. In fact, although it is clear that stressed syllables often have greater overall acoustic intensity than more weakly stressed ones, loudness seems to be the least salient and least consistent of the three parameters of pitch, duration and loudness – at least for linguistic purposes such as signalling stress (section 9.3 below).

The segmental and suprasegmental dimensions of the speech signal do not function independently of each other. In particular, there are important interactions between the segmental structure and its accompanying pitch pattern. Several studies have been devoted to the effects of voiceless and voiced consonants on the pitch of adjacent vowels (see Hombert 1978 for a review of evidence). It seems, for instance, that voiceless pulmonic egressive stops often, though not universally, result in a higher pitch on the following vowel. A major reason for the interest in such phenomena is that they explain the origins of tonal distinctions in some languages: a distinction between, say, syllable-initial voiced and voiceless stops is lost (by historical change) but a tonal distinction on the following vowel, originally conditioned by the preceding consonants, is preserved. Thus a secondary cue supplants the original primary one in the process of sound change. Hombert (1978, pp. 78–9) points to a number of south-east Asian languages, including Chinese and Vietnamese, in which such changes are reported. Figure 9.2.1 shows examples from Hombert (1978) of the conditioning of fundamental frequency by a preceding stop in English and French. The data have been normalized for comparison.

The reasons for this conditioning of pitch are not fully understood. One theory is that the larynx is often lower in voiced stops, to enlarge pharyngeal volume and maintain sufficient transglottal pressure to continue phonation during the occlusion; this lowering results in lower pitch. Conversely, the larynx remains higher for voiceless stops. Nevertheless, while there is a tendency for the pitch to be lowered during the occlusion phase of voiced stops, the evidence suggests that it is only voiceless stops that have a significant effect on the pitch in the initial part of the following vowel. An alternative theory proposes that vocal fold tension during a (voiceless) stop consonant may influence pitch at the onset of phonation in the vowel. A major problem for this explanation is that voiceless stops do not seem to have the same influence on the pitch of a *preceding* vowel. Nor do studies of muscular activity indicate that muscular tensions in the larynx are significantly correlated with stop voicing. Overall there is no really satisfactory explanation for the pitch perturbation effects of prevocalic stops, especially in the light of the fact that postvocalic stops appear to have weaker and less consistent effects.

Prenasalized stops and breathy voiced stops lower the pitch of following vowels more than plain voiced stops do. In the case of breathy stops, this is thought to be due to the lower intrinsic laryngeal muscle tensions used in breathy phonation. Implosives lower pitch less than plain voiced stops, possibly partly because glottal airflow is rapid as the larynx is lowered during implosion. It may also be that the muscular tensions required to close the glottis during the implosion counteract other

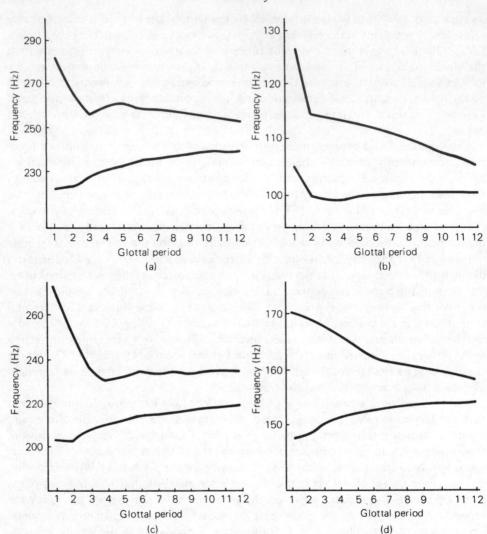

FIGURE 9.2.1   Effects of stop consonants on F_0. In each case the upper curve shows average F_0 values after *p t k*, the lower after *b d g*: (a) American English female speaker; (b) American English male speaker; (c) French female speaker; (d) French male speaker
Adapted from: Hombert 1978, p. 88.

factors tending to lower pitch in the following vowel. Generalizations are again dangerous, and Pinkerton (1986) shows that the conventional wisdom about the articulatory nature of various kinds of 'glottalized' stops (including implosives) is not always supported by careful instrumental investigation.

Postvocalic stops have little effect on tone, but a glottal stop raises the pitch of the preceding vowel, and a rising tone may in time replace the syllable-final glottal stop.

By contrast, postvocalic /h/ causes pitch lowering – presumably because of anticipatory relaxation of the laryngeal muscles – and may give rise to a falling tone. Ohala (1978) and Hombert (1978) provide details of consonantal pitch perturbation; see also section 9.4 below.

Vowels themselves tend to have an 'intrinsic' pitch which correlates with vowel height: high vowels have high pitch and low vowels have low pitch. According to Lehiste (1970) and Ohala (1978) the difference may be as great as 20–25 Hz, but Ladd and Silverman (1984) suggest that intrinsic pitch effects are not as strong in running speech as those observable in test words in citation sentences. There are several hypotheses about the causes of this effect, two of which will be noted here. The first is that the narrow constriction of high vowels causes an 'acoustic loading' of the vocal folds, which means that F_0 tends to be pulled towards the F_1 of the vowel. In high vowels, F_1 is quite low and in many cases within the speaker's pitch range. The second hypothesis is that there is 'tongue-pull', in other words that the mechanical coupling between the tongue root musculature and the larynx influences the height of the larynx and its phonatory adjustments. On this hypothesis, tongue raising will cause larynx raising. According to Lindblom and Sundberg's evidence (1971), if the mandible is fixed, there is more extrinsic tongue muscle contraction in high vowels, and the pitch difference between low and high vowels is thus enhanced. Silverman (1984) reviews the evidence for and against this hypothesis and others, and concludes that the evidence is not adequate to support any single explanation based on acoustic or physiological factors. He argues that although these factors may contribute to intrinsic vowel pitch, comparable effects may be, in part at least, phonologically motivated aspects of the speech production process and may be demanded by the perceptual expectation of the listener.

PITCH PATTERNS are essentially either steady, rising or falling, and it is changing pitch that has the greater perceptual salience. Evidence reviewed by Ohala (1978) suggests that falling pitch is more common in language than rising pitch, and that falling pitch uses a wider range of F_0 movement. It also seems that speakers can produce falling pitch more readily than rising pitch, and can achieve downward pitch movements more rapidly than upward movements. On the basis of this evidence, Ohala very tentatively hypothesizes that falling pitch is more salient perceptually and is more likely to be accomplished within a single syllable (1978, p. 31). But this is debatable, and significant pitch movement is not necessarily constrained within specific syllables of polysyllabic words, even when its main function is to mark major prominence on a single syllable.

DECLINATION is the term for what appears to be an almost universal tendency in language, namely a moderate progressive fall in pitch from the beginning to the end of any sequence of speech of appreciable length (Vaissiere 1983). The term DOWNDRIFT is sometimes used with the same meaning, for example by Hyman (1975, pp. 225ff.), who distinguishes between this 'automatic' process of lowering and the tonal phenomenon of DOWNSTEP. But there is potential confusion between 'downdrift' and 'downstep' in some authors, and we will reserve the term 'declination' for the phonetic pattern of F_0 behaviour. Figure 9.2.2 illustrates declination.

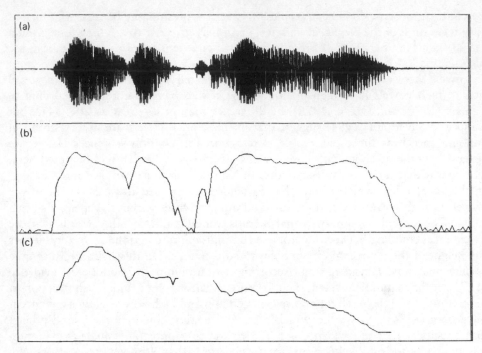

FIGURE 9.2.2 Declination of F_0 in overall sentence contour *We went to Woolloomooloo*; (a) time domain waveform; (b) intensity contour; (c) F_0 contour

Declination can generally be observed over identifiable units of the intonation system, often corresponding to clauses or clause complexes. There are of course constraints and exceptions, for example where the speaker selects a rising pitch pattern to signal that the utterance is a query. Declination occurs in both tonal and nontonal languages, and although listeners are not usually conscious of the effect, Breckenridge (1977) and Pierrehumbert (1979) have shown, for English at least, that listeners do compensate for its presence in judging pitch height. Ohala (1978) believes it to be a deliberately controlled part of the articulatory organization of breath groups.

There has been considerable debate about the status and causes of declination. Some researchers have argued that it is essentially an involuntary or automatic process, probably due to interaction between the larynx and the respiratory system. (This physiological explanation does not of course deny that declination can be deliberately suppressed or overridden for functional purposes.) Others have suggested that it is essentially the observable consequence of a phonological lowering of pitch on successive accented syllables. Ohala (1978) and Vaissiere (1983) review the explanations that have been put forward, focusing on those related to speech production mechanisms. Ladd (1984) discusses declination in some detail: he makes the case that declination need not be a distinct component of pitch patterning, and that declination effects might be included in phonological behaviour rather than in quasi-intrinsic phonetic behaviour. In other words, the phonological rules of the language would include the generation of pitch declination (if required), and it would be wrong to assume that declination was an underlying pattern on which phonological pitch was superimposed.

It has also been suggested that declination effects are observed mainly in formal reading aloud, oriented to prose sentences, and that they are much less noticeable in the patterns of informal speech. Certainly, declination effects can be suspended (Hyman 1975, pp. 227–8, Cruttenden 1986, pp. 163–4, 167–8), and an essentially phonological explanation has strong appeal; but the debate is not resolved.

9.3 The systemic organization of prosody

Understandably, many terms used in describing prosody take on a particular meaning within particular languages: just as terms such as 'noun' and 'verb' or 'consonant' and 'vowel' cannot be expected to have identical reference across different languages, so also the terminology of stress and pitch needs to be carefully interpreted in the context of its use. In this section we review some of the more common terms and the uses to which they are put, as background to subsequent sections dealing with some of the types of prosodic system that have been classically recognized.

The term TONE has a general sense in which it is almost synonymous with 'pitch'. We can say, for example, that the English word 'no' may be uttered either with falling tone (in which case it is likely to count as a definite refusal or denial) or with rising tone (as a query, checking whether a denial or refusal is indeed intended). More precisely, we can identify a number of distinct pitches or pitch patterns in a language such as English, which may be considered to be 'the tones' of English. Here the term takes on a systemic value, since we recognize only a finite number of discrete tones – such as high, low, falling, rising – which are functional in the language. In this sense, tone is not synonymous with pitch, since a tone in a linguistic system will be realized in such a way that it contrasts with other tones in the system while varying according to context. In the case of English, tones are part of what is usually called intonation (to which we return in a moment) but in many languages tones are more directly associated with syllables or lexical items. Thus in Mandarin Chinese, what might seem to English speakers to be a single lexical item /ma/ is in fact four different words, depending on the associated tone (McCawley 1978, p. 120):

ma^1 (with high level pitch)	'mother'
ma^2 (with high rising pitch)	'hemp'
ma^3 (with low, or falling then rising pitch)	'horse'
ma^4 (with falling pitch)	'scold'.

Languages such as Chinese, in which differences of pitch serve to distinguish word meanings, are called TONE LANGUAGES (section 9.4 below).

The term STRESS similarly has wider and narrower senses in linguistic description. Some writers (e.g. Trager and Smith 1951) have particularly related stress to loudness; one might then be able to distinguish the stress of a syllable (its perceived relative loudness, reflecting force of articulation) from its tone (the perceived pitch, whether relative height or a movement such as falling or rising, reflecting fundamental frequency). More commonly, stress is a conventional label for the overall prominence of certain syllables relative to others within a linguistic system. In this sense, stress does not correlate simply with loudness, but represents the total effect of factors such as pitch, loudness and duration. It is in this sense that we say that the English words *over, supper, China* and *broken* are all stressed on the first syllable, while words such as *ahead, before, suppose* and *career* are stressed on the second. Where words have their own stress pattern or potential in this way, the stress is often called WORD-STRESS or LEXICAL STRESS.

Patterns of stress are highly important in a language such as English: this is not so much because the patterns are significant in distinguishing one word from another, although there are instances where this is true in English (e.g. *content* meaning 'pleased, satisfied' versus *content* 'that which is contained'); rather it is because the rhythm of spoken English is to a very large extent determined by strong beats falling on the stressed syllables of words. Thus a typical spoken utterance of English will consist of a number of rhythmic units, each of which is dominated by the beat of the stressed syllable. In verse, the wording is characteristically and deliberately organized to yield a regular rhythm, and the units of this rhythm are commonly called 'feet'; but the term FOOT is no less applicable to ordinary spoken English, even though the feet may not be consciously constructed. In a normal reading of, for example,

Wanda's joining the parade,

the rhythm is determined by the stress patterns of the words 'Wanda' and 'joining' (stressed on the first syllable) and 'parade' (stressed on the second syllable). The words 'the' and 'is' are normally unstressed, so much so that 'is' can be pronounced without any vowel at all and written as a single consonant (s) tacked on to the preceding word. The resulting rhythm of the utterance can be informally conveyed as

WAN-da's JOIN-ing-the-pa RADE.

This kind of rhythm puts a characteristic stamp on the nature of spoken English. Normal tempo is such that unstressed syllables are greatly reduced ('swallowed' as some critics would have it) and simply form a tail of varying length in each foot. There is even a tendency to equalize the duration of each foot, so that in the above example the three unstressed syllables following JOIN are likely to be the most rapidly articulated, while the final stressed syllable RADE (which happens to have no unstressed syllables following it) may be given extra length. Thus each foot, whether a single syllable or several, will tend to take – very roughly – the same amount of time. This ISOCHRONY (equal timing) based on stress is often commented on – although the evidence for it is not entirely satisfactory (see Cruttenden 1986, pp. 24–6 and section 8.9 above). It is related to the frequent description of English as a STRESS-TIMED language. Less commonly but more appropriately, English and languages sharing this characteristic are called FOOT-TIMED (Halliday 1985a, pp. 271ff.). By contrast many of the world's languages are SYLLABLE-TIMED. In syllable-timed languages there is no strong pattern of stress, at least not to the extent that unstressed syllables are markedly reduced or hurried, and the total duration of an utterance is dependent more on the number of syllables it happens to contain than on the number and position of stressed syllables. Readers may like to test their sense of spoken rhythm by articulating (or getting another to articulate) an English utterance while tapping out the rhythm of the major beats. If the beats occur at more or less regular intervals, regardless of the number of syllables in each foot, the result is likely to sound like reasonably normal English. Deliberate variations in this pattern – for example, making each syllable a full beat, or adopting a simple alternating rhythm in which odd numbered syllables are stressed and even numbered syllables unstressed – should demonstrate that other rhythmic patterns are quite feasible but that they are foreign to normal English. At the very least, the difficulty of this exercise should underline the way in which timing and rhythm are essential to the nature of spoken language.

The term ACCENT is sometimes used loosely to mean stress, referring either to prominence in a general way or more specifically to the emphasis placed on certain syllables. (What we have mentioned above as WORD-STRESS or LEXICAL STRESS is sometimes called WORD ACCENT.) The term PITCH-ACCENT, like tone, has a particular use in describing certain languages which are, in a sense, limited tone languages. If, for example, a language has restricted tonal options such that two-syllable words are either high–low (high tone on the first syllable, low on the second) or low–high, then we might well simply say that words carry a (high pitched) accent which falls either on the first or on the second syllable. In general functional terms, this is tantamount to saying that words are stressed on either the first or second syllable, particularly if we bear in mind that the word-stress of languages like English is often signalled by pitch. Thus although most languages described as 'pitch-accent languages' are rather more complicated than this simple example, it is debatable how far they constitute a definite type, distinct from both 'tone languages' and 'stress languages' (section 9.5 below).

The term 'accent' is also used by some writers to refer to relative prominence within longer utterances. English is noteworthy for the way in which a stressed syllable (already prominent within the normal rhythmic pattern determined by word-stresses) can be further accentuated relative to other stressed syllables. Thus in the English utterance 'Hector started running' each word has its own (lexical) stress pattern, in this case on the first syllable in all three instances; normally the last of these three stresses will be the most prominent, but it is possible to put the 'accent' on the first or second stress, usually by ensuring that the major pitch movement falls across that syllable. Suppose – with considerable oversimplification – that a falling pitch is placed somewhere in this utterance and that the rest of the utterance is relatively level. If the fall (marked below) occurs over the first syllable of 'Hector' and the pitch of the rest of the utterance is relatively unchanging and lower than the starting point, English speakers will perceive emphasis on the first syllable:

\   -   -   -   -

HECTor started running.

This pattern invites the hearer to attend specially to the first word. Instead of ACCENT, terms such as SENTENCE STRESS and CONTRASTIVE STRESS are sometimes used, the latter because the functional meaning is often one of contrasting the accented word with alternatives, for example where the speaker is contradicting the addressee ('you say that Rupert started running but I assert that HECTOR started running') or going against the likely assumption ('you would not have expected it but it was HECTOR who started running'). It is of course also possible to put the 'accent' on the second word, in which case we have – again in a simplified version – something like:

-   -   \   -   -   -

Hector STARTed running.

Here the function may be to correct the impression that Hector did not run at all or to indicate that he only started to run but quickly decided to walk instead.

Given that this phenomenon of 'sentence stress' or 'accent' in English is (often) a matter of the location of a tone rather than some heightening or intensification of the degree of stress, it is preferable to place it within the wider context of the English INTONATION system. While this term is also open to various interpretations – including some deplorably vague ones that imply that intonation is the idiosyncratic imposition of personal emotions on to a base of consonants and vowels – it can usefully be taken as a cover term for several subsystems of which the least controversial are TONE (the choice of a pitch pattern or melody), TONE PLACEMENT (location of the selected tone, called 'accent' or 'sentence-stress' in some descriptions) and TONE STRUCTURE (organization of the utterance into units, including both the basic level of rhythmic feet determined by 'word-stress' and a higher level of units dominated by a major 'accent'). We will give a broad outline of this approach by dealing with 'word-stress' and 'intonation', with special reference to English, in separate sections below (9.6–9.8).

In general, the terms reviewed here should be approached with caution. The terms STRESS and ACCENT in particular are notoriously ambiguous, and it would be misleading to suggest that there are standard definitions. Certainly in the description of English, the phenomena to which the terms usually refer are best understood within an analysis of intonation, but it remains important, given the enormous attention that has been devoted to the prosody of English, not to assume that what is true of English is necessarily true of other languages. (For an overview of terms see Cutler and Ladd 1983, pp. 140–6.)

9.4 Tone languages

Many of the world's languages are traditionally recognized as 'tone languages'. The precise definition of a tone language is controversial but it is common among linguists to stress lexical relevance: in a tone language, tone is 'a feature of the lexicon, being described in terms of prescribed pitches for syllables or sequences of pitches for morphemes or words' (Cruttenden 1986, p. 8); or, more informally, pitch 'distinguishes the meanings of words' (Pike 1948, p. 3). This is in contrast to a language such as English, where pitch is certainly functional and where one can equally speak of distinctive tones, but where the tones cannot be directly associated with lexical meaning. Speakers of tone languages can be expected to regard tone as a significant part of a syllable (or morpheme or word). Most of the world's languages are in fact tonal in this sense, including major east Asian languages such as Chinese, Vietnamese, Burmese and Thai, as well as a substantial proportion of the languages of Africa, the Americas and Papua New Guinea. Pike (1948) remains a classic introduction to the nature of tone languages and strategies of analysis and description. Otherwise most information is available in papers dealing with particular languages or with general problems of theory and description; a particularly useful collection was published as Fromkin (1978).

Pike is responsible for a distinction between REGISTER (or LEVEL-PITCH) tone systems and CONTOUR (or GLIDING-PITCH) systems. In a register system there are distinctive pitch levels, often two or three and probably never more than four. These levels will of course be relative to each other rather than absolute values, so that a high tone, for example, will be perceived as high relative to any adjacent mid or low tone syllable. In fact, it may not be possible to distinguish a two-syllable word with two high tones, uttered in isolation, from a two-syllable word with two mid or two low tones. On the other hand, in a contour system it is the pitch movement or glide that is characteristic: the contrast will be among patterns such as falling, rising and 'dipping' (fall–rise) rather than among relative heights or levels.

For Pike, it was important to differentiate these two types of tone language because of the method of analysis. While it may be possible to identify the distinctive tones of a contour tone language merely by listening to them, a register system will generally require points of reference against which the relative levels can be judged. Thus single syllables bearing high, mid or low level tone will not be clearly identifiable unless adjacent to a 'marker' level. Hence Pike emphasizes the importance of tonal frames that provide a fixed context. Suppose, for example, that we have already established in a tone language that a certain prefix, meaning 'my', always carries low tone. If we then use this prefix as a frame, getting a native speaker of the language to utter various phrases such as 'my house', 'my garden', 'my vegetables', and so on, we can judge the tone of each noun relative to the low tone prefix. If the initial syllable of the noun is at (more or less) the same pitch level as the prefix, we can identify it as low tone; if it is noticeably higher, it must be mid or high. The use of another frame, say a prefix bearing mid tone, will enable us to sort out the mids from the highs, and to check the lows, which should now be identifiably lower than the preceding mid tone. The procedure is clearly laborious, since one must identify suitable frames to begin with and then run extensive lists of items through them, but it offers a principled way of basing a tonal description on reasonably solid evidence.

The two types of tone language are nevertheless not quite as distinct as this account may suggest. In the first place, register systems rarely if ever consist of a few perfectly level and consistent tones. The effects of declination (section 9.2 above) may be such that what is in theory a sequence of identical tones may actually fall in pitch, and there may be quite specific assimilatory processes whereby a mid tone is realized as a rising tone between a low and a high, or a high tone is realized as a high fall if before a low, and so on. In fact the literature on tone languages suggests that interactions among tones are typical rather than unusual, and Pike himself devotes major attention to what he calls PERTURBATIONS of tone or tone SANDHI. He describes such phenomena in detail for two languages of southern Mexico, namely Mixteco and Mazateco (1948, chs 7, 8).

Moreover, it often seems to be the case in register tone languages that tonal options on individual syllables are constrained by word patterns. For example, Leben (1978, pp. 186ff.) suggests that there are five basic word patterns in Mende, a language of Sierra Leone. The five are (1) high; (2) low; (3) high–low; (4) low–high; (5) low–high–low. But these five patterns may be distributed over words of varying length, so that a monosyllabic word carrying pattern (3) actually has a falling pitch, while a three-syllable word with the same pattern will have high–low–low. Examples of pattern (4) on words of different length are (Leben 1978, p. 186):

mbu ('rice')   (monosyllable with rising pitch)
fande ('cotton') (first syllable low, second high)
ndavula ('sling') (first syllable low, others high).

Thus pitch glides or contours are by no means excluded from register tone languages: what is significant is that these glides can be analysed as realizations of (sequences of) level tones.

On the other hand, contour systems frequently if not always include level or near-level tones. One of the four tones of Burmese, for example, is described as low level. Indeed, although the pitch is probably always the dominant cue, other factors, such as duration and abruptness, are relevant. The four tones, as described by Tun (1982, p. 80) are (1) low level; (2) high rising–falling; (3) high falling; (4) high falling, with abrupt ending. No fewer than three of the five tones of Thai are traditionally labelled high, mid and low. Gandour (1978, p. 42) lists the tones as (1) mid; (2) low; (3) falling; (4) high; (5) rising. As with register tone languages, it is the system within which these tones function that is significant, rather than a simple categorization of stable or gliding tones. Gandour (1978, pp. 43ff.) refers to experimental evidence suggesting that Thai listeners readily distinguish all five tones in isolation, without any frame of reference of the kind that seems necessary in the analysis of a register system.

In fact, the crucial difference between the two kinds of tone system may be that in contour systems tone is a property of syllables and in register systems tone is a property of larger units such as words. Hombert (1986, pp. 180ff.) reports a word game experiment in which speakers of tone languages were asked to transpose parts of words (either vowels or syllables). Thus if the game were applied to English, participants would be asked either to reverse the vowels of, say, *fifteen* (yielding presumably, *feef-tin*) or to swap the syllables (yielding *teen-fif*). Speakers of three west African languages (Bakwiri, Dschang and Kru) and four east Asian languages (Mandarin Chinese, Cantonese, Taiwanese and Thai) were asked to participate in the experiment. In the traditional classification, the African languages would be regarded as register tone languages, and the Asian as contour systems. Although Hombert points out that the results are not quite straightforward, it does seem that speakers of the four Asian languages tended to carry the tone with a transposed syllable, whereas the African participants moved the segmental component but left the tone behind, so to speak. Cruttenden (1986, pp. 8–9) also comments that many African languages have 'characteristic tone', in which the tone is sensitive to word structure and affixation, as opposed to the more narrowly 'lexical tone' of languages such as Chinese.

Apart from research of this kind exploring the nature and diversity of tonal systems, considerable attention has been paid in recent years to the way in which tone patterns can be explained by rules. This is not just a matter of formulating rules to explain assimilatory adjustments and perturbations of sequences of tones, but also a more fundamental question of how tone is mapped on to segmental structures. Leben (1978), for example, uses data such as the Mende words given earlier in this section to support the notion that tone is a separate prosodic component of phonological representation. Certainly where a language, like Mende, has patterns that distribute themselves over words of varying structure, there is an obvious case for treating tone as something independent of, but associated with, segmental structure (Leben 1978, pp. 177–80). Schuh (1978, especially pp. 251–2) relates the elaboration of tone rules to the question of typology, again making a distinction between the African and Asian type. Explorations of this kind, prompted by analysis of tone, are in turn related to more general issues in phonology which have been taken up in 'autosegmental' and 'metrical' phonology (sections 11.12 and 11.13 below).

A further perspective on the description of tone comes from the investigation of its historical development, including its origin or TONOGENESIS. It is clear for many languages that tone has arisen where pitch differences, originally conditioned by consonants, have become distinctive when the consonants have been changed or lost. In Vietnamese, for example, rising tones seem to be a consequence of lost glottal stops: a final glottal stop must originally have conditioned a rise in the pitch of the preceding vowel, and when final glottal stops were dropped, the rising pitch became a distinctive tone (Hombert 1978, pp. 92–3). It is not surprising that tones interact not only with each other but also with their segmental context (section 9.2 above); Hyman (1978) provides a summary of ways in which tonal changes may be motivated, and Ohala (1978) and Hombert (1978) are useful reviews of evidence.

There is no standard way in which tones are marked, either in conventional orthographies or in linguists' representations. In traditional Chinese orthography, tones are implicit in the characters and there is no particular symbol or diacritic to indicate each tone; on the other hand, many of the world's tone languages, in Africa and the Americas, have relatively modern spelling systems devised by missionaries or linguists, in which tone, if indicated at all, is usually marked by some kind of diacritic within an alphabetic writing system. Pike (1948, pp. 36–9) notes various ways of using accents in practical orthographies. Linguists themselves sometimes resort to pictorial representations of tone, based either on a plot of fundamental frequency or on an impressionistic trace of the perceived pitch. This is particularly helpful in displaying contour tones, which may differ in the duration and slope of a pitch movement and not just in direction of movement. Such displays are of course cumbersome as a regular notation, but a system devised by Chao (1930) for Chinese is an interesting compromise between pictorial accuracy and alphabetic convenience. In this system, an iconic shape representing the tone is attached to a vertical marker line at the right of each symbol. Examples are

mid level tone   ⊣
rising tone   ⟋
falling tone   ⟍

The system is quite often used (e.g. McCawley 1978, p. 120).

Three other notational strategies are common among linguists. Firstly, simple diacritics, notably accent marks, may be used. While the shape of the accent can usefully indicate pitch movement (e.g. acute for a rising tone), it is often convenient to be even more conventional and to use acute for high tone and grave for low. Various other semi-arbitrary conventions are often adopted, such as use of a bar above or below a vowel to indicate mid or low level tone. A second strategy is simply to number the tones and mark each syllable with its number, e.g. $[ma^1]$ or $[ma^2]$. Pike uses this notation for Mazateco (1948, ch. 8): there are four contrasting level tones, which he numbers 1–4 from highest to lowest. In the same work, Pike uses accents for the three tones of Mixteco (acute for high tone, bar or macron for mid and grave for low; 1948, ch. 7). Thirdly, tones may be represented by letters, e.g. H for high, or L for low. This notation has become popular in recent work in which tone is assumed to constitute a separate layer or component mapped on to segmental structure, as in e.g.

   H L
[b a m a] (high tone followed by low) or
   HL
[b a :] (falling tone).

Two brief and readable accounts of tone in particular languages can be found in Fudge (1973a): an extract from Kratochvil (1968) describes the tones of Chinese with details of the nature of the four tones and their relationship to stress, and Smith (originally 1968) deals with tone in the west African language Ewe. The reader may find both accounts informative about how tone functions in language and illustrative of methods of description and notation. Comrie (1987) also includes accounts of several tone languages, with concise notes about the tonal system, notably: Hausa, Yoruba and other west African languages (chs 35, 49, especially pp. 707, 711, 974, 977); Thai (ch. 38, especially pp. 761–3); Vietnamese (ch. 39, especially p. 783); Chinese (ch. 41, especially pp. 814–16); Burmese (ch. 42, especially p. 842).

9.5 Pitch-accent languages

Several of the world's languages are said to have PITCH-ACCENT: these include Japanese, Norwegian, Swedish and Serbo-Croatian. As already noted (section 9.3) they are in a sense on the fringes of fully fledged tone systems. Pike refers to such languages as 'word-pitch' systems and describes them as 'utilizing pitch in the differentiation of the meaning of various lexical items, but with the placement of the pitch limited to certain types of syllables or to specific places in the word' (1948, p. 14).

In Swedish, there are two tones or accents, and about 500 pairs of words are distinguished by this tonal contrast. The word *anden* 'the duck', for instance, has falling tone on the first syllable, whereas *anden* 'the spirit' has a double-peaked pattern with a fall on the second syllable as well as the first (Gandour 1978, pp. 53–4; Cruttenden 1986, p. 11). From an English speaker's point of view, the first word sounds as if it is stressed on the first syllable, the second as if it has stress on both syllables. (But, as Cruttenden points out, the precise realization of these accentual patterns varies both according to the context in which the words appear and according to the dialect of Swedish.) Thus there are only two options but these may be considered to constitute a simple tonal system. The system is highly constrained – it does not apply, for example, to monosyllabic words, which always carry the fall as the normal accent.

Serbo-Croatian (Browne and McCawley 1973, Gandour 1978, pp. 49–53) is usually described as having four tones or 'accents', namely (1) short rising; (2) short falling; (3) long rising; (4) long falling. But vowel length is distinctive in unaccented as well as accented syllables, so that the tonal contrast is essentially one of fall versus rise, intersecting with an additional opposition of length. There are again limitations on the exercise of the options – the falling accent is restricted to initial syllables (including monosyllabic words), while the rising accent is restricted to nonfinal syllables. A system of this kind is open to more than one analysis (as demonstrated by Browne and McCawley) but one can again speak of a limited tonal system.

In Japanese, on the other hand, the variable is the point at which pitch falls. In the following examples (from McCawley 1978, p. 113) this point is marked by \, showing that the preceding syllable bears the high pitch accent and that the following syllable (if any) drops to a lower level. (A word or phrase may also be unaccented, in which case there is no fall; and the pitch of any syllable preceding the accented one is predictable, since a word-initial syllable is low and any other syllables before the accent are high.)

ka\ki ga ('oyster')	H L L (first syllable accented)
kaki\ ga ('fence')	L H L (second syllable accented)
kaki ga ('persimmon')	L H H (unaccented).

Since there is really no tonal option – i.e. no opposition of tone type, such as high versus low, or rise versus fall – but only a choice as to where the 'accent' is located, Cruttenden (1986, p. 13) argues that Japanese is a true pitch-accent language, in contrast to languages like Swedish and Serbo-Croatian which make restricted use of tonal contrasts.

McCawley's discussion of Japanese and other languages (1978) leads him to a rather different conclusion. He points out that any language will exhibit a combination of characteristics, including

1 whether tones or accents are integral to lexical items and if so whether this is a matter of tone type (as in Chinese) or accentual pattern (as in Japanese);
2 what effect the rules of the language have, for example by limiting the options of the system;
3 what units are relevant in the operation of the system, for example whether tones or accents are carried by syllables or words.

This leads McCawley to reject simple classifications of the kind that typify languages as 'tone languages' or 'pitch-accent languages'. As we shall see below in connection with English intonation (section 9.8) it is indeed important to bear in mind that systemic organization is such that every language has its own character. Nevertheless, prosody, like other global systems, comprises subsystems – such as choice of tone type and placement of tone (or accent) – which can certainly be compared and may show similarities, even among otherwise dissimilar languages. In that light, while simple categorization of linguistic types always runs the risk of superficiality, specific phenomena and functional mechanisms are worth study. Hyman (1975, ch. 6) and Cruttenden (1986, ch. 1) are useful in this regard, both as overviews and as pointers to more detailed literature.

9.6   Stress in English

The phenomenon of lexical stress in English has received considerable attention and is probably best described as a word pattern or potential. Halliday (1970) speaks of 'word accent' as the potential salience of certain syllables within certain words; Gimson includes a detailed description of the 'accentual patterns' of English words within his more general treatment of English pronunciation (1980, especially ch. 9); and Fudge introduces his book-length treatment of English word-stress (1984) by referring to the way in which one syllable in a given word is picked out or singled out.

Some authors (e.g. Trager and Smith 1951) particularly associate (lexical) stress with loudness. In their treatment of English stress, Chomsky and Halle (1968, pp. viii, ix, 15) say they are concerned with 'stress contours', not with pitch, although they do not explicitly claim that stress is purely a matter of loudness (cf. Crystal 1969, pp. 113–20 and 156–61). In fact under normal circumstances English stress is signalled by pitch as well as by supporting factors, notably loudness and duration. Thus if the word 'sugar' is uttered on its own – say in reply to the question 'what's in this container?' – the first syllable of the word is likely to have higher pitch than the second as well as being (relatively) loud and long. Our perception is in fact likely to be more responsive to the pitch pattern than to the other factors. All of the factors are of course relative, and integrated within the intonation system. Hence, for example, if the speaker opts for rising pitch, to signal a query ('Sugar? Is that what you said?'), the second syllable will be higher than the first, but the *change* of pitch, in the context of a rising pattern, coupled with the relative loudness and duration of the first syllable, will normally be perceived as stress on the first syllable. Indeed, in longer utterances it is often the point at which the pitch level changes substantially that signals stress placement, rather than the level itself. Moreover the integrated nature of the system is such that loudness (or duration) may become a primary cue for stress where pitch has been pre-empted for some other function (Crystal 1969, p. 120).

Despite the persistence of the terms 'word-stress' or 'lexical stress', the patterning of spoken English is not based on words – or at least not on words in a grammatical or orthographic sense. Phrases such as 'the table' or 'a party' or 'leave it' will normally have the pattern of single words, with only one prominent syllable. In fact, there is normally no difference in spoken English between single words such as 'array' or 'arise' and two-word combinations such as 'a ray' or 'a rise'. Some writers therefore redefine the word for phonological purposes, as a PHONOLOGICAL WORD (e.g. Chomsky and Halle 1968, pp. 367–8), or use some other term such as STRESS GROUP (Fudge 1984, p. 1) or FOOT (section 9.3 above; Halliday 1970, p. 1, and 1985, pp. 271–3). The latter term is helpful in indicating the significance of word-stress patterns in determining the characteristic metre or rhythm of spoken English.

The corollary of this concept of foot or stress-group is that certain English words (grammatical or orthographic words) are characteristically unstressed. We must distinguish those monosyllabic words that normally are stressed in connected speech from those that are not. The latter are a small minority but are words of very high frequency, including articles and prepositions such as 'the', 'a', 'at' and 'to', pronounced virtually as prefixes to the following word, and pronouns such as 'he', 'him' and 'them' pronounced as suffixes of the preceding word, as well as diverse other items such as 'and', 'than' and 'that'. A full list is given by Gimson (1980, pp. 261–3). English intonation does allow the option of stressing these words, but the stress is then meaningful, in contrast with the normal or unmarked pronunciation. Compare a normal reading of

Joe was angry (two feet, each with stress on the first beat)

with a reading in which 'was' is stressed

Joe WAS angry (three feet, with each of the first two syllables constituting a separate foot).

The second reading signals that the speaker is contradicting a previous statement or implying that Joe was angry but no longer is. Many of these normally unstressed words have a reduced segmental shape as well: for example 'he' has no initial [h] in 'did he?' (= 'diddy') or 'was he?' (= 'wozzy'). Some speakers of English have unnecessary misgivings about such reduced pronunciations, and, especially in formal situations, produce fully stressed versions where the normal unstressed version would be more communicative. (Note for instance the effect of an over-careful reading of 'numbers one to four': a speaker who stresses the word 'to' runs the risk of causing confusion with 'two'.)

Gimson (1980) comments that the accentual pattern of English words is free, in the sense that there is no simple rule that lexical stress always falls on a particular syllable of the word (say the last or the penultimate). But there is a large measure of predictability about English stress (section 9.7 below) and Gimson himself comments that stress is also fixed, in the sense that the stress falls (almost always) on the same syllable of any given word (1980, p. 221). Gimson illustrates the variety of patterns in some detail (pp. 226–30), including those instances where the position of the stress is grammatically distinctive, such as in the nouns *conduct* and *rebel* as opposed to the corresponding verbs *to conduct* and *to rebel* (p. 233). Fudge likewise notes that, subject to certain exceptions, 'the place of word-stress within the word remains constant' (1984, p. 3); he also gives a comprehensive list of those words that do have distinctive stress (mostly noun–verb pairs, pp. 189ff.)

The exceptions to which these authors refer are cases where the stress pattern of a word may vary according to context, and where other aspects of English prosody may be said to override the 'normal' word-stress pattern. An example is the word 'afternoon', which usually has major lexical stress on the last syllable (e.g. in 'in the afternoon') but has the stress on the first syllable in phrases such as 'afternoon tea' or 'afternoon sun'. Other words that vary in similar fashion are 'fifteen' (compare 'at three-fifteen' and 'fifteen teachers') and, at least in a conservative variety of English, 'princess' (compare 'a princess' and 'Princess Margaret'). But the word 'princess' also demonstrates that lexical stress patterns may vary among individuals and groups, for many speakers of English consistently stress 'princess' on the first syllable, regardless of context. Indeed, there is considerable 'instability' of lexical patterning in English (Gimson 1980, pp. 230–2). A common tendency, for example, is for speakers to stress the second syllable of certain longer words that were traditionally stressed on the first syllable:

INtegral	or	inTEGral
COMMunal	or	coMMUNal
FORmidable	or	forMIDable
CONtroversy	or	conTROVersy.

Pronunciations in the first column may generally be considered conservative, those on the right increasingly the norm. The change may reflect a preference for a pattern in which the major stress is surrounded by unstressed syllables, rather than an initial stress followed by two or three unstressed syllables. It is probably safe to say that most younger speakers of English would regard 'FORmidable' as an awkward pronunciation. Examples such as these are not necessarily unstable within the speech of an individual – although some speakers, knowing the alternatives, may be hesitant about their pronunciation – but are another reminder that English phonology is not a single system, uniform across all groups and regions.

The normal accentual pattern of a word may be systematically overridden by the placement of the major tone (what some writers call 'sentence stress', here dealt with as part of the intonation system in section 9.8 below). The tones or characteristic pitches of English utterances usually fall on syllables that are potentially stressed by virtue of word-stress patterns. Thus when the placement of the tone is varied in the following sentence, it is the (lexically) stressed syllable of the relevant word or foot that is selected:

Joanne	wanted	Louise	to join	the paRADE
Joanne	wanted	Louise	to JOIN	the parade
Joanne	wanted	LouISE	to join	the parade
Joanne	WANTed	Louise	to join	the parade
JoANNE	wanted	Louise	to join	the parade.

But in certain cases, a syllable which does not normally receive lexical stress may be selected, for example when the syllable is specifically contrasted, as in

	ThirTEEN girls and thirTY boys
compare:	THIRteen girls and FOURteen boys

or

	I said 'MYology' not 'BIology'
compare:	I need a book about myOLogy.

So far we have spoken in terms of accentual patterns in which one syllable is stressed, relative to the other unstressed syllables of the foot. But some writers recognize intermediate degrees of stress in English. The following words, for instance, all seem to have the major stress on the first syllable; but some speakers pronounce the words on the right with a second syllable that seems to bear some degree of stress. The transcriptions represent a typical Australian pronunciation:

collar /'kɒlə/   follow /'fɒloʊ/
lacquered /'lækəd/   placard /'plækad/
conquered /'kɒŋkəd/   concord /'kɒŋkɔd/.

Likewise many words of three or more syllables may be perceived as having a syllable which is intermediate between stressed and unstressed. Compare words with initial stress and two unstressed syllables (on the left below) and those with major stress on the initial syllable and minor stress on the final (on the right). The transcriptions again represent Australian pronunciation:

numerous /'njumərəs/   universe /'junəvɜs/
quantity /'kwɒntəti/   pedigree /'pɛdəgri/
delicate /'dɛləkət/   indicate /'ɪndəkeɪt/

On the basis of pronunciations such as these, some linguists recognize degrees of stress, in particular PRIMARY and SECONDARY stress. Thus the word 'universe' can be said to have primary stress on the first syllable, no stress on the second syllable, and secondary stress on the final syllable. Formally, this amounts to a three-level system (in which zero or unstressed is the lowest level).

Not all speakers of English will agree that these examples demonstrate an intermediate level of stress. Some American speakers, for instance, may pronounce 'conquered' and 'concord' identically (and with syllabic /r/ in the second syllable rather than a vowel); and many speakers, whether from North America or not, may judge 'quantity' and 'pedigree' to have exactly the same stress pattern. Certainly it is true that the distinction between a syllable with secondary stress and an unstressed syllable almost always hinges on the occurrence of schwa, the so-called indeterminate vowel [ə]. In English, this vowel can be considered to signal minimal or zero stress. A syllable containing any other vowel quality, but not given prominence by the normal devices of English stress-marking, will then count as having secondary stress. With the exception of 'pedigree' (which is in any case disputable), all of the examples of secondary stress given above are open to this interpretation. Nevertheless, many writers recognize even more than three levels of stress (e.g. Trager and Smith 1951, Chomsky and Halle 1968; cf. Crystal 1969 p. 157) although the instances that seem to require four or more degrees of stress are, as we shall see (section 9.7), complex structures such as compounds and phrases.

In this context it is not surprising that the notation of lexical stress in English is far from standardized. The use of numbers above the relevant syllables is common in North American publications and is an attractively easy way of indicating several levels of stress. Within the tradition of the IPA, and especially in British descriptions, the marks ['] (primary stress) and [,] (secondary stress) are widely used. For convenience, an accent above or after the stressed vowel (as used in many dictionaries) or capitalization of the stressed syllable are simple and handy devices, but they do not lend themselves to systematic display of different levels of stress. For accuracy, indication of pitch, loudness and duration can be combined in a stylized pictorial display, often known as 'tadpole' notation. Illustrating these possibilities we have (assuming secondary stress on the third syllable of 'pedigree')

```
  1 3 2                              ⌢
                                          •
pedigree    'pedi,gree    pédigree    PEDigree    pedigree
```

9.7 Stress assignment

The extent to which the placement of lexical stress in English can be explained by rule remains a controversial issue. In many languages the patterns of lexical stress seem to be governed by relatively simple principles. Thus it may be possible to predict the occurrence of stress from phonological structure, as in the statement that words are always stressed on the initial syllable in Finnish (Comrie 1987, p. 598) or on the final syllable in Turkish (Comrie 1987, p. 628) or on the penultimate in Polish (Comrie 1987, p. 354). Sometimes stress rules are not strictly a matter of phonological structure, but are sensitive to grammatical structure as well. For example both Farsi (Persian) and Turkish are said to have stress on the last syllable of words, but in both languages certain suffixes do not count as part of the word for this purpose (Comrie 1987, pp. 529, 628). For such languages the stress rule may be better phrased as assigning major stress to the last syllable of a (grammatically defined) stem or root. In Polish also, certain words break the rule of penultimate stress, but these exceptions are predictable from their grammatical form. Indeed many languages of which it may be said that stress is regular or predictable are actually subject to several rules. In Italian, for example, stress commonly falls on the second syllable of three-syllable words:

aMIco ('friend')   voLAre ('to fly');

but note also

CApito ('I turn up')   capiTO ('s/he turned up').

These forms reflect other rules, such as one that puts stress on the final syllable of verbs meaning 's/he . . . ed'. This of course undermines the simple distinction sometimes drawn between languages in which the position of stress is predictable by rule and those in which its position is contrastive or meaningful. In Italian the stress on the second syllable of *amico* is predictable, but the final stress on *capito* is meaningful. Several principles of this kind can be observed in English: for example, the position of lexical stress serves to distinguish noun from verb in words such as *conduct*, *insert* and *reject*, where the rule is that stress is on the first syllable of the noun and on the second syllable of the verb; while stress can also be said to fall on the root, regardless of prefixes and suffixes in examples such as

FRIEND   DECK   BOARD   RISE
beFRIEND   beDECK   aBOARD   aRISE
FRIENDly   DECKing   BOARDer   aRISen.

An adequate account of English lexical stress must in fact recognize three relevant factors in relation to each word: firstly its origin (e.g. whether it is of Greek or Latin origin); secondly its phonological structure (e.g. whether it contains certain kinds of vowel and consonant combinations); and thirdly its grammatical organization (e.g. whether it is a compound noun, or a root plus suffix, and so on).

The fact that English words of Latin origin tend to follow the Latin rules of stress has long been noted (Chomsky and Halle 1968, p. 59, n. 3). Since words of Greek origin also show some 'non-English' stress characteristics, Kingdon (1958) made a tripartite division of English vocabulary into words of Greek, Romanic and English origin, as part of an explanation of English word-stress. Interacting with this distinction are structural considerations, notably the effects of what Chomsky and Halle call 'strong' and 'weak' clusters (1968, p.29). A weak cluster is a sequence consisting of a short vowel followed by at most one consonant; a strong cluster consists either of a short vowel followed by at least two consonants or of a long vowel or diphthong followed by any number of consonants. Now this structural difference is relevant in a stress rule (more or less reflecting the stress patterns of Latin) which applies to words such as the following, which end in a weak cluster and have stress on the penultimate syllable:

deVElop   deLIver   inHERit   inHIbit   EDit;

whereas those that end in a strong cluster have stress on the final syllable:

eLOPE   comPLETE   reVEAL   aLLOW   exIST.

But morphological factors are also relevant – in particular certain suffixes have their own effect on the stress pattern. Thus the suffix *-ance* or *-ence*, although it ends in a strong cluster, does not attract the stress when added to the above words, i.e.

deLIVer   deLIVerance
inHERit   inHERitance
aLLOW   aLLOWance
exIST   exISTence.

On the other hand, the suffix *-ion* requires stress on the preceding syllable, which in some cases causes a shift of stress:

inHIBit   inhiBItion
EDit   eDItion
DEDicate   dediCAtion

Furthermore, if word-stress rules are intended to cover the patterning of compounds and phrases, they must account for the English tendency to stress the first element of a compound but the final element of a phrase. Note examples of contrast such as

a BLACKbird   a black BIRD
a BLACKboard   a black BOARD
a BLACKberry   a black BERRy.

The significance of this distinction is actually quite subtle, and not always reflected in the spelling (as one word or two). Thus many speakers treat the following as compounds, with stress on the first word:

COFFee table
BIRTHday party
BIRD'S nest
CHURCH Street
the WHITE House (the presidential residence in the USA);

but not the following:

garden SHED
leather JACKet (but note the fish: LEATHerjacket)
Church ROAD
the white HOUSE (a house which happens to be white).

Notice that word stress is preserved within the larger context of a compound or phrase: when *berry* or *jacket* is stressed as the second element of a phrase, the stress falls on the first syllable of the word because that is where it normally falls in these words. Hence we have structure within structure, which can be displayed by bracketing, for example:

loganberry = [[logan] [berry]].

Within the innermost brackets (surrounding each word) there is a lexical stress assignment that determines which syllable of the word is most salient; at the higher level of the outer brackets (taking the two words together as a unit) there is a further stress assignment that determines which of the two lexical stresses will be heightened – the first if the unit is a compound, the second if it is a phrase.

A formalized version of this stress assignment procedure is set out in some detail by Chomsky and Halle (1968, pp. 15–27; see also section 5.6 above). They argue that it follows a CYCLIC principle, such that the same rules (say a compound rule heightening initial stresses and a phrase rule heightening final stresses) may be repeated at each level of constituency, working up from the innermost bracketing to the outer. Thus they take examples such as the following:

1 blackboard eraser (i.e. the thing for cleaning a blackboard)
   = [[[black] [board]] [eraser]].
   Innermost brackets enclose the single words; the next level up is the bracketing of [black board] as a compound; and the outermost brackets enclose
   all three words as a compound. Hence the total structure is of a compound
   noun, the first part of which is itself a compound of an adjective and a
   noun.
2 black board-eraser (i.e. a board-eraser which is black)
   = [[black] [[board] [eraser]]].
   Innermost brackets enclose the single words; the next level up is the bracketing of [board eraser] as a compound; and the outermost brackets enclose
   all three words as a phrase. Hence the total structure is of a phrase, consisting of an adjective preceding a compound noun.

Now Chomsky and Halle assume several degrees of stress in English. Conveniently,
they number them, taking 1 as the maximum degree, and they adopt the convention
that any rule that assigns stress actually lowers the stress on all other syllables. This is
as if we start with the assumption that every syllable is (potentially) numbered 1: we
then assign stress to, for example, the first word of the compound *blackboard* by
lowering the second by one degree, yielding the stress pattern 1 2.

A simplified summary of what happens to example (1) under this scheme is as
follows:

1 (i)   Input   [[[black] [board]] [eraser]].
   (ii) Lexical stress assignment (within innermost brackets); for simplicity we
         ignore unstressed syllables of words:

              1   1   1
           [[black   board]   eraser].

   (iii) At the next level, only the compound rule applies (within the now
         innermost bracketing [black board]), heightening the first word of the
         compound:

              1   2   1
           [black   board   eraser].

   (iv) At the next and highest level, the compound rule again applies, now
         strengthening the first word of the entire structure (i.e. lowering all
         others by one degree):

              1   3   2
            black   board   eraser.

The usual reading and perception of this compound should indeed be with greatest
stress on the first word and least on the second.

The second example will, in response to its different grammatical structure,
acquire a different stress pattern from the same procedural routine.

2   (i) Input   [[black] [[board] [eraser]]].
    (ii) Lexical stress assignment (within innermost brackets);
        1   1   1
        [black   [board   eraser]].
    (iii) At the next level, only the compound rule applies heightening the first
    word within the now innermost bracketing [board eraser]:
        1   1   2
        [black   board   eraser].
    (iv) At the next and highest level, the phrase rule now applies, strengthening
    the last major stress of the entire structure (note that this is 'board', as
    'eraser' has been weakened to a lower level on the previous cycle):
        2   1   3
        black   board   eraser.

This should again accord with our usual reading and perception of the phrase.

This generative routine is often referred to in literature as the STRESS CYCLE or PHONOLOGICAL CYCLE, and a useful simple account (under the latter name) can be found in Schane (1973, pp. 100–4). Schane's analysis of the phrase *Spanish American history teacher* (following Chomsky and Halle) presupposes five levels of stress and several alternative interpretations of the phrase. With the major stress on *history*, for example, we have

2 5   5   4 55   1 5 5   3   5
Spanish American history teacher

Schane's point is that this reading significantly reflects the structure, yielding the meaning 'a teacher of American history who is of Spanish nationality'. Alternative readings, namely 'a history teacher who is Spanish American' and 'a teacher of Spanish American history', will have different stress patterns reflecting the different interpretations.

It remains an open question how far this is truly a stress system, independent of intonation, and how far Chomsky and Halle can justify their assertion that they deal with 'stress contours', not pitch (1968, pp. viii, ix, 15). It is doubtful whether English speakers control the stress pattern of such phrases independently of the wider context of tone choice and placement within larger units of language. Certainly if 'word-stress patterns' are taken to be relevant within relatively small domains, it is unnecessary to recognize more than three levels of stress at most (including unstressed). Given the role of the vowel [ə], a simple two-way opposition of stressed and unstressed may be descriptively adequate.

Fudge (1984) is a thorough examination of word-stress in English. Fudge rejects the cyclical explanation (pp. 11–12) except for the treatment of certain suffixes (pp. 46–9) but is attentive to the details that make English lexical stress complex. He includes (at the end of each chapter) useful pointers to background reading. Goldsmith (1989, especially ch. 4) includes discussion of recent treatments of stress in the generative tradition.

9.8   Intonation in English

The importance of English intonation, both as an area of difficulty for the foreign learner and as a challenge to theory and description, has been acknowledged in a number of classic studies. Among the works prompted by the needs of learners are Pike's outline of American English intonation (1945) and treatments of British intonation by O'Connor and Arnold (1973) and Halliday (1970). Pike (1945, pp. 3–18) includes a survey of work prior to his own, and Crystal (1969) is a detailed account of English, which spans a wide range of prosodic features and pays thorough attention to relevant work both inside and outside linguistics. More general accounts of intonation are Lieberman (1967), Bolinger (1972) – which is a collection of papers that includes extracts from works mentioned above as well as treatments of languages other than English – and Cruttenden (1986). In recent years, several researchers have turned their attention to the role of intonation in discourse: this perspective is reflected in, for example, Brazil et al. (1980), Brown et al. (1980) and Johns-Lewis (1986).

Intonation is often described, somewhat impressionistically, as a matter of 'musical features' or speech 'tunes or melodies' (O'Connor and Arnold 1973, p. 1). While this may be a useful nontechnical pointer, it is sometimes linked with a conception of intonation as something superimposed upon the intrinsic meaning of words themselves, conveying the speaker's attitude rather than any fundamental meaning (Pike 1945, p. 21; O'Connor and Arnold 1973, p. 2). It is true that the prosodic features of utterances – including such aspects as tempo and overall pitch setting – signal what may loosely be summarized as 'attitudinal' factors, such as the speaker's anger or tiredness. It would nevertheless be an injustice to English intonation to suggest that it does no more than provide an overlay of feelings or emotions. It is in fact a crucial part of the English language, carrying important semantic functions. These functions may be 'attitudinal' in the sense that they express, for instance, definiteness or tentativeness, but these meanings are no more superimposed or extrinsic than other functional options such as whether to ask a question or make a statement or whether to qualify a statement by including the word 'probably' or 'possibly'.

If we narrow the concept of intonation to exclude both basic rhythm (as determined by lexical stress patterns, section 9.6 above) and overall settings (such as faster or slower rate of utterance and higher or lower pitch range), there remain three functional ingredients that are central to English intonation: TONE, or pitch pattern, TONE PLACEMENT ('sentence stress' in section 9.6 above) and TONE GROUP STRUCTURE. The first of these is a matter of tonal options, or the pitch patterns available in the system; the second and third can be taken together as aspects of TONICITY or the structural organization of utterances into units within which prominences are positioned.

The fundamental tonal choice of English is between rise and fall. The selection is highly functional and in the normal case is marked on the last lexical stress of an utterance. Thus the following (with fall marked \preceding the relevant syllable) are complete or definite:

She lent him her \ CAR
Would you leave the \ ROOM
Do be \ QUIET.

Notice that although the wording of these structures is quite different, the final falling tone is significant in determining the interpretation. In particular, the second example is ostensibly a question but with falling tone is likely to count as an authoritative demand. But our rather vague assertion that these utterances are complete or definite becomes more meaningful when we consider the opposition between fall and rise. If the utterances have a rising tone (/), they will be interpreted as open-ended or indefinite, usually inviting response or reaction.

She lent him her / CAR
Would you leave the / ROOM
Do be / QUIET.

The first utterance is now likely to convey a surprised query ('did she really?'), and the second will be tentative or polite, as if the speaker is hesitant or unsure of the right to make the request, or at least willing to qualify that right. The third utterance will also sound tentative – despite the wording, which on the face of it, is pretty blunt. Indeed, it is precisely the kind of utterance that school teachers are well advised to avoid with an unruly class: it has the appearance of authority but the rising tone will surely signal hesitancy or uncertainty. Of course, it is somewhat artificial to isolate this simple choice between rise and fall from all the other options at a speaker's disposal, for we normally combine resources if we can. Thus, to achieve a polite request, we are unlikely to rely only on a rising tone but may add wording such as 'please' or 'would you mind . . .', and so on. Nevertheless, even the examples given here should be enough to suggest the inadequacy of comments to the effect that questions always have rising pitch and statements falling pitch. The system is both simpler than that – in that the fundamental opposition is between what Halliday calls the 'certainty' or 'polarity known' of the falling tone, and the 'uncertainty' or 'polarity unknown' of the rising tone (1970 p. 23; 1985a p. 281) – and more subtle, in that this fundamental choice is combined with all the other options of wording that yield different interpretations of certainty and uncertainty.

The tonal options are not limited to simple rise and fall. They may be combined, for example in a falling then rising pattern (fall–rise tone) in which the rise so to speak cancels or qualifies the definiteness of the fall (Halliday 1985a, pp. 281–3). Compare

She doesn't lend her car to \ ANYone (definite statement)
She doesn't lend her car to / ANYone? (querying the statement)
She doesn't lend her car to V ANYone (qualified statement).

The implication of the fall–rise is that she doesn't lend her car to everyone ('not just ANYone') but may lend it rarely and exceptionally, say only to very close friends. In this sense, the definiteness of the fall is maintained but the open-endedness of the rise is added. Again, although these meanings might conceivably be described as attitudinal, there is nothing vague or idiosyncratic about systemic distinctions which English speakers clearly use and recognize and which convey precise information about whether someone will or will not lend her car.

Tonal choices are expressed within a highly organized structure. In the first place, the fundamental rhythm of spoken English is determined by the foot (section 9.6 above) and tones are normally realized on lexical stresses – indeed the occurrence of the tone is part of what signals that the lexical stress pattern is maintained. But since the foot may contain unstressed syllables following the stress, the tone may spread over these unstressed syllables. Hence a fall, for example, still marked below as before the relevant syllable, may actually be realized by successively lower pitch on each syllable of the foot. Compare:

Take the \ CAR
Take the \ CAMera
Take the \ CARamel

where in the last example the fall may be realized as three descending pitches over three syllables.

Secondly, the tone itself characterizes a TONE GROUP, in which other feet will be subordinate to the foot containing the tone. The number of tones in an utterance and its division into tone groups thus go hand in hand, again with functional value. A simple and common instance in English is where a descriptive word or phrase, in apposition, forms a separate tone group echoing the one before. The boundary between the two groups (here marked ||) is likely to be represented by a comma in written English:

He has two \ BROTHers|| in \ BRISbane.
  (He has two brothers, who live in Brisbane.)

You mean his / FRIEND|| the / ARchitect?
  (You mean his friend, who happens to be an architect?)

Contact the \ MANager|| who deals with com\PLAINTS.
  (Contact the manager – he deals with complaints.)

If these utterances are spoken as single tone groups, the second element will no longer be in apposition as a kind of addition or afterthought but will be interpreted as a restrictive specification:

He has two brothers in \ BRISbane.
  (He has two brothers in Brisbane – and possibly other brothers elsewhere.)

You mean his friend the / ARchitect?
  (You mean the architect friend? – He may have other friends who are not archi-
  tects).

Contact the manager who deals with com\PLAINTS.
  (Contact the manager who deals with complaints – not any of the other man-
  agers.)

Compare also the following, with two tone groups

I didn't \ TELephone‖ because I was \ ANGry

and the single tone group

I didn't telephone because I was V ANGry . . .

In the first case the two tones, each ending a group, serve to divide the utterance so
that it makes a statement (the speaker did not telephone) and gives the reason for this
(the speaker was angry). In the second case, the single group brings the reason within
the scope of the negation, so that it is the reason that is denied, not the telephoning.
This interpretation is reinforced by the fall–rise which signals a qualification – as
Halliday puts it, 'there's a but about it' (1985a, p. 282). Hence we take this utterance
to mean something like 'I telephoned, not because I was angry, but . . . '
  At the same time, the structuring of English intonation allows flexible placement of
the tone itself. While tone on the final lexical stress can be taken as the normal or
unmarked case, the tone can actually be placed on virtually any syllable (sometimes
called 'sentence stress'; 9.6 above). If it is not on the final syllable, the tone usually
has a 'contrastive' value, e.g.

He has \ TWO friends in London   (not just one)
He has two / BROTHers in Toronto?   (not sisters?)
He doesn't live \ IN Auckland   (but nearby).

Structural organization goes beyond the fundamentals noted here, and there is considerable complexity within the tone group. Lexical stresses may still be maintained
and given greater or lesser salience within the tone group, even though subordinate
to the overriding prominence of the tone, and tones themselves may form what is
usually called a COMPOUND tone, with, say, a rise separated from, but linked to, a
following fall, as in

Do you want a / SNACK or a \ MEAL?

  The kind of notation adopted here, with tones shown by conventionalized devices,
and tone groups separated by boundary markers, is adequate to show the basic
options. It does not reveal the details of how a pitch fall may be distributed over

several syllables, or of what is happening in the rest of the tone group, nor does it cope well with background variables, such as a general raising or widening of the pitch range over certain stretches of discourse. For such purposes, more intricate notations may be used, mirroring more closely the actual contours but at the risk of obscuring the systematic choices underlying them. Pike (1945) provides extended passages of English marked with a line notation, more or less as follows

Can you see me?

Pike couples this with a numbering system, in which the numbers 1–4 indicate relative pitch height. Numbering remains common in American publications, not without some confusion between levels of stress and levels of pitch. British authors, such as O'Connor and Arnold (1973) and Gimson (1980) have generally preferred the 'tadpole' notation (more correctly 'interlinear tonetic') for relatively detailed transcription. Crystal (1969), however, offers a notation which is based on simple stylized symbols (such as / and for tones) but also includes pitch range markings (such as arrows to indicate raising or lowering) and even allows for musical-style signatures (such as 'forte' and 'crescendo') at the beginning of an utterance.

The brief overview of English intonation in chapter 8 of Halliday (1985a) is a readable introduction which has the further merit of placing intonation within its proper grammatical context. The papers in Johns-Lewis (1986) give useful indications of the range of issues currently popular with researchers, including experimental approaches to the perception of intonation, and Cruttenden (1986) is a general introduction to the subject. The classic descriptions of English mentioned at the beginning of this section are also worth study, and Cruttenden gives a fairly full bibliography which includes references to work in autosegmental and metrical phonology (sections 11.12 and 11.13 below).

Exercises

   1 Give a brief summary of the speech production mechanisms that contribute to English prosody.

   2 What are the reasons for and against separating segmental phonology from suprasegmental?

   3 Discuss the relationship between pitch and segmental features, including the 'intrinsic' pitch of vowels and factors relevant to 'tonogenesis'.

   4 What are 'register tone languages' and 'contour tone languages'? Why is the distinction debatable?

   5 Why is it an oversimplification to equate stress with loudness?

   6 Distinguish between syllable-timing and stress-timing (or foot-timing). Note the suggested demonstration in 9.3.

   7 List as many examples as you can of English words which can have different stress patterns (such as *integral* stressed on either the first or second syllable). In your experience, can you relate the different stress patterns to differences in the speakers' age, sex, social background or regional origins?

8 How extensive is vowel reduction in your own speech? You may like to check your pronunciation of, for example:

the first vowel in *obtain, consider correction,*
and the second vowel in *hostel, carpet, item.*

How does vowel quality (reduced or not) affect your perception of stress in such words?

9 Summarize the discussion of English stress assignment in 9.7. Extend the discussion by examining a variety of English words and checking the extent to which the stress pattern of a word can be predicted from the phonological structure and morphological composition of the word.

10 Review the prosodic difference between 'a black bird' and 'a blackbird' (9.7). Collect some additional examples of both patterns, including contrastive pairs such as 'the north gate' versus the name 'Northgate'.

11 Explain the role of the phonological cycle in accounting for English stress.

12 What is tonicity in English intonation?

13 Choose some utterances to illustrate the functions of intonation in English. Note especially instances of contrast (such as 'I thought it would rain' implying 'and I was right' versus the same wording implying 'and I'm surprised it hasn't'). In general it is advisable to concentrate discussion on functional distinctions that can be relatively easily recognized and confirmed by other speakers; otherwise there is a risk that the exercise will degenerate into subjective speculation.

14 It is sometimes claimed that children begin to learn intonation even before they acquire most consonant and vowel distinctions. If this is true, we might expect an infant's pitch patterns to be significant before any words are clearly recognizable. For example, an infant might seem to be producing relatively inarticulate noises but nevertheless making a distinction between rising pitch (meaning perhaps something like 'I want that' or 'can I have that?') and falling pitch (meaning perhaps something like 'this is mine' or 'I like this'). If you have the opportunity to observe any infants, check whether you can find any evidence of this kind of 'proto-intonation'.

10   Feature Systems

Much of this book refers to features, understood as components of speech. This chapter reviews and explores the concept of features. After a general introduction (10.1), various kinds of feature – or ways of conceptualizing features – are explained:

– acoustic features (10.2)
– articulatory features (10.3)
– perceptual features (10.4)
– distinctive features (10.5)
– cover features (10.6)
– abstract features (10.7).

The issue of the accuracy and universality of such features is then taken up in 10.8 and 10.9.

The latter part of the chapter emphasizes the discreteness of features (10.10) and then moves on to two related issues that have been prominent in recent phonological discussion:

– the hierarchical organization of features (10.11)
– the notion of feature geometry (10.12).

An overview concludes the chapter (10.13).

10.1   Introduction

Features or components have long been implicit in the description of speech. Even descriptions which focus on segmental sounds frequently recognize characteristic features of these sounds: for example, the description of [p], [t] and [k] as voiceless plosives implies shared features of 'voicelessness' and 'plosiveness', contrasting with other sounds which are not voiceless or plosive. Indeed, most of the earlier chapters of this book have assumed phonetic components of this kind, such as voicing and nasality, and in chapter 5 in particular we made explicit use of features in phonological rules, in keeping with the tenets of generative phonology.

Explicit attention to features has been driven by a number of motives. In the earliest records of speech description, from ancient India, sounds are labelled and classified by various criteria. The term *dantya*, for example, was used by the Sanskrit grammarians in much the same way as modern phoneticians use its English equivalent 'dental', to refer to the point of articulation of certain consonants. Many of the terms used in Sanskrit grammar have a similarly direct reference to articulation (and have influenced the terminology of modern phonetics) but others may have been motivated more by systemic considerations than by articulatory accuracy. The Sanskrit sound usually transcribed as *v*, for example, may well have been pronounced (as the symbol suggests) as a labio-dental fricative, yet the grammarians' description of it was as a 'labial semivowel', suggesting [w] rather than [v] (Whitney 1889). The reason for this is that there are regular alternations between semivowels and vowels in Sanskrit, such that, for instance, a word-final *u* will be rewritten as *v* (i.e. [w]) if followed by a dissimilar vowel (e.g. *madhu iva*, written as *madhv iva*; cf. section 3.13 above). Moreover, the Sanskrit classification of sounds such as [w] and [j] as 'intermediate' may be due simply to their position in the sequential tabulation of sounds and not intended to indicate their 'semivocalic' nature (Whitney 1889, section 51). Thus features are not uncontroversial labels for objective characteristics of speech but may be used in various ways to indicate the nature, status and function of sounds within a linguistic system.

10.2 Acoustic features

A speech sound wave (or some visual display of it, such as a spectrogram) can be analysed in terms of its acoustic properties. Acoustic phoneticians normally describe these properties in terms of measurable scales or parameters, such as intensity or frequency of spectral components (e.g. Fant 1973, p. 26). It should be noted, however, that some characteristics lend themselves fairly readily to simple two-way choices (e.g. presence or absence of fundamental frequency) and that overall pattern (e.g. distribution of formants) may be at least as significant as more easily quantified measures (chapter 7 above).

Partly for this reason, acoustic features are rarely systematized fully independently of articulation and perception. Presence of a fundamental component (F_0) is, for example, readily related to the articulatory feature of voicing, and formant patterns may be similarly related to perceived vowel qualities (section 7.15 above). Some analysts have nevertheless tried to take account of acoustic properties in drawing up sets of features (as in the classic concept of distinctive features; section 10.5 below).

10.3   Articulatory features

Articulatory terminology is in fact far more common than acoustic, largely because observation of the movements and positions of articulatory organs is less crucially dependent than acoustic analysis on instrumentation, and because there is a long tradition of regarding articulation as the ultimate substance of speech.

Articulatory features are again often regarded as physical scales (e.g. Ladefoged's physiological parameters: 1982, p. 254), but the terminology is reasonably varied. The fairly rough and ready traditional terms, such as the dimension of consonant place, with values bilabial, labio-dental, dental, etc., have been refined both by improved accuracy of measurement of physiological phenomena and by general revision of perspective (for instance, by describing palatal and velar consonants in terms of tongue configuration rather than point of articulation).

Of the two best known feature systems that use articulatory terms, Ladefoged's 'traditional features' (1982, pp. 244, 254ff.) are clearly anchored in measurable values, while Chomsky and Halle's 'phonetic features' (1968, pp. 293ff.) are actually treated as articulatory correlates of more abstract features. In fact neither system is strictly articulatory: Ladefoged deliberately includes features such as 'sonorant' and 'grave' that are defined by what he calls an acoustic scale (1982, pp. 261–2), while Chomsky and Halle introduce (by footnote) a feature of 'syllabicity' which is almost certainly intended to be perceptual rather than articulatory (1968, pp. 302, 353–4).

Generative phonologists continued to pay some attention to the articulatory basis of features during the 1980s. Halle (1983) suggested that features should be taken to be neural commands which activated certain articulators with specific muscular gestures. This continuing interest in articulation also took note of the way in which features need to be related to each other. It is clear that some articulatory movements, such as laryngeal setting and lip rounding, are relatively independent of each other. On the other hand, features specifying tongue position, such as 'high', 'back' and 'low' – originally listed in Chomsky and Halle's scheme as if they were independent variables – are related by the fact that they are all gestures or settings of the dorsum of the tongue.

To represent the relationships among these articulatory features, generative phonologists have developed a 'feature tree' (figure 10.3.1). Figure 10.3.1 shows both how features are related to articulators (such as tongue root and soft palate) and how they are hierarchically ordered (such that, for example, the selection of values for [high], [low] and [back] is possible only for dorsal sounds and not for labials or coronals). The model is explained in Halle (1992) and a detailed account can also be found in Kenstowicz (1994, especially chapters 4.3 and 9.1). We will return to some of the implications of the model in 10.11 and 10.12 below.

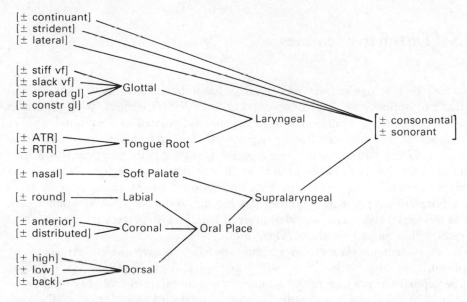

FIGURE 10.3.1   Articulatory feature tree
Source: Kenstowicz 1994, p. 452; based on Halle 1992.

10.4   Perceptual features

It would be possible to characterize speech in terms of its auditory qualities, and it is noteworthy that most languages do have terms to describe perceived qualities of speech sounds. Some of these terms may be auditory descriptives used also of non-speech sounds, such as 'hiss' or 'buzz'; others represent synesthetic impressions, such as 'dull', 'heavy' or 'sharp'. Australian Aborigines, for instance, seem to describe the postalveolar 'retroflex' consonants of their languages as 'heavy', as opposed to 'light' alveolar consonants. In common usage, terms like these are not likely to be employed for systematic description or analysis. There are some striking, if individual, examples, such as Rimbaud's sonnet in which the vowels A, E, I, O, U 'correspond' to the colours black, white, red, green and blue, and there is of course a substantial tradition of discourse within literary studies about the esthetics of sounds, including onomatopeic effects (see e.g. Ullmann 1970, pp. 82–91, 129–30). Phoneticians and linguists have done little with these impressionistic terms other than adopt some of them for their own purposes.

Of relevance here is the fact that human beings do not normally perceive speech for the purpose of identifying overt qualities analogous to textures or colours. Speech perception is focused on differences or distinctions, not as ends in themselves, but in order to discriminate utterances. Hence perceptual features are usually treated systematically as 'distinctive features' rather than as auditory properties.

10.5   Distinctive features

It has long been recognized that any language has a limited number of phonological contrasts or oppositions. For example, Jakobson (1939, 1949), drawing on earlier phonological concepts of de Saussure and Hjelmslev, pointed to the limited number of 'differential qualities' or 'distinctive features' that appeared to be available to languages. Given that no two languages are phonologically identical, distinctive features must be, to some extent at least, language-specific. Nevertheless Jakobson's interest was in showing how oppositions – as the constitutive features of relations among phonemes – reflected a hearer's response to an acoustic signal. Just as this signal contains a limited number of variables, so perceptual response to it operates with a limited number of categories.

The most famous elaboration of this approach is expounded in works by Jakobson, Fant and Halle (1952) and Jakobson and Halle (1956). This scheme uses perceptual terms which reflect acoustic cues rather than articulatory mechanics. Thus in 1939, Jakobson had already taken up Grammont's terms 'acute' and 'grave', representing opposite ends of a scale that measures the predominance of upper or lower components of the acoustic spectrum. The 'acute–grave' feature distinguishes both high front vowels from back vowels and palatal consonants from velar consonants. Inasmuch as both high front vowels and palatal consonants show greater high-frequency predominance, they may be termed 'acute' in opposition to back vowels and velar consonants, which are relatively 'grave'.

Jakobson and Halle employed only 12 features, which were listed with articulatory ('genetic' or 'motor') correlates as well as acoustic cues (1956, pp. 29ff.). The features are listed in table 10.5.1, and given in more detail in Appendix 2.1. All of the features are polar oppositions, allowing relative values. Hence the acute vowels of one language need not be identical in nature with the acute vowels of another, provided that they are more acute than the grave vowels to which they are opposed. Moreover the same acoustic effect (and perceptual impression) can be achieved by different articulatory means. Lip rounding, pharyngealization and retroflexion, for instance, may all be covered by the one distinctive feature of 'flatness'. Hence the 12 features allow for considerable articulatory diversity. Each feature is nevertheless binary, with only two opposed values along a single dimension, although a third 'unmarked' value is sometimes implied. Thus in a language like Russian, with distinctive palatalization of consonants, some consonants are 'sharp', others 'plain'; in a language like English, where there is no such distinction, consonants may be considered redundantly 'plain', but on one interpretation of distinctive feature theory, this amounts to saying that consonants are neither 'sharp' nor 'plain'. Tables of feature values sometimes enshrine this interpretation by leaving some features blank or marking them as zero. Table 10.5.2 gives a selection of English consonants marked for their distinctive feature values, including 0 where the feature may be judged redundant or irrelevant.

Table 10.5.1 *Distinctive features (each feature is listed as a pair of opposed terms, which are to be interpreted relative to each other)*

1 Vocalic/nonvocalic	Distinguishes vowels and vowel-like sounds from nonvocalic sounds like stops and fricatives
2 Consonantal/nonconsonantal	Distinguishes sounds with low energy and relatively substantial obstruction in the vocal tract from nonconsonantal sounds; thus, for example, a typical vowel can be considered vocalic and nonconsonantal, a plosive nonvocalic and consonantal, an approximant such as a lateral both vocalic and consonantal, and a glottal stop nonvocalic and nonconsonantal
3 Compact/diffuse	Refers to the acoustic spectrum and distinguishes sounds with energy concentrated in the central region of the spectrum (such as low vowels and velar consonants) from those with a more 'diffuse' spread of energy (such as high vowels and labial and alveolar consonants)
4 Tense/lax	
5 Voiced/voiceless	
6 Nasal/oral	
7 Discontinuous/continuant	
8 Strident/mellow	Distinguishes 'noisy' sounds like sibilant [s] from more 'mellow' fricatives like [θ]
9 Checked/unchecked	Refers to the higher rate of energy discharge in glottalized sounds and therefore distinguishes ejectives from pulmonic sounds
10 Grave/acute	Refers to the acoustic spectrum and distinguishes sounds with more energy in the lower frequency ranges (such as back vowels and labial and velar consonants) from those with greater concentration of energy in the upper frequencies (front vowels and alveolar consonants)
11 Flat/plain	Refers to the lowering or weakening of upper frequencies created by some kind of narrowed aperture: distinguishes lip rounded sounds from nonrounded, as well as other articulations with comparable acoustic consequences, notably pharyngealized consonants from their 'plain' counterparts
12 Sharp/plain	More or less the opposite of 'flat/plain' and refers to the upward shift of upper frequencies characteristic of palatalized consonants

Source: Jakobson and Halle 1956; see Appendix 2.1 for further details

Table 10.5.2　Distinctive feature values of some English consonants

	p	t	k	b	d	g	f	s	v	z	h	m	n	ŋ
Vocalic	–	–	–	–	–	–	–	–	–	–	–	–	–	–
Consonantal	+	+	+	+	+	+	+	+	+	+	–	+	+	+
Compact	–	–	+	–	–	+	–	–	–	–	0	–	–	+
Tense	+	+	+	–	–	–	–	–	–	–	0	–	–	–
Voiced	–	–	–	+	+	+	–	–	+	+	–	+	+	+
Nasal	–	–	–	–	–	–	–	–	–	–	–	+	+	+
Discontinuous	+	+	+	+	+	+	–	–	–	–	–	–	–	–
Strident	–	–	–	–	–	–	+	+	+	+	–	–	–	–
Checked	0	0	0	0	0	0	0	0	0	0	0	0	0	0
Grave	+	–	+	+	–	+	+	–	+	–	0	+	–	+
Flat	0	0	0	0	0	0	0	0	0	0	0	0	0	0
Sharp	0	0	0	0	0	0	0	0	0	0	0	0	0	0

10.6　Cover features

The Jakobsonian concept of distinctive features revives a prospect already entertained in Sanskrit phonetics (section 10.1 above), and certainly perpetuated by twentieth-century linguists such as Sapir (1925), namely that, within a particular linguistic system, sounds may be classified by criteria that transcend acoustic or articulatory properties.

In describing a language, it is often convenient to refer to classes of sounds that are not well defined by features. In English, for example, the consonants / l r w j / have some functional characteristics in common – they are the only English consonants that can form clusters with preceding voiceless plosives (as in *click*, *crick*, *quick*; *clue*, *crew*, *cue*, etc.), and they show a common tendency to devoicing in this environment. Nevertheless there is no acoustic, articulatory or perceptual feature specification that neatly unites them, other than the negatively phrased 'non-obstruent non-nasal consonants'. There is no single feature available of the kind that specifies all voiced sounds or all nasal consonants.

Now the extent to which classes of sounds are neatly described by one or two feature values will obviously depend on the particular feature system being used. Chomsky and Halle include in their scheme a feature 'anterior', which refers to sounds articulated in front of the palato-alveolar region. This feature would (if necessary) allow easy characterization of a class of consonants including [p] [t] [b] [d] [f] [s] [v] [z] but excluding [k] [g] [x]. In Ladefoged's scheme, which does not employ 'anterior', the specification would not be as straightforward. The question is, of course, whether 'anterior' sounds do constitute a class that needs to be identified in this way.

In fact the term 'cover feature' has a critical overtone and was originally intended to refer to precisely those features which had no measurable phonetic correlate but which 'covered' a class of sounds (Sommerstein 1977, pp. 96, 111). In its narrowest sense 'cover features' can be taken to mean only features which provide convenient labels for combinations of other features. For example, the term 'sonorant' may provide a label for the class of sounds that are neither stops nor fricatives – the label is convenient and applies to a specifiable class even though its precise phonetic meaning is controversial (Ladefoged 1982, pp. 253, 261). Many traditional categories are in fact of this kind: the class of consonants in many languages includes syllabic consonants and vowel-like approximants which may not be readily identifiable as consonants on acoustic or articulatory grounds; or the term 'vowel' may cover not only vocalic sounds but also syllabic consonants (section 3.14 above). In a wider sense, 'cover feature' may apply to any feature required in the description of a language, including *ad hoc* features which have little or no phonetic basis at all. We will deal with the latter as 'abstract features'.

10.7 Abstract features

Sapir's contention (1925, p. 19) that there are criteria by which one can determine the 'place' of a sound in a system 'over and above its natural classification on organic or acoustic grounds' argues for a certain abstraction in phonological description. The suggestion is that the sounds of language need not be characterized in the apparently 'concrete' terms of acoustics and articulation.

Total divorce of phonological features from a phonetic basis is in fact rarely if ever entertained. We could, in theory, describe the three vowels of many Australian Aboriginal languages with three *ad hoc* features: /i/ is 'sharp', /a/ 'dry' and /u/ 'soft'. It is hard to imagine any reason for an abstraction of this kind, and the features would in any case have to be mapped on to genuine features to make phonetic sense – for example, 'soft' means perceptually 'grave', or articulatorily 'back and lip-rounded', and so on.

There may nevertheless be linguistic justification for abstraction of the kind that is responsive to systemic criteria, such as patterns of distribution and assimilation. Suppose for example, that the nouns of a language end in /p/ /t/ /m/ or /n/ and that their plurals are signalled by the changes in the final consonant: p → f, t → s, m → b, n → d. Here we might justify treating /p t m n/ and /f s b d/ as two parallel classes of sounds, even labelling them, say, 'hard' and 'soft', so that /p/ and /f/ are hard and soft counterparts, and so on. We might expect that speakers of the language would find this classification quite reasonable, given their sense of how sounds function in the language, despite the fact that 'hard' and 'soft' do not directly correspond to straightforward phonetic qualities.

Sapir himself explicitly defended the notion that sounds could be 'felt' by native speakers to be other than what they were phonetically. Arguing in terms of segments rather than features, he maintained, for example, that English speakers feel [ŋ] to be a sequence of two consonants, [ŋg]. This apparent defiance of articulatory reality is justified not by the spelling *ng* but by the restricted distribution of English [ŋ] which, for instance, does not appear in syllable-initial position, as the true nasal consonants [m] and [n] do (see Sapir 1925 for this and other examples).

In fact the traditional grammars of many languages enshrine classifications of this kind, often applied, by way of spelling rules, to letters rather than sounds. In Arabic, for example, 14 of the letters are classified as 'sun' letters by the criterion of assimilation of the preceding definite article. (The definite article *al-* becomes *as-* before *s*, *an-* before *n*, etc., and /ʃams/ 'sun' begins with one of the 14 letters that trigger such assimilation.) The term 'sun' is clearly nonphonetic but is almost equivalent to 'dental/alveolar', 'apical' or 'coronal'. Note, however, that [d] and [ʒ] *are* 'sun' consonants, while the affricate [dʒ] is not. Historically, this affricate is derived from [g], and a generative treatment of Arabic might regard it as underlyingly velar; but in terms of current pronunciation (in most dialects of Arabic) the class of consonants that triggers assimilation is not neatly specifiable.

Other examples of traditional classifications include the Slavonic terms 'soft' and 'hard' and the Celtic (Irish) 'slender' and 'broad', correlating (more or less) with palatalized (or palatal) and nonpalatalized consonants. And the history of English spelling is such that ten of the English vowels are often presented as five 'long' and five 'short' paired values of the letters A E I O U, even though the opposition within each pair (e.g. long A [eɪ] versus short A [æ]) is certainly not merely one of duration.

10.8   Accuracy and universality

Descriptive accuracy requires that we recognize the principled distinction among different kinds of features. This point has been emphasized by Fudge (1967; 1973b, especially p. 174), particularly with respect to acoustic, articulatory and perceptual (auditory) features, each of which represents a different perspective on speech.

Nevertheless, some phonologists, especially in the generative tradition, are opposed to this differentiation. In their view, features should not be of different kinds at different levels. Thus the features of Chomsky and Halle's system serve both as a universal descriptive inventory and as the elements of a language-specific classification. The feature 'tense', for example, is supposedly a universal label referring to acoustic and articulatory properties, but is also the means of identifying a functional class of tense vowels within the phonology of English. An important principle of this tradition of feature analysis is the concept of NATURAL CLASS: it is expected that the classes of sounds that are relevant in the description of particular languages will be natural, in the sense that they have a clear phonetic foundation.

Examples of natural classes in English include the following. An English syllable can begin with various combinations of /s/ and some other consonant:

sp	e.g.	spy, spear, spoon
st		sty, steer, stool
sk		sky, scare, school
sf		sphere, sphinx
sθ		sthenia, sthenic
sm		smile, smear
sn		sneer, snare
	etc.	

But a group of sounds is systematically excluded from following /s/ at the beginning of a syllable, namely voiced stops and fricatives. There are no words beginning /sb/, /sd/, /sg/, /sv/ etc. We call this a systematic restriction because speakers of English are likely to consider the excluded sequences unpronounceable, or at least foreign to normal English patterns of speech. It is a different matter with sequences such as /sf/ and /sθ/ – these are admittedly rather rare but they are admissible in a way that /sb/ and /sv/ are not. The excluded consonants are of course a natural class, given that they can be defined as voiced obstruents. A second example from English concerns the vowels that can occur in open monosyllables: *paw, bee, may, toe*, and so on. One class of vowels cannot occur in this position, and this again proves to be a natural class, namely short (or 'lax') vowels. The number and quality of these vowels varies regionally, but in RP we have six such vowels, illustrated below in closed monosyllables. Note that there are no corresponding open monosyllables containing these vowels, e.g. no /bɪ/ alongside /bɪt/ and /bɪn/:

bit, bin, lick	ɪ
bet, pen, peck	ɛ
bat, ban, lack	æ
foot, book, look	ʊ
but, bun, luck	ʌ
pot, lot, lock.	ɒ

A third example from English is that of the consonants that require a vowel in the plural suffix. For most nouns, the plural suffix is /s/ or /z/ depending on the voicing of the preceding segment: *bits, locks, cliffs* and *moths* all have /s/ following a voiceless consonant, *bids, logs, buns* and *seas* all have /z/ following a voiced sound. But after a sibilant fricative or affricate, the plural suffix is /əz/ or /ɪz/, as in

masses, losses
buzzes, mazes
rashes, dishes
riches, ditches
ridges, judges.

It is in fact not just the plural suffix that is affected but any suffix of the same shape: the same pattern is observable with the possessive suffix (*Trish's book*, *the judge's opinion*) and with affixation of the verb in the third person singular (*she judges*, *he washes*). The relevant consonants are again a natural class (sibilants).

Largely because of this commitment to natural classes, many phonologists do not distinguish among features, especially at the 'higher levels' of perceptual, distinctive and linguistic (systemic) features. It nevertheless seems necessary to draw a line between perceptually distinctive features of the kind that represent the hearer's categorical discrimination, and linguistic features that characterize classes of sounds defined within a linguistic system. For English speakers, for example, there is a difference between the perceptual separation of the vowels themselves (as reflected in a speaker's ability to distinguish rhymes) and the potential classification of vowels into categories such as 'tense' and 'lax' (as reflected in the speaker's awareness of distributional or grammatical criteria that identify particular sets of vowels).

Moreover, much of the terminology of features slides between different criteria of description, not always in a way that clearly and explicitly represents any particular theoretical commitment. The term 'voiced' or 'voicing', for example, is probably no longer regarded as specifically acoustic or perceptual and may be applied to (1) the characteristic component of the acoustic signal (the 'voice bar'), (2) the periodic vibration of the vocal cords ('voicing'), and (3) the perceived 'buzz' of relevant sounds ('voiced' sounds). (See for example Jakobson, Fant and Halle's description of voicing: 1952, p. 26.) In many cases, a certain looseness does no great harm: 'click' is presumably a perceptual term in origin but is now readily used in the context of describing the suction mechanism (Chomsky and Halle 1968, p. 322; Ladefoged 1982 pp. 255–8). On the other hand, some features are controversial: vowel height often purports to refer to the position of the highest point of the tongue but in fact refers more appropriately to auditory quality and acoustic properties. (Hence Ladefoged's insistence on 'vowel height' rather than 'tongue height', 1982, p. 201; cf. sections 2.7 and 7.15 above.) And, while generative phonologists may make a principle of using a single set of features for all levels of description, the terminology does often point to one criterion rather than another. In the Chomsky and Halle scheme, feature labels like 'anterior' and 'coronal' are evidently based on articulatory reality; but those like 'strident' and 'sonorant', in name at least, suggest an acoustic or perceptual foundation.

To some extent, this apparent slippage between categories of description indicates that different aspects of speech are integrated. However important it is analytically to distinguish acoustics, articulation, perception and so on, these different levels of reality are integrated under linguistic control. Thus while an acoustic signal must be analysed in its own terms (intensity, frequency, etc.), the criteria by which features and parameters are selected and assigned values must refer to linguistic activity. In short, acoustic features are treated as correlates or realizations of other features. The values of formants within an acoustic spectrum are measured not because they are objective properties of acoustic reality but because they are believed to reflect articulatory settings and to serve as cues in human perception. A similar point can be made about articulatory features. If phoneticians set up a parameter of lip rounding, it is precisely in order to measure the physiological correlate of an acoustic property or of a linguistic feature of certain speech sounds. If phoneticians do not measure the extent to which the nose is wrinkled or the eyebrows are raised during speech, it is because these gestures are judged irrelevant to phonological distinctions (although they may be meaningful *non*speech gestures).

Notwithstanding this integration, some phonologists are rather too glib about the concept of natural classes. It is obviously true that the classes of sounds that are functional in language often have a basis in the nature of articulation or perception. It is entirely to be expected, for example, that the class of sounds that conditions a particular assimilatory process will have some property or properties that explain the assimilation. There are nevertheless reasons to remain cautious about natural classes. In the first place, there is enough evidence about the variability of articulation and perception to raise doubts about simple equations between phonological classes and their phonetic correlates. We have already noted the example of English 'voiced' stops and fricatives that may be signalled by the length of a preceding segment rather than by voicing. In other words, the difference between *send* and *sent* or between *feed* and *feet* may be, in terms of articulation and perception, more a matter of the length of the preceding segment [n] or [i:] than of the voicing of the stop itself. Now if there is still justification for talking about the voiced stops and fricatives of English as a class of sounds – as presumably there is – the relationship between this natural class and its characteristic property of voicing is, to say the least, indirect. Similarly, the 'back rounded' vowels of a language may not always be back and rounded; and so on.

Secondly, the classes of sounds that prove relevant in linguistic description are sometimes phonetically irregular because of historical changes. An example already mentioned is that of Arabic, where [g] has become [dʒ] by a process of sound change, but has not thereby entered the class of sounds that condition assimilation of the definite article. It would appear that [dʒ] ought to occasion assimilation, since a phonetically comparable sound like [ʒ] does so; but it does not. A second example of this kind can be taken from those varieties of English in which postvocalic *r* is no longer pronounced, unless linked to a following vowel. For most speakers from south-eastern England, Australia or New Zealand, the long vowels and diphthongs fall into three classes, depending on how they are linked to a following vowel. Vowels such as long /i/ and diphthongal /aɪ/ have a linking /j/, as in

me-y-and my-y-uncle

while long /u/ and diphthongal /aʊ/, for instance, have linking /w/, as in

you-w-are now-w-over Kangaroo-w-Island.

But a third group of vowels take linking /r/. These vowels are

/a/ as in spa; a spa-r-in Germany
/ɔ/ as in law; law-r-and order

/ɜ/ as in her; her-older brother
/ə/ as in Cuba; Cuba-r-is an island

Diphthongs ending in /ə/ (as in *hear* and *hair*) also behave in the same way. Now the vowels that take linking /j/ can be considered front vowels (including diphthongs that move towards a front vowel) and those that take linking /w/ are back rounded vowels (or diphthongs that move towards a back rounded vowel). But the group that takes linking /r/ is by no means an obvious natural class: it includes back rounded /ɔ/ as well as central vowels, and may also include front vowels, for many Australians and New Zealanders pronounce the vowels of *hear* and *hair* as long front vowels with little or no centering offglide. That this group of vowels continues to take linking /r/, despite its articulatory and auditory diversity, argues that patterns may be set up in language that do indeed, as Sapir would have it, transcend natural classification. The point should not be exaggerated – much of phonological organization is natural in the sense under discussion – but it is at least evident that a sound change does not always lead to reorganization in accordance with what linguists take to be natural principles.

10.9   Universal feature systems

The classic feature systems such as Jakobson and Halle's (1956) and Chomsky and Halle's (1968), have put considerable emphasis on universal validity. Chomsky and Halle say of their feature system: 'The total set of features is identical with the set of phonetic properties that can in principle be controlled in speech; they represent the phonetic capabilities of man and, we would assume, are therefore the same for all languages' (1968, pp. 294–5). In the light of the preceding section it should be noted that this approach to universal properties assumes that they are under (linguistic) control and that it is indeed possible to correlate features of different levels.

Chomsky and Halle relate 'physical' properties to potentially language-specific features by distinguishing description from classification. A single feature value, say [+round], may be used to *classify* the vowels of a language, i.e. to specify those vowels which are distinctively or functionally rounded. In this role, the feature may be considered an abstract or functional property of the phonological system. In assessing the acoustic or articulatory correlates of this property we may use the feature as a *descriptive* parameter: it is then possible to measure the range of articulatory lip rounding (and its acoustic correlate) which will count as [+round] for this language. Notice that this approach allows for features to be binary within the system (vowels are either [+round] or [−round]) but to be multivalued scales in their articulatory or acoustic realization (lip position may vary from fully spread to fully rounded, and the feature might have values from [0round] to, say, [5round]).

It remains controversial, however, whether a linguistic feature value is necessarily realized by a single articulatory or acoustic scale. Suppose, for example, that

[+round] vowels were actually signalled, in articulation, by a rather complex inter-action of tension, compression and protrusion of the lips. Nor is it clear whether feature labels must be appropriate across all correlates – for example whether there is any principled objection to the possibility that phonological *lip rounding* correlates with articulatory *lip protrusion*, perceptual *graveness* and acoustic *flattening* (of certain formants). (The point here is of course not to assert the truth of this correlation but to question whether the possibility should be ruled out in principle).

In general, phonologists seem to be motivated not only by economy of descrip-tion – by a reluctance to multiply terms for different aspects of a feature – but also by caution about abstract features. Principles of 'naturalness' have been taken to mean that phonological features must have genuine phonetic meaning (sections 5.8 and 5.9 above). The effect of this constraint is that in cases such as the Sanskrit [v] (functionally a [w]), or English [ŋ] (functionally [ŋg] according to Sapir and others), there is no possibility of inventing entirely *ad hoc* features, such as 'semifricative' to classify a [w] which is actually articulated as a [v]. The result of this strategy is that the burden of explaining the discrepancy between levels of reality falls on rules that derive one feature specification from another, rather than on the feature system itself. The trend, at least in classic generative phonology, has been to favour rule complex-ity within a unified feature system; and *The sound pattern of English* (Chomsky and Halle 1968) not only embraces Sapir's proposal that [ŋ] be specified as a cluster of nasal consonant plus [g] (p. 171 n.), but, for example, also takes [ɔɪ] to be a front rounded vowel, which is of course converted into a diphthong by phonological rules (pp. 191–2). More recently, attention has turned away from rule complexity to the representation of features – and particularly to richer concepts of structural organi-zation (sections 10.10 and 10.11 below). (For further discussion of classic approaches to features, see Chomsky and Halle 1968, pp. 293–9; Sommerstein 1977, especially pp. 92–7, 108–13; and Ladefoged 1982, pp. 241–5.)

10.10 Features and discreteness

Differences among languages are such that if there are universals of human speech they are found not in a universal inventory of phonetic properties but in the universal nature of sound waves and articulatory organs, and in the universality of systematic discreteness. Since sound waves and articulatory movements are continua, it is human response to them which brings the discreteness of a linguistic system.

This discreteness is both paradigmatic and syntagmatic. Paradigmatically, the continua of acoustics and articulation are converted, via perceptual choices, into a finite set of sounds. As Jakobson puts it: 'Where nature presents nothing but an indefinite number of contingent varieties, the intervention of culture extracts pairs of opposite terms' (1949, p. 321). Syntagmatically, this discreteness entails linear seg-mentation of speech. Extending Jakobson's point, Halle notes that humans are cap-able of listening to speech ('a continuous flow of sound, an unbroken chain of movements') and recording it as a sequence of discrete written letters (1954, especially pp. 333, 337–8).

It is not necessarily a consequence of this discreteness that features are perfectly in phase with each other. We may represent the English word *pan* as a sequence of three sets of features, for example, as in figure 10.10.1. We know nevertheless that the onset of voicing after an English voiceless stop will be somewhat delayed, creating the effect of aspiration, that the coupling of the nasal cavity for [n] may substantially precede the consonant, even to the point where the vowel is fully nasalized by anticipatory assimilation, and so on. Indeed given the continuous nature of articulation, it would be surprising if all articulatory gestures and acoustic cues could be assumed to be contained within segmental boundaries (section 3.1 above).

This point has been emphasized in some approaches to phonology. Firth made it a virtue of 'prosodic phonology', in which prosodies included features that extended over more than one segment, for example nasality extending over vowels adjacent to nasal consonants (Robins 1957, Palmer 1970, Sommerstein 1977, ch. 3; and section 11.8 below.) More recently, autosegmental phonology has paid particular attention to phenomena such as vowel harmony (in which all vowels within a word may have to agree in respect of features such as 'back' and 'round') and suprasegmental assignment of tone (in which tonal distinctions may be mapped on to one or more segments, depending on the structure available). CV phonology has similarly addressed questions of the linear organization of speech. Both autosegmental and CV phonology envisage a structured representation of speech such that features are not automatically contained within segmental units but are mapped, in various ways, on to a segmental 'skeleton' (Goldsmith 1979, 1989; section 11.12 below).

These approaches question the traditional status of the segment – and revive a constant worry in phonology: that our interest in segmental transcription and representation is driven more by tacit emulation of alphabetic writing systems than by genuine insight into the nature of phonological organization. In this light, features or components may indeed be a more realistic model of the smallest or most fundamental units of speech. But the contention does not undermine discreteness as such. In short, although there is room for debate about the formal representation of linear organization, there is little dispute about the fundamental principle that the units of language are discrete, despite the continuousness of speech.

$$
\begin{array}{ccc}
\text{p} & \text{æ} & \text{n} \\
\begin{bmatrix} -\text{voice} \\ +\text{labial} \\ +\text{stop} \\ -\text{nasal} \\ -\text{high} \\ -\text{back} \end{bmatrix} &
\begin{array}{c} +\text{voice} \\ -\text{labial} \\ -\text{stop} \\ -\text{nasal} \\ -\text{high} \\ -\text{back} \end{array} &
\begin{array}{c} +\text{voice} \\ -\text{labial} \\ -\text{stop} \\ +\text{nasal} \\ -\text{high} \\ -\text{back} \end{array}
\end{array}
$$

FIGURE 10.10.1   Example of a feature matrix: English *pan*

10.11   Hierarchical organization of features

Classic feature systems – such as the distinctive features of Jakobson, Halle and Fant, or Chomsky and Halle's system – assume that a segment is realized as, or can be rewritten as, a set of features, but they recognize no internal grouping of the features within a segment. In this respect figure 10.10.1 above is representative of most approaches, in that each segment is represented as an array of features, with no significance attaching to the order in which the features are listed down the array, and no explicit grouping of the features as 'point of articulation features' or 'vowel quality features'.

Features have nevertheless often been implicitly categorized in some way or other. Schane's summary of features, for example, which to some extent follows Chomsky and Halle, presents features under headings 'major class features', 'manner features', 'place of articulation features', 'body of tongue features' and 'subsidiary features' (Schane 1973, ch. 3). These headings scarcely provide consistent categories ('body of tongue features' actually includes lip rounding, for instance) and, more importantly, they are not intended to play any part in formal description. From the 1980s, however, there has been renewed interest in categorizing features in ways that show their interrelatedness or interdependency. We have already mentioned the generative phonologists' interest in 'feature trees' (10.3 above). In this section we will deal with a rather different approach to dependency developed by Anderson and Ewen (1987) and known simply as 'dependency phonology' (see also 11.15 below). In the next section (10.12) we will return to the generative interest in what is now being called 'feature geometry'.

Dependency phonology draws on classic thinking about features – it assumes, for example, that features should be natural, that they should make sense phonetically. But it allows far more diversity among the features themselves than most approaches. In dependency phonology, some features are scalar, allowing several values along a continuum; others are binary. Moreover, binarity is taken in an older sense to represent a choice between presence and absence of a feature, rather than in the orthodox generative sense of + and −. At the same time, the features are in some ways reminiscent of the classic distinctive features of Jakobson, Fant and Halle: components such as 'lowness' (or 'sonority') and 'roundness' (or 'gravity') for example, may be relevant to consonants as well as to vowels. These features may also be relative, in the traditional functional sense: a particular feature value implies an opposition within the relevant language without implying that the opposition is phonetically constant across all languages.

Most of the terms used in dependency phonology are familiar enough, including for instance 'consonantality', 'apicality' and 'nasality'. What is of particular interest is the way in which the concept of dependency contributes to description. Dependency phonology emphasizes the importance of functional subgroupings of features and of the internal organization of features within segments. In Chomsky and Halle's scheme, for example, assimilatory processes – such as assimilation of a nasal consonant to the point of articulation of a following consonant – require reference to all the relevant features, say 'anterior', 'coronal' and 'high'. But if features are grouped, so that all point of articulation features form a natural sub-group, it is possible to describe an assimilation simply as agreement of that set of features. It is interesting in this regard that Chomsky and Halle do in fact group their features under headings such as 'major class features' and 'cavity features'; but they make no use of this in describing the structure of the segment itself.

Not only does dependency phonology explicitly group features within the segment, it also recognizes the relative preponderance of various components within the segment. Thus the basic dimensions of vowels (often described as height, backness and lip rounding) are accounted for by three components, namely 'frontness', 'lowness' and 'roundness'. Departing from customary notation, dependency phonology represents these three not as bracketed labels but as the elements |i|, |a| and |u|. But these three may be combined, so that a vowel phoneme such as /e/ may be represented as {|i,a|}, combining frontness and lowness, or /y/ as {|i,u|}, combining frontness and roundness. Moreover, the notation of dependency phonology allows for components to 'preponderate' to a greater or lesser extent. Where a language distinguishes /e/ from /ɛ/, the higher vowel may be represented with frontness preponderant over lowness, the lower with lowness preponderant over frontness. Using arrows to indicate the preponderance, we have {|i$\rightarrow$a|} for /e/ and {|a$\rightarrow$i|} for /ɛ/. If it were necessary to make a further distinction, we could distinguish

{|i$\rightarrow$a|} = /e/
{|i$\leftrightarrow$a|} = /ɛ/
{|i$\leftarrow$a|} = /æ/

Thus although the components are universal, their function may be language-specific. The /e/ phoneme of a language distinguishing only two front vowels /i/ and /e/ is not functionally equivalent to the /e/ of a language which distinguishes four front vowels /i/, /e/, /ɛ/ and /æ/.

Classes of sounds can be specified by the components, but the implications of Anderson and Ewen's bracketing need to be carefully noted (1987, p. 127). {a} refers to any segment containing |a| and therefore includes all nonhigh vowels (i.e. it includes vowels in which |a| is present in any combination), whereas {|a|} refers to a segment containing only |a|. The negation of {a}, namely {~a}, refers to any segment containing a component other than |a|; and {| ~a|} refers to a segment containing only a component other than |a|. The other notational conventions of dependency phonology are available as well, so that {a,} refers to segments containing |a| and some other component, {a,~a} refers to segments containing |a| and a component other than |a|; and so on.

With considerable phonetic realism, dependency phonology categorizes features as gestures. The two basic gestures are the CATEGORIAL and the ARTICULATORY. The categorial gesture is divided into the subgestures of PHONATION and INITIATION, which between them include the components corresponding to what traditional phonetics would call the selection of airstream mechanism, the consonant–vowel

Table 10.11.1   Components in dependency phonology

Gesture	Subgesture	Components
Categorial	Phonation	consonantality (a scale ranging from |C| to |V|)
	Initiatory	|O| degree of glottal opening
		|G| glottalicness
		|K| velaricness
Articulatory	Locational	|i| frontness
		|a| lowness
		|u| roundness
		|ə| centrality
		|l| linguality
		|t| apicality
		|d| dentality
		|r| retracted tongue root
		|λ| laterality
	Oro-nasal	|n| nasality

Source: Anderson and Ewen 1987, chs 4–6; see also Appendix 2.4.

parameter of periodicity, and phonatory settings. The articulatory gesture is also divided into two subgestures, the LOCATIONAL and the ORO-NASAL. The first of these includes all the components relating to point of articulation and tongue configuration, such as 'frontness', 'lowness', 'linguality', 'dentality' and 'laterality'. The oro-nasal subgesture separates nasal coupling from the other articulatory settings and refers simply to the component of nasality. Thus the four subgestures correspond broadly to major articulatory categories recognized in phonetics, although there is certainly room for argument about, for example, the appropriateness of treating tongue posture as part of the locational subgesture or about the exact nature of the distinction between phonation and initiation.

The case in favour of dependency phonology is argued at some length by Anderson and Ewen (1987, especially part II, 'Phonological gestures and their structure'); and there is some convergence between dependency phonology and other recent work in autosegmental and CV phonology (Anderson et al. 1985; sections 11.12, 11.15 below). The components of dependency phonology are listed in table 10.11.1 (more detail is given in Appendix 2.4).

10.12   Feature geometry

The term 'feature geometry' has become common in discussion of the way in which phonological features are grouped or structured. In his survey of generative discussion of this topic, Kenstowicz draws on the classic Jakobsonian concept of phonological segments as 'bundles of distinctive features' (10.5 above), adding that these bundles are 'internally structured' and that the behaviour of segments 'can be understood from the elucidation of this internal feature structure' (1994, p. 451). Kenstowicz comments on the similar interest underlying other work, such as dependency phonology, but also points out that there is a difference between postulating feature structure within segments and treating some segments as elements within others (as in dependency phonology, where [e] may be analysed as [i] plus [a], 10.11 above). As Kenstowicz puts it, this is 'one of the most active and unsettled areas of current phonological theory, with many competing proposals' (1994, p. 451).

We have already seen (10.3 above and figure 10.3.1) that many generative phonologists now model features as a tree, designed to reflect the way in which features are interrelated. Thus, apart from what we might call 'nonlocalized' features such as [consonantal] and [strident], features are grouped as laryngeal or supralaryngeal; laryngeal is further divided into two articulators, namely the glottis (contributing mainly to phonation) and the tongue root (contributing mainly to pharyngealization), and supralaryngeal is divided into the soft palate (as the articulator governing airflow through the nasal cavity) and three 'oral place' articulators, namely labial, coronal and dorsal.

This tree organization carries through, so to speak, to the specification of individual segments, so that the feature representation of [s], for example, might be displayed as in figure 10.12.1, rather than as a simple array of unordered features.

It must be said that this kind of structure remains controversial. For example, it is not self-evident that [lateral] should be treated as a stricture feature, independent of place, rather than as a feature selected only in conjunction with certain articulatory settings; and it is similarly debatable whether [pharyngeal] should be a feature

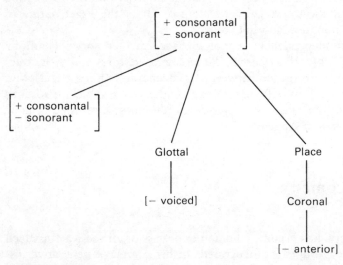

FIGURE 10.12.1   Tree representation of [s]

representing an additional category of articulatory place, alongside [labial], [coronal] and [dorsal]. There has been considerable argument in generative phonology about such questions, some of the debate intersecting with discussion of the linear arrangement of features (including the question of how to represent complex segments such as affricates, as well as the question of how to model syllabic organization and phenomena such as vowel harmony). This debate is picked up again in chapter 11, especially from section 11.12 on; for a detailed account of the problems tackled under the heading of feature geometry, see Kenstowicz (1994, ch. 9).

10.13 Overview

Within phonetics and speech research, acoustic and articulatory features are frequently dealt with as scales, parameters or articulatory gestures. Ladefoged's attempt to relate such 'physical' features to linguistic features and his evaluation of other feature systems from a phonetic point of view is comprehensive (1982, especially ch. 11). Jakobson, Fant and Halle's work (especially 1956) remains influential, partly because of their unusual attention to perception. The greatest subsequent influence is that of Chomsky and Halle (especially 1968, ch. 7), whose system of features has become a touchstone. Their system has, however, been substantially modified, even by those who have considered themselves to be firmly in the generative tradition; and even modified versions now face some competition from a more radically phonetic system as represented by dependency phonology (Anderson and Ewen 1987).

Many introductions to phonology devote some attention to the Jakobson, Fant and Halle scheme before surveying the Chomsky and Halle features. Useful reviews can be found in Anderson (1974, appendix), Hyman (1975, ch. 2), Sommerstein (1977, ch. 5), Kenstowicz and Kisseberth (1979, ch. 7), Hawkins (1984, ch. 3) and Lass (1984, especially ch. 5). Among these, Anderson and Kenstowicz and Kisseberth concentrate on Chomsky and Halle's features; neither survey is uncritical, but Anderson's list should be read with care, as he introduces modifications without identifying precisely where he differs from Chomsky and Halle. The most detailed discussions are found in Sommerstein and Lass. Anderson et al. (1985), Goldsmith (1989) and Kenstowicz (1994, especially chapters 1, 4 and 9) include more recent perspectives.

Features have also been investigated psycholinguistically under the heading of 'experimental phonology' (section 11.16 below) and Jaeger provides an interesting example of a test to see what kind of 'concept' native speakers have of the feature [voicing] in English (1986, pp. 227–8, 230–1). Fischer-Jørgensen (1985) provides a good example of the way in which features need to be evaluated in the light of linguistic evidence. A summary of the major feature terms and their usage can be found in the tables of Appendix 2.

Exercises

1 What is the significance of 'distinctive' in the term 'distinctive features'?

2 What assumptions underlie the concept of a 'natural class' of sounds?

3 What justification is there for cover features and abstract features in phonological description?

4 Evaluate Sapir's contention that sounds can be 'felt' to be other than what they are in articulatory or acoustic terms. (If you wish, assess the specific suggestion that English speakers 'feel' [ŋ] to be a sequence of two consonants.)

5 Consult Appendix 2 and the four feature systems summarized there. Show how each of the following sounds would be specified by the features of each of the four systems:

[p] [n] [z] [x] [l] [i] [o] [a]

6 Depending on the feature system used, classes of sounds may be characterized in different ways. For example, vowels may be [+vocalic] in one system, or
$\begin{bmatrix} -\text{consonantal} \\ +\text{syllabic} \end{bmatrix}$ in another.

With the help of Appendix 2, show at least two different ways of specifying each of the following classes of sounds:

voiced obstruents
laterals and r-sounds
high vowels
back rounded vowels

7 How does dependency phonology incorporate hierarchical organization of features?

8 Compare and evaluate the four feature systems outlined in Appendix 2, with particular reference to these questions:

How far does the system integrate acoustic, articulatory and perceptual features?
To what extent do the features take on different meanings when applied to different languages?

11 The Progress of Phonology

Introduction

This chapter draws the book together, by surveying the theoretical development of the subject. The introductory section (11.1) calls attention to the theoretical underpinnings of phonetics and phonology. Subsequent sections proceed more or less historically through perspectives and schools.

The classic perspectives and terminology were developed in the late nineteenth century and first half of the twentieth (11.3–11.8). The second half of the chapter deals mainly with generative phonology (11.9) and elaborations of it or reactions to it (especially 11.10–11.14). The emphasis here is on currents of theory: other chapters give more details of phonemics (ch. 4) and generative phonology (ch. 5).

The topics of the sections are

- phonetics and phonology before the twentieth century (11.2)
- phonemic phonology (11.3)
- the traditions of phonetics (11.4)
- early North American phonology (11.5)
- the Prague School (11.6)
- glossematics and stratificational phonology (11.7)
- prosodic phonology (11.8)
- generative phonology (11.9)
- natural generative phonology (11.10)
- natural phonology (11.11)
- autosegmental and CV phonology (11.12)
- metrical phonology (11.13)
- lexical phonology (11.14)
- dependency phonology (11.15)
- experimental phonology (11.16).

The conclusion emphasizes the fundamental nature of theoretical discussion in any scientific approach to reality (11.17).

11.1   Currents of theory

We began this book on a functional footing, declaring that language has the ultimate function of conveying meaning and that the task of analysis is to investigate how that function is achieved through subsidiary functions, such as articulation and perception (section 1.2 above).

Functional linguists commonly emphasize the systemic and structural organization of language: language functions by virtue of the choices available to speakers, whether choice of words, selection of options within the grammatical system, or exploitation of phonological distinctions. The term 'system' indicates that we operate with the finite options available to us within the language we are using, and the significance of any particular selection within a system rests in the contrast between what is selected and what could have been selected. In a phonological system, for example, the choices are limited and make sense only by reference to the system itself, a point which has long been recognized in discussion of the 'phonemic principle' or 'phonological distinctiveness' (section 4.2 above). The term 'structure' is less precise, being used sometimes in much the same way as 'system', to indicate that choices are made within a 'structured' scheme or framework, but sometimes to refer to the linear organization of language. In this second sense, structure can be contrasted with system, reflecting the two dimensions of linguistic organization that are often referred to as 'syntagmatic' and 'paradigmatic'. Syntagmatic relations are linear or sequential, operative for example in the coarticulation or assimilation of adjacent sounds or in the organization of alliteration or rhyme across longer stretches of language. Paradigmatic relations are those that exist among the options in a system, for example between a word in a text and other words that might have been used in its place or between a phoneme and the other phonemes to which it is opposed. (For a current and influential functional view of language, set in a respectable tradition of functional linguistics, see Halliday 1978, 1985a; see also Sampson 1980, ch. 5, for a general account of functional linguistics.)

The essential role of theory in such description of language is underlined by the frequent use of '-isms', as in functionalism, structuralism and systemicism. These words are often employed to declare or reject a theoretical standpoint. Loosely, one may acknowledge the importance of linguistic structure by aspiring to 'structuralism' or describing oneself as a 'structuralist'. More strictly, '-isms' may define theoretically limiting positions, so that 'structuralism' may profess a belief that structures are the only true reality and that all meaning and value is achieved within structures. A structuralist in this sense may believe, for example, that human society – as well as language – is a structure, and that concepts or values such as justice, beauty and truth are functional or meaningful only by virtue of their expression within such a structure. Ultimately, when fundamental beliefs of this kind are explored and exposed, they must indeed be revealed as beliefs, resting on human faith or commitment of one kind or another. And this does not mean that we can somehow purify ourselves of any such belief and stick to solid facts and obvious truths. Rather, all human undertakings ultimately rest on commitment, and even our notions of what counts as science, and of how facts can be shown to be solid, and of which truths are obvious, are themselves reducible to beliefs – to a belief, for example, in the power and primacy of human reason, or in the self-contained and self-justifying nature of the world, or in a reality that is ultimately beyond human understanding and explanation.

That modern science often fails to probe these underlying beliefs is itself a matter of theoretical commitment. Scientific enquiry, as practised in industrialized countries, has been strongly influenced by a belief that concrete reality is the only reality of life, or, less arrogantly, by a belief that it is only material reality that is amenable to scientific investigation or that human experience provides the only valid data of science. The most famous versions of such beliefs are characterized as materialism, empiricism and positivism. Those who explicitly defend these beliefs may set them against what they negatively describe as metaphysics, mentalism or transcendent beliefs – speculation going beyond the evidence of the human senses, for example, or a willingness to accept the existence of that which cannot be directly observed, such as mental concepts or the human mind itself. Positivism is particularly associated with the name of Auguste Comte (1798–1857), a French philosopher who began a modern obsession with the 'positive' data of human experience, but positivism draws on a long tradition of empiricist thinking that makes human experience the determinant of reality. Via such philosophers as Bertrand Russell (1872–1970), a version of positivism (usually known as 'logical positivism') remains pervasive and influential. It bears at least some responsibility for the widely held view that esthetics, ethics and religious beliefs are entirely a matter of individual self-satisfaction or social convention, and that national and political ambitions cannot go beyond an ill-defined pursuit of material well-being for a reasonable number of citizens. For logical positivism allows only logic and mathematics as legitimate undertakings that transcend sensory experience: truth is what can be shown to be true by universal logic (and mathematics) or by observation. Moral and esthetic judgments are not so much wrong as meaningless, for they are neither logically true nor derived from observation.

While positivism can be blamed for many of the woes of modern industrial society – for example for that kind of materialist medicine which treats human beings as purely physical organisms and struggles to find any moral ground on which to base concepts of caring and service – it has undoubtedly had some beneficial effects, particularly in pointing to the limits of human knowledge and the need to study language carefully. Paradoxically, the very search for certain knowledge, based firmly on logic and experience, led to the realization that statements about causation, scientific law and generalizations from experience were just as vulnerable to positivist puritanism as were moral and esthetic judgments. As a consequence, it is now recognized in orthodox science, though not always in popular presentations of it, that one cannot prove a generalization by scientific methods of observation and experiment. One cannot prove, for instance, that a cricket ball thrown in the air will always return to earth: repeated experiments will presumably confirm our experience and demonstrate that the ball keeps coming down, but they cannot *prove* that this is what will always happen, indefinitely and without exception. At best, the conclusion must be in terms of probability and expectation rather than certainty about the future (always assuming one remains a positivist, unwilling to admit a measure of faith in the predictability of the universe). What *can* be shown by experimental means, quite decisively, is that a generalization is *not* true. Thus the hypothesis that a cricket ball is lighter than air can, if necessary, be *dis*proved by a single experimental trial. Hence positivist science has introduced a note of caution into our formulation of truth, a reminder of the provisional nature of human knowledge. Partly because of this attention to the phrasing of statements, many twentieth-century philosophers, particularly in the English-speaking world, have devoted much of their time to the analysis of language, so much so that for some of them philosophy and linguistic analysis became synonymous.

The important questions are often the ones that nobody will admit into discussion, and linguists, in common with other scientists, have at times taken a theoretical position for granted, as if no alternative were even conceivable. But theoretical debate has at times been vigorous and prominent. Leonard Bloomfield (1887–1949), highly influential in the 1930s in North America, explicitly argued for what he called a 'materialistic' or 'mechanistic' explanation of human behaviour, as opposed to a 'mentalistic' view (1933, pp. 32ff.). Bloomfield's explanation belonged within behaviourism, itself an application of positivist thinking to psychology which sought to describe human behaviour entirely in terms of stimuli and responses. This behaviourism denied the existence of nonphysical factors such as ideas and intentions, except to the extent that they could be reinterpreted as physical states or changes in the human organism.

In another instance of theoretical debate, behaviourism itself came under overt attack when Chomsky (1959) reviewed Skinner's account of what he called 'verbal behaviour' (1957). Chomsky not only criticized the behaviourist explanation of language – some would say demolished it once and for all – but provided a spirited exposition of a new mentalism, unashamedly talking of the organization of the human *mind* and concepts. Chomsky's mentalism is more accurately described as rationalism, for it makes reason, or the rational organization of the mind, the central characteristic of human beings. Here again, an '-ism' can be taken in a restrictive or reductionist sense, for rationalism can be accused of overlooking other, nonrational aspects of human life, especially the extent to which reason is constrained and shaped by social motives and structure.

These brief remarks can hardly be regarded as a history of modern philosophy of science but are meant to suggest that philosophical issues are crucial. Even the assumption that one can survey various perspectives or schools of thought presupposes a certain vantage point. It is not uncommon for university teachers to give courses of precisely the kind that pretend to look fairly but critically at all major points of view; but it has to be asked of such surveys where the viewer is meant to be standing. It may be that a degree of superior objectivity is implied, perhaps unstated because it would be too arrogant to express, or that scrutiny of everyone else's views sits oddly with unwillingness to adopt any position of one's own. Or reluctance to grapple with incompatible alternatives may be dignified by yet another '-ism' as eclecticism. Having said that, we shall attempt a survey of our own, but without any claim to give equal value to everything that has been written about phonetics and phonology, and without any attempt to hide from the reader our own commitment to a functional view of language in which system and structure are foundational. Readers who wish to delve further into theoretical assumptions are urged to consult at least one or two major overviews of the development of modern linguistics such as Robins (1979) or Sampson (1980). These works and their bibliographies give more than adequate pointers to further reading.

11.2 Phonetics and phonology before the twentieth century

Interest in pronunciation is far older than the pursuit of phonetics and phonology as academic subjects. Several centuries before Christ, Indian scholars were devoting themselves to the description of Sanskrit and achieving remarkable accuracy in articulatory phonetics. Although their primary concern seems to have been to maintain the correct pronunciation of what was already becoming a classical language, their observations about points and manners of articulation and other aspects of pronunciation reveal an interest that qualifies as scientific in the best sense of the term (Allen 1953).

Progress is not inevitable: many who came later remained ignorant of this early work in phonetics and did not equal it, let alone improve on it. Modern European civilization owes many debts to Ancient Greece and Rome, but phonetics is not one of them. The Greek grammarian Dionysius Thrax, for example, bequeathed a curious misunderstanding of the nature of voicing. Writing around 100 years before Christ, he recognized that the spoken Greek of his time had both voiceless aspirated and voiceless unaspirated plosives, i.e. both /p t k/ and /p^h t^h k^h/. But he considered voiced plosives /b d g/ to be 'middle', intermediate between the two voiceless types. The resulting habit of labelling voiced consonants with the misleading Latin term *mediae* persisted well into the nineteenth century.

While Greek and Roman scholars did not match the phonetic and phonological brilliance of ancient India, they were interested in related issues, such as the orthographic representation of spoken forms, and it should not be forgotten that the modern European style of alphabetic writing has its roots in the Greek adaptation of Phoenician symbols. The Greek innovation was to develop separate vowel letters alongside the consonants, thus establishing a convention which is now standard in modern European orthographies. By contrast, many other writing systems still use symbols which stand for entire syllables or morphemes or treat vowels as diacritic or subsidiary features of consonants. The Japanese *Hiragana* syllabary, for example, has in principle a distinct symbol for each syllable of the language; and various Semitic writing systems – including the one which the Greeks adapted – either omit the vowels or write them above or below the preceding consonant. (If English were to follow the Semitic practice, we might write something like $b^a n^a n^a$ or *b'n'n'* rather than the familiar *banana*.) Whether the Greek alphabetic innovation is entirely beneficial remains an open question: we have noted already (especially in sections 3.1 and 10.10) that many of our worries about segmenting speech may be inappropriately influenced by our familiarity with an alphabetic writing system.

Most societies which have developed or adopted a writing system have shown some degree of interest – even if meagre or misguided – in pronunciation or phonological analysis. While spoken language is typically unconscious, writing is far less so, for the product remains before us for inspection and reconsideration (Halliday 1985a, pp. xxiii–xxv, 1985b). The existence of a written form of expression not only invites reflection on the relationship between speech and writing but also creates a distance between speakers and their language that encourages them to treat language as an object of analysis. In China, a system of written characters was in use by 2000 BC, and by the time Chinese scholarship became known to Europeans there was a long Chinese tradition of linguistic studies. Even though the use of characters can scarcely have encouraged segmentation, the Chinese developed an analysis of syllables into 'initials' and 'finals', where the 'final' corresponds to what we might describe as the rhyming portion of a syllable. (Under this kind of analysis, English *sea*, *flee*, *suit*, *flute* might be considered to consist of initials /s-/ and /fl-/ and finals /-i:/ and /-u:t/. It is worth noting that some phonologists are now recognizing units of this kind in languages other than Chinese; see section 11.13 below.) In Korea, Chinese characters were long used to write Korean but an indigenous alphabet, said to have been commissioned by King Sejong, came into use in the middle of the fifteenth century. This alphabet, apparently a genuine local invention and not an adaptation of an existing alphabet, represented a break with character writing, as its 28 letters included separate symbols for vowels as well as consonants. Sensitivity to pronunciation is revealed in the relationship among the symbols – for example, the symbols for fortis voiceless obstruents are essentially doubled versions of the symbols for the corresponding lenis obstruents.

It is of course important not to confuse phonology and spelling. All human languages are spoken languages and can be analysed and described phonologically; but many of them have no written form or have only recently begun to be written. And in any case, some writing systems do not neatly match phonological organization. As we have already had cause to note, English spelling often obscures the patterns of phonological organization. The written form of words such as *psalm* and *psychic*, for instance, suggests that English words can begin with the consonant cluster /ps/, whereas in fact these words begin, in spoken English, with a single consonant /s/, and indeed it is a systematic feature of the phonological structure of English that words cannot begin with clusters of consonant plus /s/. On the other hand, English structure does tolerate words that end with sequences of voiceless plosive plus /s/, i.e. /ps/ /ts/

and /ks/. But this regularity is again obscured in written English, by orthographic devices such as the 'silent *e*' on *apse* and *copse*, or the use of a single letter *x* to represent /ks/ in *fox* and *six*. Nevertheless, written and spoken language are not entirely unrelated to each other, and discussion of the written may sometimes – though certainly not always – reflect insight into the spoken.

In many cases, little survives to testify to the insights and achievements of previous generations. We are fortunate to have any record at all of the work of an Icelandic grammarian of the twelfth century. His main aim was to reform the spelling of Icelandic, which was already being written in an adaptation of the Roman alphabet, but his discussion does indicate some thinking about the phonological organization of the language, and suggests a clear grasp of what we would nowadays call phonemic contrasts, minimal pairs and allophonic variants. The name of this scholar is no longer known and his treatise was not published until the nineteenth century. In quite a different part of the world, Sequoyah (1760–1843), a half-Cherokee Indian who never learned to speak or read English, succeeded in designing a syllabary for the Cherokee language. He experimented with pictographs before finally adopting various letters from English, Greek and Hebrew (without knowing what these symbols stood for in the source languages) to represent Cherokee syllables. His syllabary was widely used for some time, and seems to be based on a sensible phonological analysis of Cherokee syllables, but we know next to nothing of Sequoyah's thinking in devising the system.

11.3   The phoneme

By the latter part of the nineteenth century, phonetics had been established as part of the modern European scientific enterprise. Interests in spelling and pronunciation were now benefiting from technological advances that made it possible to investigate speech by instrumental methods. At the same time, horizons widened. Where scholars had previously tended to focus on their own languages, the nineteenth century brought, particularly in Germany, a flowering of historical phonology that tried to encompass all the sound changes that had taken place in the development of Indo-European languages. And accompanying this expansiveness was a growing interest in the various spoken dialects of Europe and in hitherto unwritten languages outside Europe, many of which were spoken in areas now under the control of the European colonial powers.

The concept of the phoneme became important not only for its relevance to practical problems such as how to represent the pronunciation of dialects and languages that had never been transcribed before, but also as a keystone of modern phonological theory. In a sense, the word 'phoneme' merely provided a technical term for a concept that was already known – for example to Sanskrit scholars and the Icelandic grammarian. Yet the origin of the term is somewhat obscure, and its meaning continues to be controversial.

The term is usually ascribed to Baudouin de Courtenay (1845–1929), a Polish linguist who taught in Russian universities from 1870. He actually seems to have taken the term over from Kruszewski, a fellow Pole who studied under him from 1878 at the University of Kazan. But the Swiss linguist Ferdinand de Saussure (1857–1913) had already used the French version of the term 'phoneme' in an article published in 1878, and he in turn had adopted the word from French predecessors who had almost certainly used it as a convenient translation of the German *Sprachlaut*, 'language sound'. It would be wrong to suppose that all of these early users of the term meant exactly the same by it. The common thread is the need to treat discernibly different sounds as a single sound for functional or descriptive purposes; but it is evident that early usage, foreshadowing continuing disagreement, was not uniform (Anderson 1985, pp. 65–82).

Baudouin de Courtenay, whose own use of the term 'phoneme' seems to have shifted during his lifetime, fell back on what is now commonly described as a 'psychological' or 'intentional' definition of the phoneme. This definition proposes that the phoneme represents a mental image or intention and that variants or alternate realizations of the phoneme are to be regarded as different actualizations of a single underlying 'ideal' or 'intended' sound. This mentalism – or versions of it – achieved some popularity among European scholars and was kept alive in North America by Sapir (section 11.5 below), who wrote unapologetically of the 'psychological reality' of phonemes. It was nevertheless overshadowed by alternative conceptions before being revived by modern generative phonology in the 1960s. Chapter 3 of Anderson (1985) provides a detailed account of the work of Baudouin de Courtenay and Kruszewski.

11.4   The traditions of phonetics

In Britain in particular, phonetics was already a creditable pursuit in the sixteenth and seventeenth centuries. No doubt encouraged by – and contributing to – the strong empiricist flavour of the British scientific tradition, phoneticians such as Henry Sweet (1845–1912) and Daniel Jones (1881–1967) were more interested in the description and transcription of speech than in the concept of the phoneme as a matter of theory. Sweet was aware of German linguistic scholarship and reportedly somewhat hostile to it. He did not use the term 'phoneme' at all, but did distinguish between 'broad' and 'narrow' phonetic transcription: broad transcription recorded speech in symbols that were sufficient to convey the relevant distinctive differences, whereas a narrow transcription included phonetic information of the kind which was not contrastive within the system but which might be of importance to the dialectologist noting precise details. Thus a broad transcription of English RP might show simple voiceless plosives; a narrow transcription might show that these plosives are also markedly aspirated. Sweet's broad transcription is at least roughly equivalent to a phonemic transcription, and Sweet's notion of the phoneme (if it can be called that) is of a functionally distinctive unit rather than a psychological entity.

Jones maintained Sweet's use of 'broad' and 'narrow' and was familiar with the development of phonology in Europe. Under his leadership, University College London became a centre of practical phonetics, and Jones himself was renowned for his documentation of English pronunciation and his attention to training in articulatory and auditory skills. He tended to regard phonology as subsidiary to phonetics and is considered to be the author of the 'phonetic' view of the phoneme. In this he retreats even from Sweet's recognition of distinctiveness and describes the phoneme as a set of similar sounds that are in complementary distribution. The extreme empiricist flavour is not surprising but it must be said that Jones was not entirely consistent and that he continued, for example, to recognize the practical importance of minimal pairs, which clearly reflect phonemic contrasts (section 4.2 above). Jones's successors have continued his high standards of phonetics, often still oriented to 'ear training' and the teaching of English pronunciation to foreign learners, but have been generally less suspicious of phonological theorizing. Gimson's work on English phonetics (1980, first published in 1962), essentially a successor to Jones's *An outline of English phonetics* (first published in 1918), straightforwardly acknowledges the phoneme as a contrastive unit.

Jones's own views are set out in a paper on the history and meaning of the term 'phoneme' (Jones 1957) as well as in a book-length treatment of the phoneme (1962).

11.5 Phonology in North America

Franz Boas (1858–1942) was born and educated in Germany but settled in the United States after he had begun to study American Indian culture. An anthropologist rather than a linguist, he stressed the need to respect the diversity of culture and to study a cultural system (including language) on its own terms. He laid the foundation for phonetic and grammatical studies of American Indian languages, and influenced men like Edward Sapir (1884–1939) and Leonard Bloomfield (1887–1949), who combined high standards of scholarship with an enthusiastic interest in recording and analysing unwritten languages. Sapir's phonology was explicitly 'mentalist' (section 11.3 above), while Bloomfield allied himself with the new behaviourist psychology and began a tradition of linguistic description which, taken at its worst, can be accused of studying linguistic forms without proper regard for meaning.

Sapir's understanding of phonology is set out in two influential papers. The first, on 'Sound Patterns in Language' (1925), promotes the psychological reality of sounds within a linguistic system and contends that there are ways of determining the 'place' of a sound in a system that go beyond the articulatory and acoustic nature of the sound (cf. section 10.7 above). The second paper (1933) is explicitly entitled

'The Psychological Reality of Phonemes' and appeals to evidence from field work on North American Indian languages. Sapir's examples are well worth study and reflection. In one account he describes how a speaker of Sarcee (Alberta, Canada) felt that two words in his own language differed in pronunciation even though he could not substantiate this from the pronunciation itself; Sapir shows how he later came to understand that this was because the two words differed morphophonemically and compares this with the way in which even English speakers who pronounce *soared* and *sawed* identically might still 'feel' a difference between the two words because of their awareness of related forms such as *soaring* and *sawing*. In effect, Sapir is suggesting that we can hear what is not there in the phonetic record, by what he calls 'collective illusion'.

Bloomfield's views, as set out in his major work *Language* (1933, especially ch. 5), have proved more influential than Sapir's but are in some ways contradictory. He professes a materialist concern with 'actual speech' but none the less refers to the distinctiveness of phonemes in ways that would be acceptable to Prague School functionalists (section 11.6 below). Chapter 6 of *Language* is a survey of articulatory processes entitled 'types of phonemes', which risks some confusion between the phoneme as a distinctive unit within a system and the speech-sound as a convenient descriptive device of general phonetics, although he does speak of some sounds as 'variants' and others as 'separate phonemes'; and he concludes the chapter by noting the possibility that the 'same phoneme' may be produced by quite different articulatory mechanisms. Bloomfield's rather programmatic view of phonology and the ways in which it was taken up and elaborated are further discussed in Fischer-Jørgensen (1975) and Anderson (1985, chs 10, 11).

In the 1940s and 1950s followers of Sapir and Bloomfield vigorously debated and applied the principles of phonology. Some of the exchanges – for example about whether phonemes were 'physical' or 'fictitious' or whether one could analyse a language phonologically without knowing any of the grammar – may strike the modern reader as pedantic. Nevertheless, much of our modern terminology, such as 'allophone' and 'complementary distribution', was elaborated in this period, and the American experience of analysing and discussing American Indian languages has proved normative for much comparable work done elsewhere, for example on indigenous languages of Australia and Papua New Guinea.

The continuing interest in developing analytical techniques is reflected in Kenneth Pike's *Phonemics* (1947), significantly subtitled *A technique for reducing languages to writing*. The book remains unusually thoughtful and comprehensive, and has been studied by hundreds of field linguists, many of them missionary linguists working with Wycliffe Bible Translators, an organization which Pike helped to found.

Though it was certainly not Pike's intention to restrict phonology to a matter of analytical technique and orthographic design, questions of transcription have often been dominant in modern phonology, especially in the English-speaking world. Sometimes neatness seems to become an end in itself. A classic North American example, originally proposed by Trager and Bloch in 1941 but later modified, is an analysis of English vowels into six, namely /i e a o ə u/ representing the vowels heard in *pit*, *pet*, *pat*, *pot*, *cut* and *put*. Additional vowels are accounted for by postulating that each vowel may be followed by /j/ /w/ or /h/, so that, for example, *beat* can be represented as /bijt/, *boat* as /bowt/ or /bəwt/ and *law* as /loh/. Thus we have an array of 24 vowels, as shown in table 11.5.1.

Table 11.5.1   Trager and Bloch's vowel transcription system (originally due to Trager and Bloch 1941)

simple vowel	i	e	a	o	ə	u
vowel + j	ij	ej	aj	oj	əj	uj
vowel + w	iw	ew	aw	ow	əw	uw
vowel + h	ih	eh	ah	oh	əh	uh

While there may be a certain appeal in economizing on symbols and making a symmetrical table, it has to be conceded that not all of the possibilities occur in any one variety of English. Trager and Bloch are reduced to noting that /əj/ occurs in a New York City pronunciation of *bird*, but not in General American, that /əh/ occurs in (some varieties of) British English (*burr, furred*), and so on. Thus the transcription becomes a general notational scheme for varieties of English rather than an analysis or description of a phonological system, and its attractiveness rests in the neatness and potential of the notation rather than in systemic validity.

Further details of Trager and Bloch's analysis, which has remained influential in the USA, can be found in Trager and Bloch's 1941 paper (Makkai 1972, pp. 72–89, with notes on pages 4, 72). See also Gleason's adaptation of the system and commentary (1961, pp. 27–39, 320–5).

11.6   The Prague School

By the 1920s, the terms 'phoneme' and 'phonology' were well known to European linguists. More importantly, de Saussure (section 11.3 above) had left a legacy of modern structuralism which greatly influenced linguistics in general. Working within this structuralist tradition were, among others, a group of scholars known from 1926 as the Linguistic Circle of Prague. In phonology, two members of the Circle stand out: Roman Jakobson (1896–1982), who began his career in Moscow but moved to Czechoslovakia and worked there in the 1930s before fleeing via Scandinavia to the USA; and Nikolai Trubetzkoy (1890–1938), also of Russian origin, who was a professor in Vienna from 1923 until his death.

Following de Saussure's emphasis on the differential function of linguistic elements, both Jakobson and Trubetzkoy attached great importance to the OPPOSITIONS among phonemes rather than to the phonemes themselves. Thus to say that English has phonemes /s/ and /z/ is a statement about a distinction which English speakers make and recognize rather than a claim about phonemes as mental images or phonetic entities. This was a significant insight, which seemed to accord with linguistic experience. By the very nature of spoken language, a speaker is aware of differences and reacts to mispronunciation or interference with the system of oppositions ('Was the name *Buss* or *Buzz*?', 'Did you say *sip it* or *zip it*?', and so on). But the isolation of individual phonemes from their spoken context is neither a typical nor an easy task. Most speakers seem incapable of doing it in any systematic way, and, in literate societies, usually resort to naming letters and spelling out a word rather than attempting to articulate separate phonemes.

Jakobson (and others of the Prague School) published actively during the 1920s and 1930s, but it was Trubetzkoy who provided the School's most comprehensive and widely consulted work on phonology, *Grundzüge der Phonologie* (Principles of Phonology), which first appeared in 1939, the year after his death. Besides discussing the nature of distinctive oppositions in theoretical terms, Trubetzkoy also surveys analytical procedures ('rules' for determining the phonemic system of a language) and gives extensive examples of the different oppositions of various languages. He follows through the implications of the structural approach in a number of ways, particularly in the classification of oppositions. For example, some oppositions within a language are 'proportional', i.e. distinguish more than one pair of phonemes, while others are 'isolated', i.e. are restricted to just one pair. In English, for instance, the voicing distinction is proportional (relevant for p/b, t/d, k/g, f/v, etc.) whereas the l/r opposition is isolated (no parallel cases). Trubetzkoy is also responsible for the concepts of 'neutralization' and 'archiphoneme' (section 4.9 above), which are consistent with a functional view of the phoneme. For, if the phoneme is characterized by its opposition to other phonemes, then it follows that the /p/ in words such as *spin* and *spa* (where there is no potential opposition to /b/ in *sbin* or *sba*) is of different functional status from the /p/ in words such as *pin* and *par* (where there *is* opposition to /b/ in *bin* or *bar*).

Jakobson and Trubetzkoy also initiated modern distinctive feature theory. The notion of component features is already implicit in the idea of opposition: /n/ is nasal by opposition to /d/, alveolar by opposition to /m/, and so on. The notion was made explicit by Jakobson's and Trubetzkoy's recognition of such features as 'differential qualities' or 'relevant properties' (section 10.5 above). This further strengthened their point that phonemes represented points in a system rather than physical or mental entities. It was now possible to conceive of the phoneme as a 'bundle' of distinctive features, a simultaneous set of oppositions. (For further details of the Prague School phonologists and their concerns, see Fischer-Jørgensen 1975, ch. 3; Anderson 1985, ch. 4).

11.7   Glossematics and stratificational phonology

Glossematics is much more than an approach to phonology. It is a general theory of language, elaborated by two Danish linguists, Louis Hjelmslev (1899–1965) and Hans Jorgen Uldall (1907–57). Glossematics is neither popular nor widely understood, but has exercised some influence on the development of phonology (which within glossematics is termed 'phonematics'). Hjelmslev's presentation of this theory at the Congress of Phonetic Sciences in London in 1935, which drew approval from Jakobson, affirmed that a phoneme must be defined by means of its function in language, not by physical or psychological criteria. For Hjelmslev, linguistic function included more than distinctive opposition, and he was not averse to classifying and interpreting sounds on the basis of their distribution and alternation. Accordingly, he entertained such possibilities as analysing French /ɛ:/ as /ɛə/ and Danish /ŋ/ as /ng/ (Fischer-Jørgensen 1975, p. 134). His tolerance of a high degree of abstraction is also evident in the positing of a phoneme /h/ in French (Anderson 1985, p. 158): the /h/ is entirely abstract in that it is never pronounced, but it serves to account for lack of elision. Thus words on the left below begin with a vowel (despite their orthographic *h*) and the preceding article *le* is reduced to *l'*; those on the right also begin with a vowel but show no such elision and are therefore credited with an initial /h/ which is unpronounced but blocks the elision:

l'habit ('the clothes')   le havre ('the harbour')
l'harnais ('the armour')   le haricot ('the bean')
l'homme ('the man')   le homard ('the lobster').

Stratificational phonology is, again, part of a wider theory of language. Developed in the USA in the 1960s, it falls within the broad tradition of Saussurean structuralism and shows particular influence from glossematics, notably the emphasis on language as a network of relationships rather than a set of elements. The stratificational view is that language is organized on distinct levels or 'strata', the one of most relevance to phonology being the 'phonemic stratum'. The units of this stratum, phonemes, are represented as points in a network which links each phoneme in three directions. Oversimplifying somewhat, phonemes are

1   realizations of morphemic elements;
2   subject to the phonotactics (i.e. the pattern specifying how phonemes can be sequentially combined);
3   realized as (combinations of) features.

In a full display of relationships, the English phoneme /k/ would therefore be linked to

1   each element which it realizes (the first segment of the morpheme *cat*, the second of *sky*, the first and last of *critic*, and so on);
2   the tactic pattern determining that /k/ can follow initial /s/, can precede /r/, and so on;
3   the various features by which it is realized, i.e. [voiceless], [dorsal], etc.

In fact the network is even more complex than this suggests, for realizations are mediated via alternation patterns. Viewed from the morphemic stratum, the first and last elements of the morpheme *critic* are not identical: the first is always realized as /k/ but the last may be either /k/ (as in *critic*) or /s/ (as in *critic-ism*). Such alternation is handled by saying that the segmental components of morphemes are 'morphons' (not phonemes) and that morphons are realized as phonemes. In English there will be one morphon which is realized only by the phoneme /k/, another which is realized by /k/ and /s/ in alternation with each other.

Elaborations of this kind make stratificational phonology intricate both in its terminology and in its diagrammatic displays (see Lamb's foundational work, 1966a, b). Whether for this reason or because it was overshadowed by the greater popularity of generative phonology in the USA in the 1960s and 1970s, it has relatively few champions today. Nevertheless, stratificational phonology is an impressive outline of a structuralist perspective which incorporates many important concepts such as levels of organization, phonemes and phonetic features. Its bold attempt to formalize the entire network of relationships (including phonotactics and alternations, not just phonemic oppositions and allophonic realizations) is an improvement upon the simpler varieties of North American phonemics, and it deserves better than to be submerged in the shifting of the phonemic concept itself towards a more morphophonemic notion.

Both glossematics and stratificational phonology receive detailed attention in Makkai (1972), under the heading of 'The Copenhagen School and stratificational phonology', and in Fischer-Jørgensen (1975). In addition, glossematic phonology is evaluated in considerable detail by Anderson (1985, ch. 6) and stratificational phonology is reviewed by Sommerstein (1977, ch. 4).

11.8   Prosodic phonology

Like stratificational phonology, prosodic phonology offered thought-provoking insights into phonology but never achieved a wide following. Unlike stratificational phonology, it questions the centrality of the phoneme as a segmental unit.

The founder of prosodic phonology was J. R. Firth (1890–1960), who held a chair at the School of Oriental and African Studies in the University of London from 1944 to 1956. Firth himself wrote only a few papers on phonology but his ideas were developed and applied by pupils and successors, and prosodic phonology is some-times referred to as part of 'Firthian linguistics' or 'the Firth School'.

Firth broke with the English tradition of Sweet and Jones (section 11.4 above) and tried to take English phonology away from its preoccupation with phonetic description and segmental transcription. His starting point was solidly structuralist. He recognized systems as reflections of paradigmatic oppositions (a set of phonemes in opposition to each other is a system) and structures as reflections of syntagmatic relations (a syllable, for example, is a sequential structure). But he disputed the traditional concern with systems (especially phonemes) at the expense of structures. He drew attention to the subphonemic components of speech and to the extent to which such features may spread across successive segments. In this respect he and his followers have something in common with others who, from the 1930s on, were increasingly interested in features as the ultimate elements of phonological description.

The thesis of the prosodic school is that various components of the flow of speech do not lend themselves to analysis into discrete segments. This point has always had force regarding intonation and other such 'suprasegmental' phenomena (chapter 9 above), but the prosodic school extended it to other features such as nasality and lip rounding. A favourite example to demonstrate the point is the pattern of vowel harmony found in languages such as Turkish and Hungarian. In general, vowel harmony means that successive vowels agree in certain features. Under Turkish vowel harmony, a vowel other than the first in a word may be low unrounded or high: other features of these noninitial vowels are simply taken from the first vowel. For example, 'my house' is *evim*, 'my nation' *ulusum*, 'my arm' *kolum* and 'my rose' *gülüm*. In all four examples, the high vowels of noninitial syllables copy their backness and roundedness from the first syllable. All four also end in what is grammatically the same suffix meaning 'my'. Other examples can be found in table 4.7.1 above, where the plural suffix is seen as *-ler* after front vowels and *-lar* after other vowels, and the genitive suffix (like the suffix 'my') has different high vowels agreeing with the backness and roundedness of the preceding vowel. Table 4.7.2 (repeated below as table 11.8.1 for convenience) shows the vowels as two systems, reflecting the way in which the phonemic options are constrained by the operation of harmony. The notion that the vowels constitute two (sub)systems is itself in keeping with Firthian thinking.

Vowel harmony is of course not just a matter of vowel articulation, but of pervasive tongue or lip settings that must affect intervening consonants as well, even if less audibly. Hence a prosodist would argue that the fronting and rounding of the vowels is not located in the vowels but extends throughout the relevant stretch of speech. (Compare remarks on coarticulation in section 4.1 above.) To capture this in the notation, we can extract the pervasive features and show them as 'prosodies' of the word (or other appropriate unit). Notice that this implies that

Table 11.8.1   Turkish vowels

(a) FULL SYSTEM (in first syllable of a root)

	Front		Central/back	
	Unrounded	Rounded	Unrounded	Rounded
High	i	ü	ı	u
Low	e	ö	a	o

(b) SUBSYSTEM (in noninitial syllables, including suffixes)

High	I
Low	A

I is realized as /i/, /y/, /ɨ/ or /u/ according to harmony
A is realized as /e/ or /a/ according to harmony

the vowels themselves do not carry any marking as (non)front or (un)rounded but simply take on these values from the prevailing prosody. Using /V/ for a high vowel (unspecified for frontness or rounding) and superscript /y/ for frontness and /w/ for lip rounding, we might then transcribe *ulusum* as /ʷVlVsVm/ and *gülüm* as /ʷʸgVlVm/. Under such an analysis there is only one other segmental vowel besides /V/ – let us call it /A/. This vowel is low (or nonhigh), again taking its specification as (non)front from the prevailing prosody. Thus the analysis differs sharply from one that recognizes eight vowel phonemes subject to certain constraints on their sequential cooccurrence. Here there are two phoneme-like units and two prosodies. The phoneme-like units are in fact termed PHONEMATIC UNITS within prosodic theory, underlining their difference from the phonemes of, say, North American phonemics or the Prague School.

Prosodies in the Firthian style are not limited to extensive components but also include demarcative phenomena of various kinds, such as the English 'intrusive' /r/ in e.g. *draw(r)ing* or *banana(r)oil*, or the German glottal stop in a word such as *Be[ʔ]amte* ('official'), where the consonantal element may be thought of as a boundary marker between two successive vowels or syllables, rather than as a phoneme of the same status as other consonants. And a further difference from most versions of phonemics is that prosodic phonology is explicitly polysystemic, in the sense that the set of phonematic units need not be considered a single undifferentiated set. In prosodic analysis, the vowels of Turkish are clearly not a single system of eight phonemes (although they do turn out, arguably, to be a single system of two phonematic units). More generally, wherever there are restrictions on the distribution of phonemes within units such as syllables or words, sets of phonemes occurring in specific positions may constitute distinct subsystems. Thus in English the system of consonants standing syllable-initial before /r/, namely

/ p t k b d g f θ ʃ /,

is not the same as the system that applies syllable-initial before /l/, namely

/ p k b g f s /.

Sommerstein gives a helpful outline of prosodic phonology (1977, ch. 3) and Lyons contrasts the prosodic approach with North American phonemics (1962). Both authors explain the relevance of Turkish in further detail and give references to works by Firth and other prosodists.

11.9   Generative phonology

After moving to the USA, Roman Jakobson (section 11.6 above) continued a distinguished career as a linguist, and in the 1950s joined forces with Morris Halle (also in the USA) and Gunnar Fant (working in Sweden) in the development of distinctive feature theory (section 10.5 above). In the 1960s Halle and Chomsky, at the Massachusetts Institute of Technology, elaborated a new approach to phonology which came to be known as generative phonology (chapter 5 above).

Generative phonology belonged to a new school of linguistics, transformational–generative theory. Those who embraced this theory were critical of prevalent interests, particularly in North America, and Chomsky himself accused his 'structuralist' predecessors of undue concern with inventories of elements and a classificatory or 'taxonomic' approach to linguistic analysis. Instead, linguistic description ought to aim to construct a grammar that would 'generate' linguistic forms. The phonological component of such a grammar would be a set of phonological rules applying to the underlying forms of the language and yielding surface phonetic representations. Since both underlying and surface forms were represented in features, the rules essentially changed feature specifications (section 5.3 above), and the shape of a phonological description was indeed radically different from a typical inventory of phonemes and allophones. Moreover, the attention to the formal conventions governing rules and their operation (sections 5.4–5.6 above) went hand in hand with a new interest in what was phonologically possible and what impossible in language. The formalism, often offputting to the newcomer, did bring explicitness to hypotheses about phonological organization and supported a new emphasis on claims about the nature of human language.

Orthodox generative phonology is part of a model of language (more strictly a model of 'linguistic competence') which proposes that underlying representations are converted into surface representations by the application of rules. The model went through several modifications in the 1960s, and one version of it is presented in figure 11.9.1. The model shows phonology as a component 'fed' by a syntactic component that generates grammatical sequences of the language. These grammatical structures – so-called 'surface structures' – are complete with lexical items and reflect the grammatical rules of the language. The lexical items in surface structures bring with them their underlying phonological representations in the form of feature matrices. The surface structures serve as input to the phonological rules, which, responding both to underlying phonological representations and to their syntactic and phonological contexts, generate a phonetic representation.

The model is an idealization in that it portrays the competence of an 'ideal speaker–hearer'. Indeed, generative scholars explicitly contrasted competence and performance, excluding 'performance factors' from consideration (Chomsky and Halle 1968, pp. 1–3). Competence is viewed as knowledge, and the generative model is meant to have psychological import. Thus a grammar (in one sense of the word) is competence represented as rules: the grammar is 'internalized' by speakers, constructed from data in the process of acquisition, that is, and used in linguistic performance (Chomsky 1964, pp. 8–10). Chomsky and Halle specifically propose that phonological representations 'are mentally constructed by the speaker and the hearer and underlie their actual performance in speaking and "understanding"' (Chomsky and Halle 1968, p. 14).

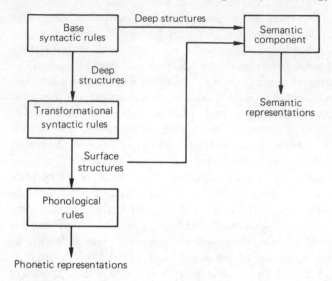

FIGURE 11.9.1   A generative model of grammar

Details of the generative approach have been given in chapter 5 above, and it is sufficient here to note that the abstraction and mentalism of orthodox phonology were contentious. Particularly in the USA, generative phonology was followed by a number of reactive movements. None of these could afford to ignore the pre-eminence which generative linguistics achieved in the 1970s: some of them stressed their disagreement with aspects of the generative orthodoxy, others claimed rather to be modifying or refining the generative model. But whatever their stance, these phonological programs brought fragmentation into the generative tradition, and, in one way or another, undermined the generative thrust against the more traditional concerns with distinctiveness and structure. Several of these postgenerative movements are reviewed in the following sections.

11.10   Natural generative phonology

Natural generative phonology (NGP) emerged from a number of papers by Vennemann in the early 1970s and is most comprehensively expounded by Hooper in a 1976 book (Vennemann 1972, 1974a, b; Hooper 1976). As the title of this 'school' suggests, its proponents do not claim to depart radically from the mainstream of generative phonology. They describe their school as 'based in part on transformational generative theory as developed since the mid-1950s' but point to a major difference concerning the 'abstractness of phonological representations and rules' (Hooper 1976, p. xi).

In fact, NGP is quite radical in its attack on abstractness, though less now than in its earliest formulations. At one stage, Vennemann had proposed to rule out any underlying form that was not identical to a surface form: if a morpheme showed no alternation, then its underlying form must be identical to its surface form; if there was alternation, then the underlying form must be identical to one of the surface allomorphs. Hooper herself assesses this proposal and states that it goes too far (1976, pp. 117 ff.). Consider, for example, pairs of words showing different vowels reduced to [ə], depending on where the stress falls, such as

melody ['mɛlədi]   melodic [mə'lɒdɪk]
heretic ['hɛɹətɪk]   heretical [hə'ɹɛtɪkəl]
demon ['dimən]   demonic [də'mɒnɪk]
telephone ['tɛləfoun]   telephonist [tə'lɛfənɪst].

A strict constraint on abstractness would mean that one of the surface forms would have to be chosen as underlying. But, of each pair of forms given above, neither seems genuinely underlying in the context of a generative description: if the term 'underlying form' has any value at all, the root should not contain any occurrence of [ə], as this vowel is derived by reduction from other vowels.

Hooper's solution is to abandon abstract underlying forms altogether – although she does revive the concept of archiphonemic representation of the kind entertained by Trubetzkoy and the Prague School phonologists (sections 4.9 and 11.6 above). Rules are now to be regarded as generalizations across surface forms rather than as the means of *generating* surface forms. Hence Hooper is able to say that within NGP, rules and representations are directly related to surface forms and that phonological analysis is more concrete and more realistic than in SPE (Hooper 1976, pp. xi–xii, 1–11, 119ff.; 1979, pp. 106–7). As she puts it: 'The major claim of natural generative phonology is that speakers construct only generalizations that are surface-true and transparent . . . An important property of surface-true generalizations is that they are all falsifiable in a way that the more abstract generalizations of generative phonology are not' (1979, p. 106). The formal apparatus of NGP offers no prospect of highly abstract underlying forms, undercutting much of the discussion engendered by SPE about the ordering and interaction of rules. In a sense, NGP directs phonology back towards the more concrete concerns of phonemics. This point is underlined by Hooper's recognition of a distinction among rules that virtually revives the traditional categorization into phonetic (allophonic) and morphophonemic rules. Hooper distinguishes between rules that refer only to phonetic information and reflect the 'automatic' pronunciation habits of a speaker (which she terms P-rules), and rules that refer to grammatical or lexical contexts and often do admit exceptions (MP-rules) (Hooper 1976, p. 15; 1979, pp. 107–8). A comparable distinction is made by many of those who have reacted against orthodox generative phonology and will emerge again in different guises below.

11.11   Natural phonology

Though similar in name to natural generative phonology, natural phonology represents a more dramatic departure from the mainstream of generative phonology. It has its origins in David Stampe's dissertation on natural phonology (submitted to the University of Chicago in 1973 and published in 1979). Stampe begins his dissertation in the context of children's acquisition of phonology and draws attention to what he calls 'phonological processes'. A phonological process is 'a mental operation that applies in speech to substitute, for a class of sounds or sound sequences presenting a specific common difficulty to the speech capacity of the individual, an alternative class identical but lacking the difficult property' (1979, p. 1). These processes are not rules of the language, acquired as the child masters language, but reflections of what we might call the child's inbuilt tendencies. Thus, by the very nature of the human articulatory and perceptual organism, a child will prefer to articulate plosives as voiceless rather than voiced (because of the relative difficulty of maintaining voicing while the supraglottal tract is closed off) or will prefer to nasalize vowels next to nasal consonants (again for reasons of articulatory ease). Processes are revealed in the consequent substitutions which children make in the early stages of acquisition – for example, when they neutralize the voicing distinction of English by substituting voiceless plosives for voiced.

The application of phonological processes is not as straightforward as simple examples might suggest. Not only are there many such processes, but some of them are contrary to others. For example, a process of vowel denasalization reflects the goals of articulatory ease and auditory distinctness in vowel production; but this is to some extent countered by the process of nasalizing vowels next to nasal consonants (Stampe 1979, pp. 17–23). In early stages of language acquisition, the unconstrained operation of natural processes will tend to reduce every potential utterance to something like a monosyllabic [pa] (Stampe 1979, pp. xvii, 2). As the child comes closer to an adult competence, processes will be suppressed or limited in response to the demands of the phonological system. Hence, if acquiring a language in which nasalized vowels are distinctive, a child will have to suppress the relevant natural processes and thus achieve control of vowel nasalization; but in a language in which vowel nasalization is not distinctive, the natural process of nasalizing vowels next to nasal consonants may persist as an 'allophonic rule' of adult speech (Stampe 1979, pp. 27–8).

Stampe appears to turn generative phonology on its head. What we thought of as rules constituting a phonological system are now seen as processes motivated by the nature of production and perception. Phonological acquisition is a matter of suppressing or constraining innate tendencies rather than of learning rules. Stampe does leave room for phonological rules, however. These are indeed acquired, but they differ sharply from processes. The English alternation of /g/ and /dʒ/ (as in, for example, *analogous* with [g] but *analogy* with [dʒ]) is governed by an acquired rule. Unlike a natural process, such a rule is open to exceptions and easily suspended:

many speakers fail to apply the rule consistently and pronounce *analogous* with [dʒ] or *pedagogy* with [g], for example, and even those who follow the rule could easily produce the 'wrong' pronunciations if they wished. By contrast, the phonetic consequences of natural processes, such as aspiration of voiceless plosives and lengthening of vowels before voiced obstruents, are much harder for native speakers to discern and overcome (Stampe 1979, pp. 45–7).

Among the various North American 'schools' of phonology which represent reactions to orthodox generative phonology, natural phonology is the least inclined to proclaim its faithfulness to generative principles. In their useful outline of natural phonology, Donegan and Stampe (1979) appeal to phonological traditions that are much older than SPE: 'Natural phonology is a modern development of the oldest explanatory theory of phonology . . . Its basic thesis is that the living sound patterns of languages, in their development in each individual as well as in their evolution over the centuries, are governed by forces implicit in human vocalization and perception' (1979, p. 126).

Donegan and Stampe claim that their theory is natural because it seeks to explain why language is the way it is. The theory offers genuine explanation by presenting language not as merely conventional but as a 'natural reflection' of the needs, capacities, and world of its users' (Donegan and Stampe 1979, p. 127). Donegan and Stampe are critical of positivism, which gives priority to exhaustive scientific description (p. 127; cf. section 11.1 above). They reject (underlying) morphophonemic representation in favour of a more traditional phonemic representation (which, following Sapir, they interpret as reflecting the phonological intention of speech; pp. 158ff. and especially 163–7). And they conclude that although both structuralist and generative phonology have a well-developed methodology, neither of them is a theory in the true sense, since neither is genuinely open to falsification by data (pp. 167–8).

11.12   Autosegmental and CV phonology

The phrase 'autosegmental phonology' is the title of Goldsmith's dissertation submitted to the Massachusetts Institute of Technology in 1976 and published in the same year. Goldsmith's initial concern is with what may seem to be a limited and particular problem, that of segmental organization, or more particularly, that of phenomena which have 'evaded segmental classification' (Goldsmith 1976, p. 6). The longest chapter in the thesis is devoted to the 'tonology' of Igbo, a west African tonal language, and Goldsmith includes substantial attention both to other tonal languages and to stress and intonation in English.

Goldsmith's work nevertheless goes beyond tone and intonation, and the implications of his thesis have been increasingly extended and elaborated. His thesis announces a claim about the 'geometry' of phonetic representations (p. 6) in the context of what he calls 'the absolute slicing hypothesis' (the hypothesis that speech can be phonologically represented as successive discrete segments, pp. 16–17). His fundamental point is that speech, observed as articulatory activity, consists of gestures – such as tongue movement, lip movement and laryngeal activity – which are coordinated, but which by no means start and finish all at the same instant. The point is a familiar one in modern phonetics (sections 4.1 and 7.17 above) and Goldsmith's reiteration of it leads him to what he calls a 'multilinear phonological analysis in which different features may be placed on separate tiers' (1979 p. 202). The tiers are connected to each other by 'association lines', which allow for the fact that there may not always be a neat one-to-one mapping between tiers. Thus an autosegmental notation can show tonal features on a different tier, represented below segmental features, e.g.

Disyllabic word with high tone on each syllable: baka

$$\begin{matrix} | & | \\ H & H \end{matrix}$$

Disyllabic word with high tone then low tone: baka

$$\begin{matrix} | & | \\ H & L \end{matrix}$$

The vertical lines are the normal association lines mapping tones on to syllables. In many tonal languages, however, a high tone becomes, by anticipatory assimilation, a falling tone when followed by a low tone. If so, this can be shown as the consequence of both the high tone and the low being mapped on to a single syllable:

baka

$$\begin{matrix} \diagdown\!\!\!| \\ H\ L \end{matrix}$$

This provides a flexible way of associating tones with segmental features, such that tones are not, as it were, swallowed up within a strictly segmental notation (cf. section 9.4 above).

The approach can be extended to other features. Nasality, for instance, may also be represented on a separate tier, allowing for similar spreading across segmental boundaries. Where a consonant is prenasalized and the preceding vowel nasalized, we may represent

[dāmba] as   d a b a

$$\diagdown\!\!\!| $$

N

Goldsmith himself remarks that the system of analysis itself was 'originally suited to fit the intricacies of African tone languages' (1979, p. 212), but various papers developing the autosegmental perspective (Goldsmith 1979, 1985; Clements 1977, 1981, 1984, 1985) show how similar notation can be applied to other phenomena, especially vowel harmony, where the spread of vowel features across segmental boundaries can be treated analogously to the examples of tone and nasality shown above.

If separate tiers are indeed a reflection of the parallel articulatory activities of speech, then we may expect features to be generally autosegmental – independent of each other, that is – in the early stages of a child's phonological acquisition. In acquiring their mother tongue, children must 'deautosegmentalize' (Goldsmith 1976, pp. 160ff.; 1979, pp. 214ff.). In other words, it is necessary for a child to learn the appropriate language-specific restructuring of the phonetics into segments (1979, p. 214) or to learn 'which sets of feature-specifications on separate tiers may be merged together to form an acceptable segment in that language' (1976, p. 164).

The notion of tiers is reminiscent of Firthian prosodic phonology (section 11.8 above), and Kenstowicz – who gives a useful general assessment of autosegmental phonology – comments on the way in which generative phonology is 'recapitulating in part some of the insights of the Firthian School' (1994, p. 311). Lass (1984, p. 269) doubts whether autosegmental phonology, 'despite its formal sophistication', is 'much more than a notational variant of prosodic analysis'. Goldsmith certainly acknowledges an affinity and seems to take Firth to be an ally against American phonologists who have too rigidly adhered to segmental discreteness (1979, pp. 203–4). He argues nevertheless that Firthian prosodies are a more limited set than the features of an autosegmental analysis, and places autosegmental phonology within the generative tradition of formalism, maintaining a discourse of 'rules' and 'well-formedness conditions', even though his theme is (auto)segmental organization rather than feature-changing processes.

The concept of tiers is also found in CV phonology, which arose from work by Kahn on syllabic organization and by McCarthy on Semitic languages (McCarthy 1981; Kahn 1980; Clements and Keyser 1983; Kenstowicz 1994, ch. 8). The original contribution of CV phonology is the postulation of a CV tier, a tier of C and V 'slots' which are filled by segments. Often segments (or the set of features represented by a segment) can be mapped straightforwardly on to these CV positions. Charting the relationships in similar fashion to autosegmental notation, we might represent English *map* and *landed* as

But, just as autosegmental phonology allows other kinds of mapping, so CV phonology offers the possibility of capturing the special nature of complex segments that traditionally require structural interpretation (section 3.14 above). Thus a diphthong

can be shown as two vowel qualities functioning as, or filling the position of, a single vowel; or a lengthened or geminate consonant can be represented as a single segment spreading over two C positions:

$$
\begin{array}{ccc}
\text{V} & & \text{C} \quad \text{C} \\
\diagdown & = [ai] & \diagdown\diagup \quad = [t{:}] \\
a \quad i & & t
\end{array}
$$

In keeping with their generative antecedents, both autosegmental and CV phonology incorporate derivational processes into their phonological modelling. Thus phenomena such as lengthening of underlying short segments and secondary articulations derived from underlying adjacent segments are captured by reallocation of association lines. In Luganda, for instance, some nouns take the prefix /mu-/ in the singular and /ba-/ in the plural (Goldsmith 1989, ch. 2, based on work by Clements). Examples are

mukazi ('woman')   bakazi ('women')
mulimi ('cultivator')   balimi ('cultivators')

But in some forms we find a slightly different pattern:

mweezi ('sweeper')   beezi ('sweepers')
mwaana ('child')   baana ('children').

Here the prefixes appear as /mw-/ and /b-/, and the vowel following the prefix is always long. These forms can be derived from 'regular' underlying forms. For 'sweeper(s)', the underlying forms are

As sequences of vowels like /ue/ and /ae/ are not tolerated in Luganda, rules of the language dissociate the first vowel and associate the second to the vacated V slot:

If the dissociated vowel is high, it can combine with the preceding consonant as secondary labialization; otherwise, if it remains dissociated, it will not be realized

phonetically. And in either case, the following vowel, having now been associated to two V positions, will be realized as a long vowel.

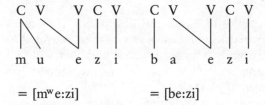

$$= [m^w e{:}zi] \qquad\qquad = [be{:}zi]$$

The CV tier, also referred to as the 'skeletal' tier or 'timing' tier, now forms part of what Clements and Keyser call 'a universal theory of the syllable' (Clements and Keyser 1983, p. 25; cf. section 11.13 below). The tier not only defines the timing of segmental organization (by, for example, determining that a vowel occupies two V slots) but also takes over the role of the feature [syllabic] (Clements and Keyser 1983, pp. 10–11): syllabic organization is shown by a tree structure dominating the CV tier.

For instance, /mweezi/ might be represented as two syllables as follows

where the C and V units constituting a syllable are dominated by a single node. This model allows for interesting and useful possibilities, such as assigning a consonant to two successive syllables, as in English *penny*, where it is phonologically appropriate to take the /n/ to be both final in the first syllable and initial in the second syllable:

The model has affinities with metrical phonology, to which we turn in the following section, and Goldsmith (1989) suggests that the convergence of autosegmental, CV and metrical phonology is yielding 'a new synthesis'.

11.13   Metrical phonology

Yet again, metrical phonology has its origins in a doctoral dissertation (Liberman 1979). Just as autosegmental phonology began with tone and was then extended to other phenomena, metrical phonology began as a theory of stress and later widened its horizons. As noted by van der Hulst and Smith (1982b, p. 30), metrical theory has now 'invaded' the territory of autosegmental phonology.

The starting point of metrical phonology is an assumption about the nature of stress and its representation, namely that stress patterns reflect an underlying structure in which stronger and weaker constituents are juxtaposed. To say that a certain syllable is stressed is to make a judgment about its strength relative to adjacent syllables (cf. sections 9.3 and 9.6 above). Using the kind of tree structure noted in the preceding section, we can display the stress patterns of disyllabic words as either

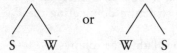

where S and W simply indicate stronger and weaker constituents. Much of metrical theory is then devoted to explaining how more complex patterns are derived from these basic patterns within certain postulated constraints. It is assumed, in some versions of metrical theory, that the relationship between S and W is binary, so that polysyllabic patterns entail subsidiary branching, e.g.

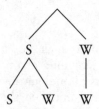

and not

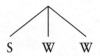

Attempts to draw up procedures for the assignment of English stress under such a model (usefully surveyed by van der Hulst and Smith, 1982b, pp. 30ff.) confronted various criteria. These were related both to the formal nature of the process (whether stress assignment proceeds from right to left throughout all words, and how subsidiary branching is organized, for instance) and to the properties of a word which may be said to affect stress assignment (such as morphological structure, syllabic structure and the presence of specific segments such as 'tense' vowels). This discussion was part of a revival of interest in the concepts of feet and syllables, an interest evident also within autosegmental and CV phonology (section 11.12 above). In the new formalism, the foot, traditionally recognized in English poetry and used also by writers such as Halliday (sections 9.3 and 9.6 above), could also be identified as a tree structure. Thus the word 'catastrophic' has two feet revealed as

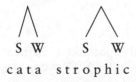

S W   S W

c a t a   s t r o p h i c

By the mid-1980s, the syllable – having been totally ignored within standard generative phonology – was attracting considerable attention in North America. It was argued that the syllable was a significant unit which must be recognized within phonological theory, and, in keeping with the spirit of generative phonology, efforts were made to formalize the structure of the syllable. Using fairly traditional terms (reminiscent of those used in Chinese linguistics; section 11.2 above), we can take a syllable to consist of a RHYME preceded (usually) by an ONSET. The rhyme may in turn consist of a PEAK or NUCLEUS, sometimes followed by a CODA. Interestingly, this structure can be handled by the general formula originally proposed for stress patterns. Compare the two patterns below:

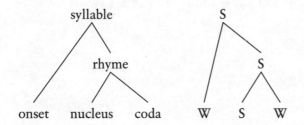

Metrical phonology offers an alternative way of expressing such structures, in the form of a so-called METRICAL GRID. Suppose we take a tree of the sort shown above, and convert it into a grid by making entries at levels corresponding to the levels of the tree. The tree on the left below reflects the stress pattern of the word *Parramatta*, with greatest stress on the third syllable, and minimal stress on the second and fourth syllables. The tree can be mapped on to a grid, as shown on the right, in which the x-entries correspond to nodes on the tree: the grid thus provides an alternative visual display, with the greatest degree of stress represented by the column having the greatest number of entries.

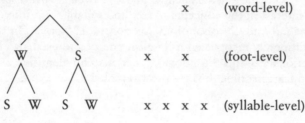

Parra matta

The illustration here is of the simplest possible kind. A detailed exposition of metrical theory, in coursebook style, can be found in Hogg and McCully (1987). Van der Hulst and Smith (1982b) offer a thorough evaluation and comment on the 'competition' caused by the expansion of both autosegmental and metrical theory to include the linear organization of speech in general (1982b, pp. 42–5). They refer to a number of possibilities – including Halle and Vergnaud's suggestion (1981) that there are two kinds of harmony, 'metrical' and 'autosegmental' – but they admit they are unable to offer a unified theory. Anderson et al. (1985, p. 203) are slightly more optimistic that the various models of suprasegmental representation, including autosegmental and metrical phonology, are less different than appears at first sight and that a single model may 'perhaps be developed from the various frameworks'. And Goldsmith, in a detailed assessment of the different schools (1989), takes a highly positive view of a new integrated perspective. Kenstowicz (1994) also sets recent work on syllabic organization and stress in its wider context: chapter 6 of his book is a survey of the major results of generative research on the syllable, and chapter 10 discusses the phenomenon of stress and a series of analyses inspired by metrical theory.

11.14   Lexical phonology

Among all the attempts to modify and extend orthodox generative phonology in North America, lexical phonology reflects most clearly the concerns of pregenerative phonemics. Originally developed by Strauss, Kiparsky and Mohanan, it shows a revived interest in morphology and asserts a level of representation which is comparable to that of taxonomic phonemics (Strauss 1982, Kiparsky 1985, Mohanan 1985, 1987; Goldsmith 1989, ch. 5).

In a useful overview, Kaisse and Shaw (1985) point out that despite the willingness to recognize value in traditional phonemics, lexical phonology is not as concrete as, say, natural generative phonology or natural phonology (sections 11.10 and 11.11 above). Lexical phonology does allow for abstract underlying forms and in that light is 'a standard generative phonology' (Kaisse and Shaw 1985, p. 3). What the title of the school reflects is a distinction between 'lexical' and 'postlexical' components of description. Lexical rules are fed by the morphology (itself a subject of considerable debate in the postgenerative era): the morphological component supplies the various affixed and compounded forms of the language, and lexical rules then apply, to modify these forms in accordance with the phonological requirements of the language. In English, a lexical rule might ensure that the final consonant of stems such as *logic, critic* and *electric* is 'softened' to /s/ before the suffixes *-ism* and *-ity*; or another lexical rule might apply to the suffix *-ed* to devoice the /d/ in forms like *tapped* and *licked*, in conformity with the patterning of English consonant clusters. At this stage of derivation, only distinctive features are relevant (in the classic sense of 'distinctive'), and lexical representations and lexical rules make no reference to redundant or 'allophonic' features (such as, in English, the voicing of nasal consonants or the aspiration of voiceless plosives). The postlexical rules, applying to the output of lexical rules, include those that apply to larger domains than words – rules, for instance, that need to refer to phrasal structure or that apply across word boundaries. In English, the assimilation of /s/ and /z/ to /ʃ/ and /ʒ/ before /j/ must be postlexical, since it applies not only within words (as in *tension* and *usual*) but also across word boundaries (as in *I miss you* or *as you wish*). Rules of the postlexical component also fill in the redundant features that have been unspecified in the lexical component.

It is noteworthy that lexical rules are by and large 'morphophonemic' in traditional terms, including the rules familiar from SPE which apply to tense and lax vowels (*sane, sanity,* etc.). Postlexical rules are similar to Stampe's natural processes (section 11.11 above) or the allophonic processes of traditional phonemics (section 4.3 above). Thus postlexical rules do not tolerate exceptions, can apply across word boundaries and may yield phonetic values such as 'heavily aspirated' or 'partially devoiced'. The consequence is that the output of lexical rules – termed 'lexical representation' – is in some respects quite similar to a traditional phonemic transcription. It is recognized by lexical phonologists as a significant level within phonology, one which is likely to be real to native speakers in the sense that, for example, they are conscious of the different vowels in *sane* and *sanity* determined by lexical rules, but unaware of the extent to which they voice the plosive or nasalize the vowels in *sanity* (Kaisse and Shaw 1985, pp. 4–8).

It is tempting but unfair merely to dismiss lexical phonology as the generativists' rediscovery of phonemics. Lexical phonology is clearly generative in its style of theoretical modelling and its commitment to rule-based description (including even the principle of cyclic rule application; section 5.6 above). Early proponents of generative phonology who made a point of being scornful of taxonomic phonemics might have some cause to be embarrassed but there have always been those within generative phonology who remained open to phonemic insights (for example Schane 1971 and Hyman 1975). Moreover, lexical phonology continues to grapple with the problems of describing English morphology and morphophonemics. These problems are real, given the extent of morphophonemic alternation in English and the difficulty of determining what is truly patterned or rule-governed (by genuine processes such as assimilation) and what is odd irregularity (such as the forms of 'to be').

Volume 2 of the *Phonology Yearbook* (1985) contains, in addition to Kaisse and Shaw's overview, a number of papers devoted to lexical phonology, including contributions by Kiparsky and Mohanan themselves. Goldsmith (1989) also includes a chapter on lexical phonology which again holds out some promise of a synthesis of postgenerative trends in phonology. Kenstowicz (1994, ch. 5) provides a thorough outline of lexical phonology, concluding with a detailed review of some of the 'unresolved problems' that confront this model (pp. 227 ff.).

11.15   Dependency phonology

Dependency phonology (Anderson et al. 1985, Anderson and Ewen 1987) shares much of the modern interest in structures such as feet and syllables and in the organization of features below the level of the segment. We have already noted the way in which features are treated in dependency phonology (section 10.11 above) and we review here the wider concept of dependency that underlies this work.

It is possible to model the structural organization of speech in a way that is reminiscent of metrical tree structures (section 11.13 above) but different in important respects. A monosyllabic word like English *print* might be displayed as follows:

p r ɪ n t

As in other kinds of tree diagram, the single node at the top can be said to dominate the structure, defining the unit – here a syllable in which the vowel serves as head or nucleus. But in dependency phonology there are no category symbols (such as the S and W used in metrical models), and structural relations are shown by 'dependency' alone, reflected in the tree diagram. Thus the vowel in our example is most prominent, and the consonants are subordinate or dependent. But dependency extends further than this, for the diagram shows the vowel both as head of the syllable and as head of the rhyme /ɪnt/. Moreover, /r/ is shown to be head of the initial consonant cluster, and /n/ head of the final cluster; conversely /p/ is dependent on /r/, /t/ on /n/ and both clusters are dependent on the nuclear vowel.

Anderson and Ewen (1987, pp. 96ff.) use this kind of notation for much larger structures. One of their examples is given in figure 11.15.1, where the structural levels reflected in the diagram are labelled on the right. The utterance 'run to Daddy' is shown to be a single tone group, two feet, and four syllables. The diagram models prominence relations in direct fashion, incorporating points that are now standard in

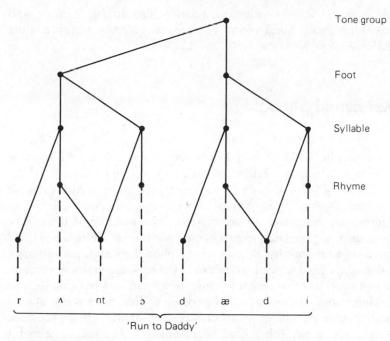

FIGURE 11.15.1   Dependency structure of an English utterance *Run to Daddy*
Adapted from: Anderson and Ewen 1987, p. 101

modern phonology, such as the recognition that a consonant can belong to two
syllables (as the second /d/ in 'Daddy' does).

We saw earlier (section 10.11) that features or components can also
'preponderate' in dependency phonology. Where a language distinguishes /e/ from
/ɛ/, the higher vowel may be represented with frontness preponderant over lowness,
as {|i⇉a|}, the lower with lowness preponderant over frontness, as {|a⇉i|}. But
Anderson and Ewen (1987, pp. 127ff.) point out that this relationship of preponderance can also be portrayed in a similar way to prominence relations within linear
structure. Hence |i| dominating |a| can be shown as

A diphthong such as [ai] can be shown with the first target predominant:

As Anderson and Ewen put it, preponderance relationships among features, and prominence relationships among linear elements are parallel: 'preponderance is the intrasegmental analogue of prominence' (1987, p. 128).

11.16   Experimental phonology

While many phonologists in the 1970s and 1980s may seem to have been reacting to generative phonology – Anderson refers to 'a variety of knights-errant' (1979, p. 2) – some maintained or developed quite different perspectives. A striking example is the emergence of what is generally known as 'experimental phonology'.

Experimental phonology represents an attempt to draw together at least three research styles: experimental phonetics, experimental psychology and phonological theory. The intention is to submit hypotheses about phonological organization to testing and validation of the kind which is standard in the experimental sciences, and which has been taken over, to some extent at least, by researchers in fields such as psychology, psycholinguistics and instrumental phonetics. This move is not always free of the implication that phonology is speculative and that evidence obtained experimentally is superior to any other kind of evidence. Thus Ohala begins his 'Consumer's guide to evidence in phonology' with the words: 'For the past 30 years phonologists have speculated on how sound patterns in language are represented in the human mind (Chomsky and Halle 1968: viii). The claims made, of course, are only as good as the evidence they are based on' (Ohala 1986, p. 3). In a sense, then, experimental phonology is after all a reaction against generative phonology, or if not a direct reaction, then a reassertion of pregenerative interests. Ohala stresses the importance of evidence in evaluating theories and appeals to the example of physics, in which, he argues, evidence has enabled modern physicists to discard inadequate theories (such as the Ancient Greek hypothesis that all matter consists of only four elements; Ohala 1986, p. 5). In fact, he maintains that 'physics, chemistry and biology first became mature disciplines (with an accompanying marked increase in the rate of successful applications of their theories) when they started relying on and insisting on experimental evidence for claims' (p. 11). Similarly, Ohala and Jaeger express the hope that phonology is developing into 'an experimental discipline' (1986, p. 1) and again refer to the importance of the experimental method as it has been defined in modern Western science (pp. 1–6).

Proponents of experimental phonology take a rather generous view of what constitutes an experiment, and emphasize observation and careful refinement of one's beliefs rather than reliance on instrumental investigation or statistical processing of results (Ohala 1986, p. 10; Ohala and Jaeger 1986, pp. 2–3). The two collections of papers referred to here, for example, give some prominence to word games (Ohala 1986, pp. 9–10, Campbell 1986, Hombert 1986). Both Campbell and Hombert suggest that evidence from word games provides a test of the 'psychological reality' of phonological rules and structures. Hombert describes a word game in Bakwiri, a

Bantu language which has no consonant clusters other than sequences of nasal followed by homorganic voiced stop. The word game involves reversing the two syllables of two-syllable words, so that e.g. [moko] would become [komo] and [lowa] would become [walo]. Now words such as [komba] and [kondi] are reversed as [mbako] and [ndiko], suggesting that the syllabic structure is [ko.mba] and [ko.ndi] rather than [kom.ba] and [kon.di]. Evidence of this kind has long been used in phonology (as noted by Hombert himself) and can hardly be described as experimental, unless the analysis extends to inventing word games and asking speakers to perform new operations on words (Hombert 1986, pp. 175–6 and 180ff.)

Other investigations reported in Ohala and Jaeger (1986) include instrumental studies of articulation and perception, such as Pinkerton's measurements of intra-oral air pressure in the production of various kinds of glottalized stop in the Quichean languages of central America, and Kawasaki's study of the degree of vowel nasalization perceived in subjects listening to controlled stimuli. These studies continue the kind of work already being carried out by phoneticians and psycholinguists – and demonstrate very clearly the need to test impressionistic judgments of speech. What is new about such work is not so much its nature but its location in a setting of explicitly phonological questions. In Ohala and Jaeger's own words (1986, p. xi), it is the intersection of traditional phonological questions and experimental means that gives their book a claim to noteworthiness. Many of the contributors can be said to share this perspective: Lindblom (1986, p. 13) puts his modelling of the vowel space and distance among vowels (sections 2.7 and 7.15 above) in the setting of what he calls a 'functional perspective', namely that 'language form is forged by the sociobiological conditions of its use'; while Nearey and Hogan (1986, p. 141) begin their experimental study of categorical perception with a firm assertion that experimental phonetics is 'inextricably linked with phonology' (cf. section 8.5 above).

It is refreshing that phonetics and phonology are meeting each other in this way – that experimental phoneticians are aware of the theoretical assumptions and implications of their work, and that phonologists are aware of empirical methods and the need for evidence. Some caution is warranted, however, and the importance of experimental methodology in modern science should not delude us into thinking that knowledge gained through experiments is absolute. Ohala and Jaeger themselves go some way towards this recognition: 'The primary purpose of experimentation is not to create knowledge . . . It is, rather, a way of refining our knowledge. Following Popper (1959), one might even say that in a sense experiments actually destroy knowledge; at least they help to show which of our beliefs about the workings of the world do not agree with observation and hence should be discarded' (1986, p. 2). If taken seriously – as it should be – this view of scientific method as a procedure of disproving false hypotheses rather than proving true ones means that experiments never yield certainty (cf. section 11.1 above). Equally seriously, an experiment is limited by its very conditions. An experiment in which subjects are asked, for example, to listen to artificial stimuli and record or report what they hear, tests precisely what it purports to test, namely the hearing of particular stimuli under particular conditions. It does not test the subjects' perception of the utterances of daily discourse under normal conditions. Now of course if an experiment is well designed it should be possible to make useful inferences from it about normal speaking and hearing. But we should be wary of describing such inferences as 'solid evidence' or 'proof'. Taking relevant examples, we might note that word games do not necessarily reveal more than the rules of the games: it *may* be that the organization of segments and syllables which is exploited in word games is in fact not the organization that is relevant in the actual production of speech. We have referred earlier, for instance, to the observation that speakers of English may regard the vowel complex in *few* both as a diphthong and as a sequence of consonantal /j/ followed by vocalic /u/, depending on which perspective they adopt (section 3.14 above). There is no principled reason why speakers should use the same perspective in word games as in all other aspects of their language use. Likewise, when experimental subjects are tested on their ability to classify sounds according to their auditory similarity, we may reasonably assume that the subjects are drawing on their experience of speaking and hearing under normal conditions and that the experimental results therefore convey something about normal phonological knowledge. But this is not quite the same as saying that experimental results conclusively demonstrate the categories and operations of everyday usage. Nevertheless, subject to such reservations, experimental phonology reflects a proper scepticism about speculative pronouncements and a commendable interest in integrating empirical investigation with phonological analysis and theory.

11.17   Conclusion

Readers may well ponder the ancient wisdom that 'there is no new thing under the sun' but that 'of making many books there is no end'. Certainly some of the controversies of modern phonology seem to lead in circles, and the recent habit of labelling new trends and emphases as 'schools' exaggerates the impression of proliferation and underplays both the persistence of fundamental issues and the reemergence of old themes in new dress. Nevertheless, tempting as it is for textbook writers to consolidate and simplify, the truth is that there are genuine differences of theoretical perspective, in phonology as in any field of scholarship.

Seen in this light, the custom of quoting one's antecedents – if done adequately and seriously – is not only a useful indication of historical background but also a declaration of one's place among competing theories. For example, Chomsky appeals to Descartes and seventeenth-century rationalism, Donegan and Stampe to Plato and natural explanation, and Ohala and Jaeger to Popper and the development of modern science (Chomsky 1966, Donegan and Stampe 1979, Ohala and Jaeger 1986). We cannot simply reconcile these different appeals in an all-embracing review, but should welcome the acknowledgement that theory does matter and cannot be ignored without distorting the nature of research and scholarship.

We have already declared our own preference for a view of phonology which, we believe, draws on a long and healthy tradition of thinking in terms of functions, systems and structures (section 11.1 above). We suggest that those whom we might call the earliest phonologists (section 11.2), even if they did not always expound their theoretical framework, recognized that pronunciation was systematic, that choices ('contrasts' or 'oppositions') mattered, and that phonological choices were finite and constrained (within systems and structures). The contribution of many of the classic figures of twentieth-century phonology has been to develop and refine such insights within a functional perspective. Once de Saussure had explored the concept of language as system, the way was open for elaboration of phonological description within a broadly structuralist tradition, and scholars such as Trubetzkoy, Jakobson, Hjelmslev, Pike, Firth and Lamb (sections 11.5–11.8) – all with their own emphases – explored phonological analysis as a means of revealing the organization of language as it is spoken and heard. While this tradition was somewhat overshadowed in the 1960s and 1970s by generative phonology and its aftermath (sections 11.9–11.14), it has remained strong, often forming the backdrop to work that was thought to be outside phonology itself, such as experimental phonetics, psycholinguistics and speech pathology, and often assumed rather than defended in detail by writers whose focus of attention was not phonology itself. The work in 'functional' or 'systemic' linguistics led by Halliday in the 1970s and 1980s, for example, falls within this tradition: Halliday himself argues for a (social-) functional approach to language in general, and specifically appeals to the general perspective adopted by Hjelmslev, the Prague School and Firth (Halliday 1978, esp. pp. 21, 39).

Advocacy for the generative view of phonology that emerged in the 1960s is increasingly rare. Even one who is prepared to defend the orthodox 'revised standard theory' begins by raising the question of whether he has a position to defend (Anderson 1979, p. 2). Nevertheless, many phonologists still consider themselves to stand in the generative tradition – including some of those contributing to experimental phonology (section 11.16 above) – but few if any of them accept the classic generative phonology proclaimed in *The sound pattern of English*. Kenstowicz (1994) is a remarkably detailed and comprehensive survey of how generative phonology has developed, and it demonstrates not only that generative phonology can be seen as an evolving theoretical enterprise but also that the evolution has been substantial. If Goldsmith (1989) is right, recent trends in autosegmental, CV, metrical and lexical phonology (sections 11.12–11.14 above) are converging towards a new generative model. This model will be radically different from SPE in a number of respects, but perhaps most fundamentally in its concern with structures such as syllables and feet, and in the shift of focus away from complex derivational processes (applying to relatively abstract underlying forms) towards sophisticated representational models (especially multitiered and hierarchically organized structures). Anderson et al. (1985, p. 203) are also cautiously optimistic about a new synthesis along these lines; and Basbøll's overview of phonological theory, without covering up the impression of postgenerative fragmentation, does also speak of a 'positive evolution away from the danger of extreme fragmentation' (1988, p. 211).

Of course the prospect of genuinely blending all currents in phonology – particularly structural–functional approaches with (post)generative approaches – is unrealistic. More is at issue than just notation and terminology, and as long as some of those who work in the generative tradition are still prepared, for example, to see linguistics as cognitive psychology (e.g. McCawley 1986, pp. 37–8) or to assume a model of ordered rules within various components of a grammar (e.g. Shattuck-Hufnagel 1986, pp. 145–6), there will remain fundamental differences of theoretical commitment.

There is no room here for an eclecticism which claims to take the best from each approach: the idea that one can pick a few choice fruits while ignoring the trees tends to superficiality rather than omniscience. Neither the investigation of phonetic and phonological questions themselves nor the application of phonetic and phonological insights to fields such as speech pathology and language teaching can profit from the illusion that there are facts and truths independent of their derivation and expression. Thus if there is scientific maturity in modern phonology (Ohala 1986, pp. 3–5), it is not because there is an agreed unified theory or even a consensus about theoretical issues, and certainly not because there is some body of facts accepted once and for all, but rather because scholars are willing to discuss and explore their theoretical assumptions. The nature of speaking and hearing will continue to be a proper subject of human curiosity, and phonetics and phonology will continue to be relevant wherever speech and hearing need to be explored and understood. What makes phonetics and phonology exciting – perhaps no more than other fields of specialized enquiry, but decidedly no less either – is that we cannot separate the exploration of what lies behind the everyday and the obvious from the confrontation with questions that are fundamental to science in its widest sense.

Exercises

1   What do you understand by the following?

syntagmatic and paradigmatic relations
phonological opposition
broad and narrow phonetic transcription
autosegmental
the skeletal tier
a metrical grid

2   Identify as many different definitions or views of the phoneme as you can. Is it fair to say they represent different perspectives on the same reality or do they reflect differences in fundamental theorizing?

3   What does it mean to say that the words *wide* and *width* share a common underlying form?

4 Review Sapir's notion of 'collective illusion' and discuss his example of *soared* and *sawed* (11.5). Suggest other examples of this kind.

5 Apply the notation of table 11.5.1 to your own variety of English.

6 Distinguish between natural phonology and natural generative phonology.

7 If you have the opportunity, listen to and record a sample of the very early stages of infant speech. How far does your observation bear out Stampe's claim about the unconstrained operation of natural processes?

8 Distinguish between lexical and postlexical rules in lexical phonology.

9 What do Anderson and Ewen mean by their assertion that 'preponderance is the intrasegmental analogue of prominence'?

10 What do Ohala and Jaeger mean by an 'experimental discipline'?

11 Indicate the importance of each of the following to the development of modern phonology:

Baudouin de Courtenay
Bloomfield
Boas
Chomsky
J. R. Firth
Halle
Hjelmslev
Jakobson
Daniel Jones
Kruszewski
Pike
Sapir
de Saussure
Henry Sweet
Trubetzkoy.

Appendix 1: Phonetic Symbols

1.1 Vowel symbols (see section 2.7)

(a) UNROUNDED

	Front		Central		Back
High or close	i	ɪ	ɨ		ɯ
High-mid or half-close	e		ə	ɜ	ɤ
Low-mid or half-open	ɛ				ʌ
	æ				
Low or open	a				ɑ

(b) ROUNDED

	Front		Central		Back
High or close	y	ʏ	ʉ	ʊ	u
High-mid or half-close	ø				o
Low-mid or half-open	œ				ɔ
Low or open	Œ				ɒ

Diacritics commonly used with vowels

   ᪿ fronted, e.g. [u̜] or [u<] for a fronted version of [u]
   > retracted, e.g. [e̠] or [e>] for a retracted version of [e]
   ᶺ raised, e.g. [e̝] or [eˆ] for a raised version of [e]
   ˅ lowered, e.g. [e̞] or [ĕ] for a lowered version of [e]
   – may indicate a centralized vowel (as in [ɨ] and [ʉ])
   : long, e.g. [uː] or [eː]
   · slightly lengthened, or 'half-long', e.g. [u·] or [e·]
   ₀ voiceless or whispered, e.g. [ḁ] or [u̥]
   .. with breathy voice, e.g. [a̤] or [ṳ]
   ~ with creaky voice, e.g. [a̰] or [ṵ]
   ~ nasalized, e.g. [ã] or [ũ]

1.2 Consonant symbols

	Bilabial	Labio-dental	Dental (apico- or lamino-)	Alveolar (apico- or lamino-)	Postalveolar (apico- or lamino-)	Apico-palatal	Lamino-palatal	Velar	Labio-velar	Uvular	Pharyngeal	Glottal
With pulmonic airstream:												
Voiceless Plosive	p		t̪	t		ʈ	c	k	k͡p	q		ʔ
Voiced Plosive	b		d̪	d		ɖ	ɟ	g	g͡b	ɢ		
Voiceless Central Fricative	ɸ	f	θ				ç	x		χ	ħ	h
Voiced Central Fricative	β	v	ð				ʝ	ɣ		ʁ	ʕ	ɦ
Voiceless Grooved Fricative			s̪	s	ʃ	ʂ	ɕ					
Voiced Grooved Fricative			z̪	z	ʒ	ʐ	ʑ					
Voiceless Lateral Fricative				ɬ								
Voiced Lateral Fricative				ɮ								
Voiced Central Approximant		ʋ			ɹ	ɻ	j	ɰ	w			
Voiced Lateral Approximant			l̪	l		ɭ	ʎ	ʟ				
Voiced Nasal	m	ɱ	n̪	n		ɳ	ɲ	ŋ	ŋ͡m	ɴ		
Voiced Flap or tap				ɾ		ɽ						
Voiced Trill				r						ʀ		
With ejective airstream:												
Voiceless Stop	p'		t̪'	t'				k'				
Voiceless Central Fricative		f'						x'				
Voiceless Grooved Fricative				s'								
Voiceless Lateral Fricative				ɬ'								
With implosive airstream:												
Voiced Stop	ɓ			ɗ			ʄ	ɠ				
With velaric airstream:												
Voiceless Central Click	ʘ		ʇ			ʗ						
Voiceless Lateral Click				ʖ								

Alternative symbols

In some works, [ι] and [ɷ] are used in place of [ɪ] and [ʊ]

Notes on consonant symbols

1. *Airstream mechanisms* (see chapter 2.5). Only a selection of ejective, implosive and click sounds is given, but the symbolization can be readily extended by analogy (e.g. [q'] for a uvular ejective stop, [ɖ] for an apico-palatal voiced implosive stop).

2. *Place of articulation and tongue position* (see chapter 2, sections 10 and 11, and table 2.11.1). Dental sounds are often symbolized as shown here, regardless of whether they are apico-dental or lamino-dental; if necessary lamino-dentals can be distinguished by symbolizing them as fronted alveolars, e.g. [t̪] or [n̪] (following a convention in Ladefoged 1971).

The symbols for dental and alveolar sounds normally imply apical articulation, and there is no well-established convention for distinguishing between apico-alveolars and lamino-alveolars, nor between apico-postalveolars and lamino-postalveolars; if necessary, lamino-alveolars can be represented as if they were retracted alveolars (e.g. [t̠] or [n̠] and lamino-postalveolars as fronted lamino-palatals (e.g. [c̟] or [n̟].

Labio-velar is included as a point of articulation, although it is a double articulation and only the most common of several possible double articulations (section 3.8). Except for [w], all double articulations can be represented by the two components, as in [k͡p].

3. *Manner of articulation* (see section 2.12). It is rarely necessary to distinguish between voiced central fricatives and voiced central approximants. In some cases, distinct symbols are available (e.g. labio-dental fricative [v] versus labio-dental approximant [ʋ]); in other cases, the same symbol may be used (e.g. [j] for both lamino-palatal fricative and lamino-palatal approximant); and if necessary the approximant may be distinguished by a diacritic (as in approximant [ɹ̩] versus fricative [ɹ]).

A single symbol covers the alveolar tap and flap. Taps are sometimes distinguished by writing them as plosives with a diacritic (e.g. [d̆]).

Consonant diacritics

    ' ejective, as in [p'] or [s'] (see section 2.5)
    ∘ voiceless, if no separate voiceless symbol is available, as in [m̥] or [r̥] (see section 2.6); may also be used to indicate partial devoicing of a voiced sound, as in [b̥] or [z̥] (see section 2.16)

ˌ dental, if no separate symbol is available, as in [d̪] or [l̪] (see section 2.10)
ˎ approximant (see note 3 above, and section 2.12)
: length, as in [t:] or [n:] (see section 2.15)
ʰ aspiration, or delayed voice onset, as in [pʰ] or [kʰ] (see section 2.16)

Alternative symbols

The grooved fricatives [ʃ] and [ʒ] are often represented alternatively as [š] and [ž].

The lamino-palatal approximant [j] may be represented as [y] (in line with the English spelling convention). Since [y] is used in the cardinal vowel system to indicate a high front rounded vowel, those who use [y] for the approximant normally adopt some other convention to represent front rounded vowels, often using [ü] and [ö] instead of [y] and [ø].

Postalveolar or apico-palatal consonants are sometimes written as alveolars with a subscript dot, e.g. [ṭ] or [ṇ].

The representation of r-sounds is particularly problematic. Various conventions have been used, including the use of [ř] for an alveolar flap, [r̃] for an alveolar trill, and a subscript dot for articulations further back than alveolar (e.g. [ṛ] for a post-alveolar approximant, or [r̃] for a uvular trill). The reader is warned that in many phonetic descriptions of particular languages, the terminology is vague and the symbolization *ad hoc*.

1.3 Diacritics and conventions for complex articulations

~ above a vowel or consonant: nasalized, e.g. [ã], [w̃] (see section 3.3)
~ through a consonant: velarization or pharyngealization, e.g. [ɫ] or [s̴] (see section 3.6)
w beneath a consonant: simultaneous labialization, e.g. [k̫]; superscript following a consonant: transitional labialization, e.g. [kʷ] (see section 3.4)
ʲ beneath a consonant: simultaneous palatalization, e.g. [ɲ]; superscript following a consonant: transitional palatalization, e.g. [nʲ] (see section 3.5)
ɹ superscript following a vowel: vowel retroflexion, e.g. [ɔɹ] (see section 3.9)
ˌ beneath a consonant: syllabic, e.g. [m̩], [l̩] (see section 3.11)

Vowel onglide and offglide and diphthongs can be represented by combinations of vowel symbols, e.g. onglide [əi], offglide [ɔᵊ], diphthong [ai͡] or [aⁱ] (see sections 2.8 and 3.10).

Prenasalized consonants can be represented with an appropriate preceding nasal symbol, e.g. [m͡b] or [ᵐb]; and postnasalized with a corresponding following nasal, e.g. [p͡m] or [pᵐ] (see section 3.3).

Affricates can be represented by symbols for the appropriate stop and fricative components, e.g. [t͡s] or [tˢ]. For the affricates [t͡ʃ] and [d͡ʒ], the special symbols [č] and [ǰ] are also available (see section 3.7).

Double articulation – sounds involving two simultaneous places of articulation – can be represented by two component symbols, e.g. [k͡t] for an alveolar-velar plosive, or [ŋ͡m] for a labio-velar nasal (see section 3.8).

1.4 Symbols used in transcription of English

Vowels

Unless otherwise indicated, English examples in this book assume the kind of pronunciation heard in south-eastern England and Australia. In this variety of English – unlike English spoken in Scotland, Ireland and most of North America – words such as *hard*, *hoard* and *heard* contain long vowels with no r-sound following them. Words such as *fear* and *fare* likewise have no r-sound and are pronounced with centering diphthongs. This is also a version of English in which words such as *put* and *look* are pronounced with a short vowel distinct from the long vowel in *boot* and *Luke*, and in which words such as *rod* and *pot* have a short rounded vowel distinct both from the vowel of *broad* and *bought*, and from that of *hard* and *part*.

For full exemplification of this vowel system, each vowel is listed below with some sample words. The first symbol on the left is the one generally preferred in this text. These symbols omit vowel length, on the grounds that length can be predicted from the vowel quality; but we show the long symbols (with :) as alternatives and use these symbols in the text when it seems necessary to draw attention to the vowel length. Other symbols in common use are also included below: those incorporating /y/ and /w/ are widely used in North American publications.

It should be noted that these symbols provide for a broad or phonemic transcription (in the sense outlined in chapter 4) and each symbol may therefore cover a number of variants. In Australian English, for example, a vowel can be quite noticeably influenced by a following /l/, so that the vowel in *bowl* and *dole* may sound different from the vowel in *boat* and *dough*. It is nevertheless assumed that such differences can be included as context-sensitive variants implied by a single symbol. But the symbols do *not* cover all varieties of English, given that some varieties have quite different vowel systems.

The sequence /ju/ is included as a diphthong although there are reasons for taking it to be simply the vowel /u/ preceded by the consonant /j/. It is worth noting that some varieties of English have /u/ instead of /ju/ in many words.

Vowels	Sample words
Short	
/ɪ/	hid, bit, lick
/ɛ/ /e/	head, bet, wreck
/æ/	had, bat, lack
/ʌ/	thud, but, luck
/ɒ/	rod, pot, lock
/ʊ/	hood, put, look
Long	
/i/ /i:/ /iy/	heed, beat, bee
/ɜ/ /ɜ:/	heard, pert, burr
/a/ /a:/	hard, part, bar
/ɔ/ /ɔ:/	hoard, bought, pore, poor, paw
/u/ /u:/ /uw/	food, boot, boo
Diphthongs	
/eɪ/ /ey/	fade, bait, bay
/aɪ/ /ay/	hide, bite, buy
/ɔɪ/ /oy/	void, quoit, boy
/oʊ/ /əʊ/ /ow/	hoed, boat, dough
/aʊ/ /aw/	loud, bout, bough
/ɪə/	feared, beard, beer
/ɛə/	fared, bared, bare, bear
/ʊə/	toured, lure
/ju/ /ju:/	hewed, cute, due, dew, few
Indeterminate (only in unstressed syllables)	
/ə/	(first syllable of:) above, parade, correct
	(second syllable of:) China, better, carrot

Consonants

Compared with the vowel system, English consonants show much less variation, either regionally or socially, and there is relatively little controversy about a broad or phonemic transcription. Within the English of south-eastern England and Australia, a few consonants do vary substantially according to context, notably /l/ and /r/, but the use of a single symbol does not deny the existence of such context-sensitive variation.

Alternative symbols are again included. Sample words are in three groups, illustrating (where possible) the consonant in (1) initial, (2) medial and (3) final positions.

Consonants	Sample words		
	(1)	*(2)*	*(3)*
Voiceless plosives			
/p/	peer, paw	leper, rapid	rip, loop
/t/	tier, tore	letter, baton	writ, loot
/k/	core, keel	wrecker, icon	rick, Luke
Voiced plosives			
/b/	beer, bore	pebble, rabid	rib, cube
/d/	dear, door	redder, idol	rid, rude
/g/	gear, gore	beggar, eagle	rig, dog
Voiceless affricate			
/tʃ/ /č/	cheer, chore	lecher, catcher	rich, pouch
Voiced affricate			
/dʒ/ /ǰ/	jeer, jaw	ledger, badger	ridge, rage
Voiceless fricatives			
/f/	fear, four	heifer, offer	whiff, roof
/θ/	thaw, theme	method, Ethel	myth, tooth
/s/	sear, saw	lesser, acid	miss, loose
/ʃ/ /š/	sheer, shore	pressure, ration	dish, gauche
/h/	hear, hoar	—	—
Voiced fricatives			
/v/	veer, vaunt	ever, liver	live, move
/ð/	there, thy	leather, other	lithe, soothe
/z/	zeal, zone	resin, dozen	fizz, lose
/ʒ/ /ž/	—	measure, closure	—
Nasals			
/m/	mere, more	lemon, simmer	rim, room
/n/	near, nor	venom, sinner	win, spoon
/ŋ/	—	hanger, singer	ring, rang
Approximants			
/l/	leer, law	melon, miller	will, rule
/r/ /ɹ/ /ɹ̩/	rear, raw	heron, mirror	—
/w/	weir, war	away, bewilder	—
/j/ /y/	year, your	beyond	—

Appendix 2: Features

2.1 Jakobson and Halle's distinctive features (based on Jakobson and Halle 1956, pp. 29ff.)

The features are defined in both acoustic and articulatory terms. Each feature is an opposition between two relative values; for example, vocalic sounds have a *relatively* clear formant structure in comparison with nonvocalic sounds.

Feature	Opposed to	Acoustic description	Articulatory description
1 Vocalic	Nonvocalic	Sharply defined formant structure	Voiced, with free passage of air through vocal tract
2 Consonantal	Nonconsonantal	Low total energy	Obstruction in vocal tract
3 Compact	Diffuse	Energy concentrated in central area of spectrum	High ratio of front resonance chamber to back
4 Tense	Lax	High energy with greater spread across spectrum and longer duration	Greater deformation of vocal tract from its rest position
5 Voiced	Voiceless	Periodic low frequency excitation	Vocal cord vibration
6 Nasal	Oral	Additional formants and less intensity in existing formants	Coupling of nasal cavity

(cont'd)

(cont'd)

Feature	Opposed to	Acoustic description	Articulatory description
7 Discontinuous	Continuant	Interruption or abrupt transition	Rapid closure and opening of vocal tract
8 Strident	Mellow	High intensity noise	'Rough-edged' effect at point of articulation
9 Checked	Unchecked	Higher rate of energy discharge	Glottalized
10 Grave	Acute	Energy concentrated in lower frequencies	Peripheral (towards front or back of vocal tract)
11 Flat	Plain	Downward shift or weakening of upper frequencies	Narrowed aperture (e.g. by lip rounding)
12 Sharp	Plain	Upward shift of upper frequencies	Reduced oral cavity and widened pharynx

2.2 Chomsky and Halle's universal set of phonetic features (based on Chomsky and Halle 1968, pp. 298ff.)

The features are described principally in articulatory terms, although Chomsky and Halle also refer (occasionally) to acoustic and perceptual correlates. Each feature is a 'physical' scale defined by two points, e.g. sonorant–nonsonorant. The features are binary for linguistic description – e.g. all sounds are functionally either [+voiced] or [−voiced] – but may have several values when taken as physical or phonetic scales. Where only one of the two functional values is given below, the other is a simple negative – e.g. nonvocalic, nonconsonantal.

Feature	Articulatory description
Major class features	
1 Sonorant	Produced with vocal tract cavity configuration in which spontaneous voicing is possible
(Nonsonorant = obstruent)	
2 Vocalic	Constriction does not exceed that of high vowels, and position of vocal cords allows spontaneous voicing
(Syllabic)	(Proposed renaming of vocalic)
3 Consonantal	Radical obstruction in mid-sagittal region of vocal tract

Feature	Articulatory description
Cavity features	
4 Coronal	Produced with blade of tongue raised from neutral position
5 Anterior	Produced with obstruction in front of palato-alveolar region
6 High	Tongue body above neutral position
7 Low	Tongue body below neutral position
8 Back	Tongue body retracted from neutral position
9 Round(ed)	Narrowing of lip orifice
10 Distributed	Constriction extends for some distance along direction of airflow
11 Covered	Pharynx walls narrowed and tensed and larynx raised (in vowel production)
12 Glottal constriction	Constriction of vocal cords
13 Nasal	Lowered velum
14 Lateral	Lowered side(s) of mid-section of tongue
Manner of articulation features	
15 Continuant (Noncontinuant = stop)	Primary constriction in vocal tract does not block air flow
16 Instantaneous release	Instantaneous release (of stops)

(Chomsky and Halle's discussion, 1968, pp. 318–22, suggests two release features:
16a Instantaneous versus delayed release of primary closures
16b Instantaneous versus delayed release of secondary closures)

17 Velar(ic) suction	Velar closure producing suction (clicks)
18 Implosion	Glottal closure producing suction (implosives)
19 Velar(ic) pressure	(Velar closure producing pressure – no evidence of use in language)
20 Ejection	Glottal closure producing pressure (ejectives)
21 Tense	Deliberate, accurate, maximally distinct articulation (of supraglottal musculature)
(Nontense = lax)	
Source features	
22 Heightened subglottal pressure	Tenseness in subglottal musculature producing greater subglottal pressure
23 Voiced	Vocal cord vibration (induced by appropriate glottal opening and airflow)
(Nonvoiced = voiceless)	
24 Strident	Turbulence (in fricatives and affricates) caused by nature of surface, rate of airflow and angle of incidence at point of articulation
Prosodic features	(listed but not discussed in Chomsky and Halle 1968)
25 Stress	
26 Pitch (high, low, elevated, rising, falling, concave)	
27 Length	

2.3 Ladefoged's 'Traditional Features' (based on Ladefoged 1982, pp. 254ff.)

Each feature (except 'syllabic') relates to a physical scale, either articulatory or acoustic. The features are not binary in principle and may have two or more values. Where only one value is listed, the feature *is* binary (e.g. 'click' implies +click versus −click).

Feature	Values	Description of physical scale
1 Glottalic	Ejective Pulmonic Implosive	Upward or downward movement of the glottis
2 Velaric	Click	Degree of suction of air in mouth
3 Voice	Glottal stop Laryngealized Voiced Murmur Voiceless	Degree of glottal stricture
4 Aspiration	Aspirated Unaspirated Voiced	Delay in onset of voicing
5 Place	Bilabial Labio-dental Dental Alveolar Retroflex Palato-alveolar Palatal Velar Uvular Pharyngeal Glottal	Location of articulation
6 Labial	Labial	Approximation of centres of lips
7 Stop	Stop Fricative	Degree of approximation of articulators
8 Nasal	Nasal	Lowering of soft palate
9 Lateral	Lateral	Amount of airflow over sides of tongue
10 Trill	Trill	Vibration of articulator
11 Flap	Flap	Rate of articulatory movement

(Ladefoged notes uncertainty about the characterization of flaps)

Feature	Values	Description of physical scale
12 Sonorant	Sonorant	Amount of acoustic energy
13 Sibilant	Sibilant	Amount of high-frequency energy
14 Grave	Grave	Ratio of low- to high-frequency energy
15 Height	4 height 3 height 2 height 1 height	Inverse of frequency of first formant (distinguishing four degrees of vowel height)
16 Back	Back	Difference between frequencies of formants two and one
17 Round	Round	Inverse of distance between corners of lips
18 Wide	Wide	Advancement of tongue root
19 Rhotacized	Rhotacized	Lowering of frequency of formant three
20 Syllabic	Syllabic	(No agreed physical scale)

2.4 Components in dependency phonology (based on Anderson and Ewen 1987, chs 4–6)

Articulation is resolved into gestures, subgestures and components. Some components are scales or continua, others may be simply present or absent. In the characterization of particular sounds, components may 'preponderate' to a greater or lesser extent. The vowel [e], for example, may combine the components |i| and |a|, with |i| preponderant; [æ] may combine the same two components, with |a| preponderant.

Gesture	Subgesture	Components
Categorial	Phonatory	Consonantality or periodicity: a scale ranging from |V| 'relatively periodic' to |C| 'periodic energy reduction'
	Initiatory	Degree of glottal opening: a scale encompassing aspiration as well as voicing, represented by the extent to which a component |O| is prominent; |O| is absent in the glottal stop
		|G| glottalicness (in glottalic sounds, absent in pulmonic)
		|K| velaricness (present in clicks, absent for other sounds)

(cont'd)

(cont'd)

Gesture	Subgesture	Components
Articulatory	Locational	|i| frontness (acuteness, sharpness)
		|a| lowness (sonority)
		|u| roundness (gravity, flatness)
		|ə| centrality
		|l| linguality (present in sounds in which the blade or body of the tongue is active)
		|t| apicality
		|d| dentality
		|r| retracted tongue root (present in pharyngeal consonants and in vowels with narrowed pharynx)
		|α| advanced tongue root (relevant only to languages which distinguish vowels with advanced tongue root from vowels with neutral tongue root posture)
		|λ| laterality
	Oro-nasal	|n| nasality

References

Abbreviations

ACLS American Council of Learned Societies
ANPE Archives Néerlandaises de Phonétique Expérimentale
AUMLA Australasian Universities Modern Language Association
IEEE-TA International Institute of Electrical and Electronics Engineers, Transactions on Acoustics, Speech and Signal Processing
IJAL International Journal of American Linguistics
IPO Instituut voor Perceptie Onderzoek (Institute for Perception Research), Eindhoven, Netherlands
JASA Journal of the Acoustical Society of America
JIPA Journal of the International Phonetic Association
JP Journal of Phonetics
JSHR Journal of Speech and Hearing Research
LInq Linguistic Inquiry
MIT Massachussetts Institute of Technology
MIT-QPR Research Laboratory of Electronics, MIT, Quarterly Progress Reports
MQSLRC Macquarie University Speech and Language Research Centre, Working Papers
PMLA Publications of the Modern Languages Association
STL-QPSR Speech Transmission Laboratory, Royal Institute of Technology, Stockholm, Quarterly Progress and Status Reports
UCLA-WP University of California at Los Angeles Phonetics Laboratory, Working Papers in Phonetics
WP-SILAAB Working Papers of the Summer Institute of Linguistics, Australian Aborigines Branch
ZP Zeitschrift für Phonetik

Abbs, J. H. 1986. Invariance and variability in speech production. In Perkell and Klatt 1986: 202–18.
Abbs, J. H., Gracco, V. L. and Cole, K. J. 1984. Control of multimovement coordination: sensorimotor mechanisms in speech motor programming. *Journal of Motor Behavior* 16: 195–231.

Abbs, J. H. and Welt, C. 1985. Structure and function of the lateral precentral cortex: significance for speech motor control. In Daniloff 1985: 155–192.

Abercrombie, D. 1967. *Elements of general phonetics*. Edinburgh: Edinburgh University Press.

Abercrombie, D., Fry, D. B., MacCarthy, R. A. D., Scott, N. C. and Trim, J. L. M. (eds) 1964. *In honour of Daniel Jones*. London: Longman.

Aitchison, J. and Straf, M. 1982. Lexical storage and retrieval: a developing skill? In Cutler 1982: 197–241.

Allen, J., Hunnicutt, M. S. and Klatt, D. 1987. *From text to speech: the MITalk system*. Cambridge: Cambridge University Press.

Allen, W. S. 1953. *Phonetics in Ancient India*. London: Oxford University Press.

Allen, W. S. 1978 (2nd edn). *Vox Latina: a guide to the pronunciation of classical Latin*. Cambridge: Cambridge University Press.

Allen, W. S. 1987 (3rd edn). *Vox Graeca: a guide to the pronunciation of classical Greek*. Cambridge: Cambridge University Press.

Amerman, J. D. and Daniloff, R. G. 1977. Aspects of lingual coarticulation. *JP* 5: 107–13.

Amerman, J. D., Daniloff, R. G. and Moll, K. L. 1970. Lip and jaw coarticulation for the phoneme /æ/. *JSHR* 15: 179–95.

Ananthapadmanabha, T. V. 1984. Acoustic analysis of voice source dynamics. *STL-QPSR* 2–3: 1–24.

Anderson, J. M. and Ewen, C. J. 1987. *Principles of dependency phonology*. Cambridge: Cambridge University Press.

Anderson, J. M., Ewen, C. J. and Staun, J. 1985. Phonological structure: segmental, suprasegmental and extrasegmental. *Phonology Yearbook* 2: 203–24.

Anderson, S. R. 1974. *The organization of phonology*. New York: Academic Press.

Anderson, S. R. 1978. Tone features. In Fromkin 1978: 133–75.

Anderson, S. R. 1979. On the subsequent development of the 'standard theory' in phonology. In Dinnsen 1979: 2–30.

Anderson, S. R. 1985. *Phonology in the twentieth century: theories of rules and theories of representations*. Chicago: University of Chicago Press.

Anderson, S. R. and Kiparsky, P. (eds) 1973. *Festschrift for Morris Halle*. New York: Holt, Rinehart and Winston.

Arkebauer, H. J., Hixon, T. J. and Hardy, J. C. 1967. Peak intraoral air pressures during speech. *JSHR* 10: 196–208.

Asher, R. E. and Henderson, J. A. (eds) 1981. *Towards a history of phonetics*. Edinburgh: Edinburgh University Press.

Bach, E. and Harms, R. T. (eds) 1968. *Universals in linguistic theory*. New York: Holt, Rinehart and Winston.

Baken, R. J. 1987. *Clinical measurement of speech and voice*. Boston: College Hill Press.

Basbøll, H. 1988. Phonological theory. In Newmeyer 1988 (vol. 1): 192–215.

Bell, A. and Hooper, J. B. (eds) 1978. *Syllables and segments*. Amsterdam: North-Holland.

Bell-Berti, F. 1980. Velopharyngeal function: a spatio-temporal model. In Lass 1980 (vol. 4): 291–316.

Benguerel, A. P. and Cowan, H. 1974. Coarticulation of upper lip protrusion in French. *Phonetica* 30: 41–55.

Beranek, L. 1949. *Acoustic measurements*. New York: McGraw-Hill.

Bernard, J. R. L. 1967. Length and the identification of Australian vowels. *AUMLA* 27: 37–58.

Bernard, J. R. L. 1970a. Towards the acoustic specification of Australian English. *ZP* 23: 113–28.

Bernard, J. R. L. 1970b. A cine X-ray study of some sounds of Australian English. *Phonetica* 21: 138–50.

Bernard, J. R. L. 1985. Some local effects of postvocalic /l/. In Clark 1985: 319–32.

Bernard, J. R. L. and Mannell, R. H. 1986. A study of /h-d/ words in Australian English. MQSLRC 1986: 1–106.

Bladon, A. 1987. The auditory modelling dilemma, and a phonetic response. *Proceedings of the XIth International Congress of Phonetic Sciences* 4: 319–24.

Bladon, R. A. W. and Lindblom, B. 1981. Modeling the judgement of vowel quality differences. *JASA* 69: 1414–22.

Bless, D. M. and Abbs, J. H. (eds) 1983. *Vocal fold physiology: contemporary research and clinical issues*. San Diego: College Hill Press.

Bloomfield, L. 1933. *Language*. New York: H. Holt & Co.

Blumstein, S. E. and Stevens, K. N. 1979. Acoustic invariance in speech production: evidence from measurements of the spectral characteristics of stop consonants. *JASA* 66: 1001–17.

Blumstein, S. E. and Stevens, K. N. 1980. Perceptual invariance and onset spectra for stop consonants in different vowel environments. *JASA* 67: 648–62.

Bolinger, D. 1964. Around the edges of intonation. *Harvard Educational Review* 34: 282–93. Reprinted in Bolinger 1972: 19–29.

Bolinger, D. (ed.) 1972. *Intonation: selected readings*. Harmondsworth: Penguin.

Borden, G. J. 1980. Use of feedback in established and developing speech. In Lass 1980 (vol. 3): 223–42.

Borden, G. J. and Harris, K. S. 1980. *Speech science primer: physiology, acoustics and perception of speech*. Baltimore: Williams and Wilkins.

Bouhuys, A. 1974. *Breathing: physiology, environment and lung disease*. New York: Grune and Stratton.

Bouhuys, A. 1977. *The physiology of breathing: a textbook for medical students*. New York: Grune and Stratton.

Bradley, D. (ed.) 1982. *Papers in Southeast Asian linguistics No 8: Tonation*. Canberra: Pacific Linguistics.

Brame, M. K. (ed.) 1972. *Contributions to generative phonology*. Austin: University of Texas Press.

Brame, M. K. 1974. The cycle in phonology: stress in Palestinian, Maltese and Spanish. *LInq* 5: 39–60.

Brazil, D., Coulthard, M. and Johns, C. 1980. *Discourse intonation and language teaching*. Harlow: Longman.

Breckenridge, J. 1977. The declination effect. *JASA* 60: S90.

Bright, W. (ed.) 1992. *International encyclopedia of linguistics*. Oxford: Oxford University Press.

Broad, D. J. 1973. Phonation. In Minifie et al. 1973: 127–68.

Broad, D. J. 1979. New theories of vocal fold vibration. In Lass 1979 (vol. 1): 203–56.

Broad, D. J. and Wakita, H. 1977. Piece-wise planar representation of vowel formant frequencies. *JASA* 62: 1572–82.

Brown, G., Currie, K. L. and Kenworthy, J. 1980. *Questions of intonation*. London: Croom Helm.

Browne, E. W. and McCawley, J. D. 1973. Serbo-Croatian accent. In Fudge 1973a: 330–5.

Bryden, M. P. 1982. *Laterality: function and asymmetry in the intact brain*. New York: Academic Press.

Busch, A. C. and Eldridge, D. 1967. The effect of differing noise spectra on the consistency of identification of consonants. *Language and Speech* 10: 194–202.

Buxton, H. 1983. Temporal predictability in the perception of English speech. In Cutler and Ladd 1983: 111–20.

Campbell, L. 1986. Testing phonology in the field. In Ohala and Jaeger 1986: 163–73.

Carlson, R., Fant, G. and Granström, B. 1975. Two-formant models, pitch and vowel perception. In Fant and Tatham 1975: 55–82.

Catford, J. C. 1964. Phonation types. In Abercrombie et al. 1964: 26–37.

Catford, J. C. 1968. The articulatory possibilities of man. In Malmberg 1968: 309–33.

Catford, J. C. 1977. *Fundamental problems in phonetics*. Edinburgh: Edinburgh University Press.

Catford, J. C. 1981. Observations on the recent history of vowel classification. In Asher and Henderson 1981: 19–32.

Chafe, W. L. 1968. The ordering of phonological rules. *IJAL* 34: 115–36.

Chao, Y. R. 1930. A system of tone letters. *Le Maître Phonétique* 45: 24–7.

Chao, Y. R. 1934. The non-uniqueness of phonemic solutions of phonetic symbols. *Bulletin of the Institute of History and Philology, Academia Sinica* 4: 363–97. Reprinted in Joos 1958: 38–54.

Chistovich, L. A., Sheikin, R. L. and Lubinskaja, V. V. 1979. 'Centres of gravity' and spectral peaks as the determinants of vowel quality. In Lindblom and Ohman 1979: 143–57.

Chomsky, N. 1959. Review of Skinner 1957. *Language* 35: 26–58. Reprinted in Fodor and Katz 1964: 547–78.

Chomsky, N. 1964. *Current issues in linguistic theory*. The Hague: Mouton.

Chomsky, N. 1966. *Cartesian linguistics: a chapter in the history of rationalist thought*. New York: Harper & Row.

Chomsky, N. 1967. Some general properties of phonological rules. *Language* 43: 102–28.

Chomsky, N. 1968. *Language and mind*. New York: Harcourt, Brace & World.

Chomsky, N. and Halle, M. 1968. *The sound pattern of English*. New York: Harper & Row.

Clark, J. E. 1983. Intelligibility comparisons for two synthetic and one natural speech source. *JP* 11: 37–49.

Clark, J. E. (ed.) 1985. *The cultivated Australian: Festschrift in honour of Arthur Delbridge*. Hamburg: Helmut Buske.

Clark, J. E., Lubker, J. and Hunnicutt, S. 1987. Some preliminary evidence for phonetic strategies in communication difficulty. In Steele and Threadgold 1987: 162–80.

Clark, J. E. and Palethorpe, S. 1982. Dynamic auditory masking during vowel production. *MQSLRC* 1982: 96–125.

Clark, J. E. and Palethorpe, S. 1986. Sources of invariance and variability in temporal properties of speech. In Perkell and Klatt 1986: 458–62.

Clark, J. E., Palethorpe, S. and Hardcastle, W. J. 1982. Analysis of English lingual fricative multimodal data using stepwise regression methods. *MQSLRC* 3: 1–91.

Clements, G. N. 1977. The autosegmental treatment of vowel harmony. In Dressler and Pfeiffer 1977: 111–19.

Clements, G. N. 1981. Akan vowel harmony: a nonlinear analysis. *Harvard Studies in Phonology* 2: 108–77.

Clements, G. N. 1984. Vowel harmony in Akan: a consideration of Stewart's word structure conditions. *Studies in African Linguistics* 15: 321–37.

Clements, G. N. 1985. The geometry of phonological features. *Phonology Yearbook* 2: 225–52.

Clements, G. N. and Keyser, S. J. 1983. *CV phonology*. Cambridge, Mass.: MIT Press.

Coker, C. H. 1973. Speech synthesis with a parametric articulatory model. In Flanagan and Rabiner 1973: 135–9.

Comrie, B. (ed.) 1987. *The world's major languages*. London: Croom Helm.

Cooper, F. S., Delattre, P. C., Liberman, A. M., Borst, J. M. and Gerstman, L. J. 1952. Some experiments on the perception of synthetic speech sounds. *JASA* 24: 597–606. Reprinted in Fry 1976: 258–72.

Cooper, W. E. and Sorenson, J. M. 1981. *Fundamental frequency in sentence production*. New York: Springer-Verlag.

Couper-Kuhlen, E. 1986. *An introduction to English prosody*. London: Edward Arnold.

Crompton, A. 1982. Syllables and segments in speech production. In Cutler 1982: 109–62.

Cruttenden, A. 1986. *Intonation*. Cambridge: Cambridge University Press.

Crystal, D. 1969. *Prosodic systems and intonation in English*. Cambridge: Cambridge University Press.

Crystal, D. and Quirk, R. 1964. *Systems of prosodic and paralinguistic features in English*. The Hague: Mouton.

Cutler, A. (ed.) 1982. *Slips of the tongue and language production*. Amsterdam: Walter de Gruyter/Mouton.

Cutler, A. and Ladd, D. R. (eds) 1983. *Prosody: models and measurements*. Berlin: Springer Verlag.

Daniloff, R. 1973. Normal articulation processes. In Minifie et al. 1973: 169–210.

Daniloff, R. (ed.) 1985. *Speech science*. London: Taylor and Francis.

Daniloff, R., Schuckers, G. and Feth, L. 1980. *The physiology of speech and hearing: an introduction*. New York: Prentice Hall.

David, E. E. and Denes, P. B. (eds) 1972. *Human communication: a unified view*. New York: McGraw-Hill.

Delattre, P. 1951. The physiological interpretation of sound spectrograms. *PMLA* 66: 864–75.

Delattre, P., Liberman, A. M., Cooper, F. S. and Gerstman, F. J. 1952. An experimental study of the acoustic determinants of vowel color: observations on one- and two-formant vowels synthesized from spectrographic patterns. *Word* 8: 195–210. Reprinted in Fry 1976: 221–37.

Delattre, P., Liberman, A. M. and Cooper, F. S. 1955. Acoustic loci and transitional cues for consonants. *JASA* 27: 769–73. Reprinted in Fry 1976: 273–83.

Denes, P. B. and Pinson, E. N. 1963. *The speech chain*. New York: Bell Telephone Laboratories

De Saussure, F. 1916. *Cours de linguistique générale* (publié par C. Bally et A. Sechehaye, avec la collaboration de A. Riedlinger). Paris: Payot. Revised edn 1972, *Ferdinand de Saussure: Cours de linguistique générale* (édition critique préparée par T. de Mauro). Paris: Payot. English translation with introduction and notes by W. Baskin 1959, *Course in general linguistics*. New York: The Philosophical Library. Reprinted 1966, New York: McGraw-Hill. Page references in the text are to the 1962 French edition (Paris: Payot).

Dickson, R. D. and Dickson, W. M. 1982. *Anatomical and physiological bases of speech*. Boston: College Hill Press.

Dingwall, W. O. (ed.) 1971. *A survey of linguistic science*. College Park: University of Maryland Press.

Dinnsen, D. A. (ed.) 1979. *Current approaches to phonological theory*. Bloomington and London: Indiana University Press.

Disner, S. 1980. Evaluation of vowel normalization procedures. *JASA* 67: 253–61.

Dixon, R. M. W. 1972. *The Dyirbal language of North Queensland*. Cambridge: Cambridge University Press.

Dixon, R. M. W. 1977. Some phonological rules in Yidiny. *LInq* 8: 1–34.

Donegan, P. J. and Stampe, D. 1979. The study of natural phonology. In Dinnsen 1979: 126–73.

Dressler, W. U. and Pfeiffer, O. E. (eds) 1977. *Phonologica 1977*. Innsbruck: Innsbrucker Beiträge zur Sprachwissenschaft.

Dunn, H. K. 1950. The calculation of vowel resonances, and an electrical vowel tract. *JASA* 22: 151–66.

Dunn, H. K. and White, S. D. 1940. Statistical measurements on conversational speech. *JASA* 11: 278–88.

Eimas, P. D. and Corbit, J. D. 1973. Selective adaptation of linguistic feature detectors. *Cognitive Psychology* 4: 99–109.

Elman, J. L. and McClelland, J. L. 1986. Exploiting lawful variability in the speech wave. In Perkell and Klatt 1986: 360–80.

Erikson, D., Baer, T. and Harris, K. S. 1983. The role of strap muscles in pitch lowering. In Bless and Abbs 1983: 279–85.

Essner, C. 1947. Recherches sur la structure des voyelles orales. *ANPE* 20: 40–77.

Fant, G. 1960. *Acoustic theory of speech production*. The Hague: Mouton.

Fant, G. 1966. A note on vocal tract size factors and non-uniform *F*-pattern scalings. *STL-QPSR* 4–66. Reprinted in Fant 1973: 84–93.

Fant, G. 1968. Analysis and synthesis of speech processes. In Malmberg 1968: 173–277.

Fant, G. 1973. *Speech sounds and features*. Cambridge, Mass.: MIT Press.

Fant, G. 1979. Voice source analysis: a progress report. *STL-QPSR* 3–4: 31–3.

Fant, G. and Tatham, M. A. A. (eds) 1975. *Auditory analysis and perception of speech*. London: Academic Press.

Firth, J. R. 1948. Sounds and prosodies. *Transactions of the Philological Society 1948*: 127–52. Reprinted in Makkai 1972: 252–63.

Fischer-Jørgensen, E. 1954. Acoustic analysis of stop consonants. *Miscellanea Phonetica* 2: 42–59.

Fischer-Jørgensen, E. 1975. *Trends in phonological theory*. Copenhagen: Akademisk Forlag.

Fischer-Jørgensen, E. 1985. Some basic vowel features, their articulatory correlates, and their explanatory power in phonology. In Fromkin 1985: 79–99.

Flanagan, J. L. 1958. Some properties of the glottal sound source. *JSHR* 1: 99–111. Reprinted in Fry 1976: 31–51.

Flanagan, J. L. 1972 (2nd edn). *Speech analysis: synthesis and perception*. Berlin: Springer Verlag.

Flanagan, J. L., Rabiner, L. R., Christopher, D., Bock, D. E. and Shipp, T. 1976. Digital analysis of laryngeal control in speech production. *JASA* 60: 446–55.

Flanagan, J. L. and Rabiner, L. R. (eds) 1973. *Speech synthesis*. Stroudsburg, Pa: Dowden, Hutchinson and Ross.

Fletcher, H. 1953. *Speech and hearing in communication*. New York: Van Nostrand.

Florentine, M., Buus, S. and Mason, C. R. 1987. Level discrimination as a function of level for tones from 0.25 to 16 Hz. *JASA* 81: 1528–41.

Fodor, J. A. and Katz J. J. (eds) 1964. *The structure of language*. Englewood Cliffs, NJ: Prentice-Hall.

Folkins, J. W. and Abbs, J. H. 1975. Lip and jaw motor control during speech: responses to restrictive loading of the jaw. *JSHR* 18: 207–20.

Fowler, C. A. and Smith, M. R. 1986. Speech perception as vector analysis: an approach to the problem of invariance and segmentation. In Perkell and Klatt 1986: 123–36.

Fromkin, V. A. (ed.) 1978. *Tone: a linguistic survey*. New York: Academic Press.

Fromkin, V. A. (ed.) 1985. *Phonetic linguistics: essays in honor of Peter Ladefoged*. Orlando: Academic Press.

Fry, D. B. 1958. Experiments in the perception of stress. *Language and Speech* 1: 126–52.

Fry, D. B. (ed.) 1976. *Acoustic phonetics: a course of basic readings*. Cambridge: Cambridge University Press.

Fry, D. B. 1979. *The physics of speech*. Cambridge: University of Cambridge Press.

Fry, D. B., Abramson, A. S., Eimas, P. D. and Liberman, A. M. 1962. The identification and discrimination of synthetic vowels. *Language and Speech* 5: 171–89.

Fucci, D. and Petrosino, L. 1981. The human tongue: normal structure and function and associated pathologies. In Lass 1981 (vol. 6): 305–74.

Fudge, E. C. 1967. The nature of phonological primes. *Journal of Linguistics* 3: 1–36. Reprinted in Makkai 1972: 500–21.

Fudge, E. C. (ed.) 1973a. *Phonology*. Harmondsworth: Penguin.

Fudge, E. C. 1973b. On the notion 'universal phonetic framework'. In Fudge 1973a: 172–80.

Fudge, E. 1984. *English word-stress*. London: Allen and Unwin.

Fujimura. O. 1961. Bilabial stop and nasal consonants: a motion picture study and its implications. *JSHR* 4: 233–47.

Fujimura, O. (ed.) 1973. *Three dimensions of linguistic theory*. Tokyo: TEC.

Gandour, J. T. 1978. The perception of tone. In Fromkin 1978: 41–76.

Gay, T. 1978. Effect of speaking rate on vowel formant movements. *JASA* 63: 223–30.

Gerstman, L. H. 1968. Classification of self-normalized vowels. *IEEE-TA* 16: 78–80.

Gilbert, H. R. 1973. Oral airflow during stop consonant production. *Folia Phoniatrica* 25: 288–301.

Gimson, A. C. 1980 (3rd edn). *An introduction to the pronunciation of English*. London: Edward Arnold. (First published 1962.)

Glass, A. and Hackett, D. 1970. *Pitjantjatjara Grammar*. Canberra: Australian Institute of Aboriginal Studies.

Gleason, H. A. 1961 (2nd edn). *An introduction to descriptive linguistics*. London: Holt, Rinehart and Winston.

Gold, B. and Rabiner, L. R. 1969. Parallel processing techniques for estimating pitch periods of speech in the time domain. *JASA* 46: 443–8.

Goldsmith, J. A. 1976 (mimeo). *Autosegmental phonology*. Bloomington: Indiana University Linguistics Club.

Goldsmith, J. A. 1979. The aims of autosegmental phonology. In Dinnsen 1979: 202–22.

Goldsmith, J. A. 1985. Vowel harmony in Khalka Mongolian, Yaka, Finnish and Hungarian. *Phonology Yearbook* 2: 253–75.

Goldsmith, J. A. 1989. *Autosegmental and metrical phonology: a new synthesis*. Oxford: Basil Blackwell.

Greenberg, J. H. 1966. *Language universals*. The Hague: Mouton.

Greenberg, J. H. (ed.) 1978. *Phonology* (Vol. 2 of *Universals of human language*.) Stanford, Ca.: Stanford University Press.

Gudschinsky, S. C., Popovich, H. and Popovich, F. 1970. Native reaction and phonetic similarity in Maxakalí phonology. *Language* 46: 77–88.

Halle, M. 1954. The strategy of phonemics. *Word* 10: 197–209. Reprinted in Makkai 1972: 333–42.

Halle, M. 1959. *The sound pattern of Russian*. The Hague: Mouton.

Halle, M. 1962. Phonology in generative grammar. *Word* 18: 54–72. Reprinted in Fodor and Katz 1964: 334–52; and in Makkai 1972: 380–92.

Halle, M. 1964. On the bases of phonology. In Fodor and Katz 1964: 324–33. Reprinted in Makkai 1972: 393–400.

Halle, M. 1973. The accentuation of Russian words. *Language* 49: 312–48.

Halle, M. 1983. On distinctive features and their articulatory implementation. *Natural Language and Linguistic Theory* 1: 91–105.

Halle, M. 1992. Phonological features. In Bright 1992 (vol. 3): 207–12.

Halle, M., Hughes, G. W. and Radley, J.-P. A. 1957. Acoustic properties of stop consonants. *JASA* 29: 107–16. Reprinted in Lehiste 1967: 170–9.

Halle, M., Lunt, H. G., Maclean, H. and van Schooneveld, C. H. (eds) 1956. *For Roman Jakobson: essays on the occasion of his sixtieth birthday*. The Hague: Mouton.

Halle, M. and Stevens, K. N. 1964. Speech recognition: a model and a program for research. In Fodor and Katz 1964: 604–12.

Halle, M. and Stevens, K. N. 1971. A note on laryngeal features. *MIT-QPR* 101: 198–213.

Halle, M. and Vergnaud, J. R. 1981. Harmony processes. In Klein and Levelt 1981: 1–23.

Halliday, M. A. K. 1970. *A course in spoken English: intonation*. London: Oxford University Press.

Halliday, M. A. K. 1978. *Language as social semiotic*. London: Edward Arnold.

Halliday, M. A. K. 1985a. *An introduction to functional grammar*. London: Edward Arnold.

Halliday, M. A. K. 1985b. *Spoken and written language*. Geelong, Victoria: Deakin University Press.

Hammarberg, R. 1976. The metaphysics of coarticulation. *JP* 4: 255–363.

Hardcastle, W. J. 1976. *Physiology of speech production*. London: Academic Press.

Harms, R. T. 1968. *Introduction to phonological theory*. Englewood Cliffs, NJ: Prentice-Hall.

Harris, J. W. 1973. On the order of certain phonological rules in Spanish. In Anderson and Kiparsky 1973: 59–76.

Harris, K. S. 1958. Cues for discrimination of American English fricatives in spoken syllables. *Language and Speech* 1: 1–7.

Harris, M. S. and Umeda, N. 1987. Difference limens for fundamental frequency contours in sentences. *JASA* 81: 1139–45.

Harris, Z. S. 1951. *Methods in structural linguistics*. Chicago: Chicago University Press.

Harshman, R., Ladefoged, P. and Goldstein, L. 1977. Factor analysis of tongue shapes. *JASA* 62: 693–707.

Hawkins, P. R. 1984. *Introducing phonology*. London: Hutchinson.

Heffner, R-M. S. 1964. *General phonetics*. Madison: University of Wisconsin Press.

Heiberger, V. L. and Horii, Y. 1982. Jitter and shimmer in sustained phonation. In Lass 1982 (vol. 7): 291–332.

Heinz, J. M. 1958. Model studies of the production of fricative consonants. *MIT-QPR* 15 July: 146–7.

Heinz, J. M. and Stevens, K. N. 1961. On the properties of voiceless fricative consonants. *JASA* 33: 589–96.

Hess, W. 1983. *Determination of speech signals*. Berlin: Springer Verlag.

Hirano, M. and Kakita, Y. 1985. Cover-body theory of vocal fold vibration. In Daniloff 1985: 1–46.

Hirano, M., Kurita, S. and Nakashima, T. 1981. The structure of the vocal folds. In Stevens and Hirano 1981: 33–41.

Hirose, H. and Gay, T. 1972. The activity of the laryngeal muscles in voicing control. *Phonetica* 25: 140–64.

Hixon, T. J. 1966. Turbulent voice sources for speech. *Folia Phoniatrica* 18: 168–82.

Hixon, T. J. 1973. Respiratory function in speech. In Minifie et al. 1973: 73–126.

Hixon, T. J. 1987. *Respiratory function in speech and song*. London: Taylor and Francis.

Hixon, T. J., Goldman, M. and Mead, J. 1973. Kinematics of the chest wall during speech production: volume displacements of the rib cage, abdomen, and lung. *JSHR* 16: 78–115.

Hixon, T. J., Mead, J. and Goldman, M. 1977. Dynamics of the chest wall during speech production: function of the thorax, rib cage, diaphragm and abdomen. *JSHR* 19: 297–356.

Hixon, T. J., Shriberg, L. D. and Saxman, L. H. (eds) 1980. *Introduction to communication disorders*. Englewood Cliffs, NJ: Prentice-Hall.

Hoard, J. E. 1978. Syllabication in Northwest Indian languages, with remarks on the nature of syllabic stops and fricatives. In Bell and Hooper 1978: 59–83.

Hockett, C. F. 1955. *A manual of phonology*. Baltimore: Waverley Press. (Indiana University Publications in Anthropology and Linguistics, Memoirs II: Part 1 of *IJAL* 24, 4).

Hogg, R. and McCully, C. B. 1987. *Metrical phonology: a coursebook*. Cambridge: Cambridge University Press.

Hollien, H. 1983. In search of vocal control mechanisms. In Bless and Abbs 1983: 361–7.

Holmes, J. N. 1986. Normalization in vowel perception. In Perkell and Klatt 1986: 346–57.

Hombert, J-M. 1978. Consonant types, vowel quality, and tone. In Fromkin 1978: 77–111.

Hombert, J-M. 1986. Word games: some implications for analysis of tone and other phonological constructs. In Ohala and Jaeger 1986: 175–86.

Honda, K. 1983. Relationship between pitch control and vowel articulation. In Bless and Abbs 1983: 286–99.

Hooper, J. B. 1976. *An introduction to natural generative phonology*. New York: Academic Press.

Hooper, J. B. 1979. Substantive principles in Natural Generative Phonology. In Dinnsen 1979: 106–25.

Hudson, J. 1978. *The core of Walmatjari grammar*. Canberra: Australian Institute of Aboriginal Studies.

Hughes, A. and Trudgill, P. 1979. *English accents and dialects: an introduction to social and regional varieties of British English*. London: Edward Arnold.

Huxley, H. E. 1958. The contraction of muscle. *Scientific American* November 1958: 3–14.

Hyman, L. M. 1975. *Phonology: theory and analysis*. New York: Holt, Rinehart and Winston.

Hyman, L. M. 1978. Historical tonology. In Fromkin 1978: 257–69.

International Phonetic Association 1949. *The Principles of the International Phonetic Association* (being a description of the International Phonetic Alphabet and the manner of using it, illustrated by texts in 51 languages). London.

Isshiki, N. 1964. Regulatory mechanisms of voice intensity variation. *JSHR* 7: 17–29.

Isshiki, N. and Ringel, R. 1964. Airflow during the production of selected consonants. *JSHR* 7: 233–44.

Jaeger, J. J. 1986. Concept formation as a tool for linguistic research. In Ohala and Jaeger 1986: 211–37.

Jakobson, R. 1939. Observations sur le classement phonologique des consonnes. *Proceedings of the Third International Congress of Phonetic Sciences (Ghent)* 34–41. Reprinted in Jakobson 1962: 272–9 and in Makkai 1972: 305–9.

Jakobson, R. 1949. On the identification of phonemic entities. *Travaux du Cercle Linguistique de Copenhague* 5: 205–13. Reprinted in Jakobson 1962: 418–25 and in Makkai 1972: 318–22. Page references in the text are to Makkai.

Jakobson, R. 1962. *Selected writings*. The Hague: Mouton.

Jakobson, R., Fant, C. G. M. and Halle, M. 1952. *Preliminaries to speech analysis: the distinctive features and their correlates*. Cambridge, Mass.: MIT Press. (MIT Acoustics Laboratory Technical Report 13.)

Jakobson, R. and Halle, M. 1956. *Fundamentals of language*. The Hague: Mouton.

Jamieson, D. G. 1987. Studies of possible psychoacoustic factors underlying speech perception. In Schouten 1987: 220–30.

Jespersen, O. 1904. *Lehrbuch der Phonetik*. Leipzig: B. G. Teubner.

Jespersen, O. 1922. *Language: its nature, development and origin*. London: Allen and Unwin.

Johns-Lewis, C. (ed.) 1986. *Intonation in discourse*. London: Croom Helm.

Jones, D. 1957. The history and meaning of the term 'phoneme'. London: International Phonetic Association (supplement to *Le Maître Phonétique*). Reprinted in Fudge 1973a: 17–34 and in Jones and Laver 1973: 187–204.

Jones, D. 1960 (9th edn). *An outline of English phonetics*. Cambridge W. Heffer & Sons. (First published 1918.)

Jones, D. 1962 (2nd edn). *The phoneme: its nature and use*. Cambridge: W. Heffer & Sons.

Jones, W. E. and Laver, J. (eds) 1973. *Phonetics in linguistics: a book of readings*. London: Longman.

Joos, M. 1948. Acoustic phonetics. *Language* 24: 1–136.

Joos, M. (ed.) 1958. *Readings in linguistics*. Chicago: Chicago University Press.

Kachru, B., Lees, R. B., Malkiel, Y., Pietrangeli, A. and Saporta, S. (eds) 1973. *Issues in linguistics: papers in honor of Henry and Renée Kahane*. Urbana: University of Illinois Press.

Kahn, D. 1980. *Syllable-based generalizations in English phonology*. New York: Garland. (Published version of doctoral dissertation MIT 1975.)

Kaisse, E. M. and Shaw, A. 1985. On the theory of lexical phonology. *Phonology Yearbook* 2: 1–30.

Kaplan, H. M. 1971 (2nd edn). *Anatomy and physiology of speech*. New York: McGraw-Hill.

Karjalainen, M. 1987. Auditory models for speech processing. *Proceedings of the XIth International Congress of Phonetic Sciences* 2: 11–20.

Kawasaki, H. 1986. Phonetic explanation for phonological universals: the case of distinctive vowel nasalization. In Ohala and Jaeger 1986: 81–103.

Kaye, J. D. and Piggott, G. L. 1973. On the cyclic nature of Ojibwa T-palatalization. *LInq* 4: 345–62.

Kelly, J. L. and Lochbaum, C. 1962. Speech synthesis. *Proceedings of the 4th International Congress on Acoustics* G 42.

Kennedy, J. G. and Abbs, J. H. 1979. Anatomic studies of the perioral motor system: foundations for studies in speech pathology. In Lass 1979 (vol. 1): 211–70.

Kenstowicz, M. 1994. *Phonology in generative grammar*. Oxford: Basil Blackwell.

Kenstowicz, M. and Kisseberth, C. 1979. *Generative phonology: description and theory*. New York: Academic Press.

Kent, R., Wiley, T. and Strennen, M. 1979. Consonant discrimination as a function of presentation level. *Audiology* 18: 212–24.

Kewley-Port, D. 1983. Time-varying features as correlates of place of articulation in stop consonants. *JASA* 73: 322–35.

Key, M. 1967. *Morphology of Cayuvava*. The Hague: Mouton.

Kim, C. W. 1965. On the autonomy of the tensity features in stop classification (with special reference to Korean stops). *Word* 21: 339–59.

Kingdon, R. 1958. *The groundwork of English intonation*. London: Longman.

Kinsbourne, M. 1980. Cognition and the brain. In Wittrock 1980: 325–43.

Kiparsky, P. 1968. Linguistic universals and language change. In Bach and Harms 1968: 170–202.

Kiparsky, P. 1971. Historical linguistics. In Dingwall 1971: 576–649.

Kiparsky, P. 1972. Explanation in phonology. In Peters 1972: 189–225.

Kiparsky, P. 1973a. How abstract is phonology? In Fujimura 1973: 5–56. (Revised version of a paper distributed by the Indiana University Linguistics Club, 1968.)

Kiparsky, P. 1973b. Abstractness, opacity, and global rules. In Fujimura 1973: 57–86.

Kiparsky, P. 1985. Some consequences of lexical phonology. *Phonology Yearbook* 2: 85–138.

Kisseberth, C. W. 1970. On the functional unity of phonological rules. *LInq* 1: 291–306.

Kisseberth, C. W. 1972. Cyclical rules in Klamath phonology. *LInq* 3: 3–33.

Kisseberth, C. W. 1973. Is rule ordering necessary in phonology? In Kachru et al. 1973: 418–41.

Klatt, D. H. 1979. Synthesis by rule of segmental durations in English sentences. In Lindblom and Ohman 1979: 287–99.

Klatt, D. H. 1981. Lexical representations for speech production and perception. In Myers et al. 1981: 11–31.

Klatt, D. H. 1989. Review of selected models of speech perception. In Marslen-Wilson 1989a: 169–226.

Klatt, D. H., Stevens, K. N. and Mead, J. 1968. Studies of articulatory activity and airflow during speech. *Annals of the New York Academy of Sciences* 155: 42–54.

Klein, W. and Levelt, W. (eds) 1981. *Crossing the boundaries in linguistics*. Dordrecht: Reidel.

Koenig, W., Dunn, H. K. and Lacy, L. Y. 1946. The sound spectrograph. *JASA* 18: 19–49.

Kohler, K. J. 1966. Is the syllable a phonological universal? *Journal of Linguistics* 2: 207–8.

Kopra, L. L., Blosser, D. and Waldron, D. L. 1968. Comparison of Fairbanks Rhyme Test and CID Auditory Test W-22 in normal and hearing-impaired listeners. *JSHR* 11: 735–9.

Kratochvil, P. 1968. *The Chinese language today*. London: Hutchinson.

Kurita, S., Nagata, K. and Hirano, M. 1983. A comparative study of the layer structure of the vocal fold. In Bless and Abbs 1983: 3–21.

Ladd, D. R. 1984. Declination: a review and some hypotheses. *Phonology Yearbook* 1: 53–74.

Ladd, D. R. and Silverman, K. E. A. 1984. Vowel intrinsic pitch in connected speech. *Phonetica* 41: 31–40.

Ladefoged, P. 1962. *Elements of acoustic phonetics*. Chicago: Chicago University Press.

Ladefoged, P. 1967. *Three areas of experimental phonetics*. London: Oxford University Press.

Ladefoged, P. 1968. *A phonetic study of west African languages*. Cambridge: Cambridge University Press.

Ladefoged, P. 1971. *Preliminaries to linguistic phonetics*. Chicago: Chicago University Press.

Ladefoged, P. 1980. What are linguistic sounds made of? *Language* 56: 485–502.

Ladefoged, P. 1982 (2nd edn). *A course in phonetics*. London: Harcourt Brace Jovanovich.

Ladefoged, P. and Broadbent, D. E. 1957. Information conveyed by vowels. *JASA* 29: 98–104.

Ladefoged, P., DeClerk, J., Lindau, M. and Papcun, G. 1972. An auditory motor theory of speech production. *UCLA-WP* 22: 48–76.

Ladefoged, P. and Harshman, R. 1979. Formant frequencies and movements of the tongue. In Lindblom and Ohman 1979: 25–34.

Ladefoged, P., Harshman, R., Goldstein, L. and Rice, L. 1978. Generating vocal tract shapes from formant frequencies. *JASA* 64: 1027–35.

Ladefoged, P. and Traill, A. 1980. The phonetic inadequacy of phonological specifications of clicks. *UCLA-WP* 49: 1–27.

Lamb, S. M. 1966a. *Outline of stratificational grammar*. Washington: Georgetown University Press.

Lamb, S. M. 1966b. Prolegomena to a theory of phonology. *Language* 42: 536–73. Reprinted in Makkai 1972: 606–33.

Lass, N. J. (ed.) 1976. *Contemporary issues in experimental phonetics*. New York: Academic Press.

Lass, N. J. (ed.) 1979–82. *Speech and language: advances in basic research and practice*. New York: Academic Press. (1979: volumes 1 and 2; 1980: volumes 3 and 4; 1981: volumes 5 and 6; 1982: volumes 7 and 8.)

Lass, R. 1984. *Phonology: an introduction to basic concepts*. Cambridge: Cambridge University Press.

Laver, J. 1968. Voice quality and indexical information. *British Journal of Disorders of Communication* 3: 43–54.

Laver, J. 1979. *Voice quality: a classified research bibliography*. Amsterdam: Benjamins.

Laver, J. 1980. *The phonetic description of voice quality*. Cambridge: Cambridge University Press.

Laver, J. and Hutcheson, S. (eds) 1972. *Communication in face to face interaction: selected readings*. Harmondsworth: Penguin.

Laver, J. and Trudgill, P. 1979. Phonetic and linguistic markers in speech. In Scherer and Giles 1979: 1–32.

Leben, W. R. 1978. The representation of tone. In Fromkin 1978: 177–219.

Lehiste, I. (ed.) 1967. *Readings in acoustic phonetics*. Cambridge, Mass.: MIT Press.

Lehiste, I. 1970. *Suprasegmentals*. Cambridge, Mass.: MIT Press.

Lehiste, I. 1976. Suprasegmentals. In Lass 1976: 225–39.

Lehiste, I. 1977. Isochrony reconsidered. *Journal of Phonetics* 5: 253–63.

Lenneberg, E. 1967. *Biological foundations of language*. New York: Wiley.

Leon, P. R., Faures, G. and Rigault, A. (eds) 1970. *Prosodic feature analysis*. Montreal: Didier.

Li, C. N. and Thompson, S. A. 1978. The acquisition of tone. In Fromkin 1978: 271–84.

Liberman, A. M., Cooper, F. S., Shankweiler, D. S. and Studdert-Kennedy, M. 1967. Perception of the speech code. *Psychological Review* 74: 431–61.

Liberman, A., Delattre, P., Cooper, J. and Gerstman, L. 1954. The role of consonant–vowel transitions in the perception of stops and nasal consonants. *Psychological Monographs* 68: 1–13.

Liberman, A. M., Delattre, P. C., Gerstman, L. J. and Cooper, F. S. 1956. Tempo of frequency change as a cue for distinguishing classes of speech sounds. *Journal of Experimental Psychology* 52: 127–37.

Liberman, A. M., Ingemann, F., Lisker, L., Delattre, P. C. and Cooper, F. S. 1959. Minimal rules for synthesizing speech. *JASA* 31: 1490–9. Reprinted in Fry 1976: 445–66.

Liberman, A M. and Mattingly, I. G. 1985. The motor theory of speech revised. *Cognition* 21: 1–36.

Liberman, M. Y. 1979. *The intonational system of English*. New York: Garland. (Published version of doctoral dissertation, MIT 1975.)

Lieberman, P. 1965. On the acoustic basis of the perception of intonation by linguists. *Word* 21: 40–54.

Lieberman, P. 1967. *Intonation, perception, and language*. Cambridge, Mass.: MIT Press.

Lieberman, P. and Blumstein, S. E. 1988. *Speech physiology, speech perception, and acoustic phonetics*. Cambridge: Cambridge University Press.

Liljencrants, J. and Lindblom, B. 1972. Numerical simulation of vowel quality systems: the role of perceptual contrast. *Language* 48: 839–62.

Lindau, M. 1978. Vowel features. *Language* 54: 541–63.

Lindau, M. 1979. The feature expanded. *JP* 7: 163–76.

Lindau, M. 1985. The story of /r/. In Fromkin 1985: 157–68.

Lindblom, B. 1963. A spectrographic study of vowel reduction. *JASA* 35: 1773–81.

Lindblom, B. 1967. Vowel duration and a model of lip–mandible coordination. *STL-QPSR* 4: 1–29.

Lindblom, B. 1983. On the teleological nature of speech processes. *Speech Communication* 2: 155–8.

Lindblom, B. 1986. Phonetic universals in vowel systems. In Ohala and Jaeger 1986: 13–44.

Lindblom, B., Lubker, J. and Gay, T. 1979. Formant frequencies of some fixed-mandible vowels and a model of speech motor programming by predictive simulation. *Journal of Phonetics* 7: 147–61.

Lindblom, B. and Ohman, S. (eds) 1979. *Frontiers of speech communication research*. New York: Academic Press.

Lindblom, B. and Studdert-Kennedy, M. 1967. On the role of formant transitions in vowel recognition. *JASA* 42: 830–43.

Lindblom, B. and Sundberg, J. 1971. Acoustical consequences of lip, tongue, jaw, and larynx movement. *JASA* 50: 1166–79.

Lindqvist, J. 1970. The voice source studied by means of inverse filtering. *STL-QPSR* 1: 3–9.

Lindsay, P. H. and Norman, D. A. 1977. *Human information processing*. New York: Academic Press.

Lisker, L. 1978. Segment duration, voicing, and the syllable. In Bell and Hooper 1978: 133–40.

Lisker, L. and Abramson, A. S. 1964. A cross-language study of voicing in initial stops: acoustical measurements. *Word* 20: 384–422.

Lisker, L. and Abramson, A. S. 1971. Distinctive features and laryngeal control. *Language* 47: 767–85.

Lubker, J. F. 1975. Normal velopharyngeal function in speech. *Clinics in Plastic Surgery* 2: 249–59.

Ludlow, C. L. and Hart, M. O. (eds) 1981. *Proceedings of the Conference on the Assessment of Vocal Pathology, Bethesda, Maryland, 1979*. Rockville, Md: American Speech–Language–Hearing Association.

Lyons, J. 1962. Phonemic and non-phonemic phonology: some typological reflections. *IJAL* 28: 127–34. Reprinted in Makkai 1972: 275–281 and in Fudge 1973a: 190–9.

McCarthy, J. 1981. A prosodic theory of nonconcatenative morphology. *LInq* 12: 373–418.

McCawley, J. D. 1968. *The phonological component of a grammar of Japanese*. The Hague: Mouton.

McCawley, J. D. 1978. What is a tone language? In Fromkin 1978: 113–31.

McCawley, J. D. 1986. Today the world, tomorrow phonology. *Phonology Yearbook* 3: 27–43.

McMinn, R. M. H. and Hutchings, R. T. 1988 (2nd edn). *A colour atlas of human anatomy*. London: Wolfe Medical.

MacNeilage, P. F. 1981. Feedback in speech production: an ecological perspective. In Myers et al. 1981: 39–44.

MacNeilage, P. F. and Sholes, G. N. 1964. An electromyographic study of the tongue during vowel production. *JSHR* 7: 207–32.

Maddieson, I. 1984. *Patterns of sounds*. Cambridge: Cambridge University Press.

Maddieson, I. 1986. The size and structure of phonological inventories. In Ohala and Jaeger 1986: 105–23.

Makkai, V. B. (ed.) 1972. *Phonological theory: evolution and current practice*. New York: Holt, Rinehart and Winston.

Malmberg, B. (ed.) 1968. *Manual of phonetics*. Amsterdam: North-Holland. (Revised and extended version of L. Kaiser (ed.) 1957 *Manual of Phonetics*).

Mandelbaum, D. G. (ed.) 1949. *Selected writings of Edward Sapir*. Berkeley: University of California Press.

Mann, M. D. 1981. *The nervous system and behaviour*. Philadelphia: Harper & Row.

Markel, J. D. and Gray, A. H. 1976. *Linear prediction of speech*. Berlin: Springer Verlag.

Marslen-Wilson, W. D. 1985. Speech shadowing and speech comprehension. *Speech Communication* 4: 55–73..

Marslen-Wilson, W. D. (ed.) 1989a. *Lexical representation and process*. Cambridge, Mass.: MIT Press.

Marslen-Wilson, W. D. 1989b. Access and integration: projecting sound onto meaning. In Marslen-Wilson 1989a: 3–24.

Marslen-Wilson, W. D. and Welsh, A. 1978. Processing interactions and lexical access during word-recognition in continuous speech. *Cognitive Psychology* 10: 29–63.

Martinet, A. 1955. *Economie des changements phonétiques*. Berne: Francke.

Martinet, A. 1965. De la morphonologie. *La Linguistique* 1: 16–31. Excerpt in Fudge 1973a: 91–100, translated by E. C. Fudge.

Mill, P. J. 1982. *Comparative neurobiology*. London: Edward Arnold.

Millar, J. B. and Ainsworth, W. A. 1972. Identification of synthetic isolated vowels and vowels in h-d context. *Acustica* 27: 278–82.

Miller, G. A. and Nicely, P. E. 1955. An analysis of perceptual confusions among some English consonants. *JASA* 27(2): 338–52.

Miller, R. L. 1953. Auditory tests with synthetic vowels. *JASA* 25: 114–21.

Miller, R. L. 1959. Nature of the vocal cord wave. *JASA* 31: 667–77.

Minifie, F. D. 1973. Speech acoustics. In Minifie et al. 1973: 235–84.

Minifie, F. D., Hixon, T. J. and Williams, F. (eds.) 1973. *Normal aspects of speech, hearing and language*. Englewood Cliffs, NJ: Prentice-Hall.

Mohanan, K. P. 1985. Syllable structure and lexical strata in English. *Phonology Yearbook* 2: 139–55.

Mohanan, K. P. 1987. *The theory of lexical phonology*. Dordrecht: Reidel. (Published version of doctoral dissertation, MIT 1982.)

Moll, K. L. and Shriner, T. H. 1967. Preliminary investigation of a new concept of velar activity during speech. *The Cleft Palate Journal* 4: 58–69.

Monsen, R. B. 1981. The use of a reflectionless tube to assess vocal function. In Ludlow and Hart 1981: 141–50.

Moore, B. C. J. 1982. *Introduction to the psychology of hearing*. London: Academic Press.

Moore, B. C. J. 1989 (3rd edn). *An introduction to the psychology of hearing*. London: Academic Press.

Moore, B. C. J., Peters, R. W. and Glasberg, B. R. 1993. Detection of temporal gaps in sinusoids: effects of frequency and level. *JASA* 93: 1563–70.

Morton, J., Marcus, S. M. and Frankish, C. R. 1976. Perceptual centres (P-centres). *Psychological Review* 83: 405–8.

Myers, T., Laver, J. and Anderson, J. (eds) 1981. *The cognitive representation of speech*. Amsterdam: North-Holland.

Nearey, T. M. 1977. *Phonetic feature systems for vowels*. Doctoral dissertation, University of Connecticut.

Nearey, T. M. and Hogan, J. T. 1986. Phonological contrast in experimental phonetics: relating distributions of production data to perceptual categorization curves. In Ohala and Jaeger 1986: 141–61.

Newmeyer, F. J. (ed.) 1988. *Linguistics: the Cambridge survey*. Cambridge: Cambridge University Press.

Newton, B. E. 1972. *The generative interpretation of dialect*. Cambridge: Cambridge University Press.

Nolan, F. 1983. *The phonetic bases of speaker recognition*. Cambridge: Cambridge University Press.

O'Connor, J. D. 1973. *Phonetics*. Harmondsworth: Penguin.

O'Connor, J. D. and Arnold, G. F. 1973 (2nd edn). *Intonation of colloquial English*. London: Longman. (First published 1961.)

O'Connor, J. D., Gerstman, L. J., Liberman, A. M., Delattre, P. C. and Cooper, F. S. 1957. Acoustic cues for the perception of initial /w, j, r, l/ in English. *Word* 13: 24–43.

Ohala, J. J. 1970. Aspects of the control and production of speech. *UCLA-WP* 15: 1–167.

Ohala, J. J. 1978. The production of tone. In Fromkin 1978: 5–39.

Ohala, J. J. 1986. Consumer's guide to evidence in phonology. *Phonology Yearbook* 3: 3–26.

Ohala, J. J. and Jaeger, J. J. (eds) 1986. *Experimental phonology*. Orlando: Academic Press.

Ohman, S. E. G. 1966. Coarticulation in VCV utterances: spectrographic measurements. *JASA* 39: 151–68.

O'Neill, J. J. 1975. Tests for hearing. In Singh 1975: 219–52.

O'Shaughnessy, D. 1987. *Speech communication*. Reading, Mass.: Addison-Wesley.

Ottoson, D. 1983. *Physiology of the nervous system*. London: Macmillan.

Palmer, F. R. (ed.) 1970. *Prosodic analysis*. Oxford: Oxford University Press.

Perkell, J. S. 1969. *Physiology of speech production: results and implications of a quantitative radiographic study*. Cambridge, Mass.: MIT Press.

Perkell, J. S. and Klatt, D. H. (eds) 1986. *Invariance and variability in speech processes*. New Jersey: Lawrence Erlbaum.

Perkins, W. H. and Kent, R. D. 1986. *Textbook of functional anatomy of speech, language and hearing*. London: Taylor & Francis.

Peters, S. (ed.) 1972. *Goals of linguistic theory*. Englewood Cliffs, NJ: Prentice-Hall.

Peterson, G. E. and Barney, H. L. 1952. Control methods used in a study of vowels. *JASA* 24: 175–84.

Peterson, G. E. and Shoup, J. E. 1966a. A physiological theory of phonetics. *JSHR* 9: 5–67.

Peterson, G. E. and Shoup, J. E. 1966b. The elements of an acoustic phonetic theory. *JSHR* 9: 68–99.

Pickett, J. M. 1957. Perception of vowels heard in noises of various spectra. *JASA* 29: 613–20.

Pickett, J. M. 1980. *The sounds of speech communication*. Baltimore: University Park Press.

Pickett, J. M. and Rubenstein, H. 1960. Perception of consonant voicing in noise. *Language and Speech* 3: 155–63.

Pierrehumbert, J. B. 1979. The perception of fundamental frequency declination. *JASA* 66: 363–9.

Pierrehumbert, J. B. 1981. Synthesizing intonation. *JASA* 70: 985–95.

Pike, K. L. 1943. *Phonetics*. Ann Arbor: University of Michigan Press.

Pike, K. L. 1945. *The intonation of American English*. Ann Arbor: University of Michigan Press.

Pike, K. L. 1947. *Phonemics: a technique for reducing languages to writing*. Ann Arbor: University of Michigan Press.

Pike, K. L. 1948. *Tone languages*. Ann Arbor: University of Michigan Press.

Pinkerton, S. 1986. Quichean (Mayan) glottalized and nonglottalized stops: a phonetic study with implications for phonological universals. In Ohala and Jaeger 1986: 125–39.

Pisoni, D. B. 1977. Identification and discrimination of the relative onset times of two component tones: implications for voicing perception in stops. *JASA* 61(5): 1352–61.

Popper, K. R. 1959. *The logic of scientific discovery*. London: Hutchinson.

Postal, P. M. 1968. *Aspects of phonological theory*. New York: Harper and Row.

Potter, R. K., Kopp, G. A. and Green, H. C. 1947. *Visible speech*. New York: Van Nostrand.

Purcell, E. T. 1979. Formant frequency patterns in Russian VCV utterances. *JASA* 66: 1691–702.

Rabiner, L. R. and Schafer, R. W. 1978. *Digital processing of speech signals*. Englewood Cliffs, NJ: Prentice-Hall.

Repp, B. H. 1979. Relative amplitude of aspiration noise as a cue for syllable-initial stop consonants. *Language and Speech* 22: 947–50.

Rietfeld, A. C. M. and Gussenhoven, C. 1985. On the relation between pitch excursion size and prominence. *Journal of Phonetics* 13: 299–308.

Riordan, C. J. 1977. Control of vocal tract length in speech. *JASA* 62: 998–1002.

Robins, R. H. 1957. Aspects of prosodic analysis. *Proceedings of the University of Durham Philosophical Society* 1: 1–12. Reprinted in Makkai 1972: 264–74.

Robins, R. H. 1979 (2nd edn). *A short history of linguistics*. Harlow: Longman.

Rose, P. J. 1982. Acoustic characteristics of the Shanghai-Zenhai syllable types. In Bradley 1982: 1–53.

Rubenstein, H., Decker, L. and Pollack, I. 1959. Word length and intelligibility. *Language and Speech* 2: 175–8.

Russ, C. V. J. 1978. *Historical German phonology and morphology*. Oxford: Clarendon Press.

Russell, J. 1980. Some problems of phonological analysis in Moba. *MQSLRC* 2 (5): 37–69.

Sampson, G. 1980. *Schools of linguistics: competition and evolution*. London: Hutchinson.

Sampson, G. 1985. *Writing systems*. London: Hutchinson.

Samuel, A. 1981. Phonemic restoration: insights from a new methodology. *Journal of Experimental Psychology* 110: 474–94.

Sapir, E. 1921. *Language*. New York: Harcourt Brace.

Sapir, E. 1925. Sound patterns in language. *Language* 1: 37–51. Reprinted in Mandelbaum 1949: 33–45 and in Makkai 1972: 13–21. Page references in the text are to Makkai.

Sapir, E. 1933. La réalité psychologique des phonémes. *Journal de Psychologie Normale et Pathologique* 30: 247–65. English version: The psychological reality of phonemes. In Mandelbaum 1949: 46–60; reprinted in Makkai 1972: 22–31.

Sawashima, M. 1974. Laryngeal research in experimental phonetics. In Sebeok 1974: 2303–48.

Sawashima, M., Gay, T. and Harris, K. S. 1969. Laryngeal muscle activity during vocal pitch and intensity changes. *Haskins Laboratories Status Report on Speech Research* 19/20: 211–20.

Schane, S. A. 1971. The phoneme revisited. *Language* 47: 503–21.

Schane, S. A. 1973. *Generative phonology*. Englewood Cliffs, NJ: Prentice-Hall.

Scherer, K. R. and Giles, H. (eds) 1979. *Social markers in speech*. Cambridge: Cambridge University Press.

Schneiderman, C. R. 1984. *Basic anatomy and physiology in speech and hearing*. London: Croom Helm; San Diego: College Hill Press.

Schouten, M. E. H. (ed.) 1987. *The psychophysics of speech perception.* Dordrecht: Martinus Nijhoff.

Schuh, R. G. 1978. Tone rules. In Fromkin 1978: 221–56.

Schultz, M. C. 1964. Word familiarity influences in speech discrimination. *JSHR* 7: 395–400.

Scott, N. C. 1964. Nasal consonants in Land Dayak (Bukar-Sadong). In Abercrombie et al. 1964: 432–6.

Scully, C. 1979. Model prediction and real speech: fricative dynamics. In Lindblom and Ohman 1979: 35–48.

Sears, T. and Newsom-Davis, J. 1968. The control of respiratory muscles during voluntary breathing. *Annals of the New York Academy of Sciences* 155: 183–90.

Sebeok, T. (ed.) 1974. *Current trends in linguistics* (vol. 12). The Hague: Mouton.

Shattuck-Hufnagel, S. 1986. The representation of phonological information during speech production planning: evidence from vowel errors in spontaneous speech. *Phonology Yearbook* 3: 117–49.

Shepard, R. N. 1972. Psychological representation of speech sounds. In David and Denes 1972: 67–113.

Shoup, J. E. and Pfeiffer, L. L. 1976. Acoustic characteristics of speech sounds. In Lass 1976: 171–224.

Shuy, R. and Bailey, C. J. (eds) 1974. *Towards tomorrow's linguistics.* Washington: Georgetown University Press.

Siebs, T. 1961 (18th edn, edited by H. de Boor and P. Diels) *Deutsche Hochsprache.* Berlin: Walter de Gruyter.

Silverman, K. E. A. 1984. What causes vowels to have intrinsic fundamental frequency. *Cambridge Papers in Phonetics and Experimental Linguistics* 3: 1–15.

Singh, S. (ed.) 1975. *Measurement procedures in speech, hearing and language.* Baltimore: University Park Press.

Skinner, B. F. 1957. *Verbal behavior.* London: Methuen.

Slis, I. H. and Cohen, A. 1969. On the complex regulating the voiced–voiceless distinction. *Language and Speech* 12: 80–102; 137–55.

Small, A. M. 1973. Acoustics. In Minifie et al. 1973: 11–72.

Smith, N. V. 1968. Tone in Ewe. *MIT-QPR* 88: 290–304. Reprinted in Fudge 1973a: 354–69.

Smith, N. V. 1973. *The acquisition of phonology.* Cambridge: Cambridge University Press.

Sommerstein, A. H. 1977. *Modern phonology.* London: Edward Arnold.

Sondhi, M. M. 1975. Measurement of the glottal waveform. *JASA* 57: 228–32.

Sonesson, B. 1968. The functional anatomy of the speech organs. In Malmberg 1968: 45–75.

Sprigg, R. K. 1978. Phonation types: a reappraisal. *JIPA* 8: 2–17.

Springer, S. P. and Deutsch, G. 1985. *Left brain, right brain.* New York: Freeman.

Stampe, D. 1969. On the acquisition of phonetic representation. *Papers from the Fifth Regional Meeting of the Chicago Linguistic Society*: 443–54. Reprinted as preface to Stampe 1979.

Stampe, D. 1979. *A dissertation on natural phonology.* New York: Garland. (Published version of doctoral dissertation, University of Chicago 1972.)

Stathopoulos, E. T. and Weismer, G. 1985. Oral airflow and air pressure during speech production: a comparative study of children, youths and adults. *Folia Phoniatrica* 37: 152–9.

Steele, R. and Threadgold, T. (eds) 1987. *Language topics.* Amsterdam: John Benjamins.

Stetson, R. H. 1951 (2nd edn). *Motor phonetics.* Amsterdam: North-Holland.

Stevens, K. N. 1972a. The quantal nature of speech: evidence from articulatory-acoustic data. In David and Denes 1972: 51–66.

Stevens, K. N. 1972b. Airflow and turbulent noise for fricative and stop consonants: static considerations. *JASA* 50: 1182–92.

Stevens, K. N. and Halle, M. 1967. Remarks on analysis by synthesis and distinctive features. In Wathen-Dunn 1967: 88–102.

Stevens, K. N. and Hirano, M. (eds) 1981. *Vocal fold physiology.* Tokyo: University of Tokyo Press.

Stevens, K. N. and House, A. S. 1955. Development of a quantitative description of vowel articulation. *JASA* 27: 484–93.

Stevens, K. N. and House, A. S. 1963. Perturbations of vowel articulations by consonantal context; an acoustical study. *JSHR* 6: 111–28.

Stevens, K. N., House, A. S. and Paul, A. P. 1966. Acoustical description of syllabic nuclei: an interpretation in terms of a dynamic model of articulation. *JASA* 40: 123–32.

Stewart, J. Q. 1922. An electrical analogue of the vocal organs. *Nature* 110: 311–2.

Stokes, J. 1981. Anindilyakwa phonology from phoneme to syllable. In Waters 1981: 139–81.

Strange, W., Jenkins, J. and Johnson, T. 1983. Dynamic specification of coarticulated vowels. *JASA* 74: 695–705.

Strange, W., Verbrugge, R. R., Shankweiler, D. P. and Erdman, T. R. 1976. Consonantal environment specifies vowel identity. *JASA* 60: 213–24.

Strauss, S. L. 1982. *Lexicalist phonology of English and German.* Dordrecht: Foris.

Strevens, P. 1960. Spectra of fricative noise in human speech. *Language and Speech* 3: 32–49. Reprinted in Fry 1976: 132–50.

Studdert-Kennedy, M. 1976. Speech perception. In Lass 1976: 243–93.

Sundberg, J. and Gauffin, J. 1979. Waveform and spectrum of the glottal voice source. In Lindblom and Ohman 1979: 301–20.

Tent, J. and Clark, J. E. 1980. An experimental investigation into the perception of slips of the tongue. *JP* 8: 317–25.

't Hart, J. 1979. Explorations in automatic stylization of F_0 curves. *IPO Annual Progress Report* 14: 61–5.

't Hart, J. 1981. Differential sensitivity to pitch distance, particularly in speech. *JASA* 69: 811–21.

Thomason, S. G. 1976. What else happens to crazy rules? *Language* 52: 370–81.

Trager, G. L. and Bloch, B. 1941. The syllabic phonemes of English. *Language* 17: 223–46. Reprinted in Makkai 1972: 72–89.

Trager, G. L. and Smith, H. L. 1951. *An outline of English structure.* Studies in Linguistics, Occasional Papers 13. Reprinted by ACLS.

Tribe, M. A. and Eraut, M. R. 1977. *Nerves and muscle.* Cambridge: Cambridge University Press.

Trim, J. L. M. 1951. German h, ç and x. *Le Maître Phonétique* 66: 41–2.

Trubetzkoy, N. S. 1939. *Grundzüge der Phonologie.* Travaux du Cercle Linguistique de Prague 7. Reprinted 1958, Göttingen: Vandenhoeck & Ruprecht. Translated into French by J. Cantineau 1949 as *Principes de phonologie,* Paris: Librairie Klincksieck. Translated into English by C. A. M. Baltaxe 1969 as *Principles of phonology,* Berkeley: University of California Press.

Trudgill, P. (ed.) 1978. *Sociolinguistic patterns in British English.* London: Edward Arnold.

Trudgill, P. 1983. *On dialect: social and geographic perspectives.* Oxford: Basil Blackwell.

Tryon, D. T. 1970. *Conversational Tahitian.* Berkeley: University of California Press.

Tuller, B. and Kelso, J. A. S. 1984. The timing of articulatory gestures: evidence for relational invariants. *JASA* 76: 1030–6.

Tuller, B., Kelso, J. A. S. and Harris, K. S. 1982. On the kinematics of articulatory control as a function of stress and rate. *Haskins Laboratories Status Report on Speech Research* 71/72: 81–8.

Tun, U Thein 1982. Some acoustic properties of tones in Burmese. In Bradley 1982: 77–116.

Ullmann, S. 1970. *Semantics: an introduction to the science of meaning.* Oxford: Basil Blackwell.

Vaissiere, J. 1983. Language-independent prosodic features. In Cutler and Ladd 1983: 53–66.

van den Berg, J. 1958. Myoelastic-aerodynamic theory of voice production. *JSHR* 1: 227–44.

van den Berg, J. 1960. Vocal ligaments versus registers. *Current Problems in Phoniatrics and Logopedics* 1: 19–34.

van den Berg, J. 1962. Modern research in experimental phoniatrics. *Folia Phoniatrica* 14: 81–149.

van den Berg, J. 1968. Mechanisms of the larynx and laryngeal vibrations. In Malmberg 1968: 278–308.

van der Hulst, H. and Smith, N. 1982a. *The structure of phonological representations.* Dordrecht: Foris.

van der Hulst, H. and Smith, N. 1982b. An overview of autosegmental and metrical phonology. In van der Hulst and Smith 1982a: 1–45.

van Hattum, R. J. and Worth, J. H. 1967. Airflow rates in normal speakers. *Cleft Palate Journal* 4: 137–47.

Vennemann, T. 1972. Rule inversion. *Lingua* 29: 209–42.

Vennemann, T. 1974a. Phonological concreteness in natural generative phonology. In Shuy and Bailey 1974: 202–19.

Vennemann, T. 1974b. Restructuring. *Lingua* 33: 137–56.

Wakita, H. 1976. Instrumentation for the study of speech acoustics. In Lass 1976: 3–40.

Wang, M. and Bilger, R. C. 1973. Consonant confusions in noise: a study of perceptual features. *JASA* 54: 1248–66.

Wardhaugh, R. 1986. *An introduction to sociolinguistics.* Oxford: Basil Blackwell.

Warren, D. W. 1976. Aerodynamics of speech production. In Lass 1976: 105–37.

Warren, R. M. 1970. Perceptual restoration of missing speech sounds. *Science* 167: 392–3.

Warren, R. M. 1982. *Auditory perception.* New York: Pergamon.

Warren, R. M. 1984. Perceptual restoration of obliterated sounds. *Psychological Bulletin* 96: 371–83.

Waters, B. 1979. *A distinctive features approach to Djinang phonology and verb morphology.* WP-SILAAB Series A, Vol. 4.

Waters, B. (ed.) 1981. *Australian phonologies: collected papers.* WP-SILAAB Series A, Vol. 5.

Wathen-Dunn, W. (ed.) 1967. *Models for the perception of speech and visual form.* Cambridge: Mass.: MIT Press.

Weismer, G. 1985. Speech breathing: contemporary views and findings. In Daniloff 1985: 47–72.

Wells, J. C. 1982. *Accents of English* (3 volumes). Cambridge: Cambridge University Press.

Wendahl, R. W., Moore, G. P. and Hollien, H. 1963. Comments on vocal fry. *Folia Phoniatrica* 15: 251–5.

Westermann, D. and Ward, I. C. 1933. *Practical phonetics for students of African languages.* London: Oxford University Press.

Whitney, W. D. 1889 (2nd edn). *A Sanskrit grammar.* Oxford: Oxford University Press; Harvard: Harvard University Press.

Wickelgren, W. M. 1966. Distinctive features and errors in short term memory for English consonants. *JASA* 39: 388–98.

Williams, C. E. and Hecker, M. H. L. 1968. Relations between intelligibility scores of four test methods and three types of speech distortion. *JASA* 44: 1002–6.

Witten, I. H. 1982. *Principles of computer speech*. London: Academic Press.

Wittrock, M. C. (ed.) 1980. *The brain and psychology*. New York: Academic Press.

Wood, A. B. 1964. *A textbook of sound*. London: Bell & Sons.

Wood, A. 1966. *Acoustics*. New York: Dover Publications.

Wood, S. 1979. A radiographic analysis of constriction locations for vowels. *Journal of Phonetics* 7: 25–43.

Yallop, C. 1977. *Alyawarra: an Aboriginal language of Central Australia*. Canberra: Australian Institute of Aboriginal Studies.

Yallop, C. and Abdurrahman, S. 1979. A brief outline of Komering phonology and morphology. *NUSA Linguistic Studies in Indonesian and Languages in Indonesia* 7: 11–18.

Zemlin, W. R. 1968. *Speech and hearing science*. Englewood Cliffs, NJ: Prentice-Hall.

Zemlin, W. R. 1981 (2nd edn). *Speech and hearing science: anatomy and physiology*. Englewood Cliffs (NJ): Prentice-Hall.

Zonneveld, W. 1976. A phonological exchange rule in Brussels Flemish. *Linguistic Analysis* 2: 109–14.

Zwicker, E. 1962. Subdivision of the audible frequency range into critical bands (Frequenzgruppen). *JASA* 33: 248.

Zwicker, E. and Fastl, H. 1990. *Psychoacoustics: facts and models*. Berlin: Springer-Verlag.

Index